D1004014

This book provides a new account of one of the most famous men of the English middle ages: Simon de Montfort. It traces his career from his origins as the younger son of a French noble family, through his elevation in England as the close friend and counsellor of King Henry III, to his break with the king, his rise to royal power, and his death in battle at Evesham in 1265. Montfort was a creature of contradictions. A superb soldier, an ardent religious idealist, and a forcefully able politician, he won the friendship and loyalty of some of the greatest men of his day; yet he was also ambitious and avaricious, and determined to build a position for himself and his family from the opportunities which came with power. Through the chronicles, the public records and the remains of Montfort's family archives, this biography offers not only a narrative of his life but a more unusual study of character and temperament which can hardly be attempted for any other nobleman of the period.

SIMON DE MONTFORT

SIMON DE MONTFORT

J. R. MADDICOTT

Fellow of Exeter College, Oxford

Published by the Press Syndicate of the University of Cambridge
The Pitt Building, Trumpington Street, Cambridge CB2 1RP
40 West 20th Street, New York, NY 10011–4211, USA
10 Stamford Road, Oakleigh, Melbourne 3166, Australia

© Cambridge University Press 1994

First published 1994
Reprinted 1995, 1997

Printed in Great Britain at the University Press, Cambridge

A catalogue record for this book is available from the British Library

Library of Congress cataloguing in publication data
Maddicott, John Robert.
Simon de Montfort / by J. R. Maddicott.
p.   cm.
Includes bibliographical references and index.
ISBN 0 521 37493 6
1. Montfort, Simon de, Earl of Leicester, 1208?–1265. 2. Great
Britain – History – Barons' War, 1263–1267. 3. Revolutionaries – Great
Britain – Biography. 4. Nobility – Great Britain – Biography.
I. Title.
DA228.M7M33 1994
942.03′4′092 – dc20
[B] 93–33224 CIP

ISBN 0 521 37493 6

WD

I think it to be most necessary for you to study diligently and repeatedly chapters 29, 30 and 31 of the Book of Job.

Adam Marsh, letter to Simon de Montfort, c. 1251

If I have walked with vanity, or if my foot hath hasted to deceit,
Let me be weighed in an even balance, that God may know mine integrity.

Job, 31, vv. 5–6

Contents

Illustrations

xi

FIGURES

Preface

Together with William the Conqueror, Henry VIII and Oliver Cromwell, Simon de Montfort remains a man whom anyone with a smattering of historical knowledge is likely to have heard of, even today. Some may be able to go further and to equip him with actions and achievements. Drawing on the garbled tailend of nineteenth-century traditions, they may remember him as the founder of parliament or as the defender of popular liberties against royal oppression; and if they happen to live at Evesham, where he died and is commemorated, they may find that his reputation continues to have a powerful local resonance. But generally speaking little about him besides his name is at all familiar, and outside the universities he remains at best a fringe performer in the folklore of English history. Despite his one-time fame, there has been no new biography of him for more than thirty years.

However ill-known he may now be, Simon de Montfort deserves to survive as one of those large and luminous historical figures whose abilities and ambitions made them the masters of their times. Like a Cromwell or a Gladstone, he needs a biography once every half century or so, as knowledge increases and a new generation of historians comes to see him in new ways. In Montfort's case there are particular reasons for maintaining the tradition of periodic reassessment. Simply considered as a story, his career is an intensely dramatic one, full of movement, passion and tragedy: a younger son crosses from France to England, makes good, marries the king's sister, turns against his former patron, effectively displaces him, but dies in battle, a defeated man. This personal story is entwined with an equally intense political drama. Montfort was a leading actor in one of the longest and most profound periods of turbulence in the history of the English State between the Norman Conquest and the Civil War of the seventeenth century. It was a time when the assumptions on which royal government rested were challenged root and branch, and when attempts were made to check the king's powers with an astonishing radicalism unparalleled before the days of the parliamentarians. Unlike most other medieval movements of reform and rebellion – but like that of the seventeenth century – this one raised the deepest issues of conscience and principle. It saw magnates attempting to curtail their own privileges, the emergence of an oath to reform as the rallying-point for men of conscience, and the support of some of the most scrupulous and altruistic of contemporary churchmen given to reformers and rebels. Montfort was at the centre of this movement and became its leader. Yet his participation in it was by no means an unambivalent matter, for it was distorted by appetites, greeds and grievances which cast a shadow over his motives and which raise for any historian the most difficult questions about his ultimate ambitions.

In trying to answer these questions we are fortunate to be able to draw on evidence which allows us to explore Montfort's personality with exceptional fullness and sensitivity. Through the rich flotsam of documentation left behind by his private affairs and by his quarrel with the king, he speaks to us more directly than any other lay magnate before the age of the Pastons. The use of the first person singular is characteristic. 'The king says that he did me a great boon when he took me for his man, since I was not the eldest . . . then afterwards he gave me his sister . . . three years later I returned from Outremer to Burgundy . . . I order that the wrong which I have done in whatever way shall be amended . . . the great men of the land bear me such ill-will because I uphold [the king's] rights and those of the poor against them . . .'.[1] Here is an individual voice, speaking with an immediacy and a vividness almost unique in the sources for the period. What it reveals about Montfort's temperament and ambitions can be extended by other information about his tastes and habits which again is abnormally extensive. We know something about the books he read, the clothes he wore, the prayers he prayed, the sins that burdened his conscience, and perhaps even a little about the sexual side of his relationship with his wife. Through the correspondence of the churchmen who were his intimate friends, we know something too about his moral character, his vices and virtues. Altogether it is possible to observe Montfort's emotions, his *mentalité* and the springs of his actions, more closely than those of any other medieval noble. His presence has a freshness and a sharpness denied to a Ranulf of Chester or a Thomas of Lancaster or a John of Gaunt. Outside the familiar succession of kings, no more

---

[1] Bémont, *Montfort* (1st edn), pp. 332–3, 328, 267.

worthwhile subject from the English middle ages is likely to come the way of a biographer.

It is not, of course, a new subject, nor can any biographer expect to fashion Montfort in an entirely new image. From at least the seventeenth century, when echoes of his own days were all around, Montfort has rarely been absent from the historian's agenda. Seen first as the personification of discord and as a would-be dictator, then as the visionary initiator of representative government, he was regularly made to serve the causes of others' times. With the rise of academic history in the late nineteenth century, and the wider use of record sources alongside the opinionated accounts of the chroniclers, it became possible to see him in a more objective though never entirely dispassionate way. Yet the scholars' Montfort, essentially the creation of William Stubbs in England and of Charles Bémont in France, was almost as much the prisoner of the new school of constitutional history as he had been of the partisans who had claimed him in the past. Only with the work of Sir Maurice Powicke and his pupils at Manchester and Oxford between the wars was the whole age and Montfort's part in it considered afresh, this time with a novel concentration on the unpublished archives of royal government, whose neglect had partly vitiated the researches of Stubbs and his contemporaries. One of the most durable products of this revival has been R. F. Treharne's *The Baronial Plan of Reform, 1258–63* (1932). Though too indulgent towards Montfort, sometimes to the point of hero worship, this remains the best detailed narrative of the early years of the reform movement. A second offshoot was M. W. Labarge's Oxford thesis of 1939 on the personal quarrels of Simon de Montfort and his wife with the king. Drawn on rapidly by Powicke and used later in Mrs Labarge's biography of 1962 – the last before the present one – her study was the first to give Montfort's private grievances the importance that they deserved. Despite his own distance from the archives which his pupils exploited so effectively, Powicke himself provided what was for its time the culminative treatment of the entire period in his *King Henry III and the Lord Edward* (1947). So definitive did this appear to be that in its wake a kind of historiographical torpor settled over much of the thirteenth century, which temporarily put Montfort too to sleep. Only in the last two decades has this begun to be dispersed, by a vigorous flow of theses and articles which remain to be gathered together into a new synthesis.

In what follows I have, of course, drawn on this long tradition of historical writing. I have made particular use of the documents printed in the original edition of Bémont's *Simon de Montfort* (1884), which first made available, from the detritus of the Montfort family archives, many of the documents essential for any biographer. But in general I have written directly from the sources and have sought to avoid anything resembling a commentary on Treharne, Powicke *et al.* The reader will find that four particular aspects of Montfort's career occupy the foreground of the picture, where the sources have placed them for me. First, I have given more than customary weight to his role in France and to his standing as a French noble, since I have come to believe that recent writing has perhaps exaggerated the extent of his Englishness. Secondly, I have stressed his concern for the establishment of his family, a factor often neglected in previous discussions of his motives; and so his wife, his sons and the problem of his sons' endowment, have all been given some prominence. Thirdly, I have tried to bring out the importance of his financial position and of his financial claims against the king. Closely related to his plans for his family, this peculiarly involved subject provides a main key to his actions. Finally, I have explored in some detail his religious convictions, again because they take us to the roots of his conduct, personal and political. There may seem to be a jarring inappropriateness in bringing together these two latter and apparently contrasting impulses, material and spiritual; but this is not so. Together they enable us to follow Montfort through the complexities of the reforming period, when his private claims and financial grievances interlocked bewilderingly and at every point with public principles which were ultimately grounded on religious beliefs. The extent to which those grievances affected his politics is one of the main themes of the book.

In moving towards its completion I have become conscious of two special weaknesses, both sins of omission; no doubt others will be able to spot many more. Despite my emphasis on the importance of Montfort's French activities, I have done little here beyond searching the main French printed sources and the main collection of Montfort family documents in BN, MS. Clairambault 1188. What Montfort was doing during his long sojourns in France is often a mystery. It might be solved, at least in part, by an intensive search of French local archives, particularly perhaps those at Rouen and Evreux. This I have not attempted. Nor have I attempted to analyse in anything more than a superficial way the English provincial support which was vital to Montfort's authority during the reforming years. How the knightly class divided between royalists and Montfortians, and how allegiances shifted, largely remains to be discovered, despite some invaluable preliminary studies by Dr Clive Knowles and Dr Jeremy Quick. Until this has been undertaken, the subterranean dynamics of the reform movement, below the level of its leader's actions and convictions, will remain to some extent obscure.

My work has been greatly eased by the help and guidance of many friends and scholars. At an early stage Dr David Crouch generously made available to me his notes and transcripts of Montfort's charters. I have since gone back to the originals, but I should have been unaware of many of these had it not been for Dr Crouch's assistance. I am also grateful to the authors of a number of theses, who, with equal generosity, allowed me to make use of their unpublished work: Dr Paul Brand, Dr David Burton, Dr Jean Ellis, Dr Peter Golob, Dr Clive Knowles, Mrs Margaret Wade Labarge, Dr Jeremy Quick, Dr Huw Ridgeway and Dr Hilary Wait. Dr Knowles was additionally good enough to read the whole of an early draft and to offer valuable comments. References and advice on particular points have been kindly provided by Dr Paul Brand, Dr Pierre Chaplais, Reverend John Cowdrey, Dr Jean Dunbabin, Mr Mark Page, Professor William Rothwell, Miss Elizabeth Rutson and Dr Nicholas Vincent. To all these, humble and hearty thanks.

Two particular scholars have given me more help than I had any right to expect. To Dr David Carpenter and Dr Margaret Howell I owe far more than will appear from the few inadequate references to their help in the footnotes. Both of them read a first draft of the book, commented extensively, offered salutary criticisms, put up valuable ideas, saved me from innumerable blunders, and in correspondence and conversation provided that mixture of friendly encouragement, exhortation and advice of which anyone who has tried to write a book will know the value. If the finished product has any merits, they should share in the credit. My additional and more conventional debt to David Carpenter's published work will be obvious throughout what follows.

For all mistakes I take sole responsibility.

I have some other, more personal, debts which cannot be properly repaid. While I was writing this book my father died. He knew nothing of the middle ages, but he had a strong sense of the past and had encouraged my own historical efforts from almost as far back as I can remember. He remained a great encourager, with an interest in whatever his family did and a pride in whatever they achieved. To have

Abbreviations

Ann. Burton	*Annales Monasterii de Burton, 1004–1263*, *Ann. Mon.*, i.
Ann. Cestr.	*Annales Cestrienses*, ed. R. C. Christie (Lancashire and Cheshire Rec. Soc., xiv, 1886).
Ann. Dun.	*Annales Prioratus de Dunstaplia A.D. 1–1297*, *Ann. Mon.*, iii.
Ann. Lond.	*Annales Londonienses, Chronicles of the Reigns of Edward I and Edward II*, ed. W. Stubbs (2 vols., Rolls ser., 1882), i.
Ann. Mon.	*Annales Monastici*, ed. H. R. Luard (5 vols., Rolls ser., 1864–69).
Ann. Oseney	*Annales Monasterii de Oseneia, 1016–1347*, *Ann. Mon.*, iv.
Ann. Tewk.	*Annales Monasterii de Theokesberia*, *Ann. Mon.*, i.
Ann. Wav.	*Annales Monasterii de Waverleia, A.D. 1–1291*, *Ann. Mon.*, ii.
Ann. Wigorn.	*Annales Prioratus de Wigornia, A.D. 1–1377*, *Ann. Mon.*, iv.
Ann. Wint.	*Annales Monasterii de Wintonia, 519–1277*, *Ann. Mon.*, ii.
Baronial Plan	R. F. Treharne, *The Baronial Plan of Reform, 1258–63* (2nd edn, Manchester, 1971).
Bémont, *Montfort* (1st edn)	C. Bémont, *Simon de Montfort* (1st edn, Paris, 1884).
Bémont, *Montfort* (2nd edn)	C. Bémont, *Simon de Montfort*, trans. E. F. Jacob (2nd edn, Oxford, 1930).
BIHR	*Bulletin of the Institute of Historical Research*

BL	British Library
BN	Bibliothèque Nationale
Book of Fees	*The Book of Fees, Commonly Called Testa de Nevill* (3 vols., H.M.S.O., 1920–31)
BRUO	Emden, A. B., *A Biographical Register of the University of Oxford to A.D. 1500* (3 vols., Oxford, 1957–59)
CChR	*Calendar of Charter Rolls*
Chs. of Earls of Chester	*The Charters of the Anglo-Norman Earls of Chester, c. 1071–1237*, ed. G. Barraclough (Lancashire and Cheshire Rec. Soc., cxxvi, 1988).
CIM, i	*Calendar of Inquisitions Miscellaneous*, i, *1219–1307* (H.M.S.O., 1916).
CIPM	*Calendar of Inquisitions Post Mortem* (H.M.S.O., 1904–).
CLR	*Calendar of Liberate Rolls* (H.M.S.O., 1916–).
Councils and Synods	*Councils and Synods*, II, *1205–1313*, ed. F. M. Powicke and C. R. Cheney (2 vols., Oxford, 1964).
CPL	*Calendar of Papal Letters*, i, *1198–1304* (H.M.S.O., 1893).
CPR	*Calendar of Patent Rolls* (H.M.S.O., 1906–).
CR	*Close Rolls, Henry III* (H.M.S.O., 1902–).
Cron. Maior.	*De Antiquis Legibus Liber. Cronica Maiorum et Vicecomitum Londoniarum*, ed. T. Stapleton (Camden Soc., 1846).
CRR	*Curia Regis Rolls* (H.M.S.O., 1922–).
DBM	*Documents of the Baronial Movement of Reform and Rebellion, 1258–67*, ed. R. F. Treharne and I. J. Sanders (Oxford, 1973).
Dipl. Docs.	*Diplomatic Documents Preserved in the Public Record Office*, i, *1101–1272*, ed. P. Chaplais (H.M.S.O., 1964).
DNB	*Dictionary of National Biography*

EHR	*English Historical Review*
Fasti Lincoln	Le Neve, J., *Fasti Ecclesiae Anglicanae, 1066–1300, iii: Lincoln,* comp. D. E. Greenway (London, 1977).
Flores Hist.	*Flores Historiarum,* ed. H. R. Luard (3 vols., Rolls ser., 1890).
Foedera	*Foedera, Conventiones, Litterae et Acta Publica,* ed. T. Rymer, new edn, ed. A. Clark and F. Holbrooke (Record Comm., 1816).
Ger. Cant.	*The Historical Works of Gervase of Canterbury,* ed. W. Stubbs (2 vols., Rolls ser., 1880).
Grosseteste Epistolae	*Roberti Grosseteste Episcopi Lincolniensis, 1235–53, Epistolae,* ed. H. R. Luard (Rolls ser., 1861).
Guisborough	*The Chronicle of Walter of Guisborough,* ed. H. Rothwell (Camden ser., lxxxix, 1957).
Hist. Res.	*Historical Research*
HMC	*Historical Manuscripts Commission*
Jacob, *Studies*	E. F. Jacob, *Studies in the Period of Baronial Reform and Rebellion* (Oxford, 1925).
King's Works	Brown, R. A., Colvin, H. M. and Taylor, A. J., *The History of the King's Works: The Middle Ages* (2 vols., London, 1963).
Labarge, *Montfort*	Labarge, M. W., *Simon de Montfort* (London, 1962).
Lanercost	*Chronicon de Lanercost,* ed. J. Stevenson (Maitland Club, 1839).
Layettes	*Layettes du Trésor des Chartes,* ed. A. Teulet, H.-F. Delaborde and E. Berger (5 vols., Paris, 1863–1909).
Mon. Franc.	*Monumenta Franciscana,* ed. J. Brewer and R. Howlett (2 vols., Rolls ser., 1858–82).
Nichols, *Leicester*	Nichols, J., *The History and Antiquities of the County of Leicester* (4 vols. in 8, London, 1795–1815).

Oxenedes	*Chronica Johannis de Oxenedes*, ed. H. Ellis (Rolls ser., 1859).
Paris	*Matthaei Parisiensis, Monachi Sancti Albani, Chronica Majora*, ed. H. R. Luard (7 vols., Rolls ser., 1872–83).
Peerage	Cockayne, G. E., *Complete Peerage of England, Scotland, Ireland, Great Britain and the United Kingdom*, ed. V. Gibbs and others (12 vols. in 13, 1912–59).
Powicke, *King Henry III*	Powicke, F. M., *King Henry III and the Lord Edward* (2 vols., Oxford, 1947).
PR	*Patent Rolls of the Reign of Henry III* (H.M.S.O., 1901–03).
Recs. Bor. Leics.	*Records of the Borough of Leicester, 1103–1603*, ed. M. Bateson (3 vols., Cambridge, 1899–1905).
Rishanger, *De Bellis*	*The Chronicle of William de Rishanger of the Barons' Wars*, ed. J. O. Halliwell (Camden Soc., 1840).
RL	*Royal and Other Historical Letters Illustrative of the Reign of Henry III*, ed. W. W. Shirley (2 vols., Rolls ser., 1862–6).
Robert of Gloucs.	*The Metrical Chronicle of Robert of Gloucester*, ed. W. A. Wright (2 vols., Rolls ser., 1887).
Rot. Hund.	*Rotuli Hundredorum* (2 vols., Record Comm., 1812–18).
Rot. Litt. Claus.	*Rotuli Litterarum Clausarum*, ed. T. D. Hardy (2 vols., Record Comm., 1833–34).
Song of Lewes	*The Song of Lewes*, ed. C. L. Kingsford (Oxford, 1890).
Southern, *Grosseteste*	Southern, R. W., *Robert Grosseteste: The Growth of an English Mind in Medieval Europe* (Oxford, 1986).
TCE	*Thirteenth Century England: Proceedings of the Newcastle upon Tyne Conference*, ed. P. R. Coss and S. D. Lloyd (4 vols., 1986–92).

Treaty R.	*Treaty Rolls,* i, 1234–1325 (H.M.S.O., 1955).
TRHS	*Transactions of the Royal Historical Society*
VCH	*Victoria County History*
Wykes	*Chronicon vulgo dictum Chronicon Thomae Wykes, 1066–1288, Ann. Mon.,* iv.

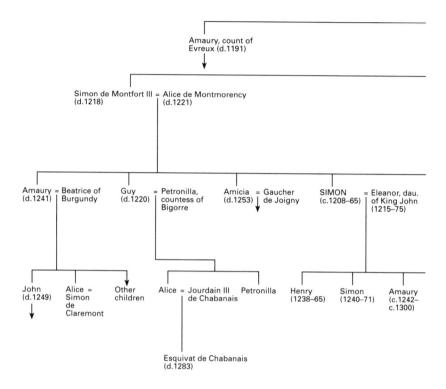

Fig. 1. Montfort's pedigree: uncles, brothers, sisters, cousins, nephews, nieces.

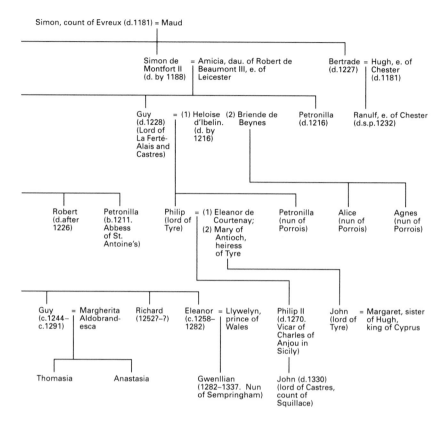

CHAPTER I

Going places, c. 1208–48

(A) FAMILY BACKGROUND AND EARLY LIFE

'I went to England and asked my lord the king to give me my father's inheritance.' So begins the remarkable fragment of autobiography in which Simon de Montfort set out his grievances against King Henry III.[1] Looking back from the early 1260s, he had, not surprisingly, a clear memory of what had happened some thirty years earlier to put him on the road first to advancement and then to a bitter separation from his former patron. For his purposes it was not necessary to go farther back into the past. Yet the departure for England in 1230 of this young French noble, equipped with little more than great expectations and his own abilities, was far from being the start of the story; for even more than is the case with most of our lives, Simon de Montfort's life took its direction from his inheritance and upbringing. 'Family background' is not just the biographer's conventional setting of the scene, but an essential part of the plot.

Montfort was born into one of the great aristocratic dynasties of northern France.[2] His father, another Simon, had his seat at Montfort l'Amaury, about thirty miles west of Paris and the same distance from the boundary which, until the loss of Normandy in 1204, had separated the Norman lands of the kings of England from the domain of the French Crown (Fig. 2). In the twelfth century the feudal rivalries of this frontier had been the chief influence on the affairs and fortunes of the Montforts. But latterly the more powerful and emotional force of the crusade had come to give another identity and a new sense of mission to

---

[1] Bémont, *Montfort* (1st edn), p. 333.

[2] The best account of the earlier Montforts will be found in *Peerage*, VII, pp. 708–17 ('The Ancestors of Simon de Montfort'), and of the elder Simon in ibid., pp. 537–40. For his exploits in the south, see especially J. Sumption, *The Albigensian Crusade* (London, 1978), pp. 100–98. All unreferenced statements in the following paragraphs derive from these works.

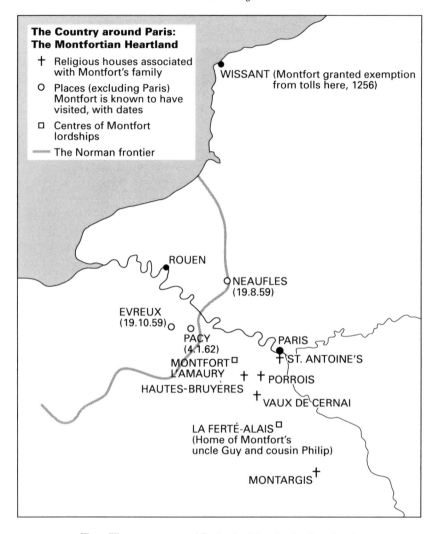

The Country around Paris:
The Montfortian Heartland

† Religious houses associated
  with Montfort's family

O Places (excluding Paris)
  Montfort is known to have
  visited, with dates

□ Centres of Montfort
  lordships

── The Norman frontier

WISSANT (Montfort granted exemption
         from tolls here, 1256)

ROUEN

O NEAUFLES
  (19.8.59)

EVREUX
(19.10.59) O   O
             PACY
            (4.1.62)
       MONTFORT □
       L'AMAURY   + + PORROIS
  HAUTES-BRUYÈRES   +
                         VAUX DE CERNAI

PARIS
† ST. ANTOINE'S

LA FERTÉ-ALAIS □
(Home of Montfort's
uncle Guy and cousin Philip)

MONTARGIS †

Fig.2. The country round Paris: the Montfortian heartland.

the family, and a different field of action to its leader. The elder Simon's
brother, Guy, had gone with Philip Augustus on the Third Crusade in
1191 and married in the Holy Land. Simon himself had taken part in
the Fourth Crusade, fought with distinction in the east, and returned to
play a much larger part in a different sort of holy war. From 1209 he led
the armies of northern France against the Albigensian heretics of the

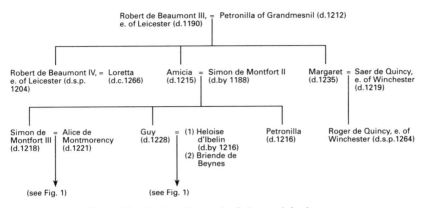

Fig. 3. Montfort's pedigree: the Leicester inheritance.

south. There he became famous as a general, built up a great territorial empire, and acquired a reputation for acquisitive brutality which was to dog his son's footsteps in that part of France more than thirty years later. After his death outside the walls of Toulouse in 1218 the advantage returned to the south, forcing his elder son, Amaury, to abandon his father's gains. In the end it was the French monarchy, under Louis VIII, which took over Simon's lands and which was the legatee of his successes.

It was the elder Simon's connections farther north which were eventually to bring our Simon on to the English political stage. The mother of Montfort senior had been Amicia, sister and coheiress of Robert de Beaumont, earl of Leicester, who had died childless in 1204. Through Amicia, the elder Simon inherited a claim to the earldom of Leicester (Fig. 3), which seems to have been recognised by the Crown after Simon had visited England in 1205 or 1206; and in 1207 the lands were divided between Amicia's heir and the second co-heiress, her sister Margaret, wife of Saer de Quincy, earl of Winchester. The partition of 1207 brought Simon only a notional advantage, for his status as a French subject gave him no hope of obtaining the lands; instead, King John committed them to a series of keepers. Yet despite his lack of a territorial footing in England, Simon was evidently a greatly respected figure on this side of the Channel. In 1210 it was plausibly rumoured that John's enemies among the barons had chosen him as king,[3] more probably in tribute to the prestige brought by his crusade

[3] *Ann. Dun.*, p. 331.

and his war against the Albigensians than to any impression made on his brief visit to England. But, of course, the rumour came to nothing. The elder Montfort remained little more than a phantom member of the English baronage, with a title and a reputation unmatched by the tangible assets of land or power.

Our Simon was probably born about 1208, the third of his father's four sons. It is the historian's misfortune, as it was Simon's, that he was a younger son, with no obvious prospects and therefore of no interest to the chroniclers. The bare fact of his existence is first revealed in a grant made by his mother, Alice de Montmorency, in 1217, to which he and his brothers assented;[4] but after that almost nothing certain is known about him until 1230, when he set out for England. It is likely that he spent his most impressionable years with the rest of his family in the south. His mother Alice was present with her husband through most of his campaigns. She was not far away when the eldest Simon won his two greatest victories, over Raymond, count of Toulouse, at Castelnaudary in 1211 and over King Peter of Aragon at Muret in 1213, and she was present, too, at the siege of Toulouse in 1217–18, where Simon was killed. Peter de Vaux-de-Cernai, the chronicler of the crusade, tells us that at Toulouse were not only Alice, but Amaury and Guy, her two elder sons, and the 'numerous children', sons and daughters, of both Simon and his brother, another Guy. The younger Simon's probable presence among these 'numerous children' is as near as we can get to conclusiveness concerning his whereabouts at any stage of his boyhood or youth.[5]

If Montfort did indeed grow up in his parents' household in the south he would have passed his formative years in an atmosphere of intense piety, crusading fervour and military excitement. Even by the standards of the day, the elder Montfort was an exceptionally devout man. With a genuine religious enthusiasm he combined ambition and rapacity, in a mixture which we find hard to comprehend but which, in a less heightened form, characterised the outlook of many members of the medieval nobility. His fervent orthodoxy made him both obedient to the pope and receptive to the new forces which were emerging to shape the future of the Church. When Pope Innocent III had prohibited an assault on the Christian city of Zara in Dalmatia on the crusade of

---

[4] BN MS. Clairambault 1188, f. 26v; Bémont, *Montfort* (2nd edn), p. 1, n. 2 (wrong foliation cited).
[5] *Petrum Vallium Sarnaii Monachi Hystoria Albigensis*, ed. P. Guébin and E. Lyon (3 vols., Société de l'Histoire de France, 1926–29), i, pp. 146, 185, 257; ii, 142, 294–5, 305.

1202, Simon, unlike the other crusaders, had withdrawn. He was, too, a close friend and benefactor of St Dominic, whose southern preaching tours, aimed at the conversion of heretics, formed a more pacific counterpoint to Simon's own campaigns. It was Dominic who had baptised Simon's daughter Petronilla in 1211 and who blessed the marriage of his son Amaury to Beatrice of Burgundy three years later.[6] In aligning himself with the crusade, the suppression of heresy, and the friars, he turned his family in a new direction, away from the feudal politics of northern France and towards a wider horizon promising both salvation and profit.

The outlook of the elder Montfort was precisely mirrored in that of his wife: a remarkable woman, whose qualities had been overlooked until Monique Zerner recently brought them into the light.[7] Alice de Montmorency was born into another of the great noble families of the north and was descended on her mother's side from an illegitimate daughter of Henry I of England. (Though our Simon de Montfort probably did not know it, and though the distinction must have been diluted among many, he was in fact the great-great-great-great-grandson of William the Conqueror.) His social equal, Alice was also her husband's partner not only in the Albigensian crusade but in his piety. In the years around 1200 both of them had come under the influence of Foulques de Neuilly, the evangelist and moral reformer, who had been as famous for his work among the prostitutes of Paris as for his inflammatory preaching of the crusade.[8] It was to the Parisian nunnery of St Antoine's, founded by Foulques and later attached to the Cistercians, that Alice consigned her ten-year-old daughter Petronilla, the child of the crusade, in 1221.[9] Like her husband, she was, too, a patron of the early Dominicans and a benefactor of the house founded by Dominic at Prouille for Albigensian women converts. But for the most part her devoutness, like her husband's, was more militant than monastic or quietist. She had participated in the counsels of the

[6] Fratris Gerardi de Fracheto, *Vitae Fratrum Ordinis Praedicatorum*, ed. B. M. Reichert, i (Monumenta Ordinis Fratrum Praedicatorum Historica, Rome and Stuttgart, 1897), p. 322; W. A. Hinnebusch, *The History of the Dominican Order*, i (New York, 1966), p. 31.

[7] M. Zerner, 'L'épouse de Simon de Montfort et la croisade albigeoise', *Femmes – Mariages – Lignages, XIIᵉ–XIVᵉ Siècles. Mélanges offerts à Georges Duby*, ed. J. Dufournet, A. Joris and P. Toubert (Brussels, 1992), pp. 449–70. All unreferenced statements in this paragraph derive from Zerner.

[8] For Foulques de Neuilly, see esp. J. W. Baldwin, *Masters, Princes and Merchants: The Social Views of Peter the Chanter and his Circle* (2 vols., Princeton, 1970), pp. 36–8, 136–7.

[9] For Petronilla and her brother Simon, see below, pp. 102, 174–5.

crusaders, recruited reinforcements for them in France, and taken the initiative in imprisoning the Jews of Toulouse in 1217. As much at home on the back of a horse as among bishops and friars, she personified the vigorous, aggressive and enterprising religion of the crusaders whom her husband led and which would later be found in the life of her third son.

The twelve-year caesura between the child Simon's appearance with his mother outside Toulouse and his re-emergence as a young man in 1230, on the eve of his first visit to England, forms the most frustrating gap in our knowledge of his career. After her husband's death Alice had returned to the family's estates near Paris.[10] When she too died in February 1221 Simon was probably taken under the wing of Amaury, now his only surviving elder brother after the death of his second brother, Guy, at the siege of Castelnaudary in 1220. In the decade of the 1220s he appears only twice in the sources, in May 1222 and February 1226, on both occasions confirming his brother's charters in northern France.[11] He must certainly have been on close terms with Amaury immediately prior to his departure for England, for the two of them had by then worked out a deal by which Simon was to claim Amaury's English inheritance. There is a strong probability that in the meantime he had been introduced to arms during the renewed Albigensian crusades of 1226–29, in which both Amaury and the brothers' uncle Guy took part.[12] One of the puzzling features of Montfort's English career is his early reputation for military ability, which rests on little in the way of known exploits;[13] and if he first saw action during these campaigns he would have had some grounding in the military expertise with which he was later credited, a little mysteriously, in England. Was he present, for example, at Louis VIII's siege of Avignon between June and September 1226, where the besiegers' use of artillery and boats puts one strongly in mind of the tactics used at his own siege of Rochester in April 1264?[14]

Almost complete though our ignorance is about the events of Montfort's early life, the influences on its future direction are fortunately

---

[10] Zerner, 'L'épouse', p. 465.

[11] *Necrologe de l'Abbaie de Notre Dame de Port-Roial des Champs* (Amsterdam, 1723), p. 101; A. Rhein, *La Seigneurie de Montfort en Iveline* (Versailles, 1910), pp. 206, 213.

[12] Sumption, *The Albigensian Crusade*, pp. 209–10, 216.

[13] Montfort's military reputation is considered more fully below, p. 109.

[14] For the siege of Avignon, see C. Petit-Dutaillis, *Étude sur la Vie et le Règne de Louis VIII (1187–1226)* (Paris, 1894), pp. 302–9, and for that of Rochester, Rishanger, *De Bellis*, pp. 25–6.

visible enough. Foremost, of course, was the example of his father, whose near-legendary status as a man of war and defender of the Church did much to fashion the attitudes of the next generation towards his son. It was in the mind of the taunting Henry III when, in 1252, he told Montfort to return to Gascony, 'where you will find war enough and bring back your merited reward, as your father did'. It was in the minds, too, of the French nobility when, in the following year, they offered Simon de Montfort the stewardship of France. If enemies and friends saw Montfort in his father's image, how much more is his own self-image likely to have been shaped by what he knew and had seen of his father? He may have known that the elder Simon had come close to acquiring the throne of England in 1210. He must have known how much his father had achieved as a man of courage, energy and military ability, who had been prepared to seize his chances. In 1258 he was to react with violent anger when one of his enemies told him that his father had been a traitor.[15] His own status, not only as a younger son, but as one who had lost both parents by the time he was about thirteen, made him independent at an early age and free of the leading strings with which medieval kings and nobles were apt to tie the hands of their offspring. Paternal example without paternal constraint, combined with the need to make his own way in the world, nourished the fierce ambition which was to be one of his most consistent principles of action. It was a principle complemented rather than countered by the sort of religion which he had learnt from his father and, as we can now conjecture with some certainty, from his mother too. The hard and combative faith, the friendship with ecclesiastics and holy men, the sense of mission which combined self-interest with what was almost a sense of divine vocation, were all features of his parents' lives which were to be replicated in his own. We do not need the facile arts of the psychohistorian to see that Simon de Montfort's career was set on course by the powerful and enduring exemplars and ideals of his childhood and youth.

(B) THE KING'S GREAT BOUNTY, 1230–38

Montfort's first footing in England came when he acquired the honor of Leicester in August 1231. He owed his establishment as an English magnate to his own initiative, to Henry III's generosity, and to the concurrence

---

[15] Paris, v, pp. 313, 372, 677; below, p. 154.

of two other men who, like Henry, had good cause to weigh up the likely consequences of his elevation: his elder brother Amaury, and his father's successor in the honor, Ranulf, earl of Chester. Through careful planning, adroit diplomacy and a firmly controlled ambitiousness, he was able to reconcile his own claims with the interests of these various benefactors in a way which was to be surprisingly harmonious.

His father's rights in the earldom of Leicester provided him with an opening. Amaury had already petitioned Henry for the elder Simon's inheritance, but his standing as constable of France, one of the great vassals of the French Crown, and Henry's life grant of the Leicester lands in 1227 to Ranulf of Chester, their custodian since 1215, both stood in the way of success. Rejected by Henry, Amaury had made over to Simon his rights in the Leicester lands, in return for Simon's inherited lands in France (unknown to us in location and extent) and in all probability for a large sum of money. Amaury had emerged from the Albigensian wars loaded with debt – Pope Gregory IX estimated that he and his father between them owed £10,000 – and he must have seen his younger brother's ambitions in England as a providential opportunity to be exploited. In 1234 he was claiming £1,500 paris, or about £500 sterling, from Simon. These transactions are likely to have taken place in 1229 or early in 1230, perhaps shortly after Simon's coming of age. They were to saddle him with a debt lasting for many years and with financial difficulties which came to characterise much of his career. Out of a colourable but hopeless claim Amaury had managed to extract a substantial benefit, to his brother's advantage too, but also at his expense.[16]

Armed with Amaury's commendations and letters of renunciation, Simon paid his first visit to England, probably in February 1230. That his initial negotiations with the king were conducted through one Amaury de Misternun, who was almost certainly his brother's knight, was another mark of Amaury's eagerness to forward his claim.[17] According to his own later recollections, written in 1262, when his bitterness with Henry ran deep, his request for his inheritance had been turned down. In fact the records show that before he returned to France

---

[16] Bémont, *Montfort* (1st edn), p. 333, (2nd edn), p. 4; *Layettes*, ii, Nos. 2088, 2366; L. W. V. Harcourt, *His Grace the Steward and Trial of Peers* (London, 1907), pp. 107–8; *PR, 1225–32*, p. 124; *Les Registres de Grégoire IX*, ed. L. Auray and others (4 vols., Paris, 1896–1955), iii, No. 3926. For the £ paris/sterling exchange rate, see P. Spufford, *Handbook of Medieval Exchange* (London, 1986), pp. 172, 209.

[17] *CR, 1227–31*, p. 316; Harcourt, *His Grace the Steward*, p. 113.

he had succeeded in obtaining all that Henry was yet able to offer: a grant of the reversion of the Leicester lands, to take effect when the estates had been released by Ranulf. That Ranulf was a witness to this grant suggests that some collusive settlement was in the offing. In the meantime his expectations were kept warm by a further royal grant to him, in April 1230, of 400 marks a year, in exchange for his service until the estate should fall in. But Simon could not wait. Late in 1230 or early in 1231 he approached Ranulf at his castle of St James de Beuvron in Brittany and persuaded him to agree to the early transfer of the inheritance. Some such arrangement, rather than the reversion of the estate which would naturally follow from Ranulf's death, had perhaps been in Henry's mind when he made his initial concession to Simon. In August 1231 the two men returned to England together and travelled to Painscastle on the Welsh marches, where Henry took Simon's homage for the Leicester lands.[18]

Montfort's quick and easy success in inducing all three of the men who had an interest in his English inheritance to stand aside owed much to his political deftness and perhaps to a persuasiveness of speech which can now only be imagined. His 'pleasant and courteous way of speaking' would later be recalled as one of his most admirable qualities.[19] All those whose goodwill he needed had reason to listen to him, for each had something to gain, or not much to lose, by his promotion. The financial inducement offered to Amaury has already been mentioned. A debt of £200 which Montfort owed to Ranulf of Chester at the time of the earl's death in 1232 suggests that he too may have been bought out, though here money did not tell the whole story. Ranulf was over sixty in 1231, an elderly man, lacking children and with only a life interest in the Leicester lands; so his generosity did no large disservice to himself and none at all to his heirs. It may have been stimulated by family ties – for Ranulf was the cousin of Montfort's father – and by a large-minded willingness to recognise the superiority of Montfort's claim. That at least was how Montfort saw things some thirty years later, at the time of his quarrel with the king.[20]

---

[18] Bémont, *Montfort* (1st edn), p. 333; *Layettes*, ii, No. 2151; Harcourt, *His Grace the Steward*, p. 110; *Foedera*, I, i, p. 206; *PR, 1225–32*, p. 325; *CR, 1227–31*, pp. 316, 543; R. Eales, 'Henry III and the End of the Norman Earldom of Chester', *TCE*, i, pp. 106–7.

[19] Rishanger, *De Bellis*, p. 6; below, pp. 350–1.

[20] Bémont, *Montfort* (1st edn), p. 333; *CPR, 1232–47*, p. 185; *RL*, ii, p. 379. For Ranulf's birth in 1170, see *Ann. Cestr.*, p. 25, and for his relationship with Montfort's father, *Peerage*, III, p. 167, VII, p. 709.

It was, however, disingenuous of Montfort then to make out that he owed his good fortune more to the complaisance of Amaury and Ranulf than to the 'great bounty' which Henry claimed to have showed him in accepting his homage.[21] Henry's friendly co-operation underpinned the whole series of transactions by which Montfort became an English magnate. His landlessness – or at least his holding no land from the king of France[22] – was an initial advantage, for it meant that there was no bar to his acceptance by Henry. But there are likely to have been other more positive reasons for his reception of this impecunious younger son. Henry's birth in 1207 meant that the two men were almost of an age. Montfort's intelligence and abilities, gifts difficult for us to assess in any medieval noble but suggested in this case by, for example, the later offers to him of high position in the Holy Land and France, may already have been evident.[23] Even if Montfort was a younger son, his father had been a famous man and Henry may have believed that his qualities ran in the blood. He came to England at a particularly opportune moment. In the early months of 1230 Henry was about to embark on the first foreign expedition of his reign, with the object of regaining Normandy from the French.[24] He needed manpower and service, both of which Montfort could provide. The king's grant of the 400-mark fee in April was made some three weeks before Henry sailed from Portsmouth and in return for service 'as much in England as elsewhere'; while Montfort's presence later in the campaign with Ranulf of Chester in Brittany suggests that he had joined Henry's forces in France. Though the army was diverted south to Poitou and achieved nothing, its recruiting may have given Montfort his opening. Henry's favours for foreigners were handed out less capriciously than has sometimes been thought, and it is likely that he saw in Montfort both a useful volunteer and a man whose family connections on the borders of Normandy might possibly be turned to advantage.

Montfort's induction into English affairs was not entirely troublefree, for he found himself and his inheritance immediately caught up in factional rivalries which had originated in Henry's minority and which continued to divide his court in the early 1230s. In those rivalries

[21] Bémont, *Montfort* (1st edn), p. 333.
[22] *Layettes*, ii, no. 2088; Harcourt, *His Grace the Steward*, p. 108.
[23] Below, pp. 30, 76, 121.
[24] For Henry's objectives, see Paris, iii, p. 190, and *Robert of Gloucs.*, ii. p. 720.

Montfort's connections and new acquisitions forced him to take sides.[25]
When he arrived in England in August 1231 the dominant royal
minister was Hubert de Burgh, earl of Kent and justiciar, whose
enterprise in the civil war of 1215–17 and loyal service throughout the
minority had helped to preserve Henry's kingdom. Hubert's modest
origins, influence with the king, and vigorous defence of royal rights had
made him many enemies. Chief among these were Ranulf of Chester,
Montfort's patron, and Peter des Roches, King John's former henchman, Hubert's predecessor as justiciar, and bishop of Winchester. After
being forced to the sidelines of the court in 1223–24, Peter had left on
crusade in 1227, a defeated man. But in July 1231 he returned, joining
Henry at Painscastle only a few days before the arrival of Montfort and
Ranulf. What followed was a long duel for power between Hubert de
Burgh and Peter des Roches, in the course of which Montfort's interests
were drawn into conflict with those of the justiciar.

The story has been well told by Dr Nicholas Vincent. It went back
to John's reign, when one of the sub-tenants of the honor of Leicester
had defected to the French, allowing the Crown to claim his two
Leicestershire estates of Illston on the Hill and Thurnby as *terra
Normannorum*, escheats at the king's disposal until their original holder
returned to his former allegiance. By 1228 these lands were held by John
de Narford, cousin of Hubert de Burgh and son of Robert de Narford,
former governor of Dover castle under the justiciar. Dying in 1231,
John was buried at the Augustinian priory of Creake in Norfolk, with
which his family had been closely associated, and in July 1231 the king
granted to the canons of Creake his two Leicestershire estates, almost
certainly at the instigation of Hubert. In doing so Henry took advantage
of the absence in France of Ranulf of Chester, then lord of Leicester,
who in 1227 had been granted the right to all escheats within the
honor.[26] The king's new grant plainly overrode the earl's rights and was
made at his expense. Nevertheless on 25 August 1231, about a fortnight
after Montfort had done homage for Leicester, Henry confirmed by
charter his earlier grant to Creake, thus depriving the new lord in
perpetuity, so it seemed, of what had once constituted a sub-tenancy
within his honor. His pretext appears to have been that the privilege of

[25] D. Carpenter, 'The Fall of Hubert de Burgh', *Journal of British Studies*, 19 (1980), pp. 1–17, is the
best account of these factional conflicts.

[26] *A Cartulary of Creake Abbey*, ed. A. L. Bedingfield (Norfolk Rec. Soc., xxxv, 1966), pp. xv, 1–2; *PR,
1225–32*, p. 124; N. C. Vincent, 'Simon de Montfort's First Quarrel with King Henry III', *TCE*,
iv, p. 4.

1227 had been granted to Ranulf, then the holder of the honor, and did not extend to Montfort, to whom the honor had now come. Ranulf's angry departure from Painscastle in mid August, recorded in the Chester annals, was probably occasioned by his knowledge of this impending grant, made contrary to his rights and to those of his protégé, and in favour of an institution under the patronage of his enemy, Hubert de Burgh.[27]

After leaving Painscastle, Ranulf journeyed north to Chester, probably taking Montfort with him, but in the following month he was persuaded to return to court. On 22 September, shortly after his return, Henry ordered that Montfort be given 'such seisin [of his lands] as his father had on the day when he left England and as King John had after Simon's departure'. He thereby showed that he had changed his mind, that he recognised the irregularity of his earlier grants of Illston and Thurnby, and that he now confirmed them to Montfort (though not in so many words). By 15 October, however, he had changed his mind again, ordering the sheriff of Leicestershire to give seisin of the disputed lands to the canons of Creake and explicitly setting aside his earlier promise of 1227 not to grant away lands escheated to the Crown as *terra Normannorum*. On this occasion he stated openly that the concession made to Ranulf was made to him alone and not to Montfort.[28]

It looks as if Henry was being pulled in different directions by the contending claims of Ranulf of Chester and Hubert de Burgh. Here the tedious dispute over Illston and Thurnby reflected both the general division among Henry's entourage at this time and the king's own vacillations. Suggestible and irresolute, he was not yet his own man. But by the winter of 1231–32 the balance of power at court was moving in favour of the justiciar's enemies, who were able to exploit his supposed responsibility for the fiasco of Henry's Normandy expedition, the failure of his Welsh policy, and the financial crisis which culminated in Hubert's inability to secure a tax grant from the great council in March 1232. Despite a long rearguard action, the justiciar was finally dismissed from court at the end of July.[29] These were the circumstances in which Montfort's claims were finally vindicated. On 27 May 1232 he secured a third confirmation of his rights to his father's lands. The king's

---

[27] *CChr, 1226–57*, p. 139; *CR, 1227–31*, pp. 550, 570; *Ann. Cestr.*, pp. 56–9; Vincent, 'Simon de Montfort's First Quarrel', p. 5. For an alternative explanation of Ranulf's departure from court, see Eales, 'The End of the Norman Earldom', pp. 107–8.

[28] *CR, 1227–31*, pp. 560, 570; Vincent, 'Simon de Montfort's First Quarrel', pp. 5–6.

[29] Carpenter, 'The Fall of Hubert de Burgh', pp. 6–7.

statement, in his letters patent, that these lands pertained to Amaury by hereditary right and that the confirmation had been made at Amaury's request, was perhaps intended to make Montfort unshakeably secure in his new holdings. In July he was given free disposal of the *terra Normannorum* pertaining to his lands: the privilege conceded to Ranulf in 1227, now, of course, giving Montfort undisputed control of Illston and Thurnby. The story came to an end in early July 1232, just prior to Hubert's fall, when Montfort was with the court in Norfolk. There, in a charter witnessed by all the most prominent of Henry's *curiales*, including Peter des Roches and Hubert de Burgh, he confirmed the canons of Creake in their possession of the two Leicestershire estates.[30] Now that his own rights had been so conclusively confirmed he was not averse to appearing as their benefactor: a role which Hubert himself, to judge by his presence as a witness, may have persuaded him to take on.

The political affiliations and sympathies which were to guide Montfort's activities during his early years in England were sharpened and clarified by this apparently trivial quarrel. That is the reason for treating it at greater length than its intrinsic importance might seem to warrant. Montfort had been adventitiously drawn into the dispute by his association with Ranulf of Chester, his benefactor and Hubert's antagonist. His relationship with Ranulf remained close. He witnessed the earl's foundation charter for the borough of Salford, probably in August or September 1231, as well as a second charter made in September or October 1232, very shortly before Ranulf's death. In both charters he was placed high among the list of witnesses, above such prominent barons and comital followers as William de Ferrers, William de Cantilupe and Payn Chaworth.[31] His position as Ranulf's favoured protégé, and his struggle for his Leicestershire escheats, set him against Hubert and inclined him towards Peter des Roches, in a court which provided the forum for the manoeuvrings of the two rival factions. In the highhanded and unpopular regime of des Roches and his nephew Peter des Rivaux which emerged after Hubert's disgrace in July 1232 and Ranulf's death in October, he was nothing like a central figure; but there is enough evidence to suggest that he was on easy terms with its leaders. He was with the court at Norwich on 28 June 1232, when a series of grants was made to des Rivaux; he was present too at the Christmas court in December 1232 when, according to Roger of

---

[30] *PR, 1225–32*, pp. 476, 481; Vincent, 'Simon de Montfort's First Quarrel', pp. 7–8, 11.
[31] *Chs. of the Earls of Chester*, Nos. 310, 435.

Wendover, Henry dismissed many native courtiers and replaced them with the alien followers of Peter des Roches; and in April of the following year he was entertained, in company with the count of Brittany, on Peter's episcopal manor of Farnham.[32] We catch an equally informal glimpse of his presence at the centre of affairs in his observing the work of the central court of the Bench in a case concerning Evesham abbey and supposedly making an implausibly prescient forecast of his own death in the abbey's neighbourhood more than thirty years later. This may have been in Michaelmas term 1232.[33]

But, fortunately for him, he was as yet too much the bystander to be deeply implicated in the arbitrary and autocratic government which provoked Richard Marshal's revolt against the curialists and which eventually brought down the bishop of Winchester in May 1234, after the Marshal's death in Ireland. He came closest to being drawn into these *émeutes* around Christmas 1233, when Richard Siward, the Marshal's ally, sacked and burnt Stephen of Segrave's chief major of Seagrave, only eight miles north of Leicester. Justiciar from 1232 to 1234, Segrave had been a tenant and close friend of Ranulf of Chester, who had almost certainly had a hand in his appointment; and his leading judicial position in a regime notorious for its disregard for justice made him an obvious target for attack. But, like other former tenants of Ranulf, Segrave was also a friend of Montfort, into whose affinity he probably passed after Ranulf's death and whose charters he sometimes witnessed in the 1230s.[34] Their association created another link between Montfort and the government of Peter des Roches. Even so, to judge by its neglect in the chronicles, the link was neither particularly strong nor widely recognised. Young, unfamiliar with England and the English language,[35] relatively inexperienced and relatively poor, Montfort's inconspicuous place on the regime's periphery allowed him to swim free from its wreckage and to begin a more rapid ascent to power after its demise.

For his first few years in England Montfort appears to have been as

---

[32] c.53/26, m. 5; c.53/27, m. 13; Paris, iii, p. 240; Vincent, 'Simon de Montfort's First Quarrel', pp. 8–9.

[33] *Lanercost*, p. 77. The only recorded case before the Bench concerning Evesham in this period comes in Michaelmas term 1232: *CRR*, xiv, *1230–32*, No. 2304.

[34] Paris, iii, p. 264; BL MS. Harley 4714, ff. 44v–45; *Recs. Bor. Leics.*, i, pp. 39–40; *CChR, 1226–57*, p. 241; Eales, 'The End of the Norman Earldom of Chester', pp. 104–5. For the general background to these events, see Powicke, *King Henry III*, pp. 122–43. For Montfort and the Segraves, below, pp. 16, 63, 71.

[35] *Lanercost*, p. 77.

concerned to establish his lordship over his new lands as to climb higher in a volatile court which was dangerously alienated from magnate opinion. After witnessing two royal charters in 1232, he witnessed none in 1233 or 1234, and throughout this period Leicester was probably the centre of his interests. Before he was formally granted the earldom in 1239, it was as 'lord of Leicester' (*dominus de Leicestr'*), the *caput* of his honor, that he spoke in his early charters. His activities there revealed some of the aspects of his character which were to become prominent later in his career: religious zealotry, an acquisitive eye for his own advantage, and a more conciliatory awareness of the need for friends and supporters. What was perhaps the earliest of his English *acta*, to be dated between August 1231 and October 1232, showed all these traits. It announced the expulsion of the Jews from Leicester (Plate 1).[36] Although this measure was presented as one for the salvation of Montfort's soul and for the relief of the burgesses from Jewish usury, it could be seen too as an extension of his family's earlier crusading anti-Semitism in the south of France. It may also have been influenced by Capetian directives against the Jews, which, during des Roches's ministry, were beginning to be imitated in England. But the approval of Robert Grosseteste, then archdeacon of Leicester, for the Jews' expulsion should warn us against regarding this action merely as a deplorable piece of fanatical intolerance. Overbearing though it may seem, it was not impossible to justify, either in terms of the threat which the Jews offered to the faith or of traditional condemnations of usury.[37] From Montfort's point of view, it was also an act of lordship and patronage, a favour from the new ruler of Leicester to his people.

In the event the Jews moved no further than the eastern suburbs of the town, held not by Montfort but by Margaret, countess of Winchester, Montfort's great-aunt and the coheiress of the original earldom of Leicester at the time of its partition in 1207. Their reception by Margaret may have partly underlain Montfort's attempts, dating from the earliest days of his lordship, to take over some of her lands,

[36] The charter is printed in Nichols, *Leicester*, 1, i, appendix, p. 38; cf. *Recs. Bor. Leics*, iii, p. 457. Grosseteste, writing as archdeacon of Leicester, approved of the action (*Grosseteste Epistolae*, p. 33), and since he had left office by 1 November 1232 (*Fasti Lincoln*, p. 34), the expulsion must have taken place by then.

[37] C. Roth, *A History of the Jews in England* (3rd edn, Oxford, 1974), pp. 57–8; R. W. Southern, *Robert Grosseteste: The Growth of an English Mind in Medieval Europe* (Oxford, 1986), pp. 244–9; Zerner, 'L'épouse', pp. 461–2 (for the actions of Montfort's mother against the Jews of Toulouse); N. C. Vincent, 'Jews, Poitevins and the Bishop of Winchester, 1231–34', *Christianity and Judaism*, ed. D. Wood (Studies in Church History, Vol. 29, Oxford, 1992), pp. 129–30.

including those in the Leicester suburbs. In January 1232 the sheriff of the county had to be told that the king's orders for Montfort's instatement in his father's lands gave him no cause to disseise Margaret of other lands which were rightfully hers under the terms of the partition.[38] This proved to be a long-running dispute. Brought up in the Leicester eyre of June 1232, it was summoned before the Bench at Westminster and then taken before the king himself, when it disappears from view in Michaelmas term 1232, apparently unsettled.[39] The rights and wrongs of the case cannot now be decided. But its summoning *coram rege* may suggest, not just the usual royal response to a quarrel between two aristocratic families, but the possibility of Henry's favour for his new man.

The only other of Montfort's early recorded acts shows him stepping more smoothly into the place formerly occupied by Ranulf of Chester. In 1231 or 1232 he granted the Leicestershire village of Kegworth to Gilbert of Segrave, son of Stephen of Segrave, and a loyal *curialis*. Like his father, Gilbert had also been prominent in Ranulf's service. Montfort's grant of Kegworth to him must be seen as a bid for the allegiance of a family closely attached to his predecessor.[40] If the expulsion of the Jews brought a disruptive intemperance into the affairs of the honor, the grant to Segrave marked a more conventional attempt to maintain traditions, ensure continuity, and put down roots.

Sustaining though they were, Montfort's activities in his new lands hardly gave him complete security. As yet he held only the honor of Leicester, half the estate of his Beaumont predecessors prior to the partition of 1207, and worth some £500 a year.[41] This was a substantial sum, but not a fortune. Against it had to be set the large debts already mentioned: about £500 owed to his brother Amaury and £200 to Ranulf of Chester (later to his executors), both probably arising from the need to buy out prior claims to his inheritance. The sense of financial strain which is one of the main themes of his career was there right from the start. Even his title remained uncertain. He was not yet earl of Leicester, and his brother had reserved the right to the reversion of the Leicester lands should Simon die without heirs.[42]

---

[38] *CR, 1231–34*, pp. 18–19; *Grosseteste Epistolae*, pp. 33–4.

[39] *CR, 1231–34*, pp. 79, 122; *CRR*, xiv, *1230–32*, No. 1974.

[40] Gloucestershire County Record Office, D.225/T.7 (Denison Jones deeds); BL MS. Egerton 3789, f. 101r; Nichols, *Leicester*, I, ii, p. 850. It is W. Dugdale, *The Baronage of England* (2 vols., London, 1675–6), i, p. 673, who dates this grant to 15 Henry III, 1231–32.

[41] Below, pp. 47–9.

[42] *Layettes*, ii, Nos. 2151, 2190.

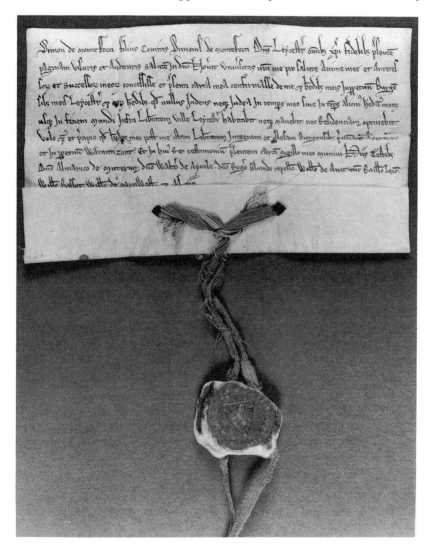

Plate 1. Montfort's charter expelling the Jews from Leicester, 1231–1232.

A limited endowment, debt, and the residual claims of Amaury, all meant that Montfort's position in England was to a degree precarious in these early years. Marriage, with the prospects of wealth and an heir, would greatly improve it, and Montfort now made two bids for wealthy women. Probably about 1235 he was pursuing Mahaut, countess of

Boulogne, the widow of Philip Augustus's son. Then, in 1236 or 1237, he set his sights on Joanna, widow of Ferrand of Portugal, and countess of Flanders in her own right. Both marriages were blocked by Blanche of Castile, queen mother and regent of France until 1234, who was unwilling to let such great fiefs pass into the hands of one who had done homage to Henry III; but not before Montfort's courting of Joanna, at least, had made sufficient progress for her to be driven, in April 1236, to swear before Louis IX and his council that she had neither married nor would marry him.[43] The episode shows Montfort aiming characteristically high, for a marriage with Joanna would have given him Flanders and made him into a European prince. But it also reveals something of the ambiguous standing which would shadow the rest of his career. An Englishman to the French, he was not necessarily regarded in the same way in England.

From 1234 Montfort's more frequent appearances in the records begin to reflect a rise to prominence at court which would culminate in a marriage more splendid than either of those he had already attempted. In October 1234 he was present when the great council of barons and royal advisers inaugurated a long and famous debate as to whether bastards legitimised by the subsequent marriage of their parents could succeed to estates. At this council meeting, the first he is known to have attended, he was listed immediately after the earls and before the other barons; and when he next witnessed a charter in January 1235 he was given the same precedence.[44] He was clearly a coming man.

But it was from the time of Henry's marriage to Eleanor of Provence in January 1236 that Montfort consolidated his position in a regime which came to be almost as detested as the earlier government of Peter des Roches.[45] A distrusted court, a financial crisis and constitutional grievances combined, as they would do again in the mid 1250s, to create a two-year period of intermittent political tension. The marriage had brought to England the queen's uncle, William of Savoy, bishop-elect of Valence, who rapidly became a leading councillor – perhaps *the* leading councillor[46] – of the king. Shortly afterwards an

---

[43] *Layettes*, ii, No. 2492; Bémont, *Montfort* (2nd edn), pp. 53–4. For the position of Joanna, see E. L. Cox, *The Eagles of Savoy* (Princeton, 1974), p. 56.

[44] *CRR*, xv, *1233–37*, No. 1178; c.53/28, m. 17.

[45] For this paragraph, see esp. R. C. Stacey, *Politics, Policy and Finance under Henry III, 1216–45* (Oxford, 1987), pp. 92–118.

[46] *Ann. Dun.*, pp. 145–6.

unsuccessful attempt was made to deprive Ralph Neville of the custody of the seal, to which he had been appointed by 'common counsel' during Henry's minority.[47] These conciliar manoeuvres were soon overshadowed by Henry's financial problems and the unpopular solutions which they necessitated. The marriage of his sister Isabella to the Emperor Frederick II in 1235 had called for an enormous dower payment of £20,000. Despite the grant of an aid on knights' fees, Henry could not find the money without expedients which seemed arbitrary, oppressive, and contrary to Magna Carta. Lands alienated by royal charter from the royal demesne were resumed, the forests exploited more effectively, lapsed customary payments revived and stringently enforced. These measures threatened security of tenure but proved financially inadequate, and in January 1237 Henry had to ask his magnates in parliament for a levy of a thirtieth on movables. This he gained, but only at the price of confirming Magna Carta, revoking the most intolerable of his fiscal innovations, and adding three baronial nominees to his council.

Montfort was dangerously near to the centre of Henry's unpopular government at this time. Between May 1236 and December 1237 he and John de Lacy, earl of Lincoln, were second only to William of Savoy in the number of royal charters that they witnessed, and after William temporarily left the court in February 1237 the two rose still higher in Henry's favour. In October 1236 Montfort had even gone so far as to issue a charter in his own name as 'earl of Leicester' for the first time: a large presumption on the king's goodwill, since he had not yet received the title.[48] He was a frequent attestor of the king's writs and a recipient of his gifts, giving good service in exchange.[49] In the early months of 1237 he and William of Savoy were nominated to negotiate with the Scots. Though the mission was cancelled, both men were present in the large and splendid gathering at York in September 1237 when Henry and Alexander II of Scotland met to conclude an Anglo-Scottish peace. It was probably during this gathering that Henry despatched the two of them to inspect the northern castles at Bamburgh and Newcastle; and the subsequent implementation of their recommendations for

[47] Compare Stacey, *Politics, Policy*, p. 100, with D. A. Carpenter, 'Chancellor Ralph de Neville and Plans of Baronial Reform, 1215–58', *TCE*, ii, p. 70.

[48] *CRR*, xv, *1233–37*, p. xxxv, n. 5; *CChR*, *1226–57*, p. 230; Stacey, *Politics, Policy*, p. 115; Vincent, 'Simon de Montfort's First Quarrel', p. 9.

[49] *CPR*, *1232–47*, pp. 155, 175–6; *CR*, *1234–37*, pp. 292, 318–19, 324, 452, 562–3; *CR*, *1237–42*, pp. 3, 10, 11; *CLR*, *1226–40*, p. 287; *CChR*, *1226–57*, pp. 216, 230.

refortification and repairs was perhaps a testimony to the store set by
Montfort's military advice in particular.[50] Meanwhile, in June, Henry
had been unwilling to allow peace negotiations with the Welsh to go
forward because he could not secure the presence of his brother Richard
of Cornwall, William of Savoy, Montfort and other *fideles*.[51] In all this we
can sense the degree to which Henry was coming to rely on Montfort
and to value the practical sagacity, in counsel, diplomacy and warfare,
which was always to mark him out among the nobility.

There is not much doubt about the hostility which his position at
court attracted. Together with John de Lacy and Brother Geoffrey the
Templar, Henry's almoner, Montfort was denounced by Paris as one of
Henry's 'infamous' and 'suspect' councillors, responsible for the king's
unwelcome decision to bring in a papal legate, Cardinal Otto, in 1237.[52]
He may have been additionally tainted by his peripheral association
with the earlier and now discredited government of Peter des Roches.
Paris again tells us that in May or June 1236 two key members of that
government, Peter des Rivaux and Stephen of Segrave, were restored
to favour and that shortly afterwards Richard Siward was arrested and
briefly imprisoned at the instigation of Montfort and des Rivaux. The
story is largely corroborated by the Dunstable annals. It is tempting
to see this move as a vengeful splutter by a remnant of the former
curialists against one who had been active in destroying their property,
and especially Segrave's property, in the rebellion of 1233–34. Since
Segrave was one of Ranulf of Chester's executors, to whom Montfort
owed £200 at this time, Montfort may have had a special reason for
acting on behalf of his *familiaris*, the former justiciar. A reconciliation
followed, under the legate's auspices, in 1237; but the episode, brief
though it was, had shown how thoroughly Montfort was now caught up
in the politics of the court.[53] Others too may have had their private
grievances against him. At the king's marriage in 1236, for example,
Roger Bigod, earl of Norfolk, had claimed the rights of the steward of
England, traditionally attached to the Leicester inheritance and
exercised at the marriage by Montfort.[54] Compromised by his past, he
probably also shouldered a full load of the grudges borne by any rising
man.

---

[50] *CPR, 1232–47*, p. 177; *Foedera*, I, i, pp. 233–4; *CLR, 1267–72*, p. 289; *King's Works*, ii, pp. 556, 746.
[51] *CR, 1234–37*, p. 536.
[52] Paris, iii, pp. 411–12, 418.
[53] Paris, iii, pp. 264, 369, 403–4; *Ann. Dun.*, p. 144; *CPR, 1232–47*, p. 185.
[54] Harcourt, *His Grace the Steward*, pp. 82–3.

In these years Montfort was thus as close as anyone to Henry. Owing his establishment in England largely to the king's support, he had survived two palace revolutions, and the ousting first of Hubert de Burgh and then of Peter des Roches, to emerge by 1237 as a leading figure, perhaps *the* leading figure, at Henry's court. His rise was not due to royal favour alone, sometimes capriciously given and subject to conflicting pressures. If he was fortunate to stand only on the edge of politics during the years of greatest danger between 1230 and 1234, he had also got what he could from association with important men – Ranulf of Chester, Stephen of Segrave – without ever being fatally drawn into their quarrels. Beyond his own survival and promotion, no underlying principles can be detected in his actions, and certainly not the principled opposition to arbitrary government, in defence of the spirit of Magna Carta, which had characterised Richard Marshal's public stance. He was not yet more than a particularly skilful climber, whose considerable talents allowed him to climb high. There was nothing to foreshadow the future defender of the Provisions of Oxford.

(c) MARRIAGE, 1238–39

Even Montfort's place at court hardly qualified him for the prize which he received in January 1238: marriage to Eleanor, the king's sister. This event, which would change Montfort's position entirely, was as extra-ordinary in the manner of its realisation as in its conception. It took place virtually in secret (Paris calls it a 'matrimonium clandestinum'), 'in the little chapel in the corner of the king's chamber' at Westminster; the celebrant was no great prelate but one of the king's chaplains; the magnates were not consulted about it; even Richard of Cornwall, Eleanor's brother and Henry's, did not know of its happening. The immediate reaction came with a flash revolt, led by Richard and by Gilbert Marshal, earl of Pembroke, and over by the end of February. Into this rising were swept other grievances – against the parallel marriage of John de Lacy's daughter to the boy Richard de Clare, earl of Gloucester, against the papal legate, against aliens at court – but the overriding issue was the clandestine marriage of the king's sister.[55]

---

[55] Paris, iii, pp. 470–1, 475–6. The privacy of the venue for the marriage is well brought out in *King's Works*, i, pp. 497–8. For the revolt, see N. Denholm-Young, *Richard of Cornwall* (Oxford, 1947), pp. 497–8, and Stacey, *Politics, Policy*, pp. 118–24. My views on Montfort's marriage owe a great deal to the most helpful comments of Margaret Howell.

It is easy to see why this should have been so. Eleanor was the most valuable asset at the king's disposal. Aged about twenty-three in 1238, she had been previously married to William Marshal, earl of Pembroke, elder brother of Richard and Gilbert, who had died in 1231. This earlier marriage had been preceded by intense discussion. It had been pointed out to Henry that he had 'no greater treasure' than his sisters' marriages, which could be used 'so that we might have great alliances in foreign parts'; and it was the advantage to be gained from linking the royal family with the great political and landed authority of the Marshal, in England, Wales and Ireland, which had led to the match. A similar debate, occupying the great council for three days, had preceded the marriage of Henry's other sister, Isabella, to the Emperor in 1235.[56] Eleanor's marriage was a blatant breach of these conventions. Not only that, it was also ecclesiastically irregular, since Eleanor had taken a vow of chastity, in the presence of Archbishop Edmund of Canterbury, after her first husband's death.[57] An important piece of state business, and a morally questionable one in which the Church also had an interest, had been disposed of by Henry as no more than a family matter. The king's sister, whose marriage could have been a strong card in Henry's dealings with other powers, had been disparaged by marriage to one who was a foreigner by origin, who owed all that he had in England to royal favour, and who seemingly had nothing to offer in exchange for his prize except dubious counsel. Montfort's position at court is likely to have associated him with financial and administrative measures which had seemed to place Magna Carta in danger; just as, in a parallel way, the marriage itself ran counter to the traditions of consultation and consent which were ultimately grounded on the Charter. The marriage exemplified all Henry's most characteristic shortcomings: his failure to consult the magnates on important political matters, his patronage of aliens, his promotion of family interests above those of the kingdom, his lack of judgement in lightly entering into the most far-reaching commitments. It was an unforeseeable irony that the recurrence of these failings in the 1250s would help to initiate a reform movement led, among others, by Simon de Montfort.

That indictment reflects the viewpoint of the king's baronial opponents. It was a just one; but except in the banal terms of royal

---

[56] *Dipl. Docs.*, i, No. 140; *RL*, i, pp. 244–6, 459–60; Paris, iii, pp. 318–19; Powicke, *King Henry III*, pp. 157–8.

[57] Paris, v, p. 235; *Lanercost*, p. 39.

favour for a favoured *curialis* it does little to explain what Henry was about when he consented to so disadvantageous a match. To discover some possible answers we have to move forward, to the king's violent denunciation of Montfort which came nineteen months later in August 1239. This *bouleversement* broke quite without warning, for in the marriage's aftermath the position of Montfort at court had seemed impregnable. In March 1238 he had left for Rome to seek papal confirmation of the marriage and no doubt to allow domestic opposition to it to subside. Contrary to Paris's report that the king had turned against him, Henry in fact wrote to the pope and cardinals to ask them to support him in his mission.[58] Clearly Montfort had not lost Henry's friendship. Indeed, his return to England in October, with his mission accomplished, initiated a period of dominance at court of the kind which he had not quite enjoyed before and would never enjoy again. Henry welcomed him back and was present at Kenilworth in November when Eleanor's first son was baptised. It was another mark of an exceptionally close relationship that the baby was named Henry,[59] and not Simon or Amaury or Guy, names which had run monotonously in the Montfort family for generations. In the following February Montfort was at last given the earldom of Leicester, all claim to which was formally relinquished by his elder brother Amaury on a visit to England in April.[60] His political influence matched the favour that he enjoyed. According to one chronicler, he was the king's leading councillor from the time of his return, no longer overshadowed by William of Savoy, who had left England for good in May 1238. Between January and July 1239 he witnessed more royal charters than anyone else: some twenty-five compared with eleven for the earl of Hereford and ten for Lincoln, the two other earls most frequently about the court. In July 1239 he was one of three earls present at the baptism of Henry's firstborn son Edward,[61] who was to bring him down at Evesham twenty-six years later.

---

[58] Paris, iii, pp. 479–80; *CPR, 1232–47*, p. 214.

[59] Paris, iii, pp. 478, 518; *CPL*, i, p. 172; Stacey, *Politics, Policy*, p. 124, n. 168. There does not seem to be any contemporary warrant for the story that Henry acted as the baby's godfather, as most of the secondary authorities state.

[60] Paris, iii, p. 524; *Layettes*, ii, No. 2789; Harcourt, *His Grace the Steward*, pp. 112–14. *Peerage*, VII, p. 545, asserts that Paris misdates Montfort's investiture to 2 February, on the grounds that it could not have taken place until Amaury had surrendered his rights in April. But the witness-lists on the charter roll (c.53/32, m. 6) show that Montfort began to witness as earl of Leicester after 2 February.

[61] *Flores Hist.*, ii, p. 229; c.53/32, mm. 2–7; Paris, iii, pp. 539–40.

For the moment Montfort was thus supreme. He had married the king's sister, faced down baronial opposition and gained an earldom. But there was a hidden contrast between his public pre-eminence and the private insecurity which resulted from his growing financial difficulties, the immediate cause of his breach with the king. Not for the last time, Montfort's financial affairs were almost unfathomably complicated, and we cannot see the whole picture; but we can make out enough to discern his weaknesses. We have already noted that he owed £200 to the executors of Ranulf of Chester. This debt the executors had made over to Peter of Dreux, count of Brittany, in June 1237, in order to settle an earlier debt owed by Ranulf to Peter. Probably by September 1237 the £200 had become part of a much larger debt of 2,800 marks (£1,866) owed by Montfort to Peter. The reasons for Peter's loan are unclear, but it is possible that he had lent money in Brittany in 1230–31 to enable Montfort to meet his obligations to Amaury. In 1238 Peter was pressing for payment, since his impending departure on crusade meant that he needed all the money he could lay hands on; and Montfort, whose failure to pay Peter was jeopardising the departure of a *crucesignatus*, was threatened with excommunication by the pope. In May 1239, when the debt was still unpaid, the excommunication was put in hand by the bishop of Soissons, though it is not known whether it yet took effect.[62]

At this stage another party became involved: Thomas of Savoy, the queen's uncle. By the late summer of 1239 Montfort owed Thomas 2,000 marks, a claim which Thomas was pursuing in the Roman curia. It seems almost certain, though impossible to prove, that this sum constituted the bulk of the 2,800 marks formerly owed by Montfort to Peter of Dreux and now transferred by Peter to Thomas, so that Thomas stood in the place of Peter as Montfort's creditor. Did Thomas, scenting a profit, perhaps offer Peter a cash settlement at a discount to facilitate his departure on crusade in July 1239? This we cannot tell; but it is certain that the whole debt was not transferred to Thomas, since in December 1239 Peter too had a plea in the curia against Montfort, presumably for the recovery of the amount still owing. The substantial sum of £330 remained outstanding until Montfort settled with Peter's executors in 1258. Montfort next made what seems to have been an unprincipled misjudgement. Driven presumably by financial

[62] *CPR, 1232–47*, p. 185; *RL*, ii, p. 379; Bémont, *Montfort* (1st edn), pp. 263–4; Labarge, *Montfort*, p. 54.

desperation, he named Henry as security for the payment of the money which he now owed to Thomas. He acted without the king's knowledge and, according to Henry's later accusation, 'by false witness', implying that he had told Thomas that Henry had consented to the arrangement. Thomas's belief that Henry stood behind Montfort may help to explain why he had accepted the debt in the first place. In August 1239 he paid a short visit to England, probably with the intention of collecting his money, and it must have been during this visit that Henry discovered that his name had been taken in vain.[63]

Henry had recently treated Montfort with great generosity, advancing him – in what was another mark of the earl's financial plight – some £1,565 to meet his expenses in Rome. It was perhaps this treatment, as well as his position at court, which had encouraged him to presume on the king's goodwill. It was a bad mistake. In these circumstances Montfort had enemies who were quick to move against him. Paris speaks of 'certain envious men' who accused him before Henry, and it would be surprising if his continuing supremacy had not provoked continuing resentment. The reaction came on 9 August, when Montfort and Eleanor were in London for the queen's churching. There Henry erupted. Barring the couple from the festivities, he called Montfort an excommunicate and denounced him angrily. 'You seduced my sister before her marriage', Paris makes him say. 'When I discovered this I gave her to you, though unwillingly, to avoid scandal.' He then brought up the question of Montfort's unpaid debts, which had resulted in his excommunication, and, 'your crowning wretchedness', the false pledging of the king's name. So great was Henry's fury that his attempt to commit Montfort to the Tower was only frustrated by the intervention of Richard of Cornwall. Montfort and his pregnant wife were forced to flee, down the Thames and across the Channel.[64]

Although Paris gives priority among the king's charges to the new issue of Eleanor's seduction, it is clear, given Thomas of Savoy's presence in England at this time, that it was the debt question which had set Henry off. Both charges illuminate Montfort's position at the moment of crisis and are worth a little more exploration. The

---

[63] Bémont, *Montfort* (1st edn), pp. 333–4; *CR, 1237–42*, pp. 234–5; BN MS. Clairambault 1188, f. 10v; Paris, iii, pp. 566–7, 616–17; *CLR, 1226–40*, pp. 394, 409, 472; Cox, *Eagles of Savoy*, p. 99.

[64] *CLR, 1226–40*, pp. 311, 312, 410; Paris, iii, pp. 566–7; Paris, *Historia Anglorum*, ed. F. Madden (3 vols., Rolls ser., 1866–9), ii, p. 424; Bémont, *Montfort* (1st edn), p. 334; Stacey, *Politics, Policy*, pp. 126–7.

accusation that Montfort had seduced Eleanor takes us back to our starting-point: Henry's reasons for forwarding their marriage. It is an accusation that cannot be summarily dismissed and one that was never specifically denied by Montfort. Faced with it, he had retired *confusus*, according to Paris, and in his own later recollections of the episode, covering all Henry's charges, he would speak only of 'the king's grievous and shameful words, which are hard to record'. If Montfort had seduced Eleanor, and still more if she was believed to be pregnant, as Henry's words about avoiding scandal seem to imply, much that was peculiar about the marriage would fall into place: its odd mismatching of the king's sister with a foreign adventurer, and its celebration secretly and hurriedly – so hurriedly that even the king's brother, who had been present with Montfort at court only a month before, apparently knew nothing about it.[65] If Montfort had forced the king's hand in this way, Henry might well have resented the position in which he had been placed, leaving him in effect with no choice but to surrender his sister.

The strongest argument against this view lies in the favour which Montfort and Eleanor continued to enjoy after their marriage. If Henry consented only unwillingly, as he stated in August 1239, he certainly bore no grudges in the months that followed, and his support for Montfort in Rome suggests that he was determined to do all he could to support the couple. The circumstances of the marriage can perhaps be explained in ways which do not depend on Eleanor's putative seduction. Henry was probably anxious to do his best for two people whom he cared for greatly and who may have shown signs of being indiscreetly close to one another, particularly in view of Eleanor's vow. The seduction story may be false, but 'no smoke without fire' is not an entirely unsafe principle of historical deduction. He knew that the impending marriage, were it to be publicly announced, would be fiercely opposed, not only by the magnates but by the Church, and especially by Archbishop Edmund, the witness to Eleanor's vow of chastity. The best way to proceed might be to present all possible antagonists with a *fait accompli* and then to seek a *post hoc* regularisation of the marriage from the pope. Crucial here was a hitherto unnoticed factor, the departure of Archbishop Edmund for Rome about 20 December 1237. His absence created an opportunity which Henry seized, and the marriage took place within weeks. Henry knew very well what the consequences would

---

[65] Paris, iii, pp. 475, 566–7; Bémont, *Montfort* (1st edn), p. 334; *CLR, 1226–40*, p. 299.

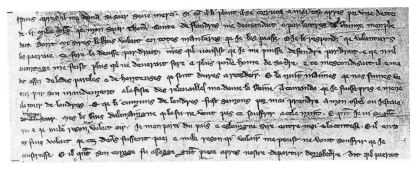

Plate 2. Montfort's quarrel with the king, 1239. Looking back from 1262, he describes his marriage to Eleanor and its consequences.

be, but by standing firm in the face of his brother's revolt, by paying handsomely for the papal dispensation, and by confronting Archbishop Edmund, on his return in August 1238, with a marriage now legally celebrated and generally accepted, he had gained all that he wanted.[66] Politically inept and constitutionally dubious though it may have seemed, Henry's promotion of the marriage can also be viewed, not as an example of the king's lack of foresight, something entered into lightly and unadvisedly, but as a carefully calculated move designed to advance the interests of those dearest to him with the least danger to all. Rarely sagacious, Henry was often both resourceful and sharp-witted.

Montfort's financial difficulties, however, suggest that the marriage had by no means solved all his problems. If in some ways it had compounded them, by forcing him to raise a large sum from his own resources as well as from the king's for the papal dispensation, the roots of those difficulties clearly lay further back: in the modest income of about £500 a year which, as we shall see, was all that he had from the Leicester lands, and in obligations which, even with Henry's support, were beyond his means to meet. His final establishment in England probably did not come cheap. In addition to the earlier payments promised to his brother Amaury, he may have had to pay more to persuade Amaury to make the final cession of his rights in England in April 1239. Paris speaks of Amaury having to be 'pacified lest he raise any question about this'; and Amaury's imminent departure on crusade

---

[66] For Archbishop Edmund's itinerary, see Paris, iii, p. 470, and C. H. Lawrence, *St. Edmund of Abingdon* (Oxford, 1960), p. 184.

(he left in July 1239, with Peter of Dreux) must have provided a strong financial incentive for him to make the best terms he could. Indeed, the crusade explains many of the pressures bearing upon Montfort at this time: the threats of papal excommunication, Peter of Dreux's demand for repayment, the fateful transfer of his debt to Thomas of Savoy, and perhaps Montfort's own increasing need for money, for he himself had taken the cross at some point before February 1238.[67] In the end these pressures compromised him where he had been strongest, at court, as Henry turned on him over his debt to Thomas. For the first time his private financial difficulties had become caught up with his place in politics and public affairs: a pattern of events which was to be frequently repeated in his later career.

Whether he was seen to be morally compromised is more difficult to say. In Henry's eyes, of course, he was. Even setting aside Eleanor's possible seduction, the king felt deeply wronged by Montfort's unauthorised pledging of his credit. Yet Montfort's own side of the story is less clear. As he told it some twenty-three years later, Henry had denied him a fair hearing, unjustly preempted the verdict of the curia on his debt to Thomas of Savoy, and then acted with vindictive unreasonableness. Both his own case and Henry's, presented by Paris, are *ex parte* statements, but there is a more neutral witness in Robert Grosseteste, bishop of Lincoln, Montfort's close friend but also a sternly just man. In 1238 Grosseteste had not flinched from rebuking Montfort fiercely when he had extorted money from a Leicester burgess in order to fund his journey to Rome. In 1239, probably soon after his flight abroad, Montfort wrote to the bishop in some anguish about his treatment by the king, and Grosseteste replied in a sympathetic letter which offered spiritual and scriptural consolation, but also the promise to intervene on the earl's behalf with Henry, as Montfort had asked.[68] Other episodes in Montfort's later life were to show that he was a persuasive advocate. Even so, such a letter is hardly likely to have been written by such a man to the seducer, excommunicate and perjurer whom Henry had condemned.

In the short term the breach that occurred in August 1239 was disastrous for Montfort. Henry was vengeful and unforgiving, levying 1,500 marks from Montfort's lands to meet his obligations to Thomas of Savoy, just when Montfort's own finances were coming under even

---

[67] Below, pp. 47–9; Paris, iii, pp. 479–80, 524; *CPL*, i, p. 167.
[68] Bémont, *Montfort* (1st edn), pp. 333–4; *Grosseteste Epistolae*, pp. 243–4, 141–3; Paris, iii, p. 479.

greater strain as he raised funds for his imminent crusade. When the king wrote to his proctors in Rome in December 1239 to support Thomas in his plea of debt against Montfort, his reference to 'our beloved uncle and *fidelis*' contrasted coldly with his unadorned mention of 'S. de Montfort'.[69] In the long term, however, his position was transformed by the events which culminated in what proved to be only a temporary break with Henry. Marriage to Eleanor brought him a new standing, new lands, a much larger income, a son and heir and, with all this, a firmer security in his adopted country. No longer an *arriviste*, he had arrived. The marriage similarly enhanced his links with France and gave him a new place in the relationships between the leading families of the West. Henry III, now his brother-in-law, was also the brother-in-law of Margaret of Provence, Louis IX's queen, and of the Emperor Frederick II. But it was in England that these new relationships mattered most. After January 1238 Montfort was, from the king's point of view, one of the family – difficult, obstreperous, sometimes a danger, sometimes in disgrace, but nevertheless an insider, who could not be disregarded or cast off. Strong and bitter though the differences between the two men often were, until 1258 these unspoken assumptions underlay them all.

(D) EXILE, CRUSADE AND RESTORATION, 1240–48

Montfort's enforced departure from England in August 1239 may have focused his ambitions more sharply on the crusade. In taking the cross, probably shortly before his marriage, he had identified himself both with a family tradition and with the crusading enthusiasm which gripped other English magnates in the mid 1230s. Here was one point of contact and common interest between Montfort and the native English nobility. During a brief return to England in April 1240 to raise money for his expedition, he was welcomed by the king in a reconciliation which signified a characteristically rapid change of mood on Henry's part. Then, later in the summer, he set out from southern Italy with a mixed contingent of English, French and Burgundian followers. His pregnant countess was left behind at Brindisi, in quarters provided by the Emperor.[70] About the same time a much larger party

---

[69] Bémont, *Montfort* (1st edn), p. 333–4; *CR, 1237–42*, pp. 234–5.

[70] Paris, iv, pp. 7, 44–5; S. Lloyd, *English Society and the Crusade, 1216–1307* (Oxford, 1988), pp. 83–4. For a gift to Montfort from the queen, probably made at the time of his April visit,

led by Richard of Cornwall departed from Marseilles. That the two forces were entirely separate may indicate Montfort's high sense of his own standing and his unwillingness to play second fiddle to the king's brother. Both had been preceded to the east in 1239 by a more substantial French army led, among others, by Amaury de Montfort; and it was the French, before the arrival of the English, who made such limited territorial gains as the crusade achieved. Nothing is known of Montfort's doings in the Holy Land, but neither he nor Richard of Cornwall appear to have seen any fighting, and the expedition cannot have contributed much to Montfort's military reputation or to that of his family. Amaury, captured at Gaza in November 1239 and subsequently held prisoner for a time in Egypt, died at Otranto on his way home in November 1241.

All the more surprising, then, is the one indisputable piece of evidence which the crusade produces for Montfort's prestige. In June 1241 'the barons, knights and citizens' of the kingdom of Jerusalem wrote to Frederick II asking him to appoint Montfort as their governor until the arrival of the Emperor himself or until his appointment of a replacement.[71] The request, which had no discernible result, may have owed something to the local standing of Montfort's cousin, Philip, lord of Tyre, and to Montfort's own position as the brother-in-law of Richard of Cornwall, whose enormous wealth had already done much to sustain the crusaders in the east. It represented, too, an attempt by one faction in the Holy Land, the Ibelins, to curtail imperial authority. But it must also reflect the high regard in which Montfort himself was held, both by the leading men of the kingdom and by the Emperor, to whom he could otherwise hardly have been commended. His particular qualities – energy perhaps, and enterprise and political intelligence – are not always clear to us. But they may have been as plain to the leaders of the families of Outremer in 1241 as they had been to Henry III just over ten years earlier.

Montfort probably left Syria in the autumn of 1241, in company with

see *CLR, 1240–45*, p. 100. For the history of this crusade, see esp. S. Painter, 'The Crusade of Theobald of Champagne and Richard of Cornwall', *A History of the Crusades*, ed. K. M. Setton (6 vols., Madison, Wisconsin, 1969–89), ii, pp. 463–85, and C. Tyerman, *England and the Crusades, 1095–1588* (Chicago, 1988), pp. 101–8.

[71] The letter is printed in *Manners and Household Expenses of England in the Thirteenth and Fifteenth Centuries*, ed. T. H. Turner (Roxburghe Club, 1841), pp. xviii–xix. For the background, see J. Riley-Smith, *The Feudal Nobility and the Kingdom of Jerusalem, 1174–1277* (London, 1973), pp. 207–9, and P. Jackson, 'The End of Hohenstaufen Rule in Syria', *BIHR*, 59 (1986), pp. 20–36.

Hugh IV, duke of Burgundy. He was in Burgundy when Henry summoned him back to his service in the following summer.[72] What proved to be the occasion for an uncomfortable meeting was the king's involvement in Poitou. The recovery of Poitou had been a central aim of Henry's foreign policy since its loss to the French in 1224.[73] This was part of his more general aim of reconstituting the whole of the old Angevin Empire. It seemed to have come a step nearer in 1241, when Henry's step-father, Hugh de Lusignan, count of La Marche, appealed for his help against Louis IX, who had recently invested his brother, Alphonse, as count of Poitou, contrary to the interests of the local nobility who were the region's real rulers. Although the magnates refused Henry a tax for his campaign in the parliament of January 1242, leaving him with inadequate resources in men and money, he nevertheless sailed for Poitou in May. When the existing truce with Louis finally collapsed in the following month, Henry summoned reinforcements from England, and it was at this stage that Montfort was recalled from Burgundy. He came grudgingly, joining Henry in July, when he was immediately caught up in the king's humiliating and pellmell retreat from Taillebourg to Saintes in the face of Louis's advancing army. He was one of a number of nobles who, according to Paris, fought hard and well outside Saintes, but this was no more than a rearguard action. Defeated and out of money, Henry pulled back to Bordeaux, where he remained until September 1243.

Henry's Poitou expedition was a watershed in Anglo-French relations. It marked the English Crown's irrevocable loss of Poitou, to the ultimate benefit of the French; it was a point in the growth of a more powerful France and a more insular England. In the smaller and more personal history of Henry's relations with Montfort, the campaign brought about a reunion without a reconciliation. Despite the signs of royal goodwill apparent in April 1240, Montfort still nursed a fierce grievance over Henry's distraining on his lands to meet the debt owing to Thomas of Savoy. It was only partly appeased by Henry's new promise to compensate him for these losses (where the king was as good as his word) and to grant him an additional hundred marks, in order to secure Montfort's service in Poitou. Henry's actions, so the earl later

---

[72] Jackson, 'End of Hohenstaufen Rule', p. 33; Bémont, *Montfort* (1st edn), p. 334.
[73] Stacey, *Politics, Policy*, pp. 160–200, is the best modern account of the Poitou campaign and its background. The best contemporary account is Paris, iv, pp. 181–92, 197–9, 202–31, 236–7, 242–5, 254–5, from which the following summary derives.

claimed, had forced him to sell lands to raise money for the crusade, and for that he had got no compensation.[74] After the fiasco outside Saintes Montfort had told Henry, in a moment of violent exasperation, that he ought to be taken and locked up, like the Carolingian, Charles the Simple, imprisoned after the battle of Soissons in 923.[75] It was an insult which Henry remembered for years.

Although Montfort was apparently with Henry until his return to England, remaining in Gascony after many other of the English nobles had left for home, he witnessed only one charter (on 3 August 1242) during Henry's entire sojourn in western France, and relations at Bordeaux were evidently strained. The differences between the two men were deliberately inflamed by Raymond of Toulouse and James I, king of Aragon, both present at court, whose families had been among the leading victims of Montfort's father in the south.[76] Yet Henry's foreign ambitions made it hard for him to do without Montfort. He needed the earl's advice and military intelligence; possibly, too, he needed his contacts with France and the manpower which he could provide. The bribe given to Montfort to re-enter his service was to be paralleled again, in similar circumstances but on a much larger scale, in 1253.[77] But the two men still found it difficult to live in peace. Already weakened by the king's treatment of his lands, the reluctant sense of loyalty that had brought Montfort back to the side of his lord, patron and relative, was attenuated further by Henry's military incompetence. Montfort's insult at Saintes showed how relations had deteriorated and how little respect Henry inspired. No one would have spoken in those terms to the king's father.

What healed this vendetta was Henry's capricious generosity, so often a cause for grievance but now a salve for old wounds. When Montfort returned to England in the autumn of 1243, after an absence of nearly four years, he and Eleanor were lavishly restored to favour. Henry's change of heart, difficult to explain, may have owed something to Beatrice of Savoy, Henry's mother-in-law, who came to England in November 1243 for the marriage of her third daughter, Sanchia, to Richard of Cornwall. It was Beatrice who, according to Montfort himself, persuaded Henry to grant Eleanor and her husband a fee of

---

[74] Bémont, *Montfort* (1st edn), p. 334; (2nd edn), p. 65 and n. 3; *CLR, 1240–45*, p. 153.
[75] Bémont, *Montfort* (1st edn), p. 341; Powicke, *King Henry III*, p. 215 and n.
[76] *CPR, 1232–47*, p. 314; Paris, iv, pp. 228–9, 231.
[77] Below, pp. 122–3.

500 marks as a marriage portion, lacking since the time of their marriage. This grant, and the concurrent arrangements for the payment of dower to Eleanor as William Marshal's widow, both considered in more detail below,[78] were the most valuable of the new gains to come the way of the couple; but they were not the only ones. In January 1244 Henry pardoned £1,000-worth of their debts; a further £834-worth of debt was pardoned in February; and in the same month Montfort was given custody of the great midland castle at Kenilworth, henceforward his principal seat.[79] Later, in July, he was pardoned a further debt of £110, owed to the great Jewish moneylender, David of Oxford, whose recent death had brought many of his loans into the king's hands. This debt, contracted on Montfort's behalf by two of his *familiares* in February 1243, while he was in Gascony, had been a mark of the earl's former financial embarrassments, now substantially resolved by Henry's liberality.[80] For the first time since his arrival in England he probably felt prosperous. As we might expect, he was often about the court in these months: between July 1244 and December 1245 he was second only to Richard of Cornwall in the number of royal charters he witnessed.[81]

Was the earl's return to favour reflected in his political role? The period from Henry's return in 1243 until Montfort's departure for Gascony in 1248 was one of intermittent disputes between Henry and some sections of the nobility, and a gathering accumulation of grievances against his government. The failure of the Poitou campaign did much to revive the sporadic discontents of the late 1230s. Undertaken without consent, as the magnates told Henry,[82] it saddled the king with a debt of some £15,000, creating financial difficulties which were exacerbated by a Welsh campaign in 1245 and by lavish spending on ceremony, display and building.[83] There was no overwhelming financial crisis, and costs were partly met in ways that were politically unobjectionable, by loans from Richard of Cornwall and by Jewish tallages. But from 1244 a series of more oppressive measures was

---

[78] Paris, iv, pp. 261, 263; Bémont, *Montfort* (1st edn), p. 335; below, pp. 54–5.

[79] *Excerpta E Rotulis Finium, 1216–72*, ed. C. Roberts (2 vols., Record Comm., 1835–6), i, p. 410; *CR, 1242–47*, p. 159; *CPR, 1232–47*, p. 419.

[80] *CPR, 1232–47*, p. 433; *CR, 1242–47*, p. 185; *Calendar of the Plea Rolls of the Exchequer of the Jews* (5 vols., Jewish Historical Society of England, 1905–92), i, ed. J. M. Rigg, p. 96; C. Roth, *The Jews of Medieval Oxford* (Oxford Hist. Soc., N.S., ix, 1951), pp. 54–6.

[81] c.53/36, mm. 1–2; c.53/37, mm. 1–7; c.53/38, m. 11.

[82] Paris, iv. p. 183.

[83] Stacey, *Politics, Policy*, pp. 198–200, is the best guide to Henry's finances in these years.

introduced: the harsher administration of the royal forests, more
frequent eyres (the provincial tours by the king's justices which had a
partly fiscal purpose), the renting out of lands held in serjeanty tenure,
the revival of inquests into the *terra Normannorum*, with the implied threat
that such lands might be confiscated, the imposition by the exchequer
of larger fiscal demands on the sheriffs and thence on the men of the
counties. It was this last group, freeholders, gentry and lesser barons,
upon whom all these measures fell especially heavily. Had Henry been
able to obtain a grant of direct taxation, their position and his would
have been easier; but the magnates' refusal of a tax grant in 1242 for the
Poitou expedition was followed by other refusals in 1244 and 1248. In
both these latter years there were attempts by those in parliament – now
the recognised forum for political debate – to secure some control over
Henry's government, beyond the merely negative influence given by
denial of direct taxation. In 1244 they asked for the chancellorship and
the justiciarship, then vacant, to be filled by men chosen with their
consent, and in 1248 they made the same request. In the 'Paper
Constitution' of 1244 (which may be no more than a visionary plan of
reform) they appear to have gone further, asking for the appointment
of four elected councillors to act as 'conservators of liberties' and for
consent to the appointment of other central officials.[84]

From 1237, when they had secured the addition of three barons to the
king's council, through to the parliaments of 1244 and 1248, Henry's
critics thus took a consistent line towards his government. They wanted
a share in it; and they saw the existence of independent and respectable
ministers, to whose appointment they had consented and who could
exercise some control over royal policy, as one means of securing a
voice, if only a vicarious one, in that government. They were opposed
to expensive foreign ventures, such as the Poitou campaign, and to the
oppressive fiscal measures necessary to pay for spendthrift policies,
whether at home or abroad. It is a harder question to know
precisely who wanted these things. Virtually our only source for the
parliamentary debates where attitudes were clarified is Paris, and he
does not name names. But it is unlikely that the higher nobility were
among them. From the 1240s onwards Henry tried hard to maintain
the loyalty of this group, and by and large he succeeded. The earls
were almost all *curiales*. Six of them had served in Poitou, making it
improbable that they had been among those in the preceding

---

[84] Paris, iv, pp. 363, 366–8, v, pp. 6–8, 20–1.

parliament who had opposed the expedition. Richard of Cornwall, the greatest of them, was the Crown's most dependable supporter; Richard de Clare, earl of Gloucester, was a rising power from the time of his knighthood in 1245; Norfolk and Hereford were both firmly attached to the court. Opposition to the Crown almost certainly came not from these men but from the unfavoured: the country gentry and the wider and lesser baronage in parliament, who were exposed to the growing voracity of Henry's government and who lacked the resources to sustain it. These were the men who had most to gain from the appointment of a chancellor and a justiciar to check extravagant gifts or the issue of unjust writs and whose collective aspirations were to come into the open as the reform movement developed in 1258–59.[85]

Montfort's place was not with these men, but with the other leading earls of the king's circle. If the scale of Henry's grants to him in 1244–45 could not be maintained, this is not to say that he lost favour. He was exempted from the feudal aid of 1245 and given wide liberties in his lands.[86] Henry continued to rely on his advice. In June 1244 the king went to Geddington in Northamptonshire to discuss the deteriorating situation in Wales with Montfort 'and others', and in 1247 Henry sent him abroad, in company with Richard of Cornwall, to see if Louis IX could be induced to surrender Normandy prior to his departure on crusade.[87] The perpetuation of Henry's imperial ambitions in France continued to make him dependent on a leading magnate and relative who had a foot in both camps.

It is highly unlikely, therefore, that Montfort played any part in the formulation of political grievances during these years. He owed everything to Henry, and the resentments which were to surface again later – over his dismissal in 1239 and over Henry's treatment of his lands in 1240 – were of the kind which could be forgotten when the going was good. The sporadic parliamentary confrontations of the period had earlier antecedents in which Montfort cannot have shared. When a section of the magnates had sought and gained the nomination of three councillors in 1237, Montfort himself had been one of the king's closest

---

[85] Stacey, *Politics, Policy*, pp. 192, 254–6; D. A. Carpenter, 'King, Magnates and Society: The Personal Rule of King Henry III, 1234–58', *Speculum*, 60 (1985), pp. 52–62; Carpenter, 'Chancellor Ralph de Neville', pp. 78–80.

[86] Carpenter, 'King, Magnates and Society', pp. 55, 68.

[87] *Calendar of Ancient Correspondence Concerning Wales*, ed. J. G. Edwards (Cardiff, 1935), p. 10; Paris, iv, pp. 645–6; *Flores Hist.*, ii, p. 344; Denholm-Young, *Richard of Cornwall*, p. 60; Bémont, *Montfort* (2nd edn), p. 71 and n.

friends, against whom the baronial attack had been directed. When Henry's covert marriage of his sister Eleanor provoked a baronial revolt, Montfort had been the beneficiary of Henry's failure to consult, not one of the excluded. When the barons had complained in the parliament of 1242 at Henry's similar failure to obtain consent before committing himself to a foreign campaign, Montfort had been out of the country. After his return the first major baronial protest came in the parliament of November 1244. Here Montfort's behaviour may appear to have been a shade more ambiguous, for he was one of a committee of twelve appointed to consider Henry's demand for a tax from the laity. Yet the other members of the committee were men such as the earls of Cornwall and Norfolk, who, like Montfort, had strong court connections and were improbable reformers. Montfort's further appearance in this parliament as the only earl among the deputation chosen by the king to put his request for a tax to the clergy points still more conclusively to his position as the king's ally.[88] He would hardly have been exempted from the feudal aid which was all that Henry managed to secure from the next parliament had he been anything else.[89]

If Montfort did not oppose, it remains true that between 1244 and 1248 he moved from the centre of the court towards its periphery. His position in Henry's inner circle appears to have been maintained for no more than two years after his return from Poitou. After October 1245 he witnessed royal charters much more rarely, and outside parliament time he was much less frequently with the king. In 1246, for example, he witnessed only seven charters, two of them during parliaments. By contrast, Richard of Cornwall witnessed on twenty-seven occasions, the earl of Gloucester nineteen, Norfolk fifteen and Hereford fourteen. In 1247 he witnessed only four charters, compared with twenty-four for Gloucester, fifteen for Norfolk and twelve for Richard of Cornwall. Royal gifts of timber and deer, another indicator of the king's regard, were made to him on 19 November 1244 and on 12 February and 10 July 1245, but not thereafter until December 1249.[90] He remained on the margins of favour, his various sorts of expertise still useful to the king, as his part in the French negotiations of 1247 showed. Yet though there was no dramatic rupture, there appears to have been an unobtrusive withdrawal by Montfort from the life of the court. Its

---

[88] Paris, iv, pp. 362, 365; Stacey, *Politics, Policy*, pp. 249–50.
[89] Paris, iv, pp. 372–3; Carpenter, 'King, Magnates and Society', p. 55.
[90] C.53/38, mm. 1–10; C.53/39, mm. 8–14; *CR, 1242–47*, pp. 268, 288, 326; *CR, 1247–51*, p. 249.

chronicler, Matthew Paris, mentions him only twice in 1246 and 1247. In these years, as at other stages of his career, his chief interests probably lay elsewhere: in his personal affairs, his lands, his affinity and the means to his eternal salvation. These are the subjects which we must next examine.

CHAPTER 2

'Familia' and fortune

(A) FAMILY

Born about 1215, King Henry's sister Eleanor was some seven years younger than her second husband, Simon de Montfort: twenty-three to his thirty at the time of their marriage in 1238.[1] One of the difficulties in the way of our imaginative recreation of their life together is that we have no idea of what they looked like. Common to virtually all medieval biographies except those of kings, this barrier means that their attributes cannot be pictured in the mind's eye, but remain as words on the page, descriptive yet unilluminating. When the Lanercost chronicler says that Montfort was 'a strenuous knight, tall in body and handsome in face', and Paris that it was Eleanor's beauty (*elegantia*) as well as her wealth and royal descent that attracted Montfort, we have no reason to doubt either writer.[2] But these conventional phrases, all that we have, do not get us very far.

The physical provides an appropriate introduction to a relationship that from the start had perhaps an unusually strong sexual charge behind it. If groundless, Henry's accusation concerning Montfort's premarital seduction of Eleanor is not likely to have been entirely implausible, and its substance may have contributed to the general sense of moral unease about his marriage which seems to have afflicted Montfort in the late 1240s and possibly earlier.[3] Any clerical

---

[1] The date of Eleanor's birth is nowhere stated in any primary source, but most secondary authorities give 1215, without citing evidence. Eleanor was the younger sister of Isabella (see, for example, *Foedera*, i, i, p. 160), who had reached her twenty-first year at the time of her marriage in 1235 (Paris, iii, p. 319). She was therefore probably born in 1214 and Eleanor in the last eighteen months of John's reign in 1215 or, less probably, 1216. The point was nearly made by M. A. E. Wood (Mrs Green), *Lives of the Princesses of England* (6 vols., London, 1849–55), ii, pp. 1–4, which provides what is still much the best account of Eleanor's life.

[2] *Lanercost*, p. 39; Paris, iii, p. 471.

[3] Above, pp. 25–6; below, pp. 86–7.

writer seeking to account for Montfort's drawing Eleanor into the denial of her vow of chastity is likely to have looked to carnal desire for an explanation. Yet the Franciscan whose work underlay the Lanercost chronicle, and whose explanation this is, seems to have been close to one who knew both partners, and for this reason his words should be given a little more credence than those of a more remote commentator.[4] Once married, however, Montfort remained a faithful husband, so far as we know, and entirely free from the sort of scandal that gathered around his womanising brother-in-law, Richard of Cornwall.[5] It is difficult enough to tell anything about other people's marriages, let alone one so distant in time. But to all appearances, at least, the marriage of Simon and Eleanor was a stable and happy one.

Montfort's fidelity gave its own strength to a relationship which rested more obviously on similarities of temperament and interest, and on the close involvement of husband and wife in each other's affairs. Like Montfort, Eleanor was an independent. Unlike his independence, however, hers was grounded, firstly, on her rank as the king's sister and, secondly, on the wealth which came from her first husband's dower. Although both she and Montfort judged the dower to be insufficient, as we shall see, and although her dower lands were effectively under the management of her husband, these two factors none the less raised Eleanor well above the level of most aristocratic wives. They may even have encouraged the occasional and unspecified acts of marital insubordination for which she was rebuked by Adam Marsh. If Montfort's energy, ambition and lack of inherited advantages drove him to make his own way forward, never less than his own man, Eleanor remained very much her own woman, capable, for example, of running a great household, pursuing her family interests in Angoulême, and bargaining with the king for her rights after her second husband's death. She was King John's daughter to the last.

At the same time she was closely engaged with her husband's activities. When in England, Eleanor spent most of her time at the former royal castle of Odiham in Hampshire, which Henry had settled on her for her residence in 1236, or at Kenilworth, where she lived intermittently from 1238 and where two of her children were born. Henry's grant of both places to the couple for life in 1253 was a mark of

[4] *Lanercost*, pp. 39–40; below, p. 86.
[5] *Wykes*, p. xxx, n. 2; *The Political Songs of England*, ed. T. Wright (Camden Soc., 1839), p. 69.

the king's continuingly close relationship with his sister.[6] But she also shared more adventurously in some of Montfort's foreign journeys and projects, accompanying him as far as Brindisi in southern Italy when he went on crusade in 1240, taking the cross alongside him in 1248, and journeying with him to Gascony in 1249–50 and again in 1251.[7] He in turn showed his confidence in her, and his sense of her business abilities, when he put her in charge of the execution of his will, under the guidance of his own advisers and allies. As his attorney she was 'to act in such a way as a good lady ought to do for her lord who trusts in her'.[8] The mutual dependence glimpsed in these episodes became part of a public issue in 1258–59, when earl and countess stood together on the question of their financial grievances against the Crown, playing as their trump card Eleanor's refusal to renounce her claims in Normandy.[9] An essential element in the stability of their marriage, their reliance on each other remained compatible with the independence of each of them.

The strongest bond between the two was probably that of religion. As a young widow Eleanor had been under the supervision of the pious and learned Cecilia de Sanford, 'a most saintly woman', who seems to have been instrumental in persuading her to take her ill-advised vow of chastity.[10] After her remarriage both she and her husband came to share a circle of religious friends whose membership and activities will be discussed more fully in the next chapter. To its leading members, the Oxford Franciscan Adam Marsh and Robert Grosseteste, bishop of Lincoln, she was almost as close as he was. At one level her relationship with these luminaries was a social one, amicably and even amusingly convivial. When Grosseteste borrowed Eleanor's cook, subsequently asking Marsh to see that Eleanor did not take it amiss if the bishop retained him, Marsh reported Eleanor's reply that if she had the best and most necessary of servants she would rejoice at the chance to put them at the bishop's disposal. (Mrs Wood's comment on this incident, 'It is not every notable housewife that would smile away a disappoint-ment in reference to a favourite domestic', is wryly evocative of a Victorian middle-class life in some ways closer to the lives of Simon and Eleanor than to ours.)[11] At a deeper level, however, the relationship was

[6] *CPR, 1232–47*, p. 166; *1247–58*, p. 250; Paris, iii, pp. 480, 498, 518; Wood, *Lives of the Princesses*, ii, pp. 73–4, 104.
[7] Paris, iv, p. 44; v, pp. 1, 263; E. Boutaric, *Saint Louis et Alfonse de Poitiers* (Paris, 1870), p. 72.
[8] Bémont, *Montfort* (2nd edn), p. 276.
[9] Below, pp. 155–6, 181–3, 185–6.   [10] Paris, v. p. 235.
[11] *Mon. Franc.*, i, p. 170; Wood, *Lives of the Princesses*, ii, p. 93.

a didactic one, in which Eleanor, like her husband, looked to Marsh and Grosseteste for religious direction, spiritual advice and practical help. In 1251 Marsh wrote to Grosseteste to say that both the earl and the countess greatly desired his 'salutary counsel'. In 1252, pregnant and about to be confined, Eleanor spoke with Marsh about both spiritual and temporal affairs, and in the same year she went to see him personally to support her husband's request that Marsh should cross to Boulogne to advise him in particularly difficult negotiations.[12] Marsh, for his part, saw Eleanor's influence as a means by which Montfort could be checked and corrected. It was her duty, he told her during the time of the earl's harsh rule in Gascony, 'in the spirit of gentleness to direct him to more prudent ways in future by the moderation of your counsels'. To work through the wife in order to persuade the husband to do good was a recognised tactic of thirteenth-century confessors;[13] here it confirms from another viewpoint the particularly close relationship between Montfort and Marsh which we shall soon consider. Although Marsh's reports and injunctions are invariably vague, they show something of the mental world, spiritually intense and morally prescriptive, yet softened by friendship, in which Eleanor and the other *dramatis personae* of these letters lived their lives.

One of those persons was the queen, Henry's Eleanor, to whom Montfort's Eleanor was for some time very close. We know of their friendship only in one particular year, 1252–53, when a few of the queen's household accounts survive coincidentally besides Marsh's letters, but it is likely to have extended beyond this limited term. Although they were widely different in age, the countess about thirty-seven in 1252 and the queen only twenty-eight, their positions as the mothers of young families and their mutual attachment to Adam Marsh provided the makings of common ground. A shared piety and general outlook was certainly one bond between them: Marsh shows them coming together to pacify the king's anger against Montfort, probably at the time of his trial in the summer of 1252, and, in an echo of a projected enterprise which Grosseteste and Montfort intended to undertake in partnership, to discuss 'the salvation of souls'. Queen Eleanor's household accounts exemplify the more mundane and quotidian side of their relationship: the regular despatch of messengers to the countess at Kenilworth and

---

[12] *Mon. Franc.*, i. pp. 107, 262, 336, 339.
[13] *Mon. Franc.*, i, p. 298; S. Farmer, 'Persuasive Voices: Clerical Images of Medieval Wives', *Speculum*, 61 (1986), esp. pp. 517–18.

Odiham, enquiries after her health, a handsome reward of 40s. given to Montfort's barber who brought the news of the birth of Eleanor's child in the autumn of 1252, presents of jewellery and furs.[14] We can glimpse a small and busy world of comings and goings, shared pleasures and common aspirations, which political differences would soon and painfully dissolve.

Encouraged in her widowhood by her governess, and seen in her maturity through her friendships, Eleanor's piety came to be closely aligned with that of her husband. She was, for example, a friend to other Franciscans besides Marsh, persuading her brother Henry to contribute to the building of the Franciscan chapel at Leicester, and also a friend to the Cistercians. The Waverley annalist writes feelingly of this 'most sincere lover' of his house, who, on a visit with her husband and two sons on Palm Sunday 1245, had entered the church at the moment of the elevation of the host, heard a sermon in the chapter house, been present for the procession and mass, adored the cross, and retired edified, later to give generously to the house's endowment and building fund: an attractively circumstantial vignette of a devout family at its devotions.[15] But for all her devoutness Eleanor had some of the same failings as her husband and, like him, was subject to criticism from her advisers. Marsh wrote frankly to her, probably during her time in Gascony: she should moderate her extravagance in dress, control her temper, do all she could to assist her husband, reform her ways, especially towards her husband, children and household, and behave in a careful, reasonable and peaceful manner, according to the example of holy matrons.[16] Unspecific though all this is, it suggests that Eleanor shared some of her husband's fierceness and almost destructive energy. The yoking together of two such difficult characters might produce domestic rows, as Marsh implies, but their temperamental similarities were also a sort of bond. The later defence of what they regarded as their rights was to show that both were equally uncompromising.

In her religious friendships, active piety, interest in the crusade, and close involvement with the work of her husband, Eleanor resembled Montfort's mother, Alice de Montmorency, the vigorous defender of the elder Simon's cause during the years of the Albigensian crusade. The

---

[14] Paris, iii, p. 335 (for the queen's age); *Mon. Franc.*, i, pp. 393–4, 290; E.101/308/1; E.101/349/18; Wood, *Lives of the Princesses*, ii, pp. 104–5. For the 'salvation of souls', see below, pp. 98–9.

[15] *CR, 1254–56*, p. 244; *Ann. Wav.*, p. 336.

[16] *Mon. Franc.*, i, pp. 294–6, 299.

two women were alike, too, in their fecundity: Alice had six known children, Eleanor seven. When were they born? Since the rapid growth of his family, and the need to support it, were factors which bore heavily on Montfort's political and financial calculations, this is an important question; but it is not an easy one to answer. The only child whose date of birth is known with any certainty is the eldest, Henry, born about 26 November 1238.[17] Eleanor was pregnant again when she fled abroad with her husband after his disgrace in August 1239, and still pregnant at the time of his brief return to England in the following April, so her second son, Simon, cannot have been born much later than April 1240. He is likely to have spent his earliest months at Brindisi, where his mother waited for her husband's homecoming.[18] Next came Amaury, the third son. According to Amaury's own impeccable authority, recorded in his own hand as part of the colophon to a theological treatise written by this the most scholarly of the Montfort children, he was in his thirty-fourth year when he completed his work in April/May 1276. He must therefore have been born between April/May 1242 and 1243, the first child to be conceived after his father's return from the crusade in the autumn of 1241. This would fit well enough with his first appearance in the sources as a young pupil of Robert Grosseteste in 1250.[19] Amaury's own record of his age demotes his brother Guy from the customary third place assigned to him to fourth among the sons. Guy first appears as joint leader, with his brother Henry and others, of a division of his father's army at the battle of Lewes in May 1264; and after the battle he was old enough to be given custody of Devon and Cornwall.[20] For positions demanding some maturity and experience he can hardly have been less than twenty, and we shall not go far wrong if we place his birth about 1244.

There were two other children who survived, Richard and Eleanor, neither of whom is mentioned until near the end of their father's life. Richard makes a brief and puzzling appearance as a hostage in 1264, and was given deer to stock his park in 1265.[21] He was probably the child born at Kenilworth in 1252, whose arrival was foreseen in one of Marsh's

---

[17] Paris, iii, p. 518; Stacey, *Politics, Policy*, p. 124, n. 168.

[18] Paris, iii, p. 567, iv, pp. 7, 44.

[19] The vital colophon is printed in L. E. Boyle, '*E Cathena et Carcere*: The Imprisonment of Amaury de Montfort, 1276', *Medieval Learning and Literature: Essays presented to R. W. Hunt*, ed. J. J. G. Alexander and M. Gibson (Oxford, 1976), p. 384; see below, p. 97, Plate 6. For Amaury as a pupil of Grosseteste, see *Mon. Franc.*, i, p. 163, and for his later scholarly career, below, pp. 95–6.

[20] *Guisborough*, p. 193; Battle chronicle, in Bémont, *Montfort* (1st edn), p. 377.

[21] *Ger. Cant.*, ii, p. 236; *CR, 1264–68*, p. 26.

letters and welcomed by the queen. Eleanor, like Richard, remained attached to her mother's household in 1265, when she still had a nurse but was old enough to have a breviary and portiforium bought for her.[22] The likelihood is that she was then about seven, and so born about 1258. We hear of one other daughter, who died, and was probably born, in Gascony during Eleanor's sojourn there between 1248 and 1251. She was buried at the Dominican house in Bordeaux.[23]

About the upbringing of these children almost nothing is known. Prior to 1258 they appear only fleetingly in the records and chronicles: the boy Henry as the household companion of the young Edward, the king's son, his cousin; Henry and Simon at Waverley with their parents in 1245; Henry and Amaury as Grosseteste's pupils; and Henry crossing to Gascony with his father in 1252 and to France with one of his father's retainers in 1256. We know too that by 1258 neither of the two elder sons had yet been knighted.[24] But even as early as the mid 1240s the problem of their endowment must have loomed much larger for Montfort and Eleanor than their near invisibility in the sources would suggest. If our deductions are right, by 1245 Montfort already had four sons after only seven years of marriage; Eleanor was still only thirty and there was a strong likelihood of an eventually much larger family. There is every sign – though the signs are later – that Montfort was particularly close to his sons and exceptionally determined to advance their interests. 'If all the world should desert me', he was to say as his fairweather friends drifted away from him in the difficult autumn of 1263, 'I and my four sons will stand firm for the just cause to which I have sworn'.[25] But to provide for those sons he would have to depend largely on private resources. These were frustratingly inadequate.

(B) LANDS AND FINANCES

The political weight of any magnate depended partly on the size of his estates. In providing income, following, and the local influence which

---

[22] *Mon. Franc.*, i, pp. 262, 293; E.101/308/1; *Manners and Household Expenses*, ed. Turner, pp. 9, 18, 24.

[23] C. Douais, *Les Frères Prêcheurs en Gascogne au XIIIme et au XIVme Siècles* (Paris and Auch, 1885), pp. 265, 276.

[24] *Willelmi Rishanger Chronica et Annales*, ed. H. T. Riley (Rolls ser., 1865), p. 37; *Ann. Wav.*, p. 336; *Mon. Franc.*, i, pp. 110, 129, 163; *CPR, 1247–58*, p. 493; *Flores Hist*, ii, p. 456.

[25] Rishanger, *De Bellis*, p. 17. He had presumably ignored the child Richard.

Eleanor de Montfort

Henry

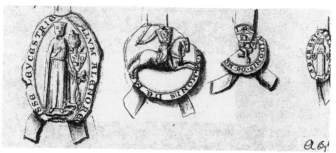

Eleanor   Simon junior   Guy   Eleanor junior

Amaury

Plate 3. The seals of Montfort's wife and children: drawings made in the eighteenth century from lost originals

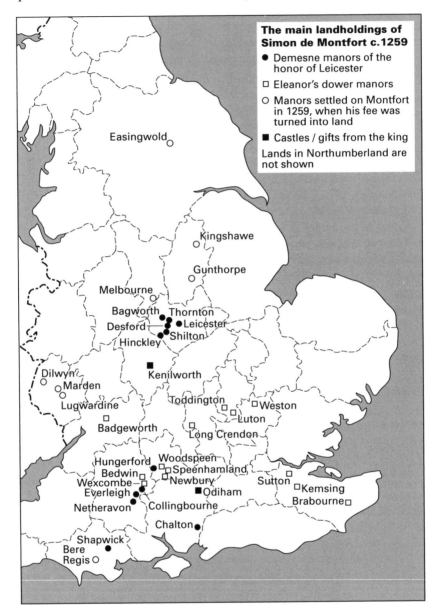

The main landholdings of
Simon de Montfort c.1259

● Demesne manors of the
honor of Leicester

□ Eleanor's dower manors

○ Manors settled on Montfort
in 1259, when his fee was
turned into land

■ Castles / gifts from the king

Lands in Northumberland are
not shown

Easingwold○

Kingshawe
○

Gunthorpe
○

Melbourne
○

Bagworth Thornton
Desford ●Leicester
Hinckley ●Shilton

Dilwyn?
○ ○Marden
Lugwardine
□

Kenilworth ■

Toddington
□ □Weston
Luton
Badgeworth
□ Long Crendon
□

Hungerford Woodspeen
Bedwin□ □Speenhamland
Wexcombe□ □Newbury Sutton□
Everleigh ●Odiham □Kemsing
Netheravon Collingbourne Brabourne□

Chalton●

Shapwick
Bere ●
Regis○

Fig. 4. The main landholdings of Simon de Montfort.

Main acquisitions

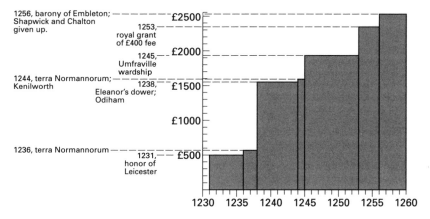

Fig. 5. The growth of Montfort's landed wealth.

both reflected and conferred influence at the centre, his property was a measure of his power, and so its description makes a necessary part of his biography. Montfort's landed resources, however, have a special importance which transcends this conventional requirement. Their deficiencies gave rise to private grievances, intensified by the need to support a growing family, which underlay much of his periodic antagonism to Henry III and which manifested, often in an extreme form, the self-interest which has to be set against his idealism. Financial preoccupations became almost as ingrained a part of his general attitudes as his religious life, and as idiosyncratic a feature of his career.

The ancestral core of Montfort's estate was the honor of Leicester, handed over in 1231, and consisting of the borough of Leicester, five demesne manors (Hinckley, Shilton, Bagworth, Thornton and Desford), all within a dozen miles of the borough, some six other demesne holdings in central southern England, and at least sixty knights' fees dispersed through twenty-two counties and providing an occasional revenue in scutage and feudal windfalls: escheats, wardships, reliefs, marriages. Since the original twelfth-century honor had been partitioned in 1207 between Montfort's father and Saer de Quincy, earl of Winchester, and his wife Margaret, this was only half of what his Beaumont ancestors had possessed.[26] The yield of the honor's Leicestershire heartland, which came to the Montforts, is set out on the pipe roll for 1210, when this part of the honor had been in royal custody. The total, £688 for the year, can hardly be representative of the average annual income. It included the exceptional levy of £200 in tallage from Leicester, which could be taken only when the king tallaged his own lands, a huge entry fine of £100 from an heir, and various other non-recurrent profits. The dependable annual income, comprising rents and farms from Leicester and the five demesne manors, amounted to £220, of which Leicester produced £172. It is reassuring to find that these figures roughly correspond with others derived from later inquisitions, held after Montfort's death in 1265, into the value of rebels' lands. At that later date Leicester and its five manors were valued at £243, of which Leicester itself produced £154.[27]

One or two further points have to be borne in mind before we can estimate possible income at the time of Montfort's accession to the estate. First, the 1210 figure represents actual yield, while the 1265 figure derives from jurors' estimates, which are notoriously prone to under-valuation. Second, these two considerations, as well as what we know of thirteenth-century inflation, suggest a rising trend in income. And, third, at least some of the incidental profits of 1210 – for example, £20 from perquisites of court – might be expected in any year. To set against these maximising factors there is one minimising one. Montfort later complained that the estates had been wasted when they were in royal custody, a complaint borne out by the very large sum of £107 from sale of wood recorded in the 1210 account.[28] All things considered, a figure of, say, £270 for the annual yield of the Leicestershire property in 1231 is not likely to be far out.

But this was not the full value of Montfort's inheritance. At the time of the pipe roll account the honor of Leicester had been depleted by provision for two surviving dowagers: Petronilla, widow of Robert de Beaumont III (d. 1190), and her daughter-in-law, Loretta, widow of Robert de Beaumont IV (d. 1204). By the time of Montfort's entry, after Petronilla's death in 1212 and Loretta's retirement to live as a recluse about 1220, these dower lands had been divided between the Quincy

---

[26] Above, pp. 3, 15–16; L. Fox, 'The Honor and Earldom of Leicester: Origin and Descent, 1066–1399', *EHR*, 54 (1939), pp. 391–4; *CR, 1237–42*, p. 491.

[27] *Pipe Roll 12 John*, ed. C. F. Slade (Pipe Roll Soc., n.s., xxvi, 1951), p. 96; *CIM*, i, No. 772. In this and the following discussion all figures have been rounded to the nearest £.

[28] Bémont, *Montfort* (1st edn), p. 333; *Pipe Roll 12 John*, p. 96.

and Montfort halves of the original honor, rejoining the Beaumont inheritance in its two divergent lines. They lay in southern England. From Petronilla's dower Montfort regained Shapwick, in Dorset, and Collingbourne, Everleigh and half of Netheravon, all in Wiltshire, and valued in 1212 at £18, £20, £23 and £4 respectively. From Loretta's dower he took over the large Hampshire manor of Chalton, worth £50 in 1219 and £80 in 1265, and the Berkshire borough of Hungerford, worth £20 in 1219. At the least this amounts to a minimum income of £135. But most of these valuations are early, and the two for Chalton again suggest a rising trend, so it might be reasonable to mark this up to, say, £180.[29]

Our provisional estimate, then, must be that the Leicestershire properties of Montfort's inherited honor were worth some £270 and the southern properties some £180, making a total income of £450. This figure for the estate's yield in a normal year might sometimes be boosted considerably by such a boon as tallage and by feudal profits, so it must be regarded as a minimum one. It would be safe to suggest £500 as a final figure for the average annual yield of the honor. This total was augmented, quite soon after Montfort's arrival, by royal grants from the *terra Normannorum*. The lands of Richard de Harcourt, which Montfort thus acquired in 1236, brought him the Warwickshire manor of Ilmington, worth £30 a year, and the Leicestershire manors of Sileby and Borstall, also jointly worth £30. In 1244 came the further unvalued grants of Barton and Gretton in Cambridgeshire, part of his lavish restoration to royal favour in that year. Altogether Montfort's holdings from 'the lands of the Normans' may have been worth perhaps £100: a maximum figure, since some of these holdings were later granted out again to his supporters.[30]

Montfort's profits from this source were trivial by comparison with those brought to him by Eleanor. His marriage gave him an income which dwarfed even that derived from his ancestral honor and transformed his position as a landed magnate. As the widow of the immensely wealthy William Marshal, Eleanor possessed a large dower which should by law have amounted to a third of her former husband's

---

[29] *Rot. Litt. Claus.*, i, pp. 130, 626, 651; *Book of Fees*, i, pp. 92, 254, 257, 298; *CIM*, i, No. 692; *CR, 1227–31*, p. 162; F. M. Powicke, 'Loretta, Countess of Leicester', *Historical Essays in Honour of James Tait*, ed. J. G. Edwards, V. H. Galbraith and E. F. Jacob (Manchester, 1933), pp. 254–7, 262. The figures for Petronilla's manors do not include the value of stock, given on the close roll, since this was capital rather than income.

[30] *CR, 1234–37*, pp. 318–19; *1242–47*, p. 226; *Book of Fees*, ii, pp. 1282, 1394; below, p. 72.

lands. In England the dower lay scattered through the southern and south-midland counties: three manors in Kent (Sutton, Brabourne and Kemsing), three in Berkshire (Newbury, Speenhamland and Woodspeen), two in Bedfordshire (Luton and Toddington), two in Wiltshire (Wexcombe and Bedwin, plus Kinwardestone hundred), and single manors in Gloucestershire, Hertfordshire and Buckinghamshire (Badgeworth, Weston and Long Crendon). Some of these were actually manors settled on Eleanor by Henry as her marriage portion during her first marriage. According to a valuation probably drawn up at the time of the dower's partition among the Marshal heirs after Eleanor's death in 1275, the whole ensemble was worth some £534 a year. The figure would perhaps have been lower at the time of her marriage in 1238, but, in counterbalance, would have been augmented by occasional income from over seventy knights' fees which also formed part of the dower.[31]

Eleanor also had a claim to dower from her former husband's considerable lands in Wales and Ireland. Here the position was more complicated and, as it turned out, more contentious. In 1233, after she had been dowered with the Marshal's English lands, Eleanor had given up her right to further dower lands from his estates in Wales and Ireland in return for an annual payment of £400. This sum had been fixed by agreement between Henry, her brother, and Richard Marshal, William's brother and heir. But Eleanor never found it easy to extract the dower fee from Richard and the successive Marshal heirs, and in January 1244 Henry made himself surety for the annual payment from Walter Marshal, to whom the Marshal lands had descended, guaranteeing that if Walter defaulted, then he would pay and recover against Walter. From 1246 Henry went further and took direct responsibility for the payment, royal orders for which now began to be sent regularly to the exchequer. The king then reclaimed the money from the Marshal heirs. From Eleanor's point of view, this was a much more satisfactory arrangement: she could now rely on her brother's word and the resources of the exchequer to provide what was due to her.[32]

---

[31] The partition is transcribed and discussed in M. M. Wade (Labarge), 'The Personal Quarrels of Simon de Montfort and his Wife with Henry III of England' (Oxford B.Litt. thesis, 1939), pp. 29–43, 115–16. This is more accurate than Labarge, *Montfort*, p. 42 (where '£400' should read '£500'), p. 279 (which includes among the Montforts' lands some which left Eleanor's possession before her remarriage, which calls Badgeworth, Glos., 'Begworth' and which assigns Speenhamland and Woodspeen to Bedfordshire). See pp. 281–2 for the valuation.

[32] *CR, 1231–34*, p. 310; *CPR, 1232–47*, pp. 125–6, 415–16; *CLR, 1245–51*, pp. 85, 118.

If we now review Montfort's financial position in these early months of 1244, what we find is this. He had an annual income of some £1,530, comprising £500 from the honor of Leicester, £100 from the *terra Normannorum*, £530 from Eleanor's dower lands in England, and £400 from her dower fee for the Marshal lands in Wales and Ireland. This statement of the account shows how very dependent he was on Eleanor, whose dower income of £930 was nearly twice that from his ancestral honor and not far short of two-thirds of the total sum. In Eleanor's disproportionate contribution to his fortune lay Montfort's predicament.[33] Large though it was, Eleanor's dower, like any other widow's dower, was neither alienable nor heritable. The law, for example, forbade the sale of its woods, an expedient that Montfort was several times forced to adopt on his own lands in order to raise money quickly.[34] Much more seriously, his interest in these lands lapsed at Eleanor's death. If she predeceased him the annual payments would terminate, the dower lands would revert to the Marshal heirs, and Montfort's holdings would shrink back essentially to the Leicester inheritance. Tenure by curtesy, the custom by which a husband could in certain circumstances continue to have a life interest in his deceased wife's lands, extended only to lands which she had held in fee or to lands held in *maritagium* where the wife had an heir or heirs by her first husband. It gave the second husband no claim to a life interest in her dower once she had died.[35] If, on the other hand, Eleanor survived him, then again the dower would revert to her first husband's heirs on her death.

Montfort's reliance for the greater part of his income on lands which hung on his wife's life, and which his children could not hope to inherit, was the crucial weakness of his and his family's position. It meant that the establishment of those children was precariously dependent on any settlement which their father could make for them from his own more limited stock of land held in fee, or on the uncertain chances of endowment by marriage. His awareness of this uncomfortable prospect, shown by his subsequent acts and demands, must have been sharpened by his knowledge of the inevitable consequences of Eleanor's premature death, in an age when even the greatest ladies lived dangerously in their child-bearing years, and by the rapid enlargement of his family. By

---

[33] The essential point in what follows was first made by D. A. Carpenter, 'Simon de Montfort: The First Leader of a Political Movement in English History', *History*, 76 (1991), pp. 17–18.

[34] *Bracton on the Laws and Customs of England*, ed. S. E. Thorne (4 vols., Cambridge, Mass., 1968–77), iii, p. 405; Paris, iv, p. 7; v, p. 294; below, p. 56.

[35] *Bracton*, iv, p. 360. I am very grateful to Dr Paul Brand for advice on this point.

1244–45 he was already distinguished and burdened by four sons. It was at just this stage, in the shadow of a growing family which it was beyond his means to endow, that he and Eleanor chose to question the propriety and justice of Henry's financial dealings with his sister. In doing so they raised arguments which would reverberate through Simon de Montfort's relationship with Henry III for the remainder of Montfort's career.

There were two essential points of difference between the Montforts and Henry. First, they claimed that the £400 dower fee, settled between Henry and Richard Marshal in 1233, was inadequate compensation for one-third of the Marshal's lands in Wales and Ireland. Second, they claimed that Henry had failed to give Eleanor the customary *maritagium* at the time of her marriage to Montfort. The matter of the dower was first raised in January 1244, when Henry undertook to assign Eleanor her dower land in Ireland should Walter Marshal default on his payment of the £400 fee. Later, on 2 May 1244, Montfort was granted an annual fee of 400 marks (£267) because Eleanor 'is not fully dowered of the lands of W. Marshal formerly her husband'.[36] From these favours we can deduce that the Montforts had complained about the inadequacy of the dower, that they had broached the possibility of a full settlement in land, that Henry had recognised their case, and that he was even prepared to contemplate giving them what they wanted by assigning Irish land to Eleanor, at Walter Marshal's expense. Shortly afterwards, in 1247–48, they went one stage further, asserting in a legal action that at the time of Eleanor's first marriage William Marshal had dowered her with a full third of his lands, including lands in the Welsh lordship of Pembroke. When this plea came to nothing they shifted their attack, considerably later in 1259, by pressing for a much more generous money settlement. They claimed once again that Eleanor had originally been dowered with lands in Wales and Ireland, adding that Henry's subsequent settlement with Richard Marshal had been made without Eleanor's consent, when she was under age and in the king's power. The true value of the dower in west Wales and Ireland, they said, was 2,000 marks (£1,333) or more a year.[37]

We have had to anticipate here the working out of a long story, to be told later in its proper place, in order to bring into view the full extent of the Montforts' claims. Did they have justice on their side? To a large

---

[36] *CPR, 1232–47*, p. 416; *CLR, 1240–45*, p. 231.
[37] KB.26/159, mm. 2d–3d; *Treaty R*, i, *1234–1325*, p. 48; below, pp. 130–1, 183.

extent, the answer is yes. When the Marshal lands were finally partitioned in 1247, after the death of the last male in the direct line, those in Ireland were reckoned to be worth £1,716, and those in west Wales, centred on Pembroke but including Haverford, Narbeth and other minor lordships, were valued at £594. Their total value was thus £2,310. The widow's third should have given Eleanor £770 rather than the £400 with which she had been fobbed off. It is possible that the disparity between what was given and what should have been given was even greater, for these calculations take no account of the Marshal's lands in south-east Wales, centred on the lordship of Usk and worth some £485, according to the partition.[38] By an agreement between Gilbert Marshal and Eleanor in 1234, Eleanor had been dowered here with the manor of Magor, near Caerleon and worth £90, to provide what was due to her; but even if this grant had taken effect Magor was no longer in her possession in 1247.[39] In 1259 the claim was for dower only in Ireland and *west* Wales. But if Eleanor had a colourable claim to dower in Usk as well, then she was owed some £930 a year. Neither figure approaches the Montforts' claim for £1,333. But they suggest the extent to which, in June 1233, Henry had been outmanoeuvred by Richard Marshal, at a time when the true value of the Marshal lands was almost certainly unknown and when Richard's imminent move towards rebellion left Henry unable to impose himself on his sister's brother-in-law.[40]

The Montforts' justifiable resentment over the insufficiency of Eleanor's dower was compounded by their related grievances over her *maritagium*. The *maritagium*, or marriage portion, was a gift of land normally settled by a father on his daughter at the time of her marriage in order to provide for the children of that marriage. In the absence of children the gift reverted to the donor or his heirs.[41] In the case of Eleanor, whose father was dead, the responsibility for her *maritagium* fell to her brother Henry; but Henry had made no such provision for her. If he seemed niggardly, it was perhaps because he had already granted her various lands as a *maritagium* during the course of her first marriage, though to complicate matters most of these subsequently came to be

---

[38] G. H. Orpen, *Ireland under the Normans* (4 vols., Oxford, 1911–20), iii, p. 79; Wade, 'The Personal Quarrels', pp. 110–11. The names of the co-parceners in the undated partition transcribed by Wade suggest that the partition dates from 1247.

[39] KB.26/159, m. 3d; Wade, 'The Personal Quarrels', p. 111.

[40] For the political situation at the time of Henry's settlement with Richard Marshal, see Powicke, *King Henry III*, pp. 125–9.

[41] F. Pollock and F. W. Maitland, *The History of English Law* (2 vols., 2nd edn, Cambridge, 1952), ii, pp. 15–16; T. F. T. Plucknett, *The Legislation of Edward I* (Oxford, 1949), pp. 125–34.

regarded as part of Eleanor's English dower from her first husband.[42] Whatever its causes, Henry's economy denied Montfort what he most wanted in the early years of his marriage. A generous *maritagium* would have given him the land to endow his sons. To that extent it would have had advantages over Eleanor's dower, in which his family could have no more than a life interest.

Eleanor's initial lack of a *maritagium* was raised by Montfort during the course of his later quarrel with the king, probably in 1261. But, as he then noted, partial amends had been made by Henry in 1244–45, at the prompting of Henry's mother-in-law, Beatrice of Savoy, just as similar concessions had then been made over the dower.[43] On 28 May 1244 the king granted Montfort and Eleanor an annual fee of 500 marks (£333) until they could be found wardships and escheats of a similar value. Of this sum, £200 was settled on their heirs, again with the promise of later wardships and escheats. In other words they had obtained a £200 *maritagium*, a life grant of £133, and an undertaking that both would be turned into land. In June of the following year this undertaking was partly put into effect when Montfort 'bought' the wardship of the newborn son and heir of the magnate Gilbert de Umfraville for 10,000 marks, agreeing to pay this off at 500 marks a year. In effect, therefore, he gave up the 500-mark fee in exchange for the Umfraville wardship, which carried with it extensive new lands in Northumberland and must have been reckoned to be of an equivalent value.[44] This was not wholly to his advantage. The grant made on 2 May 1244 of 400 marks a year for dower losses apparently lapsed after one payment, perhaps because it was regarded as having been subsumed in the second and larger fee of 500 marks, granted on 28 May, for which the Umfraville wardship had now, in June, been substituted. This may explain the apparent confusion about the purpose of this second fee. Eleanor's enemies, so Montfort was later to complain, alleged that this fee was intended to compensate for the dower losses; whereas, as he correctly pointed out, this was not stated in the charter which had granted it.[45] Yet if the fee and the Umfraville wardship which superseded it had been granted as a *maritagium*, as Montfort rightly assumed, the arrangement was an abnormal and not entirely satisfactory one. When the Umfraville heir came of age in 1266, Montfort's control of his lands would, of course,

---

[42] *CChR, 1226–57*, p. 102; *CR, 1227–31*, p. 518.

[43] Bémont, *Montfort* (1st edn), p. 335; above, pp. 33, 50.

[44] *CChR, 1226–57*, p. 278; *Excerpta E Rot. Fin.*, ed. Roberts, i, pp. 436–7; *CLR, 1245–51*, p. 2.

[45] Bémont, *Montfort* (1st edn), p. 335.

lapse, and, in default of any intervening grants of land in fee from Henry, he might still find himself lacking the permanent landed provision for his family which a *maritagium* was intended to supply.

These difficulties were, however, prospective ones. In terms of immediate gain the Umfraville wardship can be reckoned to have raised Montfort's landed income from £1,530 in 1244, calculated above, to some £1,860 in 1246. To this figure should be added at least another £50 for Odiham and, according to a much later valuation, perhaps £15 for Kenilworth, both of which were held for life only.[46] The grand total for income in the mid 1240s was, therefore, about £1,950, as the graph on p. 47 shows. Where did this place Montfort in the social hierarchy of landed power? Certainly among the richest half dozen of the earls, though perhaps in the second rank: below Richard of Cornwall, whose income may have been as much as £5,000–£6,000 a year, Richard de Clare, earl of Gloucester (c. £3,700), Walter Marshal, earl of Pembroke (c. £3,500), and probably Roger Bigod, earl of Norfolk, but well above such comital small fry as William de Ferrers, earl of Derby (c. £1,300) and Roger de Quincy, earl of Winchester (c. £400, excluding his Scottish lands).[47] It remained true that the largest single portion of this income came from Eleanor – £930 from her dower, £65 from the holdings set aside for her at Odiham and Kenilworth – and could not be transmitted to Montfort's heirs. Only some £800 derived from landed resources held in fee: the honor of Leicester, the *terra Normannorum*, and the promised grant of £200-worth of land, now apparently merged with the Umfraville wardship. Had it not been for Eleanor, Montfort's dependence on little more than his Leicester lands would have put him, too, among the minnows. As it was, his wife made him a very rich man, but one who could not expect his riches to outlast him and whose sons would be left with more limited prospects than their parents' marriage had seemed to promise.

The scatter of lands which came to him from his marriage did little to modify the essential concentration of Montfort's resources in Leicestershire and, to a lesser extent, Warwickshire. The grant of the Harcourt lands in 1236 and of Kenilworth in 1244 strengthened his interests in those counties. Only the Umfraville estate, consisting largely of

---

[46] *CPR, 1247–58*, p. 5; *CIPM*, iii, pp. 288–9.

[47] Denholm-Young, *Richard of Cornwall*, p. 163; M. Altschul, *A Baronial Family in Medieval England: The Clares, 1217–1314* (Baltimore, 1965), pp. 203–5; G. C. Simpson, 'The *Familia* of Roger de Quincy, Earl of Winchester and Constable of Scotland', *Essays on the Nobility of Medieval Scotland*, ed. K. J. Stringer (Edinburgh, 1985), p. 123, n. 9.

Redesdale and the twenty-four townships of the Northumbrian barony of Prudhoe, gave him a major stake in a more distant area. The main centres of his power were Leicester, Kenilworth and, less conspicuously, Hungerford for his southern lands.[48] As his most valuable single possession and the *caput* of his ancestral honor, Leicester was treated with special regard by Montfort. Five of his charters were issued in the town's favour, more than for any other single grantee. His initial expulsion of the Jews from the borough had been represented by him as a mark both of personal piety and of consideration for the towns-people.[49] In succeeding years he quitclaimed to the burgesses his rights in a piece of borough pasture, sold out various other rights to them, replaced ultimogeniture (inheritance by the youngest son) with primo-geniture at their request, and, in 1257, secured their exemption from the king's right to take cloth and merchandise at all fairs and markets.[50] As both his expulsion of the Jews and his introduction of primogeniture suggest, Montfort's authority over the town was akin to royal power. It was this, as well as the income which was the consequence of that power, that made Leicester the economic hub of the whole estate; just as Kenilworth, Montfort's frequent place of residence and one which he fortified elaborately, came to be its social and military centre (Plate 4).[51]

In the absence of manorial or household records, our knowledge of how the estate was exploited is necessarily limited. That it was often under heavy pressure we need not doubt. Despite Montfort's wealth, both political crises and foreign affairs made some exceptional and sudden demands on his resources, leaving him short of ready money and driving him to desperate measures in order to raise it. His journey to Rome in 1238, his crusade in 1240, and his period of service in Gascony between 1248 and 1252, when the king's subsidies proved inadequate for the duchy's defence, all forced him to deplete his capital resources by, for example, the sale of lands or woods. His sale of his 'noble wood' at Leicester to the canons of Leicester and the Hospitallers, prior to his crusade, brought him about £1,000, according to Paris.[52] There is an unusual insight here into the immediate remedies for 'cash flow' problems which might face any nobleman; yet the remedies may not have been typical. More normal would have been resort to the

---

[48] For Hungerford as a centre, see *CPR, 1247–58*, p. 249.
[49] Nichols, *Leicester*, I, i, appendix, p. 38; above, p. 15.
[50] *Recs. Bor. Leics.*, i, pp. 38–9, 46–50; *CPR, 1247–58*, p. 557.
[51] *Flores Hist.*, ii, pp. 489, 504; Rishanger, *De Bellis*, p. 87.
[52] Paris, iii, p. 479; iv, p. 7; v, pp. 208–10; Bémont, *Montfort* (1st edn), p. 334.

Plate 4. Two views of Kenilworth Castle. (a) The castle today, looking north.
Montfort took over the twelfth-century keep (top centre) and probably built the Water
Tower (with window, bottom right) and the western stretch of the curtain wall (far
left). (b) The castle Montfort inherited. An artist's impression of the castle left by
King John.

Jews, but Montfort appears to have gone in this direction only once, in 1243.[53] A combination of his own religious scruples and the unwillingness of the Jews to lend to one who, after his expulsion of the Leicester Jews, must have been known as their enemy, may have limited his access to Jewish credit, at the ultimate expense of the capital value of the estate.

It would be natural to assume that his peasant tenants took the strain, too, and were often the victims of these exigencies. If we again lack the documentation to prove the point, there are certainly indications that this was so: in Paris's remark that he extorted much money 'wherever he could' before his journey to Rome; in Adam Marsh's injunctions to him to control his household and ministers; and in the unusually personal language of his will, where he spoke of what he had unjustly taken from 'the poor people of my land . . . namely the cultivators, whose goods I have had many times'.[54] Under the pressure of circumstances that were not always easy, his unrelenting nature may have been as evident in the management of his estates as in his management of Gascony or, in 1264–65, of the kingdom.

His everyday exploitation of resources is more visible in the records of royal government, through the usurpation of rights and privileges at its expense, than in the squeezing of peasants which may have been equally commonplace. Throughout his scattered lands Montfort sought to curtail the Crown's authority and whenever possible to appropriate it for himself. So in Northumberland he absorbed outlying villages and hamlets into the Umfraville liberty of Redesdale, depriving the Crown of escheats and pleas, and withdrew the suits which his men owed to the county court; in Berkshire he refused to allow the king's bailiff to enter Hungerford to distrain for debt; in Warwickshire he withdrew various settlements from the public obligations to which they had been subject in the geldable part of the county; and in Leicestershire and Buckinghamshire he forcibly and successfully resisted, through his bailiffs, the Lord Edward's men in 1255 when they came to take over the manors of Gilbert of Segrave, Montfort's deceased tenant, whose lands had been granted to Edward.[55]

We do not, of course, know that the initiative here always lay with the

---

[53] Above, p. 33.

[54] Paris, iii, p. 479; *Mon. Franc.*, i, pp. 261, 264, 276; Bémont, *Montfort* (2nd edn), p. 277; below, pp. 58, 100, 176.

[55] *Three Early Assize Rolls for the County of Northumberland*, ed. W. Page (Surtees Soc., lxxxviii, 1891), pp. 325–6, 352; *Rot. Hund.*, ii, pp. 17–18, 225; *The Roll and Writ File of the Berkshire Eyre of 1248*, ed. M. T. Clanchy (Selden Soc., xc, 1973), pp. xxviii–xxix, 309; *CR, 1254–56*, p. 200; Carpenter, 'King, Magnates and Society', pp. 64, 68.

earl, rather than with his over-zealous officials; we do know that his or his ministers' actions were in no way unique. In the fifteen years or so prior to 1258 the usurpation of royal rights in the countryside by the greatest of the magnates, often with the king's connivance, gathered pace. That was part of the price which Henry paid for good relations with these men. Montfort kept company here both with future reformers such as Roger Bigod, earl of Norfolk, and with the future enemies of reform, such as Richard of Cornwall and William de Valence.[56] There were only two unusual features in his case: first, the contrast between the distinctive highmindedness of his private beliefs and the conventional pursuit of his private interests which was that of his kind; and, second, the insufficiency of royal favour – for example, the exemption from legal process granted to the king's Lusignan half-brothers[57] – which prevented him from carrying the process to extremes. The constraints on his taking liberties were not so much moral as practical.

(c) THE AFFINITY

Like the estates which largely supported them, a magnate's followers provided one of the springs of his power. They helped him to exploit his resources, landed and military, to maintain a *curia* for purposes both social and judicial, and to exercise the good lordship on which his standing in the local community and in the community of the realm partly depended. These considerations, commonplace but respectable, would in themselves justify some discussion of Montfort's affinity. But just as his landed resources have a significance beyond the ordinary for his career, so also does his affinity: for its leaders were to become the friends and allies who would back him unwaveringly through the period of reform and rebellion until the final catastrophe at Evesham in 1265. In looking at these men we are not only concerned with the *familia* of a typical magnate, but with what was to become a political connection, whose members would be among the main actors in a great national drama.

Montfort's following is best approached through a study of his charters, since these provide both an index to his grants and, more

---

[56] Carpenter, 'King, Magnates and Society', pp. 62–70; J. R. Maddicott, 'Magna Carta and the Local Community, 1215–59', *Past and Present*, 102 (1984), pp. 150–1.
[57] Paris, v, p. 594; Maddicott, 'Magna Carta', p. 56; below, p. 143.

importantly, through their witness-lists a guide to those who were most frequently in his company. Yet there is a difficulty in applying this traditional *modus operandi* to Montfort's affinity, and one which is in itself revealing. The corpus of Montfort's charters is quite abnormally small. For the thirty-four years of his English career he appears as grantor in only twenty-four known charters, and as grantee or party to an exchange in only another fifteen: an average, taking the 'grantor' charters alone, of 0.7 a year. Some interesting comparisons can be made with other twelfth- and thirteenth-century earls whose charters have been collected:[58]

John 'the Scot', earl of Huntingdon and Chester:
   issued 30 known charters in 5 years (1232–37)   = 6 p.a.
Ranulf, earl of Chester:
   235 charters in 51 years (1181–1232)   = 4.60 p.a.
Waleran of Meulan:
   132 charters in 46 years (1120–66)   = 2.87 p.a.
William the Marshal, earl of Pembroke:
   67 charters in 30 years (1189–1219)   = 2.23 p.a.
Roger de Quincy, earl of Winchester:
   90 charters in 45 years (1219–64)   = 2.0 p.a.
David, earl of Huntingdon:
   90 charters in 47 years (1172–1219)   = 1.91 p.a.

Some caveats are, of course, necessary. The high numbers of charters issued by earls active in the twelfth century partly denote an aristocratic generosity towards the Church more common then than later; some may derive from the chance survival of cartularies from religious houses associated with a particular earl (hence, for example, David of Huntingdon's sixteen charters for Lindores abbey); others were confirmations of earlier grants, or documents such as letters which are more properly *acta* than charters in the strict sense.[59] Yet when all such allowances have been made, the paucity of Montfort's charters, issued

---

[58] I am most grateful to Dr David Crouch for making available to me his list of Montfort's charters, the product, *inter alia*, of a systematic search through monastic cartularies. To it I have added some new discoveries. The table of other comital charters is compiled from: *Chs. of the Earls of Chester*, Nos. 202–441, 445–69; D. Crouch, *The Beaumont Twins* (Cambridge, 1986), p. xi; D. Crouch, *William Marshal* (Harlow, 1990), p. 134; K. J. Stringer, *Earl David of Huntingdon, 1152–1219* (Edinburgh, 1985), pp. 220–70; Simpson, 'The *Familia* of Roger de Quincy', pp. 123, 130.

[59] E.g. Stringer, *Earl David*, pp. 240–53; Crouch, *William Marshal*, p. 134; *Chs. of the Earls of Chester*, No. 436.

at less than half the rate of those granted by the next most illiberal of the earls, remains striking. It is especially so in view of the eventual absorption of the estate into the Duchy of Lancaster and the consequent descent of many of its muniments with the Crown, giving Montfort's grants a better than average chance of permanent record. We are almost certainly confronting here, not a poor rate of survival, but a low rate of issue. This in turn is likely to have reflected the sense of financial constraint which characterised so many of Montfort's dealings and which created a close awareness of the need to husband resources. It also reflected a related parsimony, merging into tightfistedness, which will emerge again when we look at his religious donations. In these respects charter statistics seem to reinforce what other sources tell us about his situation and mentality.

The relative scarcity of Montfort's charters, useful as an indicator of his circumstances, still leaves this body of material as an essential denominator of his following. Taken together with other evidence, the charters depict an affinity brought together from different lordships, yet overwhelmingly drawn from one region, and expanding a little in the 1240s, yet with a membership which always remained weighted towards quality rather than quantity. How was it composed?[60] Though feudal tenure by no means determined membership, some of the affinity's key members were drawn from Montfort's tenants. Two were especially prominent: Thomas of Astley and Ralph Basset of Sapcote. Astley's seat was at Astley in Warwickshire, held from the earls of Warwick, but his larger holdings in Leicestershire were held from the earls of Leicester, whom his family had long served. Thomas's grandfather had been bailiff both to Robert IV, the last of the Beaumont earls, in 1203, and also to Montfort's father during the short period prior to 1207 when the honor had been in his hands. The Astleys do not seem to have been as close to Ranulf of Chester, the subsequent custodian of Montfort's half of the honor, none of whose numerous charters they witnessed; but in Montfort's early years the old connection was resumed. First appearing as a charter witness about 1240, Thomas of Astley went on to serve Montfort in Gascony from 1248 and is once named as his steward.[61]

---

[60] Carpenter, 'Simon de Montfort', pp. 10–13, provides a brief but pioneering survey.

[61] *CRR*, iii, *1203–05*, p. 45; *Pipe Roll 9 John*, ed. D. M. Stenton (Pipe Roll Soc., n.s., xxii, 1946), p. 196; *A Descriptive Catalogue of Ancient Deeds* (6 vols., H.M.S.O., 1890–1915), iv, p. 122; *CPR, 1247–58*, pp. 31, 43; *CIM*, i, Nos. 772, 928, 929; L. Fox, 'The Honor of Leicester: A Study in Descent and Administration' (Manchester M.A. thesis, 1938), pp. 133–4. The important charter of c. 1240, a grant to Leicester abbey confirmed by the king in 1252 (*CChR, 1226–57*,

Ralph Basset of Sapcote, whose main Leicestershire manor of Sapcote was held of the honor, followed a similar course. He made his first appearance in the affinity, with Astley, about 1240, acted again with Astley as Montfort's surety for the earl's Jewish debt in 1243, and accompanied him with the earl to Gascony. He was a more frequent charter witness than all but one of Montfort's other followers. Both men were in arms with their lord during his final campaign, and Astley was to die at Evesham: a record of service which for both of them stretched back over twenty-five years.[62]

A third tenant, Richard de Grey of Codnor, in Derbyshire, was a less conspicuous but more substantial baronial follower, who probably owed his association with Montfort as much to political sympathy as to tenure. The holder of one and a half fees from the earl in Northamptonshire, and lord of the Leicestershire manor of Alvington, he witnessed no charters but was known in 1259 as a friend of Montfort and was active in his cause through the reforming period.[63]

Unlike Astley, Bassett and Grey, however, the majority of Montfort's closest followers were his neighbours but not his tenants. Here he was able to take advantage of the good fortune which had removed the leading rivals to his local supremacy.[64] Deaths, the extinction of families in the male line, and the withdrawal of potential competitors from the scene, had all cleared the ground for his isolated eminence as the one remaining magnate who could offer patronage and leadership to the minor baronage and gentry of the *patria*. These changes had begun before Montfort's accession, with the passing of the Quincy half of the honor into the hands of Margaret, widow of Saer de Quincy, earl of Winchester, in 1219, the delay until 1235 in the recognition of their son Roger as the next earl, Roger's own major interest elsewhere, in Scotland, and his relative poverty and isolation from the royal court. Though he continued to hold and exploit property in Leicestershire, he was hardly a vital force in the county. The process had continued with

---

p. 408), provides the first evidence for several associations with Montfort. It is undated, but must date from before October 1241, by which time Stephen of Segrave, a witness, was dead (*Peerage*, XI, p. 601). Since its purpose was almost certainly to alienate land in order to raise money for Montfort's crusade (Paris, iv, p. 7), it very probably dates from 1240.

[62] *Feudal Aids* (6 vols., H.M.S.O., 1899–1920), iii, pp. 97–8; *CChR, 1226–57*, p. 408; *CPR, 1232–47*, p. 433; *1247–58*, p. 31; *CIM*, i, No. 929.

[63] *Book of Fees*, ii, p. 940; *DBM*, pp. 200–1; Carpenter 'Simon de Montfort', p. 12.

[64] The point was first made, for a longer period, by D. Williams, 'Simon de Montfort and his Adherents', *England in the Thirteenth Century: Proceedings of the 1984 Harlaxton Symposium*, ed. W. M. Ormrod (Grantham, 1985), pp. 174–6.

Ranulf of Chester's handover of Montfort's part of the honor in 1231 and his childless death the following year. This delivered his personal holdings in Leicestershire and Warwickshire into the hands of his nephews, John 'the Scot', now earl of Chester and largely based there, and Hugh d'Aubigny, earl of Arundel, a minor in royal wardship. John 'the Scot' himself died childless in 1237, leaving his lands to be divided among coheirs. The further death of Thomas Beauchamp, earl of Warwick, in 1242, again without a direct male heir, completed an evacuation of local power which left Montfort dominant by virtue of survival.[65]

These circumstances brought two particular groups into the affinity, the former tenants of Ranulf of Chester and the current tenants of the largely absentee Roger de Quincy. Some of the families most closely associated with Montfort throughout his career had been in Ranulf's entourage, their links no doubt forged during the brief time when the young Montfort had himself been attached to Ranulf. This natural transfer of loyalties was best exemplified by the Segraves, whose Leicestershire manor of Seagrave had been held of the earls of Chester since the twelfth century and whose political affiliations during Montfort's early years in England have already been discussed. Stephen of Segrave, justiciar from 1232 to 1234, had partly risen through service to Earl Ranulf and had been a beneficiary of his grants. Both he and his eldest son Gilbert passed into Montfort's affinity during the 1230s and were highly enough regarded to receive substantial grants of land from him. In the next generation Gilbert's son Nicholas, under age at his father's death in 1254, went on to become one of Montfort's most dependable lieutenants in 1264–65 and to fight for him at Evesham.[66] The loyalties of a second family, the Despensers, had a similar, if more broken, descent. Like Stephen of Segrave, Hugh Despenser senior had been a *familiaris* of Earl Ranulf: Ranulf's tenant in his chief Leicester-shire manor of Loughborough, a regular witness to his charters, and probably his hereditary steward. His elder son, another Hugh, first appears in association with Montfort in 1259, but his position as a

---

[65] Simpson, 'The *Familia* of Roger de Quincy', pp. 103–4; D. Crouch, *The Image of Aristocracy in Britain, 1000–1300* (London, 1992), pp. 308–9; R. Stewart-Brown, 'The End of the Norman Earldom of Chester', *EHR*, 35 (1920), pp. 26–34; P. Coss, *Lordship, Knighthood and Locality* (Cambridge, 1991), p. 44; *Peerage*, XII, ii, pp. 365–6.

[66] *Chs. of the Earls of Chester*, Nos. 248, 266, 310, etc. (witnessings), 358, 361, 362–9 (grants); W. Farrer, *Honors and Knights' Fees* (3 vols., London and Manchester, 1923–5), ii, pp. 71–2; BL MS. Egerton 3789, fos. 100r, 101r; Dugdale, *Baronage*, i, p. 673; *CChR, 1226–57*, p. 241; *Peerage*, XI, pp. 597–604; above, pp. 16, 20.

subordinate executor of the earl's will, under Countess Eleanor and
Henry de Montfort, indicates that the two must already have been
old friends. He went on to become baronial justiciar and to die at
Evesham.[67]

In number, if not in weight, the knights from the Quincy half of the
honor made a still greater contribution to the affinity. One of the
earliest and most prominent was Thomas Menill, whose only holding
seems to have been part of a fee held from Quincy in the Leicestershire
village of Hemington, but who witnessed four of Montfort's charters, the
first in 1233, and was already his steward in 1231–32: probably the
steward of the whole estate, and not just its Leicestershire properties,
since it was as steward that he witnessed a transaction concerning the
earl's Wiltshire manor of Everleigh. He can last be seen in Montfort's
service in 1247 and may have died soon afterwards.[68] Equally prominent
but over a longer period were the two Arnolds du Bois, father and
son, whose family had been tenants of the Beaumont earls in their
Leicestershire manor of Thorpe Arnold since the early twelfth century
and 'the mainstay of Leicester honorial government'. Although Thorpe
Arnold was awarded to Quincy in the partition of 1207, and although
the family continued to have close connections with Roger de Quincy,
Arnold senior witnessed one of Montfort's charters about 1240 and
another about 1254, when he headed the witness-list. He died in 1255,
leaving a son and heir who was still higher in Montfort's favour, for he
was named as co-executor of the earl's will, with Hugh Despenser and
Peter de Montfort, in 1259. A long illness allowed him to evade the
subsequent troubles.[69] Other members of the Quincy affinity – Saer
de Harcourt, Peter le Porter, Saher of St Andrews – made a more
occasional appearance in Montfort's company; and by 1265 Saer de
Harcourt had become his knight.[70]

The evidence suggests, then, that in Montfort's earliest years in
England, and to a large extent throughout his career, his following was

---

[67] *Chs. of the Earls of Chester*, Nos. 211, 212, 258, etc.; Bémont, *Montfort* (2nd edn), p. 277; *Peerage*, IV,
pp. 259–61.

[68] *HMC, Hastings*, i (1928), p. 328; BL MS. Cotton Nero C. XII, f. 110; *CChR, 1226–57*, p. 408;
DL.35/2313; *Memoranda Roll 16–17 Henry III*, ed. R. Allen Brown (H.M.S.O., 1991), No. 2355;
JUST.1/454, m. 9.

[69] *HMC, Hastings*, i, p. 325; *CChR, 1226–57*, p. 408; *Recs. Bor. Leics.*, i, pp. 46–9; Paris, v, p. 487;
Bémont, *Montfort* (2nd edn), p. 277; *CPR, 1258–66*, p. 140; Crouch, *The Beaumont Twins*,
pp. 109–11; Simpson, 'The *Familia* of Roger de Quincy', pp. 108–9, 116.

[70] Simpson, 'The *Familia* of Roger de Quincy', pp. 108–9, 121; BL MS. Harley 4714, ff. 44v–45;
CPR, 1258–66, p. 418; Carpenter, 'Simon de Montfort', p. 11.

concentrated in Leicestershire. With the exception of Peter le Porter and Saher of St Andrews, neither of whom could be classed as *familiares*, all those mentioned so far had their main holdings in the county. Montfort's patronage of his own tenants, and his adoption of lordless men from the former Chester affinity and of others who were under the semi-detached lordship of Roger de Quincy, was one way in which he became assimilated into his English inheritance and put down roots. Yet before about 1240 the process was hardly complete. When he went on crusade in that year five of the ten bannerets who followed him were French or Burgundian, and none of his English bannerets were drawn from his earldom.[71] It was only in the 1240s, as old connections were perpetuated, new ones created and the affinity enlarged, that Montfort became more firmly fixed in the social landscape of the English midlands.

This was more than just an effect of time: it also reflected Montfort's deepening interest in Leicestershire's neighbouring county of Warwickshire. This in turn resulted from the death of Thomas Beauchamp, earl of Warwick, in 1242, and from Montfort's own more permanent hold on the great castle of Kenilworth, granted to him in custody in 1244 and for life by two grants of 1248 and 1253.[72] Beauchamp's death without male heir is likely to have confirmed the allegiance to Montfort of those who, like Astley, had held from both lords. But this consolidation and extension of his influence also gave a leading place in the affinity to a new figure who was to become one of Montfort's closest aides: Peter de Montfort.[73] No relation of his namesake, Peter had been a major tenant of the earl of Warwick and became a near neighbour of the earl of Leicester. His Warwickshire seat of Beaudesert was nine miles from Kenilworth, his manor of Whitchurch marched with Montfort's at Ilmington, and both were held of the earl of Warwick. His introduction to the *familia*, however, probably owed less to these local ties than to his uncle, William de Cantilupe II (d. 1251), and, at one remove, to Cantilupe's patron, Ranulf of Chester. William de Cantilupe II had been a trusted friend of Ranulf, whose executor he was and one of whose charters he witnessed, in company with Montfort, in 1232. Their common dependence on the earl of Chester thus initially connected

---

[71] Paris, iv, p. 44; Lloyd, *English Society and the Crusade*, p. 83.
[72] *CPR, 1232–47*, p. 419; *1247–58*, pp. 5, 250.
[73] For Peter de Montfort, see D. A. Carpenter, 'Peter de Montfort', *The Dictionary of National Biography: Missing Persons*, ed. C. S. Nicholls (Oxford, 1993), pp. 520–1.

Simon de Montfort to William. These early ties were strengthened by Montfort's friendship with William's brother Walter, the bishop of Worcester, and with his son, William de Cantilupe III, at whose funeral in 1254 Montfort was one of the chief mourners. Peter de Montfort was still more closely linked to William II, the uncle who had brought him up and in whose service he probably remained until the mid 1240s. But in 1248 he went to Gascony with Simon, the first mark of their association, and from then on he became a prominent *familiaris*, one of the executors of the earl's will, a frequent witness to his charters, and a leading political ally through the period of reform and rebellion.[74] His allegiance, like that of the Segraves and the Despensers, provided another example of the way in which the ramifications of the Chester connection spanned the whole period of Montfort's English career.

Although his estates in Leicestershire and Warwickshire provided Montfort with less than half his income, they were thus the homeland of almost all his leading supporters. His other holdings – the dispersed manors in southern England which made up both Eleanor's dower and the outlying parts of the honor of Leicester, the *terra Normannorum* outside these two counties, the Umfraville barony in Northumberland – lacked the most necessary elements for the creation of strong lordship: geographical cohesion, historical connections, and the close personal contacts with their lord which Montfort's early residence at Leicester and later at Kenilworth provided for his midlands contingent. Only two of the earl's *familiares* stood slightly apart from this connection: John de la Haye and Richard de Havering. De la Haye was an important man in Montfort's following: an occasional witness to his charters, his companion in Gascony in 1248 (as in Peter de Montfort's case, the first sign of their relationship) and in France, with Henry de Montfort and then with Montfort himself, in 1256–57. As constable of Dover castle and defender of the south-east coast, he was one of Montfort's most valuable supporters in 1263–65. He had strong links with the midlands heartland of the affinity, both through his family holding of one and a half fees of the honor of Leicester in Northamptonshire and through his marriage to Margaret, daughter of Richard de Harcourt, one of the

[74] *Book of Fees*, ii, p. 956; *VCH Warwickshire*, iii, ed. P. Styles (London, 1945), p. 45; *CR, 1247–51*, p. 119; *CPR, 1232–47*, pp. 80, 140; *1247–58*, pp. 17, 31; *Chs. of the Earls of Chester*, No. 310; *Ann. Dun.*, p. 192; *Sir Christopher Hatton's Book of Seals*, ed. L. C. Loyd and D. M. Stenton (Oxford, 1950), Nos. 56, 192; Bémont, *Montfort* (2nd edn), p. 277; *Peerage*, ix, pp. 123–6; D. A. Carpenter, 'St Thomas Cantilupe: His Political Career', *St Thomas Cantilupe, Bishop of Hereford*, ed. M. Jancey (Hereford, 1982), pp. 61–2.

foremost tenants and associates of Roger de Quincy and father of that other Montfortian, Saer de Harcourt. It may have been through his Harcourt relations that de la Haye gained an entrée to the *familia*. But his main landed holdings were the manors of Burwell and Houthorpe (Lincs.), Middleton (Sussex) and Horsemonden (Kent). Geographically speaking, they made him an outsider.[75]

This was still more true of Richard de Havering, whose position in the affinity was different from that of its other members in more ways than one. Havering was the earl's steward, financial agent and general factotum: a key man in holding together what was, beyond its midlands core, a dispersed estate, and in managing the affairs of a magnate whose finances were peculiarly tangled. He first appears as a servant (if that is how 'serviens' should be translated) of Eleanor in a legal case of 1234, passed thence into the service of her second husband, was bailiff of Newbury and Hungerford in 1241, and by the late 1240s had become Montfort's righthand man. He witnessed more of Montfort's charters than anyone else in his entourage, sometimes being described as 'steward of Leicester' or 'steward of the earl of Leicester'.[76] Montfort employed various followers as stewards at different times in his career – Menill, Astley and (as we shall see) Anketin de Martival – but the area of their responsibility, whether Leicester or the whole estate, is often unclear. Havering, however, undoubtedly had the comprehensive authority implied in the second of the titles cited above. That he was recognised as having a general oversight of the estates is clear from one of Adam Marsh's letters, in which he exhorted Montfort 'to write to Richard de Havering and forbid him to allow your officials, the guardians of your property in England, to destroy souls for whom the author of life died'.[77] We are not likely to get a more revealing glimpse of Montfort's uninhibited government of his lands or of the influence, for good or ill, which the steward could exercise over it.

Havering's responsibilities extended beyond estate management. He was also his lord's agent at the exchequer, collecting money for transmission to Montfort in Gascony in 1249 and taking delivery of

---

[75] *CIM*, i, Nos. 297, 720, 725, 735, 760, 796; *CPR, 1247–58*, pp. 31, 493, 564; *1258–66*, pp. 341, 424; *CIPM*, i, No. 291, ii, No. 59; Simpson, 'The *Familia* of Roger de Quincy', pp. 109, 118.

[76] *CRR*, xv, *1233–37*, No. 1145; *Roll and Writ File of the Berks. Eyre*, ed. Clanchy, p. xliii; *Recs. Bor. Leics.*, i, pp. 52, 58. Havering needs to be distinguished from two other contemporaries of the same name, one of whom was a prominent pleader: see P. Brand, *The Origins of the English Legal Profession* (Oxford, 1992), pp. 58, 62–3.

[77] *Mon. Franc.*, i, p. 276.

Eleanor's dower fee there in 1259. In the civil wars of 1263–65 he took on a military role, with custody of some of the castles in Montfort's hands, including Odiham and Wallingford.[78] His rewards for this multifarious activity were probably greater than those recorded. He was a knight by 1255 and built up a small estate centred on Montfort's Dorset manor of Shapwick and extending into three other manors in Berkshire, Wiltshire and Hampshire. In addition, there was probably also some patrimonial land at Havering in Essex. But the greatest gains, as so often, accrued to the second generation. When Havering died in 1267, loyal to the end but reconciled after Evesham to the restoration of royal power, he left a son, John, who became Edward I's seneschal in Gascony in 1289 and was summoned to parliament in 1299.[79] It was a classic success story of social promotion through ability and service, not unlike, *mutatis mutandis*, Montfort's own.

If we now move beyond the naming of parts to look at the affinity as a whole, we are at once struck by its smallness. In reconstructing Montfort's 'inner circle' (to use a category employed by Dr Simpson in his analysis of the Quincy *familia*) we are hard put to produce more than the dozen names already discussed. With the addition of the number of charters which each witnessed, granted either by or for Montfort, the list runs: Richard de Havering (11), Ralph Basset of Sapcote (10), Thomas of Astley (5), Thomas Menill (5), Peter de Montfort (5), John de la Haye (3), Stephen of Segrave (3), the two Arnolds du Bois, father and son (2 and 2), Hugh Despenser (2), Gilbert of Segrave (1) and Nicholas of Segrave (1). Richard de Grey, as a latecomer and non-witness, has been ignored.

This was not, of course, the full tally of Montfort's followers, for important men such as Peter de Montfort could themselves probably provide knightly sub-retinues for his service.[80] There may, too, have been a few others whose exiguous record of adherence to the earl belies their actual importance: for example, Anketin de Martival, a tenant both of Montfort and of Quincy in his Leicestershire manor of Noseley, chosen as baronial sheriff of Leicestershire and Warwickshire in 1258, named as Montfort's steward in a plea of 1261 and an undated

---

[78] *CR, 1247–51*, pp. 248–9, 254; *CPR, 1247–58*, p. 56; E.403/18; E. F. Jacob, *Studies in the Period of Baronial Reform and Rebellion, 1258–67* (Oxford, 1925), pp. 234–6.

[79] *Recs. Bor. Leics.*, i, p. 50; *CIPM*, i, No. 647; *Dorset Fines*, ed. E. A. and G. S. Fry (Dorset Records, x, 1910), pp. 162–3, 99–100; C. H. Knowles, 'The Resettlement of England after the Barons' War, 1264–67', *TRHS*, 5th ser., 32 (1982), pp. 39–40; *Peerage*, VI, pp. 405–8.

[80] Carpenter, 'Peter de Montfort', p. 520.

charter, witness to another of his charters, and his active supporter in
1265.[81] There were certainly others who acted for him occasionally and
who may have constituted an outer circle: men such as the Warwickshire knight William Trussell, who once served as his attorney, or
William Bassett, a knightly witness to four charters but otherwise
obscure.[82] During the troubles of 1263–65 the numbers of such part-
time partisans rose, as events forced the knights of the midlands to
choose between king and earl. But none of these foul-weather friends,
politically and militarily valuable as they were, augmented the
membership of our 'core' dozen. Even that low figure represents all
those known to have been leading members of the affinity over a thirty-
four-year period, and by no means all were in service at the same time.
If we took a view from 1258, say, we should have to discount Arnold du
Bois senior, Stephen and Gilbert of Segrave (all dead), Thomas Menill
(probably dead), and possibly Nicholas of Segrave, whose opposition to
the king and likely association with Montfort is traceable only from
1261.[83] At any one time his inner circle may have numbered no more
than six to eight men: a figure little larger than the group of four –
Astley, Basset, de la Haye and Peter de Montfort – who followed him to
Gascony in 1248.

Placed beside the other affinities which scholars have examined,
Montfort's *familia* looks no more than modest. It contrasts with the great
William Marshal's inner circle of about eighteen knights and Roger de
Quincy's fifteen.[84] These figures comprehend the whole span of the
earls' respective careers, so they should be compared with Montfort's
dozen, rather than the putative six to eight in service at any one time.
With these latter figures we may compare the twelve or so knights who
were annually in the service of William de Valence, Montfort's enemy
in the 1250s. The comparison with Quincy's affinity is particularly
telling. Unlike the Marshal, who was considerably richer than Montfort,
and William de Valence, whose income of c. £2,500 made him somewhat richer,[85] Quincy was a good deal poorer; yet he apparently had a
rather larger knightly following.

81 G. F. Farnham and A. H. Thompson, 'The Manor of Noseley', *Trans. Leics. Arch. Soc.*, xii
(1921–2), pp. 219–20; *HMC, Hastings*, i, pp. 41–2 (where 'Adam' should clearly read 'Anketin');
DL.42/4, f. 46; *CIM*, i, No. 648; Crouch, *The Image of Aristocracy*, pp. 146–7.

82 E.159/30, m. 18d; C.56/16, m. 19; *Recs. Bor. Leics.*, i, pp. 49–50; DL.25/1782; DL.42/2,
ff. 207–207v; Carpenter, 'Simon de Montfort', p. 13.

83 *CR, 1259–61*, p. 491.

84 Crouch, *William Marshal*, pp. 137–41; Simpson, 'The *Familia* of Roger de Quincy', p. 107.

85 H. Ridgeway, 'William de Valence and his *Familiares*', *Hist. Res.*, 65 (1992), p. 245.

Quincy had, too, a larger following of clerks, some five or six of whom were especially close to him. Montfort, by contrast, had no clerks among his intimate associates. Robert de Vielenc, *clericus*, witnessed two of his charters and is identified as a clerk in his service during his time in Gascony in 1253; 'Sir Peter the priest of Dunganac' is named as his chaplain in a charter of 1236; but that is the best we can do.[86] The absence of a strong clerical party in the *familia* is one of its most peculiar features, especially peculiar in view of Montfort's religious predilections. In his own household he does not seem to have had any particular attachment to the men of learning, education and piety whom he cultivated among the bishops and the Franciscans.

Neither its numbers nor its narrow constitution tell the whole story, however, for Montfort's affinity had a weightiness that was out of proportion to its size. Some of its members – the Segraves, Despenser, Basset, Peter de Montfort, perhaps the two Arnolds du Bois – were themselves substantial men, minor barons rather than knights. Defining the baronage is notoriously difficult in the mid-thirteenth century, before the regular survival of parliamentary summonses, and with few other indications of those whom contemporaries regarded as barons. But it is worth noting that Peter de Montfort and Hugh Despenser were members of the baronial group nominated to choose the king's councillors in 1258, that Peter de Montfort, Ralph Basset and Nicholas of Segrave were among the *barones* who agreed to submit their quarrel with the king to Louis IX's arbitration in 1263–64, and that Despenser, Segrave and Basset were summoned to Montfort's parliament in January 1265.[87] Evidence drawn from the reforming period, when it is most abundant, is, of course, suspect, since it may reflect partisanship rather than an established place in the baronial hierarchy. But it receives some support from one of the earliest rolls of arms, Glover's Roll, dating from c. 1250, which lists Arnold du Bois senior, Peter de Montfort and Gilbert of Segrave among the barons and senior county knights whom it records.[88] What we can deduce about status from these sources is partly corroborated by what we know about wealth. Peter de Montfort, Hugh Despenser, Ralph Basset and Nicholas de Segrave, for example, all had lands worth more than £120 a year, at a time when a

---

[86] DL.42/2, f. 46v; DL.25/1784; *CPR, 1247–58*, p. 258; *CChR, 1226–57*, p. 230.

[87] *DBM*, pp. 100–1, 284–5; *CR, 1264–68*, p. 86.

[88] *Rolls of Arms: Henry III*, ed. H. S. London (London, 1967), pp. 135, 137, 149. It is hard to agree with Crouch, *The Image of Aristocracy*, pp. 37, 235, that this roll distinguishes clearly between barons and knights; they seem rather to mingle promiscuously.

£20 income would make a man liable for knighthood. Even below the level of this honorial baronage there were some exceptionally prosperous men among Montfort's followers: after Evesham the lands of Thomas of Astley were assessed at £67 and those of John de la Haye at more than £57. Within the inner circle of barons and knights only Thomas Menill, part holder of a fee worth £10, came anywhere near to landlessness.[89]

The cohesion of this group, and hence partly its value to Montfort, rested on more than its members' common service to their leader. It was also founded on ties of neighbourhood and family which were perhaps stronger and more deeply felt. We have already seen how neighbourhood did more than tenure to link the earl with his followers: as with the retinue of William Marshal, feudal ties counted for less than geographical bias towards a particular *patria*,[90] in Montfort's case the *patria* of Leicestershire and Warwickshire. The social life of this compact stretch of countryside does much to explain the remarkable number of marriage connections found within so small a group. Stephen of Segrave married Rohese, sister of Hugh Despenser senior (d. 1238). Gilbert of Segrave, who was the child either of this marriage or of Stephen's subsequent marriage to Ida, widow of Henry de Hastings, married Amabil, daughter and coheiress of Robert de Chaucombe of Northamptonshire, whose other daughter, Millicent, married Ralph Bassett of Sapcote. Basset's wife was thus the aunt of Nicholas of Segrave. Thomas of Astley married Joan, daughter of Arnold du Bois, senior, making him respectively the son-in-law and brother-in-law of the two Arnolds. And we have already noticed John de la Haye's marriage to Margaret, sister of Montfort's knight Saer de Harcourt.[91] For these men, living at no great distance from each other, in a world of close legal and family relationships in some ways more akin to that of Jane Austen than to that of the romances or the *chansons de gestes*, attachment to Montfort only added another strand to an existing skein of connections. For Montfort, on the other hand, these horizontal ties contributed to the strength imparted to the retinue by the primary and vertical tie of lordship.

What price did he have to pay? It is clear that Montfort picked his

---

[89] C. H. Knowles, 'The Disinherited, 1265–80' (Univ. of Wales Aberystwyth Ph.D. thesis, 1959), pp. 7–8; *CIM*, i, Nos. 720, 772, 796, 925, 928, 929; *HMC, Hastings*, i, p. 328.

[90] Crouch, *William Marshal*, p. 138.

[91] *Peerage*, II, p. 6; XI, pp. 601, 603; Nichols, *Leicester*, IV, i, p. 59; Bodleian Lib. MS. Dugdale 15, f. 117; above, p. 67.

followers with careful discrimination, to create an affinity more influential than its numbers would suggest. Its weighting towards minor barons and major knights may have reflected, not just the desire of every powerful magnate for powerful supporters, but the deliberate choice of men whose relative self-sufficiency might be thought likely to moderate the expectations which poorer men might have had of their lord. The costs of retaining, and hence the special need for caution in taking up new obligations by one who was always a cautious giver, are suggested by what little information we have on the rewards offered by Montfort. To Richard de Havering he gave a small estate in Shapwick. To Peter de Montfort he gave £40-worth of land in fee in Ilmington, including the manor house, and another Warwickshire estate acquired by purchase. To Thomas Menill he gave the Leicestershire manors of Bagworth and Thornton until Menill could be found £30-worth of land elsewhere. On another occasion he granted Bagworth to Gilbert of Segrave (Plate 5), who had already received the village of Kegworth and by 1247 had also been given the former Harcourt manor of Sileby in Leicestershire. This holding was in the hands of Nicholas of Segrave in 1265.[92] Ilmington and Sileby were *terra Normannorum* and hence, as acquisitions, more dispensable than the earl's patrimony. Nevertheless, the alienation of these and other lands shows the process of attrition by which grants to wellwishers and supporters could eat away at the edges of an estate.

Whether there were other sorts of reward is difficult to say. Though some of the younger Simon's men were identified as rebels in 1265 by wearing his robes, there is no evidence that money fees – the concomitant of robes in late-medieval retaining – were disbursed by either father or son. The earl's anxiety in his will to see the settlement of his debts owed 'for services performed for me . . . by those who have served me' is suggestive, but could as well refer to domestic servants and tradesmen as to knights and barons.[93] Nor is there much evidence for the downward transmission of royal favours through the conduit of seigneurial patronage. John de la Haye's receiving a royal licence at Montfort's instance to lease out a manor, and Anketin de Martival's escape from knighthood and, once a knight, from the civil obligations

[92] *CIPM*, i, No. 647; *Dorset Fines*, ed. Fry and Fry, pp. 99–100; Bodleian Lib., MS. Dugdale 13, f. 256; DL.25/1784; DL.42/2, f. 46v; BL MS. Egerton 3789, ff. 100–1; Gloucs. County Record Office, D.225/T.7; *Book of Fees*, ii, p. 1392; *CIM*, i, No. 771.
[93] *CIM*, i, Nos. 705, 853; Bémont, *Montfort* (2nd edn), p. 276.

Plate 5. A follower rewarded: Montfort grants Bagworth, Leicestershire, to Gilbert of Segrave, 1230–1239.

of his rank, thanks possibly to his lord's influence, remain as rare examples.[94] For the most part the brittleness of Montfort's relationship with Henry III through the 1240s and 1250s promised no regular access to the spoils of power for his friends. If that was what was wanted, they would have done better to look elsewhere, to Richard of Cornwall, say, or Peter of Savoy. So if we ask why these men joined Montfort we cannot frame an answer entirely in terms of material gain. The less tangible attractions of his lordship also have to be taken into account; ancestral ties, the natural allegiance of local men to their local lord, and

[94] *CPR, 1247–58*, p. 631; Crouch, *The Image of Aristocracy*, p. 147.

the allure possessed by a magnate who was married to the king's sister, an outstanding military leader, and widely experienced on an international stage perhaps more glamorous than the parochial life of the English counties.

Montfort's own expectations of his followers may be more easily defined in traditional terms. What he wanted from them was service: in the management of his estates, in his foreign campaigns, and no doubt in the enhancement of his prestige and worship both locally and centrally. Their role in witnessing his charters, on occasions when the lord could be seen in the company of his *familia*, was one public expression of the honour which the affinity brought him. In the end he received much more than this, more indeed than any lord had a right to expect. Of the dozen members of Montfort's inner circle, eight were alive and active between 1258 and 1265, and all except Arnold du Bois junior, an invalid, were loyal to the last. Astley, Despenser and Peter de Montfort were all killed at Evesham; Nicholas of Segrave fought and was captured there; Basset was in arms for his lord and may also have been present; de la Haye and Havering were protecting his interests in other parts of England. Unlike the retainers of another rebel baron, Thomas of Lancaster, in similar circumstances,[95] they were not men to break and run. Their fidelity, like that of the bishops, is a sign of the respect and perhaps affection in which this hard and uncompromising man was held and of his ability to identify his men with his own interests. It is some tribute to Montfort's qualities that in these last years the affinity transcended its local background and became instead a party to a cause.

Beyond their concentration on matters central to Montfort's position as a landed magnate, the different sections of this chapter may appear to have had little underlying unity. As with any magnate, Montfort's family, lands and finances, and affinity formed the grounds of a private life which served to sustain a public role, whether in politics, war or diplomacy. In his case they also generated claims and grievances which became entwined with that role, in ways which we have already glanced at and will pursue later. Besides their common bearing on Montfort's public life, however, these subjects are linked by two other themes. First, their study suggests that Montfort was constantly on the edge of financial embarrassment. It may seem difficult to understand how any

---

[95] J. R. Maddicott, *Thomas of Lancaster, 1307–22* (Oxford, 1970), pp. 295–6.

earl with an income of some £1,950 a year could be in this position – until we remember the debts that Montfort had incurred in the 1230s, the heavy costs of his journey to Rome and his crusade, the further expenses that he was to incur in the king's service in Gascony, and above all the size of his family. A combination of occasional but acute shortages of cash, exemplified by the crusade, of the constant medium-term demands of aristocratic life (how much did it cost him to refortify Kenilworth castle, with its 'marvellous buildings' and its 'hitherto unheard of . . . machines'?),[96] and of the prospective difficulty of endowing his sons, all seem to have produced a countervailing financial caution which is reflected again and again in the history of Montfort's affairs – in the paucity of his charters, the smallness of his affinity and, as we shall see, in the exiguous number and size of his grants to religious institutions.

Secondly, these features of Montfort's private life can all be seen as aspects of his anglicisation. The acquisition and expansion of his English lands, his marriage into the English royal family (and not to one of the continental noblewomen who had first attracted his attentions),[97] his linking up with the former *familiares* of Ranulf of Chester and the current tenants of Roger de Quincy, were all central to this process of cultural assimilation. The process had gone far enough by 1258 for his antagonism towards the king's alien favourites, who were themselves sometimes moving towards assimilation by the same routes,[98] to seem not entirely incongruous.

But this view cannot go entirely unqualified. Montfort was never anything like wholly English. That he continued to hold some lands in France is suggested by Pope Gregory IX's order in 1238 to the bishop of Soissons, arising out of the earl's debt to the count of Brittany, to put his lands under interdict. He had particularly close links with Burgundy. Three Burgundians accompanied him on crusade in 1240; he probably returned in the company of Hugh IV, duke of Burgundy, who was later to grant him the castle of 'Burdelii'; and he was in Burgundy when Henry summoned him to Poitou in 1242.[99] He may have had a following in France, just as he had in England. Who, for example, was the Simon de Cauda, described as Montfort's knight but unknown to

[96] *Flores Hist.*, ii. p. 489.
[97] Above, pp. 17–18.
[98] Ridgeway, 'William de Valence', pp. 256–7.
[99] Bémont, *Montfort* (1st edn), pp. 263–4, 334; Paris, iv, p. 44.

English records, the legitimation of whose marriage he sought from the pope in 1247?[100] The offer to him of the stewardship of France, after Queen Blanche's death and during Louis IX's absence on crusade, is an indication of his standing there. Paris, who tells the story, says that he was chosen because of his great love for France and his father's reputation, 'nor was he an alien by blood'.[101] His long absences from England, his French connections, and the range of his foreign experience, all separated him from the other English nobles and made him never quite fully at home in the towns and countryside of Leicestershire and Warwickshire which provided him with a large part of his fortune and his following. In the next chapter we shall look at an equally distinctive feature of his place among the English nobility, and one still more remarkable: his religious beliefs and his ecclesiastical connections.

[100] *CPL*, i, p. 233.
[101] Paris, v, p. 366, 371–2.

CHAPTER 3

Religion and virtue

(A) LANDSCAPE WITH FRIENDS

The two impulses which gave coherence and direction to Simon de Montfort's activities were piety and self-interest. Each formed a deep and powerful part of his character. Their opposing polarities, intermittently visible from the start of his English career, became especially conspicuous after 1258, when the impossibility of reconciling them, and the counterpoint between them, gives the earl's political odyssey much of its enduring fascination. So far we have seen more of self-interest than of piety. Montfort's pushing self-assertiveness has been obvious, both throughout the narrative of his rise to power in England, and in the claims and grievances which arose from the peculiarities of his endowment and family situation. It will become more obvious still as we move towards and beyond the climacteric of the 1258–59 reform movement. Here we are chiefly concerned with the other side of the story: with a personal devoutness perhaps more fully apprehensible than that of any other layman between King Alfred in the ninth century and Henry of Lancaster in the fourteenth, and certainly as extreme in its manifestations as the pattern of conduct which was often set against it.

Montfort's religion in some ways typified the changing forms through which, in the first half of the thirteenth century, lay piety found expression. In an earlier period the layman's hopes of salvation had largely centred on the monasteries. Their intercession through the monastic life of liturgical prayer, for society in general but for benefactors in particular, had been seen as the main route to divine favour; and hence the foundation, endowment and protection of monasteries had been the most usual sorts of pious act. At the start of the thirteenth century, however, a fundamental and quite rapid shift in the outlook of the clergy began to bring the layman in from the fringes of the Christian life, where his spiritual needs had been largely catered for by monastic professionals, and to place him nearer its centre. Behind this development several influences were at work: the increasingly moral and pastoral emphasis of the teaching of the schools, especially in Paris; the general reformation of the Church set in train by Innocent III's Fourth Lateran Council of 1215, which sought to lay down the rules of Christian conduct for the laity and to provide educated priests to guide that conduct; and the advent of the friars, who formed the Church's missionary vanguard in what was essentially a campaign to convert nominal Christians into devout and observant ones. The effect was to give a new place to the laity in the life of the Church and to create new standards for lay piety: regular confession, regular reception of the eucharist, and conformity to the teachings of a pastorally-minded clergy. Naturally, this shift in religious sensibilities was not total, and older forms of piety were by no means superseded. Monasteries continued to be founded and endowed, though more sparsely, and the crusade in particular provided a road to eternal life which was travelled as enthusiastically in the thirteenth century as in the twelfth. Nevertheless, in general the salvation of the laity was coming to be seen as less dependent on the vicarious intercessory work of the clergy and more on a personal obedience to Christian norms which it was the clergy's duty to inculcate.

Montfort's spiritual outlook was shaped both by the old conventions of lay devotion and by these newer patterns which were emerging in his boyhood and youth. As it developed, it came to stand rather apart from both, by no means a mere emanation of the *Zeitgeist*, but something distinctively different from the religious lives of his contemporaries among the nobility. It is true that in some basic ways his own religious life remained entirely typical, most obviously perhaps in the central place which it gave to the crusade. The strong crusading tradition which was part of his family background fired the religious zealotry seen in his expulsion of the Jews from Leicester about 1231 and later in the attacks on the Jews which he authorised and encouraged during the troubles of 1263–65.[1] A blurring of the distinction between Jews and pagans had often disfigured the crusading movement in a similar way. After his more conventional crusade in the east during 1240–41, he took the cross again in 1247, but was prevented from going by his service as Henry's lieutenant in Gascony from 1248 to 1252. Even in these difficult years he did not lose sight of the Holy Land or cease to view it as his ultimate

[1] Above, p. 15; below, p. 268.

objective.[2] In the end, however, he came no nearer to waging another holy war than in the self-proclaimed crusade which he fought against the enemies of the Provisions of Oxford in 1263–64; one sanctioned not legally by the pope but morally by his own oath to the Provisions and by the perjury of those who opposed them.[3] Throughout his career, therefore, the crusade remained high among his priorities, and all the more so because latterly he was able to appropriate it to justify resistance to the Crown.

But the crusade was the common property of the English and French nobility in the thirteenth century, and Montfort's commitment to it differed only in its intensity, and perhaps in its perception of the movement's political possibilities, from that of other great men. Much less typical was the quietist direction taken by his religious life after his arrival in England, towards the introspective and highminded *dévot* whose enthusiasm was the chief quality uniting him with his counterpart, the militant crusader. This conversion – for that was what it amounted to – Montfort owed to the encouragement of a group of religious leaders whose preoccupations and abilities placed them at the forefront of the contemporary church. From 1258 onwards their example and teaching helped to shape his political outlook, and their friendship, with one seemingly so different in background, provided one of the most remarkable features of his career.

First among these friends, in time and importance, was Robert Grosseteste: bishop of Lincoln from 1235 until his death in 1253, and the outstanding scholar and pastor of his day. The two men became acquainted when Montfort's accession to his English inheritance in 1231 brought him the lordship of Leicester, where Grosseteste was archdeacon, with a prebendal church and other property in the town. Grosseteste's firm backing for Montfort's expulsion of the Jews suggests that they immediately saw eye to eye.[4] Their attraction was partly one between similar temperaments. Although Grosseteste was a kinder and more humane man than Montfort, both were zealots, independent-minded and disinclined to compromise. But in time, as Grosseteste took

---

[2] Above, pp. 29–31; below, pp. 106–7. For Montfort's interest in the crusade while in Gascony, see *Mon. Franc.*, i, pp. 275, 277–9; Boutaric, *Saint Louis et Alfonse de Poitiers*, p. 73.

[3] Below, pp. 247, 271.

[4] *Fasti Lincoln*, p. 34; *The Registrum Antiquissimum of the Cathedral Church of Lincoln*, ed. C. W. Foster and K. Major (10 vols., Lincs. Rec. Soc., 1931–73), iii, pp. 235–7; *Grosseteste Epistolae*, pp. 33–8. For the relationship between Grosseteste and Montfort, see also F. S. Stevenson, *Robert Grosseteste, Bishop of Lincoln* (London, 1899), pp. 269–75, and Southern, *Robert Grosseteste*, pp. 244–6.

on the role of spiritual adviser and Montfort that of confidant as well as disciple, their friendship came to rest on more than just common perceptions. Already, in 1239, Montfort could ask for Grosseteste's intercession with the king when Henry's anger broke over him.[5] Fourteen years later the overtones and undercurrents of their relationship were more clearly and subtly caught in an episode following Montfort's departure from the king's service, after what he justifiably regarded as his mistreatment by Henry in Gascony. According to Paris, it was Grosseteste's advice to the earl to render good for evil and to remember the many benefits conferred on him by Henry which persuaded Montfort to rejoin Henry in the south during 1253. Montfort, 'who regarded the bishop as a father confessor and was on terms of most intimate friendship with him, inclined his ear and heart in obedience to the request'.[6] Peacemaker and counsellor, Grosseteste had the moral authority to bring his self-willed pupil to order.

Montfort's relationship with Adam Marsh was of the same quality and equally close. A theologian with a European reputation, Marsh was the leading figure among the Oxford Franciscans, their lector (or divinity lecturer and general adviser) from 1245 to 1250, and a man whose practical sagacity drew him into public life as a diplomat and counsellor.[7] The two men were probably brought together by Grosseteste, first lector to the Oxford Franciscans from about 1230 to 1235, and a firm friend of Marsh from a still earlier time; but it was not until Montfort left for Gascony in 1248 that their friendship opens out for us in the letters that Marsh wrote both to the earl and to his countess, Eleanor. In Marsh's surviving letter-collection only Grosseteste himself and William of Nottingham, Provincial Master of the English Franciscans, received more letters than Montfort and Eleanor. Those to Eleanor we have already looked at. Those to Montfort show Marsh playing the role of informant, passing on home news, and also of spiritual director, exhorting, rebuking and encouraging; and we shall come back to them again. Even though the correspondence is one-sided, we know that Marsh's exceptional regard for Montfort was reciprocated, for in 1259 Montfort appointed Marsh as one of the two chief executors who were to advise Eleanor on the

---

[5] *Grosseteste Epistolae*, pp. 243–4; above, p. 28.
[6] Paris, v, pp. 415–16.
[7] C. H. Lawrence, 'The Letters of Adam Marsh and the Franciscan School at Oxford', *Journal of Ecclesiastical History*, 42 (1991), pp. 218–19, 228–9.

execution of his will.[8] He was not only the keeper of Montfort's conscience, but also a man of business who could be trusted.

Perhaps more easily overlooked is the third of Montfort's mentors: Walter de Cantilupe, bishop of Worcester from 1236 until his death in 1266. After Grosseteste, Cantilupe was the most distinguished bishop of his time. A university *magister*, probably from Oxford, and a forceful pastor, he may, like Marsh, have been introduced to Montfort by Grosseteste, whose ideals and friendship he shared.[9] But it is equally likely that bishop and earl were brought together by the ties of social background, affinity and neighbourhood. Member of a Warwickshire baronial family, Walter was the younger brother of William de Cantilupe II, whose association with Montfort in the *familia* of Ranulf of Chester, during Montfort's earliest years in England, we have already noticed. He was also the uncle of Peter de Montfort, Simon's close ally.[10] The earl's possession of Kenilworth, an occasional home for Eleanor from 1238 and granted to him in custody from 1244, made Walter his bishop as it made William and Peter his neighbours. Marsh's correspondence attests the close connection between Walter and Montfort from at least the late 1240s, but with the coming of reform in 1258 friendship merged into political alliance. Cantilupe was one of only two prelates on the reforming council, and during the subsequent civil wars he seems to have acted more or less as Montfort's army chaplain, confessing his troops before Lewes and Evesham and dying broken-hearted shortly after the earl's last battle.[11]

All three of these guides are brought nicely together with their protégé in a letter of Adam Marsh. 'Of all men', Marsh wrote to Montfort about 1248, 'the bishops of Lincoln and Worcester are more favourable to you in special friendship'. The high value which Grosseteste set by friendship, as both a virtue and a comfort, remains one of his most attractive qualities, and Montfort's place in what was a circle of friends transcended the formal relationship of disciple and masters.[12] There were others in the same circle about whom we would like to know more. One is Richard of Gravesend, Grosseteste's

[8] Bémont, *Montfort* (2nd edn), pp. 276–7.

[9] For Cantilupe, see the *DNB* article by Luard; *BRUO*, i, pp. 349–50; and Carpenter, 'St Thomas Cantilupe', pp. 60–3.

[10] Above, pp. 65–6.

[11] *Mon. Franc.*, i, pp. 123, 270, 277–8; *DBM*, pp. 104–5, 200–1; *Wykes*, p. 180; *Ann. Wigorn.*, p. 453.

[12] *Mon. Franc.*, i, pp. 270, 277–8; J. McEvoy, *The Philosophy of Robert Grosseteste* (Oxford, 1982), pp. 24, 39–40, 476.

archdeacon of Oxford and companion at the papal curia in 1250, dean of Lincoln from 1254, and bishop there from 1258. Like Cantilupe, Gravesend was to be one of Montfort's leading episcopal supporters during the troubles of 1263–65 and was already on intimate terms with him by 1259, when he was named with Marsh as co-executor of the earl's will; but prior to that year their relationship is almost completely obscure.[13] A second, on the other side of the Channel, was Eudes Rigaud, Franciscan scholar, regent master in the Paris schools, and Louis IX's choice for the archbishopric of Rouen in 1248. It was Marsh, Rigaud's confidant, who recommended Montfort to him and probably first brought the two together. He, too, was to prove a good friend during the rough waters of the reforming period.[14]

All these men shared some well-defined characteristics, which made them representative figures in the church of their day but also placed them among its moral and intellectual leaders. They combined an urgent sense of pastoral responsibility for the salvation of the laity with a concern for academic scholarship which again had a largely pastoral rationale. Grosseteste's extraordinarily energetic administration of his diocese, his attempts to reform its clergy and laity, his personal and often disruptive visitations of religious houses, and his emphasis on preaching and instruction as incentives to good conduct, are all too well known to need more than a mention.[15] Cantilupe regulated his diocese in a similarly vigorous way, drafting reforming statutes which were to be among the most influential of the century, and emulating Grosseteste in his severity towards the backsliding monks and abbots who came before him in his visitations.[16] Rigaud, too, carried through visitations of his see's religious houses which became a byword for thoroughness and regularity.[17] Marsh lacked the diocesan responsibilities which made the activities of his friends so exigent and practical a matter; but we have only to look at the long pastoral treatise that he addressed to Archbishop

[13] *BRUO*, ii, pp. 803–4; *Fasti Lincoln*, p. 37; Bémont, *Montfort* (2nd edn), pp. 276–7; below, pp. 173, 230, 252–3. For hints at Montfort's earlier relationship with Gravesend, see *Mon. Franc.*, i, pp. 110, 270.

[14] *The Register of Eudes of Rouen*, ed. J. F. O'Sullivan (New York and London, 1964), pp. xvii–xviii; J. Richard, *St. Louis: Crusader King of France*, ed. S. Lloyd (Cambridge, 1992), p. 222; *Mon. Franc.*, i, p. 86; below, pp. 187, 190, 198–9, 296–7.

[15] Southern, *Robert Grosseteste*, pp. 237–71, is the best survey of Grosseteste's pastoral work.

[16] *Councils and Synods*, II, i, pp. 294–321; *Ann. Tewk.*, pp. 146–7, 150, 152; *Ann. Wigorn.*, pp. 429–30, 433, 439; C. R. Cheney, *English Synodalia of the Thirteenth Century* (Oxford, 1941), pp. 90–106.

[17] *Reg. of Eudes of Rouen*, ed. O'Sullivan, pp. xxi–xxxiv; C. R. Cheney, *Episcopal Visitation of Monasteries in the Thirteenth Century* (Manchester, 1931), pp. 149–67.

Sewal of York about 1255 to realise how closely his ideals matched those of Grosseteste and the others.[18]

But the common ground that Marsh shared most completely with these men lay in the world of learning. Closely linked to the Church's mission to the laity, the learning of the Oxford schools was the focus for the academic lives of both Grosseteste and Marsh. As their first lector, Grosseteste had built up the Oxford Franciscans as a learned community, and he and Marsh later came to be seen as the outstanding figures in what both regarded as the pre-eminent branch of academic learning, the study of the Bible. They were the leading advocates of the Bible's primacy over all other texts, seeing in it more than just the fundamental cornerstone of theology and a key to salvation. It could also contribute greatly to the education of the pastors on whom the spiritual health of the laity depended, and illuminate the moral dilemmas which a more introspective and personal religion was bringing to the forefront of lay consciousness.[19] Rigaud's early position in the Paris schools showed that he, too, shared in the same pattern of interests. So perhaps, in a smaller way, did Richard of Gravesend, whose gifts to Rochester cathedral priory of books containing glosses on Isaiah and the minor prophets suggests some familiarity with the Biblical scholarship at which Grosseteste and Marsh excelled.[20]

The ability of this group of scholars and pastors to shape Montfort's religious development derived not only from their intellectual and moral examples, but from their age and social background. Their leaders were all much older than he was. Grosseteste, born about 1170, must have been around sixty when he first met the twenty-three year old Montfort in 1231. Cantilupe appears to have held his first benefice by 1208, and cannot have been born much after 1190; he was 'that old man', *senex ille*, to the disrespectful royalist chronicler of Merton, writing of the events of 1258. Marsh, perhaps the youngest, was born before 1202, in all likelihood some time before.[21] Two of the three were born into aristocratic families similar to, if less illustrious than, Montfort's own. Cantilupe's origins in the baronage of the west midlands were matched by Marsh's probable descent from a comparable landed

---

[18] *Mon. Franc.*, i, pp. 438–89; Lawrence, 'Letters of Adam Marsh', p. 219, nn. 3, 7.

[19] Southern, *Robert Grosseteste*, pp. 18, 73–5; P. Raedts, *Richard Rufus of Cornwall and the Tradition of Oxford Theology* (Oxford, 1987), pp. 122, 130, 137.

[20] *BRUO*, ii, p. 804.

[21] Southern, *Robert Grosseteste*, pp. 3, 63–4; *BRUO*, i, p. 349; *Flores Hist.*, iii, p. 254; Lawrence, 'Letters of Adam Marsh', pp. 223, 225.

family, the Mariscos of Somerset. Grosseteste's birth was much more humble, but his urbanity, courtesy, and ability to give good practical advice on matters such as estate management had won him many friends among the nobility.[22] If Montfort proved susceptible to the influence of this trio, it was partly because they differed from him greatly in age, but not so greatly in background as may at first appear. To an extent, all three were father figures.

(B) INTERESTS AND INFLUENCES

Montfort's own religious life provides a better gauge of his relationship with these men than the inevitably patchy record of their daily contacts. His friends' teaching and example did not determine all its qualities nor necessarily change him for the better, as we shall see. Yet it remains true that their moral authority helped to determine some of what he did before 1258 and much of what he was to become between 1258 and 1265. Consideration of four topics in particular will allow us to assess his debt to his mentors and to weigh it against the contributions made by other sources. Those four topics are his conscience, his devotional practices, his respect for the Franciscans, and his learning.

Pride of place must be given here to Montfort's conscience, for in the last phase of his life it supplies us with one key to our understanding of his actions. Conscience was a moral force which came to have a particularly high profile in the thirteenth century, and Montfort's friends were experts in its treatment and direction. The stimulus here came from confession. After the Fourth Lateran Council had made confession an annual obligation for all Christians, its practice took off in an almost explosive way. The rapid increase in the number of confessors' manuals, the multiplication of references to confession in contemporary *exempla* (or moral stories), and the public role of the friars in encouraging confession and themselves acting as confessors, all marked the measure of its expansion, as Alexander Murray has pointed out. The most important consequence was the growth of internal self-examination; for confession could hardly be efficacious unless the penitent sinner had examined his conscience beforehand.[23]

---

[22] Above, pp. 65–6; Lawrence, 'Letters of Adam Marsh', p. 225; Southern, *Robert Grosseteste*, pp. 19–20, 63 and n. 1, 192, 318–19.

[23] A. Murray, 'Confession as an Historical Source in the Thirteenth Century', *The Writing of History in the Middle Ages: Essays Presented to R. W. Southern*, ed. R. H. C. Davis and J. M.

At the forefront of this new movement, Montfort's spiritual advisers saw confession and the cultivation of conscience as central to their most fundamental task of instructing the laity in their Christian duties in order to save their souls. Of no one was this more true than Grosseteste. His own role as confessor during his diocesan visitations, and his use of the friars as confessors and penitentiaries on these tours, were complemented by a remarkably extensive literary programme. He left behind him the *Templum Dei*, 'one of the most popular hand books of confession', at least half a dozen other treatises on confession, and a mass of penitential writings which have proved hard to disentangle.[24] Cantilupe showed a similar and hardly less energetic concern. In his diocesan legislation of 1240 he called for confession to take place more frequently than the statutory once a year, he told parish priests that they should instruct their parishioners in how to confess and how to scrutinise their consciences ('conscientias perscrutari'), and he referred them to a separate treatise which he had written on confession.[25] Even Marsh, less actively involved in church government and lay affairs, wrote a *Summa de Penitentia*, so far unidentified.[26]

With three such guides, it would be surprising if Montfort had been unaware of the imperatives of conscience and of its necessary examination as a prelude to confession. Just once, in a conversation between Montfort and one of those guides, we can eavesdrop on this process and detect the sort of moral issue which it might raise. 'The clear circumspection of your wisdom will remember', wrote Adam Marsh to Montfort, in a letter typical of Marsh's infuriatingly obfuscatory style, 'in how many conferences, after repeated and careful examination, we drummed into each other's ears the execrable shamelessness of seductive cunning'.[27] That Montfort was both interested in and responsive to what was being drummed into his ears in these and no doubt other conferences is suggested by the one book that he is known to have owned. In 1270 the prioress of the Dominican house of Montargis, south of Paris, acknowledged the receipt from Amaury de Montfort, the earl's

Wallace-Hadrill (Oxford, 1981), pp. 278–80; A. Murray, *Excommunication and Conscience in the Middle Ages* (London, 1991), pp. 34–6.

24 Murray, 'Confession as an Historical Source', pp. 305–6; J. Goering and F. A. C. Mantello, 'The Early Penitential Writings of Robert Grosseteste', *Recherches de Théologie ancienne at médiévale*, 54 (1987), esp. pp. 52, 57.

25 *Councils and Synods*, II, ii, pp. 303–5; C. R. Cheney, *Medieval Texts and Studies* (Oxford, 1973), p. 191.

26 Lawrence, 'Letters of Adam Marsh', p. 219, n. 3.

27 *Mon. Franc.*, i, p. 267. I have used the editor's translation, p. xciii.

clerical younger son, of a copy of the *Summa de Vitiis et de Virtutibus* which had belonged to Amaury's father, Simon. This was almost certainly the *Summa* of the same name written between 1236 and 1244 by Guillaume Peyraut, prior of the Dominicans at Lyons. It was essentially an ethical handbook for confessors – one of the longest and most popular of a large class – and an exposition of the Christian life, dealing with the seven deadly sins and the various categories of virtue. Its readership seems to have been mainly one of clerks, university students and Dominicans.[28] The peculiarity of a layman's possessing what was primarily a practical manual for priests suggests that Montfort had an interest beyond the ordinary in questions of personal conduct and conscience, and in the scheme of confession through which conduct and conscience could be regulated.

There is a good deal to confirm this inference. The moral question which touched Montfort most closely sprang from his marriage to one who had taken a vow of chastity after her first husband's death. Although Montfort's marriage to Eleanor was both stable and successful, it seems to have created in his mind a sense of growing disquiet as he looked back at its circumstances. According to the *Flores Historiarum*, it was a marriage which he had entered into 'not without harm to his conscience' ('non sine laesione conscientiae'). According to the Franciscan author drawn on by the Lanercost chronicle, who was familiar with the Oxford Franciscans and who had spoken to 'a man accustomed to probe the secrets' of both Montfort and Eleanor, probably their confessor, the tenderness of his conscience on this point led him to abstain from relations with his wife for a long period. And according to Paris, it was his preying doubts about the propriety of his marriage, and his desire for absolution, which impelled him to take the cross again in 1247.[29] Although he had sought papal sanction for his marriage shortly after its celebration in 1238, he seems at that time to have had no real qualms about its rightness. Were his new doubts, ten years later, the mark of a developing

---

[28] Bémont, *Montfort* (2nd edn), p. 41, n. 2. For Peyraut, see A. Dondaine, 'Guillaume Peyraut: Vie et Oeuvres', *Archivum Fratrum Praedicatorum*, 18 (1948), esp. pp. 184–92; Murray, 'Confession as an Historical Source', pp. 309–10; and J. Dunbabin, 'The Lyon Dominicans: A Double Act', *Monastic Studies*, ed. J. Loades (Bangor, 1990), pp. 191–4. Montfort may conceivably have met Peyraut, since he visited Lyons twice during the period of Peyraut's priorate: see Bémont, *Montfort* (1st edn), 318, (2nd edn), p. 45, for his visits.

[29] *Flores Hist.*, ii, p. 227; *Lanercost*, pp. 39–40, 76–7; Paris, v, p. 1. For the Franciscan author of the chronicle from which *Lanercost* derives, and his Oxford connections, see A. Gransden, *Historical Writing in England, c. 550 to c. 1307* (London, 1974), pp. 494–6.

conscience, and one cultivated by his friends, particularly perhaps by a Franciscan confessor? To have had any doubt at all about so enduring a marriage, legitimised by the pope, canonically valid,[30] and blessed with children, points to a conscience of unusual sensitivity.

Our final piece of evidence shows us Montfort's conscience refracted through his views on that of another man. In 1252 he was put on trial for his alleged misgovernment of Gascony, and in the course of the trial he demanded that the king should keep the terms of the contract by which Gascony had been committed to him. Henry answered bluntly that he would keep no promises to a traitor and to one who had broken his own. Montfort let fly at this. 'Who can believe that you are a Christian? Have you ever confessed?' 'Indeed', replied the king. 'What use is confession', retorted Montfort, 'without penance and satisfaction?' – as if to say, our informant Matthew Paris helpfully adds, 'if you have ever confessed, you have never been contrite or offered satisfaction'. The language here is particularly interesting, if Paris can be trusted as to its accuracy. Contemporary penitentials saw penance as divided into three parts: contrition, an awareness of one's sins and a desire to abandon them; confession, a thorough admission of those sins to the confessor; and satisfaction, the punishment or penance to be undergone in expiation for the sin. All three terms came into Montfort's angry exchange with Henry, although admittedly 'contrition' is part of Paris's gloss rather than Montfort's actual words. Those words suggest a familiarity with the language of the penitentials, of the concepts embodied in the language, and of the issues of conscience raised by the whole penitential procedure.[31] The Christian kept his word. It was a point to remember in 1258.

The piety whose inward and spiritual sign was an exceptionally fastidious conscience found its outward manifestation in devotional practices which were both idiosyncratic and unusually well observed by Montfort's contemporaries. They form the second of our four topics and are described in two accounts: in the so-called *Opusculum de nobili Simone de Monteforti*, written shortly after 1285, possibly by a Franciscan, and forming part of the Melrose chronicle; and in the sketch of Montfort given by William Rishanger, monk of St Albans, in his tract on the

---

30 F. W. Maitland, 'The History of Marriage, Jewish and Christian', *Collected Papers*, ed. H. A. L. Fisher (3 vols., Cambridge, 1911), iii, p. 24.
31 Paris, v, p. 290; Goering and Mantello, 'Early Penitential Writings', pp. 58–9.

barons' wars, written (he tells us) in 1312.[32] Neither is very familiar and both are worth paraphrasing. Stripped of its flourishes and rhetorical wrappings, the Melrose *opusculum* says this. After Montfort had taken his oath to the Provisions of Oxford in 1258, he began to lead a life of self-denial. He used to rise at midnight, timing himself by the burning of a wax taper which he lit before he went to bed, and spending the rest of the night in vigil and prayer. He knew by heart the primer, the psalter and other prayers, which he repeated during the night with alacrity and devotion. By day and night he wore a hair shirt. He was frugal and temperate in food, drink and clothing. When he was with his household he was content to wear russet (the cheapest, coarsest cloth), and even when he was with other magnates he rarely wore scarlet (the most splendid and expensive cloth), but more usually bluet or burnet (medium-range blue or brown cloth). In the midst of wealth he lived a life of frugality. After his oath he even abstained from relations with his wife.

Rishanger's account has a slightly different emphasis. Montfort, he says, was 'commendably endowed with the knowledge of letters'; an avid listener to the offices of the church by day and night; sparing in food and drink; keeping vigil at night more than sleeping; and assured of the blessings of his wonderful faith. He commended himself to the prayers of the religious, with whom he asked to be fraternally associated, and he constantly prayed that divine grace might keep him free from avarice and covetousness. He had been instructed in all good teaching by Robert Grosseteste, whom he cherished with heartfelt affection and whose wholesome advice he followed in many things.

These two accounts have been either wholly ignored or treated dismissively by modern historians, and it is easy to see why. Both are late and seemingly hagiographical, the products of unreliable authors and the manifestations of a popular cult. Rishanger's tract on the barons' wars has been judged especially harshly, since its derivation from the *Flores Historiarum*, an earlier St Albans chronicle, has appeared to deprive it of any intrinsic and independent value.[33] There is, however,

---

[32] *The Chronicle of Melrose*, introduced by A. O. and M. O. Anderson (London, 1936), pp. xix–xx, 136–44; *Chronica de Mailros*, ed. J. Stevenson (Bannatyne Club, Edinburgh, 1835), pp. 207–16; Rishanger, *De Bellis*, pp. 6–7. I have disregarded the Andersons' suggestion (*Chronicle of Melrose*, p. xx) that the author of the *opusculum* was a Franciscan who became a Cistercian, since this seems so unlikely a progression and one unsupported by any real evidence.

[33] Labarge, *Montfort*, p. 11; *The St. Albans Chronicle, 1406–1420*, ed. V. H. Galbraith (Oxford, 1937), p. xxix, n. 1; A. Gransden, *Historical Writing in England*, ii: *c. 1307 to the Early Sixteenth Century* (London, 1982), pp. 4–5; C. H. Lawrence, 'The University of Oxford and the Chronicle of the Barons' Wars', *EHR*, 95 (1980), pp. 101–2.

much to be said against this sceptical approach. Both accounts are, so far as we can tell, entirely independent and were written at opposite ends of the land; yet each is sufficiently similar, and at the same time sufficiently different, to carry conviction. Both speak of Montfort's night vigils, devotion to prayer, and frugality of diet; the Melrose *opusculum* alone talks about his dress and his relations with his wife; Rishanger alone about his interest in learning and his desire to be associated with the religious. One or two details in the *opusculum* are particularly telling: the wax taper for a night clock, the precise classification of the different sorts of cloth Montfort chose for different company. These bear the marks, not of hagiographical topoi, but of direct observation; and direct observation is what each author claims for his sources. Knowledge of the earl's hair shirt, the *opusculum* tells us, was spread about by those who slept in his chamber, his *cubicularii*; other intimates, *secretiorii sui*, provided Rishanger with information about Montfort's night vigils.[34] There are useful reminders here of how public a life a thirteenth-century noble-man led and how difficult it must have been to keep secret such private devotions as Montfort's. Nor do these authors stand alone in what they say. Several others, including Robert of Gloucester, a well-informed contemporary, vouch for the hair shirt, found when Montfort's body was stripped after Evesham; and we shall see further evidence later for the 'fraternal association' with the religious orders on which Rishanger comments.[35]

A special word should be put in here for Rishanger. Although it is true that he drew heavily on the *Flores Historiarum*, at half a dozen points in his text he preserves independent information, not found elsewhere, and apparently picked up from those who were very close to the earl; for example, on Montfort's words to Henry of Almain when Henry deserted him in 1263; on his reasons for rejecting the Mise of Lewes in 1264; on his fortitude after the baronial defeat at Northampton in the same year; and on his justification for his gathering lands and castles for himself in 1264–65. In its claim to draw upon the revelations of Montfort's associates, his *secretarii* and *secretiorii*, Rishanger's description of Montfort's religious practices is closely comparable to some of these later incidents. Nor is this claim implausible. Rishanger came from a

---

[34] *Chron. Melrose*, intro. A. O. and M. O. Anderson, p. 137; *Chron. Mailros*, ed. Stevenson, p. 208; Rishanger, *De Bellis*, p. 6.

[35] *Robert of Gloucs.*, ii, p. 765; Bémont, *Montfort* (1st edn), p. 380 (Battle chronicle); F. W. Maitland, 'A Song on the Death of Simon de Montfort', *EHR*, 11 (1896), p. 318; *Anglo-Norman Political Songs*, ed. I. S. T. Aspin (Anglo-Norman Text Soc., 1953), p. 30; below, pp. 103–4.

house with which Montfort had particularly close associations. He himself was sixty-two years old when he was writing in 1312, as he helpfully tells us, and he could easily have spoken to men who had been out with their leader in the barons' wars. Both on these political episodes and on Montfort's piety he should be regarded as a primary source of high value.[36]

The composite picture presented by these two authors from Melrose and St Albans is thus probably a true one. As such it is exceptionally interesting in its portrayal of a lay magnate who led a life of devotion and austerity hard to parallel among the thirteenth-century nobility. Although the pious layman was not rare, Montfort seems to have taken to extremes some of the normal practices of his contemporaries. Knowledge of the primer, for example, the layman's prayer book, was widespread, and the first surviving examples of the books of hours, which embodied the prayers of the primer and were made for the devout laity, date from just this period, the middle years of Henry III.[37] But knowing the primer by heart and repeating it during the night are likely to have been more unusual accomplishments. Others of Montfort's practices were more clerical than lay, and hint at the possible example of those in his circle. His friend Walter de Cantilupe owned a hair shirt, later bequeathed to another Montfortian, Thomas de Cantilupe, and Archbishop Edmund of Canterbury had possessed an especially uncomfortable one.[38] But among the nobility these mortifying garments can hardly have been common. It is hard to imagine (let us say) Richard of Cornwall in a hair shirt.

The layman whose religious life compared most closely with that of Montfort was not an Englishman but a Frenchman, King Louis IX. After the failure of his crusade and his return to France in 1254, Louis's deep sense of his own sinfulness led him to adopt a penitential regime which was commented on by all who wrote about him, most fully by his confessor, Geoffrey de Beaulieu. He wore dark clothing, rejecting scarlet and other bright cloths; he abstained from sleeping with his wife, not only during the Church's penitential seasons, which was normal, but at other times as well; he wore a hair shirt, though he later laid it aside in deference to his confessor's sense of what was decent for a king; he

---

[36] Rishanger, *De Bellis*, pp. vi, 17–18, 24, 41–2.

[37] C. Wordsworth and H. Littlehales, *The Old Service-Books of the English Church* (2nd edn, London, 1910), pp. 248–54; C. Donovan, *The de Brailes Hours: Shaping the Book of Hours in Thirteenth-Century Oxford* (London, 1991), pp. 16–17, 132–56, 183–7.

[38] Carpenter, 'St. Thomas Cantilupe', p. 63; Paris, iv, pp. 328–9.

fasted for long periods, often subsisting on bread and water; and he sometimes rose in the middle of the night to hear matins with his chaplains and clerks, afterwards returning to pray before his bed.[39] Much of this is so remarkably similar to what we know of Montfort's habits (the disdain for scarlet is a particularly striking resemblance) that we are bound to suspect that Louis may have influenced Montfort's religious outlook or even been his model. This is by no means inconceivable. Between 1255 and 1258 Montfort was frequently in France, often to negotiate the terms of what was to become the Treaty of Paris. He was regularly in Louis's company and is likely to have had many opportunities to observe the conduct of a man with whom he was in any case on close and friendly terms.[40] If the Melrose author is right in saying that this life of self-denial intensified from the time of his oath to the Provisions of 1258, the reforms may have engendered in him the same mood of religious dedication as the failure of the crusade stimulated in Louis, and one all the more profound because of what he had seen of Louis's austerities in the preceding years. We shall see later that this seems in fact to have been the case, and that the reforms themselves may also have owed something to Louis's example.[41]

Our knowledge of Louis's religious life supplies an additional reason for taking seriously what we are told about that of Montfort. Geoffrey de Beaulieu's description of the practices of an exceptionally pious layman, coming as it does from an observer who knew Louis as well as anyone, suggests that there was nothing inherently implausible in the reports of the comparable regime which Louis's friend is said to have followed. But though Montfort may have been Louis's emulator in these things, it is almost equally likely that the devotions of both men had a common source in the corpus of ascetic practices and precepts lived and preached by the friars. Their influence provides our third topic in this survey of Montfort's religion and its analogues. Louis's own attachment to the friars, both Dominicans and Franciscans, needs no rehearsing, while Montfort's affection for the Franciscans was highlighted by the Melrose writer. Montfort loved the friars minor religiously, he says, and they were privy to his conscience in many things ('conscii fuerunt

---

[39] 'Vita Sancti Ludovici auctore Gaufrido de Belloloco', *Recueil des Historiens des Gaules*, 20 (Paris, 1740), pp. 5–7, 10, 13. Cf. W. C. Jordan, *Louis IX and the Challenge of the Crusade* (Princeton, 1979), pp. 128–9, for other sources bearing on the same theme.

[40] Below, pp. 140–2; *CR, 1254–56*, p. 195; *Layettes*, ii, No. 4178; *DBM*, pp. 194–5, for examples of Montfort's contacts with Louis.

[41] Below, pp. 168–9.

consciencie eius' – that word again).[42] The truth of this is borne out by more than just his relationship with Adam Marsh. Other Franciscans, too, were close to him. One such was Gregory de Bosellis, probably trained at Oxford, first lector to the Franciscan convent at Leicester from c. 1240, and later Vicar General of the English Franciscans, whose presence in Gascony was requested by Montfort and who was named by Marsh as a man able to offer him spiritual counsel. Another was Thomas of York, among Marsh's successors as lector to the Oxford Franciscans, and one of the most learned philosophers and theologians of the day, to whom Marsh passed on news of the earl and who was urged to give him good spiritual advice.[43] A third was Eudes Rigaud, Franciscan scholar and pastor, and friend of Louis IX. Here was a Franciscan circle, centred on Marsh and Oxford, extending across the Channel to Rouen and the court of Louis IX, and with Montfort firmly within its circumference.

Montfort's respect for the Franciscans may have done a good deal to inform the devotional practices which we have already discussed. Both in their general austerity and in some of their details these show characteristically Franciscan features. His night-time prayers and vigils, for example, are reminiscent of what Thomas of Eccleston tells us about those of the early English Franciscans: 'There was scarcely an hour in the night when some of them were not at prayer in the oratory. On the principal feasts they chanted with such fervour that their vigils sometimes lasted the whole night'. If that seems too general a parallel, consider Montfort's dress. The russet that the Melrose writer says that he favoured was the normal cheap cloth used for Franciscan habits; it was russet, for example, that Henry III ordered to be given to the friars minor of Reading in 1239.[44] That Montfort's Franciscan adviser had strong views on the need for such sobriety in dress was made clear in one of Adam Marsh's letters to Countess Eleanor, in which he denounced her lavish and expensive tastes in clothes and jewellery. Perhaps with reason: for although in her early widowhood Eleanor, too, had worn russet, by April 1265, at the height of her family's glory, she was buying

---

[42] Jordan, *Louis IX*, pp. 53–5, 184–5; *Chron. Melrose*, intro. A. O. and M. O. Anderson, p. 140; *Chron. Mailros*, ed. Stevenson, p. 212.

[43] *Mon. Franc.*, i, pp. 270, 276–8, 281, 308, 368–9, 388, 393–5; *BRUO*, i, pp. 223–4; iii, pp. 2139–40.

[44] *De Adventu Fratrum Minorum in Angliam: The Chronicle of Thomas of Eccleston*, ed. A. G. Little (Manchester, 1951), p. 25; J. R. H. Moorman, *A History of the Franciscan Order* (Oxford, 1968), p. 359; A. G. Little, *Studies in English Franciscan History* (Manchester, 1917), pp. 35–6; *Mon. Franc.*, i, p. 295.

scarlet for herself from an Italian merchant in London.[45] Was this a
subject on which husband and wife differed, and where the extravagant
Eleanor found it difficult to follow the plain Franciscan principles of her
husband?

It is curious that Montfort's ties seem to have been so exclusively with
the Franciscans, and that the Dominicans, who were equally favoured
by Louis IX, play so small a part in the story. If small, it may not have
been entirely negligible. He and Eleanor chose the prior of St Jacques,
the Dominican house in Paris, to represent them in their negotiations
over Eleanor's dower in 1259, and the bequest of his books to the same
house by Amaury, Montfort's younger son, thirty years later, may
suggest some family affiliation. It is probable, too, that Montfort
founded the Dominican friary at Leicester, a house which Amaury also
remembered in his will, and he was certainly a benefactor to the
Dominicans of Bordeaux, in whose house his baby daughter was
buried.[46] But there is no sign of any contact with the Oxford
Dominicans, nor of any close friendships comparable to those with the
Franciscans which are recorded both in Marsh's letters and by
the Melrose writer. Although both orders supported Montfort in the
conflicts of the 1260s, it was the Franciscans alone who appear to have
backed the reforming cause in their writings.[47] The warm relationship
between Montfort's father and St Dominic himself makes this apparent
repudiation of a family tradition all the more puzzling. It can hardly be
the case that Henry III's special affection for the Dominicans, who
supplied his confessor, John of Darlington, alienated Montfort from
them, for Montfort was more often than not a royalist at the time of
rising Dominican influence at court prior to 1258. If anything, he might
have been expected to share in Henry's tastes.[48] Perhaps it was his early
connections with Grosseteste, and thence with Marsh, which pulled him
initially towards the Franciscans, and his admiration for their way of life,
more austere than that of the Dominicans, which kept him facing firmly
in their direction.

Montfort's place in the circle of Grosseteste, Marsh and the Oxford
Franciscans associated him with a group of men whose pastoral

---

[45] Paris, v, p. 235; *Manners and Household Expenses*, ed. Turner, p. 25.
[46] *DBM*, pp. 200–1; W. A. Hinnebusch, *The Early English Friars Preachers* (Rome, 1951), pp. 92–3;
Vatican Archives, Archivio Segreto Vaticano, AA. Arm. I–XVIII, 123; Douais, *Les Frères
Prêcheurs en Gascogne*, p. 265.
[47] Below, pp. 253–4, 279–80.
[48] For Henry III and the Dominicans, see Hinnebusch, *Early English Friars Preachers*, pp. 72–5.

priorities competed with their related concern for the promotion of learning. The extent to which Montfort shared in that concern is our fourth and final topic. In its pastoral rationale he probably had no share, except in so far as familiarity with such pastoral literature as Peyraut's *Summa* might be good for his own soul; but in its general tendencies he was a committed participant. For this role he was apparently well qualified. Rishanger's remark that he was 'commendably endowed with the knowledge of letters' is immediately suggestive, for 'scientia litterarum' points not just to literacy but to a particular knowledge of Latin. That in itself may not have been a rare accomplishment among the thirteenth-century nobility, though specific examples are hard to come by.[49] In Montfort's case, however, we can fill out the words of Rishanger through the use of Marsh's letters. These seem to be essentially private letters, too personal and often too critical for any eyes but those of the recipient. If Montfort could read Marsh's tortuous and allusive Latin prose, he must have been a good Latinist, better indeed than some modern historians, who have sometimes been understandably defeated by Marsh's adeptness at disguising what he wants to say. Marsh himself expected his correspondent to read, and to read in Latin, for during the time of Montfort's tribulations in Gascony he told the earl to seek consolation through frequent study of the Scriptures; in particular, he should read chapters 29 to 31 of the Book of Job and Gregory the Great's Commentary on Job.[50] How many other of Henry III's earls, troubled in mind, could have been directed to Gregory's Commentary on Job? It was a piece of advice which linked together Montfort's spiritual needs and the study of the Bible which was Marsh's own forte, with the ability to read Latin as the bridge between the two.

A different type of intellectual interest, combined with the same facility in Latin, was assumed by the famous tract which Montfort's other adviser, Robert Grosseteste, sent to him in 1251. Part of Grosseteste's address to the papal curia at Lyons in the previous year, this pamphlet used the distinction between just rule and tyranny in order to show the injustice of the archbishop of Canterbury's current demand for uncustomary visitation fees. It was an example of the sort of hyperbole to which those in Grosseteste's circle, especially Marsh, were all too prone. But the argument had a wider application to all forms

[49] M. T. Clanchy, *From Memory to Written Record: England, 1066–1307* (London, 1979), pp. 186–7.

[50] *Mon. Franc.*, i, pp. 266–8.

of misgovernment, and its moral case was closely grounded on the Nicomachean Ethics, translated by Grosseteste, and whose author, the 'Philosopher' Aristotle, Grosseteste cites repeatedly.[51] Presumably he thought that Montfort would have no difficulty in reading what he had to say and that he would be equally able to appreciate an academic argument. The terms of the argument placed Montfort vicariously in touch with the world of Greek learning, where Grosseteste had made himself at home and with which Montfort may already have had some secondhand familiarity through his friendship with another man: John of Basingstoke, Grosseteste's learned archdeacon of Leicester from 1235 to 1252, and probably his teacher in Greek. Montfort's grief at John's death, noted by Paris, may be merely the mark of a local connection, of the sort which had originally brought him into touch with Grosseteste; but it may also be another small indication of his place in the society of his clever, cultivated and scholarly friends.[52]

The question of Montfort's learning can be approached from another direction, via his interest in education. His own education is entirely obscure, but we know something about that of his sons. Both Henry, the eldest, and Amaury were sent for a time to be educated in Grosseteste's household, which had a reputation for just this sort of work: according to an anonymous poem, taking in boys of noble birth and teaching them Latin and Greek.[53] We have no means of knowing how much they learnt, but at the very least both could write. Henry noted on his father's will of 1259 that he was the scribe, and he wrote a clear and evidently practised hand.[54] Amaury was more widely learned. Besides Grosseteste, he had for a teacher one Master Nicholas, whom Roger Bacon places among the best mathematicians of the day. He went on to study at Padua in the 1260s and to write both an alchemical tract, surviving in four manuscripts, and a notable theological treatise, of which the holograph copy is now in the Bodleian (Plate 6).[55] There is unlikely to have been any other English nobleman of the period two

[51] *Mon. Franc.*, i, p. 110; S. Gieben, 'Robert Grosseteste at the Papal Curia, Lyons, 1250: Edition of the Documents', *Collectanea Franciscana*, xli (1971), pp. 377–80; *Robert Grosseteste: Scholar and Bishop*, ed. D. A. Callus (Oxford, 1955), pp. 212–13 (a useful paraphrase); Southern, *Robert Grosseteste*, pp. 287–90; below, p. 99.

[52] Paris, v, p. 284; *BRUO*, i, pp. 126–7; Southern, *Robert Grosseteste*, pp. 185–6.

[53] *Mon. Franc.*, i, pp. 110, 163, 268–9, 298, 301; R. W. Hunt, 'Verses on the Life of Robert Grosseteste', *Medievalia et Humanistica*, n.s., i (1970), pp. 242, 248.

[54] See the facsimile in Bémont, *Montfort* (2nd edn), facing p. 278 and below, Plate 9, p. 175.

[55] Boyle, '*E Cathena et Carcere*', pp. 380–2; D. W. Singer, *Catalogue of Latin and Vernacular Alchemical Manuscripts in Great Britain and Ireland* (3 vols., Brussels, 1928–30), i, p. 41, iii, p. 912.

of whose sons wrote in their own hands works which still survive. These are scraps. But in combination with Montfort's own literary and bookish interests they suggest a degree of family respect for learning and education which was rare by the standards of the day.

Taken individually, all these features of Montfort's religious life could no doubt be faintly paralleled in the activities and attitudes of other members of the nobility. Yet taken together, and with the weight of so much evidence behind them, they bring before us a pious layman whose beliefs and practices so far exceeded the expected norms of aristocratic behaviour as to make him essentially *sui generis*. In his sensitivity to the claims of conscience, his ascetic traits, and his affection for the Franciscans, as much as in his regard for learning, Montfort was not so much a representative of a type as the accomplished and unique pupil of his clerical friends and masters. Before 1258 their relationship was grounded on these common interests and ideals. It rested much less on the common line towards questions of government in Church and State which was subsequently to emerge during the reforming period. Until the inauguration of reform, Montfort's mainly royalist position left him almost always uninvolved either in the sporadic parliamentary opposition to Henry's kingship[56] or in the opposition to the papal provisions and papal taxation which Henry often sanctioned and which so much concerned Grosseteste and the bishops. He made only two recorded interventions in these matters: in 1244, when he was a member of the king's delegation sent to ask the clergy for a tax, which Grosseteste was instrumental in refusing; and in 1246, when he sealed the letter of protest against papal exactions sent to the curia by the magnates and prelates.[57] The first of these interventions suggests no great warmth towards the claims of the clergy as an estate, and the second saw him acting merely as one member of a large group. Although he probably shared in the widespread opposition to Henry's involvement in the Sicilian business from the mid 1250s, opposition which was more certainly led from the clerical side by his friend Walter de Cantilupe, the experience did more to consolidate than to initiate his relationship with Henry's clerical opponents.[58]

---

[56] Above, pp. 33–6; below, pp. 148–9.
[57] Paris, iv, pp. 365–6, 533–4; *Councils and Synods*, ii, i, pp. 388–90, for the background.
[58] Carpenter, 'St. Thomas Cantilupe', p. 61; below, pp. 144–5.

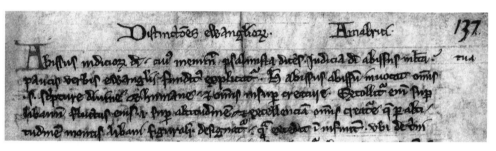

Plate 6. A learned younger son. Amaury de Montfort records his completion of a
theological treatise in prison in his thirty-fourth year, 1276, and (below) signs his name
'Amalrici'.

(C) VIRTUE

His friends came late, and only some years after Grosseteste's death, to
their view of Montfort as a public champion of the ethical principles of
justice and good government which clerical teaching embodied. Prior to
1258 they had regarded him, not as a political ally, but as an exemplar
of the type of layman whom the reformers wished to create: devout,
spiritually alert, given to prayer, attendant to conscience, and firmly set
on the road to salvation. That he was a great nobleman made his
commitment to the Christian life all the more welcome. We usually see
the Church's pastoral effort in the thirteenth century as directed chiefly
at the urban poor and at what might be called the parish laity. These are
reasonable deductions, both from the activity of the friars and from the
bishops' vigorous attempts to educate and instruct parish priests. But
they should not lead us to forget that the nobility was also targeted, and
with good reason. They were a class traditionally regarded by church
reformers as especially unregenerate: Guillaume de Peyraut, whose

book Montfort owned, saw them as proud, self-indulgent, violent men.[59] Both their reputation and their power to influence and command, for good or ill, make it easy to detect the pastoral purpose behind some episcopal leanings in their direction: in Grosseteste's education of noble children, for example, or in some of his Anglo-Norman writings, most notably the *Chateau d'Amour*, which were designed to offer entertaining instruction in Christian doctrine to a chivalric and French-speaking audience.[60] Given these aspirations towards the conversion of a class peculiarly difficult to convert, Montfort must have seemed an especially valuable catch. He was a great layman who took the reformers' message seriously.

But he was not only that. His secular qualities, his energy, his wide experience and his military expertise, all made him more than a *dévot*, fitting him rather for his father's role as a leader of the Church militant. Montfort's commitment to the crusade, already touched on, aligned him with an enterprise which was very close to the hearts of his friends. Grosseteste and Cantilupe were the two bishops chosen by Innocent IV in 1247 to raise funds for the projected crusade to which Montfort bound himself shortly afterwards. Marsh, too, was intensely interested in the fortunes of the crusaders in the east, as his letters to Montfort show.[61] In partnership with Grosseteste, Montfort even contemplated some related but more unusual project. About 1251 Grosseteste suggested that the two of them should join forces on an arduous journey for 'the liberation of souls', as Marsh put it, with his usual tantalising vagueness. The suggestion was welcomed by Montfort.[62] Just what was under discussion remains unclear. But perhaps the most plausible suggestion is a mission to rescue or relieve the Christians of central Asia who lived under Mongol rule, either as native communities or as captives carried off from eastern Europe. Their misfortunes moved Louis IX, then in the Holy Land, to envisage some such mission at just this time, and their plight may have been made known in England by a party of Christian Armenian refugees who stayed for a while at St Ives, in Grosseteste's diocese, in 1250.[63] Montfort certainly had a later interest in the Mongols,

[59] A. Murray, *Reason and Society in the Middle Ages* (Oxford, 1978), pp. 274–5, 331–7, 353.
[60] For the *Chateau d'Amour*, see M. D. Legge, *Anglo-Norman Literature and its Background* (Oxford, 1963), pp. 222–4, and Southern, *Robert Grosseteste*, pp. 225–30.
[61] *CPL*, i, pp. 234–5; *Mon. Franc.*, i, pp. 275, 277–9. The best account of Grosseteste's interest in the crusade is Stevenson, *Robert Grosseteste*, pp. 250, 260–3.
[62] *Mon. Franc.*, i. p. 111.
[63] Paris, v, pp. 116, 340–1; Richard, *St. Louis*, pp. 283–4. Cf. *Mon. Franc.*, i. p. 376.

for a tract on their way of life ('de vita et moribus Tartarorum') was passed on to him in 1258.[64] Marsh's allusive words seem to open up the prospect of the earl's activity on some much wider stage than the household setting of his personal piety or the academic and diocesan world of his religious friends.

The expectations of those friends thus rested heavily on Montfort: a Christian layman who was both privately devout and publicly committed to the Church's cause. Yet he fell some way short of fulfilling them. His conversion was never more than partial, and his pilgrim's progress was too erratic for even his closest sympathisers to regard it with unqualified satisfaction. In Montfort's mentality there was always a tension, more marked than in most of us, between the promptings of conscience and the demands of self. His father's example, which combined piety with an aggressive, self-serving, acquisitive zeal, may have continued to count for a good deal, even when the examples of Grosseteste and Marsh were nearer to hand and seemingly more compelling. After all, this younger son partly owed his establishment in England to just these qualities; though they were ones which often compromised his religion and stifled the virtuous behaviour which should have been its pledge.

Montfort's greatest moral failing, persistent throughout his career, was an overbearing harshness, which pastors had often seen as one of the characteristic sins of the nobility. It was often combined with greed and greed's negative counterpart, meanness. Both vices, but especially the first, were regularly censured by his spiritual advisers. His extortion of 500 marks from a Leicester burgess before he went to Rome in 1238 earned him a devastating rebuke from Grosseteste, supported by a catena of biblical quotations on the need for mercy and the punishment reserved for those who preyed on the poor, and ending with the demand that he should be 'an example of clemency and mildness, and not a master of cruelty'.[65] Grosseteste's despatch to him, some thirteen years later, of his tract on the distinction between just rule and tyranny was surely an equally pointed if more subtle rebuke, for it held up for condemnation the tyrannical practices of oppression and extortion which seemed to inform Montfort's government of Gascony at just this time. Marsh's letters are more consistently revealing. Although their general tone is affectionate and full of praise for the services to the

---

[64] *Oxenedes*, p. 217; Bémont, *Montfort* (2nd edn), p. 151, n. 2.

[65] Paris, iii, p. 479; *Grosseteste Epistolae*, pp. 141–3; above, p. 28.

Church of one 'most devoted to Christ', they often sound a warning note of remonstration. Marsh's most frequent criticisms were of Montfort's failure to control the excesses of his household and ministers, a fault for which he was also condemned by Grosseteste.[66] Typically of Marsh, his grounds for criticism are as unspecific as those for praise; but they do not suggest that before 1258 Montfort attached much importance to the principle of restraint on officials, baronial as well as royal, which was to be one of the themes of the Provisions of Oxford. We have already seen how financial constraints and sudden expenses drove him to bear down hard on his estates. Occasionally his actions clashed with the pastoral ideals of his mentor. When, with characteristic highhandedness, he carried off the parish priest of Odiham to serve him in Gascony, he drew from Marsh a reproachful letter which ended with a plea for the return of the shepherd to his sheep.[67] Self-restraint was the virtue most frequently preached to him. 'Better is a patient man than a strong man and he who can rule his temper than he who storms a city.'[68] Embodied perhaps in the injunctions of the confessional is the strong suggestion that the confessor had got the measure of his man.

Montfort's attitude to wealth, often grasping and tightfisted, has left a fainter impression on the writings of his advisers, perhaps because what was frequently a sin of omission proved less easy to spot and correct than one of commission. Yet it seems to be inferable, if only negatively, from the accounts of his spiritual life. What is missing from the sketches given both by the Melrose writer and by Rishanger is any word about good works: religious donations, hospitality and almsgiving and, above all, generosity to the poor. There is a curious contrast between the apparent austerity of Montfort's private life and the lack of much sign that surplus wealth was directed towards the needs of others. This was one factor which set him apart from the two other men in his society whose religious life we know most about, Henry III and Louis IX, both of whom were almost obsessive in their concern for the poor.[69] Of course, the omission was not total. In the confraternity agreement which he made with St Albans, discussed below, Montfort made arrangements for the feeding of the poor after his death, and the household accounts for Countess Eleanor in the months before Evesham in 1265 show the

[66] *Mon. Franc.*, i. pp. 86, 103–4, 261, 264, 276.
[67] *Mon. Franc.*, i, pp. 262–3.
[68] *Mon. Franc.*, i, p. 264.
[69] H. Johnstone, 'Poor Relief in the Royal Households of Thirteenth-Century England', *Speculum*, 4 (1929), pp. 153–7; Richard, *St. Louis*, pp. 80, 240–3.

regular distribution of food and drink to *pauperes*.[70] But prospective generosity was an easy virtue; and in the thirteenth century it would have been a very peculiar magnate household that failed altogether to support the poor. The most we can say is that Montfort's charity towards the poor does not appear to have been anything out of the ordinary or to have matched his religious convictions. Only with the coming of reform in 1258, and Montfort's oath to the Provisions of Oxford, can we see signs of a change of heart, as the play of his conscience moved beyond such interior anxieties as the validity of his marriage to touch both the welfare of the king's non-noble subjects and that of his own tenants.

But the charitable inclinations of any great nobleman are less likely to be traceable in any possible generosity to the poor than in his benefactions to the religious. Montfort's primordial connections here were with France rather than England, and in particular with a group of houses in and around Paris with which his family had close ties as founders and benefactors. With the chief of these, the abbey of Hautes-Bruyères, belonging to the order of Fontevrault and lying a few miles south-east of Montfort l'Amaury, his own links were slight. This was the burial place of his paternal grandparents, his father and mother, and his brother Guy; yet his only recorded association with the abbey came after his death, when the monks kept the anniversary of 'Earl Simon of Leicester, who died in England'.[71] In the case of three other houses, however, the family links were maintained into Montfort's own generation and remembered by him and his descendants. First among the three was Porrois, later famous as Port Royal, a house of Cistercian nuns founded in 1203 by his mother's uncle, Matthew de Montmorency. His father, his uncle Guy, and Guy's son, his cousin Philip, were all among the house's benefactors; another cousin, Petronilla, Philip's sister, was a nun there by 1231, and her half-sisters, Alice and Agnes, by 1259; and his niece, also Petronilla, daughter of his brother Amaury, became abbess before her death in 1275.[72] Second

[70] Below, p. 104; *Manners and Household Expenses*, ed. Turner, pp. 20–3, 29, 36, 41, 53–4.

[71] *Obituaires de la Province de Sens*, ed. A. Milinier and A. Longnon (4 vols., Paris, 1902–23), ii, pp. 224–5.

[72] *Cartulaire de l'abbaye de Porrois*, ed. A. de Dion (Paris, 1903), pp. 34, 94–5, 128, 260–1, 322; *Necrologe de l'Abbaie de Port-Roial des Champs* (Amsterdam, 1723), pp. 57, 139, 252; Zerner, 'L'épouse de Simon de Montfort', p. 468. Guy married (1) Heloise d'Ibelin, dead by 1216 (Balme and Lelaidier, *Cartulaire ou Histoire Diplomatique de Saint Dominique* (2 vols., Paris, 1893–97), ii, pp. 42–3), and (2) Briende de Beynes (*Cart. Porrois*, ed. de Dion, pp. 94–5; *Necrologe de . . . Port-Roial*, p. 57). Philip and Petronilla were the children of the first marriage, Alice and Agnes of the second.

came St Antoine's, in Paris, another Cistercian nunnery, where Montfort's sister, a third Petronilla, had been placed by her mother in 1221, when she was ten, and which by 1254 she ruled as abbess.[73] Finally, his second sister, Amicia, widow of Gaucher de Joigny, had founded a convent of Dominican nuns at Montargis, south of Paris, dying there as a nun in 1252. After Evesham it was to Montargis that Eleanor retired, and it was there, too, that Amaury, her son and Simon's, made his will in 1289.[74]

Montfort cared for this circle of devout sisters and cousins, and in various small ways he did what he could for them. In 1254 he was able to persuade Innocent IV to order the modification of the oppressive new rules which the senior house of Vaux de Cernai wanted to impose on its dependents at Porrois, where, as the pope noted, the abbess was Montfort's kinswoman. Visiting St Antoine's in 1258, perhaps to see his sister, he arranged for the house to receive money which he owed to the executors of Peter Mauclerc, former count of Brittany, in repayment of a debt. In the following year he successfully backed his cousin Philip's request to his son, another Philip, to hand over to the Porrois nuns Agnes and Alice, the elder Philip's half-sisters, their share in the family inheritance from the Albigensian conquest, for the benefit of the house.[75] Both religious piety and family *pietas* drew him towards these nunneries of the Ile de France, in which his close relatives had invested so much of their lives and property. The same sympathies took him to the Cistercian general chapter at Cîteaux in 1242, during his stay in Burgundy after the crusade, and led him on several occasions to ask the Cistercians to celebrate the anniversaries of his father, mother and dead brothers.[76] A more than dutiful son, he was still a figure in the ancestral landscape of northern France which was the continuing setting for the religious life of his extended family.

South of the Channel, however, the exiguousness of his property meant that he had little besides influence to offer these monastic houses.

[73] Bémont, *Montfort* (2nd edn), p. xxx, n. 1; Zerner, 'L'épouse de Simon de Montfort', pp. 465–6; Balme and Lelaidier, *Cart. de Saint Dominique*, i, pp. 239–40.

[74] Bémont, *Montfort* (2nd edn), p. xxx, n. 1, p. 258 (where the foundation is misdated to 1207); Hinnebusch, *History of the Dominican Order*, i, p. 381; M.-D. Chapotin, *Histoire des Dominicains de la Province de France* (Rouen, 1898), pp. 348, 360–3.

[75] *Les Registres d'Innocent IV*, ed. E. Berger (4 vols., Paris, 1881–90), iii, No. 7618; *Cart. Porrois*, ed. de Dion, pp. 260–1; *Nécrologe de . . . Port Roial*, p. 139; BN MS. Clairambault 1188, f. 10v; below, pp. 174–5.

[76] *Statuta Capitulorum Generalium Ordinis Cisterciensis*, ed. J. M. Canivez, ii (Louvain, 1934), pp. 249, 349, 378, 390.

In England he could do rather more. His status as a newcomer meant that there was no particular house like Hautes-Bruyères in which he had deep roots. The Augustinian abbey of Leicester, founded by Robert de Beaumont II, earl of Leicester, his great-great-grandfather, in 1143, came nearest to it. But Montfort showed no special affection for Leicester abbey, and his one large grant of 320 acres of land to the canons, made c. 1240, may be a concealed sale, intended to finance his crusade, rather than a gift. Henry III's detention of the abbey's advowson, another item in Montfort's long catalogue of grievances against the king, perhaps weakened what ought to have been a special relationship.[77] His other grants were small and, to all appearances, mostly indiscriminate. The ten virgates of land granted to the nuns of Nuneaton in Warwickshire may have deliberately echoed his family's generosity to Hautes-Bruyères, for Nuneaton was one of only four English houses belonging to the same order of Fontevrault; though it was also another foundation of his ancestor, Robert de Beaumont II.[78] The rest of the tally is short and reveals no special pattern: 10s. a year granted to the Leicestershire leper house of Burton Lazars;[79] two minor grants to the Premonstratensian houses of Durford and St Radegund's, Bradsole, both in Kent;[80] confirmation of grants by his predecessors and others to the canons of Leicester and the nuns of Sopwell in Hertfordshire;[81] twenty tree trunks given to the Dominicans of Wilton;[82] a rich cloth offered on the altar of St Albans when he was a visitor there in 1260;[83] and the demesne tithes of Luton given to the same house on 11 November 1257.[84] This last was probably donated in exchange for the letters of confraternity which the abbot of St Albans conferred on him next day. In a slightly more emphatic way than most lay grants to the religious in the middle ages, the grant of the Luton tithes was charitable, but not quite disinterested.

Montfort's affection for the religious, the value he placed on

[77] *CChR, 1226–57*, p. 408 (for the date, see above, p. 61, n. 61); Paris, iv, p. 7; Bémont, *Montfort* (1st edn), p. 333; A. Hamilton Thompson, *The Abbey of St. Mary of the Meadows, Leicester* (Leicester, 1949), pp. 2, 17.

[78] BL Add. Ch. 47593; Crouch, *The Beaumont Twins*, pp. 203–4.

[79] BL MS. Cotton Nero C. XII, f. 110, summarised in *The Burton Lazars Cartulary*, ed. T. Bourne and D. Marcombe (Nottingham, 1987), p. 60.

[80] BL MS. Cotton Vespasian E. XXIII, ff. 51v, 77; Bodleian Library, MS. Rawl. B. 336, f. 12.

[81] c.56/16, m. 19; Bodleian Library MS. Laud Misc. 625, f. 102; *Cat. Anc. Deeds.*, iii, p. 136.

[82] *CR, 1242–87*, pp. 325–6; Labarge, *Montfort*, p. 79.

[83] *Flores Hist.*, ii, p. 443.

[84] BL MS. Cotton Otho D. III, f. 111.

monastic prayer, and his desire for 'fraternal association' with monastic houses, all commented on by Rishanger, are undoubted. Preserved among the remains of his family archives are the confraternity letters from St Albans, which provided for an elaborate programme of posthumous prayers and masses for the souls of himself, his wife and his benefactors, accompanied by the regular feeding of the poor.[85] In 1263 he received similar confraternity rights from the Benedictine house at Dunstable.[86] Yet it is doubtful whether his enthusiasm for these benefits was quite equalled by his generosity. It should not surprise us that he is not known to have founded any religious house, with the probable exception of the Dominican friary at Leicester. By the thirteenth century the passion for monastic foundations had passed, and the few lay founders were usually men of exceptional wealth. Montfort was not in the same league as, for example, Richard of Cornwall, that contemporary Maecenas, who set up the Cistercians at Hailes. But even at the more humble level of grants and confirmations, the record remains thin, as we might have guessed from the small tally of Montfort's twenty-four extant charters. Of those charters, only eleven record donations to religious houses, and some of the eleven – the large grant to Leicester abbey about 1240, the grant of the Luton tithes to St Albans – are unlikely to be the unencumbered gifts that they seem. To some extent parsimony was the order of the day, as lay benefactions of all sorts to the religious tailed off at this time; the same closeness is observable a generation earlier in the frugal giving of David, earl of Huntingdon.[87] But when all allowances have been made, both for the incompleteness of the record and for the spirit of the age, the strong impression remains that for a man with Montfort's religious reputation the scale of his charitable disbursements is a good deal smaller than we might expect. This was in part the reflection of his circumstances: the tying up of much of his wealth inalienably in Eleanor's dower, and the pressures of all kinds, from the endowment of his family and the rewarding of his affinity, to the expenses of his crusade and of his government in Gascony, which bore on his limited resources. But it also reflected his own not over-generous nature. Openhandedness, an aristocratic virtue as well as a religious one, was what he most singularly lacked.

---

[85] BN MS. Clairambault 1021, f. 42. I am very grateful to David Carpenter for drawing my attention to this document and for generously sending me a transcript.
[86] *Ann. Dun.*, p. 226.
[87] Stringer, *Earl David of Huntingdon*, pp. 141–3.

The general record of Montfort's relations with the religious, of which his grants form only a portion, reminds us that his piety had a deeply conventional side. It is easy to see him as a precursor of the devout nobility who seem to proliferate after about 1350: penitent men and women, often ascetic in outlook and habits, their sensitive consciences trained by confessors and their faith strengthened by devotional reading. There is indeed much in Montfort's religious life which foreshadows that of a Henry of Lancaster or a Henry, Lord Scrope.[88] He was perhaps the first, and certainly the pre-eminent, example of the type of devout layman created by the Fourth Lateran Council and its agencies, who was later to come into his own in the age of the Lollards. In Montfort's case the instrument which brought him into conformity with these larger developments in the Church was a group of proselytising and particularly pious friends. Yet in his case there was none of the concomitant turning away from the old norms and institutions of established religion which was beginning to become apparent by the later fourteenth century. By conviction and upbringing he remained firmly rooted in his family's traditions of veneration for the monastic ideal and for the crusade.

Both varieties of religious experience, the new and the old, combined in Montfort to create a *dévot* of an unusually extreme kind, but one whose nature and temperament could not sustain the demand for the wholehearted conversion that his teachers must have hoped for. When he prayed to be delivered from avarice and covetousness, as according to Rishanger he did pray,[89] he showed a degree of self-knowledge which was not always matched by the moral improvement that confessors expected from their penitents. So far we have only glimpsed this side of his character: in his treatment of the unfortunate burgess of Leicester, in the harsh behaviour of his officials, in his no more than ordinary interest in the poor, and in his apparent illiberality towards the religious. It will become plainer as we move towards and beyond 1258, when the conflict intensified between his public and religious ideals and his private interests.

---

[88] For these examples, and for the subject in general, see J. Catto, 'Religion and the English Nobility in the Later Fourteenth Century', *History and Imagination: Essays in Honour of H. R. Trevor-Roper*, ed. H. Lloyd-Jones, V. Pearl and B. Worden (London, 1981), esp. pp. 51–3.

[89] Rishanger, *De Bellis*, pp. 6–7.

CHAPTER 4

Simon de Montfort's road to reform, 1248–58

(A) MONTFORT IN GASCONY

The best-known period in Simon de Montfort's life began in 1258, when he and other leading magnates initiated a reform movement which would eventually bring him to supreme power and then to disaster at Evesham in 1265. The movement marked the coalescence of the general and local resentments of clergy, gentry and baronage with the particular and private grievances of some members of the higher nobility. None had grievances which were more deeply held than Montfort. Although their origins dated back to the time of his marriage, as we have seen, they grew in number and intensity in the years after 1248. It was then that old disputes about Eleanor's dower were aggravated by others arising from Montfort's rule in Gascony between 1248 and 1252, a novel set of financial claims against the king, and new factional rivalries at court. In this chapter, therefore, we shall trace the history of Montfort's personal grievances against a background of widening discontent at the exercise of Henry's kingship.

At the turn of the year 1247 the direction of these events had hardly been visible. It looked then as though the quiet time which Montfort had enjoyed since his return from Gascony in 1243 would be terminated, not by any disagreement with Henry, but by a new crusade. The fall of Jerusalem in 1244, Louis IX's subsequent crusading vow, and Innocent IV's later declaration of a crusade, had produced a response in England which paralleled that in France. In May 1247 William Longespee and other nobles took the cross, to be followed later in the year by Simon de Montfort.[1] In his case there were special reasons for participating, beyond those arising from the needs of the Holy Land and the initiatives

---

[1] Paris, iv, pp. 629–30, v, pp. 1–2. Paris says that Montfort took the cross around Christmas 1247, but the pope spoke of him as a *crucesignatus* in mid November: *CPL*, i, p. 239. For this crusade, see Tyerman, *England and the Crusades*, pp. 108–10.

of the pope and the French king. His family's long crusading traditions, the role of his close friends and spiritual advisers, Robert Grosseteste and Walter de Cantilupe, as the ecclesiastical managers of the English enterprise, charged with the collection of crusading funds, and, if Paris is right, Montfort's own religious doubts about the validity of his marriage,[2] all combined to intensify the natural attractions of an undertaking which so great a noble could in any case hardly ignore. For Montfort the new crusade was both a penitential exercise and the Church's cause.

Yet in the end he did not go. What brought him fully back into public life was not the crusade but his appointment in May 1248 as Henry's lieutenant in Gascony for a period of seven years.[3] In retrospect this can be seen to have marked the beginning of troubles, and a turning-point in Montfort's relations with Henry. At the time, however, it showed the need to give priority to Gascony over even the most compelling alternative goals. English control of the province was threatened by dangers which only a bold and active man could overcome. In the best of circumstances Gascony was not an easy land to govern. Its towns and nobles had far more independence than their English counterparts. The towns, especially Bordeaux, were riven by faction, and the nobles, many of whom held their lands freely and not by feudal service, had only a tenuous allegiance to their duke, who was also king of England. They had little in common besides their determination to defend regional customs and private rights, such as the right to make war, which were themselves violently inimical to good order. The greatest of them, men such as Gaston de Béarn, ruled what were in effect independent frontier lordships and were well placed to intrigue with enemies beyond the frontier. Ducal sovereignty over this fragmented political landscape hardly existed, and ducal authority rested less on force than on conciliation, respect for urban privilege, and the distribution of fees to the nobility. In a region where ducal castles were few, ducal demesne scattered, and the importing of troops from England prohibitively expensive, any more thoroughgoing policy was out of place.[4]

---

[2] W. E. Lunt, *Financial Relations of the Papacy with England to 1327* (Cambridge, Mass., 1939), pp. 436–7; above, p. 86.
[3] Bémont, *Montfort* (1st edn), pp. 264–5.
[4] For conditions in Gascony, see Powicke, *King Henry III*, pp. 208–14; J. P. Trabut-Cussac, *L'Administration Anglaise en Gascogne sous Henry III et Edouard I de 1254 à 1307* (Geneva, 1972), pp. xi–xxv; M. W. Labarge, *Gascony: England's First Colony, 1204–1453* (London, 1980), pp. 10–14;

In 1248 the routine problems facing English rule in Gascony were exacerbated by external threats. The kings of Castile and Aragon both had dormant claims to the territory, arising from their descent from Henry II's daughter Eleanor, which could be activated at any time. More immediately, the king of Navarre, whose land projected across the Pyrenees, was making incursions along Gascony's southern frontier, and French power had moved dangerously close to the northern frontier since the establishment in Poitou of Alphonse of Poitiers, Louis IX's brother, following the failure of Henry III's campaign there in 1242–43. The imminent expiry of the five-year truce with France, made after that campaign, was awaited apprehensively. If any of these threats materialised, the Gascon nobility, whose feuding and disorderliness had increased in recent years, might well take advantage of their new opportunities to collaborate with the invaders; in particular, Gaston de Béarn and the king of Navarre were natural partners. As Montfort himself later pointed out, there was a real danger that Gascony would be lost, with disastrous consequences for Henry.[5] The only remaining continental fragment of the Angevin empire, the province was seen as both an outlying part of England's defence system and an important source of funds (though we now know that its maintenance cost more than its revenues brought in).[6] Considerations of ancestral honour, royal prestige and the national interest seemed to be closely bound up with its security.

In these circumstances Montfort's task was essentially a military one: he was appointed to bring the Gascons to heel and to meet the dangers looming after the expiry of the French truce. The terms of his commission reflected these objectives. He was to have control of the province for seven years, full disposal of its revenues for purposes of defence, and reimbursement for any expenditure on castles; while Henry was to take responsibility for external warfare against the four kings and to supply him with 2,000 marks and 50 knights for a year's service. In the subsequent disputes between the two men these terms assumed great importance. As Montfort repeatedly stressed, they made him no mere bailiff, removable at Henry's will, but a lieutenant in the literal sense, acting in the king's place for a fixed period; only if he had

---

and M. Vale, *The Angevin Legacy and the Hundred Years War, 1250–1340* (Oxford, 1990), pp. 80–3, 112–24.

[5] Bémont, *Montfort* (1st edn), p. 341.

[6] Paris, iv, p. 594, v, p. 368; Stacey, *Politics, Policy*, pp. 174–6.

the independence conferred by the province's revenues and by a long stint of service would he be able to bring Gascony to order. That Montfort was pressed to take up office by the king, the queen and the council, and was apparently able to lay down these conditions, shows how desperately Henry needed his help.[7]

Why did Henry turn to Montfort? The answer is given by Matthew Paris: 'because he was a warrior (*vir Martius*), famous and experienced in warfare'.[8] Montfort's military reputation, attested by other chronicles besides Paris,[9] is a minor mystery in the story of his career and one worth dwelling on for a moment. By 1248 he was certainly 'experienced in warfare'. We have surmised that he may have fought his first campaign against the Albigensians in 1226–29; he had more clearly taken part in Henry's Brittany expedition of 1230; Paris tells us that he had campaigned briefly with the Emperor on his journey to Rome in 1238; he had been on crusade in 1240–41; he had fought with distinction at Saintes in 1242 and accompanied Henry on the Welsh campaign of 1245.[10] In some respects, however, this record is less impressive than it may seem. In Brittany, on crusade and in Wales there was very little fighting; no specific actions by Montfort are anywhere related; and at Saintes he was one of a number of nobles named by Paris as sharing in whatever glory was available on that inglorious occasion. One vital quality of contemporary generalship, skill at fortification, he certainly possessed: he rebuilt Kenilworth castle with such ingenuity that in 1266 it was able to withstand a six-month siege, the longest in English history.[11] He was also a resourceful recruiting officer and paymaster, as events in Gascony were to show. Yet daring deeds are nowhere much in evidence in his early career. Perhaps his outstanding reputation as a soldier owed something to that of his father, who had fought and won two great battles,[12] and to the simple fact of his own participation in so many campaigns. Perhaps, too, there were exploits in Montfort's past that are unknown to us. Did he, for example, make his name at tournaments, like that other great warrior, William Marshal?

---

[7] Paris, v, p. 293; Bémont, *Montfort* (1st edn), pp. 264–5, 335–6, 341–2. But note that the terms of office of Richard de Grey, the seneschal appointed in March 1248, whom Montfort superseded, had been similar, though not identical: *CPR, 1247–58*, p. 10.

[8] Paris, v, p. 293.

[9] E.g. Guillaume de Nangis: 'a man strenuous in arms and most skilled in the science of arms' (*Recueil des Historiens des Gaules*, 20, p. 414).

[10] Paris, iii, pp. 479–80, iv, p. 213; *Ann. Cestr.*, pp. 64–5; above, pp. 6, 10, 29–31.

[11] *Flores Hist.*, ii, p. 489; Paris, v, p. 697.

[12] Above, p. 4.

Whatever its basis, Montfort's military reputation made him seem the obvious man for Gascony in 1248. But that was not his only qualification. His family's standing in France and his own diplomatic experience equipped him to deal more peaceably with the immediate threats to Gascony's security. After crossing the Channel he was able, between September and November 1248, to negotiate an extension of the truce with France and to reach an agreement with the king of Navarre by which the king's quarrels with Henry were to be submitted to arbitration.[13] With an invasion prevented, and one of the main objects of his mission fulfilled, he could turn to the much more difficult task of reimposing order and ducal authority within Gascony.

Here he was hampered both by his father's reputation for greed and brutality, acquired during the Albigensian crusade a generation earlier and still bitterly remembered,[14] and by his own lack of the personal qualities necessary for success. He came as a military governor, bringing with him a force of knights, drawn mainly from his own household and the king's, which was probably rather larger than the fifty originally agreed on. It was easy to see him, as Paris saw him, as a man preparing to follow in his father's footsteps and to rule by force of arms.[15] In denying the Gascon nobility the prescriptive liberty of disorder which they had previously enjoyed, he rode roughshod over cherished local customs, took sides in local feuds and imposed arbitrary punishments.[16] Local malefactors were arrested without trial, deprived of their castles and held to ransom. The vicomte de Gramont, who, like many of his peers, combined the status of a noble with the profession of a brigand, was taken and kept in prison for six years without judgement. Burgesses whose municipal privileges entitled them to a visit from the king's lieutenant when oaths of fealty were to be sworn were instead made to visit him. In Bordeaux, where violent feuding broke out in 1249 between the rival families of Colom and Delsoler, the earl sided with the Colom, imprisoning supporters of the other party, seizing their goods

---

[13] *Foedera*, I, i, p. 269; Bémont, *Montfort* (1st edn), pp. 265–6.

[14] Bémont, *Montfort* (1st edn), p. 298; Powicke, *King Henry III*, p. 219.

[15] *CPR, 1247–58*, p. 31; *CR, 1247–51*, p. 119; Paris, v, p. 104.

[16] For the rest of this paragraph, see Bémont, *Montfort* (2nd edn), pp. 77–93. Though not always accurate, this is the fullest and most accessible account in English of Montfort's rule in Gascony. But it needs to be supplemented by J. Ellis, 'Gaston de Béarn: A Study in Anglo-Gascon Relations, 1229–90' (Oxford D.Phil. thesis, 1952): an invaluable work which has been entirely ignored by historians of Gascony.

and invoking ecclesiastical sanctions against their clerical allies. Much of this activity found a sort of justification in his contract, which had bound him to recover the king's rights, liberties and possessions; but it is clear, too, that Montfort sought his own ends as well as Henry's. As well as ransoming those he captured, he took possession of the county of Bigorre, intervening in a complicated succession dispute to bar the interests of Gaston de Béarn, lord of the neighbouring county, and a rival claimant. Gaston, the chief of his enemies and the greatest single threat to the peace throughout his time in Gascony, was the leader of the first concerted rising against Montfort's rule in the last months of 1250.

Montfort's methods gradually turned Henry against him. The king came to be increasingly offended by his harsh rule, by the complaints which it provoked, by his inability to govern within the financial constraints of his commission, and by the paradox that order could be achieved in Gascony only at the risk of rebellion. Montfort, on the other hand, saw his authority subverted by the interference of a monarch largely ignorant of local problems, yet willing to pass judgement on them, and liable to be imposed upon by the guile of rebels. Both sides found in the end that the contract of 1248, which had defined Montfort's revenues but not his powers, could not be maintained. This gathering distrust progressively undermined Montfort's relations with Henry between 1248 and 1252. During his first return visit to England in December 1248 he was feted as a hero: after no more than a few months in Gascony he had not only made peace with France and Navarre but also temporarily brought Gaston de Béarn to terms.[17] But by November 1249 Henry was receiving representatives of the aggrieved Delsoler faction, and although they were arrested and sent back to Gascony for trial, the king had at the same time given a discreet warning to Montfort about the severity of his conduct.[18] In the following month came a much more serious subversion of the earl's position. Gaston de Béarn, captured and sent to England by Montfort, was pardoned and restored to his lands by Henry at the request of the queen, whose cousin he was. In exchange for his clemency, Henry received Gaston's homage, which he may have seen as a step towards the pacification of Gascony. Nevertheless, his was an act of repudiation, directly contrary

---

[17] Paris, v, p. 48; Ellis, 'Gaston de Béarn', p. 113.
[18] *CR, 1247–51*, pp. 343–4.

to the Crown's real interests, and later a cause of special bitterness to his lieutenant.[19]

Like Machiavelli, Montfort knew that men do not rule states with paternosters in their hands. Good order, achieved at some cost in terms of disregard for established rights and liberties, was the measure of his success; and despite Gaston's rehabilitation Montfort *had* restored order in Gascony. The chaplain of Alphonse of Poitiers, who was hardly a partisan observer, told his lord, after visiting Montfort in February 1250, that 'he holds Gascony in good estate and all obey him and dare not undertake anything against him'.[20] But although Montfort had spoken optimistically to the chaplain about his intention to go on crusade by midsummer, he must have known that his achievement was very fragile. In March 1250 he wrote sombrely to Henry from Paris, where he had been dealing with the king's business before the Paris parlement. The great men of the land bore him such ill-will because of his maintenance of the king's rights and those of the poor that he could not safely return without speaking to Henry first. He was unable to levy the king's rents, and an army would be useless in the kind of war that was being waged, 'for they will do nothing but rob the land, and burn and plunder, and put the people to ransom, and ride by night like thieves by twenty or thirty or forty in different parts'; and then they would tell the king that he, Montfort, was the cause of the war.[21] Knowledgeable in his enemies' ways, Montfort showed in this succinct résumé both his sharp military sense and some of his more general intellectual qualities. It was a letter which passed comment on all his difficulties: inadequate finances, a kind of terrorist banditry which could not be countered by conventional military methods, and a king who was as likely to believe his enemies as his own representative.

The financial problems to which Montfort alluded were one of the main factors hastening the collapse of trust between king and lieutenant. Under the terms of his contract the revenues of Gascony had been made over to him, while Henry was to provide for the maintenance of castles. But from an early stage the Gascon revenues proved inadequate to meet Montfort's needs, and the cost of castles far more than Henry had

---

[19] Paris, v, pp. 103–4; *CPR, 1247–58*, p. 57; Bémont, *Montfort* (1st edn), p. 342, (2nd edn), p. 79, n. 3; Labarge, *Montfort*, pp. 114–15; Ellis, 'Gaston de Béarn', pp. 114–17.
[20] Boutaric, *Saint Louis et Alfonse de Poitiers*, p. 73; Bémont, *Montfort* (2nd edn), p. 87.
[21] Bémont, *Montfort* (1st edn), p. 267.

bargained for. Control of castles was vital to Montfort's policy, for the security of Gascony depended largely on the building of new ones and the capture and retention of those used as bandit strongholds by rebellious nobles.[22] This was inevitably expensive. In November 1249 the king had made over all his Irish revenues for two years for spending on Gascon castles; a further grant of some £660 followed in January 1250; in May, during the visit to England which Montfort had requested in the letter mentioned above, he received an additional £1,200, borrowed by Henry from Italian bankers, and a bond for £800 in acknowledgement of the king's debts for knights which Henry should have supplied; and in September came yet another grant of £1,000 to be spent solely on fortifying the castle of Cussac.[23]

The financial strains placed on Henry's already overstretched resources by Montfort's government of Gascony helped to propel events towards a climax. Late in 1250 there were further disturbances in the province, and in January 1251 Montfort had to return to England, hurriedly and humiliatingly, to ask for further funds. Without the means to hire mercenaries he could clearly do nothing in the face of widespread disorder. He cleverly appealed to Henry's own experiences of Gascon treachery in 1242–43, and, according to Paris, was given £2,000, though only some £300 are recorded on the chancery rolls. It was to be a future source of grievance that he continued to have to meet his expenses by drawing on his own income from his estates, probably, as we have seen, at the expense of his tenants. At the same time Henry had become increasingly uneasy about his strongarm methods of government. After having warned him about the complaints that his actions had provoked, Henry despatched two commissioners in January 1251 to settle Montfort's quarrels with the Gascons or to refer them to the king.[24] Although Henry had already received complaints against him, this was the first formal limitation of the powers conceded to him by the contract of 1248. For the moment, however, his position was unimpaired. Backed by new money, he was able to hire mercenaries, to return to the duchy in March 1251, and to reimpose order by force. The capture of his enemies' stronghold at Castillon in May marked the

---

[22] Paris, v, p. 209, for an example.
[23] *CPR, 1247–58*, pp. 55, 67; *CR, 1247–51*, pp. 254, 321; *CLR, 1245–51*, p. 288; Labarge, *Montfort*, pp. 115–16.
[24] Paris, v, pp. 208–10; *CLR, 1245–51*, p. 329; *CPR, 1247–58*, p. 85. For pressure on Montfort's estates, see above, pp. 56–8.

summit of his success. For the time being he could afford to ignore the resentments provoked by his seizure of castles, his taking of hostages, and his violent answer to violence.[25]

But not for long. In December 1251 Montfort returned to England once again. While he was with the king at York for the marriage of Henry's daughter Margaret to Alexander III of Scotland, his simmering dispute with Henry about the whole conduct of Gascon affairs became for the first time an open conflict. There were essentially two reasons for this public breakdown of relations. First, news came that the Gascons were once again in revolt, and Henry, acting on information received from the Gascons themselves, accused Montfort of having provoked the rising through his harsh government. Montfort wanted to leave England to deal with the new disturbances, but was forbidden to do so. Secondly, the old quarrels over the financing of Gascony came to a head. Montfort asked the king to reimburse him for his expenses there, but Henry declined either to do this or even to meet the cost of castles, as he was obliged to do under the terms of the contract. He gave way only after Montfort had threatened to alienate the castles in order to recoup his losses, provoking the queen to intervene. Gascony had been granted to the Lord Edward, heir to the throne, as an appanage in 1249, and Eleanor rightly judged that the loss of the castles would pose a major threat to Edward's interests there. The related question of Montfort's expenses remained unsettled, probably because Henry was unwilling to take Montfort's word on what might be a very costly commitment.[26]

In the opening months of 1252 both these outstanding issues moved towards some sort of resolution, though it was one which marked the virtual supersession of Montfort's rule in Gascony. New commissioners despatched there by the king in January were told to enquire into complaints against Montfort and to summon Gascon representatives to state their case in England. On arrival they found a land at war. Gaston de Béarn was besieging the king's castle at La Réole, and although a fragile truce was made until 22 June, there was a general refusal to attend in England if Montfort should return to the duchy.[27] Meanwhile Henry had gone some way towards meeting the earl's private claims. In March he was granted £2,000, to be collected from the king's debtors

[25] Paris, v, p. 256; Bémont, *Montfort* (1st edn), p. 271, (2nd edn), p. 94.

[26] Paris, v, pp. 266–70, 276–7; Bémont, *Montfort* (1st edn), pp. 336, 339, 342; *CChR, 1226–57*, p. 325; *CPR, 1247–58*, p. 50.

[27] Paris, v, p. 277; *CR, 1251–53*, pp. 186–8; *RL*, ii, pp. 76–81; Bémont, *Montfort* (2nd edn), pp. 98, 100–2.

overseas; arbitrators were appointed to look into his receipts and expenses since 1248; and a final balance sheet was to be drawn up. But by the same agreement he was to hand over four of the most strategically situated Gascon castles to the king. This was a further confirmation of Montfort's declining position, and one contrary to the terms of his appointment. Yet he was far from accepting retirement. About the time of the March agreement he returned briefly to Gascony, believing no doubt that he was needed to suppress the current rebellion.[28]

When he came back to England it was to confront his accusers in parliament. His 'trial', which took place before king and barons in the refectory of Westminster Abbey and lasted from early May until early June, is recorded for us both by Paris and in a letter sent by Adam Marsh to Grosseteste. Although both are highly favourable to Montfort, they are independent and on many points they concur both with each other and with Montfort's own recollections ten years later.[29] The issues were clear cut. The Gascons, led by the archbishop of Bordeaux, alleged that Montfort had acted with brutal highhandedness, sending nobles away to prison in France, extorting money from others, and arresting those who came to him under safe conduct. They supported their case with a dossier of written complaints which provides one perspective on Montfort's administration of the province. Montfort's reply was part denial, part vindication. His opponents' testimony was unreliable. He had been commissioned by the king to put down traitors and he had done so with a degree of justifiable severity. Henry, on the other hand, had disregarded the charter appointing him for a fixed term, refused to meet his expenses, and left him out of pocket.

In the recriminations which followed both men lost their tempers. The exchange which saw Montfort questioning Henry's credentials as a Christian was part of this violent quarrel.[30] But in these volleys of charge and countercharge Montfort had one great advantage: he had the backing of the magnates, while Henry and the Gascons appear to have stood alone. Between them, Paris and Marsh name the earls of

---

[28] Paris, v, pp. 277, 284; *CPR, 1247–58*, pp. 124, 132; *CR, 1251–53*, pp. 203–5; Bémont, *Montfort* (1st edn), pp. 336, 342, (2nd edn), pp. 98–9; Ellis, 'Gaston de Béarn', pp. 136–7. Montfort, 'gone on the king's service to Gascony', received a protection on 22 Feb. (*CPR, 1247–58*, p. 129), even though the agreement was not made until 10 March.

[29] Paris, v, pp. 287–96; *Mon. Franc.*, i, pp. 122–30 (there is a translation of this difficult letter in Wood, *Lives of the Princesses*, ii, pp. 447–53); Bémont, *Montfort* (1st edn), pp. 342–3.

[30] Paris, v, p. 290; above, p. 87.

Cornwall, Gloucester and Hereford, Peter of Savoy, Peter de Montfort and Walter de Cantilupe as Montfort's main allies, together with other unnamed barons and bishops. Their reasons were diverse and often personal. Richard of Cornwall himself had claims to Gascony, overridden by Henry in 1242 and more recently by the grant of the duchy to Edward in 1249;[31] Peter of Savoy, closely identified with the interests of his niece, the queen, and of the Lord Edward, probably wished to see Gascony firmly secured as the prince's appanage;[32] Cantilupe and Peter de Montfort were the earl's personal friends, and Peter had been with him in Gascony; and many shared acrimonious memories of Gascon treachery during Henry's expedition of 1242–43.[33] They may well have thought that the Gascons deserved all that Montfort had given them. Their support for him transformed the earl's private quarrel with Henry into a public cause, which temporarily set Henry apart from his great men and for once gave Montfort a central place among the higher nobility. Nor were they alone in their sympathies, for the earl was also able to call on witnesses from Gascony to justify his conduct.

Against Montfort's own convincing defence and the apparently unanimous support for him, Henry could do little, and he gave his verdict in the earl's favour, to general approval. But then, with characteristic inconsistency, he changed his mind and arguments broke out once more. Montfort and his followers had already offered to accept the verdict of the king and his justices on the charges against them; but a formal resort to law had been rejected by the Gascons, a rejection which rankled deeply with the earl for many years.[34] Now he offered a fresh compromise: he would return to Gascony, this time to govern with justice and mercy, in order to save the province for the king. If the opposition of his enemies made this impossible, he would raise troops to put them down. If the king rejected both these alternatives, he would surrender the government of the duchy, asking only to be given his expenses, to be exonerated from guilt, and to be safeguarded from reprisals. But these proposals were ignored by Henry, who on 13 June imposed his own terms. Their essentials were threefold: either the king or the Lord Edward would come to Gascony by 2 February 1253 to

[31] Denholm-Young, *Richard of Cornwall*, pp. 48–9, 75–6.
[32] H. Ridgeway, 'The Lord Edward and the Provisions of Oxford (1258): A Study in Faction', *TCE*, i, pp. 91–2.
[33] Paris, v, pp. 337–8.
[34] *Mon. Franc.*, i, pp. 125–6, is almost exactly corroborated in Montfort's own account: Bémont, *Montfort* (1st edn), pp. 336, 342.

settle the outstanding disputes between Montfort and the Gascons; in
the meantime both sides were to accept a truce; and a conservator of the
truce was to be appointed to see that its conditions were observed. This
was hardly a final settlement. As the king recognised, the trial had
merely been adjourned.[35]

Yet only in a formal sense was the trial inconclusive, for if Montfort
had been morally vindicated, he had been politically convicted. He had
some reason to feel aggrieved. He had been given full powers for seven
years to bring to heel an ungovernable people, and he had imposed
a precarious peace by methods which were inevitably rough and
expensive. Henry in return had undermined his authority by receiving
the complaints of men who were both his own and Montfort's enemies,
tried to evade his financial responsibilities, and in effect caused the
termination of his contract before the agreed date. Again and again he
was to appeal to the agreement of 1248 as the arbiter of his claims: it
gave his case its moral foundations, just as the Provisions of Oxford
would later do in a different argument. Henry saw things differently.
Montfort's rigour threatened the security of what was now his son's
appanage. Thanks to his rule, the complete loss of the province
remained almost as much a danger as it had been when he had taken
over.[36] He could not simply disregard the complaints of his Gascon
subjects, for he was their lord, with a duty to do them justice. He had
made what he thought was ample provision for Montfort's financial
needs, and in the previous three years he had added thousands of
pounds to that provision; yet all that had been achieved was a transient
stability which could be preserved only by the personal presence of his
overbearing lieutenant. Much, of course, had been unforeseen. The
contract of 1248 had made no allowance for the difficulty of suppressing
guerrilla warfare, the need to hire large numbers of mercenaries, the
almost uncontrollable expenditure on castles. One's sympathies, like
those of Paris and Marsh, are with Montfort. But Henry, too, had a case;
and both men were to some extent the victims of circumstance.

During his years in and out of Gascony, Montfort was in regular
correspondence with Adam Marsh and Robert Grosseteste. Though
Marsh's letters are too imperfectly dateable, and often too obscure in
their phrasing, to provide anything more than a very sparse commentary

---

[35] *Mon. Franc.*, i, pp. 127–8; *Foedera*, i, i, pp. 282–3; Bémont, *Montfort* (1st edn), p. 340. Ellis, 'Gaston de Béarn', pp. 140–9, provides the best analysis of the Gascons' complaints.
[36] Paris, v, pp. 277–8.

on the earl's difficulties, and though Grosseteste's are known only from allusions by Marsh,[37] even the fact of this correspondence is significant. It suggests the continuing importance to Montfort, at a particularly difficult time in his career, of religious relationships and values which are nowhere evident in the chronicle accounts and administrative records of his governorship. In its contents it suggests, too, a more troubled and diffident Montfort than the vigorous and sometimes brutally self-confident figure portrayed by Paris and by the complaints of the Gascons. His requests to Marsh for advice, and, on one occasion, his remonstrating with his friend for speaking so highly of him, point to a degree of humility which was at odds with his public actions. Marsh's replies betray Montfort's anxieties. 'If you have received the answers of broken friendship and feigned affection, what else are you suffering than what you before expected?', Marsh once wrote to him, before sending him to the Book of Job for consolation.[38] Of course, Marsh also rebuked him for his rough methods and his unruly followers, as we saw in the previous chapter;[39] but this corroboration of faults already well attested by other sources only increases the value of what Marsh discloses about the earl's most inward concerns. Behind the tough military governor stood the man in the confessional, in need of good advice. At a time when Montfort led the active life as never before, his contemplative side also comes intermittently to the surface, hinting at tensions which, in a more subdued form, were present throughout his career.

After his trial it seemed as if the earl would have to tolerate a contrasting period of inactivity. It was time for a new approach to Gascon affairs. Once Henry had imposed his terms on Montfort he took immediate steps to pacify the province by substituting conciliation for autocracy. He had Gascon approval for the renewal of his grant of Gascony and Oléron to the Lord Edward in April 1252 and for the promised royal expedition to Gascony, which in April was put in hand for October.[40] Meanwhile two conservators of the truce had been appointed, and under Henry's supervision they began to compensate the nobility for their losses. Henry himself countermanded many of Montfort's earlier orders and restored those whom the earl had cast

---

[37] *Mon. Franc.*, i, pp. 111, 269.

[38] *Mon. Franc.*, i, pp. 264–9.

[39] *Mon. Franc.*, i, pp. 261, 264, 298; above, pp. 99–100.

[40] *CChR, 1226–57*, p. 386; *CR, 1251–53*, pp. 239–40; Bémont, *Montfort* (2nd edn), p. 108; Trabut-Cussac, *L'Administration Anglaise*, pp. xxvii–xxviii.

down.[41] Montfort remained as the king's lieutenant, but in name only. The reversal of his policies marked his effective dismissal.

These plans for restoring the allegiance of Gascony were disrupted by two unforeseen contingencies: Montfort's renewed military intervention in the province, and Henry's own inability to secure support at home for his projected expedition. After unwillingly accepting the truce, Montfort had left England for France, but he stayed there for only a short while, in order to gather troops, before returning to Gascony. According to his own later account, he did so because he had heard that the castle of La Réole was under siege and that the truce was being broken; but Paris is probably more correct when he represents the earl as burning for revenge on his accusers.[42] Whatever his motives, Montfort's return provoked another savage war in which he himself was almost captured by his enemies.[43] His intervention brought an order from Henry that he should obey the truce, backed by subsequent letters depriving him of his command.[44] The earl responded by invoking the agreement of 1248, but when it became clear that Henry was prepared to buy him out Montfort gave in.[45] By an agreement made with the Lord Edward, probably in October or November 1252, he surrendered all his claims in Gascony and agreed to hand over the land and its castles to Edward in exchange for 7,000 marks (£4,667), the payment of his debts, and the right to retain all prisoners taken outside Gascony. Those taken inside the duchy were to be handed over to Edward's representatives in return for their ransoms.[46] It was an extremely generous settlement, which showed once again Montfort's expertise in promoting his own financial interests. In a difficult situation he had done very well for himself. Henry had appealed to the avarice which was deeply rooted in Montfort's nature, and secured his departure; but at a price. The king was to remember with bitterness his breaking of the truce, the war that resulted, and the extravagant terms for his withdrawal.[47]

Montfort's retirement, however, left Gascony without effective government. Henry's attempts to take an army there in October 1252 came to nothing, largely because he could get no support from the

---

[41] *RL*, ii, pp. 87–8; *CR, 1251–53*, p. 225; *CPR, 1247–58*, pp. 142, 157–9.
[42] Bémont, *Montfort* (1st edn), p. 343; Paris, v, p. 313.
[43] Paris, v, pp. 315–16, 334–5.
[44] Bémont, *Montfort* (1st edn), pp. 337, 340, 343; *CPR, 1247–58*, p. 161.
[45] Bémont, *Montfort* (1st edn), p. 337.
[46] Bémont, *Montfort* (1st edn), pp. 321–4.
[47] Bémont, *Montfort* (1st edn), pp. 340–1.

magnates in parliament. Their sympathies were again with Montfort, whom they thought had done no more than justice to the Gascons, and they refused Henry a tax.[48] In these favourable circumstances, with both the king and Montfort absent, a rebellion was launched in the spring of 1253 which drew together several powerful Gascon factions in the most concerted movement of opposition to Henry's authority yet seen. At its head, predictably, was Gaston de Béarn. But he acted this time in alliance with some of the major towns and also, much more dangerously, with Alfonso X of Castile, who had come to the throne in 1252 and who now responded to the rebels' invitation to reinvoke his ancestral claims to Gascony. In the ensuing disorders royal castles fell to the rebels, the countryside was pillaged, and Bordeaux itself was nearly reduced to starvation. These events were in one sense a vindication of Montfort's policies, as he himself was later to point out. The king, he said, had good cause to regret his freeing of Gaston in 1249 – and one can almost hear his sardonic tone of voice – when Henry himself came to Gascony in 1253, to find that Gaston had done homage to the king of Castile and was now holding La Réole against him. In showing that the Gascon nobility objected to all government, and not to the earl's alone, the rebellion provided a justification for coercive rule. But a movement which was no longer just anti-Montfortian but anti-English threatened the very survival of Henry's position in Gascony. In April 1253 the people of Bordeaux wrote to tell him that he would lose the whole province unless he acted quickly.[49]

Henry took note. At the parliament of May 1253 he secured a feudal aid from the lay magnates for the knighting of his son Edward, in exchange for the confirmation of Magna Carta. By drawing additionally on all his resources – the Irish revenues, a tallage on the Jews and the demesne, monastic *dona* – he was able to sail for Bordeaux in August.[50] There he summoned Montfort and others to appear in arms, but apparently without response from the earl. Henry was nevertheless able to initiate a remarkably successful campaign, which by the end of September had given him control of the Garonne valley and of every fortress except Benauges and La Réole. It was while besieging Benauges on 4 October that he wrote to Montfort again, asking him

---

[48] Paris, v, pp. 324–8, 330–2, 334–8.

[49] Paris, v, pp. 365–6, 368–70; Bémont, *Montfort* (1st edn), p. 342; Trabut-Cussac, *L'Administration Anglaise*, pp. xxviii–xxx; Ellis, 'Gaston de Béarn', pp. 156–60.

[50] Paris, v, pp. 373–9; *CR, 1251–53*, pp. 376, 386, 408, 411; Trabut-Cussac, *L'Administration Anglaise*, p. xxx.

to return. The tone of his letter was conciliatory, even deferential. If, having arrived, Montfort should subsequently want to leave, he would be free to do so without incurring the king's indignation and he would be given an escort of six magnates to whatever place he named. If he chose to stay, the king would defend him against all ill-wishers. By 22 October Montfort had accepted the invitation and rejoined Henry outside Benauges.[51]

As late as July 1253, on the eve of his embarkation, Henry had intended to resume Montfort's trial during his stay in Gascony.[52] In fact, his sojourn there became the occasion for a reconciliation between the two men which was both a pendant to Montfort's curtailed governorship of the duchy and also a prelude to a new phase in their relationship, one that was to last until 1258. Why, after all that had happened, did he prove reconcilable? According to Montfort himself, it was loyalty to his lord which brought him back to Henry's service: an explanation half corroborated by Paris, who says that a few months earlier Montfort had been offered the stewardship of France by the French nobility, after the death of Queen Blanche, the regent, and in the continuing absence of Louis IX in the Holy Land, but that he had refused the offer on the grounds that he could not serve two masters. Paris adds that his rejoining Henry also owed much to the advice of Grosseteste that he should remember the benefits that Henry had conferred on him and do good in return for the wrongs which he had suffered. It was the finale to their long friendship, for Grosseteste died on 9 October 1253, when his erratic disciple was probably about to set off for Benauges.[53]

Loyalty and conscience may have done much to prompt Montfort's return. But at the same time he must have realised that he was in a position to extract the most favourable terms from the king. Henry had a war on his hands. He could not afford to take the fastidious and highminded attitude to Gascon affairs which had seemed appropriate at Westminster. He had seen for himself the treachery of Gaston de Béarn, the need to capture and control castles, and the value of the terror tactics, involving the destruction of vineyards and houses, for which he had once criticised Montfort but which he now practised

---

[51] *Rôles Gascons*, ed. Francisque-Michel and C. Bémont (4 vols., Paris, 1885–1906), i, Nos. 3540, 2111 (= *CPR, 1247–58*, p. 244); *CPR, 1247–58*, p. 246; Trabut-Cussac, *L'Administration Anglaise*, pp. xxxi–xxxii.

[52] *CR, 1251–53*, p. 489.

[53] Bémont, *Montfort* (1st edn), p. 338; Paris, v, pp. 366, 371–2, 407, 415–16. For the date of Grosseteste's death, see Stevenson, *Robert Grosseteste*, p. 324.

himself.[54] His experiences had to some extent vindicated Montfort's methods; and with his half-finished campaign temporarily stalled before the rebel stronghold at Benauges, Henry desperately needed Montfort's military expertise and the manpower which he could provide. In almost exactly similar circumstances, and with the same motives, he had summoned Montfort back from Burgundy to Poitou in 1242;[55] and on both occasions he was prepared to pay for what he wanted.

The main terms for the settlement between the king and the earl were drafted on 9 November. On that day Montfort was promised £500 in compensation for his losses and expenses in Henry's service in Gascony; and Kenilworth castle, granted to Eleanor for life in 1248, was confirmed to the earl and countess jointly, together with the manor of Odiham, which Eleanor had formerly held only during pleasure.[56] But the most valuable concession was a very substantial new annual fee, again granted for his losses and expenses. It was set up in a rather complicated way. As we have seen, in 1244 Montfort and Eleanor had been granted a fee of 500 marks a year by way of a *maritagium*. When Montfort 'bought' the Umfraville wardship in the following year this fee was set against his notional annual payment of 500 marks for the wardship, so that no money changed hands. In effect, therefore, he had gained the Umfraville wardship as a *maritagium*.[57] In November 1253 these arrangements were drastically modified. First, Henry pardoned Montfort the notional annual payment of 500 marks for the wardship. This meant that the king now had to start paying the original 500-mark fee. Second, he increased the fee by 100 marks, making 600 marks (£400) in all, and conceded that the whole sum was to be enjoyed by Montfort, Eleanor and their heirs. This was a great improvement on the terms of the 1244 grant of 500 marks, of which 200 marks had been for life only. Third, he undertook to replace this new 600-mark fee with lands of an equivalent value at a later date. But the most surprising feature of the settlement lay in the arrangements made for the payment of the fee. It was to be made the first charge on the incoming revenues of specified counties and to be paid by the sheriffs of those counties: 200 marks from Warwickshire and Leicestershire, 200 marks from Nottinghamshire and Derbyshire, 100 marks from Wiltshire and

---

[54] Bémont, *Montfort* (1st edn), pp. 340–1; Paris, v, pp. 409–10.
[55] Above, pp. 31–2.
[56] *CPR, 1232–47*, pp. 166, 419; *CPR, 1247–58*, p. 250.
[57] Above, pp. 54–5.

100 marks from Berkshire. The money was to be handed over by the sheriffs twice yearly on Montfort's own lands: at Leicester for the midland counties, at Hungerford for the southern ones. Finally, Montfort was permitted to distrain upon the lands and goods of any sheriff who defaulted, to assent to the choice of sheriffs for the named counties until the 600 marks had been turned into land, and to take oaths from the sheriffs that payment would be made according to these terms.[58]

This was one of the most extraordinary financial arrangements ever made between a thirteenth-century king and one of his subjects. It gave Montfort an additional income of 600 marks a year, over and above what he derived from the Umfraville wardship, with a virtual guarantee that the money would be paid. If we are right in thinking that his ordinary annual income at this time was about £1,950, then Henry's grant raised this figure by nearly twenty per cent (as Fig. 5 on p. 47 shows). It is hard to doubt that the terms were Montfort's and that they reflected his considerable (and well-justified) doubts about Henry's ability to pay whatever might be promised. By making the fee the first charge on the county revenues he was in effect allowed to intercept those revenues before they reached the exchequer. His voice in the choosing of the sheriffs would enable him to veto those whom he thought unlikely to protect his interests, while the sheriffs' personal liability gave him a second line of defence. There was no precedent for giving any subject such a tight hold over the king's income from the counties; though eventually, when his fee had been replaced by a yet more stable and certain equivalent in land, he could expect to do better still. The prospect of such a sizeable grant in fee went some way towards tilting the balance of his estate away from life holdings and towards the heritable land needed for his family's security. The whole arrangement testified to his financial acumen, to his bargaining power, and ultimately to the military skills which that bargaining power reflected. So highly did Henry value his services that he was willing to buy them at a price which would cause contention for years to come and would influence the course of the reform movement itself.

Did Henry get value for money? Montfort later spoke as though the settlement had resolved all his differences with the king, and their new

---

[58] *Rôles Gascons*, i, Nos. 2154–57 (= *CPR, 1247–58*, pp. 249–50); Bémont, *Montfort* (1st edn), p. 338; E.159/27, mm. 15d, 16d. For other minor grants to Montfort made about this time, see Bémont, *Montfort* (2nd edn), p. 120, n. 4.

partnership was a major asset for Henry. It was virtually the first time since 1248 that the two men had made common cause in Gascony. Henry had apparently asked Montfort to stay only until early November, but in fact he remained until after Christmas and possibly until early February 1254.[59] During that time Benauges fell (on 5 November), La Réole was put under siege, rebels submitted and were despatched to England as hostages, their castles destroyed and their goods confiscated. Though nothing specific is recorded about Montfort's role in all this, his presence and his formidable following of knights and footsoldiers were, so Paris tells us, important factors in inducing the rebels to submit.[60] When he left much had been done, but much seemed still in doubt. Gaston de Béarn was still at large, the intentions of Alfonso of Castile remained uncertain, and La Réole continued to hold out. It was the town's surrender in August 1254, followed by Edward's marriage to Alfonso's half-sister, Eleanor, at Burgos on 1 November, which marked the real end of the emergency.[61] The fears of 1248 had not been realised: Gascony had been secured, even if events were to show that its security was precarious.[62] Although this result owed a good deal to Henry's Castilian diplomacy, and some-thing to his willingness to conciliate once the Gascons had submitted, it also rested on Henry's adoption of Montfort's style of warfare and military government, and on Montfort's co-operation with him during the crucial few months which marked a turning-point in the campaign. Henry's first and last wholly successful foreign expedition had in part both demonstrated and justified the price that he set on Montfort's support.

(B) POLITICS AND FINANCE

In the ten years before 1258 four questions dominated English politics. The first of these, the defence of Gascony, has already been described in relation to Montfort's career. But equally prominent were the rise of the Lusignans from 1247, Henry's increasing financial difficulties from 1253, and his commitment to the conquest of Sicily from 1254. These inter-locking themes are not simply the background to Montfort's own story:

---

[59] Bémont, *Montfort* (1st edn), p. 338. The last possible indication of his presence in Gascony is his appointment on 6 February to contract a loan on the king's behalf: *CPR, 1247–58*, p. 264.

[60] Paris, v, pp. 415–16; Trabut-Cussac, *L'Administration Anglaise*, p. xxxiv.

[61] Trabut-Cussac, *L'Administration Anglaise*, pp. xxxii–9.

[62] Below, pp. 137–8.

they were closely entwined with his own private claims and resentments against Henry III's government, which found public expression in 1258. That is the justification for their preliminary treatment here.

Henry's finances provided the leading issue of the period, and one which affected all others. Thanks largely to uncharacteristically prudent housekeeping, Henry had been able to pay his way from 1250 to 1253 and to accumulate a large treasure in gold. This he intended to use for the crusade to which he had committed himself in 1250.[63] As long as he lived in peace and refused to be lured into grandiose projects abroad, he could get by, and even achieve a surplus, as the history of his gold treasure showed. But any unforeseen demands on his resources revealed the weaknesses of his position. Fundamental among those weaknesses was his inability to gain a subsidy. His requests to parliament for extraordinary taxation, made in 1248, 1252, 1255 and 1257, were always turned down, depriving him of the £20,000–£40,000 that a subsidy might have brought in.[64] Nor was he able to compensate for this deficiency as he might once have done. Jewish tallages, for example, which had produced some £40,000 in the 1240s, became less remunerative from the mid 1250s, since the Jews no longer had the means to pay them.[65] His ordinary revenues were also depleted, though to a lesser extent, by his endowment of his son Edward in 1254 with an appanage worth perhaps £6,000 a year.[66] But what really disrupted the precarious financial stability of the early 1250s was the Gascon war. Subventions for Gascony during Montfort's time there from 1248 to 1252 had probably cost Henry between £8,000 and £10,000 in English and Irish revenues.[67] Henry's own expedition was vastly more expensive. It cost him all his gold treasure, worth about £18,900, and an additional sum of about £17,000.[68] He came home deeply in debt, to be refused a grant to pay off his debts by the parliament of April 1255

---

[63] Paris, v, p. 114; D. A. Carpenter, 'The Gold Treasure of King Henry III', *TCE*, i, pp. 68–71, 81.

[64] Paris, v, pp. 20–1, 334–7, 493–5, 520–1, 621–4 (it is not absolutely clear that a tax was requested from the laity as well as the clergy on this last occasion); Carpenter, 'Gold Treasure', p. 73.

[65] R. C. Stacey, '1240–60: A Watershed in Anglo-Jewish Relations?', *Hist. Res.*, 61 (1988), pp. 136–41; Stacey, *Politics, Policy*, p. 256.

[66] M. Prestwich, *Edward I* (London, 1988), pp. 10–20.

[67] A very rough estimate based on the records of the monies sent to Montfort: *CR, 1247–51*, pp. 248–9, 254, 321, 345, 401; *CPR, 1247–58*, pp. 55, 67, 132; *CLR, 1245–51*, pp. 226, 326, 329, 335; *CLR, 1251–60*, p. 52.

[68] Carpenter, 'Gold Treasure', pp. 71–3. In calculating Henry's additional expenditure, over and above his gold treasure, I have discounted the loans from Richard of Cornwall, since these were paid off in gold (ibid., p. 63), and I have made no allowance for Henry's borrowings while in Gascony.

and to be faced in 1257 with the need to finance a Welsh campaign. Only a loan of 10,000 marks from Richard of Cornwall allowed him to maintain his household.[69]

Henry's financial difficulties were the main cause of mounting fiscal pressure on the counties, generating grievances which helped to fire the reform movement of 1258–59 and to rally support for Montfort during his last years. They were pressures applied from the exchequer, chiefly via the eyre and the sheriffs. The eyre, the travelling commission of royal justices, had always been in part a fiscal device, but from the visitation of 1246–49 it was used more systematically to raise money by imposing amercements on individuals and local communities in entirely uncustomary ways. At the same time, and especially after 1250, the cash increments imposed on the sheriffs by the exchequer, rising since 1241–42, began to increase more sharply. Many sheriffs were thus left unable to meet their obligations without a more sustained than usual resort to extortion from their local subjects.[70] Nor was this all. Henry's fierce exploitation of the Jews placed their debtors, many of them country gentry, in a very vulnerable position, for Jews needing cash were often forced to sell cheaply bonds acknowledging debt. The result was frequently the transfer of these Jewish bonds into the hands of men about the court who had the means and opportunity to buy them, and ultimately the transfer of the land which was the security for the debt.[71] The types of men who were the victims here were also the chief sufferers from the king's order of 1256 that all those with land worth £15 or more a year should take up knighthood. Distraint of knighthood was nothing new, but its purpose was now fiscal rather than military – to raise fines from those seeking exemption from knighthood rather than to increase the number of knights – and it had never before impinged on those with such low incomes.[72]

For all these reasons Henry's government came to be increasingly resented by the middling men of the counties: minor barons, knights and major freeholders. As in the years before 1248,[73] we should probably hear their voice, rather than that of the higher nobility, behind the regular refusal of taxation in parliament. That refusal was largely a

---

[69] Carpenter, 'Gold Treasure', pp. 76–7.

[70] D. A. Carpenter, 'The Decline of the Curial Sheriff in England, 1194–1258', *EHR*, 91 (1976), pp. 21–4; Maddicott, 'Magna Carta and the Local Community', pp. 44–8.

[71] Stacey, '1240–60: A Watershed', pp. 142–3.

[72] Paris, v, p. 560; *CR, 1254–56*, p. 293; *Close Rolls (Supplementary) of the Reign of Henry III, 1244–66* (H.M.S.O., London, 1975), pp. 5–18; Carpenter, 'Gold Treasure', p. 77.

[73] Above, pp. 34–5.

cause of the government's fiscal inventiveness, though also in part its consequence; the activity of the eyre, for example, features several times among the complaints which were the usual response to Henry's request for a grant.[74] So, though more intermittently, does the activity of the Lusignans:[75] the second of the main themes of the period, and one which again affected the interests of the gentry as well as those of the magnates. Henry's four Lusignan half-brothers, William and Aymer de Valence, Guy and Geoffrey, the sons of his mother Isabella of Angoulême by her marriage to Hugh of Lusignan, had been invited to England in 1247. Henry's reasons for promoting them were not merely personal or capricious, for their friendship gave him some continuing influence in their homeland of Poitou and some security along Gascony's northern frontier, at a time when this was under threat from an expansionist France. But in terms of his domestic policy the Lusignans were a liability rather than a good investment. There were essentially two reasons for this. First, Henry endowed them on a lavish scale. William de Valence, the most favoured of all, was married in 1247 to Joan de Munchensi, one of the Marshal coheiresses, who brought with her lands worth some £700, including the lordship of Pembroke. In addition, he was given two large annual fees of £500 and 500 marks, with the promise that he would receive the equivalent in land as soon as possible. Guy and Geoffrey were similarly provided with fees of 300 marks each, later increased, and again with the promise of land. Aymer de Valence, the youngest of the four, became bishop-elect of Winchester, the wealthiest English see, in 1250. These were only the most important of a string of grants and favours which continued until 1258. They stood out all the more conspicuously because by the 1250s the lands and cash available for royal patronage were much more limited than they had been in the years around 1240, when Henry had similarly endowed the queen's relatives, the Savoyards. One particular group was now receiving a larger proportion of a declining resource.[76]

Secondly, the conduct of the Lusignans was often arrogant, violent

---

[74] Maddicott, 'Magna Carta and the Local Community', p. 48.

[75] E.g. Paris, v, p. 6.

[76] *CPR, 1232–47*, pp. 502, 505–6, 508–9; *CPR, 1247–58*, p. 3; H. W. Ridgeway, 'Foreign Favourites and Henry III's Problems of Patronage, 1247–58', *EHR*, 104 (1989), pp. 591–3, 595–7. (Ridgeway is wrong to say that 'the grant of 500 marks p.a. [to William de Valence] did not involve a specific promise of lands'. It did.) Ridgeway, 'King Henry III and the "Aliens", 1236–72', *TCE*, ii, pp. 81–4; D. A. Carpenter, 'What Happened in 1258?', *War and Government in the Middle Ages: Essays in Honour of J. O. Prestwich*, ed. J. Gillingham and J. Holt (Woodbridge, 1984), pp. 112–13.

and rapacious: they exploited their connection with the king in order to do virtually as they liked. In one notorious incident of 1252, recalled angrily by the reformers of 1258, Lambeth Palace had been virtually sacked by the followers of the four brothers, the culminating episode in a quarrel between Aymer de Valence and Archbishop Boniface of Savoy.[77] In the country Henry allowed them to run their estates without regard either for royal rights or for the rights of their tenants and neighbours; so that by 1258 local grievances against royal officials had merged with those against the Lusignans to create a demand for local reform on all fronts. All the brothers, too, were involved in the murky and unpopular business of exploiting Jewish bonds, often bonds granted to them by the king.[78] Though both Savoyards and Lusignans were aliens, and there was little to choose between them as unrelenting landlords, the Savoyards proved to be assimilable, as the Lusignans were not. The latter remained outsiders in English society, dependent for their place on royal favour and on the support of a narrow segment of the court, and a dangerous threat to political stability.

The king's susceptibility to the advice of aliens was shown by his involvement in Sicily: the last of the issues dominating the politics of the 1250s. In March 1254, when Henry was in Gascony, he had accepted the papal offer of the throne of Sicily for his second son, Edmund. Here he was the instrument both of Pope Innocent IV, who wanted to use English money and arms against the Hohenstaufen occupants of Sicily, and also of the Savoyards, who had their own reasons for favouring an English candidate there. Yet Henry's acceptance of Innocent's offer, like his patronage of the Lusignans, may not have been entirely misconceived. Sicily was wealthy; an English candidature would block a possible French one; and the conquest of the island, could it be achieved, would elevate English power against that of France and possibly provide a base for a new crusade or even a bridgehead for English expansion in the eastern Mediterranean.[79] The obstacle, of course, was cost. The papal conditions for the grant of Sicily, accepted by Henry in April 1255, obliged the king not only to send an army there, but to meet the papal debts already incurred in the Sicilian war: 135,541 marks, or nearly £90,400. These conditions became public at the

---

[77] Paris, v, pp. 348–54, vi, pp. 405–6; Carpenter, 'What Happened in 1258?', pp. 113–14.
[78] Maddicott, 'Magna Carta and the Local Community', pp. 50–1, 55–61; Carpenter, 'King, Magnates and Society', pp. 63–8; Stacey, '1240–60: A Watershed', pp. 142–3.
[79] Cox, *The Eagles of Savoy*, pp. 242–4, 264–8; M. T. Clanchy, *England and its Rulers, 1066–1272* (Oxford, 1983), pp. 235–9; Lloyd, *English Society and the Crusade*, pp. 221–9.

parliament of October 1255, where they caused consternation.[80] They entailed the diversion to Sicily of the clerical tenths raised for Henry's crusade to the Holy Land (to which Henry remained formally committed), and during the next two and a half years the Church was ruthlessly exploited to meet Henry's new debts. Though the weight of the king's financial demands for Sicily fell largely upon the clergy rather than upon lay society, the Sicilian Business provoked the bitter criticism of magnates as well as churchmen. We can appreciate Sicily's possible role in Henry's grand strategy, however impracticable it may seem, but this was hidden to contemporaries. Like the Poitou campaign of 1242, but on a much aggravated scale, Henry's acceptance of Sicily seemed to epitomise all his political failings: his neglect of the need for baronial consent before entering into onerous obligations, his lack of financial sagacity, and his distorted view of the national interest.[81]

(c) MONTFORT AND HENRY: FINANCES

Money matters had been a fundamental cause of dispute between Henry and Montfort since the time of their first quarrel in 1239. The earl's debt to Thomas of Savoy, Henry's seizure of Montfort's property before his crusade, and, above all, the question of Eleanor's dower and *maritagium*, had together loosened the bonds of lordship, kinship and mutual interest that secured their relationship. In the 1250s, however, financial issues came to play a still larger part in that relationship, contributing powerfully to the private grievances which underlay Montfort's public support for reform in 1258. For this there were a number of reasons. As we have seen, Henry's financial position deteriorated sharply from 1253, just when his need to buy Montfort out of Gascony and then to repurchase his service were imposing new financial obligations upon him. At the same time the maintenance of the Lusignans was making further demands on Henry's dwindling resources. By increasing the competition for a limited supply of royal patronage, it brought a newer element of rivalry into the relations between Montfort and the most prominent group at court. The claims of Henry's great men, and the financial debility which prevented him from meeting them, thus combined to produce a more febrile political environment.

---

[80] Paris, v, pp. 515–16, 520–1, 529–31; *CR, 1254–56*, pp. 406–7.
[81] Cf. *Ann. Burton*, pp. 387–8; *Ann. Tewk.*, p. 170.

Henry's most longstanding financial commitment to Montfort was the £400 paid annually for Eleanor's dower in Ireland and Wales. Nothing was done in this period to augment a sum whose inadequacy, already raised by Montfort in 1244, was to become a major issue in 1258–59; and Henry found it difficult even to maintain regular payments. Circumstances were partly to blame for this. Since Henry merely took responsibility for paying the dower to Montfort and Eleanor, while recouping himself from the heirs of William Marshal, Eleanor's first husband, he should not have been out of pocket. But in 1245 the last of the Marshal's brothers died childless, and the estates were then divided between his five sisters and their issue, each of whom was allocated a share in the dower payment. Henry now had the much more difficult task of collecting the dower from a large number of individuals – at least eighteen[82] – who included some of his greatest magnates. Although this should not have affected payment of the dower, in practice his general lack of money meant that his payments to Montfort and Eleanor became dependent to some extent on the payments which he himself could collect from the Marshal heirs. As early as January 1249 the failure of the earls of Norfolk and Gloucester and of William de Valence to pay their shares of the dower was being met by orders from the exchequer for the distraint of their ploughbeasts. Henry's subsequent intervention in order to respite the payments and to secure the release of the beasts shows how difficult he found it to offend a key group of magnates in the interests of his sister and brother-in-law.[83]

By this time his inability to meet the dower payments had already become evident. According to Montfort's later recollection, in 1248 the king had defaulted on the payments and had advised Montfort and Eleanor to bring an action for the whole of the dower against the Marshal heirs. By allowing them to obtain a full dower settlement in land, beyond the inadequate £400 fee, and by facilitating Henry's withdrawal from the whole arrangement, a successful plea might have solved the problems of both Henry and Montfort. But nothing had come of the ensuing action. Judgement should have been given, said Montfort, implying that it had not been.[84]

---

[82] For lists, see *CR, 1254–56*, pp. 438–9, and *CPR, 1364–67*, pp. 263–75. The complicated descent of the Marshal estates is best set out in I. J. Sanders, *English Baronies* (Oxford, 1960), p. 63.

[83] *CR, 1247–51*, pp. 134–5.

[84] Bémont, *Montfort* (1st edn), p. 335. Bémont misdates this legal action to 1256 (ibid., n. 2). Montfort says that the plea took place on the last occasion when the countess of Provence was

Here, as in other matters, Montfort's statement is almost exactly corroborated by the records. It is true that Henry's defaulting cannot be proved, and there is no break in his regular twice-yearly orders to the exchequer to pay the dower. But if the exchequer was short of funds, the king's writs of liberate may sometimes have been ignored, as certainly happened in the 1250s.[85] The issue rolls, which might have settled the point, are missing between 1246 and 1252. The legal plea, recorded on the curia regis roll, shows that in Easter term 1247 Montfort brought an action for Eleanor's dower against John de Munchensi and the other Marshal heirs, alleging that Eleanor had been dowered with lands in Pembroke and not with a money payment. The action was resumed in Michaelmas term, after John's death, against the countess of Warenne and the other heirs, and judgement was to have been given on 10 February 1248.[86] But the absence of any further record indicates that Montfort was right in saying that judgement was never passed. Henry's reluctance to proceed is perhaps understandable. A verdict against Montfort would have intensified his grievances; a verdict in favour would have antagonised all the numerous Marshal heirs, including some of the greatest magnates, on whose support Henry was dependent.

Montfort's allusion to this failed action more than a dozen years later in the 1260s shows the offence that it caused. He had followed the king's advice and then been denied satisfaction. Nor did his position improve. Although Henry continued to order payment of the dower after 1248, his special instructions to the exchequer in November 1251 to pay the current instalment 'by all means and without delay and without fail' suggest that his officials had not always complied.[87] The peremptory tone of Henry's order probably owed much to the delicacy of his relationship with Montfort over Gascony and to his anxiety not to add to the earl's financial grievances arising from his service there. It is easy to see why, in November 1253, Montfort should have demanded payment directly from the sheriffs when he stated his terms for returning to the king's service.[88] Experience had taught him that it was safer to tap the king's revenues at source rather than to rely on payments from an

---

in England after the death of her husband. This was in 1248: Paris, iv, pp. 283–4, 485, v, pp. 2–3. The countess's visit on which Bémont bases his dating was to Paris, not England, and in 1254, not 1256: Paris, v, p. 477.

[85] *CLR, 1245–51*, pp. 46, 85, 118, 142, 178–9, 214–15, 226, 285, 312, 349; below, p. 132.

[86] KB.26/159, mm. 2d, 3d; above, p. 52.

[87] *CLR, 1251–60*, p. 4.

[88] Above, pp. 122–3.

unreliable exchequer. In the mid 1250s these problems deepened, making the dower once again a major issue. Henry's insolvency after his return from Gascony in December 1254 made it harder than ever for him to pay the annual dower fee of £400 without his being able to extract the money for himself from the Marshal heirs. After October 1254, when payment was ordered for the current Michaelmas term, no further payments were put in hand until May 1256, when the exchequer was told to pay Montfort £600 to cover two terms' arrears and the instalment then due for Easter 1256. The memoranda roll shows a slightly worse situation, with nothing paid after Easter term 1254.[89]

By this time Henry's payments had patently come to wait on those made to him by the Marshal heirs. Such was Henry's poverty, however, that even when this money was to hand it was not now always made over to Montfort and Eleanor. By August 1256 two of the Marshal heirs owed the king a total of £1,543. The greatest defaulter, the countess of Lincoln, had arrears going back over seven years and amounting to more than 1,000 marks, while the earl of Gloucester owed some £427. By October 1256 the countess had undertaken to pay Montfort 1,600 marks (£1,066) to cover, so the exchequer calculated, the entire arrears from Michaelmas 1254 to Michaelmas 1256.[90] Henry's order to the treasurer to apply all the money coming in from the Marshal heirs to the payment of the dower was a clear indication that earlier receipts from the same source had been diverted to other needs.[91] When the exchequer next did its sums, in May 1257, its officials reckoned that the whole sum owing for the dower, a notional £1,000, had now been more than cleared by payments of £1,064 from the countess of Lincoln, £343 from the proceeds of Roger Thurkelby's current eyre in the northern and eastern counties, and a further £310 paid under a writ of liberate. But either Montfort disputed these calculations or Henry's financial affairs were in such confusion that the true extent of his liabilities had become entirely unclear; for the issue rolls show that early in 1258 Montfort received a further £600 to cover dower instalments for the three terms from Easter 1255 to Easter 1256.[92] Yet the exchequer's earlier calculations suggested that he had already received payments for these terms.

[89] *CLR, 1251–60*, pp. 180, 285; E.159/30, m. 4d.
[90] *CR, 1254–56*, pp. 438–9; E.159/30, m. 4d.
[91] E.159/30, m. 1d.
[92] E.159/30, m. 15; E.403/15a.

It is still less possible for us than it was for Henry III's exchequer to chart the course of the dower payments with any certainty. Nevertheless, the main components of the general picture are plain enough: the king's almost fearful concern to see that the payments were maintained, the powerlessness of the exchequer to comply expeditiously with his orders, the mounting burden of arrears, which had reached £1,000 by October 1256 and which may or may not have been subsequently paid off. The whole story shows a close and predictable connection between Henry's failing finances and his inability to meet his obligations to Montfort.

It was a connection also exemplified in the king's new commitments arising from Montfort's activities in Gascony. When he had been bought out of Gascony for 7,000 marks, in the autumn of 1252, it had been agreed that the money should be paid in two instalments, at Easter and Michaelmas 1253.[93] In fact, payment of only 5,000 marks had been ordered by the end of 1253 and the actual sum outstanding as late as February 1254 was at least 3,500 marks. Montfort's departure from Henry's camp in Gascony about this time may have owed something to the king's failure to honour his obligations. Certainly Henry thought that this debt was an especially urgent one, for on 5 February, possibly immediately before Montfort left him, he ordered the treasurer to give its repayment priority over all other debts. In May 1254, 1,069 marks was still outstanding and it is not until May 1257 that we can be sure that the whole debt had been finally cleared.[94] Other payments were made equally tardily. As part of the extravagant settlement made when he rejoined the king in the autumn of 1253, Montfort had been granted £500 for his losses and expenses in Gascony, in addition to his new fee. Payment had been promised at Easter 1254, but it was May 1257 before it was made.[95] Similarly, the king had bought from Montfort a Gascon prisoner, Donatus de Pyns, agreeing in September 1254 to pay 500 marks for his ransom at Easter 1255. But, again, as late as May 1257 the debt remained unpaid.[96]

Thus although Montfort had been lavishly compensated for his various discomforts in Gascony, Henry's financial difficulties meant that, as with the dower, the exchequer could make none of the payments

[93] Bémont, *Montfort* (1st edn), p. 322; above, p. 119.
[94] *CLR, 1251–60*, pp. 112, 154, 167; *CR, 1253–54*, pp. 210–11; E.159/30, m. 15. For the date of Montfort's departure, see above, p. 124 and n. 59.
[95] *CPR, 1247–58*, p. 249; *CLR, 1251–60*, p. 375; E.159/30, m. 15; above, p. 122.
[96] *CPR, 1247–58*, pp. 158, 337; E.159/30, m. 15.

due to him at the specified times. In some cases they remained outstanding for years. Two of Henry's obligations, however, were still more
important than those so far discussed, the one for its size, the other for
its political consequences. The first arose from Montfort's position in
Bigorre.

For the first half of the thirteenth century the county of Bigorre, south
of Gascony in the foothills of the Pyrenees, was ruled by Countess
Petronilla, the third of whose five husbands had been Guy, Simon de
Montfort's elder brother, who had died in 1220.[97] In 1248, in her old age,
Petronilla had leased Bigorre to Montfort in an attempt to protect her
land against the claims of her neighbour, Gaston de Béarn, who was
also her son-in-law. Before her death in 1251 she bequeathed the county
to Esquivat de Chabanais, the eldest son of her eldest daughter by
Petronilla's marriage to Guy, and therefore Montfort's grand-nephew.
But she also appointed Montfort as the guardian of the county until he
had been compensated for his expenses in defending it. Gaston de
Béarn's hostility to Montfort, one cause of the earl's troubles in
Gascony, is partly to be explained by Montfort's tightening grip over a
county which Gaston regarded as his. Esquivat's continuing defence of
Bigorre against Gaston was actively supported by Montfort, leaving
Esquivat deeply in debt to him.

The next complication arose in 1253, when Henry III came to
Gascony and secured the overlordship of Bigorre from the bishop and
chapter of Le Puy, its feudal suzerains. Esquivat now looked to Henry
for protection, taking service with him and leasing his castles to him in
return for payment. The result was that Henry ended up owing him
£1,000 for the lease of the castles and 1,000 marks for military service.
In February 1255 the 1,000 marks that Henry owed to Esquivat was
made over by Esquivat to Montfort, to whom Esquivat still owed
money; and in addition a 200-mark annual fee payable by Henry to
Esquivat was again made over to Montfort for the next three and a half
years. The outcome of these arrangements was thus a sudden and steep
increase in Henry's indebtedness to Montfort. The king undertook to
pay the 1,000 marks in two instalments at Michaelmas 1255 and Easter
1256, and the fee annually at Michaelmas, but he was, of course, unable
to do so. In May 1257 the full 1,000 marks and a further 200 marks

---

[97] This paragraph summarises a long and complicated story. It derives from Powicke, *King
Henry III*, pp. 220–5; Labarge, *Montfort*, pp. 128–40; and, best of all, Ellis, 'Gaston de Béarn',
pp. 381–91.

for the fee were still outstanding.[98] On the eve of the reform movement they made up the largest component in Henry's list of debts to Montfort.

But perhaps the most portentous of all Henry's obligations arose from his undertaking in November 1253 to pay Montfort a fee of £400 a year until he could provide him with lands to that value. The pipe rolls show that the fee was paid.[99] Montfort's hardheaded insistence, at a time when the king's stay in Gascony was driving him ever more deeply into debt, that the money should be secured on the revenues of the counties rather than being precariously dependent on the priorities of a near bankrupt exchequer, had made payment almost impossible to avoid. It was the parallel promise to replace the fee with lands that caused trouble. Because of the many similar competing claims to such little land as became available Henry was quite unable to keep his promise. He had made identical undertakings to his Lusignan half-brothers in 1247, three of whom had, as we have seen, been granted substantial fees with the guarantee of the equivalent in land later; and others were similarly placed.[100] But in the 1250s Henry lacked the resources to satisfy all these clients. There were no great conquests or escheats to enlarge the pool of available land; the *terra Normannorum*, a useful source of patronage in the 1230s and 1240s, had all been distributed; and the alienation of the royal demesne was coming to be increasingly restricted by the council.[101]

In these circumstances an order of precedence had to be established. First among the magnates came Richard of Cornwall, who had been granted a large fee, with the promise of land, at the time of his marriage to Sanchia of Provence in 1243. Next, from 1251 or earlier, came William de Valence, followed from 1253 by Montfort and then by Thomas of Savoy, the queen's uncle.[102] The working of what was almost a system provided Montfort with some major grievances. When he and Eleanor had been given an annual fee by way of a *maritagium* in 1244, the arrangement had been a provisional one, like the later grants already discussed, to last until they had been provided with escheats and wardships. According to Montfort himself, their claims had been given second

[98] *CPR, 1247–58*, pp. 398, 403; E.159/30, m. 15.
[99] E.372/98–102, rots. Notts. and Derbs., Warw. and Leics., Wilts., Berks.; *DBM*, pp. 196–9.
[100] Above, p. 127.
[101] Ridgeway, 'Foreign Favourites', pp. 596, 598–9; *DBM*, pp. 196–7.
[102] Denholm-Young, *Richard of Cornwall*, p. 51; *CPR, 1247–58*, pp. 119, 195; Ridgeway, 'Foreign Favourites', pp. 600–1.

place after those of Richard of Cornwall.[103] This fee had been superseded when Montfort had received the Umfraville wardship in 1245, but
it became payable again in 1253, when he was pardoned the annual 500
marks which he owed for the wardship. He now found that the claims
of William de Valence trumped his own and, moreover, that William
was able to secure a large part of his fees in land. By April 1255 William's
500-mark fee had been entirely replaced by lands, and he had received
£120-worth of land towards the settlement of his £500 fee. By 1258 this
figure had risen to £192. Montfort, on the other hand, had received
nothing in land. Even the £400 dower fee was being jeopardised by the
precedence given to others: payment of the substantial dower arrears
due at Easter 1256 was to be made only after Thomas of Savoy and
Boniface, his nephew, had been paid their annual fees.[104]

Of all Montfort's grievances, the inadequacy of the dower and
Henry's failure to replace his fee with land were those raised most forcefully and specifically in 1258–59. The fee question underlay much of his
animus against William de Valence and his brothers, successful rivals for
royal patronage, whose removal would leave the way clear for the
settlement of Montfort's own claims. Yet the size of Henry's debt to
Montfort was a barely less pressing issue. It was a testimony to the
seriousness with which Henry regarded the debt that in 1256 and 1257 it
was set out item by item in a series of statements on the memoranda
rolls. In October 1256 it totalled £874; in May 1257, £1,334; in June
1257, £1,201; and in December 1257 – the last statement before the
reform movement – £1,199.[105] These were large sums: on average
substantially more than half Montfort's estimated annual income.
There is no doubt that Montfort was putting considerable pressure on
Henry to secure payment and that Henry was anxious to comply. In
July 1256 he wrote urgently to the treasurer ordering payment of the
arrears of the dower and of the money for Bigorre, and saying that
payment had been promised by an oath on the king's soul.[106] Even more
extraordinary was the arrangement made in March 1257, when the
king's four ministers, Philip Lovel, the treasurer, Henry Wingham, the
chancellor, Robert Walerand, steward of the household, and Roger
Thurkelby, a senior justice, undertook on Henry's behalf to pay to

[103] Above, p. 54; *CChR, 1226–57*, p. 278; Bémont, *Montfort* (1st edn), p. 335.
[104] *CLR, 1251–60*, pp. 202, 281, 285; *DBM*, pp. 196–9; Ridgeway, 'Foreign Favourites', p. 595.
[105] E.159/30, mm. 4d, 15, 19; E.159/31, m. 7; *CPR, 1247–58*, p. 609.
[106] *CR, 1254–56*, pp. 426–7.

Montfort at the exchequer 514 marks owed to him by the king. In default of payment, and in order to compel it, they empowered the earl to distrain on the king's lands and goods, and they submitted themselves for excommunication and interdict.[107] These were terms of almost unprecedented humiliation: the last occasion on which the sanction of distraint had been invoked against a king in breach of his obligations had been in Magna Carta.

Between the exigence of Montfort's claims and the king's anxiety to meet them lay the void of Henry's poverty. Yet given Henry's circumstances, the earl had not done badly. His £400 fee from the county's revenues was paid, even if it could not be turned into land; and he had received, if belatedly, his 7,000 marks for leaving Gascony, together with a number of other smaller payments from the king. Between October 1256 and December 1257 his total receipts from Henry, excluding his fee from the county revenues, amounted to some £6,500–£7,000, including £1,063 made over by the countess of Lincoln and £343 from the profits of Thurkelby's eyre.[108] It was to meet claims of the sort made by Montfort on the king's revenues that the eyre continued to bear down harshly on the counties; and there was a mild irony in Montfort's joint leadership from 1258 of an enterprise which championed local interests against such instruments of royal fiscality. Indeed, royal government in these years owed a good deal of its general oppressiveness to the unrelenting demands of Montfort and others on royal resources. No more than the Lusignans was he the defender of the community of the realm. He remained a man with a just grievance and, more obliquely, the cause of grievances in others. But he had done his not inconsiderable best to protect his own interests.

(D) MONTFORT AND HENRY: POLITICS

A heavy load of debt and a latent crisis over Sicily were not the only problems that faced Henry when he returned from Gascony in December 1254. The whole complexion of foreign affairs was threatening, and remained so until the grand resolution achieved by peace with France and withdrawal from Sicily in 1258–59. Danger came from several directions: perhaps most pressingly, and surprisingly, from the direction of Castile. The Anglo-Castilian treaty of April 1254,

---

[107] *CPR, 1247–58*, p. 590.
[108] E.159/30, mm. 4d, 15, 19; E.159/31, m. 7.

preceding Edward's marriage, had bound Henry to seek papal approval for the transformation of his planned crusade to the Holy Land into a joint expedition with Alfonso to North Africa.[109] Despite Henry's further commitment to the conquest of Sicily from April 1255, his vulnerability to Castilian interference in Gascony meant that he could not afford to renounce his prior undertaking to Alfonso. Some of the most powerful Gascon rebels remained in exile at Alfonso's court, and Henry was under pressure from Alfonso to restore others implicated in the disturbances of 1253–54.[110] It was essentially Henry's concern for Gascony that prompted his fantastical assurances to Alfonso in January 1257 that once the Sicilian business had been settled he would join him on his African crusade.[111]

Relations with France were equally uncertain. The existing truce was extended for a further three years in 1255, and in 1257 negotiations began for a lasting peace: a necessity if Henry's Sicilian ambitions were to be realised. But the negotiations foundered, twice, on Henry's continuing demands for the return of his French lands, still one of the central objectives of his foreign policy.[112] Louis IX had good reason to feel threatened, not only by Henry's claims, but also by his alliance with Alfonso and by the possibility of his establishment in Sicily, which would have elevated English power in the Mediterranean.[113] He was not to know that the king's relations with Alfonso were more precarious, and his prospects in Sicily more chimerical, than he supposed. Tension between all three kings was heightened by Richard of Cornwall's election to the vacant German throne by a party of Rhineland princes in January 1257. The seeming threat posed by an English ruler on France's eastern frontier led Louis to strengthen the fortifications of Normandy, presumably against the possibility of an English landing there, and to support Alfonso's rival candidature for the Empire.[114] Henry's more immediate troubles, however, were nearer home. In Scotland his daughter Margaret and her young husband Alexander III were under the domination of a baronial faction led by the Comyns. Henry intervened to secure the Comyns' removal in September 1255,

---

109 *Foedera*, i, ii, pp. 299–300.
110 E. C. Lodge, *Gascony under English Rule* (London, 1926), pp. 48, 50; Trabut-Cussac, *L'Administration Anglaise*, pp. 20–1.
111 *CR, 1254–56*, pp. 389–91.
112 Paris, v, pp. 547–8, 659–60.
113 Paris, v, p. 516.
114 Paris, v, pp. 625–6, 636, 657.

but in October 1257 they were restored, bringing closer the civil war which threatened Scotland throughout the period.[115] In Wales war came. During the late summer of 1256 the Welsh revolted, forcing Henry to send an army there in 1257. Under all these pressures, with his hopes for Sicily failing, the Welsh in arms, and his private life overshadowed by the death of his much-loved baby daughter Katherine, it was no wonder that in the summer of 1257 Henry came near to breakdown.[116]

Henry's foreign policy between 1254 and 1258 was thus a tangle of incompatible objectives, none of them realisable without the money and domestic support which he lacked. His plans were at their most grandiose, in Sicily, France and North Africa, when his resources were most limited. The determining effect of foreign relations on Henry's affairs in this period does much to explain the political role of Simon de Montfort, for it was here that Montfort could be most useful. Initially he was more obstructive than helpful. After having left Gascony early in 1254, he returned to England in May, presumably having spent the intervening months in France. He arrived just as a parliament was meeting to consider Henry's request, sent from Gascony, for men and money to meet a threatened invasion from Castile. But Montfort, says Paris, told the truth about this to those assembled. What the truth was is left obscure. But from the nobles' reported anger at Montfort's words, the abrupt termination of the parliament, and Paris's later comment on Alfonso's inability to invade because of the hostility of Navarre and Aragon, it seems almost certain that the earl had shown the threat to be illusory and no more than a pretext for a request for funds. Here he was wrong, for Henry's fears, set off by Castilian manoeuvres directed at these two other kingdoms and not at Gascony, were real enough, though unfounded. Montfort's recent experiences in Gascony had clearly left him prepared to believe the worst of the king; and it was perhaps disingenuous of him to say later that the financial settlement of November 1253 had ended their quarrel.[117] Much may still have hung on Henry's unpaid debts and unkept promises.

Thereafter Montfort played a more positive role in Henry's diplomacy. In September 1254 he was sent on a mission to Alexander III

[115] A. A. M. Duncan, *Scotland: The Making of the Kingdom* (Edinburgh, 1975), pp. 562–71.

[116] Paris, v, pp. 632, 643.

[117] Paris, v, pp. 440, 445; Bémont, *Montfort* (1st edn), p. 338; Trabut-Cussac, *L'Administration Anglaise*, pp. xxxvii–xxxviii; Ellis, 'Gaston de Béarn', pp. 170–87, esp. pp. 178–9. For the date of the parliament, see *CPR, 1247–58*, p. 370.

of Scotland, almost certainly in connection with Henry's anxiety about his daughter's welfare.[118] His despatch to a country with which he had no known earlier associations implies that his value as a diplomat lay in his own weight and abilities, and not only in his French affiliations. But it was in France that he was most frequently employed. In May 1255 he negotiated successfully, at a later stage in partnership with Peter of Savoy, for an extension of the Anglo-French truce, finally agreed in Louis IX's presence in June.[119] In January 1256 Montfort, William de Valence and the earl of Gloucester were the three men whom John Mansel was told by Henry to consult, if necessary, before Mansel's departure on an important mission to Castile.[120] In February 1257, at the start of the negotiations for a permanent peace with France, he and Robert Walerand were the two whom Henry chose to send to Louis.[121] In June he and Peter of Savoy were appointed to advise Walter de Cantilupe, Adam Marsh and Hugh Bigod on the peace negotiations, to request the appointment of a papal legate in Rome to promote the negotiations, and at the same time to seek the alleviation of the papal conditions for Sicily.[122] The inclusion in the 'negotiating team' of Cantilupe and Marsh is a good indication of Montfort's influence at this time. The mission to Rome never took place, but, according to Paris, Montfort was also a member of yet another embassy sent to France in October.[123] In these circumstances he may have placed a special value on the charter which he had obtained in March 1256 from Mahaut, countess of Boulogne (his intended bride of twenty years earlier), granting him quittance from tolls at Wissant, the main French channel port, and other ports in the county.[124] There was no one in Henry's entourage who was more continuously occupied in the cross-channel diplomacy which would lead eventually to the Treaty of Paris.

It is easy to see why Montfort should have been given this role. His high standing in France, his long periods of residence there, his

---

[118] *CPR, 1247–58*, p. 321; *CR, 1253–54*, pp. 272–3.
[119] *CPR, 1247–58*, p. 411; *CR, 1254–56*, pp. 195–6; *Layettes*, iii, No. 4178.
[120] *CR, 1254–56*, pp. 389–91.
[121] *CPR, 1247–58*, p. 542.
[122] *CPR, 1247–58*, pp. 567–8, 594.
[123] Paris, v, pp. 649–50, 659–60. But there are some doubts about this embassy. It is not mentioned on the chancery rolls, and Montfort's itinerary shows him to have been in England on 11 Nov., 4, 5, 18 Dec. 1257 and 8 Feb. 1258: BL MS. Cotton Otho D. III, f. 111; C.53/48, m. 5; *CChR, 1257–1300*, p. 3; *The Beauchamp Cartulary Charters, 1100–1268*, ed. E. Mason (Pipe Roll Soc., n.s., xliii, 1980), No. 51.
[124] BN MS. Clairambault 1188, f. 9; above, pp. 17–18.

connections with the French nobility, and his familiarity with the Paris *parlement*,[125] all commended him to Henry at a time when a French peace was beginning to seem essential to Henry's interests. No one could rival Montfort's experience on both sides of the Channel, and Henry's need for his services was probably one factor which underlay his eagerness to settle his debts to the earl. Montfort's willingness to act, after all that had passed between him and Henry, is harder to explain, but probably had much to do with the chance of personal advantage which the negotiations offered. He had been in France, on his own business, in the first half of 1255, before being commissioned to negotiate for an extension of the truce; and when negotiations for a final peace began, in February 1257, he was authorised by Henry to receive his inheritance or any part of it which Louis might restore to him.[126] What Montfort may have had in mind here is suggested by the quit-claim which he made to Louis in December 1259, at the time of the Treaty of Paris, of all his rights in the county of Toulouse, the viscounty of Beziers and 'the whole Albigensian conquest', the county and city of Evreux and in all Normandy: in other words, his father's conquests in the south and other ancestral lands in the north. Evreux, for example, had been held by his great-grandfather, another Simon, until his death in 1181, and his Beaumont ancestors had held other Norman lands, forfeited after 1204.[127] The release of 1259 implies that these claims were still in play at the time of the negotiations of 1257–58, and the chances of their being met may have seemed less remote to Montfort than they do to us. Louis's mood of penitential reform after the failure of his crusade, his concomitant enquiries into the unjust acquisitions of his ancestors, and his resolve to do justice to the aggrieved,[128] all gave both Henry and Montfort reason to hope that what had been lost might be regained. Both in 1247 and 1257–58 it was the French nobility, rather than the king, who were most rigidly opposed to any restoration of the English lands in France. Louis himself was inclined to temporise or even to favour the English cause.[129] The possibility that both might yet profit

[125] Above, p. 112.

[126] *CR, 1254–56*, pp. 153–4, 195; *CPR, 1247–58*, p. 542.

[127] *Cartulaire Normand de Philippe-Auguste, Louis VIII, Saint Louis et Philippe-le-Hardi*, ed. L. Delisle (Caen, 1882), No. 637; *Peerage*, VII, pp. 715–16; Bémont, *Montfort* (1st edn), pp. 75–6.

[128] Odoricus Raynaldus, *Annales Ecclesiastici*, iii (Lucca, 1748), pp. 26–7; P. Chaplais, 'The Making of the Treaty of Paris (1259) and the Royal Style', *EHR*, 67 (1952), p. 238; Jordan, *Louis IX*, pp. 135–213.

[129] Paris, iv, pp. 645–6; v, pp. 649–50.

from the conscience of the king was a common bond between Henry and Montfort in 1257, and one which may do much to explain Montfort's commitment to Henry's negotiations.

Montfort may have been encouraged by the one spectacular success which he had already achieved in the south. In August 1256 Esquivat de Chabanais and his brother Jourdain, still under attack from Gaston de Béarn, granted him the county of Bigorre. Though the grant was no more than a nominal one, made in haste and subsequently ignored by Esquivat, it played up to Montfort's earlier ambitions to take over the county during his time in Gascony, and was regarded as binding by him when the Bigorre affair next surfaced in 1258.[130] If he were able to add his father's conquests to this stake in the south of France, as he may have envisaged, he would have gained a principality comparable to that which Henry was seeking in Sicily. In so far as they can be deduced from his claims, his ambitions were as large as those of the king, and perhaps even a little more practicable.

At almost the same time he was acquiring land elsewhere. In 1255–56 he secured the coastal barony of Embleton, in Northumberland, giving its holders, Hereward de Marisco and Rametta his wife, his southern manors of Shapwick, in Dorset, and Chalton, in Hampshire, in exchange. Montfort had much the best of the bargain here. Embleton and its associated manors, granted to the earl in fee, were worth some £300 a year, and augmented the considerable Northumbrian estate which the Umfraville wardship had already given him. His subsequent purchase of further holdings at Embleton, and the king's grants to him of a weekly market and annual fair there, and of the right to impark his wood at Shipley, near Alnwick in the same county, all show him setting about the development of this northern estate in an entrepreneurial way. What he conceded in exchange was relatively small. The two southern manors, worth perhaps £100–£120, were given to Hereward and Rametta for Rametta's life only, though Hereward was allowed a life interest in a house and small estate at Shapwick.[131] In terms of practical benefits the little barony of Embleton was worth more than the Pyreneean lordship of Bigorre. But the acquisition of both fiefs, almost at opposite ends of Europe, was a mark of the wide and ambitious

---

[130] Labarge, *Montfort*, p. 136; Ellis, 'Gaston de Béarn', pp. 391–2, 395–9; below, p. 173.

[131] *A History of Northumberland* (15 vols., Newcastle, 1893–1940), ii, ed. E. Bateson, pp. 16–18; *Dorset Fines*, ed. Fry and Fry, pp. 162–3; c.132/3/8; *CR, 1264–68*, p. 109; *CChR, 1226–57*, p. 460; *1257–1300*, p. 1; *CPR, 1247–58*, p. 525. For the values of Shapwick and Chalton, see above, p. 49.

sweep of territorial interests which remained one of Montfort's central preoccupations in these years.

Montfort's activities in France took him out of English affairs for much of this time, making it difficult to position him along the spectrum of Henry's intimates, friends and associates. The difficulty is increased by the loss of the royal charter roll and its witness-lists for the period from November 1255 to November 1256. What signs there are suggest that in 1255 Montfort was only on the fringes of the court, but that by 1257 he had moved much closer to its centre. In 1255 he witnessed no royal charters, though he was certainly in England for part of the time;[132] in 1257, by contrast, he witnessed on twenty-three occasions. In the same year, when he was also a member of the king's council,[133] a spate of minor favours came his way: he secured pardons for dependents and royal grants for the burgesses of Leicester, his tenure of Embleton was confirmed and he was granted the rights to a market and fair just mentioned, a commission of enquiry was appointed to look into his rights of common on a Kentish manor, and so on. There were some nine favours of this sort in 1257, compared with only three in 1256 and none in 1255.[134] His attendance on the king and Henry's regard for him, both contrasting strongly with his position in 1255, probably reflect his indispensability in the hectic French negotiations of that year, the additional prominence which may have come to him after Richard of Cornwall's departure for Germany in April 1257, and Henry's desire to placate him in the face of a royal debt that was hardly diminishing. Pardons and grants of local privileges came more easily to the king's hand than hard cash.

Close though Montfort was to Henry in 1257, at no point in these years does he seem to have been among the innermost circle of Henry's confidants. One definition of this inner group is provided by Paris's account of how, probably in November 1256, the king ordered that no chancery writ should be issued which might cause loss to Richard of Cornwall, Gloucester, Peter of Savoy or the four Lusignans. Of all the great men about the court, Montfort is conspicuously absent here. Of those given protection by the king in this way, Gloucester, followed by William de Valence, was the most frequent charter

---

[132] c.56/16, m. 19; *Recs. Bor. Leics.*, i, pp. 49–50.
[133] c.53/47, mm. 1, 4–8, 10; c.53/48, m. 5; *CChR, 1257–1300*, p. 3; *CPR, 1247–58*, p. 563.
[134] 1256: *CPR, 1247–58*, p. 493; *CR, 1254–56*, p. 297; *Recs. Bor. Leics.*, i, pp. 50–1. 1257: *CPR, 1247–58*, pp. 542–3, 557, 593–4; *CR, 1256–59*, p. 176; *CChR, 1226–57*, pp. 460, 462; *1257–1300*, p. 1.

witness in 1255, William de Valence (but now followed by Montfort) in 1257.[135]

Besides the longstanding differences between the two men, there were probably two other factors which set Henry and Montfort somewhat apart from each other: Montfort's opposition to the Sicilian Business, and his growing conflict with the Lusignans. Although his opposition to Henry's involvement in Sicily cannot be proved, it may be deduced, not only from what is known of his later attitude in 1258–59, but from his omission from the several lists of those known to have favoured such involvement. When Henry, in Gascony, had accepted the papal offer of Sicily for Edmund, in March 1254, Montfort had already left the court. Those with Henry at that time included most of the leading royalists: the Savoyards, Peter of Savoy and Peter of Aigueblanche, bishop of Hereford; the Lusignans, William de Valence and his brother Geoffrey; John de Plessis, earl of Warwick; John Mansel and Robert Walerand.[136] When the terms for Sicily were finally revealed at the parliament of October 1255, Montfort was almost certainly present.[137] But he witnessed none of the charters made at parliament time, nor was he among those councillors who, in the following month, advised Henry to accept the terms: Aigueblanche, William and Aymer de Valence, the earls of Gloucester and Warwick, Mansel and others.[138] His close friend Walter de Cantilupe was one of the leaders of the clerical opposition to taxation for Sicily and was probably dismissed from the council as a result.[139] Montfort may have had private reasons for opposing Henry's Sicilian plans, for the huge financial obligations which they entailed jeopardised his own chances of securing payment of his debts. When Henry borrowed 10,000 marks from Sienese merchants in June 1257 to meet these obligations, the escheats due to William de Valence and Simon de Montfort were among the revenues specifically exempted from those set aside for the repayment of the debt.[140] Though direct evidence is lacking, there is thus good reason to think that Montfort, like almost all the magnates, disapproved of the Sicilian venture. Henry's attempt from April 1257 to renegotiate the terms for

---

135 Paris, v, p. 594; c.53/46–48.
136 *CPR, 1247–58*, pp. 270–9, 282.
137 c.56/16, m. 19; *Recs. Bor. Leics.*, i, pp. 49–50.
138 *CPR, 1247–58*, p. 451. Mansel may have accepted the terms only reluctantly: see *Foedera*, I, i, p. 333.
139 Paris, v, p. 525; Carpenter, 'St Thomas Cantilupe', p. 61.
140 *CPR, 1247–58*, p. 562.

Sicily – an attempt in which Montfort played a part – may have been one force which moved earl and king into closer alignment at this time.[141]

Montfort's rivalry with the Lusignans presents fewer uncertainties. The lawlessness of the four Lusignan brothers, Henry's unwillingness to allow legal action against them, and their access to royal patronage, were all factors which gradually turned even the other *curiales* against them. Since the early 1250s Montfort had accumulated more reasons than most for disliking the Lusignans. When he had returned from Gascony in 1251, in company with Guy de Lusignan, Henry had welcomed Guy but snubbed Montfort.[142] In 1252, after Henry's displeasure at the magnates' defence of Montfort's actions in parliament and the king's threat to disinherit him had been made known to the earl in Gascony, he had remarked sardonically that when he had been ruined the king would enrich 'some Savoyard or Poitevin' with his earldom.[143] Henry's poverty did not prevent him from giving what he could to the Lusignans. At Michaelmas 1256, when Montfort's dower arrears amounted to £1,000, the exchequer paid out £590 in fees to William, Guy and Geoffrey, and additional sums of £100 and 80 marks as gifts to Guy and Geoffrey respectively.[144] But it was with William de Valence in particular, the leader of the four brothers, that Montfort increasingly fell out. We have already seen how William's defaulting on his share of the dower payments may have made it more difficult for Henry to pay Montfort and how William had taken precedence over Montfort in the replacement of his fee by an equivalent in land.[145] The dower may have caused other conflicts, for through his marriage William had acquired Pembroke, the lordship claimed by Montfort and Eleanor when they took legal action to secure a landed settlement in place of the dower fee in 1247–48.[146] Not only a successful competitor for royal patronage, William was also the possessor of lands which Eleanor and her husband saw as justly theirs.

If we are right to think that the need to provide for his sons was one of the sharpest spurs to Montfort's acquisitiveness, William's marriage may have provoked a further resentment. A lucrative match with a royal

---

[141] Lunt, *Financial Relations*, pp. 278–9.
[142] Paris, v, p. 263.
[143] Paris, v, p. 338.
[144] E.403/11.
[145] Above, pp. 130, 135–6.
[146] Above, pp. 52, 131; Carpenter, 'What Happened in 1258?', p. 115, n. 44.

ward would have solved at a stroke the problem of endowing one or
other of the earl's sons from an estate which for the moment still
contained an uncomfortably high proportion of land held for life only;
for the grants of land in fee promised in 1253 had yet to be made good.
In the 1240s Henry had set up a number of Savoyards in England with
just such marriages. The supply of heiresses had dwindled in the 1240s,
but the provision of Joan de Munchensi for William in 1247 had shown
that some could still be found. Nor was this the only example of royal
arrangements which elevated one or two other Poitevins at about
the same time, though Joan's value made it the most offensive.[147] No
similar arrangements benefited either of Montfort's two elder sons,
Henry and Simon, aged nineteen and seventeen respectively in 1258.
Their marriage prospects, which must have greatly concerned their
father as they grew older, are entirely obscure. In the end neither did
marry. The later contrast between the extinction of the Montfort family
in England and the continuation of William de Valence's line in the
English baronage rested on more than just the result of the battle of
Evesham.

These rancorous jealousies loured over Henry's court at a time when
there was already enough to darken its atmosphere. Matters came to a
head in May 1257, when William was the court's most influential figure.
At a gathering of the king and magnates in London a furious quarrel
broke out between the two men. According to Paris, William had
raided the earl's lands, only to see his spoils retrieved by Montfort's
steward. William accused Montfort of treachery, Montfort exploded in
anger, and the two would have come to blows had the king not
intervened. They quarrelled with similar ferocity in the parliament of
April 1258, when both Montfort and Gloucester were accused by
William of giving help to the Welsh, whose rebellion threatened his
Pembroke estates.[148] In the face of William's intemperance (a quality
which he shared with Montfort) and his elevation to a position of
supremacy at court, the fragile rapprochement of 1257 between
Henry and Montfort could not be consolidated. Its breakdown, and the
alienation of the other *curiales* from a Lusignan regime, inaugurated
the reform movement.

---

[147] Paris, iv, pp. 628–9; Ridgeway, 'King Henry III and the "Aliens"', p. 88; Ridgeway, 'Foreign
Favourites', p. 596.
[148] Paris, v, pp. 634, 676–7; below, p. 154.

(E) THE END OF THE ROAD

By 1258 Henry III's government had generated grievances which were shared by most of the higher nobility. Opposition to the Lusignans, to the Sicilian folly, and to a financial policy which brought penury out of extravagance and extortion, had created a movement in which Montfort was one participant among others. Yet his position was not strictly comparable to that of the earl of Gloucester or John fitz Geoffrey or Peter of Savoy or any other of the erstwhile *curiales* who turned against Henry in 1258. He had his own particular grudges against the king, older, more numerous and more sustained than theirs. Some, such as that arising from Eleanor's dower, stretched back over many years; but most were the product of his period of office in Gascony and its abrupt termination. His mistreatment in Gascony, as he saw it, rankled very deeply. Its various incidents would not otherwise have been so thoroughly rehearsed during his disputes with the king in the 1260s. The reconciliation of 1253 was only superficial; nothing had been forgotten. What he regarded as his dismissal in 1252 was the culmination of Henry's bad faith and, so one chronicle implies, a major cause of his opposition in 1258.[149]

In one sense Montfort's actions in Gascony were to his immediate advantage, for they won him the support of the nobility. At his trial in 1252 he had the backing of most of those who mattered – Richard of Cornwall, Gloucester, Peter of Savoy – and the nobles defended him against Henry in the subsequent parliament.[150] In response to the disorderliness of the Gascons, Montfort's policy of thorough seemed entirely justified. His return to England in May 1254 and his report on the situation in Gascony, contrary to the king's, caused the magnates to abandon all further parliamentary discussion of the tax that Henry wanted.[151] It was a testimony to his power to move and influence his equals. But Henry's double-dealing and faulty judgements in Gascony raised a storm that passed. To Montfort alone were they a continuing grievance, and one exacerbated by the king's financial obligations which arose from his service there and which Henry's own expensive intervention in the duchy made it impossible for him to meet. Though Montfort shared many of the general grievances which surfaced in 1258,

---

[149] *Flores Hist.*, iii, p. 252.
[150] Paris, v, pp. 296, 337–8; *Mon. Franc.*, i, p. 123; above, pp. 115–16, 119–20.
[151] Paris, v, pp. 440, 445; above, p. 139.

the scale of his private claims marked him off from the other reformers, with whom, as we shall see, his alliance was to some extent a tactical one.

Prior to 1258 there had been certain continuities of theme and method in the opposition to Henry III's government. They had been most visible in parliament, where on many occasions royal policy had been criticised, demands made for the enforcement of the Charters and the public nomination of the great officials, and taxes denied. In all this Montfort had, so far as can be seen, played no part, either before or after his appointment to Gascony in 1248. When the usual demand had been made for consent to the appointment of the chancellor, treasurer and justiciar, in the parliament of 1249, he had been in Gascony. When the same demand was repeated in April 1255, coupled with another for the full observance of the Charters, he was in France. When the confirmation of the Charters had been traded against the grant of a feudal aid in 1253, he had likewise been abroad.[152] He cannot be associated with the attempts to restrain royal government and to secure a baronial voice in its workings which characterised the twenty years before 1258: attempts which in any case more probably came from the clergy, the lesser baronage and the knights than from a predominantly royalist higher nobility. Restraints on royal power – of the kind, for example, that might be exercised by an independent-minded chancellor – were likely to be regarded with some ambivalence by those like Montfort who were on the prowl for royal patronage.

In Montfort's case there is some limited evidence to suggest that he was averse to any such restraints which might injure his own interests. In 1257, probably in February and at Windsor, he and other royal councillors took a new oath, whose general purpose was both to curb corruption and to alleviate the Crown's financial crisis. Two clauses were especially important: one bound the councillors not to assent to alienations from the royal demesne; a second sentenced any councillor found guilty of taking rewards or gifts, presumably in the course of his official business, to exclusion from the council and to loss of land and rent for a year. On 20 February 1257, at just this time, Montfort was permitted by the king to have the free disposition in his will of his lands and wardships 'notwithstanding any mandate, order, customs or laws of the realm to the contrary, or any statutes whereby such validity [of his disposition of his lands and wardships] might be impeded'. It looks as if

---

[152] Paris, v, pp. 73, 376–8, 494.

this was a precautionary measure, designed to circumvent, if necessary, the terms of the oath that he had recently sworn.[153]

Between 1248 and 1258 Montfort was thus playing his own game. The issues which divided him from Henry III were not constitutional but personal ones, which 'constitutional' arguments might even hinder him from pursuing. Only in 1258 did his private grievances converge both with local protests against the harshness of Henry's government and with a political movement towards radical reform which had some earlier and milder precedents in the parliamentary demands of the 1240s and early 1250s. It is difficult to feel more than a limited sympathy with his sense of injustice. True, he had been badly treated in Gascony and the king owed him nearly £1,200 at the end of 1257. But in the previous few years he had received some thousands of pounds from Henry; he was in secure possession of his £400 annual fee, even if it had not yet been turned into land; and he had acquired the barony of Embleton and, more nominally, the county of Bigorre. Almost certainly a richer man in 1258 than he had been in 1248, it was hardly economic decline that drove him towards reform.

How, finally, was he viewed by Henry? There is no doubt that Henry was almost desperately anxious to placate Montfort, at the cost of considerable humiliation. The control which Montfort gained over county revenues and shrieval appointments, the oath on the king's soul to pay him what was due, the submission to the sanction of distraint on the king's lands and goods, the threat of excommunication and interdict held over his chief ministers if he failed to make payment, all suggest a king who was prepared to go to almost any lengths to meet Montfort's demands. This is only partly to be explained by Henry's needs for Montfort's services as a diplomat and general. He remained Henry's brother-in-law, a member of the family whom Henry could hardly set aside even had he wanted to do so. But he was also a hard and irascible man, as even his best friends realised. Beholden to no one, he was not afraid to insult or even to threaten the king. His violent quarrels with Henry at his trial in 1252 and with William de Valence in 1257 and 1258 showed how easily political differences might be inflamed by contempt and anger.[154] His standing in France gave him a certain independence from the English Crown. Despite his circle of churchmen and *familiares*, and his family connections, he was in some ways an isolated figure,

---

[153] *Ann. Burton*, pp. 395–7; *DBM*, pp. 196–7; *CPR, 1247–58*, p. 543.
[154] Above, pp. 87, 115, 146.

whose grievances, abilities, and almost savage energy made him a destabilising force in politics. Paris tells a famous story of how, in July 1258, Henry was caught in a thunderstorm on the Thames and was put ashore at the bishop of Durham's palace, where Montfort was staying. The earl greeted him cheerfully and courteously and asked him what he was afraid of, since the storm had passed. 'Not jestingly and with a severe look', Henry blurted out, 'I fear thunder and lightning beyond measure, but by God's head I fear you more than all the thunder and lightning in the world'.[155] Like the lightning which Henry feared, this little scene illuminates, intensely and momentarily, the tensions and constraints in a relationship not wholly hostile but certainly full of ambivalence.

[155] Paris, v. p. 706.

CHAPTER 5

The reformer: ideals and interests, 1258–59

(A) THE BEGINNINGS OF REFORM, APRIL–NOVEMBER 1258

The reform movement of 1258 was the most radical assault yet made on the prerogatives of the Crown, and one which brought England nearer to a republican constitution than at any time before 1649. This was not a development which had at the outset been either intended or foreseen. Beginning as an attack on two specific consequences of royal policy, the dominance of the Lusignans at court and Henry's obligations to the papacy, the movement quickly led on to the effective baronial appropriation of the Crown's executive power and to the unleashing of social forces in the localities which turned a court coup into a national enterprise. At the centre of these great events from the start, Montfort became the most committed of the reformers, and one almost painfully sensitive to the moral obligations that his commitment entailed. Yet the new and principled consistency which reform appeared to give to his career was marked and distorted by his own sense of injustice. As we have seen, his private grievances were broader and deeper than those of his fellow reformers. As we shall see, for long periods Montfort gave their ventilation priority over the public issues of the day. In this final phase of his life it is more than usually difficult to be sure about the springs of his actions. The idealist and the malcontent pull together in implausible harmony.

The origins of reform reached back to the start of Henry III's personal rule in the mid 1230s. They have been sketched in the preceding chapters and were later set out with admirable clarity by the rump of the reforming party in their submission to Louis IX in 1264. There they spoke of Henry's breaches of Magna Carta, his exploitation of the Church, the favours in legal privileges, land and money given to his courtiers and to aliens, to the detriment of his other subjects and of his finances, the rapaciousness of his local officials, and the wasteful profanity of the Sicilian Business, a projected crusade against Christians at the expense of the Holy Land.[1] Valid though this case was, it concentrated largely on the issues of justice and Christian conduct which would appeal to Louis. It passed over a more political charge, less likely to win the favour of another king but equally important in explaining the need for reform: that is, Henry's persistent failure to consult and to seek consent, which had led him towards Sicily in the first place.

Henry's general incompetence and oppressive government had created an indictment here which all political society could support. Yet only in retrospect, and forensically, could these grievances be presented as a charge preferred from the start by the whole community. At the time they represented more the particular discontents of churchmen and of minor barons, rural gentry and their tenants, than those of Montfort and the higher nobility. Until the few years prior to 1258 this latter group had been much less affected by Henry's mismanagement of his kingdom. During these years, however, attitudes had changed, as the growing ascendancy of the Lusignans came to threaten other curial interests besides those of Montfort. The consequent enmity of the earls and greater magnates towards these men was the immediate cause of '1258'. Peter and Boniface of Savoy, the queen's uncles, the earls of Hereford, Gloucester and Norfolk, and John fitz Geoffrey, the powerful former justiciar of Ireland, had all crossed swords with the king's half-brothers, and it was one of these quarrels that precipitated the crisis. On 1 April 1258 a dispute between Aymer de Valence, bishop-elect of Winchester, and John fitz Geoffrey over the advowson of the church of Shere in Surrey reached a violent climax when Aymer's forces attacked his rival's men. On complaining to the king, fitz Geoffrey was refused justice by Henry, in a blatant display of partiality which epitomised Henry's failings and set off a demand for the reform of the whole realm.[2]

This was first voiced in the parliament which opened at Westminster about 9 April.[3] The military successes of the Welsh and new papal demands for men and money for Sicily, with the possibility of excommunication and interdict in the event of non-payment, created a

---

[1] *DBM*, pp. 268–79.

[2] Paris, v, pp. 708–9; Carpenter, 'What Happened in 1258?', pp. 112–16.

[3] The most detailed account of the events of April–June 1258 is given in *Baronial Plan*, pp. 65–101. The main documents are printed in *DBM*, pp. 72–113. Where references are not given in what follows they will be found in these two works.

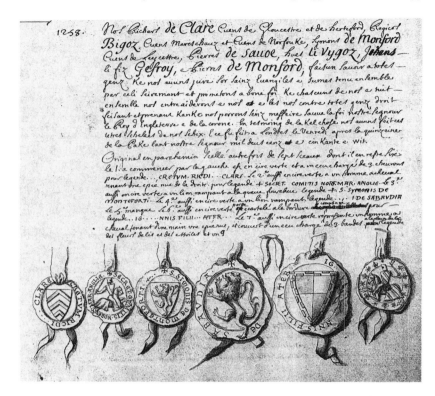

Plate 7. The confederation of April 1258. The only source is this eighteenth-century transcript of a lost original, with drawings of the confederates' seals. The seals are those of the earls of Gloucester, Norfolk and Leicester, Peter of Savoy, John fitz Geoffrey and Peter de Montfort. That of Hugh Bigod is missing.

threatening background which again reflected unfavourably on the king. But the misdeeds of the Lusignans transcended these other issues. They were the prime factor in leading seven magnates – the earls of Gloucester, Norfolk and Leicester, Hugh Bigod, Norfolk's brother, Peter of Savoy, John fitz Geoffrey and Peter de Montfort – first to join together in a sworn confederation on 12 April, and then to confront the king in arms with a demand for the expulsion of the aliens and the reform of the realm by a committee of twenty-four (Plate 7).[4] Forced to submit, Henry agreed on 2 May to the committee's establishment. It

[4] Bémont, *Montfort* (1st edn), pp. 327–8; *Ann. Tewk.*, pp. 163–5; Carpenter, 'What Happened in 1258?', pp. 106, 110, 116.

was to comprise twelve royalists and twelve baronial representatives, and to convene in parliament at Oxford on 9 June.

At this stage, therefore, Montfort was one of a group of confederates sharing common discontents. Like him, most were former royalists now alienated from the court. Partly drawn into this association by his own hostility towards William de Valence, Montfort once again quarrelled fiercely with William during the Westminster parliament, after the favourite had accused both Montfort and Gloucester of conniving at Welsh attacks on his lordship of Pembroke. When William called him a liar and a traitor to his face, Montfort had to be restrained from violence, as had happened during their earlier clash in 1257, and he was later to demand justice against him from the king.[5] Whatever their validity, William's suspicions about the earl's subversive moves against Pembroke suggest that both quarrel and demand were rooted in Montfort's continuing resentment over William's possession of this lordship: a *casus belli* matching the primordial dispute between fitz Geoffrey and Aymer de Valence over Shere. It was the convergence of these and other grievances which brought the dissidents together. But this effect was supplemented by a sense of common danger which gave Montfort a special place in what was partly a military alliance. If the baronial confederation was one for security against a possible Lusignan *revanche*, as Dr David Carpenter has stressed,[6] his skills of generalship were bound to enhance his standing among its members.

Beneath these unities of purpose, however, Montfort was already beginning to play his own game. On 5 May, only three days after Henry had consented to the institution of the reforming committee, he went on to promise to abide by the committee's decision both on the assignment of land to Montfort to replace his £400 fee and on the payment of the king's debts to him.[7] There was nothing surreptitious or underhand about Henry's undertaking, which was signified in letters patent; yet it set Montfort somewhat apart from his allies. His quarrel with William de Valence, though probably focused on the particular issue of Eleanor's dower, was only one of a number of private disputes between individual reformers and the Lusignans. But in seeking to use the machinery of reform as a means to a favourable settlement of his financial claims against the king, Montfort had revealed motives that

---

[5] Paris, v, pp. 676–7, 689; Carpenter, 'What Happened in 1258?', p. 115.
[6] Carpenter, 'What Happened in 1258?', pp. 116–17.
[7] *CPR, 1247–58*, p. 627.

were more explicitly self-regarding than those of his fellow confederates. From the outset of the reform movement the latent contradictions between his pursuit of the public good and of his private interests began to shadow his career.

Similar contradictions were soon to become visible in an area which Montfort had made his own: that of Anglo-French relations. Peace with France was the most important external issue confronting both king and barons in 1258. When the reform movement began, the broad terms of what would eventually become the Treaty of Paris had already been settled through negotiations in which Montfort had played a leading role.[8] Central to those terms was Henry's agreement to give up his claims to Normandy, Anjou, Touraine, Maine and Poitou, and to receive Gascony as a fief held from the French Crown. Although this was a humiliating reversal of the whole thrust of his previous foreign policy, which had aimed at the recovery of the lost French lands, Henry was determined to see the treaty concluded. His underlying affection for Louis IX,[9] his problems in Wales, the new demands made on him by the baronial reformers, and above all his continuing ambitions in Sicily, for which a French settlement was a necessary precondition, all gave him an urgent view of the need for peace.

The draft of the treaty included a clause which was to prove wide open to exploitation by Simon de Montfort. In it, Louis demanded that not only Henry but also his brother Richard of Cornwall and his sister Eleanor should renounce their claims to the old Angevin lands. When, on 8 May, between the Westminster and the Oxford parliaments, Henry appointed Montfort and others to negotiate once again for him in France, he undertook to try to secure these renunciations.[10] But the need now for Eleanor's co-operation before any treaty could be completed would give Montfort the chance to impede the whole progress of negotiations, providing him with a lever which he could use to extract from Henry a favourable settlement of his personal grievances. Given the large potential advantage to the Montforts from Louis's demand, and the use that they would later make of it, Henry's subsequent accusation in 1260 that Montfort had put it into Louis's head to ask for Eleanor's renunciation looks prima facie plausible. He had after all been the chief peace negotiator, and no similar renunciations

---

[8] Chaplais, 'Making of the Treaty of Paris', p. 238; above, pp. 140–2.
[9] Jordan, *Louis IX*, pp. 198–9; Vale, *The Angevin Legacy*, p. 14.
[10] *CPR, 1247–58*, p. 663; Chaplais, 'Making of the Treaty of Paris', pp. 238–9.

were demanded from Henry's daughters or from his nephew and niece, the children of his sister Isabella. Henry noted both these points.[11] Yet what weight did the king's charge carry? Montfort himself vehemently denied it, and there were other good reasons for singling out Richard of Cornwall and Eleanor. Richard, as king of Germany, and Eleanor, whose husband's ancestors as well as her own had claims and roots in Normandy, were the two members of Henry's family from whom Louis had most to fear. He may not have thought it necessary to ask for renunciations from more remote and harmless relations. But it remained true that Montfort had been given a bargaining counter, which, in a negative way, he now began to turn to account. The articles of peace resulting from his embassy, agreed in Paris on 28 May, again contained the demand for renunciations; and while Richard of Cornwall had indicated compliance even in advance of the agreement, Eleanor made no move.[12] Her consent to these arrangements had not yet been explicitly linked to the dower question, but, to judge by later events, the linkage must already have been firmly in the minds of the two Montforts. The trap had been set and was waiting to be sprung.

When the Oxford parliament met, probably on 11 June, Montfort may thus have seen the prospect of an advance on all fronts in his claims against Henry: the reforming committee was to rule on the question of the king's debts and his unfulfilled promise to provide land in exchange for Montfort's fee, while Eleanor's renunciation of her rights in France could be made conditional on a satisfactory dower settlement. This dual approach to the three main areas of contention between Montfort and Henry suggests a carefully thought-out strategy on Montfort's part. But whatever Montfort's plans may have been for his personal affairs, they were eclipsed at Oxford by the extraordinarily rapid development of the reforming programme and its expansion beyond anything likely to have been envisaged earlier at Westminster. What had begun there as a coup by a small group of disaffected magnates was now transformed into a much broader social movement, directed at the reform of local as well as central government and even at the ways of the magnates themselves.

This is likely to have been in part the accidental result of the intention to make Oxford the muster point for a new Welsh campaign: a circumstance which meant that parliament met there in the midst of a much larger and more socially comprehensive assembly. In March

---

[11] *DBM*, pp. 194–7; cf. Chaplais, 'Making of the Treaty of Paris', pp. 235–6.
[12] *Dipl. Docs.*, No. 299; Chaplais, 'Making of the Treaty of Paris', p. 240.

orders had been issued for a muster at Chester on 17 June, to which the prior assembly at Oxford was ostensibly the preliminary. One hundred and thirty-seven tenants-in-chief and their service had been summoned to Chester. If comparable numbers appeared at Oxford – and the chroniclers suggest that they did – those present would have included not only the reforming committee of twenty-four and the parliamentary magnates, but also many of the lesser baronage and knightly class.[13] These groups had a more continuous history of opposition to Henry's government than did the higher nobility. They had long wanted a more responsive judicial system and more effective restraints on the Crown's local agents. With the former curialist magnates they now shared both a general interest in the reform of royal government and a more specific opposition to the Lusignans, whose extortionate management of their wide estates made them as detested in the country as their influence over royal patronage and justice made them at court.[14] This wide cross-section of lay society assembled at Oxford was perhaps responsible for the so-called 'Petition of the Barons': a miscellaneous collection of grievances, some explicitly said to have been submitted by 'earls and barons', others emanating from 'knights and freeholders', which was probably circulated during the parliament. It marked both the expanding range of reform and the first stage in the legislative process which would lead eventually to the Provisions of Westminster.[15]

The new political alignment of the higher nobility, the lesser baronage and the gentry was one of the most significant features of the Oxford parliament. It was reflected in the Provisions of Oxford, the first and most momentous instalment of the reforms which came to constitute the reforming programme. So far as we know, the Provisions were never formally published, but took the form of a series of memoranda drawn up by a section of the committee of twenty-four.[16] They set out a scheme for the wholesale reform of the English polity through the placing of royal government under organised control for the first time. Central to that scheme was the superseding of the original

---

[13] *CR, 1256–59*, pp. 294–6, 299; *Ann. Burton*, p. 438; Paris, v, pp. 695–6; Rishanger, *De Bellis*, p. 8; *Flores Hist.*, iii, p. 253.

[14] Cf. Maddicott, 'Magna Carta and the Local Community', pp. 55–60.

[15] *DBM*, pp. 76–91; P. Brand, 'The Drafting of Legislation in Mid-Thirteenth-Century England', *Parliamentary History*, 9 (1990), pp. 244–51, 272–3.

[16] Cf. H. G. Richardson and G. O. Sayles, 'The Provisions of Oxford, 1258', *Bulletin of the John Rylands Library*, 17 (1933), pp. 25–7, reprinted in H. G. Richardson and G. O. Sayles, *The English Parliament in the Middle Ages* (London, 1971), Ch. III (same pagination). The Provisions are printed in *DBM*, pp. 97–113.

committee of twenty-four by a new council of fifteen, instituted during
the parliament. The twenty-four had been a body balanced between
royalists and reformers. It had included among the king's twelve the
four Lusignans, whose obstructiveness had made it difficult for the
committee to function effectively and probably hastened its demise.[17]
Their presence makes it seem likely that the Provisions were predominantly the work of the baronial twelve rather than the whole committee.
The new council, chosen by a complicated electoral method, was a
more partisan body, which included seven of the former baronial
twelve against only three of the king's twelve. Its commission was
correspondingly more extensive than that of the original twenty-four.
It was to oversee royal ministers and to appoint the great officials, to
sanction all non-routine writs issuing from chancery and all major royal
grants, and to remain in being for an indefinite period, perhaps for
twelve years.[18] The council was to co-operate with parliament, an
assembly meeting thrice yearly, at prescribed times, 'to deal with the
common business of the realm and of the king together', by collaboration
between the council and twelve elected representatives of the wider
baronial community. Finally, the justiciarship, vacant since 1234, was
revived in favour of Hugh Bigod. Holding it as chief justice, rather than
as the leading royal minister of the old Angevin justiciarship, he was to
provide the commodity which was at the moral centre of the reforming
movement.

These innovations came near to putting the Crown into commission.
To ensure the continuance of their work the reformers had set up
what was in effect a semi-permanent governing body for the kingdom.
Previously unwilling to consult, Henry now found not only that
consultation had been thrust upon him but that political direction had
been largely transferred from himself to the council. A prerequisite for
that direction was the council's right to appoint and supervise the king's
ministers, to whose choice and management Henry had in the past
vigorously laid claim. Essential for successful reform, this new
stipulation struck at the heart of the prerogative, and in the ensuing
struggles between the king and his opponents it was often to be the
fulcrum of their arguments. Almost as radical was the provision for
regular meetings of parliament, now to be the public forum for the
discussion of the nation's affairs. If this was a riposte to Henry's way of

---

[17] *Ann. Tewk.*, p. 171; *Ann. Burton*, p. 458; *DBM*, pp. 100–1.
[18] *DBM*, pp. 72–3, 100–5, 222–3.

taking decisions *inconsulte* with a few friends, which had led to the fiasco over Sicily, it marked a further and more general encroachment on the Crown's traditional authority.

These changes were, of course, as much to the advantage of the lesser baronage and the gentry as to that of the great magnates: the appointment of an impartial justiciar to do justice to all, the restrictions on royal grants, and the general reining in of royal power gave them what they had been pressing for in the years up to 1258. But the Provisions also made more specific concessions to provincial interests by passing a large measure of initiative over to the counties. Four knights in each county were to collect complaints, primarily against officials, for transmission to the justiciar as he toured the counties; the justiciar was to have jurisdiction over baronial as well as royal officials; and the sheriffs were henceforth to be local landowners, salaried and appointed for one year only, to discourage the abuse of power which the reformers saw as the concomitant of long-term tenure.

The Provisions promised much else – the future reform of the Church, the city of London and other towns, the Jewry, the mint and the royal household – but what had been done already was sufficiently revolutionary to be intolerable to the king's closest friends. Threatened with the loss of their lands and castles, the four Lusignans refused to take the oath to the Provisions which all present had taken at the conclusion of the parliament. They fled to Winchester, where the reformers, in 'a second parliament',[19] decreed their expulsion. In July they went overseas to France.

In these events Montfort had taken a leading role, committing himself to a course of action which would not necessarily circumscribe his private ambitions but would certainly come to dominate his public career. He had returned from France by 14 June and was present throughout the fortnight of the Oxford parliament.[20] Together with four others of the original seven confederates – the earls of Gloucester and Norfolk, John fitz Geoffrey and Peter de Montfort – he was a member of all the various groupings concerned with reform and nominated before or during the parliament: the baronial twelve on the committee of twenty-four, the later council of fifteen, and a subsidiary committee of twenty-four appointed to negotiate an aid for the king.[21]

[19] *Ann. Tewk.*, p. 165.
[20] He witnessed royal charters at Oxford on 14, 15, 17, 19, 20, 21 June, after which no further charters were enrolled until 5 November: c.53/48, m. 1.
[21] *DBM*, pp. 100–1, 104–5.

Among this inner circle of committee men the real leaders, identified by several of the chroniclers, were Montfort, Gloucester and fitz Geoffrey.[22] But the strong representation of his friends and *familiares*, both on these bodies and among the new keepers appointed for the king's castles at the end of the parliament, gave Montfort in particular a good deal of additional weight. On the baronial twelve were four Montfortians besides their leader: Walter de Cantilupe, Richard de Grey, Peter de Montfort and Hugh Despenser. All except Despenser survived the electoral process to appear on the council of fifteen, while in addition both Cantilupe and Peter de Montfort were among the twenty-four negotiators for the aid.[23] Of the new castellans, the first two commissions enrolled went to Montfortians: Grey received Dover and the Cinque Ports, and Ralph Basset of Sapcote was given Northampton, key positions for the control of the routes to France and the midlands.[24] Of course, not all these appointments necessarily reflected Montfort's influence, for men such as Peter de Montfort were important barons in their own right. But this was not invariably true. Nothing in the earlier career of Hugh Despenser, for example, seems to have prepared him for his place among the baronial twelve; and it is difficult to see what justified Basset's custody of Northampton besides Montfort's trust in him. Whatever his political standing, the reformers' chief military man is likely to have had a special say in the allocation of castles.

At this stage the reform movement was by no means Montfort's enterprise alone. Its social backing was too general, its aristocratic support too broad, and its remedies attuned to too wide a variety of discontents for it to be anything like the exclusive property of one man. Nevertheless Montfort's connections magnified his role among its leaders, to give him an unofficial influence hardly visible at the earlier Westminster parliament or rivalled by the other confederate magnates. It was appropriate that he should have taken the lead in the expulsion of the Lusignans at the end of the Oxford parliament. 'Either you will give up your castles or you will lose your head', Paris has him say to the prevaricating William de Valence. It was a scene which linked back to Montfort's earlier collisions with William, at the April parliament and before, to show how deeply and unremittingly he hated the Lusignan.

---

[22] *Robert of Gloucs.*, ii, pp. 733–4; Rishanger, *De Bellis*, p. 8; *Flores Hist.*, iii, p. 252; *HMC*, 14th Report (1896), App. 8, p. 209.

[23] *DBM*, pp. 100–1, 104–5.

[24] *DBM*, pp. 112–13; *CPR, 1247–58*, pp. 627–8.

But it also showed the foremost position which he was coming to hold in the baronial counsels. In Paris's account of the Oxford parliament, written soon after the event and long before Montfort had emerged as supreme leader in 1263, he is the only one of the reforming magnates whose particular activities are mentioned.[25]

It may seem peculiar, then, to find two chronicles, with support from a third, speaking of Montfort's ambivalence towards the oath to the Provisions which concluded the Oxford parliament. Both the Lanercost chronicle and the later French chronicle of Guillaume de Nangis say that at first Montfort declined to take the oath and had to be compelled to do so. His reluctance is explained by his realisation of the irrevocable commitment which an oath would impose and which his allies (so he believed) might later disregard, abandoning the cause and, by implication, deserting him. The chronicle of St Benet of Hulme attributed to John of Oxenedes says something similar. Although not mentioning the oath, the author reports that at Oxford Montfort initially resisted the requests of the barons that he should join them, asserting that there was no constancy in the English, who were all too likely to turn tail when in a fix. It was a gibe that was to become almost a topos in his later opinions about the English as the chroniclers record them. All three of these sources are late; but they are not related, they describe the same incident in different words, and the Lanercost chronicle derives from the work of a Franciscan familiar with Oxford and who seems to have known a good deal about the earl's private life.[26] Neglected though it has been by Montfort's later biographers, their story may well be true.

Its importance lies in its bearing on the larger question of his oath to the Provisions: a subject central to the later history of the reform movement. Montfort had good reason to be wary of oaths lightly undertaken. Eleanor's breach of her early and ill-considered vow of chastity had long troubled his conscience, and he may have known, too, of Louis IX's principled avoidance of oaths. 'Let your communication be yea, yea, nay, nay', Christ had said.[27] Added to these general

---

[25] Paris, v, pp. 697–8.

[26] *Lanercost*, p. 67; Nangis, 'Vie de St Louis', 'Chronicon Guillaume de Nangis', *Recueil des Historiens des Gaules*, 20, pp. 414, 557; *Oxenedes*, p. 225. For the sources of the Lanercost chronicle, see above, p. 86. For Montfort's later remarks about the English, see, e.g. *Wykes*, p. 160; Rishanger, *De Bellis*, pp. 16–17.

[27] 'Vita Ludovici Noni auctore Gaufrido de Belloloco', *Recueil des Historiens des Gaules*, 20, p. 5, citing Matthew 5: 37; above, pp. 86–7.

considerations was his own unwillingness to create an obligation, sacred in its intensity, from which there could be no retreat. When he eventually took the oath at Oxford, probably in the great new church of the Dominicans,[28] the circumstances must have heightened his sense of participating in more than a political compact. They are described in several of the sources. The holding of burning tapers by the king and the magnates, the excommunication by the archbishop of Canterbury and nine other bishops of those who might deny their oaths, the final 'Amen' pronounced by all as the excommunication came to an end, and the casting down of their tapers by the whole company, made him an actor in a great spiritual drama.[29] These ceremonies presented the Provisions as a religious enterprise, something 'holy and virtuous', as the barons afterwards termed them, intended to provide for all the justice which the king had failed to provide.[30] It was an appeal to which Montfort's temperament and religious sensibilities were likely to make him particularly responsive, in private and in public. According to the Melrose chronicler (who makes the point twice), it was only after his oath to the Provisions that he imposed on himself his penitential regime of midnight vigils, prayer and sexual abstinence.[31] The same oath was to provide him with a principle of public conduct for the rest of his life. Though he lost interest in the Provisions for long periods, did not always contribute much to their enforcement or extension, used them as a lever in his quarrel with Henry, and was eventually willing to consider their modification, he was never prepared to throw them over. There he was to differ from almost all who had been present with him at the Blackfriars oath-taking. Far from indicating his lukewarmness towards reform, his apparent hesitancy over his oath at Oxford suggests that he had an unsettling and almost prescient awareness of what reform might entail. As during his time in Gascony, when Adam Marsh had consoled him, so in June 1258, the everyday hurly-burly of his involvement in politics concealed a deeper stratum of spiritual beliefs, values and anxieties.

In the aftermath of the Oxford parliament and the departure of the

---

[28] Paris, v, p. 697, says that parliament met at the Dominican friary. The Dominican church, completed in 1246, was only a few hundred yards from the Franciscan house, home of Adam Marsh: *VCH Oxfordshire*, iv, ed. Alan Crossley (Oxford, 1979), pp. 30, 366.

[29] *DBM*, pp. 258–9; *Robert of Gloucs.*, ii, p. 734; *Guisborough*, pp. 185–6; *Flores Hist.*, iii, pp. 253–4.

[30] 'Provisio sive ordinacio ista sancta est et honesta': *DBM*, pp. 264–5.

[31] *Chronicle of Melrose*, intro, A. O. and M. O. Anderson, pp. 136, 139; *Chronica de Mailros*, ed. Stevenson, pp. 207, 211; above, p. 88.

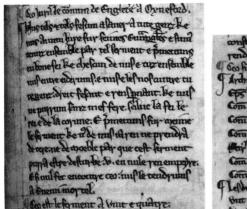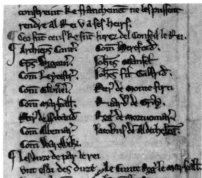

Plate 8. The Provisions of Oxford, from the Burton Annals. (a) (left) The oath of the commune of magnates, taken at Oxford. (b) (right) The new council of fifteen.

Lusignans that involvement brought into view, almost for the first time, Montfort's eldest son, Henry. Paris is our only source for the story of how, in July 1258, Henry pursued the fleeing Lusignans to France, determined to attack them and raising support by spreading the news of William de Valence's insults to his father. Taking refuge in Boulogne, his victims were eventually allowed to retreat by Louis IX.[32] Whether Henry acted with or without his father's knowledge – and Paris admitted ignorance about this – he clearly shared both in his father's political objectives and in his impulsive tendency to use force to achieve them. His actions were an early instance of that family solidarity, best exemplified in the common pursuit of Eleanor's dower rights by Montfort and Eleanor, which in the end converted the reform movement into something approaching a family enterprise.[33] But for the present they revealed one of Montfort's longstanding strengths: his reputation in France, where the *ultramarini* could not believe that Valence had dared to defame 'a man so noble in disposition, of such noble birth, and pre-eminent among all on both sides of the sea'.

The expulsion of the Lusignans, the transfer of the major royal castles to the barons and their allies, and the truce with Wales which was also made at Oxford, countered the main external threats to the survival of the new regime. The baronial council, now effectively ruling the kingdom, could operate in conditions of security. For the rest of the year

[32] Paris, v, pp. 702–3, 710. [33] Below, pp. 324–7.

three issues dominated its business: the continuing negotiations for a peace with France, the attempt to secure the despatch of a papal legate, and above all the implementation of reform. Relations with the papacy and the progress of reform can be discussed here, leaving over the French negotiations, in which Montfort again took a leading part, for later consideration.

The baronial council essentially wanted three concessions from Pope Alexander IV in the summer of 1258: the mitigation of the pope's terms for Sicily, the appointment of a papal legate, and the formal removal of Aymer de Valence, the youngest of the Lusignans, from his see of Winchester. In the first two of these objectives the king shared. Henry could not meet papal demands over Sicily; and a legate might act as both moderator and mediator, providing protection for the rights of the Crown just as Guala and Pandulf had done during his minority. The reformers looked to a legate to guide the Anglo-French negotiations to a conclusion and to confer papal approval and moral leadership on their enterprise. These motives imbued the letters which Gloucester, Montfort and others sent to the pope in July and the speech which their bearer made at the curia shortly afterwards.[34] But Alexander refused to comply. In December he cancelled the grant of Sicily to Edmund and, reluctant to confer respectability on reform, procrastinated in his response to the request for a legate.[35]

His hostility mattered less than it might have done had not the implementation of reform widened and consolidated the support which its initiators enjoyed in England. The council had the detailed oversight of the administration which was a main constituent of reform, leaving Henry with little more than a ratificatory role. His assent to reform was publicly proclaimed in August, when letters in his name were sent out for publication in the counties to make known the election of the twenty-four, the subsequent election of the fifteen, and the need for all to obey the council's decrees. Further royal letters, despatched in mid October, repeated and elaborated these injunctions.[36]

It was in the localities that reform took hold most firmly. Its instruments – Bigod's justiciarship, his eyre, the institution of county panels of knights – had all been envisaged and to some extent set up by the Provisions of Oxford. Thereafter the plan was put into operation. The

[34] *Ann. Tewk.*, pp. 170–4; *Ann. Burton*, pp. 457–68; *Baronial Plan*, pp. 106–7.
[35] Paris, vi, pp. 410–16; *Baronial Plan*, pp. 106–7.
[36] *CPR, 1247–58*, pp. 644–5; *DBM*, pp. 116–19.

justiciar began his sessions at Oxford in June and by the end of the year his court had moved in a wide sweep through southern and eastern England.[37] In early August the knightly committees were appointed in the counties to collect complaints; though the original scheme was modified, so that the complaints were to be brought up to Westminster on 6 October, before the start of the Michaelmas parliament, rather than delivered to the justiciar.[38] The parliament itself followed on from the previous assembly at Oxford as an occasion for the concerting of reform. Attended by knights from at least fifteen counties, it provided both a point of convergence for king, council and local opinion, and a source for further change. During its sessions the position of the sheriff was elaborately regulated in the Ordinance of Sheriffs, by which the king promised early redress for local grievances and placed the sheriffs under new restrictions, most of them embodied in a new oath.[39] Shortly afterwards, in late October and early November, nineteen new sheriffs, all of them local knights, were appointed for twenty-eight counties.[40]

To some extent the reformers had created expectations which they could not satisfy. The delivery of complaints to parliament rather than to the justiciar, as originally planned, marked the realisation that it would take many months for Bigod to complete his circuit of the whole country. In the Ordinance of Sheriffs Henry had to speak reassuringly to his audience, saying that wrongs that had endured for so long could not quickly be put right. Nevertheless a great deal had been achieved. The denial of justice to the victims of the Lusignans had been ended by their banishment, which had brought together magnates and gentry in a common cause. The reform of the shrievalties had taken up a central grievance of the localities in the years before 1258. The directive role of the council, and the function of parliament as a point of contact between the council and wider interests, baronial and local, suggested that the scheme envisaged in the Provisions was a practicable one. The broad spread of reform, its priorities as much local as central, was beginning to create for Montfort the constituency from which he would later draw his strongest support.

Although this last development could not have been foreseen in 1258, Montfort was already particularly closely identified with the reforming

---

[37] Jacob, *Studies*, pp. 39–41.
[38] *DBM*, pp. 112–15.
[39] *DBM*, pp. 118–23.
[40] *CPR, 1247–58*, pp. 649, 654–5; *Baronial Plan*, pp. 121–4.

cause. His aggressive stance in the Oxford parliament, the prominent place given there to his closest friends, and his own pre-eminent role in the expulsion of the Lusignans, all contributed to his special position in what remained a collective leadership. After the Lusignans' departure he was actively involved in the work of the council. On 23 July he had been among the deputation of reformers, including the earl of Norfolk and John fitz Geoffrey, who had gone to the London Guildhall to secure the assent of the city's leaders to the Provisions. Later, there were daily meetings of the baronial twelve (who seem to have had an afterlife extending beyond the appointment of the council of fifteen) at the New Temple and elsewhere 'on the reform of the usages and customs of the realm': discussions which may have marked a stage in the formulation of proposals for legislation published as the Provisions of the Barons in March 1259, and ultimately in the Provisions of Westminster.[41] Whether Montfort participated in these meetings is not known. But as a leading councillor, who could, for example, be named first among those appointed to oversee the drafting of letters on 4 August for despatch to the pope, he is unlikely to have been absent. In the same month he was among other councillors nominated to negotiate with the Scots, while his attestation of writs in July and November shows both his presence in London and his activity on routine conciliar business.[42] From May to November 1258 he was caught up in the implementation of reform as he would never be again.

If there was any distinctive Montfortian contribution to reform, it lay in the moral imperatives which were part of the driving force behind the movement. The general tone of moral rectitude which runs through so many of the reforms, exemplified by repeated injunctions 'to do and receive justice' and to accept no presents or bribes, had already been adumbrated in the councillor's oath of 1257.[43] Now it found expression in new and more practical ways: through the determination to provide justice in the localities, both against the agents of the king and, much more remarkably, against the barons themselves and their agents. This

[41] *Cron. Maior.*, pp. 38–9; Brand, 'Drafting of Legislation', pp. 251–64; Carpenter, 'Simon de Montfort', p. 5. Dr Brand seems to go beyond the evidence in assuming that these discussions were necessarily the work of Norfolk, Montfort, fitz Geoffrey and others. The 'predicti barones' of the London chronicle refers back to the baronial twelve, who are not specified, rather than to the deputation sent to the Guildhall.

[42] *CR, 1256–59*, p. 324; *CPR, 1247–58*, pp. 543, 645; *1258–66*, p. 1.

[43] To do and receive justice: Bémont, *Montfort* (1st edn), p. 327; *DBM*, pp. 100–1, 116–17; cf. D. A. Carpenter, 'The Lord Edward's Oath to Aid and Counsel Simon de Montfort, 15 October 1259', *BIHR*, 53 (1985), p. 227. Presents and bribes: *DBM*, pp. 100–3, 108–9, 120–1.

latter was a theme present from the start in the reforms of 1258. It was manifested in the undertaking made by the magnates at the Oxford parliament to observe towards their tenants all that the king had promised to observe towards the magnates; in the justiciar's commission to correct the faults, among others, of 'earls, barons and all other persons'; and in the county commissions to enquire into the misdeeds of sheriffs, bailiffs and others, including bailiffs of liberties.[44] One of the chief issues between lords and tenants may already have begun to receive more considered attention. Suit of court, the unpopular duty of attending a lord's court, had first been complained against in the Petition of the Barons and was probably among the 'usages and customs' discussed by the council in July and August.[45] Running through the response to the complaint, and through all these proffers of redress, was a principle of baronial self-denial with which Montfort was to become especially identified. In February 1259, when the backsliding Gloucester proved unwilling to offer redress to his tenants, Montfort would fall out with him over just this principle.[46]

It was a principle partly rooted in the tactical need to win the support of local knights and freeholders: men whose backing was necessary to broaden the social basis of reform, confirm its permanence, and prevent any royalist recovery of power.[47] But it was also sustained by an idealism which contributed equally to the restraints devised for royal officials and which may have had less immediate origins. Here we should perhaps consider the circles both of Grosseteste and of Louis IX: circles which overlapped, in the person not only of Simon de Montfort, but of a few others such as Eudes Rigaud, archbishop of Rouen.[48] Grosseteste had been insistent on the need to show justice to inferiors, an obligation which underlay many of the details of reform in 1258–59. In his *Rules* written for the countess of Lincoln in 1241 and in the *Statuta* which he drew up for the government of his own household, he had laid down lines of conduct for ministers which were to be echoed in the reforming period. Stewards and bailiffs were not to make tyrannical demands on the lord's tenants; there were to be no unjust extortions, for example, of tallage; redress was to be offered to the aggrieved through enquiry and compensation; no official was to take gifts, except for

[44] *Ann. Dun.*, p. 209; *DBM*, pp. 98–9, 106–7; Paris, vi, p. 399.
[45] *DBM*, pp. 86–7; Brand, 'Drafting of Legislation', pp. 251–2, 262, 264, 275–8.
[46] Below, pp. 180–1.
[47] Cf. Carpenter, 'What Happened in 1258?', p. 119.
[48] Above, pp. 79–80, 82.

moderate food and drink.[49] A similar emphasis had been evident in some of the episcopal articles of enquiry into lay conduct, drawn up in 1253, probably by Grosseteste, for use throughout England. There again, enquiry was ordered into the behaviour of lay estate officials, though only those employed by churchmen.[50] The general attitude of mind here was one reflected in the forthright rebuke which Grosseteste had delivered to Montfort himself after his extortionate behaviour in 1238;[51] and it was an attitude, rather than any specific proposals for action, which linked Grosseteste with the reforms of 1258.

In the case of Louis IX the links were perhaps more tangible. Louis's reforming activities after his return from crusade in 1254 are all well known. Within six months of reaching France he had published his *Grand Ordonnance* for the reform of the kingdom. It had as its main object the imposition of a Christian moral order through the rooting out of abuses committed by the king's agents. Many of the *Ordonnance*'s detailed stipulations were paralleled north of the Channel, both in Grosseteste's injunctions and in the later reforms of 1258–59: no gifts to royal officials except minor ones of food and drink; no extortion; no abuses of rights of hospitality; no employment of unnecessary subordinate officials; no exactions for the official's benefit.[52] All three of these last decrees were matched in the Ordinance of Sheriffs, published in October 1258: 'striking similarities', which Stacey was the first to notice.[53] The *Ordonnance* was enforced by *enquêteurs*, itinerant royal inquisitors, often friars, who were commissioned to look into abuses, make restitution to the aggrieved, and dismiss minor officials who were found wanting. Of course, the correspondences between royal activity in France after 1254 and baronial activity in England after 1258 were not precise. Louis's *Ordonnance*, with its condemnation of blasphemy, usury and gambling, had a more overtly religious and moral thrust than the baronial reforms, and its enforcement in part by friars, the instruments of the king's conscience, had no parallel in England. Nor was Louis concerned with

---

[49] *Walter of Henley and Other Treatises on Estate Management and Accounting*, ed. D. Oschinsky (Oxford, 1971), pp. 391 (*Rules*), 409 (*Statuta*).
[50] *Ann. Burton*, p. 308; *Robert Grosseteste*, ed. Callus, p. 202, n. 3.
[51] Above, pp. 28, 99.
[52] *Ordonnances des Roys de France de la Troisième Race*, ed. E. Laurière, i (Paris, 1723), pp. 65–75. For comments, see Jordan, *Louis IX*, pp. 61–3, 158–71; L. Carolus-Barré, 'La grande ordonnance de 1254', *Septième Centenaire de la Mort de Saint Louis* (Paris, 1976), pp. 85–96; and Richard, *Saint Louis*, pp. 156–63.
[53] *DBM*, pp. 118–23; R. C. Stacey, 'Crusades, Crusaders and the Baronial *Gravamina* of 1263–1264', *TCE*, iii, p. 147.

seigneurial abuses, as were the English reformers. Nevertheless, the sequence of legislation and provincial enquiry, the general aim of providing redress for those suffering from officials' misconduct, and the underlying sense of the need for justice – 'virtually shut out from the kingdom of England' before 1258, according to the reformers[54] – were all points at which Louis's aims and achievements touched those of the barons.

In surveying societies where officials were ubiquitously corrupt, where common problems of inequitable government invited common solutions, and where concepts of justice and fair dealing were debated in the schools and disseminated by bishops and friars on both sides of the Channel, we need to handle carefully the question of direct influences. In both England and France ideas about reform were in the air in the 1250s, something pervasive rather than transmitted. Though he put principles into practice only erratically, Henry III himself took a highminded line towards the obligations of the rich to the poor and of the governors to the governed.[55] That said, it remains likely that the ideals and practices of both Grosseteste and Louis IX were fed into the reforms of 1258, and more probably through the agency of Montfort than of anyone else. Not only had he been almost the spiritual pupil of Grosseteste, but he remained closely associated with Walter de Cantilupe, Grosseteste's former ally, the inheritor of his moral authority among the English bishops, and the only churchman to be at the heart of the reform movement in 1258. He had also been frequently in France and at Louis's court in the period following the 1254 *Ordonnance*, notably in the first half of 1255.[56] With the possible exception of Peter of Savoy, none of the other members of the baronial council had such close personal knowledge of the French king. We have already surmised that Louis's penitential austerities at this time may have influenced Montfort's own devotional practices.[57] Is it too fanciful to conjecture that Louis's attitude to government, to the proper role of conscience in its working, and to the methods for its reform, may have exercised a comparable influence on Montfort's thinking and, via Montfort, on the thinking of the reformers?

For once in politics, what seemed expedient also seemed right. The

[54] *DBM*, pp. 260–1.
[55] Maddicott, 'Magna Carta and the Local Community', pp. 52–4.
[56] *CR, 1254–56*, pp. 153–4, 195–6; *Layettes*, iii, No. 4178; above, pp. 140–2.
[57] Above, pp. 90–1.

reform both of royal government and of baronial estate management
represented a convergence of utilitarian and moral imperatives which
Montfort certainly supported and perhaps did much to foster. But if he
gave a moral lead in 1258 he must also have had something of a change
of heart; for, so far as we can see, until then his conscience had operated
selectively, to more effect in such private matters as the validity of his
marriage than in public affairs. Such a change of heart is what the
evidence tentatively suggests. Not only did his oath to the Provisions,
hesitantly taken and deeply pondered, create an almost oppressive sense
of new obligations, probably with concomitant effects on his devotional
life, but his will, too, testifies to the movement of his conscience into
hitherto uncolonised territory. This we shall consider shortly. He had
always been a pious man and we do not need to see him as being struck
down on the road to Damascus in 1258. But we do need to envisage his
sense of religious values being brought to bear on politics for the first
time.

This did not diminish his ardent concern for his own financial claims
or his willingness to forward them through the machinery of reform.
Indeed, we are moving into a period when his public principles and his
private interests begin to stand in striking juxtaposition to each other as
each is pressed more fiercely. The committee of twenty-four, authorised
to adjudicate at the Oxford parliament on Henry's debts to Montfort
and on the replacement of his fee by a land grant, had failed to act.
Pressure of business at Oxford is likely to have set aside all but the most
urgent matters of reform, and there was to be no full settlement of these
issues until 1259. Something was done, however, to offer at least the
prospect of the discharge of the king's debt. In April 1258 the annual
payments due for Eleanor's dower had been made good up to and
including Easter term 1256, leaving them £600 in arrears; but the
prompt payment of the £200 due at Easter 1258 at least ensured that
the debt grew no larger. More than this may have been paid but not yet
recorded, for the issue roll for Easter 1259 notes a payment of £186.10.2
prior to November 1258 for the dower of Michaelmas 1256.[58] Later in
the year significant attempts were made to clear the backlog of outstanding debt. On 4 November a writ of liberate for £200 was issued in
Montfort's favour 'in part payment of the king's debts to him' (though
the exchequer did not pay out the money until Easter 1259). Two days
later, on 6 November, the council promised him a further £200 at

---

[58] E.403/15A, 17A, 3115; above, p. 132.

Hilary 1259 and payment of the whole residue at the following Easter exchequer.[59]

These undertakings coincided in a remarkable way with a change in the treasurership. On 2 November Philip Lovel, treasurer since 1252 and a man with a bad reputation for corrupt and oppressive administration, was replaced by John Crakehall, archdeacon of Bedford. Lovel had held office in the years before 1258, when Montfort had been ineffectively pressing his claims, and had at one stage stood pledge for the payment of the king's debts to him.[60] Crakehall is likely to have been a much more congenial figure. He had been one of the closest friends of Grosseteste: his steward, his companion on his visit to Lyons in 1250, a witness to his dying, and the executor of his will. On one occasion Grosseteste had nominated him to settle a dispute between Montfort and the men of Leicester, and he had also received letters, some of spiritual advice, from Adam Marsh. He was thus very much a member of Grosseteste's entourage, one of a good number promoted during the reforming period through whom the bishop's influence was perpetuated.[61] Though there is little more than common friends and interests to connect him directly with Montfort, it seems likely that Montfort stood behind his promotion and that the immediate action in his favour which followed Crakehall's elevation, after months in which little had been done, was more than a coincidence. If he judged that he would receive more co-operation from Crakehall than he had from Lovel in the settlement of Henry's debts, he was probably right.

In the opening months of the reform movement, therefore, Montfort had identified himself absolutely with the reforming cause. But he had also done what he could to use these favourable circumstances in order to satisfy the grievances which had partly impelled him towards reform in the first place. He was not simply using reform as a means to his own ends. The commitment suggested by his routine activities on the council, by his awareness of the fearful obligations imposed on him by his oath, and by the evidence for his contribution to the keynote of moral idealism running through the reforms, all preclude such a facile conclusion. In pressing his own claims he was at best doing no more than seek for himself the justice which it was one purpose of the

---

[59] *CLR, 1251–60*, pp. 437, 441; E.403/3115; *CPR, 1258–66*, p. 3.
[60] Paris, v, pp. 714–15, 719–20; *CPR, 1258–66*, p. 1; above, pp. 136–7.
[61] *Robert Grosseteste*, ed. Callus, p. 225; below, pp. 251–2.

reformers to offer to all. At worst, however, his conduct was already beginning to cast doubt on his priorities. Were they with reform and the appeasement of his conscience – or with self-aggrandisement and the rectification of private wrongs? In the winter of 1258–59, during his time in France, these questions became still more insistent.

(B) MONTFORT IN FRANCE, NOVEMBER 1258–FEBRUARY 1259

In the autumn of 1258 two major pieces of public business still hung fire: the drafting of reforming legislation, beyond the general principles of the Provisions of Oxford, and the completion of the peace with France. Although both required Montfort's co-operation, the French peace took precedence. It had been arranged in June that the terms already settled should be published and ratified at a meeting between the two kings in November, but the barons' unwillingness to allow Henry to leave the country at that time meant that envoys had to be sent in his place. Those chosen were Montfort himself, Walter de Cantilupe, Richard of Gravesend, and Roger Bigod, earl of Norfolk. Montfort's participation, alone of those who had gone to France earlier in the summer, and in association with his two closest episcopal friends and a trusted magnate (who had named Montfort as his executor only a few months before), all suggest his controlling influence in Anglo-French affairs. If he was the council's natural choice as chief negotiator, he must also have recognised how much turned for himself on the treaty's demand for Eleanor's renunciation of her French claims. Yet neither Montfort's diplomatic expertise nor his personal stake in the embassy's outcome produced results. Because of Henry's absence Louis would not meet the English party; negotiations foundered; and Bigod had returned to England by 3 December and Cantilupe by early January.[62]

Montfort himself remained abroad, in Paris for some of the time and with his sons, Henry and Simon, and Richard of Gravesend for company. What he did there was unknown at home, but a handful of documents has survived among his family archives and those of the French Crown to reveal some of his preoccupations at this crucial stage in his reforming career. They show him concerned, not with reform, but with securing a lordship, making a will, and acknowledging a debt.

---

[62] Paris, v, pp. 720–1; N. H. Nicolas, *Testamenta Vetusta* (2 vols., London, 1826), i, pp. 48–9; *CPR, 1258–66*, p. 6; c.53/49, m. 5; Chaplais, 'Making of the Treaty of Paris', p. 242.

The lordship was that of Bigorre, already conferred upon Montfort by Esquivat de Chabanais in 1256, when Esquivat's control had been threatened by Gaston de Béarn. Bigorre now re-emerged once again as the object of his designs. On 22 November, in Paris, Esquivat regranted the county to Montfort by a second charter. Succeeding grants added other territories and promised Montfort two castles when he wished to receive them. Esquivat represented himself as unable to defend his interests from his enemies. But he was not under attack at the time, and since he soon tried to take back what he had given, it seems likely that he acted under duress or in the expectation of some momentarily tempting inducement. Perhaps the latter is more likely, since the sealing of the second territorial grant by Gravesend suggests that there was nothing sinister about these arrangements. Montfort's motives in resecuring what he apparently already held can be more easily surmised. He may have had in mind the Anglo-French agreement awaiting ratification, for this had left the question of feudal lordship over Bigorre to be decided at a later date. His own claims to lordship would be greatly enhanced if he had a firm and recent grant of title. But more important, and hitherto unnoticed, were the newly favourable terms of the 1258 grant. In 1256 Esquivat had offered the county to Montfort alone; now he gave it to Montfort 'and his heirs and assigns'. A grant vaguely cognisable as one for life had been unequivocally turned into one in fee, conferring rights on Montfort's heirs which he had consistently sought in England in order to compensate for the disproportionate share of his estate held for life only. We may suspect, more easily than we can prove, that one purpose in particular lay behind this vital amendment: the creation of an appanage for one of his sons, possibly for Henry, who would be given temporary control of Bigorre in 1259, as we shall see.[63] Bigorre may have been regarded as a new resource, to be laid under contribution in Montfort's efforts to endow a family too large for his inherited means.

The acquisition of Bigorre in fee suggests that private ambitions, family and territorial, remained central to Montfort's motivations in 1258. But if we turn to his other transactions in France we receive a different impression. On 1 January 1259 Montfort made his will, probably in Paris (Plate 9). Written in the hand of his son Henry, as the document tells us, the original remains among the debris of his family

---

[63] *Layettes*, iii, Nos. 4279, 4454–4456; Powicke, *King Henry III*, p. 224, n. 5; Ellis, 'Gaston de Béarn', pp. 396–7; below, pp. 183–4.

papers.[64] It was probably not his first, for the king had given him permission both in 1255 and in 1257 to make a will, and had promised that its execution should not be impeded by pretext of debts owed to him; but it is the only one to survive.[65] It has already been used in earlier chapters to show something of Montfort's relations with his wife, who was given charge of its execution, and with the ecclesiastical and baronial friends who were to advise her.[66] The terms of the will itself, however, have never received the attention they deserve. Three sections are especially revealing.

In the first Montfort called on his executors to pay his debts. This pious overture was a standard feature of medieval wills,[67] but in this case the language is unusually emphatic and intense. After stating that he regarded himself as most obliged to those who had served him, who were to be given priority in repayment, Montfort went on to say:

> It is my wish that those who make any claims on me be believed without difficulty, provided that they give such reasons to suggest that it is more likely that they are telling the truth than that they are lying, for it is my wish in the case of any uncertainty that the debt should be cleared on my behalf, whatever it may cost, so that I am freed from it, for I do not wish to remain in debt or under suspicion of debt to anyone.

The insistent wording, the willingness to exceed legal obligations, and the seemingly oppressive anxiety about meeting even questionable claims, all go well beyond the routine and unelaborated instructions of other thirteenth-century wills.[68]

Montfort's concerns here are remarkably reflected in another of his *acta* in France. On 2 December 1258, just a month before he made his will, he issued letters patent in Paris setting out the arrangements for the payment of a longstanding debt. The executors of Peter of Dreux, former count of Brittany, he said, had asserted that he owed the deceased count £333.6.8 sterling (500 marks). He did not wish to deny this, and had undertaken to pay £100 paris (about £22 sterling) to the nuns of St Antoine's, Paris, on whom the executors had conferred the

---

64 Printed in Bémont, *Montfort* (2nd edn), pp. 276–8, from BN MS Clairambault 1188, f. 82. It is characteristic of Bémont's quirks as a historian that he gave this engrossing document only twenty words of comment: ibid., p. 172. I am most grateful for the help of Miss E. M. Rutson and Professor W. Rothwell in translating the passages cited below.

65 *CPR, 1247–58*, pp. 399, 543.

66 Above, pp. 40, 63–4, 66, 80–1.

67 M. M. Sheehan, *The Will in Medieval England* (Toronto, 1963), pp. 155–6.

68 Compare, for example, the wills of William Longespee, earl of Salisbury, 1225 (*Rot. Litt. Claus.*, ii, p. 71), and of Hugh of Wells, bishop of Lincoln, 1233 (*Registrum Antiquissimum Lincoln*, ii, p. 73).

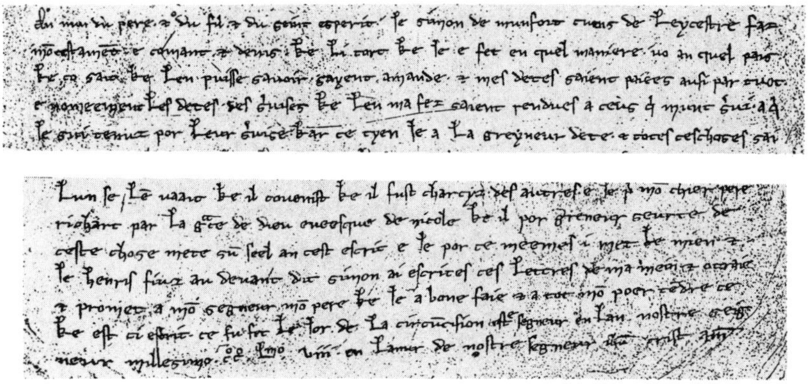

Plate 9. Montfort's will: opening and closing sections. In the penultimate sentence Henry de Montfort records his writing of the will.

debt, on 2 February every year until the debt had been cleared, save for the £160 paris (about £36 sterling) he had already paid them. The pledge was made at St Antoine's, in the presence of Henry and Simon, his sons, who consented to it.[69]

These long-term arrangements gave Montfort a good deal of leeway in clearing the debt, perhaps a sign of his lack of ready cash. But it remains striking that he should have entered into them at this particular time. Peter of Dreux had died eight years previously in 1250, returning from Louis IX's crusade, and the debt itself probably went back to the late 1230s, when Montfort's obligations to Peter had become part of a highly charged political quarrel with Henry.[70] Yet for all these years the debt had remained unpaid, to be taken in hand only on Montfort's visit to Paris in 1258–59, when his will suggests that the whole question of debt pressed hard on his conscience. The making over of the debt to the nuns of St Antoine's was in the nature of a religious benefaction, perhaps springing from his initiative; for his sister Petronilla had been abbess there in 1254 and probably was so still.[71] The lesson to be drawn here about Montfort's underlying beliefs throws an indirect and unsuspected light on his relations with Henry III, who owed *him* so much money at just this time. If he had come to regard debt almost as a sin, as the evidence suggests, it may be a little unjust to see his own

---

[69] BN MS Clairambault 1188, f. 10v. For the £ paris/sterling exchange rate, see Spufford, *Handbook of Medieval Exchange*, p. 209.

[70] *Peerage*, X, p. 803; above, pp. 24–5, 28.

[71] Above, pp. 101–2.

bitterly pursued claims against Henry entirely in terms of financial self-interest. They contained too an element of righteous anger. 'Who can believe that you are a Christian?', had he not once asked Henry already?[72]

Montfort's anxiety to see that his debts were paid was paralleled by a similar moral concern to make restitution to those whom he had wronged. Towards the end of his will he gave some revealing instructions to his executors. They were to see that 'the poor people of my land, are provided for from my goods, if they are not in serious default, and namely the cultivators (*gaaneuors*), whose goods I have had many times, and I suspect that in the eyes of some I have done harm'. In the will's final section he reverted more obliquely to the same topic, giving Eleanor power to dispose of his remaining possessions for the benefit of their children, 'so that thereby when they come to inherit the land they would have no need to make demands on their people'. Like provision for payment of debts, provision for reparations was a commonplace in contemporary wills,[73] but, again, Montfort's language here was far from commonplace. Its tone is at once introspective and remorseful, and its intention, set down in directions unmatched in other wills, partly to save his sons from the wrongs which he knew himself to have committed. Montfort had probably driven his peasant tenants hard, especially during his years in Gascony, when Paris several times spoke of burdens which office had forced him to impose on his own estates.[74] His financial difficulties prior to his journey to Rome in 1238 had occasioned similar measures. In part, these experiences may have lain behind his concern to see his children properly maintained, for their tenants would be among the gainers. The moral and religious earnestness which had often surfaced in his past now took this form of practical penitence.

We know nothing more of what Montfort did during his months in France and it may therefore be misleading to judge him by these few *acta*. Nevertheless, the evidence, so far as it goes, is consistent in suggesting a Montfort whose preoccupations were intensely personal and bound up with the future of himself and his family. His travelling abroad with his two elder sons, their consent to the payment of his debt, the possible reservation of Bigorre for Henry, Henry's role as the scribe of his father's will and prospectively as its chief executor (as the will

---

[72] Paris, v, p. 290; above, p. 87.
[73] Sheehan, *The Will*, pp. 260–1.
[74] Above, pp. 58, 113.

states) should Eleanor die, all demonstrate Montfort's desire to draw his sons into his activities. Overlapping with these tight family bonds and interests was Montfort's own sense of religious inquietude. It permeates his will, palpable not only in the will's provision for the payment of debts and restitution to tenants, but in Montfort's insistence that whichever members of his circle eventually came to execute the will – whether Eleanor or Henry or the three associates, Hugh Despenser, Peter de Montfort and Arnold du Bois – they should act with the counsel of Adam Marsh and Richard of Gravesend. It was above all the advice of his religious confidants, including one who had been as close to him as any man, by which Montfort set such store and which he invoked to guide his family and friends.

What then had happened to Montfort the reformer, who for some months before his departure for France had been at the centre of English politics? Only at one point, but a significant one, do Montfort's concerns in France interlock with those which had engaged him in England earlier in the year. His confession in his will that he had wronged 'the poor men of my land' and now wished to do right by them was a more personal expression of the public ideals of the reformers: of their promise to do justice to all, rich and poor, of the prospects for redress held out by Bigod's eyre, and of the barons' attendance to 'the clamour of the poor' which their representative reported to the pope, in an oration whose drafting Montfort had probably shared in before his departure.[75] As a guide to his convictions the evidence of the will is all the more valuable here for its inwardness. Meant for no eyes but those of his own circle, it confirms what we can deduce from the events of 1258 about his public attitudes. Concern for the grievances of the poor, stimulated by conscience, united Montfort the reformer with Montfort the testator.

Montfort's engagement with reform, however, was now more a matter of attitude than of his earlier involvement with its practicalities; and this remained true for much of 1259. His long absence was unexpected and left the baronial council 'mutilated', according to Paris: an interesting comment on Montfort's centrality in the reforming movement.[76] One sign of this mutilation may lie in the slow progress made towards new reforms. None were promulgated during his months

---

[75] *DBM*, pp. 260–1; *Ann. Burton*, p. 464. For Montfort's probable role in drafting the letters carried by the envoy who delivered the oration at the curia, see *CR, 1256–59*, p. 324; above, pp. 164, 166.
[76] Paris, v, p. 732.

away, and at the time of his return in February 1259 the most that had
been achieved was a short preliminary draft of future legislation.[77] More
immediately dangerous than the possible disillusionment of those non-
nobles who stood to benefit from change was the reformers' growing
isolation, to which Montfort's absence contributed. The return from
Germany in January 1259 of Richard of Cornwall, a man of formidable
power and intelligence, had led to fears that he would work for the
readmission of the Lusignans and the overthrow of reform.[78] The death
of John fitz Geoffrey in November, and Hugh Bigod's activity on eyre,
increasingly left Gloucester, the most royalist of the reformers, as the
dominant influence on the council. From November to February he was
the most frequent witness to Henry's charters.[79] Gloucester's main
quarrel had been with the Lusignans, who had now gone, and it is
doubtful if he had ever approved of the reform of baronial abuses
initiated in Bigod's eyre and targeted on such notoriously rapacious
landlords as himself. Without the counterweight of Montfort,
Gloucester's elevation threatened to qualify the whole baronial
enterprise.

It was no wonder then, as Paris says, that many were astonished by
Montfort's delaying abroad. No one knew the reason for it, not even this
best informed of all chroniclers.[80] That we know more than they did
about Montfort's doings in France is a reminder of how much of his life
and affairs was conducted out of the public eye. Private ambitions such
as the acquisition of Bigorre were concealed from those who surveyed
events in England and who saw only the public man of the Oxford
parliament or the baronial deputation to the Londoners. That is one
reason why even the most observant chroniclers, operating as they did
on the surface of things, can hardly tell the whole story about a man
whose ends and motives were often far from manifest.

(C) THE REFORMER IN RETREAT, FEBRUARY–DECEMBER 1259

Montfort had returned to England in time for the Candlemas parliament which opened on 9 February 1259.[81] Its session was dominated by
two issues, the French peace and the reform of baronial malpractices,

---

[77] Brand, 'Drafting of Legislation', p. 262.
[78] Paris, v, pp. 729–30.
[79] Paris, v, p. 724; c.53/49, m. 5.
[80] Paris, v, p. 737.
[81] Paris, v, p. 737. He witnessed royal charters on 10, 12 and 28 February: c.53/49, m. 5.

both of which concerned him closely. The formal renunciation of their French claims by Richard of Cornwall, Richard's son Henry, Edmund, the king's second son, and the king himself, during the course of the parliament, marked another step towards a permanent settlement, but it left the isolation of Montfort and Eleanor sharply exposed. With the exception of Edward, Henry's elder son, who had his own reasons for opposing the French peace, Eleanor was now the only party who had failed to renounce.[82] It was probably at this stage that her renunciation was first linked explicitly to the satisfaction of the Montforts' private grievances, for on 10 March Gloucester, Mansel and Walerand were authorised to settle with Montfort and Eleanor over Eleanor's dower and their other claims against the king, and to appoint arbitrators for this purpose.[83] The parliament thus saw the emergence of what were to be the main features of the coming months: the obstruction of a final peace by Eleanor's refusal to renounce, and Henry's attempts to find a way forward through arbitration on the couple's claims.

But Montfort was also involved more altruistically with the considerable reforming achievements of this parliament. These were embodied in two sets of proposals, both of them intended to limit seigneurial abuses. By the Ordinance of the Magnates, sealed on 22 February but not published until 28 March, the council of fifteen and the twelve representing the whole baronage agreed to place themselves under the same restraints as the king and his officials, freely permitting complaints against themselves and their bailiffs, allowing their misconduct to be corrected by the justiciar, and abiding by future legislation on such matters as suit of court.[84] By the Provisions of the Barons, probably already drafted in French when parliament opened but then amended and published in Latin as draft proposals only in March, the lord's right to demand suit was defined and restricted. These proposed regulations and others in the same text were to appear, somewhat revised, in the Provisions of Westminster later in the year.[85] Taken together, the Ordinance and the Provisions showed that the impetus of reform was by no means exhausted. They marked a radical extension of the commitment to correct baronial offences which had been evident from the start

---

[82] Chaplais, 'Making of the Treaty of Paris', pp. 243–4. For Edward's attitude, see below, pp. 193–4.

[83] *CPR, 1258–66*, p. 18.

[84] *DBM*, pp. 130–7. The title is conventional and has no contemporary warrant.

[85] *DBM*, pp. 122–31. But for a critique of this text, alternative versions, variant readings, and date, see Brand, 'Drafting of Legislation', pp. 251–64, 273–85.

of the movement, and a reaffirmation of the council's awareness of the needs and grievances of local society.

The progress made here almost certainly owed a good deal to Simon de Montfort. It was only a month since his sympathies for his own 'poor people' had been evinced in the making of his will, and it was only with his return to the centre of English politics that the momentum of change resumed after the long interval of his absence. He was present in parliament on 22 February when the Ordinance was enacted and when he and Gloucester appear to have sealed it on behalf of the council.[86] This was the tacit recognition of a dual leadership, but one about to be split apart by differences over the pace and content of reform. The long delay in publishing the Ordinance, and the amendment of the original French text of the Provisions of the Barons in ways favourable to magnate interests before its publication in March,[87] both point to opposition within parliament to the self-denying principles of what was proposed. Gloucester was its leader. According to Paris, his reluctance to proceed with reform, after parliament's conclusion about 26 February, led Montfort to turn on him. 'I do not want to live or have dealings with men so fickle and deceitful. For we have promised and sworn together to do what we are discussing.' Montfort then left England in disgust, while Gloucester was compelled by the other magnates to send his steward round his estates to offer redress according to the new reforms.[88]

That Paris was writing very close to these events (he died in June 1259)[89] gives his words a special value. He knew nothing of Montfort's subsequent reputation and was not looking back at his actions with a hagiographer's credulity. This quality makes his evidence the best we have for Montfort's wholehearted identification with the reforming cause and, less directly, for the continuities of principle linking him back, via his will, to the leading reformer of 1258. His oath remained a sacred obligation. Of course, his conduct was probably not wholly

---

[86] Richardson and Sayles, 'The Provisions of Oxford', p. 33. This seventeenth-century abstract of a now missing document refers to 'letters of alliance between them for the service of the king and the government of the kingdom', sealed on 22 February by Montfort and Gloucester for the council and Roger de Quincy, earl of Winchester, and Thomas de Gresley for the baronial twelve. The coincidence of the date, and of the council and the twelve as parties to the agreement, makes it unlikely that these 'letters' can be anything but the Ordinance of the Magnates.

[87] Brand, 'Drafting of Legislation', pp. 260–2.

[88] Paris, v, pp. 744–5; *Flores Hist.*, ii, pp. 424–5. Parliament must have ended by 26 February, when the king left Westminster for Windsor: *Baronial Plan*, p. 384.

[89] R. Vaughan, *Matthew Paris* (Cambridge, 1958), pp. 10–11.

disinterested. There are likely to have been social pressures from the lesser baronage and gentry which made progress with reform imperative and which are perceivable in the elaborate arrangements made for publishing the Ordinance in the counties;[90] and Montfort's own unresolved claims against the king may have given an edge to his enthusiasm. Nevertheless, it remains true that in the parliament of February 1259 his status as a reformer stood out unimpaired.

Yet, by one of those sudden shifts which make the themes of his career so difficult to reconcile, all this was to change, and for many months to come reform would no longer be Montfort's main concern. From March to October 1259 he was in France. Although Paris says that his quarrel with Gloucester was the occasion for his angry departure, he was in fact commissioned on 10 March to go abroad with Gloucester and other envoys to deal with the outstanding points which still delayed the treaty.[91] It was one of Montfort's advantages that he remained the indispensable negotiator, with opportunities as well as reasons for interposing his own claims between the wishes of both Henry and Louis for a final peace. For the rest of the year the two related questions of renunciation and claims became almost an obsession, dominating his view of both foreign and domestic affairs and driving the issue of reform to the margins of his vision. He knew that the need for Eleanor's renunciation gave him a chance which might never recur to extract from Henry far more than the king would previously have been prepared to give.

The embassy to France took place in April 1259. During its course Gloucester and Montfort once again quarrelled violently, this time over Eleanor's refusal to renounce.[92] The quarrel may have been precipitated by the demands which Montfort now put forward as preconditions for renunciation and which were taken home by the envoys when they returned in early May, leaving Montfort abroad. To judge by the concessions which were then made to Montfort, at a full meeting of the king and council in parliament,[93] they concerned the three great questions of Henry's financial obligations, the promised land grant, and Eleanor's dower. First, on 7 May Henry's debts to Montfort were fully paid, thus settling a dispute which had soured their relations

---

[90] *DBM*, pp. 135–7; cf. Brand, 'Drafting of Legislation', p. 259 and n. 92.
[91] *CPR, 1258–66*, p. 18.
[92] Paris, v, pp. 741, 745.
[93] *Flores Hist.*, ii, pp. 428–9; *Ann. Tewk.*, p. 167; *Ann. Wint.*, p. 98.

since Montfort's time in Gascony.[94] Next, on 20 May Montfort and Eleanor were granted nine manors in fulfilment of the king's undertaking to replace Montfort's £400 fee with land. From Montfort's standpoint the arrangement was not entirely satisfactory. The suspected status of the manors as royal demesne barred their outright alienation and so they were granted only temporarily (*in tenencia*), pending a permanent settlement.[95] Nevertheless, in essence he had acquired what he had energetically coveted and pursued since 1253. Eleanor's obduracy had been wholly responsible for this, for we know that she had refused to renounce until the lands had been granted. We will return later to this grant, since its protracted history offers an unusually clear view of Montfort's aims and methods.[96] Finally, there remained Eleanor's dower; and here again there was progress. On 24 May a team of arbitrators headed by Gloucester was authorised to decide whether Henry had compelled Eleanor to accept an inadequate dower settlement after the death of her first husband (as Montfort had first claimed in 1247) and whether the 500 marks p.a. granted by Henry in 1244 had been given as compensation for any shortfall in the dower or (as Montfort clearly believed) simply as a gift.[97] This was dangerous ground, soon to open and to leave an almost unbridgeable gulf between Henry, his sister and his brother-in-law.

At the end of May these terms were taken back to Montfort in France by the same envoys. More bargaining ensued. The settlement of the nine manors was amended in ways which were very much to Montfort's advantage, and it was agreed to nominate a fresh body of arbitrators to deal with the dower. When the lands had been handed over and the dower problem solved, Montfort and Eleanor agreed to renounce. On 21 July both these new terms and the articles of peace with France were formally accepted by the king and council; on 23 July Hereford, Norfolk and Philip Basset were appointed to arbitrate on the dower by 1 November; and on 28 July orders were issued for the transfer of the manors.[98] The conciliation of Montfort and the contingent progress

[94] *CPR, 1258–66*, p. 26; *CLR, 1251–60*, p. 460; *DBM*, pp. 196–7.

[95] *CChR, 1257–1300*, p. 18. For the meaning of *in tenencia*, see Stewart-Brown, 'End of the Norman Earldom of Chester', p. 26.

[96] *DBM*, pp. 196–7; *CPR, 1258–66*, p. 25; below, pp. 188–90.

[97] *CPR, 1258–66*, pp. 25–6; KB.26/159, mm. 2d, 3, 3d; above, pp. 52–4.

[98] *CPR, 1258–66*, pp. 25–6, 34–5; *Treaty R*, i, pp. 41–8; *DBM*, pp. 196–7, 200–1. Prior to Hereford's appointment, first Richard of Cornwall and then Gloucester had been named as arbitrators, but both were unwilling or unable to act: BN MS Clairambault 1188, f. 15.

towards a French peace seemed to be moving smoothly forward together.

This was far from being the case. The continuing dependence of the renunciation on an agreed dower settlement left Montfort and Eleanor with a trump card, which they now played for its full value. It was probably in late July that the three arbitrators received a written statement of the couple's demands. They claimed that Eleanor's dower in Ireland and west Wales was worth, not the 600 marks a year which the king had been paying her, but instead 2,000 marks; they claimed arrears of the 1,400 marks p.a. deficit for the previous twenty-six years, amounting to 36,400 marks; and for the future they claimed either the full 2,000 marks a year or the dower lands themselves.[99] Henry's reaction to these modest proposals must have been one of consternation. He could not remotely meet them. He had neither the money to pay so vast a sum nor, if the claim to the dower itself were to be pressed, the ability to ensure that the numerous Marshal heirs who held the lands would disgorge. The claim threatened all who had benefited from the division of the Marshal lands in 1246, including two of the reforming earls, Gloucester and Norfolk; but, more immediately, it threatened the Anglo-French peace. Henry's response was to try to steer round this obstacle. On 30 July he sent to France a version of the treaty drafted in May, and no doubt kept in reserve for just such an emergency, which omitted the clauses providing for Eleanor's renunciation. At the same time he probably offered to indemnify Louis against any claims which Eleanor might subsequently make to the French lands.[100] Henry clearly had reason to think that this new arrangement would be acceptable, for at the end of August he was preparing to cross to France for the personal meeting with Louis necessary for the final ratification of the treaty. In the event, however, the visit was suddenly cancelled when Henry received secret news from France.[101] It is likely that Louis had refused to accept the new terms and possible that he had done so at the prompting of Montfort.

By this time the relationship between Henry and Montfort had been further complicated by the recurrence of an old issue: the affairs of Bigorre. After he had been granted Bigorre in fee by Esquivat de Chabanais in November 1258, Montfort had conducted himself as the

99 *Treaty R*, i, p. 48; Carpenter, 'The Lord Edward's Oath', p. 231.
100 *CPR, 1258–66*, p. 25; *Treaty R*, i, pp. 40, 43; Chaplais, 'Making of the Treaty of Paris', pp. 244–5.
101 *Flores Hist.*, ii, pp. 431–2.

master of the county, appointing his cousin Philip as his lieutenant there in April 1259. The son of Simon's uncle Guy, Philip already held a southern lordship and was an obvious choice as custodian. But because the feudal suzerainty over Bigorre was to be decided in the forthcoming Anglo-French settlement, Henry, too, was anxious to acquire the county, as he had been once before in 1253. His anxiety gave Montfort a chance to strike a characteristically hard bargain, in negotiations which revealed something more of his ambitions for his family. On 6 July 1259 Henry de Montfort was empowered by his father to surrender Bigorre to the king and to receive it back as his tenant: the best evidence we have for the probability already mentioned that Montfort had all along intended Bigorre as an appanage for his eldest son. On 27 July, however, this arrangement was either superseded or supplemented by a new agreement between Montfort and the king. Bigorre was now to be leased to Henry III for seven years; Henry was to pay Montfort £1,000 by 1 November for his earlier costs incurred in defending the county; failure to pay was to nullify the agreement; and within the seven-year term Montfort was to be provided with other lands of an equivalent value in exchange for Bigorre. Failing this, the county would revert to Montfort and his heirs at the end of the term. It may have been intended that Henry de Montfort should remain as the king's sub-tenant. Montfort's ultimate aims here are not quite clear. But it looks as if he saw a chance to make more money from the king, in return for the leasing out of a possession which cannot have been easy for him to exploit, and with the further possibility of extracting land from Henry, perhaps in some more convenient location and perhaps for the benefit of his eldest son. The king's intense concern over the future treaty, very evident in his later bitter recriminations at Montfort's obstruction of it, had led him to lay himself under yet more obligations to his unrelenting brother-in-law.[102]

There matters rested until 13 October, when the Michaelmas parliament met at Westminster. That it was to be the focus for reforming aspirations, like the earlier parliaments of June and October 1258 and February 1259, was shown at the outset in a famous episode. When parliament opened, the 'community of the bachelors of England', probably the knights for whose attendance at parliament this is the only

---

[102] *Layettes*, iii, No. 4476; *Treaty R*, i, pp. 49–51; Labarge, *Montfort*, p. 137; Ellis, 'Gaston de Béarn', pp. 397–9. The £1,000 was intended as a single payment and not as an annual rent for seven years, as is sometimes stated (e.g. *DBM*, pp. 198–9, n. 12).

evidence, protested to the Lord Edward and to Gloucester and the other councillors that although the king had submitted to reform, the barons had as yet done nothing for the common good. They may have had in mind the slow progress of reform in the preceding months, the effective failure of Bigod's eyre, continuing through the summer, to deal with the offences of magnates and their officials, and the unfulfilled promises made in the decrees published in March. Their protest was taken up by Edward, who swore to keep the oath to reform which he had taken at Oxford in 1258; and it expedited the promulgation of the last great reforming act, the Provisions of Westminster, published on 24 October. These gave legislative authority, sometimes in amended form, to the limitations on suit of court set out in the earlier Provisions of the Barons, abolished many of the abuses practised by the eyre in the years before 1258, and dealt with other grievances – distraint, the sheriff's tourn, exemption from jury service – which mattered greatly to local society. The Provisions were to be enforced by a new eyre, on which the councillors were to be represented and for which commissions were issued in November.[103] As a comprehensive set of legal and administrative enactments, backed by the means for their implementation, the Provisions of Westminster marked the zenith of the reforming movement. Together with all the earlier enactments since June 1258, they came to be known, collectively and confusingly, as the 'Provisions of Oxford'.[104]

For all his public allegiance to the Provisions, Montfort seems to have kept entirely aloof from the practicalities of reform in this parliament. Returning to England for the first time since March 1259, he was present in parliament on 13 October, when he and the other councillors swore to accept a form of Anglo-French peace which omitted the clause demanding Eleanor's renunciation. By some means or other, possibly on the understanding that the renunciation would be dealt with in a separate document, Louis IX had been persuaded to agree to the amended treaty proposed earlier by Henry. As a councillor Montfort had no option but to accept this.[105] The new treaty, however, deprived him of his most powerful bargaining counter, and it was probably at this stage that he played the one card which remained to him: from the

---

[103] *Ann. Burton*, pp. 471–84; *DBM*, pp. 136–65; *Baronial Plan*, pp. 145–65. For the text of the Provisions, see Brand, 'Drafting of Legislation', pp. 265–70.

[104] Jacob, *Studies*, pp. 121–5.

[105] *Layettes*, iii, No. 4554; Chaplais, 'Making of the Treaty of Paris', pp. 246–7; Carpenter, 'The Lord Edward's Oath', p. 230.

French envoys who were present in parliament he demanded Eleanor's share in all King John's lost territories.[106] To refuse to renounce a claim, Montfort's previous tactic, was one thing; to activate that claim was quite another. It was now once again imperative for Louis to secure Eleanor's renunciation, allowing Montfort once again to raise the whole issue of the dower. He had never been more boldly or more blatantly obstructive.

That the dower remained uppermost in his mind is suggested by the agreement with Edward which he made on 15 October, during the course of the parliament. This has recently been published and reinterpreted by Dr David Carpenter. By it, Edward swore to aid and counsel Montfort, to maintain the baronial enterprise (meaning the reform movement), to make war on no one concerned with that enterprise except for those who refused to abide by 'the award of the king's court', and to compel any opponents of this award to accept it.[107] This agreement is full of obscurities and uncertainties. But it seems likely that its purpose was both to bind Edward to reform and to ensure his support against any who might refuse to accept the decision of the arbitrators ('the award of the king's court') which was pending on the question of Eleanor's dower.[108]

The prominence given to reform in this document, its least ambiguous feature, shows that Montfort remained foursquare behind the baronial movement. But the brevity of his visit to England can have allowed him to contribute little to its development. By 19 October, within four days of his agreement with Edward, he had returned to France; he was certainly absent when the Provisions were published on 24 October;[109] and the chronicle account of the bachelors' protest suggests that it was now Gloucester, not Montfort, who was seen as the leading councillor. At this stage his commitment to reform was to a principle sanctified by an oath rather than to the particular details of grievances and remedies. His energies were reserved for his private affairs.

After the Westminster parliament it looked as though the dower problem would prove insoluble. This was because Montfort seemed determined to make it so. The arbitration due by 1 November was never

---

[106] *DBM*, pp. 204–5; *Layettes*, iii, No. 4555; Carpenter, 'The Lord Edward's Oath', p. 230.
[107] Carpenter, 'The Lord Edward's Oath', p. 236.
[108] Carpenter, 'The Lord Edward's Oath', pp. 229–35.
[109] *Recueil des Historiens des Gaules*, 23 (Paris, 1894), p. 467; *DBM*, pp. 204–5 (cl. 26), 150–1 (cl. 4); *CR, 1256–59*, p. 459.

published, and Henry was later to accuse Montfort of having used his influence to prevent publication: an accusation that Montfort circumvented rather than denied.[110] Presumably he had discovered the terms of the award to be unfavourable. This would hardly have been surprising, since the leading arbitrator, the earl of Norfolk, was among the Marshal coheirs whose interests would have been upset by the territorial settlement of the dower which Montfort saw as one way forward.[111] On one reading of the evidence, he had earlier sought Edward's support for the arbitration, presumably in advance of the verdict. Now, when the verdict was known, he appears to have tried to suppress it. If there was consistency here, it lay only in the priority given throughout to Montfort's own interests.

Despite these unresolved questions, Henry crossed to France in mid November for the meeting with Louis necessary for the treaty's ratification and pending for so long. The two kings met on 24 November, but Montfort's continuing refusal to renounce held up proceedings for eight days or more. It was Louis himself who broke the deadlock by proposing that if the renunciations were made, 15,000 marks of the money due to Henry under the terms of the treaty should be withheld in France until the personal disputes between Montfort, Eleanor and Henry had been settled.[112] Montfort's acceptance of these terms, grudgingly given, was perhaps not so surprising as it may seem. He had nothing to gain from the old arbitration, which had in any case expired. His longstanding respect and affection for Louis were perhaps enhanced by the valuable fief-rent, worth some £110 sterling a year, which Louis may now have offered to him in order to hasten his compliance.[113] He must also have been under considerable pressure from the two kings and their councillors to give way: pressure perhaps brought to bear especially by Eudes Rigaud, archbishop of Rouen, Louis's friend and Montfort's, who had acted as Louis's representative in the making of the treaty. It was Eudes who now, on 3 December, formally read it aloud to a great assembly convened 'in the apple orchard of the king of France'.[114] So, at last, agreement of a kind had been reached. On

---

[110] *DBM*, pp. 200–3.

[111] Carpenter, 'The Lord Edward's Oath', pp. 232–3.

[112] *Reg. of Eudes of Rouen*, ed. O'Sullivan, p. 396; *DBM*, pp. 202–3; *CPR, 1258–66*, pp. 106–7.

[113] BN MS Clairambault 1188, f. 25v; *Les Olim*, ed. A. Beugnot (3 vols. in 4, Paris, 1839–44), i, p. 872. The date of Louis's grant is not known, but Bémont, *Montfort* (1st edn), p. 76, associates it with the negotiations of December 1259.

[114] Chaplais, 'Making of the Treaty of Paris', pp. 239, n. 9, 240, 242, n. 2, 245, n. 4; *Reg. of Eudes of Rouen*, ed. O'Sullivan, pp. 396–7.

4 December Eleanor made her renunciation, Montfort renounced any claims which he still had to the French lands of his father and brother, Henry did homage for Gascony, and the treaty was published.[115] One stage of Montfort's quarrel with Henry had closed and another was about to begin.

At one level Montfort's actions in 1259 are easily defensible. He was merely pursuing his undoubted rights. Henry owed him money, his fee had not been turned into land, as he had been promised, and Eleanor's dower settlement fell well short of the widow's third. In his demand for what was due in these matters, 'he did no wrong'; it was his insistent answer to Henry's later charges arising out of these protracted disputes.[116] Rights merged easily into duties, their defence a matter of familial obligation rather than the mere pursuit of profit. Yet this would be to hold a very narrow view of Montfort's activities, though it was perhaps his own view. He had taken every advantage of Henry's difficulties in order to exact the maximum possible from the king. When Henry had paid his debts and given him land – no small achievement at a time of financial stringency – he had immediately made fresh demands over the dower, claiming much more than was due[117] and more than Henry could afford to pay. In his dealings with Henry there was the same lack of scruple and of self-restraint evident at other times in his career, notably during his years in Gascony. Over the decades character and actions were all of a piece.

The grant of the nine manors in satisfaction of his £400 fee illustrates his aims and methods particularly well. Two factors make the history of this grant especially striking: the relentless extension of Montfort's demands and the king's offers, and the dubious propriety of his receiving the land in the first place. The initial temporary grant of the manors, made on 20 May 1259, was subsequently defined more precisely as part of the bargaining between Montfort, Eleanor and the king's envoys in France. The couple were very much the gainers. If the lands were found to be royal demesne, then they were to retain them until they could be exchanged for the first escheats falling into the king's hands; if they were too dispersed for easy management, then they were to have the option of surrendering them and once again taking cash

---

[115] Chaplais, 'Making of the Treaty of Paris', p. 247.
[116] *DBM*, pp. 198–9, 202–5.
[117] Above, pp. 52–3.

from the county revenues; and so on.[118] Then, on 27 July, after an enquiry into the status of the lands, the only non-demesne manor was granted outright and another Yorkshire manor was added on lease, to bring the grant up to an estimated £400.[119] After the Westminster parliament provision was made for the manors to be extended in the presence of the earl's bailiffs, so that any shortfall could be made good and any surplus revert to the king. If this had not been done by Easter 1259, then the manors were to remain with Montfort and Eleanor, to be held in fee by them and their heirs.[120] Henry clearly suspected that the manors were worth far more than their nominal value, for he wrote from France in February 1260 to press for completion of the extent, saying that he feared 'grave disinheritance and no little expense' if this was not done.[121] The extent was not delivered into the exchequer, however, until October 1262,[122] and the manors remained in Montfort's hands until his death at Evesham.

Yet it was not only the hardness of the bargain that made these grants morally questionable. The councillor's oath of 1257 had forbidden any councillor to receive or consent to any grant from the demesne. In 1260 Henry raised this point when he accused Montfort of accepting these manors contrary to his oath. 'He and others of the council swore an oath', replied Montfort, ' . . . that, *so far as he can remember it*, the ancient demesne of the crown should not be alienated'. Montfort's partial lapse of memory gives us a rare opportunity to spot a medieval magnate being disingenuous. In any case, he went on to say, since the land was held impermanently, *in tenencia*, its tenure was not contrary to his oath. This bordered on casuistry. Henry clearly thought differently, and Montfort's curious way of speaking as though the lands had been assigned to Eleanor was perhaps a legalistic way of disowning any grant to himself in the interests of a tender conscience.[123] Certainly others thought the grant difficult to justify, for Peter of Savoy and John Mansel confirmed it as members of the council only 'saving our oath to the king concerning his demesnes'.[124] The actual transfer of the lands to Montfort's bailiffs in July and August 1259 was marked in some cases by

---

[118] *CChR, 1257–1300*, p. 18; *Treaty R*, i, pp. 45–6.
[119] E.368/35, m. 3; *CChR, 1257–1300*, p. 20.
[120] *CPR, 1258–66*, p. 46.
[121] *CR, 1259–61*, pp. 237–8.
[122] E.403/18; E.159/37, m. 3d.
[123] *Ann. Burton*, p. 396; *DBM*, pp. 196–9.
[124] *Treaty R*, i, p. 46.

lawless seizures of corn and stock belonging to the occupiers which set another sort of moral question mark over the whole episode.[125] These were acts opposed to the principles of legality, conciliation and self-limitation which the reformers were seeking to promote.

Montfort's whole engagement with reform at this time was very slight. He had been away in France almost continuously from early November 1258 to early January 1260, returning only briefly for the parliaments of February and October 1259. No doubt there was much to keep him abroad: his exposition of his family claims to Louis IX, his disgust at what he regarded as Gloucester's breach of his obligations, and his participation in the agreeable social life of Paris, Normandy and the court. He was present in Paris in June 1259 when a contract was drawn up for the marriage of Amicia de Courtenay, his grand-niece, to Robert of Artois, Louis's nephew.[126] Clearly in favour with Louis, he was residing at the royal castle of Neaufles in upper Normandy when Eudes Rigaud called there for dinner on 19 August.[127] On 19 October, five days before the publication of the Provisions of Westminster, he was in Louis's company at Evreux for the consecration of the new bishop, and in the following month he partnered his cousin Philip in directing a benefaction towards the nuns of Porrois.[128] In Paris he must have been on good terms with the prior of the Paris Dominicans, who acted for him in his dealings with Henry.[129] He was present in his ancestral *pays*, among family and friends, while in England he had allies and agents enough to guard his interests. There was one significant, and perhaps morally debilitating, departure from his circle, for Adam Marsh died on 18 November 1259.[130] But others remained. It seems to have been his close associates on the council, Walter de Cantilupe, Peter de Montfort and Richard de Grey, who prevented the dower arbitration from going forward, and it was his steward, Richard de Havering, who collected the Michaelmas dower payment from the exchequer.[131] What was there to return for?

---

[125] *CR, 1256–59*, pp. 426, 433.

[126] *Cart. Normand*, ed. Delisle, No. 618. Amicia was the daughter of Petronilla de Courtenay, whose mother Amicia, the founder of Montargis, was Montfort's sister: see *Gallia Christiana*, xii (Paris, 1770), p. 256.

[127] *Reg. of Eudes of Rouen*, ed. O'Sullivan, p. 388. For Neaufles as a royal castle, see *Cart. Normand*, ed. Delisle, No. 209, and *Comptes Royaux (1285–1311)*, ed. R. Fawtier, ii (Paris, 1954), Nos. 16028, 16029.

[128] *Recueil des Historiens des Gaules*, 23, p. 467; *Cart. Porrois*, ed. de Dion, pp. 260–1; above, p. 102.

[129] *DBM*, pp. 200–1.

[130] Lawrence, 'Letters of Adam Marsh', p. 229.

[131] *DBM*, pp. 200–1; E.403/18.

The answer, of course, was reform. Montfort's conduct disabled the reform movement in several different ways. Paris's remark about the anxieties caused by his briefer disappearance in the winter of 1258–59 shows the value placed on him: he was a man of vigorous sagacity, with an almost unrivalled experience of public life and military affairs. His preoccupation with his own interests divided him from the council at home, depriving the councillors of his advice and leadership, and leading them to spend much time on his conciliation. Almost every act designed to placate Montfort, from the improved terms for the grant of manors in July to the agreement over Bigorre and the final arrangements for the renunciation in Paris in December, was sanctioned by the council.[132] Its members were as concerned as Henry to satisfy Montfort; yet his demands must have severely tried their patience and public-spiritedness, not least because they threatened a wide range of interests. The grant of manors, for example, had meant the dispossession of some powerful Savoyards and entailed the diversion of future escheats to Montfort and Eleanor; while the demand for Eleanor's dower lands was potentially much more explosive, as we have seen.[133]

Montfort had jeopardised these private interests without offering any compensating public services. He had taken no share in the drudgery of reform: the regular meetings of the council, the technical discussions which must have preceded the Provisions of Westminster, the redress of grievances in the shires. At this time he was quite detached from the local forces favouring change which he was later to exploit. Perhaps most important of all, his withdrawal from the political scene in order to pursue his own claims made possible the re-emergence of Gloucester as the dominant force on the council and irrevocably alienated the king. After Hugh Bigod, the justiciar, Gloucester and Mansel were the most frequent charter witnesses in the summer and autumn of 1259;[134] and Gloucester, the enemy of some of the essentials of the reform movement, increasingly enjoyed Henry's confidence, as events were to show. To Henry, Montfort's bad faith and obstructiveness, as the king saw them, were unforgivable, and a source of continuing bitterness. Montfort's conduct had made its own contribution to the factional conflicts which were to characterise the next two years.

---

[132] *CChR, 1257–1300*, p. 20; *Treaty R*, pp. 44–7, 51; *DBM*, p. 203.
[133] Ridgeway, 'Foreign Favourites', p. 609; H. Ridgeway, 'The Politics of the English Royal Court, 1247–65, with Special Reference to the Role of Aliens' (Oxford D.Phil. thesis, 1983), pp. 226–7, 331.
[134] c.53/49, mm. 1–4; c.53/50, m. 6.

CHAPTER 6

The decline of the reform movement, 1260–63

(A) PARTIES AND PRINCIPLES: MONTFORT IN ENGLAND, 1260

For Montfort the Treaty of Paris marked a great defeat. In the long term it threatened to push him to the margin of affairs. Prior to 1259 he had largely owed his position at Henry's court to his military and diplomatic skills and to his standing in two countries whose relations were volatile. After 1259 neither his skills nor his standing had the same value for Henry. The Anglo-French peace meant that he was no longer likely to be summoned to the rescue, as he had been in Poitou in 1242 and in Gascony in 1253, nor to remain the essential go-between. If he lost bargaining power in this direction, he lost far more by the renunciations which he and Eleanor had made, for he now lacked his best means of securing a favourable settlement on the dower issue. Louis's withholding of 15,000 marks until the dispute had been settled merely antagonised Henry without offering much to Montfort.[1] The new arbitrating committee appears once again to have comprised Hereford, Norfolk and Philip Basset, men whose verdict he had already rejected, and the two-year period set for their arbitration stretched far into the future.[2] Whatever grandiose expectations Montfort and Eleanor may once have entertained of a settlement worth thousands of marks in cash or land had now gone up in smoke.

Montfort's actions in the months following the treaty show the extent to which his grievances had been intensified by their effective dismissal. They were those of an angry and disappointed man. He left France in a temper, probably in late December 1259, offending the king by his failure to take leave of him.[3] Henry clearly thought that he was out to make trouble, for on 20 December he wrote home to Hugh Bigod,

[1] DBM, pp. 202–3.
[2] CPR, 1258–66, pp. 106–7; CR, 1259–61, p. 269; above, pp. 182, 186–7.
[3] DBM, pp. 206–7.

the justiciar, ordering him to arrest newcomers who arrived at the ports armed and unauthorised.[4] The earl's opportunity came when, in late January, Henry forbade the meeting of the Candlemas parliament until after his return to England. Unfinished business in France, which delayed his departure, and an unexpected Welsh attack on the castle of Builth in the marches, provided him with a pretext for overriding the requirement in the Provisions that one of the three annual parliaments should be held at Candlemas on 2 February.[5] This was a deliberate challenge to the Provisions, intended to put the council on the defensive and to prevent its consultation with the wider body of magnates which the reformers had seen as one of the main purposes of parliament. It was taken up by Montfort. Disregarding the king's prohibition, he arrived in London on 2 February to hold the parliament, only to be countered by the justiciar's intervention to adjourn the meeting.[6]

Montfort's defiance of the king exacerbated divisions among the reformers which Henry had initiated, cleverly and purposely, at his departure. He had taken with him to France the most royalist of the councillors: Gloucester, Mansel, Peter of Savoy, and William de Fors, earl of Albemarle. Robert Walerand, another consistent royalist, was also with the court. The two Montfortians, Richard de Grey and Peter de Montfort, who had accompanied Henry, probably returned home with their leader about the turn of the year. Together with Walter de Cantilupe, they are likely to have been among the 'other sound councillors' who, according to Montfort, supported his attempt to hold the Candlemas parliament.[7] Between these two groups stood the remaining 'home' councillors, of whom Hugh Bigod, his brother the earl of Norfolk, and Philip Basset, were the most active. To judge by Bigod's compliance with Henry's demand for the postponement of parliament, he at least was not prepared to put his allegiance to the Provisions above that to the king.

If Montfort's closest supporters were his personal friends, his most powerful ally, Edward, the king's son, was outside the council. Although Edward's actions since the start of the reform movement had not been entirely consistent, they had essentially been guided by four

---

[4] *CR, 1259–61*, pp. 228, 259.
[5] *CR*, pp. 235, 267–8; *DBM*, pp. 164–9, 110–11.
[6] *DBM*, pp. 206–7.
[7] *DBM*, pp. 170–1, 206–7; *Baronial Plan*, pp. 214–15.

principles.[8] First, he wished to free himself from the tutelage imposed by his father and maintained by the council, and in particular to have the free disposition of his lands, castles and offices. Second, he was opposed to the French peace, which he probably saw as depriving him of his hereditary rights and weakening his control of his Gascon appanage. Third, he detested the earl of Gloucester, who favoured peace with France and who had a claim, vigorously pursued, to Edward's castle at Bristol.[9] Fourth, he had a genuine, if recent, attachment to the reforming cause. It had been seen both in the desire which he expressed privately (and thus all the more tellingly), in a writ of August 1259 to one of his officials, to do justice to all men, and in his public response to the bachelors in the subsequent October parliament.[10] In the winter of 1259–60 all four of these principles set him against his father and confirmed the alliance with Montfort already clinched by the agreement which they had made in the previous October. Like his new ally, Montfort, too, was the opponent of Gloucester, the advocate of reform, and the loser from the French treaty.

Whatever his relative isolation from his fellow councillors, Montfort's partnership with Edward made him a force in politics. Edward had recently come to command a large retinue of young nobles and knights,[11] whose services might be essential in the military conflict for which both sides seemed to be preparing in the tense months following the aborted parliament. Henry continued to delay abroad, ostentatiously deferring to the home council on matters concerning the implementation of the treaty, but continuing to forbid a parliament during his absence and, on 19 February, to prohibit any new reforms.[12] By March both sides were raising troops.[13] Gloucester, sent to England to report on events, was probably responsible for spreading malicious rumours that Edward was planning to dethrone his father in a military coup.[14] Some of the preparations put in hand for Henry's return, now

[8] For a general discussion, see Carpenter, 'The Lord Edward's Oath'; Ridgeway, 'The Lord Edward and the Provisions of Oxford (1258)', pp. 88–99; and Ridgeway, 'Politics of the English Royal Court', pp. 336–46.

[9] *Ger. Cant.*, ii, pp. 209–10; Altschul, *A Baronial Family*, pp. 26–8, 77, 82–3; *Baronial Plan*, pp. 193, 336–46.

[10] Carpenter, 'The Lord Edward's Oath', pp. 235–7.

[11] Ridgeway, 'The Lord Edward and the Provisions of Oxford (1258)', pp. 97–8; Prestwich, *Edward I*, p. 27.

[12] *DBM*, pp. 164–9, 172–3.

[13] *CR, 1259–61*, pp. 250–1, 253–4, 277, 282–3; *CPR, 1258–66*, p. 121.

[14] *Flores Hist.*, ii, pp. 446–8; *Ann. Dun.*, p. 214; *Wykes*, pp. 123–4; *Baronial Plan*, p. 228, n. 11.

seemingly essential for the preservation of his authority, give a clear view of the disposition of the parties. When Henry wrote to the justiciar from St Omer on 27 March, ordering him to summon the tenants-in-chief and their knights to London on 27 April, the omissions from the list partly identified those whom he could not trust: Montfort himself, the earl of Hereford, Peter de Montfort and Richard de Grey, a group of Edward's supporters comprising Roger Mortimer, Roger Clifford, Hamo Lestrange and Roger Leyburn, and all the bishops save Salisbury, Exeter and Norwich.[15] Despite Henry's earlier prohibition, a parliament met in London in April, but Richard of Cornwall's securing of the city for the king, and the general unwillingness to resort to arms, allowed Henry to return, with a large force of foreign mercenaries, on 23 April. A full reconciliation between Edward and Henry followed in early May, and a settlement between Edward and Gloucester, devised by Richard of Cornwall, in the following month.[16]

Montfort's underlying motives throughout this period of confrontation are hard to be sure about. He himself later spoke as though he had been solely concerned to uphold the Provisions, justifying in those terms both his attempt to hold the Candlemas parliament and his military preparations to defend 'the common enterprise'.[17] This was a plausible line to take. Henry's deliberate attempts to subvert reform by delaying abroad, forbidding parliaments in his absence, and cultivating the loyalties of the royalist councillors gave Montfort a platform on which to campaign; and his enjoyment of the firm support of the bishop of Worcester and the probable support of most of the other bishops suggests that his cause could convincingly be presented as a moral one. Cantilupe went so far as to lend money to Edward, possibly to pay for troops.[18] Yet to others Montfort must have seemed an unpersuasive advocate of reform. Though he may, for all we know, have continued to proclaim his enthusiasm for reform, neither in the previous year nor in the weeks between his return to England and the Candlemas parliament had he engaged himself with its implementation. In the reforming work of the council around midwinter 1259–60 – the first sessions of the new eyre to enforce the Provisions of Westminster, the annual change of

---

[15] *CR, 1259–61*, pp. 157–8; *DBM*, pp. 180–2; *Baronial Plan*, p. 226.

[16] *Baronial Plan*, pp. 229–33.

[17] *DBM*, pp. 206–9.

[18] c.61/4, m. 3. Montfort cannot have enjoyed the support of all the bishops whom Henry failed to summon, for some, such as Peter of Aigueblanche (of Hereford) and Robert Chaury (Carlisle) were firm royalists. I am very grateful to Dr Margaret Howell for pointing this out to me.

sheriffs according to the Provisions, the conciliar supervision of justice and finance – he had taken no apparent part.[19] His alliance with Edward may have seemed to compromise his reforming principles in a more positive way, for the reinforcements which Edward was intending to bring into England included his Lusignan uncles, whose expulsion had been one of the reformers' earliest acts. Montfort himself had reached some agreement with William de Valence during his time in Paris. When Henry later charged him with this breach of principle, he was careful to note in his reply that their pact concerned only their private quarrel (perhaps over Pembroke) and not 'the common provision'.[20] Yet this episode, whatever its obscurities, suggested that he was no longer irreconcilably opposed to the chief enemy of the baronial council.

These factors make it difficult to decide whether Montfort's combative stance owed more to his personal disappointments than to his principles. His appeal to the Provisions on the holding of the Candlemas parliament, coming as it did shortly after his defeat in the Treaty of Paris, invites comparison with a later occasion in 1262, when he would again spring to the defence of the Provisions immediately after his own claims had been thwarted.[21] This is not to say that his enthusiasm for reform necessarily varied with the progress of those claims; but certainly the grievances which had always fuelled his principles did so with a particular intensity in the months after the treaty. With his central grievance over Eleanor's dower still unsatisfied, his deepening antagonism towards the king now begins to provide one of the keys to his conduct, as it would continue to do until the end of his life. The negotiations and arbitrations through which he and Eleanor had pursued their claims against Henry in 1259 had given way to outright opposition. He may indeed have tried to obstruct the arbitration proposed in the treaty, knowing that it offered him no possible gain. A letter to which Henry wrote to him on 5 February 1260 ordering him to give up to Bigod and Basset the letters of obligation issued by the king and the three arbitrators, which he was retaining, suggests that he was blocking Henry's attempts to initiate the new arbitration.[22] For the rest of the year nothing more would be heard of it.

---

[19] *DBM*, pp. 164–5; *CR, 1259–61*, p. 23; D. Crook, *Records of the General Eyre* (London, HMSO, 1982), pp. 189–90; *Baronial Plan*, pp. 196–212.

[20] *CR, 1259–61*, pp. 138, 285–6; *CPR, 1258–66*, p. 68; *DBM*, pp. 204–5.

[21] Below, p. 219.

[22] *CR, 1259–61*, p. 269.

Force, however, offered no alternative way forward, either for Montfort's principles or for his grievances. His alliances, his attempts to bring in troops, his readiness to resort to arms, all emphasised the extent to which he and Edward were the leaders of a militant faction. His separation from most of the other councillors was reinforced by his autocratic attempts to dictate to the justiciar: defying Bigod's prohibition of the Candlemas parliament, and telling him to refuse Henry the money he had requested and to order the king not to return with foreign troops.[23] Cautious men, and averse to such extremism, the councillors allowed Henry to take advantage of their passivity. By method and temperament, as in so much else, Montfort stood out among them as a dangerous maverick.

Henry's victorious return did not leave Montfort entirely isolated. Despite Edward's reconciliation with his father, Montfort still kept company with him: together with Walter de Cantilupe and Peter de Montfort, he witnessed one of Edward's charters at Mortlake on 13 May.[24] Nevertheless, Henry now felt strong enough to go for revenge and proposed to put Montfort on trial. In agreeing to this, Montfort asked only for the absence of five men, his enemies and Edward's, from the panel of judges; whereupon Gloucester, concerned about the charges which he might face, asked for the postponement of the trial until the coming July parliament.[25] Montfort's five enemies are likely to have included Gloucester, Mansel, Peter of Savoy, and Walerand, who had been in Henry's company abroad, and Gloucester's fears to have arisen from the possible exposure of his recent attempts to set Henry against Edward.

The procedure of the subsequent trial seems in part to have been suggested by Montfort himself. There was to be an investigation of the charges by an episcopal committee of six, comprising two of his friends, the bishops of Worcester and Lincoln, two royalist bishops, Norwich and Exeter, and two more neutral prelates, Boniface of Savoy, archbishop of Canterbury (the queen's uncle, but the backer of the Provisions and one of the council of fifteen) and Henry Wingham, bishop of London (the king's chancellor and one of the royal twelve in 1258, but trusted enough to have been kept in office by the reformers). The results of the enquiry were to be referred to the king and council,

---

[23] *DBM*, pp. 206–9.
[24] *CChR, 1257–1300*, p. 147.
[25] *Flores Hist.*, ii. p. 449.

by 15 July if possible.[26] The charges themselves survive and have already been drawn on extensively in this and the preceding chapter: their central attack was on Montfort's obstruction of the French peace, his acquisition of the king's demesne manors, and his resistance to Henry before the king's return to England.[27] If they showed the intensity of the king's anger against Montfort (and their antagonism was now entirely mutual), Montfort's replies, seemingly taken down verbatim, convey the gift for sharp and pointed repartee which probably characterised his way of speaking. Most of Henry's accusations he answered with a blank denial or with a justificatory appeal to the Provisions, sometimes salted with an almost insolent sarcasm. Charged, for example, with coming to the Candlemas parliament with horses and arms, he countered that he had appeared there with neither, 'except in the usual way of travelling about the country'. The opponent who faced Henry in these extraordinary exchanges was recognisably the same man who had told him at Saintes in 1242 that he ought to be taken and locked up.[28]

If nothing came of all this, it was partly because Montfort had some powerful supporters. He was helped by the presence in England of Eudes Rigaud, archbishop of Rouen, sent by Louis IX to assist in his defence. Rigaud took this opportunity to confer a prebend in his cathedral on Montfort's young son, Amaury, while at the same time the archbishop's companion on his mission, John de Harcourt, a Norman *seigneur*, was restored by Montfort to his ancestral Warwickshire manor of Ilmington, received by the earl as *terra Normannorum* in 1236. Harcourt's restoration was at the expense of Peter de Montfort, to whom Simon had previously granted Ilmington and who presumably now obtained compensation elsewhere.[29] This was not the only good turn which Montfort performed for his French allies. On 17 July he sealed a charter in Rigaud's favour, undertaking to restore to him all the rights and liberties which the earl's bailiffs of Odiham had usurped in the archbishop's neighbouring manor of Bentworth and to compel his men to attend the hundred court at Odiham no more than the

[26] E. F. Jacob, 'A Proposal for Arbitration between Simon de Montfort and Henry III in 1260', *EHR*, 37 (1922), pp. 80–2. For the positions of Boniface of Savoy and Henry Wingham in 1258, see *DBM*, pp. 104–5, 258–9, and *Baronial Plan*, pp. 58, 89.

[27] *DBM*, pp. 194–219.

[28] *DBM*, pp. 206–7; Bémont, *Montfort* (1st edn), p. 341; above, p. 32.

[29] F. M. Powicke, 'The Archbishop of Rouen, John de Harcourt, and Simon de Montfort in 1260', *EHR*, 51 (1936), pp. 108–13; *Reg. of Eudes of Rouen*, ed. O'Sullivan, pp. 418–19; above, p. 72.

customary twice a year.[30] This is a peculiarly interesting grant, pointing as it does both to Montfort's oppressively expansionist tactics as a land-lord and to his previous demand for the uncustomary suits which it was a main purpose of the baronial reformers to curtail. In making amends he was falling into line with reforming policy; but more directly he was strengthening his ties with one who was already an old friend. The whole episode provides another revealing glimpse of the bonds of friendship and favour which linked Montfort to the courtly and religious society of northern France. Together with his appeal to the bishops in the matter of his trial, it suggests that his political strength did not lie solely, or even perhaps mainly, in his position as the captain of a faction, the leader of an affinity, and the paymaster of foreign troops.

But it was none of these assets which gave him an immediate respite. On 20 July news came of the fall of Builth castle to the Welsh. The new crisis, and the need for Montfort's service in the army which was summoned on 1 August, led to the trial's inconclusive postponement.[31] In the event, however, a truce with Wales was made at the end of August, and this was one of several factors which kept Montfort out of the limelight for the next three months.[32] During this period he witnessed no royal charters, nor were he and his friends associated with any conciliar acts. His alienation probably resulted from Gloucester's continuing presence both at court and on a council whose control of royal government was slipping. As early as 5 June, in a move designed to placate Gloucester and other royalist barons, Henry was able to prorogue until Michaelmas the special eyre set up to enforce the Provisions. None of this brought any discernible reaction from Montfort, whose one remaining ally, apart from his personal friends, continued to be Edward. If he, too, was isolated from the government at this time, in his case by what he may have regarded as its pusillanimous policy towards Wales,[33] he forged another and more positive bond with Montfort out of the affairs of Bigorre.

As we have seen, Montfort had agreed to lease Bigorre to Henry in

[30] Hampshire County Record Office: Photocopy Accessions, Ph. 62c, from an original at Rouen. I am very grateful to Dr Nicholas Vincent for drawing my attention to this document and for supplying me with a copy. For the archbishop's holdings in Bentworth, see *VCH Hampshire*, iv, ed. W. Page (London, 1911), p. 68.

[31] *CPR, 1258–66*, p. 85; *CR, 1259–61*, pp. 191–4; *Flores Hist.*, ii, p. 454; *Cron. Maior.*, p. 45. H. Ridgeway, 'King Henry III's Grievances against the Council in 1261', *Historical Research*, 61 (1988), p. 231, was the first to suggest that Montfort's trial was prorogued.

[32] *Baronial Plan*, pp.241–4.

[33] *Baronial Plan*, p. 237; *CPR, 1258–66*, pp. 85, 88–9.

1259. The lease, however, seems not to have taken effect, probably because Henry failed to pay what he owed for Bigorre at the stated term.[34] By the spring of 1260 Esquivat de Chabanais, whom Montfort had replaced as lord of the county, had once again seized control, leaving Montfort only with the castle of Lourdes and the town of Tarbes. At this stage, in May 1260, Gaston de Béarn, Montfort's old enemy, wrote to announce to the earl that he was about to intervene to recover the remaining places for Esquivat.[35] Montfort could do little directly; but Edward, as lord of Gascony, was a natural ally. In early August, when Montfort was with Edward in London, he gave Lourdes to him in trust for its protection. Edward took immediate action for the defence of what was left to Montfort: the Lusignans, Guy, Geoffrey and William de Valence, were ordered to visit Bigorre and to fortify Lourdes and Tarbes; the seneschal of Gascony was to obey them; and in the truce with Esquivat which was made at Tarbes on 2 October Geoffrey and William acted as Montfort's representatives.[36] Via the mediation of Edward, necessity had once again brought Montfort and his former enemies together.

The affairs of south-west France thus gave Montfort and Edward a common interest in 1260. These wider horizons, beyond the frontiers of English politics, helped to set both men apart from the other magnates. Yet in October 1260 English politics once again became Montfort's main concern and for virtually the first time since 1258 he became fully involved in government. As Dr Ridgeway was the first to show, the occasion for his re-entry into public life was the Michaelmas parliament. Absent when parliament opened on 13 October, he was influential enough from the outset to be allowed by the council to appoint a deputy, Henry of Almain, son of Richard of Cornwall, to perform his duties as steward and to do so without waiting for the king's traditional summons: an act of disregard for the prerogative which caused Henry great offence.[37] Then from 20 October to 2 December he became a regular witness of the king's charters, as he had not been since 1258. He remained closely associated with Edward, who knighted his two sons,

---

[34] *Treaty R*, i, pp. 49–50; *CR, 1256–59*, pp. 456–7 (where 'Wigorn' should read 'Bigorr').

[35] Bémont, *Montfort* (1st edn), pp. 371–2.

[36] c.61/4, m. 3; *Roles Gascons*, ed. Bémont, i, supplement, pp. xcii–xciii; *Recueil d'Actes Relatifs à L'Administration des Rois D'Angleterre en Guyenne au XIIIᵉ Siècle: Recognitiones Feodorum in Aquitania*, ed. C. Bémont (Paris, 1914), p. 152; Ellis, 'Gaston de Béarn', pp. 399–402.

[37] *CPR, 1258–66*, p. 96; Ridgeway, 'Politics of the English Royal Court', pp. 368–72; Ridgeway, 'King Henry III's Grievances', pp. 230, 241.

Henry and Simon, in the mass knighting on St Edward's day; whose charter he witnessed on 20 October; and to whose retinue Henry of Almain belonged.[38] Much more surprising was Montfort's reconciliation with Gloucester, vouched for by a chronicle,[39] which took place in this parliament. Gloucester continued to be what Montfort had just become again, the usual witness of Henry's charters, but as well as being Montfort's associate at court he was also his partner in action against the king. In March 1261 Henry was to accuse these two 'and some other councillors' of ordering the removal of the proctors appointed by Henry to represent him at Montfort's trial: a coup which must predate the effective demise of the council in December 1260 and which points to Henry's attempt to revive the trial in October, after its abrupt curtailment in July.[40]

What did this new partnership achieve? Two developments were particularly important: the changing of the great officials and the modification of the reforming programme. During the parliament all three of the great officials were replaced. Hugh Bigod, whom Montfort may well have regarded as a broken reed after the events of the winter and spring, was superseded as justiciar by Hugh Despenser, the earl's executor in his will of 1259 and also a member of Edward's household; Henry Wingham, chancellor since 1255 and royal clerk, made way for Nicholas of Ely, who was to become treasurer, then chancellor for a second time, after Montfort's return from France in 1263; and John de Caux, abbot of Peterborough and a supporter of Edward, was appointed treasurer in place of the recently deceased John Crakehall. Given the connections of the new men, it seems likely that Montfort and Edward had a controlling voice in what was a highly contentious set of appointments. Henry was later to protest that these conciliar ministers were imposed on him against his wishes, and one of his first actions on returning to power in 1261 was to dismiss them.[41]

Did these appointments signify the triumph of a faction over a principle? That this was so is suggested by the substantial modification of the reforming programme which took place in this parliament. It had several aspects. First, the council agreed that every magnate should have

---

[38] c.53/50, mm. 1–3; c.53/51, mm. 3–4; c.61/4, m. 1; *Flores Hist.*, ii, p. 456; Ridgeway, 'Politics of the English Royal Court', pp. 368–70, 388.

[39] *Flores Hist.*, iii, pp. 254–5.

[40] Ridgeway, 'King Henry III's Grievances', pp. 231–2, 241–2.

[41] *Flores Hist.*, ii, pp. 448, 456–7; *DBM*, pp. 212–15, 222–3; Ridgeway, 'King Henry III's Grievances', pp. 239–40; Ridgeway, 'Politics of the English Royal Court', pp. 370–2.

the power to correct the offences of his own bailiffs when these were
the subject of complaint. The scheme of 1258–59, by which the justiciar
and the special eyre were to investigate baronial abuses, was thus
abandoned.[42] This innovation was linked to another: the commission-
ing in November, with conciliar consent, of an ordinary general eyre,
lacking the powers to enforce the Provisions and to receive grievances
against officials which had characterised the special eyre of 1259–60.
Finally, the yearly change of sheriffs, now due under the terms of the
Provisions, was not carried through, and the sheriffs of 1259–60 were
retained in office.[43]

These charges all had a common direction. Favouring lords against
tenants, they freed the magnates from some of the main controls
imposed upon them by the Provisions. Even the failure to change the
sheriffs can be seen in this light. Henry was later to complain in 1261 that
the baronial sheriffs had not dared to enter the lands of any councillor
to do justice, and to defend his own appointment of powerful royalists
to the office by arguing that the local sheriffs of the Provisions had been
powerless to protect small men against magnate oppression.[44] There
was probably some substance in these claims; and if they were anything
like true, they would explain the reluctance of magnate councillors to
replace men whom they had found to be either obligingly complaisant
or usefully timid in the face of their own power.

What lay behind these mutations of personnel and policies? The most
remarkable aspect of the Michaelmas parliament and of the weeks
which followed is the sudden prominence of Montfort. Defying the king
in appointing a deputy steward and in bringing the trial proceedings
against him to an end, ally of the new justiciar, and a figure at court, he
stood closer to the centre of power than at any time since the early
months of the reform movement. Yet it was at just this time that the
reform programme with which he had been so closely associated was
weakened and the Provisions modified in magnate interests. Any
explanation of these bewildering developments must take account of
Montfort's reconciliation with Gloucester. Nothing can be proved; but
it is possible that Montfort's effective readmission to the council, his way
back to power and out of the wilderness, was made conditional by
Gloucester on his willingness to modify the anti-baronial measures of

42 *CPR, 1258–66*, p. 97; *Baronial Plan*, p. 246.
43 *CR, 1259–61*, pp. 451–2; *Baronial Plan*, pp. 245, 247–8.
44 *DBM*, pp. 220–3; *Foedera*, I, ii, p. 409.

the Provisions, to which Gloucester had always been opposed. The bargain may have been made additionally attractive by Gloucester's willingness to support Montfort's efforts to obstruct the procedures for his trial: a trial which Gloucester's earlier misrepresentations of the sympathies of the Lord Edward gave Montfort's ally his own reasons for fearing.[45] Even though the two earls may have found it difficult to strike up an easy rapport, each had good cause to look to the other.

It is hard to avoid the deduction that Montfort had consented to the modification of the Provisions, if only for the best of tactical reasons and with the sanction of the other councillors. Yet it would be wrong to go further and to conclude that he had sold out. In one particular way what had happened in the Michaelmas parliament represented a reaffirmation of the Provisions rather than their dilution, for the replacement of the great officials was a firm endorsement of the principle of conciliar control of appointments laid down in June 1258.[46] This principle remained central to the whole scheme of reform and, it is worth noting, to Montfort's own chances of seeing his private grievances satisfied. Nor was reform entirely abandoned in the localities. There was no full-scale revival of the special eyre at Michaelmas, as Henry had promised in June, but in December 1260 and January 1261 Hugh Despenser heard pleas in Sussex in what proved to be the final coda to that eyre. Peter of Savoy and his agents were the chief target of the many complaints that were brought, some of them under the Provisions of Westminster, but other magnates were also indicted, including Richard of Cornwall, William de Braose and John de Warenne.[47] Despenser's position as Montfort's probable nominee for the justiciarship strengthens the case for saying that Montfort had not lost interest in reform and still envisaged its local application. What had been borne in upon him in the Michaelmas parliament was the need to compromise, perhaps as the price of his return to power. But for a little while longer reform continued, as much a matter of principle as a tactical device for Henry's frustration and control.

(B) THE RECOVERY OF ROYAL AUTHORITY, 1261

In 1261 Henry III was restored to power by a series of manoeuvres and deceptions conceived and executed with a deftness that was quite

---

[45] Above, pp. 194, 197.   [46] *DBM*, pp. 222–3.
[47] JUST.1/911, mm. 6, 8, 12; Jacob, *Studies*, pp. 109–17, 353–65.

unexpected. Their essential preliminary was the collapse of the council from late November 1260. The number of conciliar acts fell away rapidly, ceasing altogether after 28 December,[48] as Henry recreated a royalist court, purged of his opponents, whose revival was the counterpart to the council's decline. Peter of Savoy, possibly ejected from the council by his enemy Montfort in the spring of 1260, had rejoined the court by early December, after some months abroad. So also had Richard of Cornwall, who had been in Germany since June and whose return was seen by one chronicle as providing the impetus for Henry's recovery.[49] Wealthy, intelligent and unshakeably loyal, these two men, together with such other inveterate royalists as John Mansel and Robert Walerand, may have masterminded the king's restoration. This was helped by the dispersal of his former antagonists. Edward had gone abroad in November, first to tourney and then to visit Gascony, taking with him the large retinue whose presence in England might have jeopardised the coup which Henry was soon to launch.[50] Gloucester witnessed no further royal charters after 4 December and Montfort none after 2 December.[51] The triumvirate of the October parliament had disbanded. At the same time the king's retaining of Philip Basset, James Audley, Roger Mortimer, Hugh Bigod and Hugh Despenser, all councillors except the last, as his *familiares* from mid December, for robes and probably fees, showed that the rebuilding of royal support was a deliberate business.[52] Not simply dependent on random comings and goings, it also entailed the attempted suborning of some prominent members of the council.

Montfort's departure may have owed something to the re-establishment of those opposed to him: Peter of Savoy witnessed his first royal charter on 3 December and is likely to have been driven closer to Henry by being called to account before Despenser's eyre for his actions in Sussex.[53] But it probably owed more to the pursuit of his and Eleanor's private claims in France, whither he almost certainly went. Some of these claims were new. In November 1260 Eleanor, backed by her husband, had begun proceedings against her Lusignan half-brothers for

---

[48] *Baronial Plan*, pp. 249–50.
[49] *DBM*, pp. 206–7; *Wykes*, p. 124; Battle chronicle, in Bémont, *Montfort* (1st edn), p. 374; Denholm-Young, *Richard of Cornwall*, p. 107; Ridgeway, 'Politics of the English Royal Court', pp. 377–8. At his trial Montfort had denied the charge concerning Peter of Savoy.
[50] *Ger. Cant.*, ii, p. 211; *Flores Hist.*, ii, p. 456; *CPR, 1258–66*, p. 126.
[51] C.53/51, mm. 3, 4.
[52] *CR, 1259–61*, p. 317.
[53] C.53/51, m. 4; above, p. 203.

the recovery of her share in the inheritance of their mother Isabella of Angoulême, from which the Lusignans had been the main beneficiaries. The preliminary hearing of the case before arbitrators, set for January 1261 at Poitiers, may have been what took Montfort abroad.[54] At the same time he used this opportunity to reopen his older case for Eleanor's dower. On 11 January 1261, after receiving letters from Louis IX about a possible peace with the Montforts, Henry agreed to accept the arbitration of Louis himself, his queen, Margaret, and his minister, Peter le Chamberlain, both on his own 'articles' against the Montforts and on their claims against him.[55] It looks as if Montfort, in France, had asked Louis to initiate this arbitration, significant in retrospect as the first in a series of French arbitrations which would end with the Mise of Amiens.

Why did Montfort appeal to Louis for justice? In part it was because he could not expect justice in England, a point driven home by the inactivity of the English arbitrators nominated after the Treaty of Paris. But a less immediate reason allows us to consider for a moment the general tenor of Montfort's relations with Louis and the natural sympathies which drew the two men together. We have already seen many signs of those sympathies: Louis's grant of a fief-rent to Montfort, the hospitality offered to him in 1259, the place found for him in the social and ceremonial life of the French court, and the despatch of Eudes Rigaud and John de Harcourt to his aid in 1260.[56] Beneath these manifestations of friendship lay some deep and enduring common interests. Although Louis was a better Christian than Montfort, both men shared the same religious outlook: pious, austere, and given direction by the friars and by the principles of the crusade. Louis had good cause to be grateful to Montfort's father and brothers, whose crusading legacy in the south had been the extirpation of heresy and the enlargement of the French kingdom. The high favour which Simon's elder brother Amaury, constable of France, enjoyed at Louis's court in the late 1230s was partly a consequence of these services.[57] One other and more specific bond lay in their sharing strikingly similar grievances over their wives' dower rights. The dower settled on Louis's wife, Margaret of Provence, by her father Raimond-Berenger V, count of

[54] Wade, 'The Personal Quarrels', pp. 51–60, 127–9; Labarge, *Montfort*, p. 192.
[55] *CPR, 1258–66*, p. 136.
[56] Above, pp. 187, 190, 198–9.
[57] Richard, *Saint Louis*, pp. 91–2.

Provence, at the time of their marriage in 1234, had never been fully paid, either by Raimond himself or by Charles of Anjou, Louis's brother and Raimond's successor in the county by his marriage to Raimond's youngest daughter, Beatrice. The issue still divided the two brothers as late as 1266, proving itself to be an even longer running saga than that of Eleanor de Montfort's dower.[58] As Montfort must have known, Louis was well qualified to appreciate the claims and frustrations of a husband whose wife came to him with an inadequate endowment.

Montfort and Louis were perhaps closer to each other than either was to Henry, whose personal acquaintance with the French king was much slighter. Although their wives were sisters and their religious lives superficially similar, the two kings did not meet until 1254,[59] and Henry's religious convictions affected him less profoundly than those of Louis. Unlike Montfort and Louis, Henry had not been on crusade (despite his crusading vow) and was noted less for personal austerity than for ostentation and extravagance. To Louis, his Christianity of almsgiving and masses may have seemed to embody a touch of the religiosity of outward observance. Louis himself preferred sermons to masses.[60] Yet at the time when Louis's arbitration was initiated by Montfort and accepted by Henry, the English king had no reason to think that Louis would not do the justice for which he was famous.[61] Like Montfort, Henry had a good deal to play for. The 'articles' against the Montforts, which Henry's letters suggest that he himself had introduced into the arbitration, can only have been the unresolved charges of July 1260, effectively blocked by Montfort and Gloucester in October. Their revival by Henry confirms once again the depth of his resentment at Montfort's conduct in 1259–60. A successful arbitration might vindicate his position here, temper Montfort's enthusiasm for the Provisions by satisfying his private claims, and secure the release of the 15,000 marks retained by Louis until the dower problem had been solved. Both politically and financially, it could contribute to the revival of royal power.

This was a distant prospect. More immediately, Henry's object was

---

[58] Richard, *Saint Louis*, pp. 66–7, 250, 308–9; M. W. Labarge, *Saint Louis* (London, 1968), pp. 54–5, 230.

[59] Paris, v, p. 476.

[60] Paris, iv, pp. 231–2 (for Louis's remarks about Henry's religious practices); E. A. Bond, 'Historiola de Pietate Regis Henrici III', *Archaeological Journal*, 17 (1860), pp. 317–19.

[61] Richard, *Saint Louis*, pp. 170–7.

to overthrow the reforms and the council, to legitimise his programme by securing papal absolution from his oath to the Provisions, and to implement that programme by force. By the end of January John Mansel, nephew of his namesake, Henry's confidant, had left England to seek the king's absolution from Pope Alexander IV. The chronicles variously attribute this move to Richard of Cornwall, the Savoyards and the queen.[62] On 9 February Henry moved to the Tower, summoning twenty-seven mainly minor barons to come armed to the forthcoming Candlemas parliament.[63] Clearly he expected trouble; the unusual venue and the quality and quantity of his militia was a measure of the magnate discontent which he feared. Montfort and Gloucester both returned for this parliament, witnessing a charter at the Tower on 28 February, together with, among others, Richard of Cornwall, Peter of Savoy, Mansel and Walerand. In parliament the initiative lay with Henry. In a speech to the magnates which revealed the thinking behind his actions, he stressed their failure to restore his finances, as they had promised to do, their use of office to profit themselves, and their treatment of him as their minister rather than their lord.[64] These grievances against the council were set out at length and in writing on 9 March. Henry's essential charge was that the councillors had usurped his proper authority: going far beyond what had been decided in 1258, excluding him from government, letting his revenues decline while enriching themselves, and failing the king in foreign policy by allowing the Sicilian Business to lapse, Wales to be lost, and the Treaty of Paris to remain incomplete. A second and later version of this indictment brought in some new charges, of which the most important related to Montfort's conduct over the stewardship and his suspension of his own trial in the previous parliament. About 14 March the king agreed to arbitration; and a third surviving set of grievances, with the council's replies, was probably that laid before the arbitrators in late April.[65]

---

[62] *CR, 1259–61*, pp. 340, 377; Battle chronicle, in Bémont, *Montfort* (1st edn), p. 374; *Oxenedes*, p. 220. For the two John Mansels, see R. F. Treharne, 'The Personal Role of Simon de Montfort' (appendix to *Baronial Plan*, 2nd edn, Manchester, 1971), p. 428, n. 45; *York Minster Fasti*, i, ed. C. T. Clay (Yorks. Arch. Soc. Record ser., cxxiii, 1958), p. 25; and *BRUO*, ii, pp. 1217–18. Dr Margaret Howell has pointed out to me that there was a third John Mansel: one 'Master John Mansel the elder' was given protection by Montfort's government in December 1264 as a clerk willing to reside at his benefice in England: *CPR, 1258–66*, p. 394.

[63] *CR, 1259–61*, p. 457; *Baronial Plan*, p. 386.

[64] c.53/51, m. 3; *Flores Hist.*, ii, pp. 463–4.

[65] *DBM*, pp. 210–39; Ridgeway, 'King Henry III's Grievances', pp. 239–42. I have followed Dr Ridgeway's arguments on the relationship and dating of these sets of grievances.

Henry's approach was a clever one. He attacked neither the Provisions nor the council directly. Indeed, he said that even now he wished to abide by the Provisions and the council's just decrees[66] (and his summoning of the Candlemas parliament was in itself a mark of respect for the Provisions). Ostensibly, his objections were to the council's acting *ultra vires*, beyond the limits licensed by the Provisions; and there was enough in the council's past to make his case a plausible one. The councillors did not deny, for example, that they had met without him, sometimes ignored his arguments, and overridden his choice of officials.[67] With the passing of time the balance of the new constitution of 1258 had been tipped increasingly against the king. Henry's charges were intended to undermine the legitimacy of the council's proceedings here, just as his absolution would undermine the legitimacy of the Provisions. After its demise in December 1260, the council had been resurrected like a phoenix, only to have its neck wrung.

Meanwhile, during the long course of the impending arbitration, Mansel's return with the bull of absolution came nearer. Henry was playing for time; and a central part of his game was the conciliation of Montfort, whose grievances, abilities, and power to call in foreign troops made him especially dangerous. The agreement in mid March to go to arbitration on the king's political complaints was accompanied by a further agreement between Henry, Montfort and Eleanor to accept Louis's arbitration on their private quarrels, according to the scheme first put forward in January. With similar restraint Henry dropped the personal charges against Montfort from his third and final list of complaints prepared for the arbitrators.[68] He shrewdly saw, what was indeed becoming clear in 1260, that the treatment of Montfort's private claims might do much to determine his politics.

In professing his obligations to the Provisions, Henry had never acted with more duplicity. During April, at the probable time of the arbitration, he was already preparing the ground for the destruction of the whole reforming programme, granting fees to barons, knights and foreign mercenary leaders, and, in the most blatant breach of the Provisions so far, restoring to favour William de Valence, who arrived in England in the company of Edward towards the end of the

---

[66] *DBM*, pp. 236–7; Ridgeway, 'King Henry III's Grievances', pp. 234, 236, 242.
[67] *DBM*, pp. 222–5.
[68] *CPR, 1258–66*, pp. 145–6; *CR, 1259–61*, p. 465; Ridgeway, 'King Henry III's Grievances', pp. 242, 236.

month.[69] Then, during the first fortnight in May, he carried through the most daring part of his coup, moving into Kent, taking Dover castle and the Cinque Ports, replacing Hugh Bigod with Robert Walerand as their custodian, securing the other Kentish castles, and receiving oaths of fealty from the men of Kent, Sussex and Hampshire. By mid May he had returned to London, where he substituted John Mansel senior for Hugh Despenser as keeper of the Tower.[70] He had thus gained the control of the south-east which was vital for the safe arrival of Mansel junior and for the entry of troops from abroad. By 25 May Mansel was back, allowing Henry to clinch his victory at Winchester in early June. With Alexander's bull of absolution now in his hands, he proclaimed his freedom from his oath to the Provisions, and the power of his represen-tatives to absolve clergy and magnates from their oaths. At the same time he replaced Hugh Despenser with Philip Basset as justiciar, and Nicholas of Ely with Walter Merton as chancellor.[71] He was once again master in his own kingdom.

Slow to develop, the reaction to Henry's restoration eventually brought together almost all the magnates in the most impressive display of baronial unity since 1258. It was one in which the first discernible move was Montfort's and from which he was to emerge as undisputed leader. On 18 May, when he had returned to London from Dover, Henry ordered the bailiffs of the Cinque Ports to keep watch for armed aliens whom the earl was attempting to bring into the realm.[72] But it was only later, after the events at Winchester, that the barons united in arms against the king. Gloucester and Montfort, the acknowledged leaders of the new confederacy, denounced the new papal bulls; and they were joined, among others, by Norfolk, Warenne, Hugh Bigod and Hugh Despenser.[73] War seemed near. From 22 June to 30 July the king shut himself in the Tower, and it was while he was there, on 5 July, that yet another attempt was made to initiate an arbitration on his personal quarrels with Montfort. Instead of the exclusively French arbitration agreed in March, it was now decided that Philip Basset and John Mansel senior should represent the king, and Walter de Cantilupe and Peter de

---

[69] *CPR, 1258–66*, pp. 147, 150; *Flores Hist.*, ii, p. 466; Ridgeway, 'King Henry III's Grievances', p. 237.

[70] *Flores Hist.*, ii, pp. 467–8; *Baronial Plan*, pp. 257–8, 260.

[71] *DBM*, pp. 240–7; *Flores Hist.*, ii, p. 470; *Baronial Plan*, p. 261.

[72] *CPR, 1258–66*, p. 185.

[73] *Ann. Lond.*, p. 58; *Ger. Cant.*, ii, p. 211; Battle chronicle, in Bémont, *Montfort* (1st edn), p. 74; *Flores Hist.*, ii, p. 470.

Montfort the earl, with Hugh, duke of Burgundy (probably a friend of Montfort's), and Peter le Chamberlain as additional arbitrators. This same panel was also to arbitrate on the political disputes between the king and the barons. Nothing came of this. The English arbitrators failed to agree, and on 18 July Cantilupe, Simon de Montfort, Norfolk, Gloucester, Warenne and Hugh Bigod wrote to ask for Louis's personal intervention and for his help in persuading the French arbitrators to act. When they declined to do so Henry asked for their replacement by Queen Margaret. For many months no more was done.[74]

These manoeuvres showed the intense loyalties which the programme of 1258–59 continued to inspire. Despite the decline of the council, an outright challenge to the Provisions could still unite its members in arms and anger. Yet they also illustrate the inherent strengths of Henry's position. His declaration of support for the Provisions may have deceived the magnates at a crucial time, and even when his intentions became obvious he could rely on their extreme reluctance to go to war, as he had done in the spring of 1260. In appealing to Louis on 18 July – a mark of their irresolution – their leaders had given sufficient reasons for holding back when they spoke of 'the desolation, destruction and irreparable loss which threaten the whole land'.[75] Nor were they as strong as they might have been had Henry's attack come a year earlier. Edward was reconciled with his father at the end of May and left for Gascony in July, depriving the barons of an ally who had previously given some legitimacy to Montfort's cause.[76] And Montfort himself had one eye on his own concerns, as he showed by his willingness to seek arbitration on his claims even during the tensest moments of political crisis.

It was at this point that a quarrel between king and barons became part of a larger public conflict. For the first time since the protest of the bachelors in October 1259 the gentry and freeholders of local society showed their hand, transforming this narrower dispute into a national issue and giving Montfort a constituency which would support him until Evesham and beyond. As we have seen, the reforms of 1258–59 had promised a good deal to the men of the shires and had received the widest publicity. The Ordinance of Sheriffs, the Ordinance of the

---

[74] *CPR, 1258–66*, pp. 162, 169; Bémont, *Montfort* (1st edn), pp. 331–2. For Montfort's relationship with Hugh of Burgundy, see above, pp. 30–1, 75.
[75] Bémont, *Montfort* (1st edn), p. 332.
[76] Ridgeway, 'King Henry III's Grievances', p. 237; Prestwich, *Edward I*, p. 35.

Magnates and the Provisions of Westminster had all been published in the counties. Bigod's judicial enquiry of 1258–59, the special eyre of 1260, and the arrangements for giving the counties a share in the election of their sheriffs had offered a voice to a local opinion ignored and overridden in the years before 1258. Yet what had happened? The special eyre had been called off in 1260, after visiting only a dozen counties;[77] the sheriffs had not been changed in 1260, as they should have been; controls on magnate abuses had been eased; and the general eyre launched in 1260 was of the old, oppressive, fiscal sort. Some of these changes, it has been argued above, had been sanctioned by the council; but this was probably not known in the shires. Grievances had been ventilated, remedies put in hand, expectations raised; then dashed. These pent-up resentments were now to find an outlet.

As early as the parliament of February–March Henry had been uneasy about rising local discontents. Exacerbated by the extortionate tallaging of boroughs and royal demesnes in the autumn of 1260, they were in his mind when he ordered the sheriffs on 14 March 1261 to proclaim that the king cherished the magnates and the community and to arrest all those spreading rumours that he intended to exact 'uncustomary tallages and undue levies'.[78] His letters initiated bids for local loyalties by both sides which were to last for the rest of the year. More serious for him was the obstruction of the eyre set up at the end of 1260. On 2 May, while Henry was taking control of Dover, the eyre at Hertford was suspended after baronial emissaries had claimed that the proper forty-day summons had not been given and that the usual seven-year interval had not elapsed since the previous eyre. On 1 July similar opposition to the eyre erupted at Worcester, where the county court refused to receive the justices, again on the grounds that the seven-year interval had not been observed. The whole visitation was subsequently abandoned by the government.[79] These events struck at the king's reviving authority, weakened the financial recovery which was essential for its maintenance, and brought the barons and local opinion into co-operative alignment on the question of the Provisions; for it was as a breach of the Provisions, both in its superseding the special eyre of 1260 and in its disregard for the seven-year rule, that the eyre was

---

[77] Crook, *Records of the General Eyre*, pp. 189–90.
[78] *CR, 1259–61*, p. 135; *Foedera*, I, i, p. 405.
[79] *Flores Hist.*, ii, pp. 468, 472; *Ann. Wigorn.*, p. 446; Crook, *Records of the General Eyre*, pp. 126–8.

attacked. Actually the seven-year interval was not so much a rule as an approximation to existing practice, recognised yet not specifically codified in the Provisions of Westminster.[80] But in the circumstances these distinctions were academic.

Far more inflammatory than the eyre, however, was Henry's replacement of the baronial sheriffs. After his emancipation at Winchester the sheriffs represented the one part of the fabric of the Provisions that was still intact. Their removal would allow him to control local government as he now controlled central government, giving him new men whom he could rely on to make his proclamations, raise money and troops, and defend his local rights. On 9 July he acted, dismissing twenty-two baronial sheriffs in thirty-four counties and replacing them with powerful *curiales* and household knights, whose novel custody of the royal castles emphasised that this was as much a military move as a political and administrative one.[81] During the next three months there was a gathering reaction to these measures. In twenty-four counties rival baronial 'keepers of the counties', mainly local men, were put into office by the same combination of local and baronial initiative as had halted the eyres.[82] It was these appointments, more than anything else, which recreated the old alliance between the reformers and the localities; and Montfort probably had a large share in them. At least three of the new keepers were his *familiares* – Ralph Basset of Sapcote in Leicestershire, Thomas of Astley in Warwickshire, and John de la Haye in Surrey, Sussex and Kent – and the appointment of one of his own men for the south-eastern counties, whose special importance he recognised as much as Henry,[83] was particularly significant.

Montfort's activities at this time ranged well outside the English counties. With characteristic energy and decisiveness he set out to organise all possible opposition to Henry's regime. On 2 September Henry suspected him to be in France, almost certainly putting the barons' case to Louis IX and attempting to raise troops and arms.[84] Given his later alliances with the Welsh in 1263–65, it was probably he who was also responsible for the ineffectual baronial approaches now

---

[80] See *DBM*, pp. 150–1 (cl. 5); and compare *Baronial Plan*, pp. 398–406, with H. M. Cam, *Studies in the Hundred Rolls* (Oxford, 1921), pp. 83–8.

[81] *CPR, 1258–66*, pp. 162–4; *Baronial Plan*, p. 263.

[82] For the names and counties of the baronial sheriffs, see *Baronial Plan*, pp. 267–8, and *RL*, ii, pp. 192–3. For Ralph Basset's appointment 'by letters of the barons which he received', see E.368/36, m. 11d.

[83] *Ger. Cant.*, ii, p. 213.

[84] *Dipl. Docs.*, No. 330; *CR, 1259–61*, pp. 489–90.

made to Llywelyn ap Gruffudd, 'the master of native Wales'.[85] He was busy, too, at the papal curia, where Alexander IV's death in May 1261 threatened the validity of Henry's absolution. Henry was anxious to have the bulls of absolution confirmed by the new pope, Urban IV, elected in August; but the barons also had their friends among the pope's associates. In mid September 1261 one of Henry's agents wrote from Rome to say that another English clerk had received letters from 'a certain earl' (who can only have been Montfort), seeking what was contrary to the king's interests and in favour of the barons: presumably new papal bulls confirming the Provisions.[86] By the time this report was written Montfort must have returned home, for, acting with Gloucester and Walter de Cantilupe, he had summoned three knights from each county to meet at St Albans on 21 September to discuss the current discontents: a move cleverly thwarted by the king's summoning of the knights to Windsor on the same day.[87]

Montfort's enterprise in these months was one of the reformers' greatest assets. His contacts and his organising power made him the linchpin of the movement, foreshadowing the leader's role which came to him in 1263. Yet – and perhaps surprisingly – all the advantages remained with Henry, who outmanoeuvred his opponents with the same skills that he had shown earlier in the year. On 16 August he appealed for the support of the counties in a long letter justifying his new sheriffs as men better able than those they had replaced to defend the interests of his subjects.[88] If this was not entirely convincing, Henry's use of peace negotiations backed by preparations for war was ultimately much more effective. At the end of August he summoned in large numbers of foreign troops, while starting to negotiate with the barons shortly afterwards.[89] After early talks had broken down, others began in mid October, against the background provided by an armed assembly of tenants-in-chief in London. The outstanding diehards are identified by their omission from the list of those summoned: Montfort, Gloucester, Warenne, Norfolk, Despenser and Peter de Montfort.[90] Their position

---

[85] *Foedera*, I, i, p. 414; J. E. Lloyd, *A History of Wales from the Earliest Times to the Edwardian Conquest* (2 vols., London, 1939), ii, p. 729; R. R. Davies, *Conquest, Coexistence and Change: Wales, 1063–1415* (Oxford, 1987), p. 317; below, pp. 228, 263, 289–90, 337–8.

[86] *Dipl. Docs.*, No. 331; *Baronial Plan*, pp. 275–7.

[87] *DBM*, pp. 246–9; G. O. Sayles, *The Functions of the Medieval Parliament of England* (London, 1988), pp. 97–8.

[88] *Foedera*, I, i, pp. 408–9; *Baronial Plan*, p. 265.

[89] *CR, 1259–61*, pp. 487–8; *DBM*, pp. 246–9.

[90] *Cron. Maior.*, p. 49; *CPR, 1258–66*, pp. 178, 189, 191; *CR, 1259–61*, pp. 497–9; *Baronial Plan*, p. 269.

collapsed, however, when Gloucester deserted to the king, won over by promises and by the favours of Queen Eleanor, whose persuasiveness had earlier helped to win over Edward.[91] Other barons were also bribed,[92] leaving Henry in a position to impose terms.

For the reformers the resulting treaty, made at Kingston-on-Thames on 21 November and later confirmed in London, was a defeat disguised as a compromise. Three representatives for the king (the bishops of Hereford and Salisbury, and John Mansel) and three for the barons (Robert Marsh, dean of Lincoln and Adam Marsh's brother, the earl of Norfolk, and Peter de Montfort) were to negotiate on the Provisions and on the affairs of the kingdom. If they failed to agree, Richard of Cornwall was to be called in to arbitrate and then, if necessary, Louis IX. They were also to decide about the future appointment of sheriffs, with Richard of Cornwall's arbitration again being invoked in case of disagreement. On the immediate question of the current sheriffs, each county was to elect four knights from whom Henry would choose one to act as sheriff until Michaelmas 1262.[93] The Provisions had thus been resurrected, but their terms were now open to negotiation and the road to their implementation effectively blocked by Richard of Cornwall. What must have been bitterly humiliating to Montfort was the submission of even his closest friends to these conditions: Richard de Grey and Ralph Basset of Sapcote had earlier been among those whom Henry had judged it expedient to summon in arms to London; Walter de Cantilupe had sealed the treaty on behalf of the barons; Peter de Montfort was one of the arbitrators.[94] It was the one point in the reforming period when his affinity came near to failing him. In anger and scorn he left for France, saying, according to the Dunstable annals, that he would rather die landless than abandon the truth as a perjured man.[95]

Here once again Henry had been able to depend on the unwillingness of his opponents to resort to arms, just as in May and June. By the end of the year, however, circumstances had changed, for the revolt of the counties had greatly widened the range of opposition to his government.

---

[91] *Ann. Dun.*, p. 217; *Ger. Cant.*, ii, p. 213; Battle chronicle, in Bémont, *Montfort* (1st edn), p. 374.

[92] E.g. *CPR, 1258–66*, pp. 192–3.

[93] *Ann. Oseney*, pp. 128–9; *CR, 1261–64*, p. 126; *RL*, ii, pp. 197–8; Sayles, *Functions of the Medieval Parliament*, p. 98. *Foedera*, I, i, p. 415, gives the names of six different arbitrators, probably appointed at a later date than those listed in the Oseney account of the treaty.

[94] *CR, 1259–61*, p. 497; *1261–64*, p. 126; *Ann. Oseney*, p. 129.

[95] *Ann. Dun.*, p. 217. Cf. *Ann. Oseney*, p. 129, and Battle chronicle, in Bémont, *Montfort* (1st edn), p. 374.

Yet without baronial leadership local dissent remained diffuse and uncoordinated, and not quite the threat to royal authority that it appeared to be. Despite its continuing vitality at the end of the year, when baronial keepers remained in place in many counties, local initiatives by themselves were unable to keep the Provisions afloat. These lessons cannot have been lost on Montfort, whose role in the appointment of the keepers and in the summoning of the knights to St Albans had shown him to be as sensitive to local needs, and to the tactical advantages which they offered, as Edward had been at the time of the protest of the bachelors in 1259. This was the ground that he was to cultivate more thoroughly from 1263 to 1265.

If we ask to what end he acted, there is a traditional and seemingly compelling answer, supplied by his embittered departure after the Treaty of Kingston: in defence of the Provisions, to which he was sworn. No doubt this is true. He could, like some of his leading allies, have recognised defeat, fallen into line, settled for compromise, and retained his lands and position; yet he chose not to do so. Here, however, his private interests should not be forgotten. He had been abroad pursuing those interests in the crucial months before the February parliament, when the ground had been laid for the revival of Henry's kingship. At least three attempts had been made to secure an arbitration on his quarrel with Henry, in a process which, running parallel as it did to Henry's recovery of power, suggests that Henry saw Montfort's appeasement as a means to his own security. The failure of the last attempt in July came just before the earl's vigorous organisation of the opposition. Militant discontents, especially local ones, gave him a new resource in what was as much a private vendetta against Henry as a constitutional or religious cause. His defence of the Provisions was by no means a mere cover for private interests. But, as the grounds for his actions, interests and principles were becoming more than usually difficult to distinguish.

(c) MONTFORT IN FRANCE, 1262–APRIL 1263

On the face of it, the months after the Treaty of Kingston were for Henry a time of almost complacent stability. While Montfort was in France, his followers cowed and his measures discredited, Henry's control over the country and its government was confirmed and extended. The council had gone; the eyres broken off by local protests in July 1261 were resumed in January 1262; and the committee of six arbitrators set up to decide on the future method of appointing the sheriffs announced in

January its failure to agree and appealed to Richard of Cornwall, who in May restored to Henry full control over appointments and dismissals.[96] Nothing was said about the committee's other task of adjudicating on the Provisions; and after 2 May this was hardly necessary, since new bulls from Urban IV confirming Henry's absolution from his oath were then published in England.[97] With the restoration of the Lusignans too,[98] it must have seemed as if the whole experiment of the Provisions was over and that the normality of pre-1258 royal government had returned.

In fact Henry's position was far less assured than it appeared to be. Acquiesced in rather than accepted, it lacked the sanction of the public and local consent which the reformers had made into a political force. Many others besides Montfort, says the Kentish chronicler, did not consent to the Treaty of Kingston, but were unable to resist.[99] The resumption of the eyre and the decision on the sheriffs are likely to have been deeply unpopular, since they struck at the most fundamental local gains from the reform movement. The king must have been nervously aware of continuing provincial opposition, for in May he took the precaution of ordering the sheriffs to publish the news of his absolution in the counties (as he had not done with Alexander IV's bulls in 1261), to proclaim his adherence to the Charters, and to arrest those denying his rights or preaching against him: a good indication of clerical sympathies and their local influence.[100] If Henry lacked support there, he was hardly more secure at the centre, where his government was essentially curial rather than baronial.[101] To judge from the witness-lists to his charters, its leading members were the royalist bishop of Salisbury, Peter of Savoy, William de Valence, Mansel and Walerand. Philip Basset, justiciar since Henry's restoration, and Hugh Bigod, always inclined to temporise, were the only native magnates of consequence regularly at court. Gloucester was a notable absentee, perhaps through illness (he died in July 1262) or as a result of the private agreements, their contents obscure, which he is known to have made with the

---

96 *Foedera*, I, i, p. 415; *CR, 1261–64*, p. 126; Crook, *Records of the General Eyre*, pp. 130–1; *Baronial Plan*, pp. 273–4, 278–9. The account in *Wykes*, pp. 130–1, of a settlement on the Provisions between king and barons after Easter 1262 clearly refers to the negotiations preceding the Treaty of Kingston in 1261.

97 *DBM*, pp. 248–51; *Cron. Maior.*, pp. 49–50.

98 *Baronial Plan*, pp. 274–5.

99 *Ger. Cant.*, ii, p. 213.

100 *Foedera*, I, i, p. 419.

101 *Baronial Plan*, p. 273; cf. *CR, 1261–64*, p. 111.

king.[102] The other earls were present only very occasionally. Henry's lack of a powerful curialist nobility was one measure of the difference between 1262 and 1257.

Montfort's alienation, now deeper than ever, posed a more remote but potentially considerable threat to the new regime. The disturbances of 1261 had shown how masterfully he could utilise those local grievances which were now suppressed but not appeased. If trouble recurred, he could be expected to move in to exploit it and to do so the more easily because of the safe base which he enjoyed in France. That Louis was well disposed towards Montfort had been confirmed by Henry's fears in September 1261 that the French king might give a sympathetic hearing to the baronial case.[103] He was not yet the unbending defender of the common rights of monarchs that he had become by the time of the Mise of Amiens in 1264. Montfort's own continuing trust in his court was newly implied in January 1262, shortly after his arrival in France, when he and Eleanor agreed to accept the arbitration of Queen Margaret, first proposed in 1261 but then abandoned, in their quarrels with Henry.[104] Issued from Pacy-sur-Eure, their letters were themselves a testimony to Louis's friendship, for Pacy was one of the Norman castles of Montfort's twelfth-century Beaumont ancestors, which was now in Louis's hands. He was evidently enjoying Louis's hospitality, just as he had been when he entertained Eudes Rigaud at another royal castle, Neaufles, in August 1259.[105]

Montfort's initiative in reopening the arbitration provided both a new sign of his abiding preoccupation with the dower question and a way forward for Henry. He, too, was willing to accept Margaret's arbitration and by April 1262 he was preparing to go to France to state his case.[106] He did not intend, however, simply to reiterate the old charges of July 1260 concerning Montfort's obstructive tactics in 1259–60, but to launch a more comprehensive indictment, thoroughly prepared and reaching back into the distant past. The king summoned to Paris to help him both Guido de Pavia, a doctor of civil laws, and Gaillard de Solers, Montfort's old Gascon enemy, who was to give evidence about the

---

[102] c.53/52, mm. 1–5; *Foedera*, I, i, p. 420.
[103] *Dipl. Docs.*, No. 330; above, p. 212.
[104] Bémont, *Montfort* (2nd edn), p. 196, n. 3.
[105] F. M. Powicke, *The Loss of Normandy* (2nd edn, Manchester, 1961), pp. 107 n. 73, 108, 343; J. R. Strayer, *The Administration of Normandy under Saint Louis* (Cambridge, Mass., 1932), p. 94; above, p. 190.
[106] *CR, 1261–64*, pp. 120–1; *Dipl. Docs.*, No. 362.

losses sustained by Henry through Montfort's government of the duchy between 1248 and 1252.[107] Henry may have hoped to set these losses against any financial settlement favourable to Montfort which might result from arbitration. But his main aim was to discredit Montfort conclusively before the French court, and so to deprive him of the benevolent reception which he had always found in France and which made him a kind of peripheral shadow in English politics even in his absence. There were no longer to be wings for him to wait in.

Although Henry's visit to France was also intended to deal with unfinished business arising from the Treaty of Paris,[108] its chief purpose was thus to contribute to the pacification of England by destroying Montfort's position abroad. The importance that Henry attached to this was seen in his willingness to take the risks which he knew his departure entailed. Before leaving in July he transferred Horston castle in Derbyshire from one Montfortian, Hugh Despenser, forbade another, Peter de Montfort, to continue to fortify his Warwickshire seat at Beaudesert, and took steps to secure some key castles in southern England, including the Tower.[109] But neither his fears nor his hopes were realised. If local disorders failed to materialise, Henry's attempts to incriminate Montfort were inconclusive. Much of the dossier on the case survives and has already been used to fill out the picture of Montfort's early career.[110] Although his side of the case is more fully represented than Henry's, the substance of the king's accusations can be deduced from the earl's replies. They began with Henry's unrequited generosity in providing Montfort with his English inheritance in 1231, continued through the financial quarrels of the 1230s and Montfort's insults to Henry, and found their sharpest focus in his misgovernment (as the king saw it) of Gascony. Montfort for his part stressed his constant services to the Crown from the time of the Poitou campaign, the financial losses that Henry's service had brought him, and, of course, the inadequate provision for Eleanor's dower and *maritagium*.

Charge and countercharge emphasised the width of the gap which now separated the two men and the feud-like quality of their relationship, which had become increasingly apparent since the Treaty of Paris. What Queen Margaret made of these recriminations we do not know.

---

[107] *CR, 1261–64*, pp. 130–1.
[108] *Foedera*, I, i, p. 418; M. Gavrilovitch, *Étude sur le Traité de Paris de 1259* (Paris, 1899), p. 59.
[109] *CPR, 1258–66*, pp. 214–17; *CR, 1261–64*, pp. 65, 68, 73, 75–7, 129–30.
[110] Bémont, *Montfort* (1st edn), pp. 332–43. Mention of Queen Margaret as arbitrator in the preface to these documents points to a date in 1262.

In early September an epidemic struck the court, and Henry's serious illness may have temporarily halted the proceedings.[111] Our next information comes in a letter home from Henry to Basset and Merton, the justiciar and the chancellor, written on 8 October. The arbitration, wrote Henry, had broken down, and Montfort was reported to be intending to return to England to sow dissension between king and people. In the face of the danger to the kingdom from the earl's schemes they should take counsel for the preservation of the peace.[112] What follows is recorded only by the Kentish chronicler. On 12 October Montfort landed at Romsey in Kent, 'unpacified' with Henry. Arriving in London next day for the Michaelmas parliament, he published in parliament, against the justiciar's wishes, a papal bull which he had brought with him confirming the Provisions in their entirety and revoking the king's absolution. Then he swiftly returned to France from Shoreham, leaving behind him many 'associates and supporters' to forward his business.[113]

If this story is true, it describes one of the most revealing episodes of Montfort's career. It is difficult to doubt its truth. Letter and chronicle dovetail; the chronicler's details are circumstantial; we know that Montfort had been lobbying at the papal curia in September 1261 and that as recently as May 1262 baronial agents had been active there;[114] and the likelihood is that a Montfortian faction had temporarily got the upper hand and secured a bull in favour of the Provisions. Even more certainly than his holding of the Candlemas parliament of 1260 immediately after his rebuff in Paris,[115] Montfort's publication of that bull just when negotiations in France had broken down demonstrates the uncomfortable linkage between his private ambitions and his public cause. In the first half of the year, when the arbitration which he had reinitiated on his claims had been pending, he had done nothing for the Provisions; but once those claims failed he produced a bull in favour of the Provisions which he can only have been keeping in reserve for just such a contingency. The inquisitive historian is bound to wonder, unhistorically but naturally, what would have happened if, *per impossibile*, Montfort's claims had been fully satisfied. Would the bull have been consigned to some bottom drawer?

---

[111] *Baronial Plan*, pp. 288–9.
[112] *Dipl. Docs.*, No. 369.
[113] *Ger. Cant.*, ii, p. 217.
[114] *Dipl. Docs.*, Nos. 331, 364.
[115] Above, pp. 193, 196.

While Henry lingered in France, indulging himself in a long pilgrimage to Rheims in October and November, events were in train which would bring Montfort back to England, first as the champion of a faction and then as the leader of a cause. They hinged to a large extent upon accidents unconnected with political reform. Disaffection among a group of young nobles combined with the trauma of a successful Welsh revolt and the older and wider disaffection of the shires to leave both Henry's court and his government exposed to attack from all directions.

The first of these factors, noble disaffection, grew from the purge of Edward's retinue carried through by Henry and his queen between May 1261 and July 1262. Its chief victim was Roger Leyburn, Edward's steward and henchman, who was found guilty of peculation and subsequently, in July 1262, stripped of his goods and of substantial lands. At the same time Roger Clifford and other prominent members of the retinue were proscribed and their debts called in. The intention, almost certainly planned by the Savoyards at court, was to reinstitute a tight control over Edward and his finances. The effect was to separate Edward's retainers from their lord, to deprive them of patronage and money, and to create an embittered set of malcontents.[116] Henry's orders of 25 August 1262 to their leaders, including Leyburn, Clifford, John Giffard and Hamo Lestrange, not to tourney or go about in arms, suggests the threat to public order which they were seen to present.[117] Henry had made a still more powerful enemy in Gilbert de Clare, the new earl of Gloucester. After Earl Richard's death in July 1262 Henry had denied his eighteen-year-old son the early entry into his inheritance which he had hoped for, inaugurated enquiries into his father's usurpation of royal rights, and, early in 1263, proposed an allocation of dower to Gilbert's mother which took many of the prime Gloucester holdings out of the heir's hands. In March 1263 came Gloucester's riposte, in the form of his public refusal to do homage to Edward as Henry's heir.[118]

The outbreak of war with Wales made Henry's alienation of these men all the more maladroit, for most of them were marchers. Beginning with a revolt by Roger Mortimer's tenants in November 1262, a general

---

[116] *Ger. Cant.*, ii, pp. 214, 220–1; *CR, 1261–64*, pp. 117, 170–1; Prestwich, *Edward I*, pp. 37–8. The best extended treatment of this episode is Ridgeway, 'Politics of the English Royal Court', pp. 388–99.
[117] *CR, 1261–64*, p. 133; *CPR, 1258–66*, p. 227.
[118] *Ger. Cant.*, ii, pp. 215–16; *Ann. Dun.*, p. 220; Altschul, *A Baronial Family*, pp. 95–6.

Welsh rising had by the end of the year devastated lowland Hereford-shire and extended Llywelyn's power as far south as Brecon and Abergavenny.[119] This was the immediate danger which Henry faced when he returned to England on 20 December; but his underlying weakness, which the successes of the Welsh intensified, was the lack of public support for his government and the growing probability that baronial and local disaffection might unite, as they had done in 1261. John Mansel, visiting his Sussex estates in August 1262, had remarked in a letter that it would be all the better for the king if he had on his side such preachers as his opponents had;[120] and among the preachers' congregations may have been the 'associates and supporters' whom Montfort was to leave behind after his lightning visit in October. Henry's acute awareness of his vulnerability here was shown by an astonishing reversal of his previous policies. On 22 January 1263 he reissued the Provisions of Westminster (including some additions) with the greatest possible publicity. Sent for publication to the sheriffs, the two archbishops, the Bench justices, the exchequer, and the justices then on eyre in Kent, the text was prefaced by a statement that it had been issued 'purely by the free will of the king and in his full and free power'. This was clearly intended as a guarantee that Henry would not in future seek his release from the Provisions on the pretext that he had consented to them only under duress, the pretext used when he had applied to Alexander IV for absolution in 1261.[121]

Henry's concern to see the Provisions widely published shows how closely they had come to be identified with the local interests and aspirations which he hoped to mollify, vainly as it happened, by their reissue. Pressed by his council to make this move, he also undertook to observe 'other things to be provided' by Montfort, Norfolk, Philip Basset and Hugh Bigod.[122] Although this story is found only in the London chronicle, it nevertheless hints at the indirect influence which Montfort, from France, may have continued to exercise. After his return from England in October he had been occupied with the continuing plea over Eleanor's rights in Angoulême, which had been heard before the Paris *parlement* in November.[123] His affairs had been discussed by

[119] Lloyd, *History of Wales*, ii, p. 730.
[120] *RL*, ii, pp. 157–8. For the date of this letter, see Denholm-Young, *Richard of Cornwall*, pp. 172–3.
[121] *Statutes of the Realm* (11 vols., Record Comm., London, 1810–28), ed. A. Luders *et al.*, i, pp. 8n, 11n; *Cron. Maior.*, pp. 52–3; *Ann. Oseney*, pp. 130–1; *Flores Hist.*, ii, p. 477; *DBM*, pp. 244–5; *Baronial Plan*, pp. 295–6; Jacob, *Studies*, pp. 120–3.
[122] *Flores Hist.*, ii, p. 477; *Cron. Maior.*, p. 53; *Stat. Realm*, i, p. 8n.
[123] Wade, 'The Personal Quarrels', pp. 60–1, 131–3; Labarge, *Montfort*, pp. 192–3.

Henry and Louis in early December, prior to Henry's leaving for home, but their settlement only became urgent once Henry had seen the situation which confronted him in England. On 18 January 1263 he wrote to Louis exhorting him to see that the peacemaking process 'should be allowed no further relapse' because of the losses that the earl had caused to king and kingdom.[124] Coming as it did a few days before the reissue of the Provisions, this jittery letter showed how crucial Henry judged Montfort's conciliation to be for the preservation of the peace. There had never been a time when his capacity to return to England to make trouble, as he had done in January 1260 and in October 1262, had seemed more threatening.

Henry's proposals for peace were taken to Paris by his envoys in February, but despite Louis's best efforts they came to nothing. Henry was evidently the suppliant here and Montfort in a commanding position. According to Louis, Montfort had told him (surely with a touch of irony) that he knew that Henry wished him nothing but good, but that some of his council did not care much about peace.[125] On 22 February Louis reported Montfort's final rejection of Henry's proposals for his readmission to favour.[126] We have one clue as to what those proposals were. When the commission to Henry's envoys was cancelled on 22 March the documents handed over to John Mansel included one sealed by Montfort and Eleanor 'touching the restitution of manors of the king to be made under certain conditions'.[127] This must refer to the demesne manors extracted by Montfort from Henry during the negotiations of 1259 prior to the Treaty of Paris.[128] Central to Henry's accusations against Montfort in 1260, their alienation was evidently a cause of continuing bitterness and their return probably agreed to by the Montforts only on conditions which Henry was unwilling to accept, even to secure the settlement which he so much wanted.

During these negotiations in January and February nothing had been done to counter the Welsh, who by the beginning of March 1263 threatened to overrun Abergavenny and sweep into Gwent.[129] Edward's

---

[124] *BL*, ii, p. 235; *CPR*, *1258–66*, pp. 240–1 (translation corrected in *Baronial Plan*, p. 300).

[125] *Dipl. Docs.*, No. 377.

[126] *Dipl. Docs.*, No. 322, wrongly dated to 1261. For the correct date see *Baronial Plan*, p. 300 n. 4.

[127] *CPR*, *1258–66*, p. 241.

[128] Above, pp. 182, 188–90.

[129] *RL*, ii, pp. 219–21, 230–1; T. F. Tout, 'Wales and the March in the Barons' Wars', *Collected Papers* (3 vols., Manchester, 1932–34), ii, p. 65.

return to England about 24 February with a large mercenary army might have restored the situation, as it was intended to do; but in fact his arrival turned a foreign war into a civil war. The sequence of events is set out in a neglected source, the Merton version of the *Flores Historiarum*. Edward's alien followers, Burgundians, French and Champenois (says the chronicle), were promoted over his English retainers. Flying in the face of the Provisions, he bestowed offices and castles on the newcomers. Violently indignant at this, the former knights of Edward's retinue joined together with all those whom Henry's government had offended and summoned Montfort back to England.[130] Other chronicles corroborate much of this: the unpopularity of Edward's army, its return contrary to the Provisions, the unwillingness of the English to help Edward.[131]

Montfort returned to England about 25 April 1263.[132] It was almost exactly five years since the start of the reform movement and he had spent almost exactly half that time, some thirty months, in France.[133] If the Merton chronicle is right, he was called back to England by a disgruntled faction of Edward's former retainers, of whom Leyburn and Clifford (to judge from their later actions) were probably the chief. They knew that they could exploit the general detestation of Henry's government and the symbolic value of the Provisions to present his return as that of a hero in a great and popular cause. Montfort for his part must have seen that conditions had never been more favourable for his restoration. Publicly untouched by compromise and collaboration, he had behind him both a magnate party and the wider consensus, ecclesiastical, provincial, baronial and knightly, of those who favoured reform. His private negotiations with Henry had failed, and his military expertise might swing the balance in the war which seemed to be imminent. Only once more in his life, and then for a matter of days, would he return to France.[134] From the incubator of his own resentments and grievances he was now to emerge as a

---

[130] *Flores Hist.*, iii, p. 256.
[131] *Ann. Burton*, p. 500; *Ann. Winton.*, p. 100; *Flores Hist.*, ii, p. 478.
[132] *Ann. Dun.*, p. 221.
[133] Montfort's absences were: (1) c. 8 May–c. 7 June 1258 (Chaplais, 'Making of the Treaty of Paris', pp. 241–2); (2) c. 6 Nov. 1258–c. 9 Feb. 1259 (Paris, v, pp. 720, 737); (3) c. 10 March 1259–c. 13 Oct. 1259 (*CPR, 1258–66*, p. 18; *Layettes*, iii, No. 4554); (4) c. 16 Oct. 1259–c. 1 Jan. 1260 (*Recueil des Historiens des Gaules*, 23, p. 467; *DBM*, pp. 206–7; *CR, 1259–61*, pp. 228, 259); (5) c. 2 Sept. 1261 (*Dipl. Docs.*, No. 330); (6) c. 1 Dec. 1261–c. 12 Oct. 1262 (*Ann. Dun.*, p. 217; *Ann. Oseney*, p. 129; *Ger. Cant.*, ii, p. 217); (7) c. 14 Oct. 1262–c. 25 April 1263 (*Ger. Cant.*, ii, p. 217; *Ann. Dun.*, p. 221).
[134] Below, pp. 243–4.

CHAPTER 7

The return of the general, 1263–64

(A) DISORDER, APRIL–JULY 1263

Simon de Montfort's return to England in April 1263 inaugurated the final phase of his career. He now became the undisputed master of a movement which would eventually give him control of the king's government and would last until its extinction at Evesham in August 1265. From the start of the reform movement his words and actions, the range of his experience, and the entrenchment of his friends in the movement's institutions had given him a distinctive place among the reformers. When the king's restoration moved reform towards open rebellion in 1261, his activities as the impresario of resistance had anticipated his later commanding role. Yet until 1263 his presence in England had been too intermittent, his support too hesitant and fragmented, and his leadership often too factious for him to be quite the *dux baronum*[1] which he became, somewhat paradoxically, by the invitation of a faction in 1263. His response to the appeal from Edward's former followers made him the captain of a cause; but of what cause? That of the displaced persons who had summoned him back? Of the supporters of the Provisions? Or of that powerful and enduring cause, his own avaricious sense of injustice? When he resumed his career in England there were more ambiguities in Montfort's position than the simple contrast between the confederate of 1258 and the generalissimo of 1263 might suggest.

These ambiguities were not at once apparent. The immediate consequence of Montfort's return was the formation, under his auspices, of a broad but fragile coalition whose public rallying-cry was the enforcement of the Provisions. The alliance first became visible in a meeting at Oxford, shortly after his arrival, where the presence not only

---

[1] *Flores Hist.*, iii, p. 481.

of Montfort himself but of Gilbert de Clare, hitherto uncommitted, of John de Warenne and Roger Clifford, both among Edward's ousted *familiares*, and, most remarkably, of Richard of Cornwall, suggested the possible scale of the opposition to the king.[2] The choice of venue may in itself have been significant, for in 1258 Oxford had been both the intended mustering-point for a campaign in Wales and the forum for the making of the Provisions. In both respects the proceedings of 1263 referred back, perhaps deliberately, to these earlier ones. After renewing their oaths of 1258 to the Provisions, the confederates sent a letter to the king, under Clifford's seal and sometime before 20 May, demanding not only the enforcement of the Provisions but also, and still more challengingly, the denunciation as mortal enemies of all those going against them. Henry had already conceded something through the emergency reissue of the Provisions of Westminster in January 1263; but what his opponents now wanted, almost certainly, was the Provisions of Oxford *sensu stricto*, with the full range of conciliar controls instituted in 1258. This, of course, Henry could not afford to concede. Still less could he agree to denounce the contravenors of the Provisions, for this would be tantamount to allowing the proscription of the court. The demands were designed only to provoke the king's refusal, which predictably came, and to justify the violence which came next.[3]

Interposed between Montfort's exile and the revolution brought about by his return, the Oxford meeting was Montfort's Finland Station. It was followed by 'the first war of the barons', as a chancery clerk was later to call it: a short-lived but savage series of attacks on the aliens, royalists and courtiers whom the ex-Edwardians blamed for their dismissal, and Montfort and his friends for the overthrow of the Provisions. It was Queen Eleanor who had masterminded the dissolution of Edward's affinity and in consequence it was her Savoyard relatives who now found themselves most vulnerable. The war began with the capture of Peter of Aigueblanche, the Savoyard bishop of Hereford, in his own cathedral on 7 June 1263, his imprisonment, together with his alien canons, in a neighbouring castle, and the

---

[2] For the loyalties of John de Warenne, see Ridgeway, 'The Lord Edward and the Provisions of Oxford', p. 97; *Peerage*, XII, i, pp. 503–4; and Prestwich, *Edward I*, pp. 37–8. For contemporary doubts about Richard of Cornwall's loyalties at this time, see Denholm-Young, *Richard of Cornwall*, pp. 119, 122.

[3] *Ann. Dun.*, p. 221; *Cron. Maior.*, p. 53. There seem to be confused accounts of the Oxford meeting in *Guisborough*, p. 187, and *Wykes*, pp. 133–4, though the latter may be referring to a second meeting held in London in May.

Plate 10. Montfort's seal.

destruction of his estates. It continued with the seizure of Robert Walerand's Herefordshire castle of Kilpeck and the occupation of Bristol, Gloucester, Worcester, Bridgnorth and Shrewsbury. The securing of the line of the Severn, a much fought-over frontier in the next two years, points to the strategic aim of protecting the march against royal reprisals; though if Montfort's sharp eye for a military advantage can be detected here, the leaders in all these enterprises were the former Edwardians, Roger Clifford, Hamo Lestrange, John de Vaux and Roger Leyburn, together with John Giffard.[4] Disorder, however, soon spread far outside their ambit. In June and early July prominent royalists began to come under attack throughout England, their lands seized and their goods plundered. Among the chief victims were John Mansel and Simon Walton, bishop of Norwich, Henry's agents in securing papal absolution from his oath in 1262; Robert Walerand, whose estates were occupied across fifteen counties; and Peter of Savoy.[5]

Although Henry's reaction came quickly it was quite inadequate to deal with what amounted to a nationwide breakdown of order. Between

---

[4] *CR, 1264–68*, p. 512; *Robert of Gloucs.*, ii, pp. 738–9; *Flores Hist.*, ii, pp. 479–81; *Ger. Cant.*, ii, pp. 221–2; *Ann. Dun.*, pp. 221–2; Rishanger, *De Bellis*, pp. 10–11.

[5] *Wykes*, p. 135; *The Chronicle of Bury St Edmunds, 1212–1301*, ed. A. Gransden (London, 1964), p. 27; *CR, 1261–64*, pp. 249–50, 369–70; Jacob, *Studies*, pp. 225–8.

12 and 15 June he appointed military captains for the northern counties and for Kent and Sussex, replaced the custodians of seven castles, sent Edward to take the fealty of Dover and the Cinque Ports, and reissued the Provisions of Westminster for publication in the counties.[6] Then, on 19 June, he retreated to the Tower.[7] As in previous crises, he had moved rapidly to secure the south-east, vital for his links with the continent; but here, as in other respects, he was completely outmatched by his brother-in-law.

If Montfort's precise role in the early stages of the insurrection is unclear, there is enough evidence to suggest that he was its director. Immediately on his return he had allied with the Welsh, to whom the barons had already made unsuccessful overtures in 1262. Their help had made possible the capture of the Severn valley towns and, at the barons' instigation, they had also besieged, taken and demolished Edward's castle at Diserth, in north-east Wales.[8] If the Merton version of the *Flores Historiarum* can be believed, it was Montfort, too, who had selected Peter of Aigueblanche as the rebels' first victim, realising the popular support to be gained by attacking the man generally held responsible for the Sicilian Business and the heavy taxation that it had brought.[9] To have exploited this chance of winning friends would have typified Montfort's sharp political sensitivities. Yet in the marchers' short campaign he seems to have played no part. Only one chronicle, a late source, mentions his participation,[10] and it seems likely that throughout early June he remained at Oxford or, more probably, at Kenilworth to guide events and to try to build a national movement out of what was in origin the violent but inchoate anger of a party. Without some co-ordination the attacks on the royalists could hardly have spread so far and so fast – to Kent, East Anglia, Yorkshire and the south-west, besides the marches – and baronial initiatives may have ignited the latent discontents of the shires, just as they had done when the eyres had been disrupted in 1262.[11] Writing sombrely to the chancellor in mid June, Robert de Neville, Henry's new captain in the north, spoke of some whom he had judged loyal being 'by the preaching of the rebels wholly

[6] *CPR, 1258–66*, pp. 263–5. For the reissue of the Provisions, see *Stat. Realm*, i, p. 11, n. 11, and P. A. Brand, 'The Contribution of the Period of Baronial Reform (1258–1267) to the Development of the Common Law in England' (Oxford D.Phil. thesis, 1974), p. 37.

[7] *Baronial Plan*, p. 387.

[8] Above, pp. 212–13; *Flores Hist.*, ii, p. 480; iii, p. 256; *Ann. Cestr.*, p. 85; Rishanger, *De Bellis*, p. 11.

[9] *Flores Hist.*, iii, pp. 256–7; *Wykes*, p. 134.

[10] *Rishanger Chronica et Annales*, p. 17.

[11] Above, pp. 211–12.

won over to them'; and there is other evidence, most of it unfortunately undated, for the despatch of *procuratores* and *cursores*, 'agents' and 'runners', who were active on Montfort's behalf.[12]

Once the initial offensive in the marches was over, however, Montfort took public command. In a bloodless and masterly campaign lasting barely three weeks he achieved what appeared to be a complete victory for the Provisions. About 24 June letters were sent to the Londoners, under his seal, asking if they would support the Provisions.[13] Then, moving via Reading, Guildford (which he reached about 30 June) and Reigate, and dismissing an offer of negotiations from Richard of Cornwall, he made for Kent.[14] He had correctly seen the need to avoid any confrontation with Henry, Edward, and Edward's foreign knights, who were stationed at London and Windsor, until the Channel ports had been secured. By 9 July he had been joined by large numbers of Kentish knights and had won over the Cinque Ports. By 12 July, when he reached Canterbury, he had heard that the Londoners were willing to support him.[15] It was probably about this time that the lands of the absent archbishop, Boniface of Savoy, were plundered by Montfort's sons and by Leyburn, Clifford and the other conquering heroes of the marches.[16] With the entry of the barons into London on 15 July and the surrender of Dover castle, 'the key of England', a week later, the south-east was in his hands.[17]

In parallel with this triumphant progress, the political programme of Montfort and his allies had been evolving, to reach its final form in a peace made in London on 16 July. That evolution, greatly clarified by Carpenter, reveals a good deal about Montfort's objectives and the forces and pressures that he was attempting to direct and control.[18] About the time that Montfort had written to the Londoners on 24 June, the barons had sent the king a petition, probably drafted some time before that date and enclosed with Montfort's letter. It is recorded by

---

[12] *Dipl. Docs.*, No. 387; Jacob, *Studies*, pp. 229–30.
[13] *Cron. Maior.*, pp. 53–4.
[14] *RL*, ii, p. 248; Carpenter, 'Simon de Montfort', pp. 7–8.
[15] *Ger. Cant.*, ii, p. 233; *Cron. Maior.*, p. 54.
[16] L. E. Wilshire, *Boniface of Savoy, Carthusian and Archbishop of Canterbury, 1207–1270* (Salzburg, 1977), pp. 73–4, 88–9.
[17] *Cron. Maior.*, p. 55; *Ger. Cant.*, ii, p. 223; Paris, iii, p. 28; *CPR, 1258–66*, p. 270; *Baronial Plan*, p. 310.
[18] D. A. Carpenter, 'King Henry III's "Statute" against Aliens: July 1263', *EHR*, 107 (1992), pp. 925–44. In this and the following paragraph I have followed the general lines of Carpenter's interpretation, though with some additional information and changes of emphasis.

Arnold fitz Thedmar and contained the core of what was to become the
later peace.[19] In it the barons asked for the inviolable observance of
the Provisions, but undertook to withdraw anything in them found by
elected arbitrators to be prejudicial to king or kingdom, and to correct
what needed correction. Their second request was for the future
government of the kingdom by natives and not by others. This new call
for the exclusion of aliens from the country's government, which had
formed no part of the original Provisions, was subsequently taken much
further. On 29 June the bishop of Worcester, Walter de Cantilupe,
wrote to the chancellor, Walter Merton, urging him to persuade Henry
and Edward to accept a form of peace (*forma pacis*) which the bishops
of London, Lincoln, and Coventry and Lichfield were sending to
the king and his son on the barons' behalf. The terms of the *forma* were
set out by a chronicler, the St Albans author of the *Flores Historiarum*.[20]
They asked for the release of Henry of Almain, recently taken prisoner
at Boulogne while pursuing the royalist fugitive, John Mansel, who had
fled abroad about 29 June;[21] the placing of the king's castles in baronial
custody; the inviolable observance of the Provisions (with no mention of
the arbitration proposed earlier); and the permanent expulsion of all
aliens, 'never to return', save those whose continuing residence was
acceptable to the kingdom's faithful men. The chief novelty here lay in
the final uncompromising demand for the aliens' departure. The formal
treaty of 16 July incorporated all the central points of the *forma pacis*, with
the exception of the earlier request for Henry of Almain's release:
observance of the Provisions, with the reintroduction of the proposal
for their amendment by arbitration; government by natives; and the
banishment of the aliens.[22]

The most unexpected feature of this sequence of texts is not the
routine demand for the Provisions but the call for measures against
the aliens which had been grafted on to it. The prominence given to the
alien question reflected both the opposition of the marchers to Edward's
alien followers, who by the end of June were plundering the countryside
from their base at Windsor,[23] and Montfort's growing realisation of the

---

[19] *Cron. Maior.*, p. 54; Carpenter, 'King Henry III's "Statute"', pp. 929–30, 943.
[20] *Foedera*, I, i, p. 427; *Flores Hist.*, ii, p. 482; Carpenter, 'King Henry III's "Statute"', pp. 930–1,
943.
[21] For this episode, see *Baronial Plan*, pp. 305, 307, and Carpenter, 'King Henry III's "Statute"',
p. 930 and n. 4.
[22] *CPR, 1258–66*, pp. 269–70; Carpenter, 'King Henry III's "Statute"', pp. 931, 944.
[23] *Cron. Maior.*, p. 55; *Flores Hist.*, ii, p. 482.

extent to which broader and more popular feeling against the aliens could be exploited. Orchestrated though it had been, the June revolt had raised against the aliens a more spontaneous movement of local opposition, whose energies are fleetingly revealed in the remark of the *Flores* chronicler that the common people, the *vulgus*, contemptuously despised all who could not speak English.[24] Those who came into this class are not defined, but they probably included the alien clergy, the moneylenders of Cahors, attacked in London, and the ministers of such aliens as Boniface of Savoy.[25] The full vehemence of this movement may have been apprehended by Montfort and his friends only when the rising was underway. The shift from the moderate proposal for the exclusion of aliens from government to the much more thoroughgoing one for their exclusion from the kingdom, 'never to return' in the emotive words of the *forma pacis*, was probably an attempt to exploit the nationalist fervour made manifest during the rising. The terms of the *forma* were known to the Dunstable annalist as well as the St Albans chronicler, so they are likely to have been widely published.[26] In 1258 baronial opposition to the aliens had been largely directed against the king's favourites, the Lusignans, though popular opposition may have been less discriminating. But by 1263 antagonism towards aliens had deepened and become socially more comprehensive. Growing from Henry's importing of alien mercenaries, the turning of the Savoyards against reform, and the continuing presence of alien clergy and usurers, among other factors, it was to remain a force in politics until 1265 and beyond. There was here a reservoir of potential support for Montfort's cause, whose value – so these texts suggest – he rapidly came to see; just as he had previously seen the capital to be made from knightly and local grievances against royal government and from an opening attack on the detested Peter of Aigueblanche. Support here was all the more valuable because the proscription of aliens was seen, though wrongly, as an activity sanctioned by the Provisions. The chroniclers' opinions that Edward's return with foreign troops was contrary to the Provisions shows how opposition to aliens could be factitiously justified as a defence of the letter of reform.[27] Montfort's political intuitiveness and practical skill in organising these various forces made him not only 'the first sole

[24] *Flores Hist.*, ii, p. 481.
[25] *Cron. Maior.*, p. 55; *Ger. Cant.*, ii, p. 222.
[26] *Ann. Dun.*, pp. 223–4; Carpenter, 'King Henry III's "Statute"', pp. 936–7.
[27] Above, p. 223; Carpenter, 'King Henry III's "Statute"', pp. 927–8.

leader of a political movement in English history',[28] but something more remarkable: the first with any claim to have been a populist.

On the face of it, the peace of 16 July 1263 marked a stunning victory for Montfort. Shielded from military subversion or continental interference, the resurrection of the Provisions promised a return to the fullblooded restraints on royal government originally imposed in 1258. Ministerial changes which followed the peace not only reversed the consequences of Henry's coup of June 1261 but also vindicated the principle of consent to the appointment of the great officers which the Provisions embodied. Hugh Despenser was once again made justiciar and given the Tower; Nicholas of Ely replaced Walter Merton as chancellor; and Henry, prior of St Radegund's, Kent, became treasurer.[29] If the appointments of Despenser and Nicholas of Ely restored the *status quo ante absolutionem*, the reinstatement of Richard de Grey at Dover on 26 July brought back the original custodian of 1258. His was one of a number of appointments at this time by which control over the more important royal castles was transferred to baronial nominees, just as had happened in 1258.[30]

Nor were the Provisions much qualified by the undertaking to arbitrate on their terms, for the commitment was imprecise, the arbitrating body was left undefined, and in fact the arbitration seems never to have been put in hand. The omission of any such proposal from the *forma pacis*, despite its inclusion in the original baronial petition and in the final peace, suggests that it may have provoked disagreement. This would not have been surprising, given Montfort's own quickening and more evident sense of the Provisions as inviolable, a holy cause, made 'to the honour of God', as he said in his letter to the Londoners. In a theme which would become more insistent in the next few months, their defence was beginning to be seen as a crusade in an almost literal sense. One chronicler told how Montfort had responded to the barons' invitation to return to England by saying 'that he had taken the Cross and was very willing to die fighting among wicked Christians for the liberty of the land and the holy church as among pagans'. Another preserves the curious detail that he ordered his marcher supporters to be

---

[28] Carpenter, 'Simon de Montfort', p. 3.

[29] Above, p. 209; *CPR, 1258–66*, p. 271; *CR, 1261–64*, p. 242; *Ger. Cant.*, ii, pp. 223–4; *Baronial Plan*, pp. 314, 330.

[30] *CPR, 1258–66*, p. 271; *DBM*, pp. 112–13; *Baronial Plan*, pp. 74–5. As Carpenter notes ('King Henry III's "Statute"', p. 931, n. 3), the appointment of new castellans by letters patent explains why this issue, raised in the *forma pacis*, was omitted from the peace terms of 16 July.

tonsured before they set off to destroy their enemies. Like the baronial rebels of 1215, they were, in his eyes at least, akin to 'the army of God'.[31]

This was a view which may have had some initial sympathy, though never wholehearted endorsement, from one of the two groups of Montfortian allies who declared themselves about this time: the bishops. The small group of Montfortian bishops prominent in the negotiations of June–July 1263 was soon to expand and to become one of the main props of the new regime. It may already have made its mark in the proposal to arbitrate on the Provisions; and certainly its members were to be closely associated with similar proposals in the next eighteen months. Montfort's convictions about the sanctity of the Provisions make it unlikely that the suggestion was his; nor can it have been Henry's, since it appears in the baronial petition sent to him about 24 June, preceding any negotiations with the king. Its begetter may well have been Walter de Cantilupe. Trained in the schools, whose dialectic aimed at conciliation and concord, Cantilupe had already shown himself prepared to compromise on the Provisions in the Treaty of Kingston, made in 1261; and in his letter of 29 June to the chancellor he had spoken feelingly of being bound to labour with all his strength for 'the tranquillity and peace of the kingdom'.[32] He had been as good as his word at Bristol in early July, when he had arranged a short-lived truce with Edward, then preparing to make the town a base for fresh resistance.[33] Both he and his fellow bishops may likewise have been responsible for the proviso, found both in the *forma pacis* and in the final peace, that aliens acceptable to the king's *fideles* might stay in England: a concession favouring, among others, alien clergy, of whom the bishops might disapprove but whose expulsion from their livings during the revolt they could hardly condone.[34] But the bishops would not concede more than this. The memory of the Sicilian Business and of Henry's misgovernment of the Church; an attitude to kingship which recognised the king's duty to do justice and to rule for the common good, in subjection to the law; and, in the case of Cantilupe and of his fellow negotiator Richard of Gravesend, bishop of Lincoln, personal friendship with Montfort: all were factors which inclined a growing

---

[31] *Cron. Maior.*, p. 54; *Oxenedes*, p. 226; *Flores Hist.*, iii, p. 256; Tyerman, *England and the Crusades*, p. 146; J. C. Holt, *The Northerners* (Oxford, 1961), p. 8.

[32] Above, pp. 81, 214; *CR, 1261–64*, p. 126; *Foedera*, I, i, p. 427.

[33] *Flores Hist.*, ii, pp. 482–3; *Baronial Plan*, p. 310.

[34] Cf. Carpenter, 'King Henry III's "Statute"', p. 938. For the later activities of the Montfortian bishops, see below, pp. 265–6, 269–70, 275, 291–305, 320.

number of bishops to look to Montfort as one whose beliefs about what constituted just government, embodied in the Provisions, coincided with their own.

The newfound support of a second group, the Londoners, was to become another of the mainstays of Montfortian power. It grew from a combination of national and local grievances which is not easy to analyse. The mayor and aldermen who governed London, rich men and mostly royalists, had assented to the Provisions in 1258 only reluctantly; and the implementation of the reforms widened the division between these men and the *populares* whom reform benefited. Bigod's eyre in 1258–59 had given an outlet to social grievances, and procedure by *querela*, oral complaint, had been used to curb aldermanic privilege.[35] It was only in June 1263, however, that these local divisions aligned themselves for a second time with those of national politics. Two crucial events explain how this came about. First, on 29 June Edward had broken into the New Temple, seizing the private deposits of treasure held there in order to pay his alien followers at Windsor. Edward's robbery of the bank was the signal for a general rising in the city: like the parallel movement in the countryside, it was chiefly directed against aliens, royalists and courtiers, who were extensively plundered. Second, the mayor of the city, Thomas fitz Thomas, went over to the rebels, both among the Londoners and the barons. A *déclassé* patrician, fitz Thomas stood aside while the rioting was in progress, disregarded the city magnates, governed through the folkmoot (the traditional 'open' assembly of all the citizens), and gave power to the craft guilds at the expense of the aldermanic oligarchy. This internal bouleversement in London coincided with Montfort's successful appeal to the city and the subsequent arrival of the barons. It linked once again the cause of the Provisions with the cause of what was now the dominant party among the Londoners and of Thomas fitz Thomas, the party's leader. In the slippery world of Montfort's final years, when baronial friends came and went, this stable alliance offered a reassuring security.[36]

Superficially, then, the triumph of Montfort and the Provisions in July 1263 may have appeared to rest on foundations which were as substantial as those which had supported the reforming movement in

---

[35] G. A. Williams, *Medieval London: From Commune to Capital* (London, 1963), pp. 211–14.
[36] *Cron. Maior.*, pp. 55–6; *Ann. Dun.*, pp. 222–3; *Ger. Cant.*, ii, p. 223; Williams, *Medieval London*, pp. 219–22; D. A. Carpenter, 'Thomas fitzThomas', *DNB: Missing Persons*, pp. 227–8.

1258; in some ways, even more substantial. Montfort was backed not only by a large party of barons but also by bishops and townsmen whose support in 1258 had been much less evident; he had identified his cause with an anti-alien movement socially more comprehensive and politically more forceful than anything that had existed in 1258; while his hold on London and the south-east, his control of some key castles, and to a lesser extent his alliance with the Welsh, meant that the revolution seemed unlikely to be easily upset. Yet in reality his position was tangled in contradictions and cross-purposes which left him extremely vulnerable to a royalist *revanche*. The military strength which had made his coup possible largely rested on his alliance with Leyburn and the other ex-Edwardians, most of them marchers. They had called him back to England to serve as a party leader against the queen and the courtiers who had dismissed them, and the foreigners who had replaced them. But ultimately they looked beyond vengeance and compensation towards a full restoration to Edward's favour. They needed Montfort because his charismatic identification with the Provisions could bring out the disaffected men of the shires, and because his generalship would be invaluable for the coercive purge of the court which they envisaged. In neither respect did Montfort fail them. Their own supposed enthusiasm for the Provisions, therefore, was hardly more than opportunism, a specious cover for narrower ambitions. Roger Clifford, for example, the sealer of the Oxford letter demanding Henry's renewed assent to the Provisions, had been Edward's man through and through until his dismissal in 1262, and never a reformer.[37] A fuller analysis of Montfort's following will be given later;[38] but it is already evident that he was partly dependent on the continuing support of men who had no reason to give it once their own objectives had been achieved.

As an 'army of God', crusading for the Provisions, the marchers lacked all conviction. They included men such as Hamo Lestrange, later described as 'a most notorious plunderer', and John fitz Alan, whose contribution to the 'crusade' included the sacking of Bishop's Castle in Shropshire, belonging to Aigueblanche, the killing of the constable, and the profitable detention of the castle for nearly six years.[39] Clifford, their leader, had forced the abbot of Dore to buy off

---

[37] Ridgeway, 'The Lord Edward and the Provisions of Oxford', pp. 97–8.
[38] Below, pp. 248–56.
[39] *Flores Hist.*, ii, p. 502; *Registrum Ricardi de Swinfield Episcopi Herefordensis*, ed. W. W. Capes (Canterbury and York Soc., 1909), p. 86. Cf. *Ann. Cestr.*, pp. 86–7.

the threatened devastation of his Herefordshire manor of Holme Lacy for £42, though the abbot's only offence was to be a tenant of the dean and chapter of Hereford, themselves tenants of Aigueblanche. But the lawless profiteering so evident in the marches, at the time when the barons 'took the revenues throughout the bishopric of Hereford',[40] was equally evident in other parts of England touched by the rising. However carefully Montfort may have tried to direct its course, it soon degenerated into a scramble for plunder. The sufferers were often inconspicuous and uncommitted men, set upon only for their refusal to commit themselves by setting upon others. Here the testimony of the chroniclers is borne out by the long list of those victims for whom restitution was later ordered. That twenty-four of the fifty-two men who appear on it held estates in only one county suggests that among the losers had been many others besides acquisitive royalists with wide lands.[41]

Still more damaging to Montfort's cause was the onslaught on the alien clergy, already alluded to, and on the queen. In a movement which resembled that led by Robert Tweng in 1231-2, aliens and their churches were attacked, their revenues appropriated, and newcomers intruded into their livings. At Beetham in Westmorland, for example, the church had been held by an Italian, but it was seized during the troubles by William, son of Sir Roger de Lancaster, who was still holding it by armed force in January 1264 and barring the entry of the clerk presented by the rightful patron.[42] A more dangerous victim than any alien clerk was Queen Eleanor. She was deeply antagonised both by the attacks on her friends and servants, including her Savoyard uncles and her steward Matthew Bezill,[43] and by the insults offered to her person. Attempting to move upriver from the Tower to Windsor on 13 July, during the disturbances in the city, she had been driven back by a mob who bombarded her with stones, filth and insults from the safety of London bridge:[44] an episode which was to embitter Montfort's future relations not only with the royal family but also, and much more harmfully, with the queen's brother-in-law, Louis IX.

---

[40] H. M. Colvin, 'Holme Lacy: An Episcopal Manor and its Tenants in the Twelfth and Thirteenth Centuries', *Medieval Studies Presented to Rose Graham*, ed. V. Ruffer and A. J. Taylor (Oxford, 1950), pp. 32–4, 38–40.

[41] *Ger. Cant.*, ii, p. 223; *Wykes*, pp. 134–5; *CR, 1261–64*, pp. 243–53, 257, 265.

[42] *Cron. Maior.*, p. 53; *Flores Hist.*, ii, p. 481; *RL*, ii, p. 253. For Tweng, see Powicke, *King Henry III*, pp. 77–9.

[43] *Baronial Plan*, p. 302; Carpenter, 'King Henry III's "Statute"', p. 928.

[44] *Ann. Dun.*, p. 223; *Flores Hist.*, ii, pp. 481–2.

Indeed, the consequences of the disorders of 1263 were to dog Montfort almost for the rest of his life. They associated his cause with violence and injustice, impiety and private greed. These abuses could not be regarded entirely as accidents, the regrettable consequences of passionate convictions which had gone out of control. The threat of violence lay at the heart of the Provisions for which Montfort was campaigning. If the attacks on the innocent were unpremeditated, it was the Provisions themselves which had demanded the proscription as mortal enemies of all who opposed them: a clause which the chronicler Wykes and later Henry himself saw as the root of the troubles.[45] Even chroniclers who were better disposed than Wykes to Montfort, and who acknowledged the coercion that was built into the Provisions, changed course when confronted with coercion's consequences. The Dunstable annalist, for example, who had detested the Lusignans and applauded Montfort's rebuttal of the charges against him in 1260, wrote severely that the depredations were 'contrary to right and could not stand'.[46] More germane perhaps to Montfort's fortunes were the attitudes of the knights and gentry, which may have undergone a comparable shift. As Dr Knowles has revealed, at some point in the reforming period there was a marked slippage of support for Montfort among the lesser knights who had supported reform so vigorously in 1258–59.[47] Though the slippage is difficult to chart or date precisely, the disorders may have given it an additional momentum. Both the reluctant conscripts among the rebels – a group identified by the chroniclers[48] – and still more the uninvolved who had been plundered, are likely to have had mixed feelings about the benefits of the Provisions. Almost insensibly, Henry himself would soon come to stand for law, order and the rights of property: a paradoxical position for a king whose lawless and disorderly court had done much to provoke the reform movement in the first place.

To what extent was this outcome Montfort's personal responsibility? The conduct of the revolt, and the peace which had ended it, had shown his considerable skills in building a broadly based alliance. The attacks on the Savoyards, for example, struck at men who had been both the

---

[45] *Wykes*, p. 134; *DBM*, pp. 100–1, 254–5.
[46] *Ann. Dun.*, pp. 209, 215, 221–2.
[47] C. H. Knowles, 'The Disinherited, 1265–80: A Political and Social Study of the Supporters of Simon de Montfort and the Resettlement after the Barons' War' (Univ. of Wales, Aberystwyth, Ph.D. thesis, 1959), Part ii, pp. 80–3.
[48] *Ger. Cant.*, ii, p. 223; *Wykes*, p. 134.

enemies of the Provisions, closely associated with their overthrow in 1261, and also members of the queen's inner circle, responsible for the disgrace of Edward's former followers who had led the rising.[49] Yet the revolt did more to prove his keen political intelligence than to vindicate his idealism or sense of justice. The early resort to force had often characterised his campaigns, and to some extent the rising of 1263 applied to English politics the coercive tactics that he had used in Gascony between 1248 and 1252.[50] His sanctioning of the attacks on Boniface of Savoy's property in Kent, in which his sons participated (if Boniface himself can be believed), shows how deeply he was implicated in the methods of the rebels.[51] In so far as the innocent suffered along with the 'guilty', costing him support, the flames from the fire that he had lit blew back in his face. Revolt was easier to organise and to concert than to control.

Potentially more harmful still to his reputation were the first intimations, overwhelmingly confirmed in 1264–65, that he had a private interest in the prosecution of his opponents. The charge levied by the hostile but usually well-informed author of the Merton *Flores Historiarum* that he intended to pay his men from the spoiling of Aigueblanche cannot be substantiated.[52] But one of his first acts on reaching London was to give custody of the younger John Mansel's fortified manor house at Sedgewick in Sussex to his friend and ally Peter de Montfort (though Peter's tenure was brief), and shortly afterwards, on 1 August, to commit all the elder Mansel's vast lands, abandoned by their owner's flight abroad, to his second son Simon. For the first time in his career he had control of the king's government, and with it the means to create the endowment for his family which he had always sought. But the enrichment of Simon did not go unnoticed. What was the justification for it? asked an anonymous letter-writer, probably early in 1264. 'He ought not to give himself and his men plunder and rewards if he works for the common good.'[53] In the hour of his triumph all the old ambiguities about Montfort's motives, the conflicts of private and public interest that characterise his career, were beginning to re-emerge.

---

[49] Above, pp. 204, 207, 220; Ridgeway, 'The Lord Edward and the Provisions of Oxford', p. 98.
[50] Carpenter, 'Simon de Montfort', pp. 6–7; above, pp. 109, 117.
[51] Wilshire, *Boniface of Savoy*, pp. 88–9.
[52] *Flores Hist.*, iii, p. 257.
[53] *CPR, 1258–66*, pp. 269, 273, 279; *Ann. Tewk.*, p. 180.

(B) THE ROYALIST REVIVAL, JULY–DECEMBER 1263

'The first war of the barons' brought in the first administration of Simon de Montfort. It was short-lived, lasting a bare three months from mid July to late October 1263. Unlike the more broadly based baronial oligarchy of 1258, this was very much Montfort's government, in its constitution, its principles, and in the earl's influence on both. Until at least mid August he stayed near the capital, camping out in Richard of Cornwall's park at Isleworth, with the marchers close at hand.[54] It was not generally the men who had brought him to power, however, who were now promoted, but rather Montfort's personal friends, the long-standing supporters of the Provisions. If Hugh Despenser, reappointed as justiciar, clearly fell into this category, so also perhaps did the new treasurer, Henry, prior of St Radegund's, to whose house Montfort was a benefactor.[55] Five of the eight castles which changed hands in late July also went to established Montfortians: Corfe and Sherborne to Peter de Montfort, Northampton to Ralph Basset of Sapcote, Dover to Richard de Grey, and Winchester to John de la Haye, who by 7 September had also become steward of the king's household.[56]

This last appointment had a deeper significance, for it was linked with a new interpretation of Montfort's position as steward of England which bore closely on the problems now facing him. He had acquired the hereditary stewardship with the honor of Leicester in 1231, but had never made much of it until October 1260. It was then that his nomination of Henry of Almain to deputise for him at the king's feast, contrary to King Henry's wishes, first suggested a more aggressive approach to the office and its possibilities. Pursuing the same tack, he had complained to Louis IX in 1262 that many of the steward's rights had been denied to him by Henry.[57] But it was only after the coup which followed his return from France that he was able to begin to reclaim and inflate rights which had never before been defined. When the great officials were changed in July 1263, the usually reliable Kentish chronicler tells us, with provoking terseness, that 'Earl Simon of Leicester was made steward of England'. Unless Henry had previously

---

[54] *Wykes*, p. 135; Colvin, 'Holme Lacy', pp. 39–40.
[55] *Baronial Plan*, p. 330. For Montfort's undated grant to St Radegund's, see Bodleian Library, MSS Rawl. B. 336, f. 12, Rawl. B. 461, f. 17. That Leyburn was a witness to this grant suggests that it may have been made about this time.
[56] *CPR, 1258–66*, p. 271; *CR, 1261–64*, p. 259.
[57] Above, pp. 200, 207; Bémont, *Montfort* (1st edn), pp. 333, 339.

deprived Montfort of his title, which is most unlikely, this cannot have been literally true; but it may well be that at the time of his victory Montfort had secured a public confirmation of that title. The chronicler then goes on to say that Roger Leyburn was made steward of the royal household on 15 August, and a little later we find Montfort's man John de la Haye holding the same post.[58] Since there were normally two stewards of the household,[59] it looks as if Montfort had used his supposed powers to appoint two new subordinates, one a leading baron whose support he needed, and the other a trusted *familiaris*. The promotion of Leyburn was the only major concession made to a military ally outside the affinity.

His immediate purpose was probably to reform the king's household, for shortly afterwards Henry was to complain that household ministers had been imposed on him against his will. In this Montfort was doing no more than glossing the recently confirmed Provisions, which had originally declared the barons' intentions to 'amend' the household.[60] But he seems, too, to have had a larger purpose in mind, for he soon began to flaunt his title in an unprecedented way. In December 1263 he appeared as 'steward of England' among the barons agreeing to submit to Louis IX's arbitration: the first time he had displayed in a public document a title hitherto used only in some of his private charters. After the battle of Lewes in May 1264 the chancery regularly gave him the same style.[61] These were loaded statements, whose ultimate aim may have been to justify Montfort's general supervision of the kingdom's affairs; he was perhaps drawing on the model of the powerful French stewardship, suppressed in 1191, but which the French nobility had considered reviving in his own favour in 1253.[62] In this way he could legitimise his own headship of a government much less national and more personal than that of 1258. Although the country's governing body was now the council, which regularly dealt with appointments, foreign relations and other political business, this was hardly the original council of fifteen. Only four members of that earlier body remained alive and sympathetic to reform: Montfort himself, Peter de Montfort, Richard de Grey and Walter de Cantilupe. To judge by the auth-

---

[58] *Ger. Cant.*, ii, p. 224.

[59] T. F. Tout, *Chapters in the Administrative History of Medieval England* (6 vols., Manchester, 1920–33), i, pp. 201–5.

[60] *Cron. Maior.*, p. 58; *DBM*, pp. 110–11, 254–5.

[61] *DBM*, pp. 284–5; Harcourt, *His Grace the Steward*, pp. 121–4.

[62] Harcourt, *His Grace the Steward*, pp. 54–5, 120–2; Paris, v, pp. 366, 415; above, p. 121.

orisation of writs – our only guide – the most active councillors were Despenser and Montfort, assisted by Cantilupe and Peter de Montfort.[63] For all the pretensions implied in Montfort's elevation of the stewardship, the new regime achieved little. The council's revocation of the Norfolk eyre, planned for October, on the grounds that seven years had not elapsed since the previous eyre;[64] the closer supervision of the royal household; and the replacement of the great officials according to the Provisions: this was virtually the sum of reform.

Conditions were hardly propitious for more. Provincially popular but narrowly based at the centre, lacking the king's free consent, and owing its existence to a coup legitimised only by the Provisions' morally dubious proscription of their enemies, Montfort's government had more power than authority, but not enough of either. Initially, however, the threat to its survival was not chiefly a military one. The expulsion of Edward's alien mercenaries from Windsor and their subsequent repatriation at the end of July confirmed the military advantages already given by Montfort's control of London and the south-east and of some important castles.[65] The main priority now was the restoration of order and property after the spoliations of the early summer, which had seemingly been prolonged beyond the July treaty;[66] for as long as there were resentful losers, innocent or royalist, the stability needed for effective government and the implementation of the Provisions could not be achieved. It was to deal with this threat that on 20 July knights were appointed in all counties as keepers of the peace, alongside the existing sheriffs. Though the powers of these men were later extended to take in many of the sheriffs' normal duties, their appointment was in origin not so much a considered plan for the future government of the shires as an immediate response to a practical problem. They were to proclaim the peace, restore their goods to those unjustly despoiled, and prevent future disorders. Later, on 6 August, they were told to protect churchmen and to announce the invalidity of presentations to churches made contrary to custom or in defiance of rightful patrons.[67] These measures were followed through in a series of letters sent out between mid July and late September, directing the keepers to restore the property of named individuals on condition that they took an oath to

[63] *CR, 1261–64*, pp. 243–57; *CPR, 1258–66*, pp. 275–6; *Baronial Plan*, pp. 314–15.
[64] *CR, 1261–64*, p. 311; *Baronial Plan*, p. 315.
[65] *Cron. Maior.*, p. 57; *Flores Hist.*, ii, pp. 482–3; *Ann. Dun.*, pp. 223–4; *CPR, 1258–66*, p. 272.
[66] e.g. *CR, 1261–64*, pp. 245–6, 248.
[67] *CPR, 1258–66*, pp. 271–3; *Baronial Plan*, pp. 315–17.

the Provisions. The authorisation of a good number of these writs by Montfort himself showed his awareness of the need to regain both the moral advantage and the political support which the spoliations had cost him.[68]

The spoliations posed one further danger to Montfort's government. They strengthened Henry's pretext for appealing for help to Louis IX, who was not only Henry's feudal lord, for Gascony, but also the brother-in-law of Henry's queen and a natural sympathiser with the churchmen who, like Eleanor, had been among the rebels' victims. The issues of the spoliations, the Provisions, and Louis's attitude to both now began to converge on a course which would lead eventually to the Mise of Amiens. Louis had summoned Henry to France, probably at Henry's secret request, in late July or early August. Montfort's party, who knew from their experiences in 1260 that a king over the water might be much more dangerous than one at home, had sent Walter de Cantilupe and Henry of Almain, now released from captivity, to make Henry's excuses. They had been coolly received by Louis, who must have been aware of events in England, both from Henry's communications and from the flight abroad of royalists such as Mansel; and when John de Cheam, bishop of Glasgow, and John de Houton, a Templar, were sent on a similar mission in mid August Louis refused to countenance any further delay in Henry's appearance. Henry's own letter, calling on Louis to offer the barons security for his speedy return to England, spoke of Louis as 'his lord', showing clearly the feudal grounds for what was to be an appeal for both aid and justice.[69]

Before Henry's departure a final settlement was attempted in a parliament which met on 9 September. The July peace terms were published and approved, the general restitution of plundered property was put in hand, and some prominent captives were released, including Peter of Aigueblanche. If all this was a recognition of the Provisions' demand that parliament should review 'the common business of the realm', it was also an attempt to ground the settlement on the approval of a wide constituency; and to that extent it foreshadowed the later submission, in June 1264, of more far-reaching constitutional proposals to a larger parliamentary body. Montfort was always more sensitive

---

[68] *CPR, 1258–66*, p. 283; *CR, 1261–64*, pp. 243–54, 257–8, 261–2. For writs authorised by Montfort, see *CR, 1261–64*, pp. 244–5, 250, 262.

[69] *Ger. Cant*, ii, p. 224; *Ann. Dun.*, p. 225; *Flores Hist.*, ii, p. 484; *CPR, 1258–66*, p. 275; *Baronial Plan*, pp. 319–20.

than Henry to the need for consultation and consent in policy-making. Yet in the event the parliament brought not peace but discord. Montfort's own obstructive arrogance, vaguely alluded to by Wykes, may have been one reason for this; but the planned restitution of property provided a more material flashpoint. It threatened the interests of all who had gained from the rising and it probably failed to go forward, since the individual orders for restitution on the close rolls virtually cease about the time of the parliament. Yet without restitution there could be no just and lasting peace. The impossible dilemma in which Montfort now found himself made a renewal of the war seem all too probable.[70]

The difficulties facing Montfort at home make the victory which he won in France appear all the more surprising. On 23 September Henry, his wife and his two sons, crossed to Boulogne. There they met the baronial representatives – Montfort himself, the bishop of Glasgow, and Richard de Mepham, archdeacon of Oxford – together with Louis, the leading French nobles, including Charles of Anjou, and the aggrieved exiles, including Mansel, Boniface of Savoy and Peter of Savoy. Against Henry's attempt to present his case as an appeal to the court of his over-lord, the baronial argument that the court had no jurisdiction and that Henry's complaints could be adjudicated only in the English royal court carried the day.[71] Not only this, but, according to the Tewkesbury annals, Louis both approved the baronial *acta* (the Provisions?) and conceded that every kingdom should be governed by natives and not by aliens. Less ambiguously, 'Robert of Boston' says that he approved the Provisions, with the qualification that restitution should be made to the despoiled. In other words it looks very much as if Louis confirmed the July settlement, to which the Provisions and government by natives had been central. After his earlier hostility, and with the barons' enemies in attendance, this was an astonishing outcome. If it owed something to academic skills in the presentation of the argument, discussed below, it perhaps owed more to Montfort. According to the Dunstable annals, it was he who answered Henry's charges, and it seems likely that his presence, his persuasive power, and his friendship with Louis and with Charles of Anjou, all left Henry outmatched. The last

---

[70] *Ann. Dun.*, p. 224; *Wykes*, p. 136; *Ann. Tewk.*, p. 176; *Flores Hist.*, ii, p. 484; *DBM*, pp. 110–11. Orders for restitution from the end of August are as follows: 29 Aug. – five; 2 Sept. – five; 12 Sept. – two; 13 Sept. – one. Only one further order was issued, by the king himself from Boulogne on 5 Oct.: *CR, 1261–64*, pp. 257–8, 261–2; *CPR, 1258–66*, p. 283.

[71] *Cron. Maior.*, p. 57; *Ger. Cant.*, ii, pp. 224–5.

in the long sequence of Louis's favours for Montfort and his cause, the French king's verdict makes the later decision to submit to his arbitration at Amiens seem less ill-judged than it has usually been thought.[72]

The barons may have 'returned home rejoicing',[73] but their moral victory solved none of their practical problems. During the October parliament which followed the whole precarious settlement broke down and Montfort's administration effectively came to an end. As before, the parliament was riven by recriminations and disputes over the question of restitution, with Henry, Edward and the royalists pressing for justice for the despoiled, which the other magnates, presumably Montfortians, declined to provide.[74] Louis's pronouncement in favour of restitution may have sharpened the royalist case, and there was possibly a decision, even at this early stage, to refer the whole matter back to him for adjudication.[75] These arguments were cut short by Edward's seizing the initiative. About 16 October he made off to Windsor on the pretext of visiting his wife, took control of the castle, and was joined almost immediately by Henry.[76] This well-planned stratagem, typical of Edward's surefooted deviousness in these years, was all the more dangerous for Montfort because it coincided with a public change of sides by those who had propelled him into power. Their desertion had been pending for some time. As early as 18 August Clifford, Leyburn, John de Vaux, Hamo Lestrange, John Giffard and Ralph Basset of Drayton had agreed to settle their differences with Edward 'and to be his friends in all his affairs', saving the common oath which they had sworn in 1258 (a specious gesture of allegiance to the Provisions). Pardoned in September for their part in the June rising, they had been made to declare their new loyalties only by the open division between Montfort and the royalists at the end of the October parliament. Other prominent nobles crossed over at the same time: Henry of Almain, Warenne, Roger Bigod, earl of Norfolk, and his brother Hugh.[77]

---

[72] *Ann. Tewk.*, p. 176; *Ann. Dun.*, p. 225; 'Robert of Boston', in *Historiae Anglicanae Scriptores Varii*, ed. J. Sparke (London, 1723), p. 114. The chronicle of 'Robert of Boston' is in need of investigation. These references were unaccountably overlooked by Treharne. For Montfort's ties with Charles of Anjou, see *Flores Hist.*, ii, p. 502, which reports the interesting rumour that Montfort and Charles had entered into a sworn compact of brotherhood.

[73] *Ann. Tewk.*, p. 176.

[74] *Ann. Dun.*, p. 225; *Cron. Maior.*, p. 58.   [75] *Ger. Cant.*, ii, p. 225.

[76] *Cron. Maior.*, p. 58; *Ann. Dun.*, p. 225.

[77] *Foedera*, I, i, p. 430; *CPR, 1258–66*, pp. 278, 284; *Ger. Cant.*, ii, p. 226; *Ann. Dun.*, p. 225; *Wykes.*, p. 137; *Flores Hist.*, ii, pp. 484–5; iii, p. 257.

Edward had thus captured a strategically placed castle, close to London and the Channel ports, and had reconstituted his old affinity. The fragility of Montfort's position, ever since his return in April, had been effectively exposed, and only his generalship could now save anything from the impending dissolution of his government. Clifford and the other ex-Edwardians had ridden pillion, behind the Provisions, back to favour. Once the Savoyards and the queen had gone abroad and Edward's alien knights had been sent packing from Windsor at the end of July – an episode in which Montfort was the unwitting tool of Edward's interests – they had achieved their original aim. There was nothing now to prevent them from rejoining their former master, whose need for service was as great as theirs for lordship. What lordship could bring was made plain by the lavish grants which cemented their transfer of loyalties. The little-used Abingdon chronicle goes so far as to say that Edward offered each of them a charter promising £50-worth of land, adding the circumstantial detail that John Giffard first accepted the bribe, then thought better of it, surrendered the charter and returned to Montfort. This sequence of events fits what is known of Giffard's changing allegiances.[78] Other chronicles speak of the offer of Edward's honor of Tickhill to Henry of Almain and of manors and ample lands to others.[79] In the face of Edward's substantial bidding power, reinforced by that of Henry,[80] Montfort could do little to maintain his alliance with those who had brought him back. With the Crown's resources at his disposal, he had failed to use his control of the government to consolidate the vital support now drawn away from him by the patronage of the royal family.

About one of these defections, that of Henry of Almain, we know a little more, thanks to the chronicler William Rishanger. As so often, Rishanger seems to draw on the recollections of a contemporary observer to depict Montfort's actions at a uniquely close range. The earl had high hopes of Henry of Almain, with whom he had been on familiar terms since at least October 1260.[81] When they were to separate, Henry asked for his leave to go, telling him that he could no

---

[78] *The Chronicle of the Monastery of Abingdon*, ed. J. O. Halliwell (Reading, 1844), p. 15; Powicke, *King Henry III*, p. 456, n. 2; below, p. 264.

[79] Rishanger, *De Bellis*, p. 17; *Flores Hist.*, ii, pp. 484–5; *Ann. Dun.*, p. 225.

[80] For royal grants to Edward's following, see for example *CPR, 1258–66*, pp. 302–4; *Baronial Plan*, p. 329.

[81] *CPR, 1258–66*, p. 96; Ridgeway, 'King Henry III's Grievances', pp. 230, 241; above, p. 200. In December 1261 their greyhounds were being exercised together: JUST.1/911, m. 2d.

longer stand against his father, Richard of Cornwall, and his uncle, the king, but that he would never bear arms against him. Montfort replied cheerfully (*hillariter*), 'Lord Henry, I gave a warm welcome to your person, not because of your arms but because I was hoping for special constancy from you. Go and return home with your arms. I do not fear them'.[82] In this unusual vignette of the parting of friends we catch a glimpse of the emotions and feelings which so rarely clothe the bones of the records and chronicles. Perhaps we glimpse, too, something of Montfort's qualities, his plain but wry way of speaking and his response to adversity, and of the qualities which he valued. Rishanger is not alone among the chroniclers in suggesting that what he sought was what was so rarely to be found in men less singleminded than himself: the constancy in which Henry of Almain had also failed him.

In material terms Henry's desertion mattered much less than Montfort's loss of the marchers. In retrospect their secession can be seen to have marked a long stride towards Evesham. Henceforth these men were to be his bitter enemies, and his failure to conquer or contain them was a main cause of his eventual defeat. His more immediate problem lay in Henry's regaining of the initiative. Between the king's escape to Windsor in late October and his departure for France in early January, Henry's objectives emerged clearly from his actions. He sought to rebuild his financial and military support,[83] to resume control of central and local administration, to secure the south-east, to win the backing of the pope, and to feign allegiance to the Provisions while at the same time planning their destruction. This was essentially a repetition of the programme of February–June 1261,[84] and to it Montfort could react only defensively.

On 1 November, after Henry had professed his good intentions towards the Provisions, while at the same time summoning a substantial force to Windsor, a truce was made, seemingly on Montfort's initiative and with Richard of Cornwall as go-between. By it, both sides agreed to submit their disputes to Louis IX and, probably, to maintain the Provisions in the meantime.[85] The truce was thus the preliminary to

---

[82] Rishanger, *De Bellis*, p. 17, which places this episode during or after Jan. 1264. But it must date from October 1263; cf. Denholm-Young, *Richard of Cornwall*, p. 123. For Rishanger as a source, see above, pp. 89–90.

[83] For Henry's financial measures, see *Baronial Plan*, p. 326.

[84] Above, pp. 203–9.

[85] *CPR, 1258–66*, pp. 290, 292, 294, 296; *DBM*, pp. 264–5; *Baronial Plan*, p. 328; Stacey, 'Crusades, Crusaders', pp. 140–1.

Louis's arbitration at Amiens; but under its cover Henry acted to regain power, with the same enterprise that he had shown in 1261. From Windsor he moved to Oxford, 'with a great force of armed men'.[86] There he recovered control of the chancery, and within the next month the baronial chancellor and treasurer had both been ousted. Henry had already countered the baronial presence in the localities by telling the exchequer that future orders were to be addressed to the sheriffs and not, by implication, to the baronial keepers.[87] From Oxford he moved south to Winchester, where he ejected the Montfortian John de la Haye from the custody of the castle.[88] After revisiting Windsor he then advanced on Dover – as so often the key to his plans – with a large army. Despite a later disingenuous disclaimer, he clearly intended to prepare the way for the return of the exiles, including the queen, and for the admission of alien troops. He was, however, rebuffed by de la Haye, the castle's temporary custodian while Grey was away with Montfort, who cited his oath to the Provisions as justification for his refusal to comply with Henry's demand for entry. Though the king was able to appoint Leyburn as warden of the Cinque Ports, he could do no more and retired towards Windsor.[89]

Meanwhile, news of the attempt on Dover had brought Montfort south from Kenilworth where he seems to have been since late October.[90] On 11 December at Southwark, on the south bank of the Thames, he and his small force were trapped when a group of London citizens, in collusion with Henry, barred the gates of London bridge while the two armies of Henry and Edward advanced on the cornered Montfortians. This near-fatal moment for Montfort and his men was marked by a significant act of religious dedication: they confessed, took communion and had themselves signed with the crosses of crusaders. Called on to surrender, Montfort replied that he would never do so to 'perjurers and apostates'. In the forefront of his mind was still his oath to the Provisions and his abhorrence of those who treated a religious obligation so lightly. But in the event the breaking down of the gates by his London friends allowed him to avoid a battle and to slip safely into the sanctuary of the city.[91] He had held fast to his principles, but had not yet had to fight for them.

[86] *Chron. Abingdon*, p. 15.
[87] *CR, 1261–64*, p. 313; *Baronial Plan*, pp. 325, 330.
[88] *DBM*, pp. 264–5.
[89] *Ger. Cant.*, ii, pp. 229–30; *CR, 1261–64*, p. 371; *CPR, 1258–66*, p. 300; *Baronial Plan*, p. 387.
[90] *Ann. Dun.*, pp. 225–6.   [91] *Ann. Dun.*, p. 226; *Ger. Cant.*, ii, pp. 230–1.

(c) ROYALISTS AND MONTFORTIANS

During the eight-day truce which followed this incident, while Henry was at Windsor and Montfort in London,[92] the final arrangements were put in hand for the submission of the quarrel to Louis IX. The letters agreeing to Louis's arbitration, drafted by the barons on 13 December and by the king on 16 December, provide an opportunity to interrupt the narrative and to assess the relative strengths of the two sides; for in the first place the letters list the leaders of each.[93] Henry's letters named thirty-one royalists, including two members of the royal family (Edward, his son, and Henry of Almain, his nephew), three earls (Norfolk, Warenne and Hereford), two other major barons (Hugh Bigod and Philip Basset), the marchers (John fitz Alan, Roger Mortimer, William de Braose, James Audley, Roger Clifford, Hamo Lestrange and John Vaux), their Kentish associate, Roger Leyburn, and an important group of northerners (Robert Bruce, John Balliol, Henry Percy, Adam of Jesmond and Richard Foliot). Of the thirty-one, four had been on the council of fifteen in 1258 (the earls of Norfolk and Hereford, and Mortimer and Audley), six had been among the baronial twelve then appointed to negotiate with the community in parliament (Hereford, Basset, Balliol, John de Verdun, John de Grey and Roger de Somery), and one, Hugh Bigod, had been baronial justiciar from 1258 to 1260:[94] a powerful demonstration of how baronial support for the Provisions had haemorrhaged away since the sanguine days of June 1258. In addition, Henry had one further and most valuable ally in Richard of Cornwall, who, after a possible flirtation with Montfort between April and October 1263, had now returned to the king's camp: perhaps when his son Henry changed sides in October.[95]

Henry was right to say about this time that he had almost all the magnates on his side,[96] for Montfort's party was much less impressive. The twenty-four men named in the baronial letters included two bishops (Cantilupe of Worcester and Henry Sandwich of London), where the royalists had none. But Montfort was the only opposing earl, and a large proportion of his supporters consisted of family, friends and affinity: his two sons, Henry and Simon, and Hugh Despenser, Peter de

[92] *Ger. Cant.*, ii, p. 231; *Baronial Plan*, p. 387.
[93] *DBM*, pp. 280–7.
[94] *DBM*, pp. 104–5.
[95] Denholm-Young, *Richard of Cornwall*, pp. 121–4.
[96] *Foedera*, I, i, p. 433.

Montfort, Ralph Basset of Sapcote, Richard de Grey and Nicholas of Segrave – all except Segrave longstanding supporters of the Provisions. His remaining followers were mainly middling or minor barons, chiefly drawn from central and eastern England: men such as Baldwin Wake (with lands in Lincolnshire and Northamptonshire),[97] Walter de Colevill (Lincolnshire and Rutland),[98] Henry de Hastings (Bedfordshire, Huntingdonshire, Leicestershire, Northamptonshire and Suffolk),[99] and Adam of Newmarket (Lincolnshire and Yorkshire).[100] The only notable supporter absent from the list was Robert de Ferrers, earl of Derby, who was with Montfort in London in December. Wild and flighty, he was a dangerous ally, and soon ceased to be an ally at all.[101] As Wykes noted, and as Dr Knowles's researches have confirmed, a sizeable group of these men were young. Six were under thirty (Hastings, Wake, Segrave, John fitz John, Geoffrey de Lucy and John de Vescy), and two, fitz John and Humphrey de Bohun, were the respective sons of John fitz Geoffrey and of the earl of Hereford, both prominent reformers in 1258.[102]

In terms of magnate power the two sides were thus unevenly matched and clearly demarcated. The king's chief advantage lay in his hold on the higher nobility, including a preponderance of the more active earls, on his son's marcher retinue, and on a lesser group of northerners. In addition, Leyburn's support gave him a useful ally in Kent. The baronial party, by contrast, was smaller, less weighty, more circum-scribed by region, and more clearly the personal following of one man, Simon de Montfort. Knightly support is more difficult to analyse and may have ebbed and flowed over the reforming period. But to judge by the estates confiscated after Evesham, it reflected the same regional bias found among the Montfortian baronage, with most of the confiscated property lying in the midlands and in the eastern counties.[103] Two probable factors underlay this distribution. First, many of the rebel knights were attached to the households of rebel barons who held lands in those areas. It was only to be expected, therefore, that knightly and baronial rebels would be neighbours in the same *pays*.[104] Second, the demise, or temporary abeyance through minorities, of several of

---

[97] *CIM*, i, Nos. 776, 846.
[98] *CIM*, Nos. 777, 856.
[99] *CIM*, Nos. 610, 613, 632, 716, 772, 846, 895.
[100] Dugdale, *Baronage*, i, p. 436.
[101] *CR, 1261–64*, p. 371; below, pp. 322–4.
[102] *Wykes*, pp. 133–4; Knowles, 'The Disinherited', ii, p. 13.
[103] Cf. Knowles, 'The Disinherited', ii, pp. 107–10.
[104] E.g. *CIM*, i, Nos. 843 (Hastings), 627 (Wake). Cf. Knowles 'The Disinherited', ii, p. 64.

the great midland earldoms, such as Chester and Lincoln, had left many of the knights of this region leaderless, with Montfort as the only active local earl[105] and the minor baronage offering the only alternative lordship.

In the country as a whole general patterns are still harder to discern, but it seems likely that Montfort did not have the active backing of most of the knightly class. In Kent, the only county to have been studied in detail, about one-third of the seventy-nine local knights were rebels in 1264–65, about one-quarter were royalist, and the rest seem to have been uncommitted (though we must again remember that opinion may have shifted over quite short periods and that the pattern of local support in 1263 may not have been the same as that in 1265).[106] Dr Knowles's broader sweep has shown that many of those engaged in the baronial cause in 1258 had ceased to be so by 1263–65. None of the eight known baronial keepers of the peace in 1263, for example, had been among the panels of knights appointed in each county in 1258 to collect grievances. Most of the men of 1258 had simply disappeared from public life, leaving local officeholding throughout the Montfortian period to men who were often wealthier knights or lesser barons. Reluctance to shoulder the heavy burden of public duties which was one local consequence of '1258' may partly explain this.[107] But it is perhaps more likely that the disorders of 1263, the fear of the repercussions of what was becoming rebellion rather than merely a reform movement, and the inability of Montfort's short-lived government to offer much in the way of practical benefits, all do more to explain the passivity of many knights. It remains true that Montfort continued to enjoy substantial knightly backing and that to a limited extent alien mercenaries may have been able to compensate for what had been lost, though their unpopularity made them a doubtful weapon.[108] But neither among the magnates nor among the knights were the Montfortians ever in a majority. That is a simple but compelling part of the explanation for their eventual failure.

If secular support for the Montfortian cause was limited, its real strength at this stage, and to a large extent up to August 1265, lay in its

---

[105] Williams, 'Simon de Montfort and his Adherents', pp. 174–7; above, pp. 62–3.
[106] J. A. Quick, 'Government and Society in Kent, 1232–80' (Oxford D.Phil. thesis, 1986), pp. 248–51.
[107] Knowles, 'The Disinherited', ii, pp. 74, 81–3.
[108] Note the hint in *Ann. Tewk.*, p. 180, that Montfort may have been importing aliens in the winter of 1263–64.

leader's close relationship with prelates and schoolmen. They brought to his service dialectical skills, practical support in negotiating and preaching, and a reputation for probity and intellectual distinction which the royalists could not match. Foremost among them were the Montfortian bishops, who had begun to emerge as a group in the summer of 1263. The most influential was Walter de Cantilupe, whose twenty-seven years in office and long friendship with Montfort set him somewhat apart from and above the rest. In the year of the earl's return he had proved his value: as Montfort's emissary in France in July and August, his negotiator for a truce with Edward in June, with the Welsh in August and with the king in October, and as a sponsor of the baronial letter to Louis, accepting his arbitration, in December.[109] His fellow sponsor, Henry Sandwich, bishop of London, had gained his see only in November 1262 and had first come to prominence on the baronial side in the negotiations of June–July 1263. Both were *magistri*, Sandwich certainly from Oxford, Cantilupe possibly so. The Oxford connection may have been extended by the two baronial envoys, John de Cheam, bishop of Glasgow, and Richard de Mepham, archdeacon of Oxford, who journeyed to Boulogne with Montfort in September. Again, both were *magistri*, Cheam probably from Oxford, Mepham possibly so.[110] At Boulogne Louis had compared rule over a kingdom to the management of a ship in order to justify rule by natives rather than by aliens,[111] employing what sounds as if it may have been one of the common metaphors of the schools, and perhaps reproducing the arguments of Cheam and Mepham. But the most impressive figure among the baronial churchmen was Thomas de Cantilupe: Walter's nephew, son of a great marcher lord, William de Cantilupe II, cousin of Peter de Montfort, a former student at both Paris and Oxford, chancellor of Oxford from 1261 to c. 1263, and a future saint. He was soon to make his first public appearance on Montfort's side as one of his representatives at Amiens and the probable draftsman of the baronial gravamina presented there.[112]

Apart from the Oxford connections of this group, certain, probable

---

[109] *Flores Hist.*, ii, pp. 482–3; *CPR, 1258–66*, p. 276; above, pp. 230, 233. For Cantilupe's career, see *BRUO*, i, pp. 349–50, and above, pp. 81–4.

[110] For Sandwich, see *BRUO*, iii, pp. 1638–9; Cheam, *BRUO*, i, pp. 400–1; Mepham, *BRUO*, ii, pp. 1260–1. The classifications 'probable' and 'possible' are taken from *BRUO*, as is further information about these men in the following paragraphs.

[111] *Ann. Tewk.*, p. 176. Compare *Song of Lewes*, ll. 809–15.

[112] *BRUO*, i, pp. 347–9; Carpenter, 'St Thomas Cantilupe', pp. 60–3.

or possible, three of the five had another striking characteristic in common: they had held their first livings in the diocese of Lincoln during Grosseteste's pontificate. Sandwich had been rector of Helpringham, Lincolnshire, from 1227 to 1262; Cheam rector of Bucknell, Oxfordshire, from 1242/3 to 1264; and Thomas de Cantilupe rector of Wintringham, Lincolnshire, in 1245 and of Bulwick, Northamptonshire, from 1246/7. It is true that Lincoln was a large diocese and home to many clerks; but it remains an attractive probability that the outlook of these three had been influenced by the example and ideals of their one-time diocesan. Like John Crakehall, baronial treasurer in 1258–60, and Robert Marsh, Adam's brother and baronial arbitrator in 1261, both of whom had been members of Grosseteste's *familia*,[113] their careers perpetuated into the reforming period a connection with Grosseteste which may do something to explain their support for reform.

This was not only because Montfort himself had been a close friend of Grosseteste. It was also because his movement had, as we have seen, come to comprehend a broad opposition to aliens with which native churchmen are likely to have been sympathetic, though only in part and ambiguously. It has already been argued that they did not wish for the expulsion of alien clerks, nor could they condone the violence shown to them and their property in 1263. Indeed, they were to spend much of their time in 1264 trying to undo the damage then done.[114] But, like Grosseteste, they were opposed to the papal provision of aliens to English benefices and – it is a fair assumption – for the same reason: such men impeded the cure of souls which was the central duty of all good pastors.[115] Their attitude is momentarily revealed by an episode from the career of another Montfortian bishop, Richard of Gravesend, of Lincoln, Grosseteste's former archdeacon of Oxford, Montfort's trusted friend and executor, and a baronial negotiator in 1263. This dedicated man was to be suspended from office by Pope Urban IV in June 1264 because he had, *inter alia*, 'molested papal notaries by opposing their pensions and benefices in his diocese and in other parts of England'.[116] Here he was following closely in Grosseteste's footsteps, over an issue in which Montfort, too, had a personal, though not

---

[113] Paris, v, p. 719; *Ann. Dun.*, p. 216; *Ann. Oseney*, p. 129; *Robert Grosseteste*, ed. Callus, pp. 225–6, 231.
[114] Below, pp. 303–6.
[115] Cf. *Robert Grosseteste*, ed. Callus, pp. 193–7; Southern, *Robert Grosseteste*, pp. 272–81.
[116] *CPL*, i, p. 400. This episode has been overlooked by Gravesend's biographers.

entirely principled, interest. During the earl's ministry in 1263 two vacant prebends at St Paul's were given to Amaury de Montfort, his fourth son, and to Thomas de Cantilupe, at the expense of John de Ebulo, papal subdeacon and chaplain, to whom the pope had promised the next vacant prebend.[117] It looks as if Montfort had prevailed on a sympathetic bishop, Henry Sandwich of London, to override papal claims and to promote family and friends.

To the bishops who supported him, therefore, Montfort, like Grosseteste, may have seemed to stand for opposition to an intrusive and harmful element in the English church. The alliance which this common interest helped to consolidate allowed the earl and his followers, despite their inferiority in numbers and standing, to continue to occupy the moral high ground. Their entrenchment on the heights was almost certainly confirmed by ties with Oxford which reached beyond the university's alumni among the episcopate and secular clergy to include some of the most prominent of the *magistri* currently teaching there. Because Adam Marsh's correspondence with Montfort gives out after about 1253, and Marsh himself disappears in 1259, it is easy to assume, *ex silentio*, that Montfort's own links with Oxford, so strong in the years around 1250, declined thereafter. This may not have been so. If the evidence for personal connections is largely missing, the evidence for a general academic sympathy for the reforming enterprise, especially among the Franciscans, is quite strong. Take the case of John of Wales, one of Marsh's successors as lector to the Oxford Franciscans from c. 1259 to 1262. In his *Communiloquium*, dating from c. 1265, John was to justify many of the assumptions which lay behind the activities of the baronial reformers: the subjection of the prince to the law, his duty to do justice and to choose wise counsellors, and the duty of his officials to rule equitably, rejecting bribes and shunning extortion. These precepts were too much the commonplaces of the schools to allow us necessarily to see them as a direct commentary on current events. Yet at the very least they suggest that John would have approved of the aspirations of Montfort and his allies.[118]

We are on rather firmer ground with John's Franciscan successor,

---

[117] *CPL*, p. 417; John Le Neve, *Fasti Ecclesiae Anglicanae, 1066–1300*, i: *St Paul's, London*, ed. D. E. Greenway (London, 1968), pp. 7, 48, 95.

[118] J. I. Catto, 'Theology and Theologians, 1220–1320', *The History of the University of Oxford*, Vol. I: *The Early Oxford Schools*, ed. J. I. Catto (Oxford, 1984), pp. 493–4; J. Swanson, *John of Wales* (Cambridge, 1989), pp. 8–9, 76, 82–5. Cf. J. Dunbabin's review of Swanson, *Speculum*, 67 (1992), pp. 224–6.

Thomas Docking, whose lectorship from about 1262 to 1265 covers just the period which now concerns us.[119] In the early 1250s Docking, like Montfort, had been in the circle of Adam Marsh, who had thought highly of him; and Docking's voluminous biblical commentaries contain remarks that suggest his sympathies with Marsh's other friend. He censured foreign prelates, who knew 'neither the manners nor the language of the country';[120] and he can hardly have failed to have in mind Aymer de Valence, Peter of Aigueblanche and Boniface of Savoy. He asks whether 'modern princes who oppress poor country folk, orphans and widows' incur the guilt of homicide; sentiments close to those of the barons in their attempts to reform local government, set down in language remarkably similar to that used by the reformers in denouncing the Lusignans to the pope in 1258.[121] Most strikingly of all, his commentary on Galatians contains what has always been regarded as a direct commendation of Simon de Montfort's government. 'It seems to me', he says, ' . . . that if some man who is prudent and well fitted for the business of rule, seeing God's people endangered by defect of government, should aspire to the dignity of ruling solely for the love of God and the benefit of his subjects, his aim is good and he desires to do a good work'.[122]

It may seem a long way from such academic reflections, by men whose careers are as difficult to date as their impersonal and allusive writings, to the hard practicalities of politics at the end of 1263. But in fact the distance was a rather short one, bridged by actions and events. That the friars were recognised as especially inclined towards resistance was shown in November 1263, when Urban IV commissioned his legate Gui Foulquois 'to compel by ecclesiastical censures Friars Preachers, Friars Minors and other religious to do whatever he thinks will assist his mission'. In the following year we shall find more evidence for their reforming sympathies.[123] A greater and more specific interest attaches to Henry III's peculiar journey to Oxford at the end of October 1263, already mentioned. Only recorded in the neglected Abingdon chronicle, the king's visit served no obvious political or military purpose,

---

[119] Catto, 'Theology and Theologians', pp. 493–4; *BRUO*, i, p. 580.

[120] *Mon. Franc.*, i, pp. 359–60; A. G. Little, *Franciscan Papers, Lists, and Documents* (Manchester, 1943), p. 107. Docking deserves further study.

[121] *Manuscripts at Oxford: An Exhibition in Memory of Richard William Hunt (1908–1979)*, ed. A. C. de la Mare and B. C. Barker-Benfield (Oxford, 1980), p. 65. Compare *Ann. Tewk.*, p. 172.

[122] Little, *Franciscan Papers*, p. 108; B. Smalley, *The Study of the Bible in the Middle Ages* (3rd edn, Oxford, 1983), p. 327; Catto, 'Theology and Theologians', p. 494.

[123] *CPL*, i, p. 398; below, pp. 270, 279–80.

and indeed took Henry away from London and the south-east at a time when, despite the truce of 1 November, tension remained high. The precise situation at Oxford is unclear; but Thomas de Cantilupe may still have been chancellor[124] and he must already have been a prominent baronial supporter, since his appearance as a baronial representative at Amiens followed within two months. Henry travelled with so large a force, 'prepared as if for battle', that when Oxford was reached the royal party could not all be accommodated at Blackfriars, where the king himself stayed, but spilt over into the castle and the town.[125] The general predisposition of the university in favour of Montfort has been doubted;[126] yet what we know of the opposition of the friars, of the pro-baronial views of two of the university's leading men, Docking and Cantilupe, and of the baronial sympathisers who later appeared among the students in 1264,[127] suggests that such scepticism may be misplaced. It is likely that Henry's mission of 1263 was intended to overawe and call to order those *magistri* and their pupils who had given intellectual and moral support to the enemy. Blackfriars, Henry's lodging-house, was after all the place where the reform movement had started in 1258.

At this stage, with the royalists in the ascendant, how are we to explain the continuing support, both lay and ecclesiastical, for Montfort and his cause? Belief in its justice is the simplest and probably most correct answer, and one sustained by the writings of the friars. If many of the earl's followers, Peter de Montfort, Richard de Grey and the rest, were old Montfortian hands, whose backing for their leader and for the Provisions had rarely wavered, others such as the younger nobles and the minor barons of the midlands were not. It can hardly have been self-interest which led them to support him, for that would have been better served by desertion to the king, as the example of the well-rewarded marchers had shown. Indeed, Wykes draws a telling distinction between

---

[124] Cantilupe is last known to have held office at some point between March and September 1262, when he witnessed a deed as chancellor (*Oriel College Records*, ed. C. L. Shadwell and H. E. Salter, Oxford Hist. Soc., 95, 1926, p. 7). Emden's statement (*BRUO*, i, p. 347) that he had vacated it by autumn 1263 is based only on the assumption, originally made in *Snappe's Formulary*, ed. H. E. Salter (Oxford Hist. Soc., 80, 1924), p. 322, that he could not have been chancellor when he was preparing to go to Amiens, and, probably, on the need to 'fit in' the next chancellor, John de Winton, whose dates are unknown (*Snappe's Formulary*, p. 5), before Winton's successor, Henry de Chichester, who was chancellor at some date between Michaelmas 1264 and Michaelmas 1265 (*Snappe's Formulary*, p. 322). The dates of the chancellors in the early 1260s are thoroughly obscure.

[125] *Chron. Abingdon*, p. 15.

[126] Lawrence, 'The University of Oxford, pp. 111–12.

[127] *Chron. Abingdon*, p. 16.

the younger nobles, impressionable as wax, and the rougher baronial crew whom they had joined in April 1263 – men moved not by zeal for justice but by greed for gain.[128] The change of sides by most of this latter group was not all loss, for it purged Montfort's party of its most disreputable and acquisitive elements. Montfort's own acquisitiveness had not evaporated, as the grant of Mansel's lands to his son Simon and of the London prebend to Simon's brother Amaury had shown. But in this period it was forcibly checked by the decline of his power and by the emergency conditions in which that power operated. The private claims and grasping ambitions for his family which had overlain his principles in 1259–62 and would do so again in 1264–65 were less in evidence in these later months of 1263. By December 1263 the crusading role assumed by the Montfortians when they were signed with the cross at Southwark could be assumed without any obvious sense of its inappropriateness.

(D) LOUIS IX AND THE WAY TO LEWES, DECEMBER 1263–MAY 1264

In the fortnight between his agreement of 16 December to submit to Louis and his subsequent crossing to France, Henry sought to consolidate his position where he remained weakest: in the counties. On 20 December he sent letters to the sheriffs denying that he was proposing to bring aliens into the country, as was being widely preached, and that he had gone to Dover for that purpose. The levying of money to pay for men from the villages to guard the coasts against such aliens was to stop, and no one was to leave his county. He would always be willing to keep the oath which he had made at Oxford and to defend his people's rights and liberties.[129] These protestations revealed the underlying insecurity of Henry's position. He remained vulnerable to rumours – accurate as it happened and probably deliberately spread – about his intentions to import aliens and to overthrow the Provisions: sensitive issues, which could still rally local opinion against him. His concomitant orders for the wide publication of his letters, in county courts, hundred courts, and towns, showed his continuing awareness of the need to influence that opinion. Despite his control of central government and his support from the magnates, he lacked the mastery of provincial England necessary for anything approaching complete success. Indeed, his allusions to the raising of money by his opponents

---

[128] *Wykes*, p. 134.   [129] *Foedera*, I, i, p. 433.

to fund a 'home guard', for which there is some independent evidence,[130] point to the persisting authority of Montfort's 'anti-government' in the shires. It was to counter this that Henry took a second measure, appointing on 24 December royalist barons to act as keepers in twenty-two counties. Licensed to call on the armed assistance of the locals, and existing alongside the sheriffs, these men were seen as having a purely military function. That none was appointed for the fifteen counties of the midlands, eastern England and East Anglia confirms what we have already seen about Montfortian dominance in that region.[131]

The king's appointments came to be regarded as a breach of the Provisions, which were thought to have sanctioned the local election of the only sort of provincial governor known in 1258, the sheriff. But still more provocative, and intentionally so, was the attack by Roger Mortimer, apparently at the king's instigation, on Montfort's three Herefordshire manors of Dilwyn, Lugwardine and Marden in early December. This was not just another incident in the violent life of the marches but a well-conceived royalist ploy. The three manors had been among those extracted by Montfort from Henry in 1259, when his fee was turned into land: a piece of extortion which Henry had bitterly resented and had long wanted to undo. His granting them to Mortimer, reported by the Dunstable annalist, helped to secure the loyalty of one of the greatest of the marchers. Isolated from the Montfortian heartlands in the midlands, they were particularly vulnerable to marcher appropriation. But the main purpose of the attack was almost certainly to strike hard at Montfort's private interests in the hope that he could be kept occupied and at home during the crucial meeting at Amiens, when Louis might prove as susceptible to Montfort's persuasiveness as he had been at Boulogne in September. Henry must have known that Montfort's notoriously close attachment to his own interests would make him especially sensitive to such an attack and liable to give priority to its repulse. One chronicle in fact attributed the weak baronial representation at Amiens to the war in the marches, though Montfort himself was detained at home for another reason, as we shall see.[132]

Henry crossed to France on 28 December 1263. Shortly afterwards

---

130 *CPR, 1258–66*, p. 291.
131 *CPR, 1258–66*, pp. 357–8; *DBM*, pp. 264–5; *Baronial Plan*, pp. 335–6.
132 *DBM*, pp. 264–7; *Ann. Dun.*, p. 226; *Ger. Cant.*, ii, p. 232; *Ann. Tewk.*, p. 179; Powicke, *King Henry III*, p. 456; below, pp. 259–60.

both he and a small party of baronial envoys – William Marshal, Adam of Newmarket, Peter de Montfort and Thomas de Cantilupe – appeared before Louis at Amiens,[133] where, on 23 January 1264, Louis gave judgement against the Provisions. He went on to decree that the king's right to appoint his ministers should be fully restored to him, and to quash the clause in the July settlement calling for government by natives and the expulsion of aliens. By the Mise of Amiens, as it has come to be called, Henry was once again to rule unfettered.[134]

Here Louis acted entirely within his powers, for the baronial letters of submission had authorised him, without reservation or qualification, to adjudicate both upon the Provisions and upon all other disputes arising from them down to 1 November.[135] By any reckoning so open a brief was a political misjudgement by the Montfortians, and two views have emerged about the circumstances that gave rise to it. First, Treharne and Powicke have argued that Louis had been intended to arbitrate only on the details of the Provisions, leaving their fundamental validity unchallenged and, further, on the land disputes arising from the summer disorders. Yet, as Stacey has pointed out in by far the best discussion of the Mise, neither point is supported by the royal and baronial submissions to Louis, which asked for his verdict on the Provisions *tout court*. Second, Stacey himself has explained Montfort's decision in a different way, as resulting from the deterioration in his position between July and December, which left recourse to Louis as a kind of last resort: 'the only chance he had to preserve some aspects of the reform programme through negotiations'. Arbitration on the land disputes was probably intended to follow at a later stage.[136]

Yet although Montfort's position was endangered in December 1263, it was by no means hopeless. He still held London, Dover, some other castles, and sufficient control over the midlands and the east for the king to think it imprudent to appoint keepers in nearly half the counties of

---

[133] *Wykes*, p. 139; *Ger. Cant.*, ii, p. 232. The barons had appointed a larger party to represent them, including Henry de Montfort (Rishanger, *De Bellis*, pp. 122–3), and their reduced numbers may have resulted from Mortimer's incursions.

[134] *DBM*, pp. 280–91. There is no contemporary warrant for this title, which appears to have been coined by Stubbs (*The Constitutional History of England*, 5th edn, 3 vols., Oxford, 1891–98, ii, pp. 91–2), probably by analogy with the Mise of Lewes, which *is* a contemporary usage: *Wykes*, p. 152.

[135] *DBM*, pp. 284–7.

[136] Powicke, *King Henry III*, pp. 450–3; *Baronial Plan*, pp. 340–2; R. F. Treharne, 'The Mise of Amiens, 23 January 1264', *Studies in Medieval History Presented to F. M. Powicke*, ed. R. W. Hunt, W. A. Pantin and R. W. Southern (Oxford, 1948), pp. 235–7; Stacey, 'Crusades, Crusaders', pp. 142–3.

England. He still had some baronial support, a good deal of local and popular backing, and the valuable friendship of leading churchmen. Submission to Louis's judgement may have sprung, not from desperation (*pace* Stacey), but from its opposite, overconfidence. At Boulogne in September he had disarmed Louis's initial hostility and apparently secured his approval for, if not his formal confirmation of, both the Provisions and the decree for government by natives. He had no reason to believe that Louis would not stand by his earlier decision, and indeed the chroniclers who had noted that decision expressed surprise at its reversal at Amiens. On the first occasion Louis approved the Provisions, says 'Robert of Boston', and on the second he condemned them. He went from good to bad to worse, says the Tewkesbury annalist. This inconsistency may be what the Dunstable chronicler had in mind when he wrote that at Amiens Louis acted 'unmindful of his own honour'.[137] Since Montfort himself intended to be present at Amiens, he may well have judged that his own influence would carry the day, as it had done at Boulogne. Such an energetic belief in his own abilities would have been both in character and seemingly justified by experience. Louis had not failed him in the past.

These plans were set back by a mishap. On his way south from Kenilworth to take ship for France, Montfort fell from his horse and broke his leg.[138] He was now forced to stay at home, committed to an arbitration in which he could not participate. He could, it is true, feel confidence in his chief representative, Thomas de Cantilupe, whose aristocratic background, intellectual distinction, and acquaintance with Louis at the time of his earlier studies in Paris,[139] made him the best possible substitute. It was Cantilupe who probably drafted the baronial case for submission to Louis, on which so much depended.[140] If the French king were formally to confirm his previous decision in favour of the Provisions, then the verdict would go some way towards legitimising a declining regime. If he could be additionally persuaded to arbitrate on the spoliations (and some of the chroniclers suggest that this was intended, even though it was not directly a part of Louis's commission),[141] then he would take out of Montfort's hands an intractable

---

[137] *Historiae Anglicanae Scriptores Varii*, ed. Sparke, pp. 114–15; *Ann. Tewk.*, p. 177; *Ann. Dun.*, p. 227.

[138] *Ann. Dun.*, p. 227.

[139] *Acta Sanctorum* (Antwerp–Brussels, 1643–): *Octobris*, Vol. i, p. 545; Carpenter, 'St Thomas Cantilupe', p. 63.

[140] Treharne, 'Mise of Amiens', p. 234; Stacey, 'Crusades, Crusaders', p. 143.

[141] *Ger. Cant.*, ii, pp. 225–6; *Flores Hist.*, ii, p. 485.

problem on which it was impossible for the earl and his party to reach an acceptable decision. The importance of these issues was done full justice in the text prepared for Louis: a masterly defence of the Provisions, rightly described as 'a minor tour de force'.[142] Yet its advocacy by someone other than Montfort was bound to limit its effectiveness. For all his qualities, Cantilupe did not have either Montfort's experience of public life or his intimate knowledge of Louis. He lacked Montfort's weight. Possibly, too, he lacked the weight of the earl's seasoned enemies on the other side, men such as John Mansel and Boniface of Savoy. In keeping him at home, Montfort's broken leg, like the length of Cleopatra's nose, may have been one of those contingencies which change the course of history.

When the baronial submission was drawn up, probably in the last days of December, Montfort's representatives already had before them the written statement of Henry's case, which was later laid before Louis. This was brief and rested essentially on the king's claims to be free to appoint his own officials, in central and local government, in the courts and in his household: a right of which he had been deprived by the baronial councillors appointed under the Provisions and which he had always seen as the central pillar of his prerogative. In addition, he complained of the destruction brought by the recent rising, especially to churchmen and church property, and demanded monetary compensation. Finally, he asked for the Provisions to be declared null and void.[143]

The baronial case, a much more elaborate one, has already been perceptively analysed by Dr Stacey, whose arguments are largely summarised here. Essentially it turned on the validity of Magna Carta and on a view of the Provisions which saw them as grounded on the Charter, designed to remedy abuses which sprang in the first place from the king's disregard for the Charter's terms. The Charter's impregnable status rested on Henry's oath to observe it and on the grants of taxation made in 1225, 1235 and 1237 in return for its confirmation. Yet Henry had ignored it in numerous ways: by exploiting the Church, wasting escheats and wardships, selling and denying justice, disparaging heirs, taking excessive prises, levying insupportable increments on the shire farms, and appointing outsiders as sheriffs. Then, leaving behind the matter of the Charter, the indictment moved on to Henry's favour

---

[142] Stacey, 'Crusades, Crusaders', pp. 142–3.
[143] *DBM*, pp. 252–7; Stacey, 'Crusades, Crusaders', p. 141.

for alien and greedy courtiers, and his supposed commutation of his crusading vow for Sicily, at the expense of the Holy Land. This section of the submission thus contrived brilliantly both to describe the causes of the reform movement and to relate most of them to the king's violation of a Charter which was also a contract, sworn to by Henry and paid for by his subjects. Next, the election of the council in 1258 and the concomitant Provisions were shown as a remedy for Henry's broken promises; and Henry's own complaint to Louis about the council's usurpation of his right to appoint was answered by reference to the need to select trustworthy men to restore justice, solvency and equitable government in the counties. Finally, Henry's breaches of the truce made on 1 November, including Mortimer's attack on Montfort's manors, were enumerated and a remedy asked for.[144]

This was a powerful argument. It sought to defend the Provisions as 'holy and virtuous'[145] by presenting them primarily as an outgrowth of the Charter, *articuli super cartas* intended to provide for the Charter's enforcement. It was not, however, an argument which Louis was prepared to accept. In quashing the Provisions he was careful to state that he did not intend to derogate from any existing charters or liberties:[146] the barons could have the Charter, but not the Provisions. By uncoupling the two Louis provided the Montfortians with an excuse for rejecting the whole judgement; and the comments of the chroniclers show how their arguments on this point had come to be both generally known and widely accepted. '[Louis] wholly quashed the Provisions and he judged the Charter . . . from which the Provisions were drawn out (*extractae*) to be good, and in this way he erred', says the Worcester chronicler. Still more specific is Rishanger, who as usual seems to have had access to sources close to Montfort. After noting Louis's judgement against the Provisions but in favour of the Charter, he remarks that 'the earl of Leicester and others . . . held firmly to this exception in their intention to conserve the Provisions of Oxford, because they were founded on that Charter'.[147] In fact this was debatable. The linking of the Provisions to the Charter was a shade disingenuous: it had not appeared in earlier baronial arguments, and the baronial control over the executive conferred by the Provisions marked an intrusion on the

---

[144] *DBM*, pp. 256–79; Stacey, 'Crusades, Crusaders', pp. 139–42.
[145] *DBM*, pp. 264–5.
[146] *DBM*, pp. 288–9.
[147] *Ann. Wigorn.*, p. 448; Rishanger, *De Bellis*, p. 17. Stacey overlooks these references, which support his case admirably.

royal prerogative which went far beyond anything envisaged in the Charter. Yoking the two together was clever, defensible, but not entirely convincing.

But in rejecting the Provisions Louis was not, of course, merely opposing argument with argument. He was responding to pressures at his court which had built up sharply since his earlier judgement in favour of the barons. Prior to the September meeting at Boulogne his contacts with England appear to have been desultory and the knowledge that they brought limited. But during and after that meeting he became much more aware of the outrages perpetrated there during the rising. Peter of Aigueblanche, the rebels' chief victim, had crossed to France with Henry in September and was present at Amiens in January. So also was John Mansel, another leading victim, and Boniface of Savoy, whose complaints about the plundering of the Canterbury lands greeted Henry when he arrived at Amiens.[148] Most important of all, the queen, too, had arrived in September and stayed on in France after Henry's return to England. In collaboration with her sister Margaret, she took the lead in turning Louis against the barons.[149] Through the influence of these exiles the full horror of what had happened in England – the seizure of a bishop in his own cathedral, the more general attacks on churchmen and church property, Eleanor's ordeal at the hands of the London mob, the proscription of her friends, relatives and ministers – was borne in upon Louis. These were points which Henry put to good use at Amiens, in an appeal to Louis's religious sensibilities which transcended the similar appeal made by the Montfortians over Henry's more distant misuse of the crusade.[150] By November at the latest Louis had been entirely won round to the exiles' point of view, and he and Queen Margaret wrote to the pope to request the despatch of a papal legate to England. That the man appointed, Gui Foulquois, former bishop of Le Puy, was a 'trusted agent' of Louis and was now commissioned to restore Henry to full power, showed how strong a coalition – Henrician, French, papal, émigré – had formed against the Montfortians.[151] It was this factor which Montfort had overlooked, in an agreement to submit to Louis's arbitration which was the measure of his overconfidence. The French court had turned against

[148] *Ann. Tewk.*, p. 176; Rishanger, *De Bellis*, p. 17; *Flores Hist.*, ii, p. 486; *CPR, 1258–66*, p. 378.
[149] *Ann. Tewk.*, p. 177; *Ann. Wigorn.*, p. 448; *Ann. Dun.*, p. 227.
[150] *DBM*, pp. 254–5, 278–9.
[151] *CPL*, i, pp. 396–400; Powicke, *King Henry III*, pp. 454–5.

him and he did not know it. It was the end of an old alliance and a critical moment in his fortunes.

Louis had concluded his award by calling on each side to renounce all rancour towards the other. There was small hope of that. The Mise was at once rejected by the Londoners, the Cinque Ports and 'almost all the middling people of the kingdom'.[152] Though Louis had done no more than his commission allowed him, the commission's terms were probably not widely or accurately known: the Dunstable chronicler thought that he had acted *ultra vires* and even the royalist Wykes that he had been unwise.[153] What followed was the start of a civil war, though it hardly looked like one in defence of the Provisions. News of the award led Montfort immediately to re-establish his alliance with Llywelyn and to send an army under his two sons, Henry and Simon, to attack Roger Mortimer's lands in the marches. That this force was reported to be heading towards the Severn on 4 February,[154] less than a fortnight after the publication of the Mise in France, emphasises the speed of what was more a personal reaction by Montfort to Mortimer's earlier ravaging of his lands than a political response to the quashing of the Provisions. When the Dunstable chronicler wrote that Henry and Simon set out 'to avenge their father', he once again brought to the surface the tangle of private and public interests in which Montfort's career was now enmeshed.[155] While the award was pending the earl may have held his fire, hoping perhaps that any decision on the spoliations would do justice to him as to others. But its uncompromising terms freed him from restraint. Mortimer's castle at Wigmore was taken, together with others belonging to Clifford and Thomas Corbet. In an act of apparently gratuitous violence Worcester was sacked on 28 February by Robert de Ferrers, Peter de Montfort and Henry de Montfort.[156] Coming to Mortimer's rescue after returning from France ahead of his father, Edward failed to save Wigmore but joined forces with his friend at Hereford and captured Humphrey de Bohun's neighbouring castles at Hay and Huntington.[157] The first and only major confrontation came at Gloucester. John Giffard, who had taken the town for the barons, failed to prevent Edward entering the castle, but gained an apparently

[152] *Cron. Maior.*, p. 61.
[153] *Ann. Dun.*, p. 227; *Wykes*, p. 139.
[154] *Ann. Dun.*, p. 227; *Flores Hist.*, ii, p. 486; *Ger. Cant.*, ii, p. 233; *CR, 1261–64*, p. 374.
[155] *Ann. Dun.*, p. 227.
[156] *Flores Hist.*, ii, p. 486; *Ger. Cant.*, ii, p. 233; *Ann. Wigorn.*, pp. 448–9.
[157] *Flores Hist.*, ii, p. 486; Rishanger, *De Bellis*, p. 20; *Chron. Abingdon*, pp. 15–16.

decisive advantage when Ferrers and Henry de Montfort arrived from Worcester. Through the mediation of Walter de Cantilupe a truce was made, and under its terms the gullible Henry de Montfort withdrew to his father at Kenilworth, leaving Edward free to enter the town and revenge himself on its people, in complete disregard for the truce. Montfort's bitter anger at his son's folly was understandable. In letting Edward slip he had lost the immediate chance of winning the war.[158]

Despite this setback, Montfort's position in the short term was consolidated rather than subverted by the Mise of Amiens. His rejection of the verdict which he and his followers had sworn in advance to accept gave rise to no accusations of bad faith; perhaps partly because the Montfortian view that the validity of the Provisions followed from Louis's recognition of the Charter had won wide acceptance. The French king's unqualified declaration for Henry had provided the earl with a pretext to seize the military initiative, giving full play to his qualities as a general. Responding to Mortimer's provocation, he had carried the war almost with impunity into the enemy territory of the marches. Immediately after returning from that campaign his son Simon had captured Northampton, thus gaining a crucial route centre which dominated access to the east midlands from southern England.[159] Montfort's own residence at Kenilworth, perhaps enforced by his broken leg, promoted his controlling influence in the west. The Mise, too, had strengthened rather than weakened his party. John Giffard, who had been regarded as a royalist in December, had changed sides by February, a transfer which perhaps marked his rejection of Edward's bribe. His estates in Gloucestershire, centred on his castle at Brimpsfield, quite close to Gloucester and the southern marches, made him a valuable ally.[160] Still more valuable was Gilbert de Clare, earl of Gloucester, who came over in late March or early April.[161] Clare's lordship of Glamorgan, in the southern marches, and of Tonbridge castle in Kent gave him a strategic usefulness which was matched by his wealth and status. At a more popular level the Mise had confirmed Montfort's support in London, where the citizens had fortified the city

---

[158] *Robert of Gloucs.*, ii, pp. 743–6; *Ann. Dun.*, pp. 227–8; *Flores Hist.*, ii, pp. 486–7.

[159] *Wykes*, pp. 143–4; H. M. Cam and E. F. Jacob, 'Notes on an English Cluniac Chronicle', *EHR*, 44 (1929), p. 102. For the strategic importance of Northampton, see R. F. Treharne, 'The Battle of Northampton, 5th April 1264', in Treharne, *Simon de Montfort and Baronial Reform: Thirteenth-Century Essays*, ed. E. B. Fryde (London, 1986), pp. 299–303.

[160] *Ann. Tewk.*, p. 179; Powicke, *King Henry III*, p. 456, n. 2; above, p. 245.

[161] *Wykes*, p. 140.

against the king.[162] In some ways his position was insecure, as an unfriendly critic pointed out about this time. He was getting old (he was about fifty-six), he had used his public standing to promote the interests of his family, and his political survival was threatened by the approach of the legate and the possibility of an interdict or even a French invasion.[163] But to Montfort's large political following, these weaknesses were less in evidence. His embattled position made him more than ever the leader of a cause.

The initiative, however, was about to pass to the king. Although Henry was once again refused entry to Dover when he returned from France on 15 February 1264,[164] he could for the moment afford to ignore its continuing possession by the Montfortians. His aim now was to achieve a quick and decisive military advantage by breaking Montfort's control of the midlands, and he achieved this with a sureness of touch that left his rival outmanoeuvred; though whether the achievement and its planning were his or Richard of Cornwall's or Edward's is hard to say.[165] Within three weeks of his landing he had summoned an army and moved to Oxford, where he stayed from 8 March to 3 April. Ostensibly, his forthcoming campaign was aimed at Llywelyn; but this was only a feint. His order to the baronial custodian of Northampton to surrender the castle, sent immediately after his arrival at Oxford, showed the real direction of his plans.[166] He was now in a very strong position, well placed to move into the marches, to interrupt the lines of communication between Montfort's two bases in Kenilworth and London, and to go against the barons at Northampton. With Richard of Cornwall and Edward at his side, and a large army gathering behind him, he seemed to be moving towards the position of overwhelming military superiority needed for an assured victory.

That the Montfortians were now prepared to give ground was a measure of that superiority. In mid to late March talks were held at Brackley and Oxford, where the bishops of Worcester, London, Winchester and Chichester represented the barons.[167] Neither John

---

[162] *Cron. Maior.*, p. 61; *Ger. Cant.*, ii, p. 234.

[163] *Ann. Tewk.*, pp. 179–80.

[164] *Ger. Cant.*, ii, pp. 232–3.

[165] Cf. D. A. Carpenter, *The Battles of Lewes and Evesham, 1264/65* (Keele, 1987), p. 12. Carpenter provides an excellent account of the campaigns of March–May 1264.

[166] *CR, 1261–64*, pp. 377–82; *CPR, 1258–66*, p. 306; *Flores Hist.*, ii, p. 487.

[167] *Ann. Lond.*, p. 61; *Ann. Dun.*, p. 229; *CPR, 1258–66*, pp. 307–8, 310. It is unlikely that Roger Longespee, bishop of Coventry and Lichfield was among the Montfortian bishops, as the London annals state, since he was named on the patent rolls as one of Henry's proctors.

Gervais of Winchester nor Stephen Berksted of Chichester had been active Montfortians before this time. Both elected to their sees in 1262, both formerly in the circle of the saintly Richard Wych, bishop of Chichester, both *magistri*, Berksted certainly from Oxford, Gervais probably so,[168] and both now to be his friends until the end, their help showed that even in adversity Montfort was able to draw on new support from good and able men and that his rejection of the Mise had done him no moral damage. The concession which these envoys were now prepared to offer Henry was momentous: acquiescence in Louis's award, provided only that the king would remove the aliens and govern through natives. The condition emphasised how central the alien question had become to the whole baronial agenda. In implying some continuing restrictions on the king's free choice of ministers, it preserved only the bare minimum of the Provisions, which had otherwise been demoted and edged towards the margins of the reforming programme.[169] But this was more indicative of the pressures on the barons than practically important. Henry was looking for victory, and his gathering power made it unnecessary for him to accept any conditional peace.

It was perhaps in a parallel attempt to delay and divert Henry's plans that about 10 March the Londoners began to turn violently against the king, sacking Richard of Cornwall's manor at Isleworth, attacking the property of such prominent royalists as Walter Merton and Peter of Savoy in and around the capital, and taking and imprisoning royal clerks, barons of the exchequer and Bench justices.[170] Both the role of Hugh Despenser, Montfort's custodian of the Tower, who led the raid on Isleworth, and the singling out of members of Henry's court and government, suggest that this was no spontaneous outbreak but rather a tactical ploy to draw the king's forces towards London and relieve the pressure on the Montfortians in the midlands. Montfort's own move to London with a large force, after the failure of the negotiations with the king, points in the same direction.[171] Henry, however, cleverly declined to respond in the way intended. Instead of marching on London with his whole army, he merely detached a force under John de Warenne and Roger Leyburn to secure the castles at Reigate and Rochester and

---

[168] *BRUO*, i, p. 176, ii, pp. 757–8.
[169] Carpenter, 'King Henry III's "Statute"', p. 939.
[170] *Wykes*, pp. 140–1; *Flores Hist.*, ii, p. 487; *Cron. Maior.*, p. 61; Williams, *Medieval London*, p. 224.
[171] *Wykes*, p. 144; *Cron. Maior.*, pp. 61–2.

to protect the surrounding countryside from devastation by the Londoners.[172] Then, on 3 April, he led his army northwards from Oxford, and two days later he won a great victory at Northampton, taking the town and castle and capturing the entire Montfortian garrison.[173] He lingered there only briefly before moving rapidly on to Leicester, where Montfort's townsmen offered 500 marks for his favour, and to Nottingham, where he joined forces with a large party of northerners. Then he turned towards Lincoln. Edward, meanwhile, was ravaging the lands of Robert de Ferrers in Derbyshire and Staffordshire. The only minor consolation for the Montfortians was the capture of the royalists' castle at Warwick by John Giffard and Henry de Montfort, whom the earl had left in charge at Kenilworth after his own withdrawal to London.[174]

In legal terms the battle of Northampton came to be seen as the start of the civil war.[175] It could hardly have been a more inauspicious one for Montfort. He had failed to divert Henry's army or to prevent its victory. His loss of Northampton opened the way for the extension of royal control over the area where his own position was strongest. Leicester was his borough, Lincoln, Henry's destination, the seat of a friendly bishop and the chief town of a friendly county. More damaging still was the loss of manpower that he had sustained. Some eighty barons and knights were captured at Northampton, including such prominent Montfortians as the younger Simon, Peter de Montfort, Ralph Basset of Sapcote, Baldwin Wake and Adam of Newmarket, all of whom had sponsored the baronial letter to Louis in December.[176] Their number was a witness both to the continuing strength of Montfort's support in the early months of 1264 and to the scale of the disaster. The earl's reaction was stoical. Hearing that Henry had marched on Northampton, he had got as far as St Albans with a relieving force when news was brought of the king's victory. According to Rishanger, it caused consternation, 'but the earl in no way despaired, knowing it to be the law of wars that in the course of events superiority goes now to these, now to those'. To Despenser and his *secreti* he predicted that

---

172 *Flores Hist.*, ii, p. 489; Rishanger, *De Bellis*, pp. 22, 25.
173 Treharne, 'The Battle of Northampton', provides the best account, with full references to the sources.
174 *Flores Hist.*, ii, pp. 488–9; *Wykes*, p. 146; E.159/40, m. 2d; *Ann. Dun.*, p. 230; *Ann. Oseney*, pp. 144–5.
175 Treharne, 'The Battle of Northampton', p. 299.
176 Treharne, 'The Battle of Northampton', pp. 312–13; *DBM*, pp. 284–5. For Basset, see *Ann. Lond.*, p. 61.

before May was out his enemies' joy would be swallowed up by fear and confusion.[177] If the prophecy may have been set down with the advantage of hindsight, the soldier's reflection rings true to the earl's character and experience.

Montfort's return to London was followed about 7 April by the massacre and plundering of the London Jews. He and his men were heavily involved in this atrocity, largely (so Wykes says) because they needed money to sustain their army in the capital. John fitz John, having killed one of the richest Jews, Cok, son of Abraham, with his bare hands, was compelled to hand over a share of the spoils to the earl.[178] The wealth thus gained may have helped the Montfortians to confront the most immediate threat to their position: the large royalist force which Warenne and Leyburn had established at Rochester. Lying on the main road to Dover, Rochester's position might jeopardise Montfort's links with the continent, impede any attempted relief of Dover in the event of a royalist attack, and even threaten the earl's security in London.[179] Its siege by Montfort and Clare, which began on 17 April, was thus intended to eliminate a dangerous royal strongpoint; but the two earls must also have reckoned that any move against Rochester would draw Henry's army southwards, preventing the king from consolidating his control of the east midlands and leading him into territory where the advantage lay with the Montfortians. So it did, but with such speed that Montfort's plans miscarried. Henry had news of the siege at Nottingham on 20 April. Turning south immediately, he had reached Croydon, only about twenty-five miles from Rochester, by 26 April. Meanwhile the Montfortians had taken both the town and the outworks of the castle, using among other equipment fireboats devised by their leader; but the keep still defied them, despite all Montfort's skill in just this sort of warfare. 'He gave an example to the English of how assaults ought to be made on castles, of which in those days they were wholly ignorant'.[180] On 25 April he retired to London, forced back both by the king's approach and by rumours that some London citizens were planning to deliver the city to Edward.

The initiative now lay once again with the king. Henry was on the

---

[177] Rishanger, *De Bellis*, p. 24. Cf. *Guisborough*, pp. 191–2; *Ann. Dun.*, p. 230; *Ger. Cant.*, ii, p. 235.

[178] *Wykes*, pp. 141–3.

[179] For what follows, see Carpenter, *The Battles of Lewes and Evesham*, pp. 13–16, where full references will be found.

[180] Rishanger, *De Bellis*, p. 25.

brink of regaining the control of the south-east that he had lost in the rising of 1263. On Montfort's withdrawal he relieved Rochester, marched south to receive the surrender of Clare's castle at Tonbridge, and then crossed the Weald to Battle and Winchelsea. From his own orders and from the chronicles his plans are clear. He intended to blockade Dover, to secure the submission of the Cinque Ports and to turn their fleet against London, either in blockade or in attack. About 9 May he was arranging for an imminent muster at Canterbury and receiving the submission of some of the most powerful of the Kentish gentry.[181] But by this time, on 6 May, Montfort and his army had already left London to seek him out.[182] Carpenter is no doubt right to see this move as a mark of the earl's courage and confidence, but he really had little alternative if anything was to be saved of all that he had fought for. If Dover fell he would be left virtually with London alone; and even there the royalist faction, which had twice tried to betray him, was an unpredictable threat to his security. To 'have sat tight in London and seen how things developed',[183] therefore, was arguably not an option that was open to him.

This did not necessarily mean that a battle was inevitable. Before leaving London Montfort had worked out terms for a possible settlement in discussions with the bishops and his other supporters. They would offer the king financial compensation for the spoliations (as Henry had in fact demanded at Amiens), if he would agree to maintain the Provisions. Only if these terms were rejected would they chance everything on a battle.[184] Their reluctance to fight was hardly surprising. Not only would a direct engagement with the king constitute rebellion, for which the penalty was disinheritance, but the circumstances were hardly propitious. Henry had so far fought a near-faultless campaign, and although his retreat from the midlands had allowed the Montfortians at Kenilworth to join those in London, the king's forces remained much larger than those of the opposition: in cavalry, probably by three to one.[185] His consciousness of the baronial inferiority in numbers probably explains Montfort's willingness both to take the risk of delaying in London while waiting – in vain – for the

[181] *CR, 1261–64*, pp. 343, 384–5; *Wykes*, pp. 147–8; Carpenter, *The Battles of Lewes and Evesham*, pp. 16–18.
[182] *Cron. Maior*, p. 62.
[183] Carpenter, *The Battles of Lewes and Evesham*, p. 17.
[184] Rishanger, *De Bellis*, p. 27; *DBM*, pp. 254–5.
[185] Carpenter, *The Battles of Lewes and Evesham*, pp. 17, 23.

arrival of Robert de Ferrers and his men,[186] and, subsequently, to offer more to the king than had originally been contemplated.

News of Montfort's departure from London reached Henry at Battle on 9 May and set him moving quickly westwards towards the security of Warenne's castle and town of Lewes.[187] Montfort, meanwhile, had reached his own manor of Fletching, eight miles to the north of Lewes. Negotiations between the two sides took place on 12 May.[188] That they were initiated by Montfort reflected both the earl's awareness of his army's weakness and the conciliatory influence of the bishops and other churchmen who were his friends and now his envoys. Through the bishop of Chichester and a party of Dominican and Franciscan friars Montfort asked for the observance of the Provisions, while at the same time offering to submit their terms to the arbitration of bishops, canonists and other men of religion and learning. In addition, he asked for the withdrawal of the king's evil counsellors and for his adherence to the advice of faithful Englishmen. A second mission, led by the bishops of London and Worcester, offered Henry a sum of £30,000 in compensation for the spoliations. Henry was minded to accept these terms, but was dissuaded by Richard of Cornwall and by Edward. Richard correctly saw that even the looser restraints on the king which were now proposed threatened 'to disinherit the king of England and his heirs and to depress their power'.[189] The terms were therefore rejected. On the next day, 13 May, letters of defiance were exchanged, and finally the Montfortians withdrew their homage and fealty: the formal preliminary to a feudal revolt.

(E) LEWES: THE BATTLE AND THE MISE, 13–15 MAY 1264

The concessions that Montfort was prepared to make before Lewes were a mark of his critical situation. As in the earlier negotiations at Brackley and Oxford in March, the imminence of confrontation with a greatly superior force had compelled him to give ground. But the constraints on his position were not only military and political; they

---

[186] Battle chronicle, in Bémont, *Montfort* (1st edn), p. 376.

[187] Battle chronicle, in Bémont, *Montfort* (1st edn), p. 376; Carpenter, *The Battles of Lewes and Evesham*, pp. 17–18.

[188] For these negotiations, see J. R. Maddicott, 'The Mise of Lewes, 1264', *EHR*, 98 (1983), pp. 588–91, corrected by Carpenter, *The Battles of Lewes and Evesham*, pp. 19–22, where full references will be found.

[189] *Wykes*, pp. 148–9.

were also moral ones, and these set limits on what was concedable. He could not go back on his oath to the Provisions – or, at least, so the *Song of Lewes* says, he would do so only if 'the most perfect teachers of the faith' were willing to absolve him.[190] But to seek absolution would have been to follow the bad example of Henry III in 1261 and 1262. What was at stake was not so much the system of government that the Provisions embodied (for there was now small chance of that being implemented), but rather Montfort's sworn obligation, which subsisted quite irrespective of the practicability of the reforming code to which it bound him. For him the issues were ones of religion and conscience, and the battle that he faced was 'God's battle'.[191]

The chronicles suggest that the battle was fought in a spirit of religious exaltation. On the night of 13 May Montfort had moved his men forward under cover of darkness so as to occupy a commanding position on the crest of the Downs and to take by surprise the royalists who were encamped in the town. It was a daring decision, masterfully accomplished, which showed all Montfort's tactical skills: his eye for country, his sense of timing, his powers of leadership. Drawn up on the ridge above Lewes at dawn on 14 May 1264, his army was addressed by its leader. They were about to fight, he said, for the kingdom of England, the honour of God, of blessed Mary, of all saints and of Holy Church. Then all lay prone on the ground, arms extended, praying for victory. They confessed their sins, were absolved by the bishops of Worcester and Chichester, and donned the white crosses of crusaders.[192] In the history of the Provisions as a holy cause, fused from Montfort's conscience and the support of the Church, this was perhaps the culminating moment.

In the battle that followed, excellently reconstructed by Dr Carpenter,[193] Montfort's generalship proved equal to his religious commitment; though he owed his great victory to the mistakes of the royalists as well as to his own planning and direction. His troops, arranged initially in four divisions on top of the Downs, had all the advantages of their position. Both before and during the battle the configuration of the land allowed Montfort to survey the whole scene, and his men could attack downhill, towards the lower ground outside

[190] *Song of Lewes*, ll. 228–42.
[191] *Ann. Dun.*, p. 232.
[192] *Oxenedes*, pp. 221–2; *Flores Hist.*, ii, p. 495, iii, p. 262; Rishanger, *De Bellis*, p. 31. Cf. Carpenter, *The Battles of Lewes and Evesham*, pp. 26–7, and Tyerman, *England and the Crusades*, pp. 147–8.
[193] Carpenter, *The Battles of Lewes and Evesham*, pp. 22–34.

the town of Lewes where most of the fighting took place (Plate 11).
Edward, commanding one of the three royalist divisions, scored an
opening success against the Montfortian cavalry, but then blundered by
charging the Londoners whom the cavalry shielded, scattering them
and pursuing them for several miles. The troops thus removed from the
battlefield included the marchers.[194] The rest of the royalist army was
left exposed to attack from above and was devastated in heavy fighting.
Richard of Cornwall fled for refuge to a windmill, where he was
captured. Henry, much beaten about and with two horses killed under
him, was able to retreat to the Cluniac priory in the town. When
Edward returned he found his father's army defeated. Renewing the
attack, the Montfortians put to flight some of his chief supporters,
including William de Valence, Guy de Lusignan and Hugh Bigod, but
Edward himself managed eventually to join his father in the priory.

It is Carpenter again who has greatly clarified our knowledge of the
circumstances in which a settlement was now made.[195] As he points out,
Montfort's victory was by no means total. It was limited by his having
failed to capture either the king or Edward, who were now inside Lewes
priory, with a large force of barons and knights, including the marchers.
They could not be taken without a full-scale assault on the priory, which
would be extremely damaging, politically and morally, for the
Montfortians. The alternative, a long siege, might both bring in other
royalist troops to the rescue from such nearby garrisons as that at
Tonbridge, and expose the besiegers to the danger of a royalist break-
out. It was essential, therefore, to devise arrangements which would
persuade the royalists to come quietly; and though Montfort had the
upper hand such arrangements were bound to entail concessions.

Negotiated on the night of 14–15 May, the Mise of Lewes, as the
settlement was known from the start, does not survive, but its outlines
may be reconstructed from the chronicles. In the first place, the king
undertook to observe all the Provisions, to remove all traitors, English
and foreign, from his council, to pardon the barons and to restore their
lands and goods. Secondly, two panels of arbitrators were to be set up.
The first, consisting of four English bishops or magnates, was to consider
amendments to the Provisions. If the four were unable to agree, two

---

[194] *Flores Hist.*, iii, p. 260.
[195] For the circumstances of the settlement, see D. A. Carpenter, 'Simon de Montfort and the Mise
of Lewes', *BIHR*, 58 (1985), pp. 1–11, and for the terms, Maddicott, 'The Mise of Lewes'. Both
these accounts need to be read in conjunction with the additions and modifications suggested
below.

Plate 11. The battlefield at Lewes, looking from the castle towards the Downs, from a photograph of 1869. Montfort's army probably formed up on the skyline, in the vicinity of the right-hand windmill, and most of the fighting took place on the lower ground.

French nobles, Charles of Anjou and the duke of Burgundy, were to give a final verdict. The second panel, consisting of three French prelates and three French nobles named in the Mise (but now unknown to us) was to be convened, but not chosen, by Louis IX. These six were then to choose two further Frenchmen, who were to come to England and to select a third man, an Englishman, to make up a final arbitrating panel of three.[196] The purpose of this arbitration is considered below. Other clauses in the Mise dealt with the freeing of the prisoners captured at Northampton and the ransoming of the royalists captured at Lewes. Finally, the marchers who were present in the priory were to be allowed to go free, but Edward and Henry of Almain were to remain as hostages, both for their good behaviour and for the fulfilment of the Mise.

These terms were a commentary on Montfort's strengths and weaknesses in the hours following his greatest victory. Much of what he had fought for he had won. The Provisions had been put back in place, and Henry's promise to dismiss evil councillors reinforced the restraints on his free choice of ministers which was at their heart. He was also on the

---

[196] *Wykes*, pp. 152–3; *Flores Hist.*, iii, p. 261.

point of securing the persons of both the king and the heir to the throne, opening out for him the possibility of dominating the kingdom's government with a completeness uncontemplated in 1258 and unattainable even after his successful coup in 1263. But Henry's ensconcement in Lewes priory ensured that he had to pay a good deal for these things. The undertaking to consider amendments to the Provisions modified what had almost always been his previous insistence – at least in public – on their inviolability; though events were to show that this tactical response to an immediate difficulty was a concession easily evaded. One less easy to go back on was the freeing of his old enemies, the marchers. For them Lewes proved to be a momentary interruption in a course of destructive license usually pursued at Montfort's expense and lasting from April 1263 until Evesham and beyond.

The Mise of Lewes thus represented such a mixed bag of gains and losses for Montfort that the lack of publicity given to it is not surprising. He would not have wanted to advertise what was partly a temporary expedient, designed to secure the surrender of the royalists in the priory and containing too much that compromised his victory and his principles.[197] So the Mise was never enrolled in chancery, and its sparse reporting in the chronicles suggests that it did not circulate in the same way as other texts of the reforming period. Our lack of any authoritative version means that we are largely in the dark about one of its central and most puzzling features: the proposal to bring in French arbitrators, in a scheme distinct from the planned arbitration on the Provisions.

The mechanics of this scheme are worth a moment's preliminary attention, for they hint at an influence from an unsuspected quarter. The system of election proposed, with a committee of six choosing two arbitrators who were themselves to elect a third member for the final panel, parallels in a remarkable way the statutory arrangements for electing proctors at the university of Oxford. There, the two senior Masters of Arts, representing respectively the northerners and the southerners in the university, chose a panel of six electors, presumably three northerners and three southerners, who proceeded to elect the two proctors. These arrangements seem to have been in place by 1313[198] and may date from the earliest appearance of the proctors in the 1250s, or

---

[197] Cf. Carpenter, 'Simon de Montfort and the Mise of Lewes', p. 11.

[198] *Statuta Antiqua Universitatis Oxoniensis*, ed. S. Gibson (Oxford, 1931), pp. xxxix, 64–5; M. B. Hackett, 'The University as a Corporate Body', *History of the University of Oxford*, i, ed. Catto, pp. 65–6, 82–3.

even earlier. Their resemblance to what was envisaged after Lewes may, of course, be entirely coincidental. But it is tempting to see the hand here of Stephen Berksted, regent in theology at Oxford in 1255 and familiar therefore with the university's government,[199] whose prominence in the negotiations before the battle makes it unlikely that he was ignored in those that followed it; and tempting, too, to see the six nominators as having been chosen three apiece by the king and Montfort, in just such a way as the two MAs chose the six at Oxford. If this speculation is correct it would illuminate a little more brightly the university's influence on reforming politics which there is so much else to suggest.

The question of what precisely the final panel of three was intended to do can be answered only in terms which are almost as speculative. Virtually the sole direct answer is provided by the Merton version of the *Flores Historiarum*. Its author says that the arbitrators were to ordain 'as much about what ought to be confirmed or modified in the king's ruling as about all the controversies existing between the parties and about the state of England'. Wykes confirms this in a more general way by saying that they were to ordain 'concerning the state of our kingdom'.[200] It is clear that 'the king's ruling', the *dictum regis* of the *Flores*, is Louis IX's Mise of Amiens, for the chronicler has just referred to Louis as the convenor of the electoral board for the arbitration and has earlier spoken of his *dictum* at Amiens. So one purpose in appealing to France was to secure an arbitration on the Mise of Amiens. Those charged with arbitrating on the Provisions had no powers to question Louis's decision in January, which remained as the one legal and moral barrier to the readoption of reform. This deficiency the French arbitration could put right, in a process perhaps intended to run in parallel with any arbitration on the Provisions.

Beyond this, it looks as if the arbitrators were expected to devise a full peace settlement ('all the controversies existing between the parties . . . '), to supersede an interim post-battle arrangement which was more like a truce than a treaty. One important part of such a settlement may have been intended to cover the spoliations of 1263 which had so compromised the reforming cause and on which Louis IX had failed to adjudicate at Amiens. The problems that they posed, moral, tenurial and political, had been exacerbated by the further disorders brought by

[199] *BRUO*, i, p. 176.
[200] *Flores Hist.*, iii, p. 261; *Wykes*, pp. 152–3.

the civil war and were greatly to concern the bishops later in the year. Without a third party to do justice to winners and losers here, there could be no lasting peace.[201]

It is possible that one further matter was intended to come before the arbitrators: Montfort's own claims for Eleanor's full dower. Since his return to England in April 1263 there is no word in the sources to suggest that he had raised the issue of the dower. The annual payment of £400 owed by the king to the Montforts had continued into 1263,[202] but the contentious questions of the dower's supposed inadequacy and of the arrears due to the couple had apparently lain dormant. Since these questions had been central to Montfort's grievances against Henry from 1258 onwards, and Montfort's angry return to England in 1263 had been partly occasioned by the breakdown of negotiations probably on this very point,[203] it is at first sight surprising that the dower should have disappeared so completely from the story. On reflection, however, perhaps there is less reason for surprise. Once Montfort had achieved power in July 1263 the dower became a secondary issue. Even a favourable settlement would leave him only with a wasting asset, which could not last beyond Eleanor's lifetime and which was increasingly unsuitable for the endowment of his family. Now that he had got his hands on the kingdom's controls, he could do more for his sons in other ways: witness the grant of Mansel's lands to young Simon in August 1263. Yet his claims were by no means forgotten. As we shall see, they surfaced at several points in the summer and autumn of 1264, and at the end of the year the whole issue of a favourable dower settlement was raised once again by Montfort.[204] In the past he had repeatedly looked to French arbitration on these claims, and in the hours after Lewes, when victory had given him new leverage, he may well have had it in mind that any final political settlement, of the sort which the French were apparently expected to provide, should also comprehend his own personal grievances.

But none of this quite explains why he should have looked to French arbitration at all. The immediate precedent of the Mise of Amiens was hardly encouraging. Why could not all these issues have been more safely settled in England? One possible answer lies in Montfort's search

---

[201] Maddicott, 'Mise of Lewes', pp. 597–9.

[202] *CLR, 1260–67*, p. 125.

[203] Above, pp. 221–2.

[204] Below, pp. 297–8, 300, 308.

Plate 12. Montfort's counter-seal, showing his arms.

for legitimation. The victor in a civil war, his power rested on *force majeure*, even more obviously than it had done in July 1263. To turn that power into authority he needed both recognition and consent. His elevation of the stewardship in 1263, and his later attempts in June 1264 and January 1265 to ground his position on parliamentary consensus, showed how conscious he was of that need. The planned French arbitration perhaps fits into the same pattern of his thinking. If he could get Louis to initiate the arbitration, as the Mise called for, that in itself would constitute assent to the new regime. If that arbitration led to the amendment of the Mise of Amiens, the verdict would be more valuable than any mere rejection of Louis's previous ruling by Montfort's own fiat. If a final settlement could be achieved with French approval, the firm basis for a Montfortian protectorate would have been laid down. The dangers attached to this whole process had been carefully limited by the elaborateness of what had been devised. Louis was merely to convene an already chosen electoral body of six. The earl had enough friends among the French aristocracy, lay and ecclesiastical, to make for a favourable panel; it would have been surprising if Charles of Anjou, his sworn ally, and Eudes Rigaud, archbishop of Rouen, for example, had not been among the six. That the final arbitrating body of three was to include an Englishman and, unlike any previous French arbitration between Montfort and Henry, to do its work in England, ensured that its independence would be limited. The whole scheme was carefully set up to provide the maximum advantage with the minimum of risk.

But these were castles in the air. That the French arbitration hung entirely on Louis's co-operation was only one of the uncertainties attached to the fragile and imperfect settlement which followed the battle of Lewes. Qualified as it was by the king's escape from the field, Montfort's victory had allowed him to make terms but not to impose them. If what resulted was something of an anticlimax, Montfort was at least largely able to disguise its less propitious features: the resurrection of the Provisions became better known than either of the arrangements for arbitration.[205] Our own perplexities about the Mise of Lewes reflect Montfort's success in concealing what was to his disadvantage. They reflect, too, a contrast between appearance and reality, what was publicly visible and what was privately known, which is found elsewhere in the career of the champion of the Provisions and of Eleanor's claims to her dower.

[205] The chronicle evidence is set out in Maddicott, 'Mise of Lewes', pp. 592–3.

CHAPTER 8

Simon de Montfort and his kingdom, 1264–65

(A) FOUNDATIONS FOR A NEW REGIME, MAY–JUNE 1264

The successful royalist campaign which had begun at Oxford was abruptly terminated by the baronial victory at Lewes. Like other battles in the middle ages where an inferior army defeated a superior one – Courtrai in 1302, for example, or Bannockburn in 1314 – it showed how unpredictable were the fortunes of war and why even the best commanders might be reluctant to risk a fight. Half concealed and partly evadable as they were, the compromises forced upon Montfort in the Mise which ended the war did nothing to blunt the public view of what had been accomplished. Both the scale and the unexpectedness of the victory contributed to its presentation as a religious achievement, a judgement by battle in which all that Montfort stood for had been divinely vindicated. This was pre-eminently the belief of the author of the *Song of Lewes*, possibly a Franciscan in the entourage of Stephen Berksted, who wrote shortly after the event.[1] For him, God was 'on the side of justice';[2] and justice meant the triumph of the Provisions over royal autocracy and of the English over the aliens. The king's stand on his right to appoint ministers and to distribute patronage at will, to ignore the need to consult his magnates, and generally to treat the kingdom as a private estate, run for the benefit of its lord, had gone down before the ideal of the common good, promoted by the community under Montfort's leadership.[3] It was Montfort's devotion to his oath which had accomplished this, and which now opened up the prospect of a welcome peace. 'The faith and fidelity of Simon alone is become the security of the peace of all England'.[4]

---

[1] *Song of Lewes*, pp. vii–viii, xviii–xx.
[2] *Song of Lewes*, l. 370.
[3] *Song of Lewes*, ll. 479–526, 627–700, 765–8, 803–47.
[4] *Song of Lewes*, ll. 185–284.

The panegyric of the *Song of Lewes* was the most elevated expression of the religious rhetoric and forensic power which, in combination, had come to characterise the public face of the reform movement in 1263–64. Both its author's views and the views which it cited (for example, Montfort's appeal to 'the best men . . . who have read the decretals and have becomingly taught theology and sacred philosophy')[5] showed the intellectual and moral weight of the arguments for reform. Montfort's debt to, and respect for, the academic world from which the *Song* had sprung was quickly acknowledged after the battle. At the end of May the university of Oxford, which had been dispersed by the king in March, while his army was gathering in its midst, was reconvened, 'relying upon the protection of the lord Simon de Montfort'; and a little later it was pardoned what it owed to the king as a result of the peaceful settlement of an earlier dispute with the town.[6] If Montfort's restoration of the university cannot be seen crudely as a quid pro quo for its members' support for reform – support which we have already argued to have been unjustly doubted[7] – it shows at least that at a busy and difficult time the fortunes of Oxford had a place on his agenda.

Useful though it was, however, intellectual support and polemic could contribute only indirectly to sustaining Montfort's position after Lewes. To a much larger extent that position was grounded on the practical consequences of his victory. After the battle, wrote Trivet, 'he had the king and the whole kingdom in his power'.[8] His possession of Henry and his chief male relatives meant that the regime's enemies had no obvious leaders. Henry accompanied him to London at the end of May. Edward and Henry of Almain were kept in confinement, first at Dover, then at Wallingford, and Richard of Cornwall, imprisoned initially in the Tower, was also transferred to Wallingford, probably in early June.[9] The organisation of an opposition by Henry and Edward, which had curtailed Montfort's previous administration in 1263, was no longer possible. With surveillance of the king came direction of the chancery, demonstrated in Henry's later complaint that Montfort had used the seal 'at his will' after Lewes, sealing letters contrary to the king's

---

[5] *Song of Lewes*, ll. 198–9.
[6] *Ann. Oseney*, pp. 140–1; *CPR, 1258–66*, pp. 320, 328.
[7] Above, pp. 253–5. Lawrence, 'The University of Oxford', pp. 101–2, 109, n. 3, takes issue with Rishanger, *De Bellis*, p. 22; to my mind, not entirely justly.
[8] N. Trivet, *Annales*, ed. T. Hog (London, 1845), p. 261.
[9] *Cron. Maior.*, p. 63; *Ann. Dun.*, pp. 232–3; *Ann. Lond.*, p. 64.

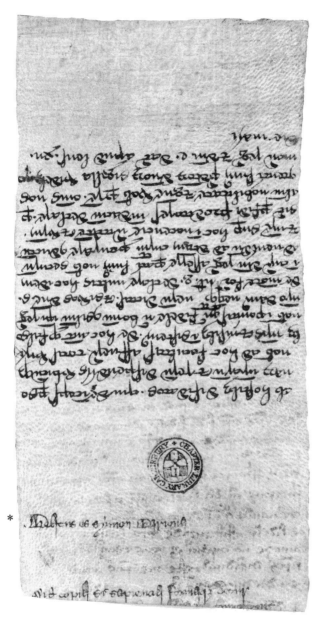

Plate 13. Montfort as saint – and the rock of the Church? To a contemporary dossier of documents from Canterbury Cathedral concerning the battle of Lewes, a scribe has added Christ's words, 'Blessed art thou, Simon Bar-jona' (Matthew, xvi. 17: asterisked).

wishes.[10] This gave him access to the whole prerogative of the Crown: to distribute patronage, summon armies, appoint and dismiss officials. John de Chishull, appointed chancellor by Henry in November 1263, was clearly no hindrance, for he was retained in office until February 1265. Never before had an opponent of the king so openly appropriated the kingdom's controls.

Despite these assets, the triumphalism of the *Song of Lewes* was misplaced and the claims of Trivet overstated. Montfort's position after Lewes was by no means impregnable. Military dangers faced him on all sides. The release of the marchers, the most telling sign of his weakness in the negotiations following the battle, created a permanent threat to his security, for which possession of the two hostages was no adequate safeguard. The northerners, led by John Balliol, had similarly been allowed to go,[11] to maintain a second unpacified royalist salient on the kingdom's periphery. Nearer the centre, the royalists continued to hold many castles. Most were subsequently surrendered, but not all, not immediately, and not without trouble. Windsor was not given up until the end of June, Nottingham until mid December.[12] The garrison at Tonbridge, told to disperse quietly, instead decamped in arms to Edward's stronghold at Bristol, which remained in royalist hands until April 1265.[13] Peter of Savoy's Sussex castle at Pevensey was never taken, despite a long siege by young Simon during the winter and spring of 1264–65.[14] It was via Pevensey that the influential royalists who had escaped from the battlefield, including William de Valence, Guy de Lusignan and Hugh Bigod, fled to France. Louis first heard of the disaster from these men, and the story was presented with embellishments which can only have hardened his attitude to the rebels. According to the London annals, they told him that Henry had been captured sleeping, unforewarned and in bed.[15] It was not surprising that Louis now gave his backing to the preparations for an invasion of England which Queen Eleanor had begun to make even before Lewes.[16]

[10] *CPR, 1258–66*, p. 436; *Cron. Maior.*, p. 76; Carpenter, 'St Thomas Cantilupe', p. 64.
[11] *CPR, 1258–66*, pp. 318, 343, 364, 374; *Flores Hist.*, iii, p. 261; *Ann. Dun.*, p. 232.
[12] *CPR, 1258–66*, pp. 318, 321–2, 324, 330; *CR, 1264–68*, p. 83.
[13] *Guisborough*, p. 196; Trivet, *Annales*, p. 261; below, pp. 319, 332, 335.
[14] *CPR, 1258–66*, pp. 333, 363, 371, 386, 392; *CR, 1264–68*, p. 80; *Ann. Wav.*, p. 363.
[15] Battle Chronicle, in Bémont, *Montfort* (1st edn), p. 377; *Ann. Lond.*, p. 64.
[16] Gavrilovitch, *Étude sur le Traité de Paris*, pp. 120–3; Labarge, *Montfort*, pp. 238–9 (the best modern account of Eleanor's activities). The proof that Eleanor was beginning to prepare for an invasion of England before Lewes comes in her letter of 7 May to Alphonse of Poitiers: Boutaric, *Saint Louis et Alfonse de Poitiers*, p. 108.

With the marchers and the northerners at large, castles still holding out for the king, and the gathering danger of invasion, the survival of Montfort's government was from the start in jeopardy. Two other internal problems weakened it still further, and indeed qualified the whole notion of the earl's 'government'. They were financial debility, and disorder. The Crown's finances were in a ruinous state. The exchequer had shut down in February 1264, probably when its staff were attacked during the London riots, and it remained closed until Michaelmas 1264: the first time that this had happened since the civil war of 1216–17. During the whole year sheriffs' payments into the exchequer of receipt totalled only £139, compared, for example, with £1,883 in 1262–3, and in some counties the Crown's local revenues were diverted into baronial hands.[17] How the administration paid its way at this time is an unsolved mystery; perhaps it was partly supported from the lands and goods of captured royalists.

Disorder was a still greater danger. The spoliations of 1263 had already left a legacy of disputes and recriminations, but the civil war had made matters much worse by licensing devastation as a way of destroying enemies. Wherever the royalist armies went, says the *Flores Historiarum*, they were accompanied by the three allies, plunder, burning and killing.[18] After Lewes one of Montfort's first priorities was to proclaim the peace and to forbid the carrying of arms, but to little effect. 'Plunderings and burnings' were generally reported, and throughout England, says the Furness chronicler, neighbour attacked neighbour and the strong oppressed the weak.[19] The suspension of the Bench from the end of Hilary term until the opening of Michaelmas term, probably again after attacks on its staff, must have contributed to these disorders by making peaceful litigation more difficult.[20] It was in these circumstances that keepers of the peace were appointed in all counties on 4 June. As with the comparable appointments in July 1263, their role was almost exclusively a policing and military one: they were literally to keep the peace, while the ordinary administration of the shires remained with the sheriffs. But the feebleness of Montfort's power here was shown

---

[17] *Flores Hist.*, ii, p. 487; M. H. Mills, '"Adventus Vicecomitum", 1258–72', *EHR*, 36 (1921), pp. 489, n. 3, 494; Jacob, *Studies*, pp. 264–9.

[18] *Flores Hist.*, ii, p. 489.

[19] *CPR, 1258–66*, pp. 325, 327, 331; *Chronicles of the Reigns of Stephen, Henry II and Richard I*, ed. R. Howlett (4 vols., Rolls ser., 1884–9), ii, pp. 544–5.

[20] *Flores Hist.*, ii, p. 487; C. A. F. Meekings, *Studies in 13th Century Justice and Administration* (London, 1981), iv, p. 182.

by further letters of 30 June, in which the keepers themselves were accused of promoting disorder by plundering and holding men to ransom, and the sheriffs were commissioned to go against those guilty.[21]

Montfort's inability to maintain the peace, the first duty of any ruler, further impaired an authority which was already very uncertain. Victory in battle may have given a divine legitimation to his power, as the author of the *Song of Lewes* believed, but it also meant that his regime had been established by force and lacked the free consent of the defeated. That the king now ruled in name only, and was almost as much a captive as his heir, were facts which nothing could disguise. The importance of the French arbitration largely lay in the hope which it offered here of recognition, and hence respectability, for his govern-ment. Yet no French arbitration was forthcoming; and this was a setback both to the standing of the new government and to the prospects for the permanent peace which the arbitration was intended to provide. The Mise of Lewes, containing in it the names of the six Frenchmen chosen as an electoral committee to initiate the arbitration, had been sent to Louis IX soon after the battle, and was followed up on 26 May with a request in Henry's name for him to induce the six to act. But Louis understandably refused to play the part assigned to him: we know from a later report by the papal legate that the request was never passed on to the electoral committee. Louis similarly ignored further anguished letters from Henry on 6 and 10 July pointing out the danger to which his silence exposed Edward and Henry of Almain, who were hostages for the completion of the Mise.[22] The successful working out of the Mise hinged entirely on French co-operation under the pressure to be applied by Montfort's possession of the hostages. Yet the scheme was ultimately futile, for if the French refused to co-operate, the status of the hostages gave them virtual immunity from reprisals. If Louis declined to convene the committee, even Montfort, never a man for half measures though he was, might have baulked at hanging the heir to the throne. For the same reason the hostages could not be used as an effective constraint on the marchers. The earl's practical inability to play the hostage card left him with inadequate leverage for the ends which he was pursuing.

That the Mise still hung fire was a consideration which helped to shape events in Montfort's famous parliament which met in London in late June. This proved to be a landmark in the history of his short

---

[21] *Foedera*, I, i, p. 442; *CPR, 1258–66*, pp. 360, 362; *DBM*, pp. 290–3.
[22] *CR, 1261–64*, pp. 385–6, 389–91; Maddicott, 'The Mise of Lewes', pp. 595, 599.

protectorate, for it allowed him to consolidate his position, both by devising a new constitution which entrenched him in power and by calling for the endorsement of local society, where his strengths had often lain. The immediate summoning of a parliament had been stipulated in the Mise.[23] None had met since October 1263, and a *post bellum* assembly would both accord with the Provisions and enable Montfort to draw support from a general discussion of 'the common business of the realm and the king' which the Provisions had defined as parliament's work. In the event the rapid alignment of all the forces which had from the start threatened the fragile peace after Lewes made the summoning of parliament a matter of urgency. The gathering of an invasion force in France was certainly known by 6 July and probably earlier.[24] Nearby in France, too, was the papal legate, Gui Foulquois, whose mission to England was discussed in parliament,[25] no doubt with an eye to the armoury of sanctions, including excommunication and interdict, which he had been given by the pope. The marchers remained contumacious, and though summoned to appear in parliament, with the prisoners whom they had taken at Northampton, failed to do so.[26] Something of the mood of apprehension growing from these dangers can be sensed in the letters of 4 June by which the new keepers of the peace were asked to supervise the election of four knights from each shire to attend parliament on 22 June 'at the latest'.[27] Both the exigent language and the short period of notice pointed to a gathering crisis.

It was probably the uncertainties of the future, as well as the non-fulfilment of the Mise, which did much to determine the form of the new constitution for which this parliament has become best known. On 23 June Henry empowered Montfort, Clare and Stephen Berksted to nominate nine councillors for the business of the king and kingdom. Two days later his authorisation was confirmed by the bishops of Exeter and Salisbury, the earl of Norfolk, and John fitz John, as representatives of the clergy, the baronage, and 'the people of the kingdom of England'.[28] Finally, on 28 June an *ordinatio* for the kingdom's

[23] *Cron. Maior.*, p. 63. Cf. J. C. Holt, 'The Prehistory of Parliament', *The English Parliament in the Middle Ages*, ed. R. G. Davies and J. H. Denton (Manchester, 1981), pp. 10–11.

[24] *CPR, 1258–66*, p. 362.

[25] J. Heidemann, *Papst Clemens IV: Das Vorleben des Papstes und sein Legationregister* (Münster, 1903), No. 14. This and subsequent references to Heidemann's edition of the legate's register follow his numeration of the documents.

[26] *CPR, 1258–66*, p. 362; *Ann. Dun.*, p. 232.

[27] *DBM*, pp. 292–3.

[28] *Foedera*, I, i, p. 444; J. P. Gilson, 'The Parliament of 1264', *EHR*, 16 (1901), p. 500.

government was sealed in parliament. It was made (so the text stated) with the consent of the king, the prelates, the earls 'and also of the community then present', and witnessed by the bishops of Lincoln and Ely, the earls of Norfolk and Oxford, Humphrey de Bohun, William de Munchensi and Thomas fitz Thomas, mayor of London.[29] By the terms of this Ordinance the three electors were empowered to nominate nine men to act as royal councillors and, if necessary, to appoint replacements. Three of the nine were always to be in attendance on the king, with whom the whole body was to settle the affairs of the realm and to sanction appointments, including those to the great offices of state, to the custody of castles, and to offices in the household. If officials misbehaved, then the king was to remove them with the consent of the nine, who were also to sanction replacements. If the councillors were in dispute, then a two-thirds majority was to carry the day, with a final power of decision lying with the three or two-thirds of them. The Ordinance was to last until the Mise of Lewes had been implemented or agreement reached on other arrangements: a probable reference to the final peace which the French arbitration was intended to provide, but which, it was envisaged, might now be made without outside intervention.

This document effectively annulled the power of the Crown. In reinstating a baronial council and calling for conciliar control of appointments, it revived the principles of the Provisions of Oxford, at the point where they touched most sensitively on the king's prerogative. But the right to consent to appointments (and therefore essentially the right to appoint) was now vested in a much narrower body than Henry had confronted in 1258, and one lacking the royalist representation (John Mansel and the earl of Warwick) which had then palliated the prospect of conciliar management for the king. The further demand for councillors to be in constant attendance at court, borrowed from the Provisions of Westminster,[30] implicitly denied him any independent initiative in the exercise of his remaining rights. It is not surprising that he had to be compelled to accept the Ordinance, so the reliable Merton chronicler says, under threat of deposition, the election of a successor, and the perpetual imprisonment of his heir: a more likely story than the

---

[29] *DBM*, pp. 295–9. The text of the Ordinance comes from its incorporation in the later Peace of Canterbury, enrolled on the patent roll in August. For the date, and the constitution of the three and the nine, see N. Denholm-Young, 'Documents of the Barons' Wars', and 'The Winchester-Hyde Chronicle', *Collected Papers* (Cardiff, 1969), pp. 158–9, 162–4, 244.

[30] *DBM*, pp. 104–5, 150–1.

Ordinance's making with his 'consent, will and precept' recorded, with transparent overemphasis, in the text.[31]

Montfort was the author of the Ordinance.[32] He had kept faith with the Provisions by re-establishing and extending their principles, while at the same time increasing his own authority. The narrow conciliar base to his government, in which sovereignty lay with an inner ring of three, by contrast with the fifteen and the king in 1258, was not only a result of the decline in baronial support for reform. It was also a measure of his own ambitions, of what might be made out of the glory that he had won at Lewes, and of the imminent dangers which made his continuing leadership imperative. He was in part the head of an emergency junta, resembling the wartime *balìe* which sometimes directed the affairs of Italian city-states in comparable emergencies during the fourteenth and fifteenth centuries. In theory, the powers of the junta were provisional, for the Ordinance on which they were grounded was to last only until the Mise had been completed or other arrangements made. But theory and practice showed every sign of diverging. What prevented the Mise's completion was the continuing absence of arbitration on the two matters for which arbitration had been looked for in the Mise: the Provisions, and the other issues to be laid before the French electoral committee. For failure in the first of these Montfort himself was responsible. As Carpenter has pointed out, once the Mise had served its immediate purpose of allowing Montfort to secure possession of Henry and Edward after the battle, he probably had no intention of carrying it through to completion by seeking arbitration on the Provisions.[33] Indeed, the Ordinance was an uncompromising restatement of the Provisions' principles. Montfort's deviation here from the Mise was noted by the chroniclers. When he had achieved power, says Trivet, 'he showed himself more reluctant (*difficiliorem*) to discuss peace according to the aforesaid form [of the Mise]'. The author of the Merton *Flores* similarly spoke of the June Ordinance as having been imposed on the king by Montfort's party, 'unmindful of the compromise of Lewes and of their oath'.[34]

It is possible, therefore, that the Ordinance was intended to last for the foreseeable future because of Montfort's own unwillingness to

---

[31] *Flores Hist.*, iii, p. 262; *DBM*, pp. 298–9. Powicke, *King Henry III*, p. 478, is mistaken in thinking that the chronicler's statement applies to the later Peace of Canterbury.

[32] *Ann. Wint.*, p. 102.

[33] Carpenter, 'Simon de Montfort and the Mise of Lewes', pp. 2–3, 10–11.

[34] Trivet, *Annales*, p. 261; *Flores Hist.*, iii, p. 261.

implement one of the conditions, arbitration on the Provisions, by which it might be abrogated. But it was also likely to be perpetuated by Louis's continuing refusal to implement the second condition by which the Ordinance might be annulled: that is to say, by setting up the electoral committee which would initiate a more wide-ranging arbitration. Without the prospect of a permanent peace which that arbitration held out, the Ordinance might come to provide for the country's government for an indefinite period. That much must have been in the mind of its maker and chief beneficiary.

Though the Ordinance was of Montfort's devising and conferred power on the small group which he headed, it did not, however, institute an autocracy. It is true that to some extent his government was that of a party. The two other members of the triumvirate, Clare and Berksted, were close associates, and the majority of the nine new councillors were loyal and longstanding supporters. Four of them – the bishop of London, Humphrey de Bohun, Peter de Montfort and Adam of Newmarket – had been among the sponsors of the baronial letters to Louis before Amiens.[35] But the nine did not, of course, constitute the whole party: even a man so central to Montfort's regency as Hugh Despenser, the justiciar, was not formally a councillor. Looking beyond the three and the nine, Montfort took great care to secure the most comprehensive consent to the Ordinance that established these bodies. The king's initial authorisation was ratified by two bishops, an earl and a baron, the Ordinance itself witnessed by two other bishops, two earls, two barons and the mayor of London. The high place given to Thomas fitz Thomas, the mayor, marked the value that Montfort rightly placed on his continuing alliance with London. Fitz Thomas kept company with him on another occasion in June and was well rewarded for his services to the regime.[36]

Most important of all, perhaps, was the assent of the knights. Though we do not know how many of the four summoned from each county actually appeared in London, the references to the 'people of the kingdom of England' and the 'community', contained respectively in the ratificatory letters of 25 June and in the Ordinance, hint at a wide sanctioning of the new arrangements. The effective revival of the Provisions and, more specifically, the new conciliar control of appoint-

---

[35] Denholm-Young, 'The Winchester-Hyde Chronicle', p. 244; *DBM*, pp. 284–5.
[36] *CPR, 1258–66*, pp. 341, 353; *CR, 1264–68*, p. 46; *Beauchamp Cartulary Charters, 1100–1268*, ed. Mason, p. 200; Williams, *Medieval London*, p. 231.

ments, including those to local offices, gave them a programme whose appeal was strengthened by other measures taken during the parliament. In late June new sheriffs were appointed in almost all counties, seemingly after local elections. They mostly held office as *custodes*, not farmers, and were presumably intended to hand over all the proceeds from their counties in return for allowances, rather than to pay to the exchequer the large fixed sums which had proved so encouraging to extortion and corruption before 1258. Both their method of appointment and the terms of their tenure, originally instituted by the reformers in 1258–59, had a guaranteed local popularity and were a further indication of Montfort's return to the Provisions. The enrolment of some of these appointments on 27 June, while parliament was still in session, suggests that the names of the new sheriffs may have been notified to the government by the shire representatives. This was the first general change in the shrievalties since 1262, though since then the royalist sheriffs had been partly superseded by the baronial keepers of the peace; and the fact that at least seven of the new appointees had been among the local knights appointed to collect grievances in 1258 points to the success of the Montfortian regime in re-establishing links with the local supporters who had been the mainstay of the reform movement in its early days.[37]

(B) THE SAVIOUR OF HIS COUNTRY, JULY–DECEMBER 1264

The parliament of June 1264 thus conferred on Montfort's government a measure of the legitimacy which it had hitherto lacked. Though his rule would never have the free consent of either Henry or Louis, it was now underpinned by a broad constituency of baronial, episcopal and local support. Vindicated in battle, Montfort had used parliament skilfully in order to consolidate his victory. He needed all the support he could muster in the great crisis that was now approaching. Immediately after parliament had ended, probably in early July, he and Clare set off against the marchers, who had not only refused to appear in parliament but were even putting to ransom the Northampton prisoners whom they should have surrendered. In a short campaign the two earls, allied with Llywelyn, were able to retake the castles of Hay, Hereford, Richard's

---

[37] *CPR, 1258–66*, pp. 327–8; *DBM*, pp. 108–9; W. A. Morris, *The Medieval English Sheriff to 1300* (Manchester, 1927), pp. 173–4; Knowles, 'The Disinherited', ii, pp. 78–80; *Baronial Plan*, pp. 182–5, 204–9; above, pp. 126, 159, 165.

Castle and Ludlow, to devastate the lands of Roger Mortimer, and to bring their enemies to terms at Montgomery, probably in late July. The truce which the king ratified on 25 August bound the marchers to hand over their prisoners, the royal castles that they held, and hostages for their own good behaviour. But they could not be kept to these conditions: the prisoners and the castles remained theirs, and no more was heard of the hostages.[38]

This unsatisfactory peace was probably forced on Montfort by the urgent need for his presence in the south-east. Before he could conclusively settle with the marchers, the danger of a French invasion had become acute. At Damme in Flanders, Queen Eleanor, 'the mightiest of warrior heroines' (*virago potentissima*),[39] acting with energy and some diplomatic finesse, had gathered together a large mercenary force from the Low Countries, France, Gascony and Savoy. She raised money from Louis IX, solicited help from Alphonse of Poitiers, his brother, and probably from Ireland, and marshalled behind her refugees, aliens and royalist exiles, including Edmund her second son, Hugh Bigod, William de Valence, Peter of Savoy and John Mansel.[40] The English response took a threefold form: military preparations; negotiations with the legate and with Louis in order to forestall an invasion and the ecclesiastical censures which might assist it; and attempts to restore order in the Church, partly so as to deprive the country's enemies of a further pretext for attack.

The military measures resulted in the raising of what is likely to have been one of the largest armies seen in England since the Conquest. Between 6 and 9 July not only was the feudal host called out, but all such extra men as the tenants-in-chief could raise. In addition, every village, according to its size, was to provide four, six or eight men, whose expenses were to be paid by their communities.[41] This immense host mustered on Barham Down, between Canterbury and Dover, in early August: 'such a multitude gathered together against the aliens that you would not have believed so many men equipped for war existed in England'.[42] Although Montfort was away in the marches for most of

---

[38] *CPR, 1258–66*, pp. 344, 362–3, 366–7, 476; Heidemann, No. 12; *Flores Hist.*, ii, pp. 498–9; Sayles, *Functions of the Medieval Parliament*, pp. 103–4; Powicke, *King Henry III*, pp. 476–7.

[39] *Flores Hist.*, ii, p. 500.

[40] *Flores Hist.*, ii, p. 499; *Wykes*, p. 154; Gavrilovitch, *Étude sur la Traité de Paris*, pp. 120–3; Labarge, *Montfort*, pp. 238–9; Cox, *Eagles of Savoy*, pp. 315–16; R. Frame, 'Ireland and the Barons' Wars', *TCE*, i, pp. 162–3.

[41] *Foedera*, I, i, p. 444; *CPR, 1258–66*, pp. 360–2; Powicke, *King Henry III*, pp. 475–6.

[42] *Flores Hist.*, ii, p. 499.

July, he kept in touch by messenger with his allies in the south-east and was seen, almost certainly rightly, as the director of the whole huge operation: summoning the local troops, setting himself to guard the ports of Kent, despatching Hugh Despenser to see to the security of East Anglia, arranging with the Cinque Ports for the keeping of the seas, initiating the raising of taxation from the clergy.[43] It was probably he who spoke through the king's letters sent to the shire communities in early July. A horde of aliens was preparing to invade the land. They would spare no one and were thirsting for English blood. At this time of crisis no one should plead the harvest or some other everyday business as an excuse for not turning out.[44] When we think of Montfort's reputation, of his posthumous cult, and of the political awareness, among peasants as among their superiors, which is so striking a feature of the reform movement, we should remember the thousands of men who must have responded to his summons and seen him in action during those summer days. Like Mr Churchill in 1940, he had given to the English a sense of common purpose and of the need to defend a great cause in the face of intense danger.

Meanwhile the barons and bishops were attempting to reach a settlement with Louis which would put a peaceful end to the threat of invasion. Their negotiations, which lasted through July, August, September and October, ran in parallel with their military preparations and may be followed in the register of the papal legate, a source hardly used by English historians.[45] Though these negotiations were tortuous, complicated and ultimately futile, they reveal the interests and opinions of both sides, and especially those of Simon de Montfort, with a clarity and directness that makes them worth studying in some detail. The Montfortians' first concern was to prevent an invasion and to avoid the publication in England of the sentences of excommunication and interdict with which the legate was equipped. That would undermine the whole moral and religious foundation for their enterprise, and place an intolerable strain on the loyalties of the bishops. So serious was the threat considered that in late July the magnates decreed the unusual penalty of decapitation for anyone bringing in or publishing such sentences against those wanting to observe their oaths to the

---

[43] Heidemann, No. 12; *Wykes*, pp. 154–5. For the clerical tax, see *Councils and Synods*, II, i, pp. 695, 698–9.

[44] *Foedera*, I, i, p. 444. Cf. D. A. Carpenter, 'English Peasants and Politics, 1258–67', *Past and Present*, 136 (1992), pp. 12–13, 32–3.

[45] Heidemann, *Papst Clemens IV* (above, n. 25).

Provisions.[46] Initially the Montfortians also wanted Louis's acceptance of the Mise and of the June Ordinance which was to lapse on the Mise's completion. When this proved unattainable, they hoped for a settlement grounded on compromise. Their most valuable bargaining counter lay in the possession of the hostages, which, as a distressed Henry recognised, made any invasion extremely dangerous to the royal family.[47] Even if the counter could not be used, the captivity of Edward and of Henry of Almain may have done something to persuade those in France to negotiate and to defer an invasion, until, as eventually happened, the failure of Eleanor's funds ended the whole enterprise. For their part, Louis and the legate wanted nothing less than the abrogation of the Provisions and the restoration of Henry to full power. It is easy to see why compromise was difficult and a settlement elusive.

Negotiations began inauspiciously in late June or early July, when the legate's envoy, a Franciscan friar named Alan, sent to prepare the way for his master's coming, failed to get beyond Dover. His subsequent report relates what happened with a vividness rare in contemporary sources.[48] On reaching Dover he had been searched and his letters taken from him. One of the searchers had said to him that if he carried a single letter directed against the kingdom, he would be killed. Eventually Henry de Montfort had arrived from London, but had told him that he could do nothing before the arrival of messengers from his father, who had gone to the marches: interesting evidence of Montfort's controlling hand. Then the bishop of Exeter had come, bearing the *forma pacis*, the Ordinance made in the recent parliament, to show to Edward (who was in captivity at Dover). The envoy had found the bishop, Henry and Sir John, the castle's custodian (presumably Sir John de la Haye) friendly and courteous, and had explained the legate's mission to them, expounding the benefits that his arrival in England would bring (an exposition unlikely to have been received quite so courteously). He had been given no firm answer about the legate's admission, though he understood that the prelates and barons were to discuss this once peace had been restored. But some men had said to him that they feared the legate's arrival because he would obstruct peace by favouring one party and putting down another; that no legate

---

[46] Gilson, 'The Parliament of 1264', p. 501.

[47] *CR, 1261–64*, pp. 390–1.

[48] Heidemann, No. 12. Cf. *Ger. Cant.*, ii, pp. 238–9, who gives this episode too early a date at the end of May.

ought to be admitted unless requested by the king and the community of the realm ('communitas regni'), which in this case had not been done; and that the kingdom had been destroyed by aliens, both laymen, who had exercised their lordship by oppressing the natives, and clerks, who held the fatter benefices ('pinguiora beneficia'). He ended by advising the legate not to come to England without sufficient security: sensibly.

Eavesdropping on these conversations in Dover castle gives us a graphic impression of the state of feeling among the Montfortians in the summer of 1264. The perceived equality of king and community, the alarm over the legate's approach, and in particular the detestation of aliens, all illuminate the political assumptions and the powerful emotions which underlay what was now national support for Montfort and his cause. The episode was concluded by Montfort himself later in July, when he wrote to turn down the legate's request for admission, to protest strongly at Louis's financial support for the queen's army, and to suggest a peace conference at Boulogne.[49] The conference never took place, however, since the baronial envoys failed to appear,[50] and on 12 August the legate moved into action. In church at Boulogne he ordered Montfort and his accomplices to admit him by 1 September. They were to free the king and the hostages, restore Henry to full power, and undertake to appear before the legate at Gravelines, there to pledge themselves to abjure the Provisions, under penalty of excommunication and interdict. The legate denied that the Mise of Lewes had ever been received by the members of the electoral committee who were to act under its terms, and stated that the three bishops on the committee had issued letters saying that at no time had they received the Mise, nor would they do so in future.[51]

The French court had thus broken silence only to reject completely the Mise of Lewes. It was probably in response to this rejection (though we cannot be sure about this) that new terms were drawn up in England and sent to Louis on 15 August.[52] Known afterwards as the 'Peace of Canterbury', where the court had arrived on 12 August, these terms went well beyond earlier constraints on royal authority. The Peace

---

[49] Heidemann, No. 14; *CR, 1261–64*, p. 396.
[50] Heidemann, No. 19.
[51] Heidemann, No. 20, esp. paras. m, n, o, p. The version of this document in the legate's register is more detailed than that in *Foedera*, I, i, p. 447. Cf. Powicke, *King Henry III*, p. 480.
[52] *CPR, 1258–66*, p. 366. The Peace of Canterbury itself bears no date. It seems probable that news of the legate's pronouncement at Boulogne on 12 August would have reached the English court in time for the despatch of the Peace, perhaps already drafted, on 15 August; especially since the legate was able to reply to the Peace as early as 17 August: Heidemann, No. 23.

incorporated the Ordinance made earlier in the June parliament, with
its establishment of the three and the nine, and its conciliar limitations
on the king's initiative; but this was now to last either until the Mise had
been carried through (as laid down in the Ordinance) or, if the Mise
remained inoperative, through the remainder of Henry's life and into
the reign of Edward, until a date to be settled. This last was a radical
new departure, which for the first time threatened explicitly to perpetuate the Crown's subjugation into the distant future. In addition, the
Ordinance was now supplemented by various new clauses. The Church
was to be reformed; the royal councillors and other officials were always
to be natives; aliens – laymen, clerks and merchants – were to be
allowed to come and go, provided they did so in peace and held no
offices; Magna Carta and the Forest Charter were to be observed, as
were the statutes concerning redress of grievances, sheriffs' tourns and
suit of court (that is, the Provisions of Westminster); and Henry, Edward
and their supporters were to forswear retribution against the barons and
their supporters for the recent disturbances.[53]

The Peace of Canterbury thus kept the fulfilment of the Mise in the
forefront of baronial demands. Its novelty lay in the inflammatory
proposal to prolong the Crown's tutelage should the Mise remain
incomplete. When the Peace was despatched on 15 August Louis had
rejected the Mise, but as yet he knew nothing of the arrangements made
in June for Henry's subjection. Part of the purpose of these
arrangements, and of the extra edge given to them at Canterbury, was
almost certainly to apply more pressure to Louis in order to secure his
co-operation in the arbitration, which was clearly still high among the
baronial desiderata. The plight of the hostages had left Louis unmoved;
perhaps the semi-permanent subjugation of the English Crown would
succeed where that ploy had failed. In return, the Peace made some
concessions, probably secured by the bishops and perhaps designed to
ease Louis's compliance. The provision for the reform of the Church –
meaning the making good of its losses during the troubles – and for
the readmission of aliens were conciliatory. In particular, there was a
notable retreat from the demand made in July 1263 for the expulsion of
all aliens except those judged acceptable.[54] At the same time the requirement that the Charters be fully observed enhanced the status of the
Provisions, which, so the barons had earlier argued, derived from
Magna Carta; while the stress laid on the Provisions of Westminster,

---

[53] *DBM*, pp. 294–301.   [54] Above, pp. 230, 233.

now, like the Charters, to be strengthened by measures 'for their better and firmer observance', was designed to appeal to the men of the shires who were both the chief beneficiaries of the Provisions and the bedrock of Montfortian support.

If the Peace of Canterbury was intended to persuade Louis to comply with Montfort's plans, it hardly had that effect. Sent to France with a request that Louis should 'accept and approve it', and persuade Henry's friends overseas to do likewise,[55] it was rejected in terms of contumelious outrage. Writing to the English bishops on 17 August, the legate expressed astonishment that they should have accepted such a peace, which abolished royal power, replaced one king by three (an allusion to the three councillors), and exposed the kingdom to so many perils and schisms. He was equally surprised that they should have expected him to induce Louis to accept a peace which overturned his own ruling – a clear reference to the Mise of Amiens.[56] A little later, in a superbly angry letter, he reported Louis's own reaction: when he had heard the terms of the Peace, the most Christian king of France had said that he would rather break clods behind a plough than have this sort of kingly rule ('quod mallet post aratrum glebas frangere, quam huiusmodi principatum habere'). It was now clear that no form of settlement which left Henry under constraint would be acceptable to Louis. Ignoring the peripheral concessions of the Peace of Canterbury, both he and the legate had seen straight through to the heart of the matter: the annulment of Henry's kingship in favour of baronial rule. 'The barons empowered, the king disabled, because such in name only' ('barones utile, rex inutile, quia tantum nominale').[57]

The outright rejection of the Peace of Canterbury seems to have confused and divided the opposition in England. The bishops were under substantial pressure to appear before the legate at Boulogne to explain themselves. They had already been cited to appear there, but had failed to do so.[58] They were cited again in the legate's letters of 17 August and again about 1 September,[59] but they probably feared that they might be prevented from returning or else made to return with the potentially explosive letters of excommunication and interdict. Towards the end of August they replied to the legate's condemnatory letter,

---

[55] *CPR, 1258–66*, p. 366.
[56] Heidemann, No. 23.
[57] Heidemann, No. 29 c.
[58] Heidemann, No. 23 a.
[59] Heidemann, Nos. 17, 23 c, 29 e.

telling him, humbly but somewhat disingenuously, that they could not see that the new measures drained the king of his power and that they had no wish for the three councillors to take his place.[60] The barons similarly expressed surprise at the legate's rejection of the Peace, 'ordained not without great deliberation and harmoniously accepted by the lord king, the prelates, all the magnates and the whole *communitas regni*'. In their eyes at least the Ordinance which the Peace embodied was sanctioned by the wide consent given to it in the June parliament.[61]

But there were clearly different opinions about what was to be done. About 4 September Henry of Almain was released from captivity to go to France to discuss peace, probably with the strong backing of the bishops, who stood surety in the huge sum of 20,000 marks for his early return.[62] His mission ran concurrently with a new scheme, drawn up on 11 September, which he was perhaps expected to promote. Under its terms the Peace of Canterbury, found wanting in France, was to be reconsidered and amended by a panel of four: the bishop of London, Hugh Despenser, Charles of Anjou and the abbot of Bec. If Charles of Anjou was unable to act, then either Peter le Chamberlain or Simon de Claremont, lord of Nesle, two of Louis's councillors then in Canterbury, was to take his place. If the four disagreed, the archbishop of Rouen was to be brought in as a fifth arbitrator. There were two conditions: none but natives were to govern the kingdom or hold office; and 'the personal and special quarrels, questions and contentions' between Montfort and Henry were to be settled before any final peace.[63]

The scheme hinted at the wide divergencies of view about how best to turn the united front presented by Louis IX and the legate. It marked a defeat for Montfort, an advance by the conciliators, probably the bishops, and a concession to the allies' opponents in France. The retreat from the earlier stand on the Peace of Canterbury meant that the whole system of conciliar supervision for the king, set out in the June Ordinance which the Peace embodied, was now to be opened to discussion. This left Montfort's position in jeopardy, for the result might be to sweep away the basis of his power. He had taken what steps he could to prevent this. The two English arbitrators were his allies; Charles of Anjou was said to be sworn to brotherhood with him; Eudes

---

[60] Heidemann, No. 28.
[61] Heidemann, No. 25 b.
[62] *Foedera*, I, i, p. 446; Powicke, *King Henry III*, pp. 480–1.
[63] *Foedera*, I, i, p. 446.

Rigaud, archbishop of Rouen, was the oldest of friends; and Simon de
Claremont, Louis's councillor, was married to Montfort's niece, Alice,
daughter of his deceased brother Amaury.[64] Yet even with such a
partisan panel, he now faced a disturbingly unpredictable situation.
Hence, we may think, his need to raise a matter which had not so far
directly entered the negotiations: his own personal quarrels with the
king, which were to be resolved in advance of any political settlement.
A draft of the scheme tells us that Louis had already been asked to
pronounce on these quarrels, perhaps in the Mise;[65] and Montfort's
purpose in making this reservation must have been to safeguard his own
interests, notably in Eleanor's dower, if power seemed likely to slip from
his hands. Once so central to his 'quarrels . . . and contentions' with
Henry, the dower had lost priority when his control of the kingdom
offered him other and much greater gains. It was now resurrected when
that control seemed at risk. The need for a prior ruling on his own
claims would ensure that so much at least could be salvaged from any
approaching political shipwreck.

In the event Montfort had nothing to fear. The project went no
further, and its abortion probably marked the renewal of his ascendancy. On 15 September it was superseded by a further peace plan
much more favourable to conciliar supremacy and the status quo.[66] The
second plan established a new body of arbitrators, comprising the
archbishop of Rouen, the bishop of London, Hugh Despenser and Peter
le Chamberlain, with the legate as a fifth member, to act in case of
disagreement. The arbitrators' commission was defined generally and
vaguely as 'the reformation of the state of the realm . . . and the
reconciliation of discords', but two specific limitations were imposed on
their work: they were not to concern themselves with the freeing of the
hostages; and they were to choose for the king councillors who were
always to be Englishmen. The powers of the councillors were then
defined: to advise the king on matters of justice, on the appointment
of officials, who were again to be exclusively English, and on the
observance of the Charters and the Provisions of Westminster; and to
supervise royal expenditure until the king was out of debt and could live
off his own, without burdening merchants and the poor. The arbitration

---

[64] Rhein, *La Seigneurie de Montfort en Iveline*, p. 75. My interpretation of the peace plans of 11 and
15 September owes a great deal to the advice of Dr David Carpenter.
[65] *Dipl. Docs.*, i, No. 393.
[66] *CPR, 1258–66*, pp. 370–1; Powicke, *King Henry III*, pp. 481–2.

was to take place in England, by Easter 1265, and when it had been completed the hostages were to be released, though only on strict conditions. If the arbitration failed, then the Peace of Canterbury was to stand.

These terms made some concessions to the legate, notably by giving the arbitrators power to choose the council and by bringing in the legate himself as a possible umpire. But the stipulation that the councillors must always be English, and the wide sweep of their powers, including the vital power to appoint officials, in effect brought back the conciliar controls which had been threatened in the earlier scheme. The reassurance that this offered to Montfort explains the disappearance of his own claims from the new agenda; for the renewed prospect of supervising Henry's activities promised far more than what could be gained from the rectification of his private grievances. Admittedly, what was proposed was not the continuance of the three and the nine instituted in June. But on any new council Montfort could expect a dominant voice, and if the arbitration failed the revival of the Peace of Canterbury would put the June constitution back in place.

Through these two contrasting routes to a final settlement we can thus trace, if only hazily, the conflicts of opinion which now prevailed among the Montfortians. The refusal of either Louis or the legate to contemplate the restraints on royal power devised in June had precipitated a minor crisis within the major crisis which loured over these months. In it, Montfort fought for the conciliar supremacy which was both the cause of the Provisions and the guarantee of his own position. Though the reservation of his private claims in the first scheme showed how closely he still cherished his own interests, the general course of his conduct remained defensible in terms of reforming principles.

Whether what he advocated remained practicable was another matter. The second peace plan was taken to France on 24 September by a strong group of envoys: the bishops of London, Worcester and Winchester, Hugh Despenser, Peter de Montfort and Richard de Mepham, archdeacon of Oxford.[67] They met the legate at Boulogne. Now that he had succeeded in bringing the baronial representatives, including the bishops, before him, the legate was able to make good use of the considerable scope for intimidation given to him by his papal commission. The envoys had to listen to a reading of the major items in that commission, including the authority given to the legate to restore

---

[67] *CPR, 1258–66*, p. 370; Heidemann, Nos. 39, 40.

Henry's power under penalty of excommunication and interdict.[68] It was probably these browbeating tactics, together with the presence of King Louis's council and of proctors for the queen and Edmund, that persuaded the Montfortians to retreat still further. The settlement drafted in England was modified. The legate's power to use his casting vote was slightly enlarged. Much more significantly, although the king's councillors were still to be English, nothing was now said about their power to advise the king on appointments, nor on the need for officials to be Englishmen, nor, finally, about a return to the Peace of Canterbury if arbitration should fail.[69]

On one central point the legate asked for clarification. Did the bishops agree with the barons that the king of England should be compelled to accept specified councillors and strictly to follow their counsel? Each of the bishops said yes. Juxtaposing as it did two irreconcilable views on whether councillors could be imposed on the king against his will, this brief exchange struck down to the essence of the conflict between Henry III and the reformers since 1258. It showed that three leading bishops stood firm on a principle vital, as they saw it, to the just government of the kingdom.[70] They had held their ground, too, in the amended plan's rather surprising acceptance of the need for English councillors: perhaps with Louis's help, for he had been sympathetic to just such an argument in September 1263 and his hand in the drafting of the revised settlement was recognised by the legate.[71] But the concessions were nevertheless too large to be ratified by the envoys alone, and the bishop of Winchester, Hugh Despenser and Peter de Montfort returned to England for consultations. The bishop was provided by the legate with letters of excommunication and interdict, directed against the barons, the Londoners and the Cinque Ports, with orders for their publication if the Montfortians would not accept what was now proposed. The terrors thus held in reserve doubtless explain why there was no outright rejection of the concessions made in France. Instead, a prevaricating response was taken back to the legate by a new

---

[68] Heidemann, No. 41.

[69] Heidemann, No. 42. There is a variant version of this scheme in Rishanger, *De Bellis*, p. 37.

[70] 'Interrogavit episcopos Angliae supradictos, an ipsi consentirent cum baronibus, quod rex Angliae ad certos habendos consiliarios et eorum praecise sequendum consilium arctaretur. Et responderunt sigillatim, quod sic': Heidemann, No. 43 a. Cf. Carpenter, 'King Henry III's "Statute"', p. 941, n. 3. For the connection between just government and the imposition of new councillors on the king, see especially the baronial submission to Louis IX before Amiens: *DBM*, pp. 262–3; and below, pp. 360–61

[71] Heidemann, No. 43 a.

group of envoys, including Peter le Chamberlain and Henry of Almain, still active and out of custody in accordance with what had been agreed earlier. En route, the envoys were attacked by the people of Boulogne, losing all their documents as a result; but they were able to report verbally the few minor amendments to the peace proposed by the barons. These amendments, however, failed to satisfy the queen because they said nothing about the release of the hostages, although the bishops offered reassurance on this point.[72]

By this time the legate's patience was running out. When the bishops of Worcester and London returned to England about 3 October, they carried with them once again the dreaded bulls of excommunication and interdict, this time to be published if the barons had not reconciled themselves to the legate within fifteen days.[73] They also brought a complicated provisional scheme laying down the conditions for the lifting of these penalties. It entailed the placing of the whole dispute in the legate's hands, further discussions with Despenser and the other baronial representatives, and, if no final agreement could be reached, the offer of pledges by both sides. The barons were to hand over to the legate Dover castle and the hostages; the queen's party was to hand over an equivalent castle in France and Eleanor's second son, Edmund. Once this had been done, and further verbal security offered, the disputes between Henry and Montfort were to be resolved and the sentences lifted.[74] The legate clearly saw that if he were to become general arbitrator, with what all must have recognised to be the certain quashing of the Provisions and Henry's full restoration, then Montfort's own private interests would have to be protected. This was what he offered. But the surrender of Dover castle and the hostages, the greatest of the baronial assets, was hardly an acceptable quid pro quo. In any case his plans were dramatically curtailed. When the bishops reached England, the bulls were taken from them at Dover, torn into pieces and thrown into the sea.[75] Shortly afterwards, on 11 October, the legate's new proposals were turned down with an equally piquant gesture when an English knight sailed to Wissant and, instead of landing, dropped into the sea a box containing formal letters of rejection. That the same box also contained the Peace of Canterbury and, separate from it, the

---

[72] Heidemann, No. 43 b, c, d, e; *Flores Hist.*, ii, p. 501; *RL*, ii, pp. 278–9.
[73] Heidemann, No. 44.
[74] 'His peractis expendientur quaestiones regis et comitis Leycestriae': Heidemann, No. 46.
[75] *Wykes*, pp. 156–7; *Flores Hist.*, ii, p. 501; *Ger. Cant.*, ii, p. 239.

June Ordinance, was almost certainly an indication that the barons intended to continue with the government of the three and the nine.[76]

Before they left France bearing the legate's sentences Cantilupe and Sandwich had made a last undertaking which showed both their fears and the pressures bearing upon them. They had promised the legate that they would procure Edward's liberation and, if this were not done, that they would return to France, to stay in a place to be decided by the count of St Pol, and that they would oppose the barons as long as Edward remained in detention. In return, Henry of Almain had agreed that the army massed on the coast for the invasion of England should stand down, presumably at his bidding.[77] This concession may have been a piece of private initiative by the two bishops, a gamble intended to trade Edward's release against the cancellation of the invasion. Offering a high price for an uncertain return, it was, like the legate's own proposals, aborted by the act of sabotage at Dover and the pantomime of the floating box. Events now moved rapidly to a conclusion. On 20 October the bulls of excommunication and interdict were finally published, but at Hesdin in Flanders, not in England, and by the legate, not by the English bishops.[78] From his point of view this was very much second best. It was also the end of the game.

Throughout these negotiations almost all the concessions had come from the baronial side. From the high point of Montfort's supremacy in the Peace of Canterbury there had been a steady retreat, which probably kept pace with the growing disquiet and division among the earl's followers. In that retreat the bishops had played a leading part. They had formed a majority among the baronial envoys who, in France, had agreed to the modification of the peace proposal drafted in England, itself a move away from the Peace of Canterbury. In the end two of them were even prepared to work for the release of Edward, without any guarantee as to the continuance of reform. Their position was as uncomfortable as it could be. Pledged though they were to the principles of the Provisions, they cannot have been happy to have set themselves up against both pope and legate. Once the legate could speak to them directly, he could play on their discomfort. His forceful

---

[76] Heidemann, No. 45.

[77] Heidemann, No. 48 (where 'proiurabimus' should clearly read 'procurabimus'). The bishops' undertaking is undated, but its making in the presence of Peter le Chamberlain and apparently of Henry of Almain, then in France (*Flores Hist.*, ii, p. 501), places it before their return to England.

[78] Heidemann, Nos. 50, 51, 52; *Foedera*, I, i, pp. 447–8; Powicke, *King Henry III*, p. 482.

reminder to the hapless Gervais of Winchester that by papal mandate he should withdraw from his alliance with the barons led the bishop to seek absolution from him then and there.[79] Nor were they all committed Montfortians. Walter Bronescombe of Exeter, for example, though he backed Montfort at the June parliament and in bringing its Ordinance to Dover for Edward's inspection, was a king's clerk by origin and was always regarded as a royalist. What forced him into the barons' camp was the need to repel a foreign invasion: it was 'to the defence of the country' ('ad defensionem patrie') that he appealed when seeking to levy in his diocese the clerical tax granted to support the army gathering in Kent. But he was a troubled man, working against the grain of his instinctive loyalties, a collaborator rather than a diehard, whose presence was more of an encouragement to waver than to stand fast.[80] Others may have been similarly placed.

But it was not only the bishops whose resolve weakened. Once in France, Despenser and Peter de Montfort had also been prepared to modify the peace proposals which they had brought, and the modifications were not rejected out of hand by those who remained in England. Clare may have been prepared to concede most, for a royal letter written on 6 October, towards the end of the negotiations, tells us that he had insisted on the delivery of the hostages.[81] The pressures for a settlement were very strong; not least, of course, the pressure exerted by the invisible army on the other side of the Channel. Desertions from the great English host assembled in Kent were causing concern as early as 6–7 September,[82] and there must have been considerable doubt about how long it could be funded and held together. Its disintegration, followed by a successful invasion from Flanders, would be the worst of all outcomes, from which nothing might be salvageable. There was much to be said for a negotiated peace, in which the delivery of the hostages was bound to have a place.

The debates among the Montfortians probably ran along these lines. But Montfort himself was set somewhat apart from those he led by the rigidity of his position. Both his power and his principles were closely bound up with the narrow constitution devised in June for the government of the country and the enforcement of the Provisions. That

---

[79] Heidemann, No. 43 b.

[80] Above, p. 195; M. Gibbs and J. Lang, *Bishops and Reform, 1215–1272* (Oxford, 1934), p. 191; *Councils and Synods*, II, i, pp. 698–9.

[81] *CPR, 1258–66*, p. 374.

[82] *CPR, 1258–66*, pp. 367–8; *CR, 1261–64*, pp. 405–6.

constitution also provided a shield, though more covertly, for Montfort's own acquisitiveness, now given the fullest of reins by his victory at Lewes, as we shall see.[83] He had every reason, therefore, to fight hard for the June constitution or – the next best thing – for general conciliar supervision of the king. Only under extreme pressure would he contemplate the sort of retreat exemplified in the scheme of 11 September; and that proved to be only a temporary aberration. Faced neither with the conflicting loyalties of the bishops nor with the proximity of the legate's thunderbolts, and courageous enough to sit out the danger of invasion, he was prepared to concede much less than some of his friends. It would not have been necessary for Clare to have insisted on the hostages' release, for example, had not this been strongly opposed; and it is hard to think that anything could have impeded their freedom had he and Montfort stood together. Since the hostages were not released, he won the argument. Likely to have been his, too, was the consistent demand for government by Englishmen. The requirement that the king's councillors, if not, in the end, his officials, should always be Englishmen was one that survived the encroachments of the legate during the negotiations and which represented a policy strongly associated with Montfort since the peace of July 1263.[84] Helped though he was by the danger from abroad, it was Montfort's achievement to have held together an uncertain coalition by imposing his own convictions upon his allies.

One further support underlay this achievement. The successful defiance of the legate depended partly on the restoration of order in the English Church. During the long time of troubles which had culminated at Lewes, ecclesiastical rights had been widely infringed. Much church land had come into the hands of laymen; clerks had been the victims and sometimes the perpetrators of attacks on church property; and the possessions of the alien clergy had proved especially vulnerable, since their holders had often fled the country. If the prelates were to maintain their alliance with Montfort, and at the same time to confront pope and legate with any confidence, they could not afford to compromise themselves by appearing to connive at these buccaneering enterprises. It was a special embarrassment that the leading offenders had sometimes been the barons themselves, of whom Clare was the most notable. In July 1264 he was still detaining lands belonging to the exiled bishop of Hereford; and about this time he was the recipient of a letter from

---

[83] Below, pp. 309–12.　　[84] Above, pp. 229–232.

Sandwich of London, in which the bishop respectfully castigated him for the depredations committed by his men against church property. These attacks, said Sandwich, might provoke complaints to the legate which would lead to the whole kingdom being placed under interdict.[85]

Sandwich had brought into the open one of the chief motives which guided those trying to make good the Church's losses. It was all the more urgent a task because of Louis's failure to initiate arbitration, either by the Mise of Amiens or by that of Lewes, which might have dealt with the spoliations and so have done the bishops' work for them. As it was, reform of the Church became part and parcel of the defence of the realm. Between June and October 1264 a series of measures to set the Church to rights ran parallel with Montfort's constitution-making and with the negotiations with the legate. At the June parliament action was set in train against clerks who had borne arms, and against both clerks and laymen who had despoiled churches or captured other clerks. It was probably Walter de Cantilupe who took the lead here,[86] as he certainly did at another assembly of prelates and magnates to consider the same matters at the end of July. Here, those who had attacked churches and churchmen were excommunicated, the bishops agreed to make enquiries into such transgressions in their dioceses, and the magnates to make satisfaction, once peace had been restored, to all those wronged. The meeting concluded with Cantilupe's appeal, as proctor for the bishops, against any sentence of excommunication or interdict which might be promulgated against them on the pretext of the injuries suffered by the Church, since those injuries were now on the point of being amended. A similar appeal *ad cautelam* was made by the king, who was made to state (by those who spoke for him) that all such pillaging was contrary to the Provisions of Oxford.[87] These precautionary appeals show how close was the perceived connection between the need to restore order in the Church and the need to avoid the impending ecclesiastical censures. The further undertaking to reform the Church, made in the Peace of Canterbury, has already been noticed.[88] At the end of October, probably shortly after the legate's sentences had been promulgated at Hesdin, a proposal was made to

[85] *Cron. Maior.*, pp. 65–7; *CPR, 1258–66*, p. 332; Bodleian Library, Oxford, MS Dugdale 20, ff. 140v–141; Denholm-Young, 'Documents of the Barons' War', p. 169.
[86] *Cron. Maior.*, pp. 65–7; *Councils and Synods*, ii, i, pp. 694–8; Powicke, *King Henry III*, p. 485, n. 1.
[87] *Ger. Cant.*, ii, pp. 239–41; *Councils and Synods*, ii, i, p. 695; Gilson, 'The Parliament of 1264', pp. 500–1.
[88] *DBM*, pp. 298–9; above, p. 294.

elect a committee of three bishops to consider reforms, to decide on the amends to be made by offenders, and to collect and safeguard the revenues from benefices held by aliens and other clergy who were temporarily in exile. Those resisting were to be distrained by the lay power, if necessary, and the justiciar was to put a force of a hundred knights and serjeants at the bishops' disposal for this purpose. In December this was followed up by the appointment of the archbishop of York and the bishops of London and Lincoln to this committee.[89]

These measures showed the extent to which the English Church in 1264 had become almost a self-governing entity, ruled, though perhaps reluctantly, by bishops working in partnership with barons. The absence abroad of the archbishop of Canterbury, the Church's *de facto* severance from papal control, the common front necessitated by the continual danger of invasion, excommunication and interdict, the attendance of the bishops at parliament and councils in June and July,[90] all emphasised the degree to which crisis had thrust a novel autonomy upon the Church. Though the degree of their commitment varied, from the qualified ardour of a Cantilupe of Worcester to the *faute-de-mieux* collaboration of a Bronescombe of Exeter, most of the bishops fell into line behind the only government available. If Berksted of Chichester, Sandwich of London, Gervais of Winchester and Cantilupe himself were still in the inner ring, they now had a wide circle of supporters. When Henry of Almain was about to leave on his mission to France in early September, he gave guarantees for his return to the bishops of London, Lincoln, Worcester, Winchester, Chichester, Coventry and Lichfield, Salisbury, Exeter, and the bishop-elect of Bath and Wells. The bishops who, in August, sought the restoration of Walter Merton's property, detained by the Londoners, included London, Lincoln, Worcester, Salisbury, Winchester, Exeter and Chichester. When all was over, after Evesham, eight bishops – Durham, London, Lincoln, Winchester, Worcester, Chichester, Ely and Salisbury – were sued *coram rege* for their transgressions during the troubles.[91] Montfort's relations with these men was not entirely free from tension: their divided allegiances, their predilection for conciliation and peace over defiance and conflict, and their necessarily censorious attitude towards baronial

---

[89] *Foedera*, I, i, pp. 443–4; *CPR, 1258–66*, pp. 375, 393; *Cron. Maior.*, p. 70; *Councils and Synods*, II, i, pp. 697–8; Powicke, *King Henry III*, p. 485, n. 1.

[90] E.g. Heidemann, No. 12.

[91] *Foedera*, I, i, p. 446; *CR, 1261–64*, p. 402; Jacob, *Studies*, p. 293.

self-help, all gave their partnership an ambivalent edge. But in general this broadening, if sometimes equivocal, foundation of ecclesiastical support was one of his greatest strengths during these difficult months.

By the late autumn the threat which had hung over England for so long was receding. The legate's period of office expired with the death of Pope Urban IV on 2 October 1264, and although he lingered in France for a few more months, whither letters were sent to him from England, he ceased to play any part in English affairs. His sentences made no discernible difference to the course of events: they seem to have been ignored and were subsequently appealed against by an ecclesiastical council held at Reading. The barons' support for this appeal, which was despatched under their seals, was a mark of their continuing co-operation with the bishops.[92] Had the legate been able to publish his denunciations in England, the story might have been a different one. As it was, the destruction of his bulls by the men of Dover had been the measure of his defeat. The danger of invasion dwindled simultaneously. Although it still loomed in early October, and the king could still write on 17 November that there was as yet no sure peace with those abroad,[93] it was within this period of about six weeks that the exhaustion of the queen's funds led to the dispersal of her forces.[94] Simply by holding a paid army at bay for so long, an achievement partly made possible by the possession of the hostages, Montfort and his allies had saved themselves, their cause and their country.

But as the threat of invasion subsided, so the older problem of the marchers re-emerged. Despite the peace made at Montgomery in July, they had still not surrendered their Northampton prisoners, nor, in September, would they join the defensive force assembled in the south-east.[95] They were all the more dangerous because the line which they held in the west had been extended by a large contingent of Edward's household knights, who had occupied Bristol.[96] In early October they once more took to arms, laying siege to Clare's castle at Hanley in Worcestershire. Henry was greatly concerned, for the new rebellion put at risk the eventual release of the hostages, which was under discussion

[92] *Councils and Synods*, II, i, pp. 694–700; Rishanger, *De Bellis*, p. 39; *CPR, 1258–66*, p. 474.
[93] Heidemann, No. 48; *CR, 1264–68*, p. 80.
[94] *Wykes*, p. 155; Battle chronicle, in Bémont, *Montfort* (1st edn), p. 378.
[95] *CPR, 1258–66*, pp. 396, 367.
[96] *Robert of Gloucs.*, ii, p. 751.

in the continuing negotiations within the legate. Since it was Clare who had insisted on their release, so Henry told the marchers on 6 October, the attack put their freedom in jeopardy.[97] This was only the prelude to a new war on the marches. The marchers plundered the countryside, sacked Hereford on 10 November, and took the royal castles of Gloucester, Bridgnorth and – in a dangerous south-easterly extension of their power – Marlborough. At some time in these chaotic weeks there was a daring but unsuccessful attempt, led by Warin de Bassing-bourne and others of Edward's knights, to rescue Edward from Wallingford castle. That it was initiated by the queen, who was in contact with Edward's followers, according to Robert of Gloucester, suggests that the two greatest threats to Montfort's government, from the rebels at home and the exiles abroad, were not entirely self-contained.[98]

Although the rescue attempt failed, it was enough to alarm the authorities. Edward, Henry of Almain and Richard of Cornwall were moved to stricter custody at Kenilworth, and the feudal army was summoned to meet at Northampton on 25 November. At the last moment the venue was changed to Oxford, where the marchers were told to appear. On their failure to do so or, probably, to take another chance offered to them to come to Warwick, the army went against them under Montfort's leadership. Although they were able to break the bridges over the Severn, the advance of Montfort's ally Llywelyn from the west compelled them to submit at Worcester in mid December.[99] The terms offered to them involved Edward and needed his assent, so Mortimer, Clifford and Leyburn were allowed to speak with him at Kenilworth. It was eventually agreed that the marchers should go to Ireland for a year and a day, returning at the end of that time to receive the judgement of their peers. In the meantime their lands were to remain in the custody of Montfort, who was also to take Chester and other lands belonging to Edward in exchange for estates of an equivalent value to be given to him elsewhere. In return, Edward was to be released; and the arrangements for his liberation were to be discussed in the Hilary parliament of 1265, for which writs were issued at

---

[97] *CPR, 1258–66*, p. 374.

[98] *Flores Hist.*, ii, pp. 502–3; *Ann. Dun.*, p. 234; *Robert of Gloucs.*, ii, pp. 751–2; *CIM*, i, No. 291; Powicke, *King Henry III*, p. 486.

[99] *Robert of Gloucs.*, ii, p. 752; *Ann. Dun.*, pp. 234–5; *Ann. Oseney*, p. 154; *Flores Hist.*, ii, pp. 503–4; *CPR, 1258–66*, p. 389.

Worcester on 14 December. Finally, it was agreed once again that the Northampton prisoners should be freed.[100]

The marchers, says the author of *Flores Historiarum*, laboured in vain against so many nobles, and especially against that 'most sagacious of warriors', Simon de Montfort.[101] The short campaign had indeed vindicated Montfort's generalship once more, impressively demonstrating his ability to raise an army, move it quickly, co-ordinate an alliance, and impose terms on his enemies. But to impose terms was not to enforce them. As events were to show, that was beyond him.

(c) hubris? december 1264–april 1265

From mid December 1264 to mid March 1265 Simon de Montfort was at the height of his power. He had thwarted an invasion, defied the papal legate, withstood his denunciations, and apparently defeated the marchers. His victory seems to have persuaded others of his enemies that the game was up: during December and January a clutch of important castles held by royalist garrisons since before Lewes, including Nottingham and Scarborough and probably Newcastle and Carlisle, were handed over, consolidating his control of England.[102] The lifting of the invasion threat had also given him an opportunity to move towards a favourable settlement of the oldest of his grievances. On 18 November 1264 Henry authorised the bishops of London and Worcester, Hugh Despenser and Peter de Montfort to enquire into Eleanor's complaints about her lack of dower from the Marshal lands in Wales and Ireland and her losses through the king's detention of what was due, and to make an assignment for both dower and losses.[103] The appointment of these sympathetic arbitrators, with a wide commission to deal with just those matters of dower lands and arrears that Montfort had raised in 1259, promised to solve the most bitterly pursued of his claims against the king. Success on every front seemed to be within his grasp. 'Fortune smiled on all that he had conceived.'[104]

---

[100] The peace does not survive and its terms have to be reconstructed, mainly from the chronicles. See *Flores Hist.*, ii, p. 504; *Cron. Maior.*, pp. 70–1; *Ann. Oseney*, pp. 156–8; *CPR, 1258–66*, pp. 394–5; *CR, 1264–68*, pp. 29–30, 84–5.

[101] *Flores Hist.*, ii, p. 504.

[102] Nottingham: *CPR, 1258–66*, pp. 392, 394–5; *CR, 1264–68*, p. 83; Scarborough: *CPR, 1258–66*, pp. 390–1; Newcastle: ibid., pp. 373, 390, 512; Carlisle: ibid., p. 399; *CR, 1264–68*, p. 37.

[103] *CPR, 1258–66*, pp. 388–9.

[104] *Flores Hist.*, ii, p. 504.

Like the younger Pitt in 1802, Montfort was now 'the pilot that weathered the storm', with a prestige and authority unequalled at any earlier period in his career. His months of supremacy coincided almost precisely with the preparations for and the proceedings of the Hilary parliament of 1265. Summoned for 20 January, and dispersing probably in mid March,[105] this parliament, the longest of the whole reforming period, has acquired a retrospective importance as the first to which knights and burgesses were jointly summoned. Its main business was to determine the conditions for Edward's release, which had been decided on as part of the peace arrangements made with the marchers at Worcester; but it was also the setting for the playing out of feuds and rivalries which, by its conclusion, had left Montfort severely weakened. These quarrels stemmed essentially from the aggrandisement of Montfort and his family, which ran side by side with the work of parliament to provide the dominant theme of the winter of 1264–65.

It was after Lewes that Montfort had first been able to promote his private interests with a vigour which had always characterised his activities but which had never before been given so clear a field. His demand in the negotiations with the legate for the satisfaction of his personal claims against Henry, in advance of any political settlement, was only the most minor aspect of his voracious quest for profit in these months. Victory had given him the opportunity to pile up wealth on a large scale, mainly from the lands and ransoms of the defeated, and often at the expense of his allies, whose grievances over the unfair division of the spoils helped to undermine his position in the spring of 1265.[106] His systematic and ruthless exploitation of his new position owed much, not only to his unchallenged leadership, but to his control of the machinery and offices of government. For some part of the crucial period after Lewes, until 23 July, Henry de Montfort was acting as escheator south of Trent, presumably by his father's appointment.[107] In that position he would have been well placed to secure the lands of vanquished royalists. It is impossible to know just what Montfort and his sons gained at this time, since grants and custodies were not systematically enrolled; but the greatest gain was probably the Devon and Cornwall lands of Richard of

---

[105] *CR, 1264–68*, pp. 84–7; *DBM*, pp. 300–3, 306–9. Parliament was still in session on 8 March and almost certainly on 14 March, when the release of Edward was announced: *Foedera*, I, i, pp. 451–3; *Cron. Maior.*, p. 71.

[106] Battle chronicle, in Bémont, *Montfort* (1st edn), p. 378; *Chronicle of Bury St Edmunds*, p. 30; *Wykes*, p. 153; *Flores Hist.*, iii, p. 1; below, pp. 312, 327–9.

[107] *CPR, 1258–66*, pp. 331, 338; *CR, 1261–64*, p. 348.

Cornwall, given in custody to Guy de Montfort.[108] It was perhaps a private convenience, as well as a public necessity, that Richard himself remained a captive through the whole period from Lewes to Evesham, his release never discussed in the negotiations with the legate, nor seemingly contemplated. His captivity allowed Montfort to put his own men into Richard's castles at Tintagel and Launceston, to lay hands on another castle and its appendant barony at Restormel, and perhaps to exploit the county's wealth in tin, from which Richard's fortune partly derived.[109] Wykes mentions another eighteen unnamed baronies which fell to him.[110] Sometimes a chance later reference alone reveals the extent of the spoils. Only after Evesham, for example, do we learn that Montfort had disseised the Kentish knight Sir Robert de Tuyt of lands in Stap 'because he was on the king's side at the battle of Lewes'.[111] In a similar way he probably came by the lands of John Balliol around Great Yarmouth, which he was holding in January 1265.[112] For ransoms the evidence is still more fragmentary; but the undertaking of Sir Robert Stuteville, imprisoned by Henry de Montfort as the king's enemy, to pay his captor £1,000 for his release suggests the scale of the possible gains there.[113]

The profits of war gave Montfort the means to buy up men and service, reinforcing a supremacy that was based on more than triumphant leadership alone. A leader who by the end of his life had accumulated more than 11,000 marks in cash – the sum later carried off by Eleanor when she fled to France after Evesham[114] – was well placed to exercise good lordship; and in the months after the December peace the size of Montfort's following began to attract comment. When he spent Christmas at Kenilworth in 1264 he was said to have had with him 140 stipendiary knights and to have been able to call on many others when he wanted to raise an army.[115] Among the latter may have been the Frenchmen and other aliens who were serving both in his retinue

---

[108] Battle chronicle, in Bémont, *Montfort* (1st edn), p. 377; *CPR, 1258–66*, p. 394.

[109] *Rotuli Selecti*, ed. J. Hunter (Record Comm., London, 1834), p. 133; *CIM*, i, Nos. 650, 834; J. P. Yeatman, *The Early Genealogical History of the House of Arundell* (London, 1882), facsimile, no. 34; C. Henderson, *Essays in Cornish History* (Oxford, 1935), p. 50. I owe the last two references to the kindness of Mr Mark Page.

[110] *Wykes*, p. 153.

[111] *CIM*, i, No. 747. Cf. Nos. 820, 930.

[112] *CPR, 1258–66*, p. 399.

[113] E.159/39, m. 1; *CPR, 1258–66*, p. 509.

[114] *CR, 1264–68*, p. 136.

[115] *Flores Hist.*, ii, p. 504.

and in the garrisons of the royal castles which were now at his disposal. His continental contacts and his skills as a general and military entrepreneur had in the past often given him access to formidable numbers of mercenaries.[116] Now these skills were augmented by a command of wealth which gave a novel bidding power both to himself and to his sons. When Henry de Montfort and his brother Simon proposed to tourney at Northampton in April 1265, they came, says Wykes, 'abounding in money and with an innumerable company of paid knights'.[117] Some documentary backing for these chroniclers' remarks is given by Eleanor de Montfort's household accounts, which show that when Montfort visited his wife at Odiham on 19 March he travelled with some 160 horses. If he had a military household of perhaps 100 to 150 knights, as the sum of the evidence tentatively suggests, he probably had more in his pay than any thirteenth-century English king. Neither John (who employed over fifty household knights), nor Henry III (thirty to seventy), nor Edward I (a maximum of 101 at the height of his military career in 1284–85) could match him.[118]

The comparison is symptomatic of the way in which Montfort had come to outstrip Henry, in power, wealth and prestige. The contrast between his elevation and Henry's debased existence as a captive in custody – words from which the chroniclers did not flinch – was widely noted. After nearly fifty years of rule, Henry was left with only 'the shadow of a name', while all his business was disposed of by the earl.[119] The extent of the king's humiliation is suggested by the 'astonishing and unprecedented words' addressed to him by Thomas fitz Thomas, the Montfortian mayor of London, when mayor and aldermen came to renew their fealty on 17 March 1265: 'Lord, as long as you will be a good king and lord to us, we will be your faithful and devoted men'.[120] If it was Henry who had formerly inverted the natural order, by raising aliens above native magnates, now it was Montfort who did so.[121] Though the evidence here comes mainly from chronicles, it suggests an underlying sense of shock at what was the culmination of a drive for profit and advancement which had from the start of his career been one of

[116] *Robert of Gloucs.*, ii, p. 752; *Ann. Wav.*, p. 358; above, pp. 109, 113, 122, 124, 250.

[117] *Wykes*, pp. 161–2.

[118] *Manners and Household Expenses*, ed. Turner, pp. xxvii, 14; D. A. Carpenter, *The Minority of Henry III* (London, 1990), p. 52; C. Given-Wilson, *The Royal Household and the King's Affinity* (New Haven and London, 1986), pp. 204–5.

[119] *Flores Hist.*, ii, p. 505, iii, pp. 1, 263; *Chrons. of the Reigns of Stephen*, p. 546.

[120] *Cron. Maior.*, p. 73.

[121] Contrast *Song of Lewes*, ll. 573–81, 966–8, with *Wykes*, pp. 153–4.

Montfort's most fundamental compulsions. Already before Lewes it had laid him open to reproof: 'he ought not to give himself and his men plunder and rewards if he works for the common good', the anonymous critic of the Tewkesbury annals had written in the winter of 1263–64. These were words which applied far more cogently a year later. Even the admiring author of the *Song of Lewes* was forced on to the defensive: 'if it was his own advantage which had moved the earl . . . he would set before him the advancement of his friends, would aim at the enrichment of his sons and would neglect the safety of the country'.[122] The need to make the point told its own story.

Montfort's obvious enjoyment of power and what it brought sits uneasily beside the frugality and austerity emphasised by those who wrote about his religious life. When he arrived at Odiham in March with 160 horses in his train, one wonders if he was wearing his hair shirt. The contrast between the hair shirt and the horses is in its way as striking as that between his defence of the Provisions and his tenacious pursuit of Eleanor's dower rights. If there were failings here, they were plainly moral ones. His public cause was hitched to another one, that of private profit and the continuing violence necessary to sustain it. He and his sons, for example, are reported to have taken a third share in the booty brought in by the piratical activities of the men of the Cinque Ports, which the Montforts encouraged.[123] But were those failings also political? In some senses they were, and with devastating results. Although grievances over the division of the spoils had arisen immediately after Lewes, the need for Montfort's leadership in the long crisis which followed had subdued criticism and shielded the earl from attack. Once peace came, however, from December onwards, he had no such protection, and it was in the months that followed, when his self-seeking reached its peak, that he lost the support both of Clare and of John Giffard. Their defections were caused essentially by the massing of power and wealth in the hands of Montfort and his sons, and, as we shall see, they played a large part in bringing him down. To that extent moral and political failings interlocked. Like any 'bad' king, Montfort had concentrated patronage too narrowly and so divided his court.

Yet these defections were the exception. Few of Montfort's party abandoned him, even of those whom he had supposedly slighted. Hugh

---

[122] *Ann. Tewk.*, p. 180; *Song of Lewes*, ll. 325–32.
[123] *Cron. Maior.*, p. 73; *Wykes*, pp. 157–9.

Despenser and John fitz John, named by Wykes as among the Montfortians who gained only a fraction of what they deserved after Lewes, were both to fight for Montfort at Evesham, and Despenser was to die there.[124] *Pace* Wykes and the rest, Montfort may have had the lion's share after the battle, but not to the exclusion of all others. Recognisances on the close rolls show both Hugh Despenser and probably Adam of Newmarket, one of the nine, raising ransoms from their prisoners.[125] The raising of ransom money, no matter to whom it was payable, might bring benefits to others besides the recipients. It was Giles de Argentein, another of the nine, to whom Robert de Stuteville, Henry de Montfort's prisoner, sold his Suffolk manor of Withersfield when he needed to find money for his ransom.[126] No one can have expected a per capita distribution of the profits, and Montfort's acquisitiveness was perhaps seen as a small price to pay for a leadership which no one else could provide. The freedom to accumulate was only what was due to this 'sagacissimus bellator'.[127]

In power as in wealth, Montfort had no rival among his followers. Yet here it would be especially wrong to see his elevation as tantamount to an unqualified hubris, 'the pride of arrogant Lucifer'[128] which went before his fall. The Montfortian cause had not lost the character of a joint enterprise, and one still governed by the spirit of the Provisions. The role of the three and the nine, initiated by him in the Ordinance of June 1264, had been opened up for discussion during the negotiations with the legate, but had been perpetuated by their failure. It was to be explicitly confirmed in the arrangements for Edward's release in March[129] and to continue until the collapse of Montfortian government in June. During this whole period royal writs were regularly authorised by the council or by its particular members, of whom Peter de Montfort, Adam of Newmarket, Giles de Argentein and Roger de St John were the most active. Peter de Montfort, for example, was with the king for 178 out of 273 days between mid July 1264 and mid April 1265, and Adam of Newmarket for 127 days over the same period. Newmarket was also household steward from July 1264 to March 1265, well placed to provide the oversight of the king's everyday expenses which the Montfortians

[124] *Wykes*, pp. 153, 174.
[125] *CR, 1264–68*, pp. 104–6.
[126] *CPR, 1258–66*, p. 509.
[127] *Flores Hist.*, ii, p. 504.
[128] *Wykes*, pp. 153–4.
[129] *Foedera*, I, i, p. 451.

had demanded in their dealings with the legate.[130] If conciliar government, allowing close supervision of the king, adhered closely to the spirit of the Provisions, so, too, did the role of the new chancellor, Thomas de Cantilupe, who replaced John Chishull on 25 February 1265 and held office until 7 May. Conscientious, immune to bribery, and responsive to the council's directions, Cantilupe played just the part which the reformers of 1258 had designed for the chancellor.[131] Montfort remained the government's impresario and director, all the more so since, of the other members of the triumvirate, Berksted was very inconspicuous at this time and Clare increasingly confined to the sidelines of power. Yet he could reasonably claim to be enforcing the Provisions and so fulfilling the programme on which he had campaigned.

Looking beyond the council, Montfort continued to be very conscious of the need for knightly support: a need which again made it politic for him to keep the Provisions clearly in view. Summoned to the June parliament, the knights had already won recognition for their interests in the new sheriffs appointed there and in Montfort's subsequent insistence on the inviolability of the Provisions of Westminster during the negotiations with the legate.[132] The same line was pursued still more vigorously through the months of his supremacy. When the king was at Worcester in mid December 1264, the Provisions were once again sent out for publication in the shires: the first time that this had been done since June 1263.[133] The protection which they provided for local interests was extended by a new stipulation, included in the complicated arrangements for Edward's release in March, that all officials, royal and seigneurial, should swear to abide by the Provisions and that no obedience was owed to those who failed to take the oath.[134] This gave fuller acknowledgement than at any time since 1258–59 to the desire of the counties for equitable government and for restraints on the officials who had so often stood in its way.

Still more may have been intended, for the Dunstable chronicle reports that one of the matters to be discussed in the Hilary parliament

---

[130] Denholm-Young, 'Documents of the Barons' Wars', p. 165; *CLR, 1260–67*, pp. 170–1; *CPR, 1258–66*, pp. 331, 371, 411; above, p. 297.
[131] Carpenter, 'St Thomas Cantilupe', pp. 63–9.
[132] *DBM*, pp. 298–9; *CPR, 1258–66*, pp. 370–1; Heidemann, No. 42; above, pp. 288–9, 294–5, 297.
[133] *Ann. Oseney*, pp. 158–9; *Registrum Malmesburiense*, ed. J. S. Brewer (2 vols., Rolls ser., 1879–80), i, pp. 42–50; above, pp. 227–8.
[134] *Foedera*, I, i, p. 451.

was the despatch of justices throughout England to enquire into robberies and other matters.[135] What may have been in prospect here was a revival of the special eyre which had lapsed in 1261. Although nothing came of this, several fragments of the same programme for local reform surfaced during the parliament. In one case, a certain J. de Gynges, an Essex landholder distrained for his failure to attend the sheriff's tourn in a hundred where he held land but did not reside, was granted exemption by a conciliar ruling of 21 February, in accordance with an earlier ruling in the Provisions of Westminster on just this issue.[136] In a second, a new writ, drafted during the parliament, was directed against lords who continued to distrain for beaupleder fines, said in the writ to be contrary to Magna Carta but actually contrary only to the Provisions.[137] Like the sworn restrictions on seigneurial officials, the writ hinted at the action against oppressive private lordship which had been one of the leitmotifs of baronial government between 1258 and 1260. But in a more general way both these measures witnessed to the detailed attention that the council was giving to local grievances, and the second also to the continuing attempt, initiated before the Mise of Amiens, to legitimise the Provisions by presenting them as mere addenda to the Charter. It was by offering redress in these ways to the J. de Gynges of provincial England that justice could be seen to be done and the reforming cause, which remained Montfort's cause, best sustained.

The return to the programme of 1258–59, marked by the revival and reinforcement of the Provisions of Westminster, was paralleled by attempts to deal with another grievance of the knightly class which the Provisions had done nothing to set right: Jewish indebtedness. The slaughter of the Jews at Worcester, London, Canterbury and elsewhere during the troubles of 1264, and the seizure and destruction of the *archae*, the chests containing the records of their loans, had shown in a frightening way the force of traditional anti-Semitism when it was driven by the bitterness of debtors and given its head by a breakdown in government.[138] Here again Montfort moved in to offer relief, though by more limited and piecemeal methods than in the field of local

---

[135] *Ann. Dun.*, p. 235.
[136] E.159/39, m. 12d; *DBM*, pp. 139–43.
[137] *CR, 1264–68*, p. 100; *DBM*, pp. 142–3; Powicke, *King Henry III*, p. 489, n. 2. For beaupleder fines, see Carpenter, 'English Peasants in Politics', pp. 27–9.
[138] *Cron. Maior.*, p. 62; *Ann. Wigorn.*, pp. 448–9; *Ger. Cant.*, ii, p. 235; *Wykes*, pp. 141–3; Roth, *History of the Jews in England*, pp. 60–2.

government. Between October 1264 and June 1265 some sixty men received royal writs pardoning debts, penalties on debts, and interest payable to the Jews. The beneficiaries were sometimes prominent Montfortians (e.g. John de Eyville) or their dependents (e.g. Fulk de Lucy, valet of Peter de Montfort) or Montfort's own retainers (e.g. Saer de Harcourt), but by no means all of them were among the committed.[139] The number and novelty of these writs suggests that there was a policy here. Its object was to gain popularity for Montfort's government, at no cost to himself, but at the expense of the Jews and of the king who was the lord of the Jews. The offer of relief was one further example of Montfort's usurpation of royal authority, and it was explicitly repudiated by Henry when he resumed power after Evesham. Like others of Montfort's actions, however, it set a precedent which would be taken up again during Henry's last years and in the early years of the next reign.[140]

It is in this context that we should see the summoning of two knights from each county to the Hilary parliament of 1265: not in isolation, but as an integral part of a more comprehensive attempt by Montfort to ground his regime on an alliance with those in the localities who had benefited most from the reform movement. We do not know how many of those summoned to parliament attended. Payment was ordered for the Yorkshire knights (and possibly for others) on 15 February, but those from Shropshire and Staffordshire, counties dominated by the rebellious marchers, had still not appeared on 23 February.[141] Nor, of course, do we know anything about the parliamentary activities of the knights. But the council's response to what was clearly a complaint from J. de Gynges, the drafting of the new writ on beaupleder fines, and the simultaneous strengthening of the Provisions of Westminster, may suggest that the demand made in the writs of summons for the counsel of the knights, as of others, should be taken seriously. They were not

[139] c.60/61, mm. 1, 2; c.60/62, mm. 3, 7, 9, 10; *CR, 1264–68*, pp. 1–40 *passim*; *CPR, 1258–66*, p. 628; *Select Pleas, Starrs and Other Records of the Jewish Exchequer*, ed. J. M. Rigg (Selden Soc., 15, 1901), pp. 43–5; Knowles, 'The Disinherited', ii, pp. 52–4.

[140] J. R. Maddicott, 'The Crusade Taxation of 1268–70 and the Development of Parliament', *TCE*, ii, pp. 101–2, 109–10.

[141] *CR, 1264–68*, pp. 89, 98–9; *DBM*. 304–9. Treharne and Sanders assume (ibid., pp. 52–3) that the issue of writs for payment on 15 February shows that the assembly was then concluded and the knights dismissed. Yet the proceedings for Edward's release were not completed until mid March and the writ to the knights for Shropshire and Staffordshire told them to attend the king on 8 March. The crisis caused by the summoning of the Dunstable tournament for 17 February (below, pp. 328–9) probably caused a break in the session about that time, and the knights may have been temporarily dismissed.

present merely to witness, but also to bring forward their grievances and to participate.

The knights would hardly have been called to the Hilary parliament had they not been judged sympathetic to the Montfortian cause, for the full list of those summoned shows how partisan an assembly this was. Writs were issued to only five earls and eighteen other magnates, almost all of them Montfortian stalwarts, such as Adam of Newmarket and Ralph Basset of Sapcote. By contrast, 120 ecclesiastics received writs, making them the largest group in the parliament. They included twelve bishops (though the delayed writ sent to the bishop of Norwich suggests some doubts about the loyalties of this rare episcopal royalist), 102 heads of religious houses and orders, and five cathedral deans. The extraordinary number of abbots and priors points to the possibility of strong support for Montfort among the religious: a topic which remains to be investigated. The burgesses were also summoned from an unknown number of towns, and no fewer than four men from each of the Cinque Ports, whose over-representation was a sign both of their defensive importance and of their alliance with the regime.[142] Taken as a whole, the summonses bear out a general pattern of allegiance to Montfort which had held good since 1263: very limited among the magnates, widespread in the Church, particularly among the bishops, and in the localities.

Montfort's supremacy in these months was thus by no means the rule of an autocrat, any more than its initial phase had been in the summer and autumn of 1264. Rather, he was the undisputed head of a narrow oligarchy, which looked for support beyond its own ranks, bypassing a largely hostile baronage, to the Church and to the country at large. The rule of the council, the promotion of the Provisions of Westminster, and the long sessions of the Hilary parliament itself, where the kingdom's affairs were discussed as the Provisions of Oxford had laid down, all emphasised the extent to which he still governed by the principles of 1258–59. Even his own self-seeking could be rationalised and justified as necessary for the Provisions' defence. In one of those telling comments by which he reveals himself almost as the mirror of the earl's mind, Rishanger writes that Montfort took control of the lands, castles and possessions of the defeated royalists because he foresaw that many of the nobles would desert him and that only thus could he maintain his dominion until the Provisions had been irrevocably secured. Such an

---

[142] *CR, 1264–68*, pp. 84–9.

argument may well have been put about by his supporters, nor was it
entirely implausible. Wykes, too, remarks on his low view of the nobility
at this time. 'Pliant, all too changeable . . . and inconstant' as they were,
only the trusted few had been summoned to parliament.[143] It would
be naive to take Montfort at Rishanger's estimation and to impute
principle where the drive for power and profit predominated; yet to
see his aggrandisement as preserving a leadership which alone could
establish the Provisions may have been a view that carried conviction
with at least some of his friends. Was it, for example, the view of the
bishops?

The main purpose of the Hilary parliament, stated in the writs of
summons, was to settle the terms for Edward's release. It is easy to see
why this should have been decided on. Formally speaking, it had been
one of the chief conditions on which peace had been made with the
marchers at Worcester. As a hostage Edward had outlived his usefulness. He had been held for the completion of the Mise of Lewes and the
good behaviour of the marchers; but the Mise had been abandoned and
the marchers, whom his captivity had conspicuously failed to inhibit,
brought to book. The possibility of invasion, against which his captivity
had also provided some security, had disappeared. There was probably
pressure from Clare and from the bishops for his release, as there had
certainly been from Clare during the negotiations. Captive, he was
likely to remain a focus for plots and escapades. Liberated, his freedom
could be paid for at a price which would bring to Montfort the greatest
possible personal advantage.

Indeed, the terms for Edward's release marked the convergence of
the twin themes of personal profit and public principle which had
characterised the whole pattern of his conduct since 1258. Some had
been settled by 14 February, when it was announced in parliament that
the king and Edward had sworn to keep the peace and the king to
observe the Charters and the Ordinance of June 1264.[144] It was not until
8 March, however, that the full terms were issued in documentary
form.[145] Essentially they entailed the acceptance by all parties of the
constitutional settlement of the previous year, arrangements for the
restoration of normal relations between the king and his subjects, and
precautions against any threat to the peace which a liberated Edward

---

[143] Rishanger, *De Bellis*, pp. 41–2; *Wykes*, p. 160.
[144] *Cron. Maior.*, p. 71; Powicke, *King Henry III*, p. 488.
[145] *Foedera*, I, i, pp. 451–2.

might offer. First came the confirmation of the Ordinance of June 1264, with its provision for the rule of the three and the nine. Next followed arrangements for the restoration of the peace. There was to be no pursuit of quarrels arising out of actions during the recent troubles; all were to oppose any man, including Henry and Edward, who acted contrary to the peace; the Charters and the Provisions of Westminster were to be kept and sworn to by all officials; and all those who had been diffidated by the king were to do homage and fealty once again, though this might once again be revoked if the king should break the agreement. Thirdly, steps were taken to bind Edward. As well as swearing to maintain the Ordinance, he was to allow his household and council to be chosen from men acceptable to the king's council; neither he nor his father was to bring in aliens without permission; he was to remain in England, where the king's writ ran (that is, not in the marches), for three years from Easter; and if he were to import aliens, he might be disinherited.

Still more important were the stipulations regarding the royal castles and lands. Those royalists currently holding castles whom the council thought suspect were to be replaced. In addition, Edward was to 'borrow' five castles from his father and to grant them to the barons as 'hostages' for his good behaviour during the next five years. These were to be maintained from the royal revenues, but neither Henry nor Edward was to have any right of entry to them, and at the end of five years they were to be returned if the peace had been kept. Neither was to seek absolution from his oath to these terms, and excommunication was laid down as the penalty for their contravention. Lastly, Edward was to give up some of his most important holdings to Montfort – the castle, town and county of Chester, Newcastle-under-Lyme, and the Peak – in exchange for lands of an equivalent value elsewhere. Until this had been carried through, the town and castle of Bristol were to be surrendered by Edward to Montfort. Having been handed back to Edward at the end of one year, during which time it was assumed that the exchanges would have been made, Bristol was to be re-surrendered for another five years as an addition to the 'hostage' castles, saving the rights of the earl of Gloucester.

All that now remained to be done was to make this elaborate settlement publicly known, to release Edward, and to arrange for the transfer of lands and castles. On 10 March Edward signified his assent to the terms, in letters sent out to the counties, and on the same day he and Henry of Almain were taken from their guardian, Henry de

Montfort, and handed over to the king at a grand ceremony in West-minster Hall. The king's letters of assent were read out, nine bishops excommunicated those going against the Charters and the Provisions, and on 14 March the king notified the counties of his assent. At the same time the Charters and the Ordinance of June 1264 were also sent out, with instructions for their twice-yearly publication in the county courts.[146] The settlement was completed a few days later. On 17 March the king transferred to Edward the five castles of Dover, Scarborough, Bamburgh, Nottingham and Corfe for five years 'in ostagium', and on 20 March Chester, Newcastle and the Peak were formally transferred to Montfort.[147]

In the complicated scheme worked out in the Hilary parliament the claims of the three and the nine to govern indefinitely were reinforced behind only the flimsiest facade of royal authority. Henry was to be recognised anew 'come seignor'; all were again to become his feudal vassals; and the plan for the transfer of the five 'hostage' castles was intended to preserve nominal royal authority over them.[148] Yet the perpetuation of the Ordinance in effect perpetuated Henry's subjection to a baronial council, while the continuing limitations on Edward's freedom were almost as restrictive as his earlier captivity. Over his household, his council, his friends and his movements, the Montfortians were to retain substantial control; and the threat of disinheritance should he fail to observe the terms showed how far they had moved beyond any concept even of partnership with the Crown. To a limited extent these actions found some justification in the Provisions of Oxford, defined broadly as the sum of the reforming legislation of 1258–59, whose principles could be made to endorse both the conciliar rule and the local reforms of the Provisions of Westminster embraced by the terms of March 1265. The regular publication of the Ordinance was intended not only to publicise the new order but to secure its recognition by the broad Montfortian constituency in the localities. The effect was to give Montfort and the council a degree of control over both Henry and his heir which was far more inhibiting than anything contemplated in 1258–59. If the March 'agreement' was an attempt to restore peace, to bury old grievances, and to bring the king's men back to their feudal

---

[146] *Foedera*, I, i, p. 452; *Cron. Maior.*, p. 71; *DBM*, pp. 308–15. That the June Ordinance was sent out is proved by the copy received in Middlesex: *Munimenta Gildhallae Londoniensis*, ed. H. T. Riley (4 vols. in 3, Rolls ser., 1859–63), II, ii, pp. 662–4.

[147] *Foedera*, I, i, p. 454; *CChR, 1257–1300*, p. 54.

[148] *Foedera*, I, i, pp. 451–2; Powicke, *King Henry III*, p. 489.

allegiance, it was also one which sought to normalise the abnormal and to achieve a settlement through a permanent cession of royal authority.

The part of the settlement which touched Montfort most personally was that providing for Edward's surrender of Chester, the Peak and Newcastle in exchange for other lands elsewhere. This had been planned as a component of the preliminary agreement for Edward's release made when Montfort came to terms with the marchers in December.[149] Although the surrender was not confirmed until March, Montfort had acted on it well before then: as early as 4 January Henry de Montfort was at Chester to take the fealty and homage of the locals and to discuss peace with Llywelyn.[150] The enormity of what Montfort was doing here has received surprisingly little comment. Chester and the Peak had formed a substantial segment of the lands granted to Edward by his father in 1254.[151] They had provided a valuable income. Farmed for 1,000 marks a year in 1253, Chester was probably worth about £1,000 a year; though its value was greatly augmented by its palatine status, which gave its lord a good deal of local autonomy.[152] The Peak – a castle and appendant honor – had been farmed for £300 a year in the 1250s,[153] and so again must have been worth rather more. Newcastle, not part of the original endowment, was worth some £100 a year.[154] The annual value of these holdings, therefore, was at least £1,400–£1,500, about a quarter of Edward's estimated income of £6,000 p.a. and perhaps treble the £500 or so derived annually by Montfort from his inherited Leicester lands.[155] Moreover, by the terms of Edward's grant they came to Montfort in fee, to be passed on to his heirs. What Edward received in exchange was relatively insignificant. As far as can be seen, he got nothing until 16 May 1265, when Montfort gave him twelve scattered manors, mainly located in Hampshire and Wiltshire and worth perhaps £500 p.a.[156] They included five of those

[149] *CPR, 1258–66*, p. 397; above, p. 307.

[150] *CChR, 1257–1300*, p. 54; *CPR, 1258–66*, p. 416; *Ann. Cestr.*, p. 91. [151] *CPR, 1247–58*, p. 270.

[152] *CPR, 1247–58*, p. 182; Prestwich, *Edward I*, pp. 13, 20.

[153] H. Wait, 'The Household and Resources of the Lord Edward 1239–72' (Oxford D.Phil. thesis, 1988), p. 60.

[154] *VCH Staffordshire*, viii, ed. J. G. Jenkins (London, 1963), pp. 12, 25; T. Pape, *Medieval Newcastle-under-Lyme* (Manchester, 1928), pp. 28, 32.

[155] Prestwich, *Edward I*, p. 20; above, p. 49.

[156] *CPR, 1258–66*, p. 424. Values can be ascertained for the following: Gunthorpe, Notts., £67; Melbourne, Derbs., £50; Kingshawe, Notts., £15; Bere, Dorset, £26; Easingwold, Yorks., £39 (*CChR, 1257–1300*, pp. 18, 20. Montfort had received these five in 1259); Chalton, Hants., £80 (*CIM*, i, No. 692); Collingbourne and Everleigh, Wilts., £95 in 1297 (*Wiltshire Inquisitions Post Mortem, Henry III–Edward II*, ed. E. A. Fry, British Rec. Soc., 1908, p. 218).

extracted from Henry in 1259 in settlement of Montfort's fee. Since Henry had long been pressing for their return, it may have given Montfort some sardonic pleasure to hand them back in exchange for a much better bargain elsewhere. A chronicler's assertion that the earldom of Leicester was handed over to Edward is unsubstantiated and entirely implausible.[157]

By this 'exchange' Montfort went a long way towards permanently dismantling the appanage of the heir to the throne. 'Simon de Montfort appropriated for himself the earldom of Chester', says the London annalist explicitly.[158] It was his most brazen step yet in securing for himself a position of overwhelming dominance among the aristocracy – no less bold in its conception for proving so short-lived in its fulfilment. It hints, too, at even greater ambitions; for having in effect disinherited Edward there could be no going back for Montfort. He cannot have imagined that Edward, as future king, would ever accept what had been done, and his ultimate aim can hardly have been less than the lasting establishment in power of himself, his family and his party. Of course, the 'exchange' was not presented in this way; and in making possible the surveillance of the marchers and their promised departure for Ireland, the acquisition of Chester at least had a kind of immediate strategic justification. But in terms of the public interest that was all there was to be said for it.

There was, however, one threat to the security of the whole scheme: the position of Robert de Ferrers, the young earl of Derby, whose arrest and imprisonment in the Hilary parliament were closely related both to Montfort's ambitions in the north midlands and to his eventual downfall. Ferrers had always been the wild card among the baronage. Never fully on Montfort's side, he had steered a course largely directed by his bitter feud with Edward, which ran through the whole period of the barons' war in 1264. Its origins are obscure, but they probably lay in Ferrers's ancestral claim to the Peveril inheritance, including the Peak, which his grandfather, William de Ferrers, had been made to surrender to the Crown in 1222 and which had become part of Edward's appanage in 1254.[159] Much of the fighting prior to Lewes, in the course of which Edward devastated Ferrers's lands in Derbyshire, Staffordshire and

---

[157] *Ann. Lond.*, p. 65.

[158] *Ann. Lond.*, p. 65.

[159] Carpenter, *The Minority of Henry III*, p. 284; P. E. Golob, 'The Ferrers Earls of Derby: A Study of the Honor of Tutbury (1066–1279)' (Cambridge Ph.D. thesis, 1984), pp. 345–6.

elsewhere, had been an episode in this feud.[160] After Lewes, with Edward a captive, Ferrers was able to strike back without fear of reprisals, and his pillaging in the north midlands had been an element in the disorderly scene which faced Montfort throughout England during that summer.[161] From the *caput* of his estates at Tutbury in Derbyshire, he had attempted the virtual conquest of Edward's lands, seizing the castle of the Peak from its royal custodian in early July, retaining it for the rest of the year, and in November sending an army against Chester and putting his opponents to flight.[162]

This was the situation when, in December, Montfort replaced Edward as lord of Chester and the Peak. As Edward's successor he inherited a feud which now threatened the integrity and the profitability of his new possessions. On 24 December, as a consequence of the settlement, Ferrers was called on to surrender the Peak to Montfort; but steps had already been taken to prise him out. The summons to the Hilary parliament, sent to him earlier on 13 December, must be regarded as a device to get him to vacate the Peak.[163] As far as can be seen, he was the only one of the barons summoned who was not a committed Montfortian, and Montfort's intention to remove the danger which he posed to his lands provides the only clear reason for the summons. That Ferrers complied was surprising; but comply he did, and with predictable results. Shortly before 23 February he was arrested in London and sent to the Tower.[164] The chroniclers provide various reasons for his imprisonment: as a half-measure taken by Montfort to placate Henry, who had wanted to see him condemned to death for his spoliations, though Montfort would have freed him;[165] as a result of his secret collusion with the marchers; by reason of a certain trespass imputed to him by Montfort.[166] This last probably comes nearest the mark. It is highly unlikely that Montfort favoured Ferrers, against Henry's demands for severity: Montfort had no need to appease the king and every reason to want Ferrers out of the way. His imprisonment must be seen as a brutally effective way of providing for Montfort's own unimpeded control of Edward's north-midland estates, made all the

[160] *Flores Hist.*, ii, pp. 488–9; *Chron. Abingdon*, p. 16.
[161] Cf. *CPR, 1258–66*, p. 359.
[162] *CPR, 1258–66*, p. 397; *Ann. Dun.*, p. 235; Golob, 'The Ferrers Earls', pp. 328–30.
[163] *CPR, 1258–66*, p. 397; *CR, 1264–68*, p. 86.
[164] *CPR, 1258–66*, p. 409; *Robert of Gloucs.*, ii, p. 753.
[165] *Robert of Gloucs.*, ii, p. 753; *Ann. Wav.*, p. 358; *Wykes*, p. 160. Cf. *Ann. Cestr.*, p. 91.
[166] *Flores Hist.*, iii, p. 263; Rishanger, *De Bellis*, pp. 20–1; *Ann. Lond.*, p. 66.

easier by Ferrers's earlier lawlessness, which allowed him to be condemned as a public enemy. Montfort had done what Edward had failed to do in his long war with Ferrers: removed him cleanly from the scene, not by the heavyhanded tactic of devastation, but by a cleverly conceived quasi-judicial coup.

The rapacious process of acquisition which culminated in Montfort's appropriation of Edward's lands may seem to have had no more disputable end than the enhancement of his own power and glory. His ambitions, however, were as much for the large family for which he had to provide as for himself. Montfort's upward progress in England had always been in part a family enterprise, in which the need to endow and establish his sons had been an abiding motive. His early search for land in fee, with the advantageous permanence that the dower lacked, his close rapport with his two elder sons, Henry and Simon, his possible attempt to secure Bigorre for Henry in 1258–59, and his conferment of Mansel's lands on Simon in 1263, all bear this out.[167] But it was only after Lewes that he found the opportunities to do as he had always wanted. Victory in a civil war gave him the means to set up his sons in ways which cannot be fully traced but were probably lavish. Almost the first references to two of the younger sons, Guy and Richard, came in November 1264 and March 1265 respectively, when each received royal (that is, Montfortian) gifts of deer for their parks: a sure sign that they now had land.[168] Guy, as we have seen, is reported to have had the custody of Richard of Cornwall's lands in Devon and Cornwall.[169] Amaury, the clerk, had already obtained prebends at Rouen and St Paul's, thanks to his father's friendship with Eudes Rigaud and Henry Sandwich, and after Lewes he profited further from his father's takeover of Richard of Cornwall's possessions. In his will he styled himself 'rector of St Wendron', one of Richard's Cornish churches and among the half dozen wealthiest in the county, which can only have come to him during the period of Richard's captivity.[170] His acquisition of his most valuable prize can be more closely dated. On 7 February 1265 he was given the treasurership of York, vacated by the death of the previous holder, John Mansel. His purloining of one of the richest benefices in England particularly rankled with Henry, and one of his first acts on

---

[167] Above, pp. 44, 51–2, 173, 183–4, 238.   [168] *CR, 1264–68*, pp. 4, 26.

[169] Battle Chronicle, in Bémont, *Montfort* (1st edn), p. 377; above, pp. 309–10.

[170] Vatican Archives, Archivio Segreto Vaticano. AA. Arm. I–XVIII, 123; *Taxatio Ecclesiastica Papae Nicolai IV* (Record Comm., London, 1802), p. 148; *Ministers' Accounts of the Earldom of Cornwall, 1296–1297*, ed. L. M. Midgley (2 vols., Camden Third ser., lxvi, lxviii, 1942), i, p. xii.

regaining his liberty after Evesham was to annul the grant, 'made against the king's will' as it had been.[171]

Of the two elder sons, Simon held not only John Mansel's lands, from July 1263, but also John de Warenne's estates in Sussex.[172] Since Mansel had also held a good deal of land in Sussex[173] and Henry de Montfort was well established in Kent, both as landholder and as constable of Dover castle, Montfort's establishment of his sons here gave him a commanding personal presence in the strategically important counties of the south-east. Young Simon was, however, in pursuit of much greater gains, for at some point between Lewes and Evesham he set out to abduct the richest woman on the marriage market, Isabella de Fors, countess of Devon and widow of the earl of Albemarle, forcing her to take refuge in Wales.[174] Even the girl Eleanor, Montfort's daughter, seemed likely to benefit similarly, for her father had reportedly betrothed her to his ally Llywelyn, though it was not until many years later, in 1278, that the marriage took place.[175]

The entrenchment of Simon junior in Sussex was strengthened by a piece of skulduggery which exemplifies the *modus operandi* of the younger Montforts in the months after Lewes. Its victim was William de Braose, royalist, marcher baron, and lord of Bramber in that county. At some point in the civil war Braose, fighting for the king,[176] had devastated young Simon's Sussex manor of Sedgewick, one of Mansel's former possessions. Simon had his revenge on 30 June 1264, probably in the final days of the parliament which had seen his father's power confirmed. Summoned several times to the Tower to answer for his offence before a 'court' headed by Hugh Despenser, the justiciar, Henry de Montfort and Henry de Hastings, Braose had failed to appear. Damages were then awarded against him in the sum of 10,000 marks, the outrageously high figure put on his losses by Simon; and Braose was

---

[171] *CPR, 1258–66*, pp. 404, 436; *York Minster Fasti*, i, ed. Clay, pp. vii–viii, 25–6; *A History of York Minster*, ed. G. E. Aylmer and R. Cant (Oxford, 1977), pp. 55, 73–4.

[172] *CPR, 1258–66*, p. 273; *CIM*, i, Nos. 700, 898; Battle chronicle, in Bémont, *Montfort* (1st edn), pp. 377–8; above, p. 238.

[173] *The Chartulary of the High Church of Chichester*, ed. W. D. Peckham (Sussex Rec. Soc., xlvi, 1946), No. 457; *Sussex Fines*, i, ed. L. F. Salzmann (Sussex Rec. Soc., ii, 1903), No. 450; *CIM*, No. 906; *RL*, ii, pp. 157–8.

[174] *Abbreviatio Placitorum* (Record Comm., London, 1811), p. 172; Labarge, *Montfort*, p. 248. Isabella de Fortibus was at Odiham, with Countess Eleanor, from 2 to 6 April, during the period of Montfort's visit, and perhaps earlier; and Eleanor was in communication with her by letter in May: *Manners and Household Expenses*, ed. Turner, pp. 15–16, 32–3.

[175] Trivet, *Annales*, p. 294; *Ann. Wint.*, p. 121; below, p. 370.

[176] *Ger. Cant.*, ii, pp. 222, 235.

told to pay this amount, or name pledges for payment, within ten days. In the meantime Simon was to retain his enemy's young heir and his Sussex castle and park at Knepp, already in his hands by a prior agreement with Braose, until payment or pledges had been proffered.[177] This was no more than a transparent device for dispossessing Braose, whose son was still a hostage, attached to Eleanor de Montfort's household, in the spring and summer of 1265.[178] But if Simon was the beneficiary, and his brother and mother his accomplices, the parallel complicity of Hugh Despenser illustrates the degree to which other members of the regime were a party to the malpractices of its leading family.

By self-help and paternal patronage Simon was thus in the way of creating a large estate for himself in a part of the country where his father looked for special security. It is the endowment of Henry de Montfort, however, which raises the most interesting problems and possibilities. Apart from some piecemeal gains taken from royalists after Lewes,[179] Henry appears to have received nothing commensurate with his standing as the eldest son. That Montfort was concerned with his endowment, and was prepared to override the law in order to achieve it, is proved by the royal confirmation, made on 12 March 1265, of Montfort's grant in fee to Henry of four of Eleanor's dower manors, three of them in Kent.[180] As dower these were, of course, held only for Eleanor's life, reverting to her first husband's heirs after her death; and it is a mark of Montfort's presumption that, in the interests of his own heir, he should have been prepared to deprive the Marshal heirs of what would one day be rightfully theirs. But Montfort's long-term plans for Henry may have been still more grand. As heir, Henry would eventually receive Edward's former lordships of Chester and the Peak, again granted to Montfort in fee; yet it is possible that Montfort intended to anticipate Henry's eventual good fortune by settling these lands on him in his own lifetime. Two pointers to this are provided by Henry's activity at Chester in January 1265, described above, and by an elliptical reference among the inquisitions taken after Evesham to Richard de Vernon, who 'was in the castle of the Peak serving (*per*) Henry de Montfort'.[181] In both Chester and the north midlands Henry

---

[177] Bémont, *Montfort* (1st edn), pp. 353–5, where the award of the court is printed. It seems to have passed without comment among historians.
[178] *Manners and Household Expenses*, ed. Turner, pp. 9–10, 65–6.
[179] *CIM*, Nos. 744, 763.
[180] *CChR, 1257–1300*, p. 54; *CPR, 1364–67*, pp. 265–6.
[181] *CIM*, i, No. 772; cf. No. 645.

may simply have been acting as his father's agent, though this would have been odd at a time when he had large responsibilities in Kent. On the other hand, there would have been a certain attractive symmetry in Montfort, who ruled in the king's place, setting up his own eldest son in lands which Henry had reserved for his.

On what had previously been the greatest of Montfort's family matters, and one whose trail through the records had until 1263 at least left far larger marks than the earl's concern for his children, there is an almost complete silence during these months. Eleanor's dower rights play no discernible part in the history of Montfort's period of supremacy. All we can be sure about is that the commission of friends whom he had appointed in November 1264 to look into the dower question and make an award had come to no effective conclusion. Nothing is heard of its work and clearly no decision was reached, for the regular and (according to the Montforts) inadequate payments of £400 a year continued until Easter term 1265, though no longer recorded on the liberate rolls. Even into the reign of Edward I, Eleanor continued to press for her dower rights here.[182] The last mention of the dower before Evesham comes on 14 April 1265, when Montfort was granted 100 marks from the Devon stannary for three years in part payment of the annual sum owed by the king.[183] There is an obvious reason for this dwindling interest in what had once been almost an obsession. Still more so than in 1263, Montfort's territorial gains in 1264–65, real and prospective, were so large as to make the dower seem insignificant. They held out the hope of his establishing hereditary control over tracts of country which no dower settlement, however favourable, was likely to rival in extent, value or permanence. Drowned by the bang caused by the acquisition of Chester, the Peak and the other spoils of victory, the great cause of the dower died with a whimper.

The promotion of Montfort's sons and the arrest of Ferrers were among the general and the particular causes for the desertion of Montfort by Gilbert de Clare, earl of Gloucester, which opened the way for the last, disastrous, phase of Montfort's career. Although Clare was the most powerful of all Montfort's adherents, his attachment to his cause was relatively recent, dating only from March–April 1264. It had been significantly weakened by Montfort's conduct after Lewes, which gave Clare special reason to find offence in Montfort's appropriation of

[182] *CPR, 1266–72*, p. 549; Labarge, *Montfort*, pp. 270–1.
[183] *CPR, 1258–66*, p. 418.

the spoils: he himself had captured Richard of Cornwall, but got the dustiest of answers from Montfort when he asked for his prize.[184] The two men also had rival claims to lands, again probably dating back to the aftermath of Lewes, and a potential cause for dispute over Bristol, where Montfort had replaced Edward, under the terms for Edward's release, in a town claimed for decades by the Clares.[185] To these personal grievances were added differences over policy. Not only had Gloucester wanted the early release of the hostages, while Montfort probably favoured their retention;[186] but he was beginning to emerge as the keeper of the public conscience on the question of the Provisions of Oxford, a role which he was to maintain even in opposition to the earl and after his death. According to Robert of Gloucester, Clare's opposition to Montfort's alien mercenaries and castellans was one reason for the summoning of the Hilary parliament, in the course of which these men were removed; and later, in April or May, he was to accuse Montfort of failing to observe both the Provisions and the Mise of Lewes.[187] His detestation of Montfort's sons exacerbated all these other grievances, to widen a breach that had been long in the making. Their greed, their arrogance and their abuse of power, exemplified in their conniving at the piratical enterprises of the sailors of the Cinque Ports, had all become common causes for the complaint which the earl of Gloucester was best placed to represent.[188]

The arrest of Ferrers brought Clare's fears and discontents to a head. The London annals report that he was 'stupified' at this, and there was a general rumour recorded by several of the chronicles that he would be the next to fall.[189] Other rumours that he was plotting with the marchers would have provided Montfort with the pretext for removing a powerful magnate who was, after Ferrers had gone, his only serious rival.[190] At the time of Ferrers's arrest Clare had been planning to tourney at Dunstable on 17 February, in the company of his younger brother Thomas, another enemy of Henry de Montfort, who was to captain the opposing side. Reflecting as it did the developing antagonisms at court, this was to have been both a grand social occasion and a formal outlet

---

[184] *Robert of Gloucs.*, ii, p. 750; *Guisborough*, pp. 196–7; *Rishanger Chronica et Annales*, pp. 32–3.
[185] *CPR, 1258–66*, p. 479; Altschul, *A Baronial Family*, pp. 77, 82–3, 127; above, p. 194.
[186] Above, pp. 302–3, 306–7.
[187] *Robert of Gloucs.*, ii, p. 752; *Cron. Maior.*, p. 73.
[188] Battle chronicle, in Bémont, *Montfort* (1st edn), p. 378; *Wykes*, pp. 157–9; *Guisborough*, p. 197.
[189] *Ann. Lond.*, p. 67; *Ann. Wav.*, p. 358; *Wykes*, pp. 160–1.
[190] *Ann. Lond.*, p. 67; *Flores Hist.*, iii, pp. 263–4.

for real and bitter conflicts. For that reason the tournament was prohibited on 16 February.[191] Montfort clearly feared that it would lead to a general breakdown of the peace and told his sons, in his usual expressive way, that if they went ahead he would put them in a place where they would enjoy the blessing neither of the sun nor of the moon.[192] It was probably at this stage that Clare left the court for Wales, finding a convenient excuse in the need to defend his lands against the current depredations of Llywelyn.[193] He had almost certainly left by 19 March, when the king wrote to him to demand the surrender of Bamburgh, which he held in joint custody and which was one of the 'hostage' castles, to be controlled by the council under the terms for Edward's release.[194] He had already been preceded to the marches by John Giffard, now a close ally, alienated from Montfort by the earl's claim to an important prisoner captured by Giffard at Lewes.[195]

Like Henry III in 1258, Montfort had allowed his court to become divided by faction. The promotion of his family, like Henry's promotion of the Lusignans, had lost him the support of important men on whom his position partly depended. The charges against the young Montforts were not unlike those against the Lusignans: greed, the excessive absorption of patronage, and a violent highhandedness which presumed on powerful connections for its toleration. 'Your presumption and the pride of your brothers had brought me to this end', he was reportedly to say to his son Henry on the field of Evesham;[196] but their presumption and pride had been given full rein by Montfort himself. Montfort's political failings here were now on the point of bringing him down. His desertion by Clare cost him not only his leading secular backer, but his only substantial ally in the marches, which were now emerging again as the seat of opposition to his government. The marchers had been able to secure successive postponements of their departure for Ireland and were still at large.[197] Montfort must have suspected that Clare would make common cause with them, as he soon did. But this was not the only source of potential trouble. Clare's men still held Bamburgh and

---

[191] *Ann. Dun.*, p. 328; *Ann. Lond.*, p. 65; Rishanger, *De Bellis*, p. 42; *CPR, 1258–66*, p. 406.
[192] *Rishanger Chronica et Annales*, p. 32.
[193] *Robert of Gloucs*, ii, p. 754; *Ann. Wav.*, p. 358.
[194] *CR, 1264–68*, pp. 33–4. Ibid., pp. 43–4, shows conclusively that he was in Wales on 6 April and suggests that he had been there for some time.
[195] *Robert of Gloucs.*, ii, p. 754; *Ann. Lond.*, p. 65; Powicke, *King Henry III*, pp. 493, 495.
[196] *Guisborough*, p. 201.
[197] *CPR, 1258–66*, pp. 398, 402, 410, 418–19.

declined to give it up;[198] Pevensey was still under siege; and there was a nervous awareness of the renewed possibility of invasion. Coinciding as it did with the final stages of the Hilary parliament, the developing crisis in the marches and elsewhere helps to explain the harshness of the terms for Edward's release and showed up the hollowness of the settlement. It sought to frustrate any possible alliance between Edward and either the marchers or the aliens; yet Montfort seemingly had little confidence in its success. When Edward was released from prison, he remained in the custody of Montfort's knights.[199] Henry of Almain was also released, only to return freely, *sponte sua* (it was said), to the custody of Henry de Montfort until 1 August. If in the meantime an alien army should land in England, his custody was to be extended until Edward's attitude to the alien invaders should have become clear.[200] In fact, Henry was sent on a new mission to Louis IX in early April,[201] perhaps with the object of persuading the French king not to support an invasion; and so he missed the concluding stages of the drama that was now unfolding.

At first it progressed slowly. On 19 March, after the termination of the Hilary parliament, Montfort arrived at Odiham to spend a fortnight with his wife and sons. Edward and Henry of Almain, escorted by Henry de Montfort, had preceded him two days previously. On 1 April he left, never to see Eleanor again.[202] The earl then moved, in company with the king and Edward, to Northampton, where a new tournament had been arranged for 20 April, in place of that planned earlier at Dunstable. Clare was evidently expected, but did not come, scenting danger, and the tournament never took place.[203] Montfort's suspicions were shown when, at Northampton on 24 April, he transferred the key castle of St Briavels, in the Forest of Dean, from John Giffard to Thomas de Clare, who was still trusted and indeed much liked by Montfort, but who seems to have been playing a double role. Though it later transpired that Giffard did not hold St Briavels, Gilbert de Clare may well have been concentrating his forces around the castle: Robert of Gloucester vouches for Giffard's raising of troops in this area.[204] Others

---

198 *CR, 1264–68*, pp. 33–4, 43–4, 112–13.
199 *Flores Hist.*, iii, p. 263.
200 *Cron. Maior.*, p. 72.
201 *CPR, 1258–66*, pp. 418, 425.
202 *Manners and Household Expenses*, ed. Turner, pp. 14–15; Labarge, *Montfort*, pp. 248–9.
203 *Ann. Dun.*, pp. 238–9; *Ann. Lond.*, p. 67; *Guisborough*, p. 197; *Wykes*, p. 162.
204 *CPR, 1258–66*, p. 419; *Robert of Gloucs.*, ii, p. 754; *Wykes*, pp. 162–3.

were also under suspicion. John fitz Alan, whose position both as the marcher lord of Clun in Shropshire and as lord of Arundel in Sussex made him a central figure in the two regions where Montfort was most at risk, was ordered either to give up his son as a hostage or to surrender Arundel castle.[205] But these precautions, taken at a distance from the seat of danger, were hardly sufficient, and about 25 April Montfort, his close friends and the royal party, left Northampton for the marches. Passing below the scarp of the Cotswolds, via Long Compton and Winchcombe, they came to Gloucester two days later.[206]

(D) NEMESIS, APRIL–AUGUST 1265

In retrospect Montfort's march on Gloucester can be seen as the beginning of his end, the first step along the short road to Evesham. Yet his move into enemy territory, away from the security of Kenilworth, London and the south-east, was not perhaps as foolhardy as it may appear to have been. He had to settle with Gilbert de Clare, by force or by negotiation, or risk the loss of the whole march and the establishment of a permanently disaffected frontier to his kingdom. His chances of doing so must have seemed good. In 1264 he had fought three campaigns in the marches, none of them conclusive (as it turned out), but none unsuccessful. Travelling westwards in company with Henry and Edward gave him a further advantage, for father and son were certainly captives[207] and in effect hostages; Edward's 'release' in March had merely transferred him from custody in a castle to custody on horse-back. Their presence conferred on Montfort – or may have seemed to confer – a degree of invulnerability which rested more heavily on armed power. Although the earl had not yet formally called out an army, he had with him a substantial force. To judge from the later casualties at Evesham, his inner ring of knightly retainers, men such as Thomas of Astley, must already have been with him, and they were probably supplemented by the large paid retinue which he had built up over the previous months.[208] He had, too, a considerable baronial following: his son Henry, four of the six baronial members of the nine (Peter de Montfort, Giles de Argentein, Roger de St John and Humphrey de

[205] *CPR, 1258–66*, p. 420.
[206] *CPR, 1258–66*, p. 420; *CR, 1264–68*, p. 114.
[207] *Flores Hist.*, iii, p. 264.
[208] *Flores Hist.*, ii, p. 504; above, pp. 310–11.

Bohun), Hugh Despenser and John fitz John.[209] With a number of other leading Montfortians left to take care of the south-east, including young Simon, Richard de Grey and Adam of Newmarket (both later captured at Kenilworth), Montfort had no reason to fear that his control of the country was irretrievably slipping away.

The need to settle with Clare nevertheless entailed some obvious risks. If not quite the mouth of the lion's den, Gloucester did not make a comfortable base for a campaign. The forces of Giffard and Clare lurked in the woods and hills around the city; forty miles to the north-west was Roger Mortimer at Wigmore; and the Edwardian knights formerly occupying Bristol had left the castle there and were now on the loose.[210] Once in Gloucester Montfort moved to deal with these threats both by military preparations and by negotiations. The county levies of Gloucestershire, Worcestershire and Herefordshire were summoned first to Hereford, then to Gloucester, while at the same time discussions opened with Clare. They resulted in an agreement on 12 May that both sides should accept arbitration to settle their differences, the substance of which was probably both political and personal. It is at this stage that fitz Thedmar speaks of Clare's charge that the Provisions and the Mise of Lewes had not been observed; but at the time of Clare's desertion the two men also had rival claims to sixteen manors, over which an enquiry was pending. Clare may also have been concerned about Montfort's treatment of Edward, for within days of the Gloucester agreement Edward received the first and only instalment of the lands promised to him by Montfort as part of the 'exchange' first arranged in December 1264. Nothing further followed from this initiative, however, perhaps partly because the majority of the arbitrators – Walter de Cantilupe, Hugh Despenser, John fitz John and William de Munchensi – were so blatantly Montfortian.[211] A little earlier, on his arrival at Gloucester, Montfort had sent off to the aged Loretta, countess of Leicester, then a recluse at Hackington in Kent, to ask for information on the 'rights and liberties' attached to the stewardship of England. The office had once been held by Loretta's former husband, Robert de Beaumont, earl of Leicester, before its descent to Montfort. He was looking once again for authority and legitimacy, on a contentious issue which had agitated him

---

209 *CPR, 1258–66*, pp. 423, 425; *CR, 1264–68*, p. 126; *Robert of Gloucs.*, ii, p. 755.

210 *Robert of Gloucs.*, ii, pp. 754–6; *CR, 1264–68*, p. 106.

211 *CR, 1264–68*, pp. 115–16; *Robert of Gloucs.*, ii, pp. 755–6; *Ann. Wav.*, p. 361; *Cron. Maior.*, p. 73; *CPR, 1258–66*, pp. 424, 479; Prestwich, *Edward I*, p. 48.

earlier in 1262, but now at a time when his quarrel with Clare would have made any reinforcement of his powers especially helpful.[212]

Clare's willingness to negotiate may have been a ruse designed to buy time while he consolidated his alliance against Montfort; for shortly before 10 May, while the negotiations were proceeding, John de Warenne and William de Valence landed in Valence's lordship of Pembroke with an armed force. The place of their landing suggests that they were well informed about events in the marches; and since Clare held the custody of the lordship – one of his few major gains from the victory at Lewes – it seems likely that Montfort's enemies were now in successful collusion.[213] Montfort's response was to march north-westwards to Hereford, where he arrived about 8 May, leaving himself well placed to intercept any combined operations between the invaders and Mortimer at Wigmore.[214] The extensive work that he put in hand on Hereford castle, including 'a building for housing engines', presumably siege engines, suggests that the city was now to become his base for a new campaign in the marches.[215] Although the landing of the exiles, who had been successfully kept at bay since their flight abroad after Lewes, marked a sharp deterioration in Montfort's position, it did not prevent his keeping up appearances. As late as 15 May he was still proposing to hold a parliament at Westminster on 1 June, precisely according to the Provisions,[216] and on 28 May the new abbot of Chester received his temporalities from Montfort at Hereford: a casual and telling revelation of the extent to which the earl had usurped Edward's authority in his appanage.[217]

But by the evening of the day of the abbot's visit Montfort's pretensions had been mortifyingly compromised by Edward's escape. For

---

[212] *CR, 1264–68*, pp. 115–16; Powicke, 'Loretta, Countess of Leicester', esp. pp. 266–7; Powicke, *King Henry III*, p. 492, n. 4; above, pp. 200, 207, 239–41.

[213] *CR, 1264–68*, pp. 119–20; *CPR, 1258–66*, p. 322; *Flores Hist.*, iii, p. 264. *Wykes*, p. 165, puts Hugh Bigod among the invaders.

[214] *Flores Hist.*, iii, p. 1; *CPR, 1258–66*, p. 424; Carpenter, *The Battles of Lewes and Evesham*, pp. 37–8. The precise chronology here is uncertain. The bulk of the letters issued from the chancery show that the king was at Gloucester until 7 May and at Hereford from 8 May. But two letters were sealed at Gloucester on 15 May, according to their – perhaps erroneous – enrolment (*CR, 1264–68*, pp. 55, 117), and *Robert of Gloucs.*, ii, p. 756, says that Montfort and Clare came to terms on 12 May (which he correctly gives as a Tuesday), before the move to Hereford. Perhaps the king preceded Montfort to Hereford. Powicke, *King Henry III*, p. 496, n. 5, identifies the problem but does not solve it.

[215] *CLR, 1260–67*, p. 175.

[216] *CR, 1264–68*, pp. 116–17. Sayles, *Functions of the Medieval Parliament*, pp. 107–9, conveniently collects together the documents relating to this parliament.

[217] *Ann. Cestr.*, p. 93.

some days Edward had been in contact with Clare, whose forces blockaded the city on three sides and whose brother, Thomas de Clare, was acting as go-between, though still a trusted Montfortian. On 23 May two of Edward's closest friends, Clifford and Leyburn, had actually been granted safe-conducts to visit him.[218] Montfort's peculiar carelessness, or perhaps overconfidence, in the matter of Edward's security was the prelude to an escape which rapidly became the stuff of tales and legends. Late on 28 May, the day arranged with his friends, Edward left the city with Thomas de Clare and an escort of knights to test their horses. After tiring out first one horse and then another, Edward finally made off at speed with the one remaining fresh mount. He was followed by Thomas and a few others. Meeting Mortimer a short distance away, they made first for Wigmore and then for Ludlow.[219] There Edward came to terms with Gilbert de Clare, undertaking to observe the ancient laws and customs and to induce the king to remove aliens from his council and his kingdom and to govern through natives:[220] an agreement which points both to the common bond of opposition to aliens which had underlain the alliance of Montfort and Clare in 1264, and to the considerations of principle, as well as self-interest, which still guided Clare's actions. To a limited extent he and Edward could now present themselves as the true continuators of the populist anti-alien tradition.

Edward's escape placed Montfort in great danger. It gave to the opposition not just a figurehead but an accomplished military leader, who for the first time since Lewes was reunited with his friends. The alliance between Edward and his marcher affinity, which had proved so damaging to Montfort between October 1263 and April 1264, was now in business again; but this time it enjoyed the additional backing of Clare and the strategic advantage of having Montfort half caught behind its lines. Edward now seized the initiative and took control over all the marches except the small remaining Montfortian sector in the southeast. At Wigmore he was joined not only by Clare and Mortimer, but by Warenne, Valence and Hugh Bigod, with their troops, by Robert

---

[218] *Ann. Wav.*, p. 362; *Wykes*, pp. 162–3; Battle chronicle, in Bémont, *Montfort* (1st edn), p. 378; *Robert of Gloucs.*, ii, p. 756; *CPR, 1258–66*, p. 427.

[219] The story of the escape is told in many of the chronicles, most vividly and minutely in the Wigmore chronicle: W. Dugdale, *Monasticon Anglicanum*, ed. J. Caley, H. Ellis and B. Bandinel (6 vols. in 8, London, 1817–30), vi, p. 351; see also *Robert of Gloucs.*, ii, pp. 757–8. The most detailed modern account, based on the Wigmore chronicle, is D. C. Cox, *The Battle of Evesham: A New Account* (Evesham, 1988), p. 6.

[220] *Wykes*, pp. 164–5.

Walerand, Warin de Bassingbourne and the former garrison of Bristol, and by substantial numbers of men from the border counties. Further north, Beeston castle in Cheshire was captured by James Audley on 31 May, and Chester castle was put under siege on 7 June. Shrewsbury, Bridgnorth and Ludlow were all taken; Worcester had fallen by 7 June; the bridges over the Severn were broken, the boats drawn up on the eastern bank, and the fords deepened and guarded.[221] This extraordinarily rapid sequence of events culminated in the fall of Gloucester. The town, and with it the bridge over the Severn, was captured on 14 June, but the castle and its Montfortian garrison held out until 29 June.[222] When it, too, surrendered the whole line of the Severn was in Edward's hands.

This was a brilliantly conducted campaign. Edward's co-ordination of his resources, his strategic sense and his rapid appropriation of enemy territory remind us of his later reputation as a chess player.[223] They were the skills which Montfort had demonstrated in his spring campaigns of 1263 and 1264. But this time he had been outgeneralled: isolated behind the Severn, cut off from his bases in the midlands and the south-east, and badly placed to secure the execution of his orders or to summon help. His immediate reaction to Edward's escape had combined vindictive anger with quick military thinking. He at once ordered Richard of Cornwall and his son Edmund, then in custody at Kenilworth, to be placed in irons, fearing perhaps that a rescue attempt might lose him these remaining valuable captives.[224] Then, on 30 May, the news of the escape was passed on to the tenants-in-chief, with orders to attend at Worcester, in arms, with all the men they could raise and with all possible speed. The venue had to be changed to Gloucester when it was known that Worcester had fallen,[225] but the fall of Gloucester, too, must have aborted the whole scheme. A better prospect of relief lay with the Montfortians stationed in the south-east. The news had almost certainly been sent immediately to Countess Eleanor and to young Simon, who were then together at Odiham, for on 1 June they suddenly left for the security of Porchester castle, where Simon was

---

[221] *Wykes*, pp. 165–6; *Ann. Lond.*, p. 68; *Guisborough*, p. 199; Trivet, *Annales*, pp. 264–5; *Ann. Cestr.*, p. 95; *Flores Hist.*, iii, p. 2; *Ann. Wav.*, p. 362; *CPR, 1258–66*, p. 487.

[222] *Flores Hist.*, iii, p. 2; *Robert of Gloucs.*, ii, pp. 758–9; *Ann. Wav.*, p. 362; *Wykes*, p. 166.

[223] Cf. Prestwich, *Edward I*, pp. 114–15.

[224] BL MS Cleopatra D. III, f. 45, the chronicle of Hailes. Since Richard of Cornwall was the founder and patron of Hailes, its chronicler was in a good position to know the truth.

[225] *CR, 1264–68*, pp. 124–5; *CPR, 1258–66*, p. 487.

constable, and then for Dover, arriving there on 15 June.[226] This looks
to have been a precautionary move, designed to allow a rapid escape to
France in case of complete disaster. Young Simon had probably been
summoned to his father's assistance, for his arrival from the east was
expected when Gloucester castle was under siege in mid June; but he
seems to have given priority both to his mother's safety and possibly to
the continuing siege of Pevensey. After spending two days at Dover, he
was at Tonbridge on 24 June, en route for London.[227] He had done
nothing to prevent the loss of the Severn bridgehead at Gloucester,
which came near to settling his father's fate.

The sustained agility of Edward's month-long campaign, and the
failure to secure help to counter it, left Montfort largely powerless
at Hereford. He was short of men, increasingly short of food, and
desperately short of money.[228] He could not relieve Gloucester, on the
east bank of the Severn, and the surrender of its garrison neutralised a
large part of his remaining forces, including two barons, Robert de Ros
and Geoffrey de Lucy, whom he had summoned to the Hilary parliament, and some 300 men.[229] On 2 June he had written to the treasurer
in London, asking him to raise 1,000 marks urgently, by borrowing
if necessary, and to deposit the money at St Frideswide's, Oxford,
probably reckoning on its collection there by his son Simon on his way
westwards. The failure of the money to reach him cannot have made
it any easier to hold together an army which was almost certainly
composed in part of 'milites stipendiarios', paid knights.[230] Nor was it
only at headquarters that his cause was failing. News of his plight must
have become widespread, for both at Gloucester and at Hereford he
had to issue proclamations denying rumours – that he was at logger-
heads with Clare, that he had moved to Hereford for some other reason
than to go against the marchers (to ally with Llywelyn?), that letters were
issued in the king's name but without his knowledge – which were in fact
largely true.[231] No doubt such rumours were assiduously cultivated by
his enemies, as Montfort's own letters stated, contributing to the decline
of the earl's power east of the Severn which was a feature of this final

[226] *Manners and Household Expenses*, ed. Turner, pp. 41–2, 48; Knowles, 'The Disinherited', i, p. 15.
[227] *RL*, ii, p. 288; *Manners and Household Expenses*, ed. Turner, pp. 50, 56–7.
[228] *CR, 1264–68*, pp. 63–6.
[229] *Wykes*, p. 166; *Flores Hist.*, iii, p. 2; *CR, 1264–68*, pp. 86, 246; Knowles, 'The Disinherited', i,
p. 8.
[230] *CR, 1264–68*, pp. 65–6; *Flores Hist.*, ii, p. 504.
[231] *Foedera*, I, i, p. 455; *CPR , 1258–66*, p. 430; *CR, 1264–68*, pp. 119–20.

summer. In Gloucestershire, William de Tracy, Montfortian keeper of the peace and hero of the local campaign against the alien sheriff Matthew Bezill in 1263, had crossed over to Clare before Evesham.[232] In Lancashire, James Audley was able to secure the submission of a large party of Montfortians, including the sheriff.[233] In Norfolk, John de Burgh, keeper of the peace, probably deserted, and in June Montfort had to write to Roger Bigod to ask him to deal with a rising there.[234] Even before Evesham, Montfort's kingdom was contracting at its periphery.

Yet what is perhaps more remarkable is the extent to which that kingdom remained largely intact. In the Montfortian heartlands, and not only there, loyalist administrators, the only group whose allegiance can be assessed, outnumbered deserters. In the south-west, in Yorkshire, in the midland counties and in London, sheriffs, keepers of the peace and other officials were strikingly constant in their fidelity. Only after Evesham, and even then not everywhere, did submissions and surrenders bring the Montfortian government of the localities to an end.[235] But support at a distance was of little use to the earl *in extremis*, for even had his friends been able to stage a rally they were separated from their leader by the impassable waters of the Severn. Montfort's own activities – the denial of rumours, the attempts to raise money and troops, the swift notification of Edward's escape to Eleanor and Simon – demonstrate that adversity had not weakened his resourcefulness or enterprise. But these qualities now had no firm ground on which to operate.

The royalist *revanche*, culminating in the siege and fall of Gloucester, and the difficulty of securing help from east of the Severn, led Montfort to look for allies to its west. On 19 June, while Gloucester castle was under attack, he came to Pipton, near Glasbury on the Wye, about twenty miles west of Hereford, and made a formal written alliance with Llywelyn: something from which he had previously refrained, despite their working partnership since 1263. So great was his plight that Llywelyn was virtually able to name his own terms.[236] Henry (who was, of course, absolutely in Montfort's control) was to pardon Llywelyn all

---

[232] *Robert of Gloucs.*, ii, pp. 736–7; *CPR, 1266–72*, p. 240; Knowles, 'The Disinherited', i, p. 10.

[233] *CPR, 1258–66*, pp. 425, 632; Knowles, 'The Disinherited', i, pp. 11–12.

[234] *CPR, 1258–66*, pp. 327, 424; *CR, 1264–68*, p. 125; Knowles, 'The Disinherited', i, p. 13.

[235] Knowles, 'The Disinherited', i, pp. 9–16, has carefully assembled the evidence for allegiances in the summer of 1265, and the helpfulness of his general discussion is gratefully acknowledged. But his conclusion 'that Montfort lost much of his hold over England in the summer of 1265' (p. 16) does not seem to me to be quite borne out by his evidence.

[236] *Foedera*, I, i, p. 457; *RL*, ii, pp. 284–7; *Dipl. Docs.*, i, Nos. 400, 401; *Ann. Wav.*, p. 363.

his offences, and to allow him to keep all the lands which he currently held (that is, including his conquests), to have the homage of the other Welsh magnates, and to control various specified lands and castles. In return for what was effectively a recognition of Llywelyn's independence and a confirmation of all his military gains, the Welsh prince was to give Henry 30,000 marks, to be paid in annual instalments of 3,000 marks, and – the matter of most immediate importance and the reason for the treaty – to give military assistance against the marchers. Not the least remarkable part of this agreement came in a supplementary document. In it Llywelyn undertook to continue to make annual payments to the king's 'heir or successor' if Henry should die before the full payment was completed 'or if by chance he should happen to go against the ordinance made in London'.[237] The full text makes it clear that the 'ordinance' refers to the arrangements made for Edward's release drawn up in London in March and incorporating the constitution of June 1264. The possibility of Henry's replacement by a 'successor' rather than an heir suggests that Montfort still envisaged the possible disinheritance of Edward, as had in fact been provided for in the March arrangements for his release.[238] But the provision for the accession of an 'heir or successor' if Henry should go against those arrangements was without precedent and almost revolutionary in its implications, for it visualised circumstances in which the king himself might be deposed.

The treaty with Llywelyn was almost as humiliating for Montfort as for Henry. The earl had to give hostages for his side of the bargain; Henry saw his entire Welsh policy since the start of the reign undone and his castle at Painscastle, built at great expense in 1231–32, demolished by Llywelyn under the treaty's terms. Llywelyn was too canny to give much help to a waning cause, and in England the agreement was denounced.[239] If it had hardly served its purpose, its conception has to be seen in relation to Montfort's next move. On 24 June, a few days after the making of the treaty and while Gloucester castle was still under siege, he left Hereford and moved south to Monmouth. His intention was to avoid the battle which would loom once Gloucester had fallen, and to cross the Severn to the friendly town and castle of Bristol, thence to link up with young Simon, while leaving Llywelyn to cover his retreat. This plan failed. Although he was able to

---

[237] *Dipl. Docs.*, No. 401.
[238] Above, pp. 319–20.
[239] Battle chronicle, in Bémont, *Montfort* (1st edn), p. 379; *Cron. Maior.*, pp. 73–4; *Wykes*, p. 168.

take Clare's castle at Usk on 2 July, Edward and Clare, now freed by the capture of Gloucester, acted with the swift decisiveness which had characterised their whole campaign. As Montfort moved south-west to Newport, in preparation for his crossing of the Severn, they swept westwards, recaptured Usk, regained Montfort's few remaining castles in the march at Hay, Huntington and Brecon, and, most seriously of all, destroyed the fleet prepared by the Bristolians for Montfort's crossing. Faced with the enemy army at Newport, Montfort avoided battle and turned back across the hills of Gwent to Hereford, where he arrived again on 16 July.[240]

Meanwhile, as Carpenter has been the first to point out, circumstances had temporarily changed in Montfort's favour.[241] Edward and Clare had been forced to withdraw east of Severn by the need to deal with young Simon's advancing army. They took up their position at Worcester.[242] At Tonbridge on 24 June, the day Montfort left Hereford, Simon had gone on to London to raise troops, before marching on Winchester. His journey thither has been seen as a move towards joining his father near Bristol,[243] but Winchester is hardly on the road from London to Bristol and it is more likely that he was drawn there by rumours of opposition among the town's citizens and by the prospects of some easy plunder. He was there on 18 July,[244] delaying for a leisurely three days to sack the town, before moving north to Oxford, thence to Northampton, and thence to the great Montfortian stronghold at Kenilworth, which he reached on 31 July. His reason for proceeding so slowly and circuitously, contemporary charges from which it is difficult to exonerate him, probably lay in his fear of meeting Edward's army.[245] That fear was realised on the following night. Simon's men, attracted by

---

240 *Wykes*, pp. 166–8; *Flores Hist.*, iii, p. 3; *Ann. Wav.*, p. 362; Battle chronicle, in Bémont, *Montfort* (1st edn), p. 379; Carpenter, *The Battles of Lewes and Evesham*, pp. 39, 47 (where new details of the king's itinerary will be found).

241 From this point onwards two very detailed narratives have been given by Carpenter, *The Battles of Lewes and Evesham*, pp. 49–66, and Cox, *The Battle of Evesham*, pp. 6–17. They differ in some respects. I have drawn on their accounts in the concluding part of this chapter, providing references to sources only when they are not provided by Carpenter or Cox or when the point is especially important.

242 D. C. Cox, 'The Battle of Evesham in the Evesham Chronicle', *Hist. Res.*, 62 (1989), p. 341.

243 *Manners and Household Expenses*, ed. Turner, pp. 56–7; Carpenter, *The Battles of Lewes and Evesham*, p. 49; Cox, *The Battle of Evesham*, p. 6.

244 E.132/1/2, m. 5, which shows him collecting £200 from his father's friend, the bishop of Winchester. I owe this reference to the kindness of Dr Nicholas Vincent.

245 *Cron. Maior.*, p. 74; Cox, 'The Battle of Evesham', p. 341; Carpenter, *The Battles of Lewes and Evesham*, p. 49.

the comforts available in the town of Kenilworth but not in the castle, in particular baths, had been imprudent enough to sleep outside the safety of the castle walls. Knowing this, Edward marched the thirty-four miles from Worcester to Kenilworth and fell upon the sleeping army. Simon himself managed to escape back to the castle with a considerable force, but a large number of leading Montfortians were captured, including Richard de Grey, Adam of Newmarket and Baldwin Wake. One of the few who died was Stephen de Holwell, Montfort's clerk, who was forcibly taken from a church and beheaded on Clare's orders: an act of brutality which may be the more explicable in view of Holwell's previous appointment by Montfort to enquire into his territorial disputes with Clare.[246]

Events were now moving towards their climax. Montfort left Hereford, probably on 2 August, knowing of his son's westward advance and intending to rendezvous with him and to join battle with Edward. He crossed the Severn near Kempsey, four miles south of Worcester, on the same day. It was there that he learnt of the disaster at Kenilworth and, more hopefully, of young Simon's escape with a force that might yet prove his salvation. His new plan was to skirt around Edward's army, now back at Worcester, and to join his son as he advanced from Kenilworth: a plan apparently agreed on by both parties, presumably through messengers. As a first stage Montfort made for Evesham, where he arrived about dawn on Tuesday 4 August. But Edward had got wind of his movements and rapidly closed in on a position where any delay for a defending force would be fatal. Evesham lies in a loop of the river Avon, which was then crossed by only one bridge. By dividing his army into three, sending one of the three divisions under Mortimer to block the bridge, and advancing under cover of the young Simon's banners, captured at Kenilworth, Edward had Montfort trapped and caught by surprise.

Montfort's forces were heavily outnumbered. The army which had left Northampton in April had been depleted by the loss of the Gloucester garrison, the flight of Thomas de Clare and others at the time of Edward's escape, the surrender of hostages to Llywelyn, and whatever further desertions may have been brought about by fear, foresight or lack of pay. A large force of Welsh infantry provided by Llywelyn was to provide scant compensation. Once Montfort knew that

[246] *CPR, 1258–66*, p. 479; *Ann. Lond.*, p. 68; *Chron. Melrose*, intro. A. O. and M. O. Anderson, p. 130; *Chron Mailros*, ed. Stevenson, pp. 198–9.

Plate 14. Evesham: the view from the abbey tower towards the battlefield, c. 1870. On the morning of the battle Montfort's army marched north along the road shown here, to encounter Edward's troops on the slopes of the hill in the middle distance.

the advancing army was Edward's and not his son's, as its banners first led him to think, he also knew that there was no way of escape. 'We are all dead men, for it is not your son, as you believed', shouted down Montfort's barber, an expert on heraldry, who had climbed the abbey tower to view the approaching troops.[247] At this point some chroniclers break into direct speech to give Montfort's reaction to the news. 'May God have mercy on our souls, for our bodies are theirs.' 'By the arm of St James, they come on well' – as he watched the enemy advance – 'they did not learn that for themselves but from me'. 'This red dog will eat us today' – an allusion to the red-haired Gilbert de Clare. 'Your presumption and the pride of your brothers has brought me to this end' – this to his son Henry.[248] Walter de Cantilupe, who had arrived in the town to speak to the king and the earl, gave him communion, confessed him and his men, and preached to them 'so that they had less fear of death'.[249] Then, probably about 8 a.m., Montfort led his troops out

[247] *Guisborough*, p. 200.
[248] *Guisborough*, pp. 201–2; Rishanger, *De Bellis*, p. 45; *Chrons. of the Reigns of Stephen*, pp. 547–8.
[249] Cox, 'The Battle of Evesham', p. 341; *Robert of Gloucs.*, ii, p. 763.

of the town towards the waiting royalists. As he did so, a great thunderstorm broke out, darkening the skies even thirty miles away at Gloucester.[250]

In the battle that followed Henry de Montfort was killed first. 'Then it is time for us to die', Montfort himself is reported to have said when he heard the news.[251] With his horse killed under him, he died dismounted, stabbed to death as he fought with his sword. 'Thank God' were his last words.[252] With him died some of his closest friends: Hugh Despenser, Peter de Montfort and the loyal knights of his retinue. Altogether some thirty Montfortian knights were killed, in an episode of noble bloodletting unprecedented since the Conquest. The king, who had been marched into battle in borrowed armour, was rescued by Edward. Montfort's own body was dismembered and the feet, hands and testicles cut off, an act of barbarity which even the royalist Wykes found shameful (Plate 15). The young Simon, advancing too late to help his father, saw his head go by on a spear and retired in mourning to Kenilworth, where for many days he would neither eat nor drink.[253]

Walter de Cantilupe, one of the most faithful and cherished of all Montfort's friends, had retired before the battle to his Cotswold manor of Blockley. There he died six months later, grieving and lamenting over the events of that day until the day of his own death. Had he not adhered so steadfastly to the earl of Leicester, says Wykes, against his fealty to the king and the pope, he might worthily have been enrolled among the saints.[254]

There is no great mystery about the immediate causes of Montfort's defeat and death at Evesham. Indeed, in retrospect his downward course seems to have been inexorable and unchecked. The withdrawal of Clare's support, Edward's escape, the rallying of a great marcher coalition against him, the loss of the line of the Severn, and the dilatoriness of young Simon's rescue bid, were its main features. Yet although we may think that Montfort's larger ambitions, notably his attempt to govern the country in the name of a captive king, were ultimately unsustainable, there was nothing predetermined about the way in which they were destroyed. Much depended on the mistakes and

[250] *Robert of Gloucs.*, ii, pp. 765–6.
[251] *Lanercost*, p. 76.
[252] *Oxenedes*, p. 229.
[253] *Wykes*, pp. 173–5.
[254] Cox, 'The Battle of Evesham', p. 341; *Wykes*, p. 180; *Ann. Wigorn*, p. 453.

Plate 15. The death and mutilation of Simon de Montfort, from the early fourteenth-century Rochester version of the *Flores Historiarum*. The surcoat in the centre bears the arms of Simon, the shield on the left those of his son Henry.

misjudgements of fallible men. If Montfort had taken more care over Edward's security and had not placed so much trust in the treacherous Thomas de Clare, Edward might never have escaped from custody. If young Simon had acted more promptly and had not taken some six weeks to move westwards after the escape, Edward's control of the Severn might have been thwarted. If he had not been so foolish as to leave his men outside the castle at Kenilworth, and so confident of the protection offered by what was by all accounts a very large army,[255] then he might have been able to join forces with his father. If Montfort himself had been more aware of the trap that was Evesham, he might have avoided the place and been able to join forces with his son. It is true that in this final stage of the war Edward's generalship and sense of strategy were near faultless. Made in his last hours, Montfort's proud, rueful, defiant comment on Edward's advancing troops, 'they learnt that from me', was in a sense a comment on the whole campaign. But Edward's qualities exploited the errors of his enemies. Without those errors the campaign might have been more protracted and a royalist victory by no means assured.

If we look beyond the events of the few months preceding Evesham, we can identify three more substantial reasons for his defeat. First, at no point during his period of power had he succeeded in taming the marchers. Re-allied with Edward from the autumn of 1263, released after Lewes, brought to terms which could not be enforced in July and December 1264, able to repudiate their proposed exile to Ireland, they could defy Montfort with impunity. Lacking much land in the marches

---

[255] *Wykes*, p. 170; *Ann. Wav.*, p. 363; *Guisborough*, p. 199.

and the powers which went with land – money, jurisdiction, lordship over men – Montfort also lacked the military power to defeat magnates whose authority not only spread over a wide area but was greatly enhanced by the breakdown of royal authority and the conditions of civil war. The restriction of Edward's movements, in the conditions laid down for his release, to 'where the king's writ runs in England', was an allusive acknowledgement of marcher independence.[256] Essentially Evesham was a victory for Edward and the marchers: there was something almost symbolic about the presentation of Montfort's head and testicles to Lady Mortimer at Wigmore after the battle.[257] When, in 1254, Henry had given his eldest son an appanage partly located in Wales and the march he had unwittingly created the circumstances which would later identify the marcher lords squarely with Edward and his interests. Their falling out in 1262–63, when Edward's retinue was purged at the queen's instigation, and their separation in 1264–65, when Edward was a captive, were only temporary interruptions in a more permanent relationship, founded on the solid ground of lordship and patronage, which Montfort was never able to counter effectively.

If the marchers were the authors of Simon's defeat, so also, if less directly, were his sons: the second factor in Montfort's decline. The ineptness of young Simon in the weeks before Evesham was only the final example of a pattern of behaviour which showed the young Montforts to have all their father's acquisitive and violent tendencies without any of the compensations offered by his political leadership, military expertise, powers of organisation, and ability to inspire respect and affection. Montfort's ambitions for his sons were ill served by their conduct, as he recognised, if the chronicler Guisborough writes truthfully, in his *cri de coeur* at Evesham. Their greed, fuelled by the offices, lands and castles which Montfort conferred on them, does not seem to have been used, as greed might properly be, to extend the patronage and connections of the family. The knights in their pay – perhaps foreigners, for we know none of their names – were a source of division rather than of strength;[258] and the tournament planned against them at Dunstable was a reflection of deep political rivalries and antagonisms.

Most important of all perhaps was the role of Henry, Simon, Amaury

---

256 *Foedera*, I, i, p. 451. Cf. R. R. Davies, *Lordship and Society in the March of Wales, 1282–1400* (Oxford, 1978), pp. 23–5.
257 *Cron. Maior.*, pp. 75–6.
258 *Wykes*, pp. 161–2.

and Guy in driving Gilbert de Clare into the marchers' camp. His alienation made a final contribution to Montfort's fall. Although Clare had many reasons for disgruntlement with the regime in which he had been a major figure but only a minor beneficiary, his detestation of Montfort's sons was among the chief. Clare's desertion, inspired by the same mixture of private grievances and public principles that drove Montfort himself, was ultimately fatal for Montfort. Not only did it cost him his one remaining magnate supporter in the marches, but it gave Edward a young ally untainted either by the politics of Henry's court (Clare had been active in politics only since 1263) or by the lawless brutality of the other marchers, and one whose identification with reform was almost as valuable an asset as his territorial power. Clare's role in securing Edward's escape through the secret plottings of his brother, his partnership with Edward in their subsequent operations along the march, and his particular success in securing the destruction of the rescue fleet which was to have ferried Montfort's army across the Bristol Channel, all showed how indispensable an ally he was. The political mismanagement which lost Montfort one of his most useful friends played a large part in his defeat. It is also one aspect of Montfort's general strengths, weaknesses and achievements which must be addressed in a conclusion.

CHAPTER 9

Conclusion: Simon de Montfort

Max Beerbohm in his later years, turning the pages of some contemporary memoirs, came upon the following sentence: 'Posterity will be puzzled what to think about Sir Edmund Gosse.' Max noted in the margin, 'Posterity, I hope, will be puzzled what to think about anybody. How baffling and contradictory are our most intimate and contemporary friends! And how many of us can gauge even himself!'[1]

Beerbohm's comment, a characteristically quizzical glimpse of the truth, could stand as an epigraph for any biography of Simon de Montfort: a figure whose motives and personality perplexed and passionately divided those among whom he lived. Was he a good man or a bad man, they asked, posing a question to which modern historians have given a more sophisticated gloss but hardly a definitive answer. We can sense some of their puzzlement, and eavesdrop on their differing opinions, in a few of the miracle stories which became attached to his name in the years after Evesham. They open windows onto a social life of conviviality and conversation which other sources rarely bring into view. At Bolney in Sussex, for example, about eighteen months after the battle, one William de la Horste was giving a dinner party where a dispute arose about Montfort's virtues. It was dramatically curtailed when one of the sceptics suffered a stroke after being rebuked by William ('Don't run down the earl!') for his vituperative criticisms. On a similar occasion, at a feast given by a Derbyshire nobleman for his neighbours, two other opponents with 'not a good word to say for the earl' were put in their place by the host's bold assertion 'that he was a good man . . . martyred for the justice of the land and for truth'. Another evening debate set the monks of Peterborough against each other: 'some said that [the earl] was a good man, others that he was not but that he

[1] David Cecil, *Max: A Biography* (London, 1964), p. 3.

346

stirred up discord'.[2] In these small gatherings, miniatures of a politically-conscious local society convulsed by Montfort's extraordinary career, the themes of a thousand later tutorials and seminars were already in the making.

It was not only in the miracle stories that Montfort's life and martyr's death were seen to demonstrate the spiritual triumph of virtue. The same theme was amplified still more loudly and insistently through other contributions to his posthumous cult: chronicles, poems and songs, and liturgical offices. Their various authors saw him as dying 'for justice',[3] 'to maintain peace and justice',[4] 'for the peace of the land and the reform of the kingdom and the church',[5] 'fighting bravely like a giant for the liberties of the kingdom',[6] 'to keep his oath and to maintain the Provisions',[7] or 'invoking the justice and equity which his conscience had defended in the Provisions of Oxford'.[8] To judge from the case histories of those who came to his shrine at Evesham, he drew his supporters from a wide area and a wide range of ranks and occupations – knights and sheriffs, an abbot and a dean, a carpenter and a fisherman.[9] To these people, as to those who eulogised him in writing, he died in a cause that was worth dying for and which made him into a kind of saint.

We do not have to go far, however, to put together the opposing case for the prosecution. The anonymous letter-writer of the Tewkesbury annals, the defensive author of the *Song of Lewes*, and the chronicler Thomas Wykes, all give us a good idea of how a less admiring audience saw him: as one who pursued his own ends under the guise of the public good, was intent on the promotion of his family, applied the rules selectively – for example, by persecuting some aliens and protecting

---

2 'Miracula Simonis de Montfort', printed as a supplement to Rishanger, *De Bellis*, pp. 89 ('Nolite detrahere comitem'), 85 ('dixerunt universa mala de comite'), 81. Cf. Carpenter, 'Simon de Montfort', p. 3.

3 Maitland, 'A Song on the Death of Simon de Montfort', p. 317; 'Miracula', Rishanger, *De Bellis*, p. 84.

4 'Lament for Simon de Montfort', *Anglo-Norman Political Songs*, ed. Aspin, pp. 30, 33.

5 *Ann. Wav.*, p. 365.

6 BL MS Faustina B. VI, part I, f. 75 (annals of Croxden, Staffs.).

7 *Chronicon Abbatie de Parco Lude*, ed. E. Venables (Lincs. Rec. Soc., i, 1891), pp. 17–18.

8 Battle chronicle, in Bémont, *Montfort* (1st edn), p. 380.

9 The best analysis of Montfort's cult will be found in D. W. Burton, 'Politics, Propaganda and Public Opinion in the Reigns of Henry III and Edward I' (Oxford D.Phil. thesis, 1985), pp. 126–46. See also R. C. Finucane, *Miracles and Pilgrims* (London, 1977), pp. 131–5, 169–70, and J. R. Maddicott, 'Edward I and the Lessons of Baronial Reform: Local Government, 1258–80', *TCE*, i, p. 4.

others – and covered his ambitions with an arrogant and intolerable self-righteousness, 'glorying in his own virtue'.[10] Other, silent, witnesses, looking at the wreckage of the countryside after the disorders of 1263–65, 'the many evils done in the burning of [the property of] the rich and the spoliation of the poor',[11] might have constructed a different but equally hostile case. They would have agreed with some of the Peterborough monks that he had indeed 'stirred up discord', living up to his reputation as 'a lover and inciter of war'.[12] Plenty of those who found themselves in the tracks of the opposing armies or set upon by the marauders who flourished during the troubles had good cause to wish that he had never lived.

Both these sets of views reflect different sides of the truth. Those who criticised Montfort were right to see the compulsive desire for profit as an essential part of his being, though they lacked the means to trace its origins and perhaps the inclination to note the ways in which it was mitigated. Brought up in the shadow of an acquisitive and brutally successful father, and shadowed, too, by the insecurities overhanging any younger son, Montfort found as a young man that his position was not entirely ameliorated by what he initially gained in England. His share in the old honor of Leicester from 1231 onwards provided him with a baronial livelihood but no more, and from the start the income which the honor yielded was depleted by debt. In these circumstances royal patronage was more than usually attractive. His marriage to the king's sister in 1238, and the conferment of the earldom which soon followed, transformed his personal standing without providing any great expectations for the large family of sons which the marriage produced. That the lands which came with Eleanor were his for no more than the term of her life qualified sharply, if only prospectively, the position of power which he built for himself in England during the 1240s. It was further qualified by what it partly rested on: a military reputation stemming not only from Montfort's skills of generalship but from his role as a condottiere, the leader and paymaster of mercenary troops whose maintenance often strained his resources. In Poitou in 1242, in Gascony between 1248 and 1254, and to some extent in England between 1260 and 1265, he owed some of his weight to the men whom he could muster, from recruiting grounds which stretched as far

---

[10] *Ann. Tewk.*, p. 180; *Song of Lewes*, ll. 325–333; *Wykes*, pp. 136, 148, 153–4.
[11] BL MS Faustina B. VI, part I, f. 75. Cf. Rishanger, *De Bellis*, p. 111.
[12] Paris, V, p. 313.

afield as the Rhine.[13] Though his wealth grew considerably in the 1250s, there was enough that was precarious about it to stimulate his resentments against the king. Henry's failure to provide adequately for him (as he saw it), either by a proper assignment of dower or by a proper settlement of debts and other obligations, became a grievance which gradually perturbed his whole relationship with his brother-in-law.

For contemporaries, however, these aspects of Montfort's situation were largely concealed from view. Only from 1263 onwards, when his headship of the government began to allow his private ambitions to operate more freely and openly, does his rapaciousness become the subject of comment in the narrative sources. The earlier issues of the dower and of his claims against the king were ignored by the chroniclers and were almost certainly unknown to them, leaving us to reconstruct their substance from Montfort's written complaints, mainly preserved in his family archives, and from the records of the Crown. Even the public consequences of these issues were hardly mentioned. The deliberate obstruction of the Treaty of Paris by Simon and Eleanor, for example, was touched on only by Wykes and Paris, and then without any mention of the dower claims which lay behind their refusal to co-operate.[14] These were perhaps the two best-informed chroniclers of the day: how much less well informed are likely to have been the knights and gentry who would later provide Montfort's following in the counties? If our attitude towards Montfort's conduct is a more probing and critical one, it is partly because we can see it in the round, as his admirers could not. Knowing what we do, we can hardly accept their panegyrics at face value.

Even if we knew nothing of Montfort's politics, at least one consideration would warn us against going to the other extreme and seeing his life as one ruled by unbridled self-interest: that is, his friendships. Montfort's closeness to some of the greatest men of his day – to Robert Grosseteste and Adam Marsh, to Walter de Cantilupe and Thomas de Cantilupe, to Louis IX and Eudes Rigaud – is one of the most striking features of his career. All these men, including their only secular representative, combined practical abilities with a commanding moral authority among their contemporaries. Two of them, Louis IX and Thomas de Cantilupe, were later canonised; Grosseteste's canonisation

---

[13] *CPL*, i, pp. 397–8; Heidemann, No. 20, para. q, p. 218.
[14] *Wykes*, p. 123; Paris, v, p. 745.

was unsuccessfully attempted;[15] Walter de Cantilupe was thought, even by the hostile Wykes, to have the qualities of a saint. The attachment of the five churchmen to Montfort cannot be explained mainly by their desire to recruit him to the cause of clerical privilege and church reform,[16] any more than can the support which he received from a larger body of prelates between 1263 and 1265. He had little interest in clerical privilege and was, if anything, hostile to it.[17] Besides, these clerical friendships formed only a segment of a broader circle of allies and confidants, comprehending such French nobles as Charles of Anjou and Hugh of Burgundy as well as the loyal *familiares* of his local following. Many of this latter group of knights and barons were later willing to die with him, in an ultimate gesture of fidelity rare in medieval rebellions. Whatever quality these men reflected on him, it was not discredit:

> Think where man's glory most begins and ends
> And say my glory was I had such friends.[18]

What was it that drew these men, most of them exceptionally high-minded and all pre-eminent in their societies, towards this ambitious and often self-seeking magnate? Part of the answer has already been given in the preceding discussion of the earl's religion. To the bishops and scholars of his circle, Simon de Montfort, whatever his faults, was an ardent Christian, a redeemable fragment of humanity among nobles who all too often looked irredeemable, a man aligned with the most vital religious forces of his age – the crusade, the friars, the schools – and one whose abilities equipped him for a leader's place in the Church militant. But besides these attributes his appeal also rested on an aspect of his personality almost wholly obscure in most of the aristocracy: that is, the manner and disposition manifested through his speech. Speaking, for a variety of ends, was clearly an art in which Montfort was especially talented. Only Rishanger (a good witness) comments directly on his 'pleasant and courteous way of speaking',[19] but the persuasive force of his words, sometimes expressed in writing too, can be deduced from many episodes in his career. Few things are more surprising about Montfort than his apparent skill in getting his friends to do the

---

[15] *Robert Grosseteste*, ed. Callus, pp. 241–6.
[16] Cf. C. H. Knowles, *Simon de Montfort, 1265–1965* (London, 1965), pp. 22, 29.
[17] Above, p. 96.
[18] W. B. Yeats, 'The Municipal Gallery Revisited'.
[19] 'Erat siquidem jocundi facetique sermonis': Rishanger, *De Bellis*, p. 6; above, pp. 9, 243.

unexpected. Grosseteste was prepared to intervene for him with the king in 1239, in a case where Montfort was at least partly at fault;[20] Eudes Rigaud, Henry Sandwich and Richard of Gravesend, conscientious bishops to a man, were prepared to confer prebends on his young son Amaury, inexperienced and unordained as he was;[21] Cantilupe was seemingly prepared to obstruct the arbitration on the dower to his advantage in 1259, and Louis IX to confirm his scheme for the government of England, after the earl's exposition of his case, in 1263.[22] We do not know what words Montfort found for his arguments, but we cannot deny their effectiveness, often, it seems, in prompting his friends to go beyond what was predictable or even proper.

Some confirmation of Montfort's talent here comes from its forensic exercise. Carried over into politics, his command of language helped to make him a formidable adversary. It is Marsh, a partisan observer, who comments on 'the clear strain of lucid reasoning' with which he 'confuted each accusation' at his trial in 1252, but Paris, too, vouches for his 'elegant answer' to the charges against him; and both agree that he was able to win the nobility over to his side.[23] So he did again in 1254, when, on arriving from France, he moved those attending parliament to turn down the king's demands.[24] It was no wonder that Henry was anxious to prevent him from appearing before Louis at Amiens in January 1264: his interventions in public arguments were all too likely to carry the day. His dexterity with words similarly informed, though to a different purpose, the quick-witted, sometimes sardonic, exchanges with which he answered his accusers at his second trial in 1260 and the sharp or ironical remarks which he directed at incompetents, blunderers or deserters – to Henry III in 1242, that he ought to be taken and kept apart, like Charles the Simple; to Henry of Almain in 1263, that it was not his arms that he had cherished, but the special constancy he had hoped for; to his sons in 1265 that he would put them in a place where they would enjoy the blessing neither of sun nor of moon.[25] A cleverer man than Henry, he possessed a verbal facility which was one mark of his intelligence and which embodied the two distinctive but opposing traits of persuasiveness and intemperance. It does something to explain why he was feared.

---

[20] Above, p. 28.
[21] For Rigaud and Sandwich, see above, pp. 198, 252–3; for Gravesend, *Fasti Lincoln*, p. 66.
[22] Above, pp. 190, 243–4.
[23] *Mon. Franc.*, i, p. 124; Paris, v, pp. 295-6.
[24] Above, p. 139.   [25] Above, pp. 32, 198, 245–6, 329.

The degree to which Montfort's appeal lay in these and other personal qualities has not always been recognised, and the image which he projected has sometimes been brusquely dealt with. Like Becket, we are told, he 'had no ease of self-expression, no pervasive charm of personality', and remained a man 'to inspire admiration, but not love'.[26] Yet his early and unforced adoption by Ranulf of Chester, and his remarkable impact on Henry in the 1230s, culminating in his marriage to Henry's sister,[27] as well as the range and loyalties of his later friends, should all make us think twice about this verdict. It would perhaps be nearer the truth to say that his unattractive features are displayed more durably in the sources than others once more sympathetic but also more evanescent. To some extent he was one of those historical unfortunates whose deep impression on many of their admiring contemporaries has proved hard for posterity to appreciate. Such reputations are not uncommon: one thinks, in worlds entirely different from Montfort's, of an Arthur Hallam or a Raymond Asquith. But they leave gaps in any biography and frustrate attempts to assess what may once have been very important. We would give much, for example, to know how the knights to whom Montfort looked for support responded to his words and his bearing in the parliaments of his last years.

But from 1258 Montfort's friendships and alliances came to depend less on these affective bonds than on the political principles defined and given shape by reform. The reform movement which made his name was the most fundamental attempt to redistribute power within the English State before the seventeenth century. It sought to establish a limited monarchy, if not indefinitely, then for a period only vaguely specified, in which the Crown's essential powers were checked and their exercise made subject to the consent of a baronial council. The king's rights to distribute patronage, summon parliament, appoint to office and choose councillors, were all taken out of his hands, in a subversion of the prerogative which was recognised by Henry for what it was. In its most extreme form, that developed in 1264 rather than in 1258, this was the princely rule that Louis IX would rather break clods behind a plough than tolerate.[28] It was more radical than anything attempted in Magna Carta, which had generally had the narrower aim of defining and curbing the Crown's rights of feudal lordship, or in the next

[26] Labarge, *Montfort*, p. 277.
[27] Above, pp. 7–13, 19–23.
[28] Above, p. 295.

movements of baronial opposition in 1296–97 and 1310–11, neither of which envisaged institutional restraints on the Crown. It was more radical in some ways than the deposition of kings in 1327, 1399 and 1461, which brought a change of management but no new statutory limitations on the Crown. It went further than what parliament attempted to do, timidly and intermittently, in the late fourteenth and fifteenth centuries through impeachment and developing notions of ministerial accountability. Only the abolition of the monarchy in 1649 trumped what was devised by the baronial reformers between 1258 and 1265.

It would be easy to see these upheavals largely as a pragmatic response to abuses of royal power. That indeed was partly the view of the reformers themselves. 'The lord king realised that the state of his realm required manifold reforms',[29] they said in 1264, with a deft but specious transfer of initiative away from themselves and towards Henry. The causes lay in Henry's misgovernment and incompetence: his reluctance to abide by Magna Carta, his failure to consult on matters of state business and foreign policy, his licence to unpopular aliens to do as they pleased, his lavish patronising of these and other favoured *curiales*, and the inflammatory contrast between his munificence to the few and the burdens that he imposed on the Church and on his provincial subjects. In disregarding the largely informal conventions of restraint, consultation and consent which Magna Carta had helped to establish, Henry had forced his opponents to turn those conventions into rules. For this there were precedents of a kind in the Paper Constitution of 1244 and in the parliamentary attempts to limit the king's choice of officials in the 1240s and 1250s. But it was only in the circumstances of 1258, with the division of the court against the Lusignans and Henry's abasement over Sicily, that the pressures for reform ceased to be containable.

That was how reform began in April 1258, with its roots deep in the fertile soil of political grievance. But it was by no means the whole story. As the movement gathered pace, from the time of the Oxford parliament onwards, it became something like a crusade, a quality which it never entirely lost, despite the backsliding, violence and self-aggrandisement which increasingly mired its course. The moral intensity of its participants' commitment separated it from almost every other movement of opposition to the Crown in medieval English

---

[29] *DBM*, pp. 256–7.

history, even allowing for the role of Archbishop Langton in 1215 and of Archbishop Winchelsey in 1310–11. Its keynote was the need for justice. Both the word and the theme resound through the most considered statement of the reformers' case, the apologia which they submitted to Louis IX in 1264. The king was bound to give justice to everyone; but instead no justice could be obtained against aliens in the king's courts, writs of common justice had been denied, sheriffs had scorned justice and sought only plunder from their offices; common justice was trampled underfoot, denied by the strong to the weak, virtually shut out from England. Hence the need for a new justiciar to do equal justice to all, both rich and poor.[30] For those who framed and supported this plea, justice meant both the practical redress of grievances and the broader principle of fair dealing which the king, through his officials, was expected to provide for his subjects: 'the constant will of giving to every man his own', to cite Hobbes's paraphrase of Justinian's classic definition.[31] That this was not mere polemic is evident from the reformers' actions: from the justiciar's eyre of 1258–59 and the special eyres of 1260, with their intention to make justice generally available, and, of course, from the limitations set by the movement's initiators on their own and other baronial officials. These things constituted an exercise in practical equity and political self-denial hard to parallel in other comparable reforming endeavours.

What were the origins of this new political idealism which surfaced in 1258 and which helped to mould the executive measures of the Provisions? In discussing its particular origins we have already noticed the examples of Grosseteste and Louis IX and argued the case for their influence on Simon de Montfort and his allies.[32] But at a more pervasive level, underlying not just the reforms of 1258 but the whole programme of the movement, the answer must lie more generally with the Church, with the bishops in particular, and with the teaching of the schools. It is customary to play down the role of churchmen in the early stages of reform and to deplore the absence of their guiding hand. 'The bishops . . . could do nothing to shape the course of the barons', says Powicke.[33] Yet this is to overlook the large and active episcopal presence at Oxford in June 1258, where nine bishops (a majority of the episcopate)[34] took

---

[30] *DBM*, pp. 264–5, 270–1, 260–3, 272–3.
[31] *Leviathan*, ch. 15.
[32] Above, pp. 167–9.
[33] Powicke, *King Henry III*, pp. 381–2. Cf. *Baronial Plan*, p. 66.
[34] Of the seventeen English sees, York was vacant in 1258.

part in the excommunication of those opposing the Provisions, and to search, vainly and mistakenly, for reforms bearing specifically on ecclesiastical abuses. These, it is true, we do not find: remedies for papal provisions, the intrusions of the secular courts, and the other distinctive grievances of the Church were not fed into the stream of reforming legislation. Instead, churchmen may have taken a wider and more humane view of what was needed, but for these reasons one which the sources make it less easy to attribute to their particular group. We know too little of the discussions which must have preceded reform to be sure of much. But the role of the bishops at Oxford, the special links between the outstanding pastor Walter de Cantilupe and Simon de Montfort, the note of altruism which runs through much of the work of the council of fifteen between 1258 and 1260, and the later role of Thomas de Cantilupe in drafting the baronial submission to Louis IX, all suggest the moral influence of ecclesiastics, on the general direction of the reforms if not on their precise codification.

Behind that influence lay the teaching of the schools, mediated not only by the bishops, among whom graduates seem to have progressed from a minority in 1258 to a majority in 1265,[35] but probably also in less formal ways: through the work of the friars, the injunctions of confessors, and the existence of such 'friendship circles' as that which brought together Grosseteste, Marsh and Montfort. It is difficult to define the political implications of scholastic teaching, and still more difficult to assess its effects on practical politics;[36] but there is enough to suggest that both implications and effects were substantial. Commentaries on the Scriptures, for example, could provide an opportunity for reflections on political themes. What is possibly the first surviving Oxford notebook, copied before 1231, contains notes on Grosseteste's lectures on the Psalms, in which he describes the qualities of good kingship.[37] It was Grosseteste, too, who was the first scholar to use Aristotle's *Nichomachean Ethics* to adumbrate the distinction between just rule and tyranny.[38] Above all, the *Song of Lewes*, written in 1264, sets down what may be regarded as the standard assumptions of the schools

---

[35] The figures can be roughly calculated from the biographies given in Gibbs and Lang, *Bishops and Reform*, *BRUO*, the *DNB*, and, for Roger Longespee, *DNB: Missing Persons*, ed. Nicholls, p. 564.

[36] There is an excellent general survey in J. Dunbabin, 'Government', *The Cambridge History of Medieval Political Thought, c. 350–c. 1450*, ed. J. H. Burns (Cambridge, 1988), pp. 477–519, esp. pp. 502, 506, 508.

[37] *History of the University of Oxford*, i, ed. Catto, plate 1, facing p. 244; Southern, *Robert Grosseteste*, pp. 113–16.　　　[38] Above, pp. 94–5.

on these problems: the duty of the king to rule according to law, with clemency and in the common interest, to avoid oppressing his subjects, to seek good counsel, and to remember his position under God, ruling a people who were also God's.[39] That these were commonplaces, lacking the forceful novelty of a Machiavelli or a Hobbes, does not argue for their insignificance. It was precisely their acceptance as norms, rather than their originality, which gave them strength and value. In the conclusions which followed from them, notably concerning the magnates' right to correct the king,[40] the applications of political thought were spelt out more plainly than in any other source for the period.

The reform movement of 1258–65 was thus much more than an attempt to remedy grievances against royal government through new laws and their enforcement. It owed its vitality partly to concepts of kingship and justice derived from the schools, and promulgated in a wider world through bishops and others steeped in the ideals which were the stock-in-trade of academic teaching. They were eminently practical men, often pursuing the practical consequences of their moral training. It was, for example, Robert Grosseteste, the promoter of the distinction between kingship and tyranny, who about 1253 prohibited the royal sheriff of Lincolnshire from holding superfluous and burdensome sessions of the local courts. His ruling, based on Magna Carta and later reiterated in the Provisions of Westminster, demonstrated at the most mundane and workaday level what was meant by justice and restraints on kingship.[41] The same connections between theory and practice informed the much more comprehensive restraints of the Provisions of Oxford. For the first time, so far as we can see, the universities, especially Oxford, their teaching and their alumni, seemed set to contribute to a powerful change in the course of public life.

In some important ways Simon de Montfort was better equipped than any other magnate to direct this change: a role which he did not fully assume until 1263 but which had been heavily foreshadowed in 1258, as we have seen. Not only was he closely associated, via Grosseteste, Marsh and Cantilupe, with the world of the schools and of reforming bishops, but from the start he had seen reform as a great moral cause, to which he was bound in conscience by his oath to the

---

[39] *Song of Lewes*, ll. 445–50, 858–72, 590–3, 609–14, 809–11, 641–54, 701–10.
[40] *Song of Lewes*, ll. 595–605, 539–46, 951–8.
[41] Maddicott, 'Magna Carta and the Local Community', p. 35; *DBM*, pp. 140–4 (cl. 4).

Provisions. Both his will, with its urgent instructions for restitution to the poor whom he had wronged, and his castigation of the earl of Gloucester for his reluctance to offer redress to his tenants, show the play of his conscience over social and political questions in the early days of reform.[42] Nor, knowing what we do of his piety and of the ideals inculcated by his religious mentors, should we be surprised at this. Until the time of his death many continued to see him as a visionary crusader: a partial view of his motives, but one justified by his adherence to his oath. The common opinion, audible through so much of the evidence for his cult, that he died for justice identified him clearly with the most powerful guiding principle of the reform movement.

Montfort's sympathy for the religious and moral substance of reform was not his only qualification to supervise its course. His aptitudes, discernment, and knowledge of the world, all fitted him for a leader's role. With the possible exception of Richard of Cornwall, no other member of the aristocracy can have been so widely travelled. By 1258 he was as familiar with Bordeaux and Paris as with Oxford and London, he had visited the papal curia at Rome and Lyon, fought beside Frederick II and crusaded in the Holy Land.[43] With the possible exception of Peter of Savoy, no other magnate can have crossed the Channel so frequently. The breadth of his experience gave him a central place in Henry's diplomacy, in Wales and Scotland[44] as well as in France. Henry's willingness to trust him with negotiations spoke for his practical intelligence and perhaps, too, for the powers of argument already noticed. To see him as a member of 'the "jet-setting" international aristocracy' prior to 1258 is only very doubtfully 'part of the story',[45] for it demeans the political weight bestowed not so much by his social position (there were other and richer earls) as by his sagacity. The small example of Henry's reluctance to settle Welsh business in 1244 without the benefit of his counsel is as revealing here as the larger one embodied in Paris's remark that the baronial counsels were 'mutilated' by his absence in the winter of 1258–59.[46] Combining great abilities both in military and in political affairs, he straddled with facility a dividing line never easy to cross. That was what made him a valuable ally and a dangerous enemy.

---

[42] Above, pp. 173–6, 180–1.
[43] Above, pp. 23, 29–30, 86, n. 28, 93, 109.
[44] Above, pp. 19–20, 35, 139–40.
[45] Carpenter, 'Simon de Montfort', p. 15.
[46] *Cal. Anc. Corr. Concerning Wales*, ed. Edwards, p. 10; Paris, v, p. 732; above, pp. 35, 177.

One of our chief difficulties in writing about medieval nobles is our lack of the means to judge their capabilities. Who knows whether Hugh Bigod was a more able man than his brother Roger, or Richard de Clare than his son Gilbert? Montfort, however, lived long enough in the public eye for us to see the high regard in which his talents were held by contemporaries: the king, the bishops, his fellow reformers of 1258. Those qualities which had helped to launch him upwards in the 1230s were fully vindicated during the period of reform and rebellion. His organisation of local and even international opposition to Henry's resumption of power in 1261, his seizing on the importance of the alien issue in 1263 as a means of attracting support, his apprehension of what might be made out of knightly grievances in 1264–65,[47] all marked him out as one who combined exceptional energy with a very quick eye for political advantage. Given a concomitant respect for his reformer's oath which at times bordered on the fanatical, his various proficiencies made him one of the most formidable opponents that any medieval English king ever had to face.

Yet in other ways Montfort was always set somewhat apart from the movement which he came to lead, and his identification with reform was never quite total. He approached the crisis of 1258 via an unusual route: not through participation in earlier parliamentary attempts to control Henry's government, nor through the anger at local abuses which fired the opposition of the minor barons, knights and gentry, nor through the scandal of the Sicilian Business and the disinterested wish for good government which mattered most to churchmen, nor even primarily through the detestation of the Lusignans which moved his fellow *curiales*. Instead, he was led towards reform by a long train of private grievances, over Eleanor's dower, the king's debts, and the complications – in which politics and finance were closely entangled – resulting from his time as Henry's lieutenant in Gascony between 1248 and 1252. Of course, at some salient points, notably resentment against the Lusignans, his complaints latterly marched in step with those of his fellow magnates. Yet the Lusignans were never the main issue for Montfort, and in 1259–60, in circumstances still unclear, he was even prepared to come to terms with their leader and, vicariously at least, to utilise their services.[48]

Committed reformer though he became in 1258, Montfort's private

---

[47] Above, pp. 212–13, 230–2, 288–9, 314–17.
[48] *DBM*, pp. 204–5; above, pp. 196, 200.

grievances continued to subsist, for all that Henry could do to appease them. They soon began to affect his whole engagement with reform. For most of 1259, through months crucial for the drafting of new reforming legislation, his energies were largely given over to extracting a favourable personal settlement from the king.[49] In the early days of 1260 he made a stand against Henry's breach of the Provisions, in postponing the Candlemas parliament, only when his own private claims had been thwarted in the Treaty of Paris.[50] In October 1262 he returned to England, with a papal bull in favour of the Provisions, only when the arbitration on his claims had broken down.[51] In April 1263 he returned again, and again as the public defender of the Provisions, only when further negotiations had failed.[52] It is hard to avoid the conclusion that although the Provisions remained a sacred principle for Montfort, and were never abandoned as others abandoned them, they were also a tactical weapon, to be used against the king in the furtherance of Montfort's private ends. Henry's own anxiety to settle Montfort's grievances through arbitration in 1261 and 1262 suggests that the king saw clearly enough how the unexploded bomb constituted by Montfort's political leadership might be defused;[53] though since Montfort's grievances were never settled, we cannot tell whether Henry judged rightly.

Montfort himself seems to have seen nothing incompatible in pursuing grievances and principles along parallel and sometimes intersecting courses; and his private concerns were too inward a matter, often disputed out of the limelight in France, to be visible to a much larger audience than the king and his councillors. They apparently detracted not at all from his public role, nor from his qualifications for leadership as contemporaries perceived them. Yet our own perceptions, clearer and more comprehensive, prevent us from seeing him as a man of principle *tout court*, Treharne's 'inspiration and . . . embodiment of the cause of reform'.[54] Nor was his attitude to the component parts of the reforming programme any less ambiguous or more amenable to a monocausal interpretation of his motives. From the start his main

[49] Above, pp. 181–91.
[50] Above, pp. 193, 195–6.
[51] Above, p. 219.
[52] Above, pp. 222–3.
[53] Above, pp. 208–10, 215.
[54] R. F. Treharne, 'The Personal Role of Simon de Montfort in the Period of Baronial Reform and Rebellion, 1258–65', addendum to *Baronial Plan* (1971), p. 431.

concern seems to have been with the control of central government, through the machinery laid down by the Provisions of Oxford in June 1258, and less with the provincial reforms of the shrievalties, the local courts and the workings of the eyre, which mattered most to his supporters in the counties. The parliament of February 1259, where he was probably instrumental in securing the publication of the Ordinance of the Magnates and the Provisions of the Barons, was the last occasion for some time on which he actively promoted what local society wanted.[55] It was not to Montfort but to Edward and Gloucester that the 'community of the bachelors' appealed for more rapid progress at the parliament of October 1259. He had no hand, so far as can be seen, in the Provisions of Westminster, issued at parliament's conclusion, which met the bachelors' grievances, or in the special eyres which took reform to the counties in the 1260s.[56] In the parliament of October 1260 he was apparently prepared to make concessions which ran against local interests on such issues as the need to change sheriffs annually and to discipline magnates' officials.[57] Only in 1261 did he take up the cause of the localities, through his probable organisation of opposition to the king's eyre, the appointment of baronial keepers of the peace, and the summoning of the knights to confer at St Albans.[58] Subsequently, during his period in power, he did all he could to offer redress to local society: calling the knights to parliament, confirming and reissuing the Provisions of Westminster in 1264, nurturing them through the difficult negotiations with the legate, implementing their rulings on such matters as beaupleder fines, and alleviating the burden of Jewish debt.[59] But this was late in the day; and it is hard to tell whether he saw such measures as part of the general defence of the Provisions or as a way of building support. Perhaps the distinction was one that he would not have recognised.

There were good reasons, public and personal, for Montfort to be more concerned with reform at the centre, and especially with the baronial nomination of the great officials and the king's councillors which was its essential feature. When he returned to power, partially and briefly in October 1261, and more confidently in 1263, baronial nominees replaced those of the king in most of the main offices of state.

[55] Above, pp. 179–81.
[56] Above, pp. 184–6, 191, 195–6.
[57] Above, pp. 201–3.
[58] Above, pp. 211–13.
[59] Above, pp. 288–9, 294, 297, 314–17.

When he took charge after Lewes, his power was buttressed by the revival and maintenance of a baronial council.[60] Located at the core of the Provisions, this form of government created the means to restrain Henry's kingship and to reorder it according to justice and equity. The bishops implicitly recognised as much when they told the legate in October 1264 that they were indeed in favour of the imposition of councillors on the king.[61] Without the primary control which these measures provided, there could be no effective secondary reforms, in the localities or anywhere else. But control of the king, and the presence of friends in high places, also brought Montfort himself nearer to the satisfaction of his private grievances. At the outset of the reform movement the committee of twenty-four had been charged to adjudicate on the king's debts to Montfort and on the replacement of his money fee by land. The settlement of both these issues in his favour in 1259 would hardly have been possible without the institution of a baronial council.[62] Some of the council's members were later said by Henry to have blocked the dower arbitration, to the earl's advantage. Later, from June 1264 onwards, the establishment of a new council which he effectively headed allowed him to forward his own and his family's interests more openly and consistently. If conciliar government and control of appointments were the practical means to moral ends, they were also the means to Montfort's own ends. The degree to which his support for Treharne's 'cause of reform' was disinterested is not easy to gauge.

A similar ambiguity, and one which also suggests a more than usually qualified view of his position, surrounds the question of Montfort's nationality. French by birth, he had become by 1258 at the very least 'an honorary Englishman': his English inheritance, his marriage to Henry's sister, his midlands affinity and his role at the royal court, all grounded him in the country where his fortunes now lay.[63] He could hardly have opposed aliens so vociferously in 1263, still less have been so insistent during the negotiations with the legate that all the king's councillors should be English, had he seen himself anything but an Englishman.[64]

Yet his assimilation was far from complete. Part of the purpose of this book has been to show that he still enjoyed a continuing role in the society of his native France, albeit one only intermittently visible. His

---

[60] Above, pp. 201, 232, 285–6, 293–4, 297–8, 313–14.
[61] Above, p. 299.
[62] Above, pp. 154–5, 170–1, 181–2.
[63] Carpenter, 'King Henry III's "Statute"', pp. 937–9.
[64] Above, pp. 229–32, 297–9.

friendships with Eudes Rigaud and Louis IX, his receipt of lands from
Louis, his connection with French nobles such as Charles of Anjou and
Hugh of Burgundy, his participation in the social life of Normandy and
the French court, his maintenance of links with a devout circle of
sisters and cousins in the religious houses of the Ile de France, the offer
of the stewardship of France to him in 1253, all prove that he had by
no means cut loose from his homeland. His long absences in France,
particularly during the early years of the reform movement, show that
he could survive comfortably outside the secure setting provided by his
English estates and following. It became easy enough to see his
Englishness as an adopted guise, which barely hid the alien beneath.
Even his admirer, the author of the Melrose chronicle, saw the
peculiarity of his position: 'the enemy and expeller of aliens, although he
himself was one of them by birth'. At moments of crisis others could be
more robustly critical. So Gilbert de Clare proclaimed in 1265 that it
was 'ridiculous that this alien should presume to subjugate the whole
kingdom'.[65] His reported statements about the treachery of the English
and of English nobles in particular do not suggest that he had been
securely absorbed into their ranks.[66] Given Gloucester's tergiversation
in 1259, Montfort's desertion even by his friends in December 1261, and
by his protégé Henry of Almain and the marchers in October 1263, his
contempt for such fairweather friends is understandable.[67] But it is
remarkable that he should have apparently expressed it in such
nationalistic terms. 'I have been in many lands and in the provinces of
divers nations, among both pagans and Christians', he supposedly said
to his *secreti* at the time of Henry of Almain's departure, 'but nowhere
have I found such deceitfulness and infidelity as in England'.[68] It was
hardly the comment of a man who was fully at home and at ease in his
adopted country.

The truth was that Montfort did not fit entirely smoothly into the
English aristocracy. Despite his English moorings, his travels through
'many lands and . . . the provinces of divers nations', as well as his
family background, placed him somewhat apart – a cosmopolitan figure
set on the edge of an increasingly insular native baronage, whose
members lacked both lands and ambitions abroad. Even when the

---

[65] *Chron. Melrose*, intro. A. O. and M. O. Anderson, p. 127; *Chron. Mailros*, ed. Stevenson, p. 195;
Rishanger Chronica et Annales, p. 32; Carpenter, 'King Henry III's "Statute"', p. 938.
[66] E.g. *Oxenedes*, p. 225; Rishanger, *De Bellis*, pp. 41–2; *Wykes*, p. 160.
[67] Above, pp. 180, 214, 244–6.
[68] Rishanger, *De Bellis*, pp. 17–18.

struggle for reform was at its most intense and absorbing, Montfort sometimes had his eye on more distant goals – Bigorre in 1258–60, Eleanor's inheritance in Angoulême in 1262–63[69] – and when the going became rough he enjoyed the possibility of withdrawal to France which was not open to his English allies. His retirement abroad in December 1261, after the Treaty of Kingston, may have marked his adamantine refusal to compromise on the Provisions, but it also signified the opportunities, open to him alone, *reculer pour mieux sauter*. In October 1262 he was similarly able to beat a rapid retreat to France after launching the papal bull in favour of the Provisions. If his English supporters were more inclined to temporise, and even a reformer like Peter de Montfort to take service with the king,[70] it was partly because such lightning comings and goings across the Channel were not an option for them; they had to live in England with the consequences of their actions. Only in 1263 was Montfort finally and fully committed to English affairs. Until then the absences permitted by his standing in France distanced him a little from reform, in body as perhaps in mind.

It is hardly possible, therefore, to see Simon de Montfort's career from 1258 onwards in uncomplicated terms as the heroic and single-minded defence of reforming principles. His commitment to the Provisions was deep, informed by conscience and safeguarded by reluctance to compromise. His oath was his lodestar, and it is impossible to doubt his horror of perjury, voiced many times:[71] the maintenance of the Provisions was the avoidance of sin. Yet this commitment was also distorted and overlaid by private ambitions and interests, and perturbed by a pedigree which meant that England was rarely the sole field of his operations, nor English politics his sole concern.

With his return to England in 1263, however, and still more with his assumption of power after Lewes, these confusions and equivocations may seem to have given way before a bolder and plainer line of conduct. It would be easy to see this last phase of Montfort's career simply as a slide into moral turpitude and an object lesson in the corrupting influence of power. A favourable dower settlement was now overtaken by other and larger ambitions, hardly confined even to the creation of a great territorial demesne for himself and his family. Though it is

[69] Above, pp. 173, 183–4, 204–5, 221–2.
[70] Carpenter, 'Peter de Montfort', *DNB: Missing Persons*, ed. Nicholls, p. 520.
[71] E.g. *Ann. Dun.*, pp. 217, 226; BL MS Faustina B. VI, part 1, f. 75.

difficult to be sure about the limits of those ambitions, they may have
encompassed the Crown itself. Montfort's appropriation of a large part
of Edward's appanage, the provision for his possible disinheritance in
the settlement of March 1265, and the references to Henry's 'heir or
successor' in the earl's treaty with Llywelyn, all show him moving
towards the permanent exclusion of Edward from the throne.[72] It is
quite possible that Montfort may have had it in mind to displace him in
favour of his own son Henry, whose possible succession may have been
contemplated as early as 1259.[73] Henry was the probable successor of
Edward in the northern sector of the prince's appanage and, like him,
the grandson of King John. The chance of the Crown tentatively held
out to Montfort's father in 1210[74] would finally have been realised in his
son. If this was his vision of the future it was cut short only by his own
misjudgements and by the alienation of some powerful supporters. In
these terms Montfort's fate can be seen almost as a classic tragedy: the
story of a great man who overreached himself and was ultimately
brought down by his own moral failings.

   This again would be too simple. Montfort's aggrandisement in
1264–65 was not a sudden and unexpected deviation from some earlier
and more altruistic norm, but the culmination of a drive for self-
advancement which had characterised his whole career. It was of a
piece with the exceedingly advantageous financial settlement which he
had forced on the king in Gascony in 1253, with his exaggerated claims
for Eleanor's dower, with his relentless and unscrupulous pressure for
land in exchange for his money fee in 1259, and with his successful
attempts to acquire Bigorre. All that happened in 1264–65 was that
circumstances now gave fuller play to his ambitions than had been
possible before. His victory at Lewes and his role as a national leader
both licensed and facilitated his acquisitiveness. Yet whatever his failings
Montfort never lost sight of what had been instituted in 1258 or of the
obligations which he had then assumed. As we have seen, he remained
an advocate of the Provisions, and one of his last acts before the collapse
of his government was to summon a parliament for 1 June, precisely
according to their terms. Despite such brutalities as his putting down of
Robert de Ferrers, his support from the bishops and from the Church in
general was as strong as ever. In March nine bishops had excommuni-

---

[72] Above, pp. 319, 321–2, 338.
[73] *Wykes*, p. 123.
[74] Above, pp. 3–4.

cated those contravening the terms for Edward's release, the same number as had excommunicated those going against the Provisions in 1258; and, in a novel way, the June parliament was to have been attended by two canons from the cathedral church of York and presumably from other cathedrals as well.[75] The planned experiment suggests that Montfort's government had not lost its expectations of religious encouragement. The continuing service of Walter de Cantilupe, and the reappearance of his nephew Thomas, this time as Montfort's chancellor, gives no grounds for thinking that the earl's supremacy was viewed through the lens of moral disapproval which might have been held up to it. Once again, his friendships with the best of men inhibit too censorious an approach to his government. If the end was seen as the establishment of a benevolent oligarchy, headed by an opulent Montfort ruling a peaceful country according to the Provisions, that may not have been unwelcome.

But the end, of course, was something quite different. The termination at Evesham of whatever hopes had rested on Montfort brought in a period of nationwide disorder, impoverishment and general misery.[76] Following on from Henry's restoration, the disinheritance of the rebels in September 1265 – a shortsighted and vindictive move – threatened to perpetuate these conditions almost indefinitely. They were only gradually ameliorated after the Dictum of Kenilworth, in October 1266, had allowed the Montfortians to repurchase their lands and after the conciliatory work of the papal legate Cardinal Ottobuono, the envoy of Pope Clement IV, who, as papal legate himself, had been successfully defied by Montfort in 1264. The resettlement of the kingdom owed a great deal to a papacy conscious of its special links with England and of the blessedness of peacemakers. The same had been true after the earlier civil war of 1215–17. Yet it was a decade before the antagonisms raised by reform and rebellion were finally pacified, debts for the reacquisition of lands largely paid off, and the Montfortians reabsorbed into public life. And it was well into Edward II's reign before Simon de Montfort himself ceased to be a popular hero and an exemplar for the Crown's opponents and became instead a figure from history.

But Montfort's legacy was neither wholly negative nor confined to the provision of a model for would-be emulators, such as Thomas of

---

[75] *Cron. Maior.*, p. 71; *Guisborough*, p. 186; Sayles, *Functions of the Medieval Parliament*, p. 109.

[76] For what follows, see Knowles, 'The Resettlement of England', pp. 25–41, and Maddicott, 'Edward I and the Lessons of Baronial Reform', pp. 1–9.

Lancaster.[77] It is true that the Provisions of Oxford, narrowly defined in terms of what had been ordained in June 1258, failed utterly. Conciliar limitations on the Crown's choice of officials and on its other prerogatives were not attempted again; indeed, the collapse of the experiment may have persuaded Edward I's opponents in 1296–97 and Edward II's in 1310–11 to avoid its repetition. The impossibility of 'imposing an acceptable form of baronial direction on a sane king in his majority'[78] was a lesson that had been learnt, and one which pointed the way towards the deposition of kings as an alternative.

In other ways, however, what had happened between 1258 and 1265 altered the tone and direction of royal government for a generation.[79] Though formal limitations on the Crown were rejected, the reform movement forced both Henry III in his last years and Edward I in the first half of his reign to acknowledge the informal and unstated restraints on their kingship. They tacitly recognised the need to govern through conciliation rather than confrontation, to make policy after consultation and consent, to curb their officials, and to defend their prerogative rights without flaunting them. This style of government, quite uncharacteristic of Henry III's rule before 1258, was most visible in the localities, where the reformers achieved their most lasting success. By the Statute of Marlborough of 1267 the legislative and administrative reforms of the Provisions of Westminster, on such matters as the sheriff's tourn, suit of court, and the eyre, passed into law.[80] Edward I was more consistently attentive to the grievances of the shires, collecting local complaints in the Hundred Roll enquiries of 1274–75, legislating against abuses in the Statute of Westminster of 1275, and seeking to enforce his legislation through the eyres which began in 1278, in a sequence of measures which directly paralleled the reformers' work between 1258 and 1260. The same groups which these reforms were designed to benefit were increasingly represented in parliament. In the assemblies of Henry III's last years, preceding Edward's departure on crusade in 1270, the knights attended more frequently than in any comparable earlier run of parliaments and were able to influence and delay the grant of a tax. Prolonged as they were beyond Evesham, the bitter conflicts of the Montfort years had shown the need for a less partial and more eirenic

---

[77] Maddicott, *Thomas of Lancaster*, pp. 224, 292, 321–2.

[78] J. C. Holt, review of *DBM*, *EHR*, 91 (1976), p. 366.

[79] For the afterlife of reform, see esp. Maddicott, 'Edward I and the Lessons of Baronial Reform', and Maddicott, 'The Crusade Taxation of 1268–70', esp. pp. 112–16.

[80] *Stat. Realm*, i, pp. 19–25; *DBM*, p. 58, n. 2. Cf. Holt, *EHR*, 91 (1976), p. 364.

approach to kingship. If the impulse behind this was more political than altruistic, it nevertheless went some way towards satisfying the ideals of justice which had underlain the work of the reformers.

The afterlife of reform hardly lasted beyond the 1280s. Its perpetuation was both hindered by the structural defects of English local government – amateur and unpaid officials, inadequate central supervision, magnate power – and halted by the wars of Edward's later years. Yet despite the impermanence of the reformer's particular prescriptions 'for the honour of the lord king and the common advantage of the kingdom',[81] the course of events during the reform period had an enduring significance. It lay rather in what had been demonstrated than in what had been achieved. Between 1258 and 1265 the *communitas regni*, that slogan of thirteenth-century political discourse, had taken on an existence more material and more socially comprehensive than ever before. It had come to embrace not just the magnates but also the knights and gentry, and, more surprisingly, numbers of the peasantry, who had benefited from the Provisions, responded to the exhortations of Montfortian preachers, fought on the Montfortian side in the wars of 1263–65, and may even have had some notion of the *communitas* of which they were a part.[82] Such grievances as those against the Lusignans or, later, against all aliens, cut across social divisions and produced common demands for action and redress. Of course, there was no national consensus on these and other reforming issues: the Crown always had a party, and neither among the magnates nor among the knights, let alone among the peasantry, did the Montfortians ever form a committed majority. Nevertheless, their movement was far from being that of a baronial faction and its attendant knightly affinities. The demand for change, and the violence which eventually came to back it, emanated from the larger and more vocal public created by the impact of Henry III's misgovernment on a politically educated society, a crowded and close-knit countryside tightly organised by vill and hundred and shire. This was much more than an aristocratic competition for power. Springing as it did from the unique intensity of English political conditions, the reform movement of 1258–65 would have been inconceivable in any other European state.

Such an environment does much to explain the posthumous

---

[81] *DBM*, pp. 264–5.
[82] Carpenter, 'English Peasants and Politics', esp. pp. 1–19. This paragraph draws heavily on Carpenter's fine article.

reputation of Simon de Montfort. The people who flocked from all parts to his shrine at Evesham, the monks and country neighbours who debated his merits in the cloister or at dinner parties, bore witness to the social breadth of the English political community. Few members of that community can have been left entirely untouched by his career. In his lapidary judgement on Montfort, Stubbs wrote of 'the idea of representative government' that 'ripened under his hand'.[83] Although the earl did indeed unwittingly do much to promote the future role of the commons in parliament, Stubbs's verdict, in its priorities and language, is of its time. Montfort's importance lies not so much in the stimulus that he gave to parliamentary institutions, but more generally, in the voice which he helped to give to those outside the aristocracy who had previously been heard in English politics only locally and intermittently. Despite all his vigorously pursued private ambitions – clearer in any case to us than to contemporaries – he was seen as their representative. Stripped of his teleological role and seen in the context of his day, he has more standing in their world than in the future world of parliamentary government.

    That Montfort himself had rarely given precedence to the needs of local society, or seen their satisfaction as more than an aspect of reforming justice and a means to win support, was only one among the many paradoxes of his life. He was a person whose nature inspired both devotion and mistrust, and who could as well be seen as a hypocrite as a hero. Like his friend Robert Grosseteste, he was very much his own man, an uncomfortable presence whose actions were often a reminder of principles beyond compromise. His practical grasp of affairs, his mastery of men and armies, his sharp but winning tongue, and the courage and decisiveness exemplified in his march on the Cinque Ports in June 1263 or in the ascent of the Sussex Downs in the darkness before Lewes, all made him a daunting figure to his enemies. To all appearances he was boldly self-confident; yet in some ways he remained restlessly insecure, materially and perhaps spiritually, despite his wealth and his faith. His angularity and rigorous expectations hindered the co-operation of those who saw more sides to an argument than he did or who could not ignore the moral faultlines which cut across a far from straightforward political career. He was both an idealist and an adventurer, a man whose conscience as a Christian was continually at odds with his drive to appropriate. He kept company with men whom

83 Stubbs, *Constitutional History*, ii, p. 503.

his contemporaries thought to be saints and carried to extremes the piety that he learnt from them and from his parents. But his self-interest was equally extreme and never successfully subjugated. He knew his own failings; or why else should he have prayed to be delivered, of all deadly sins, from 'avarice and the desire for earthly things'?[84] But he could not entirely disguise them by the claim, partly self-deceptive, that all he sought for himself was the justice that should be freely available to all and the supremacy needed to guarantee the Provisions. The austerities that he practised did little to moderate his greed or to generate the spiritual humility seen in the life of his friend and mentor Louis IX. The tug of war between conscience and self-will which informs the lives of us all was more apparent in him because the forces pulling in both directions were so strong and because the contest took place on the stage of public affairs and not in the unobservable recesses of the heart. For all the justice that he strove for, he brought great suffering to his adopted country, causing a civil war which outdid all the excesses of Henry III's unreformed rule in its destructiveness. His commanding qualities, harsh and overbearing yet compellingly attractive to many, made him one of the greatest men of his age, but led him in the end to a violent death on a battlefield, characteristically surrounded by his friends.

In what he had perhaps most wanted to achieve Montfort failed more completely than in his struggle to secure and perpetuate the Provisions. His desire to establish his family with a substantial English inheritance had predated his commitment to reform and reached its apogee with the elevation of his sons in his final months. But his death ended all these hopes, exterminating his family as a force in English affairs and scattering its members to the winds.[85] Eleanor, the senior survivor of the catastrophe, was allowed to leave for France in October 1265, in company with her young daughter and namesake. She had been preceded there by two of her sons, Amaury and Richard, and never returned to England, retiring instead to the Dominican nunnery of Montargis founded by her dead husband's sister Amicia. There she died

---

[84] Rishanger, *De Bellis*, pp. 6–7; above, p. 88.

[85] There is a large literature on the later history of the Montforts. Unless otherwise stated, what follows is derived from W. H. Blaauw, *The Barons' War* (2nd edn, London, 1871), pp. 327–50; Bémont, *Montfort* (2nd edn), pp. 259–73; F. M. Powicke, 'Guy de Montfort (1265–71)', *TRHS*, 4th ser., 18 (1935), pp. 1–23; Powicke, *King Henry III*, pp. 518–19, 606–12; Labarge, *Montfort*, pp. 260–73; Boyle, '*E Cathena et Carcere*', pp. 379–91.

in 1275. Richard, whom Eleanor had intended to send to Bigorre, disappears from the records after 1266 and may have died in the south. Amaury had a longer and more distinguished career. After going on to study at the universities of Bologna and Padua, he attempted to return to England in 1275, in company with his sister Eleanor and in preparation for Eleanor's marriage to Llywelyn of Wales, to whom, years before, she had been betrothed by their father. But their homeward-bound ship was captured, and brother and sister taken into custody by Edward I. Eleanor was eventually released in 1278, after the first Welsh war, and went on to marry Llewelyn, with Edward's blessing; but she died in childbirth four years later. Amaury had been liberated in the previous year. He was in Paris in 1286, acting as the executor of his mother's will, made his own will at Montargis in 1289, and then possibly travelled to Italy again,[86] dying there about 1300. The flourish of titles displayed in his will – papal chaplain, treasurer of York, canon of Rouen, Evreux, London and Lincoln, rector of the church of St Wendron, by hereditary right earl of Leicester and Chester and steward of England[87] – was more a testimony to his father's former power and to his episcopal friendships than to the real expectations of this disappointed exile.

The two other surviving sons, Simon and Guy, became the most notorious. Simon left Kenilworth in November 1265, and after various adventures escaped abroad in the following year. Guy, wounded at Evesham, had also managed to escape to France. By 1268 both the brothers were in Italy, serving Charles of Anjou in the campaigns which led to his conquest of Sicily in the same year. Both were handsomely rewarded by Charles, who may have recognised his obligations towards the sons of one who had been his sworn brother,[88] and by 1270 Guy was acting as Charles's Vicar-General in Tuscany. On 13 March 1271, however, the reascent of the two brothers was cut short by one of the most infamous crimes in European history: Guy's murder, with Simon's collusion, of Henry of Almain, Richard of Cornwall's son and heir, who was set upon and stabbed to death by Guy while he was hearing mass in church at Viterbo. This was a passionate and probably unpremeditated act of revenge for Henry's desertion of Montfort in

---

[86] Bémont, *Montfort* (2nd edn), pp. 262–3, is the authority for Amaury's sojourn in Italy, but he cites no source and may simply be drawing an inference from *Flores Hist.*, iii, p. 67.

[87] Vatican Archives, Archivio Segreto Vaticano, AA. Arm I–XVIII, 123.

[88] I am very grateful to Dr Pierre Chaplais for this suggestion.

1263 and for the bloodshed at Evesham (though Henry had not been present there). 'I have taken my vengeance', said Guy, as he left the church, and, as the dying Henry cried for mercy, 'You had no mercy on my father and brothers', Guy replied. Simon died later in the same year, in a castle near Siena, 'like Cain, cursed by God, a wanderer and a fugitive'.[89] Guy, after a long imprisonment, took service again with Charles in 1281, but was captured during an Angevin attack on Sicily in 1287 and died in a Sicilian prison about 1291. For his crime Dante placed him among the murderers, in the seventh circle of Hell, submerged to the throat in a river of boiling blood:[90] a unique and infelicitous point of contact, if only a vicarious one, between the life of Simon de Montfort and the high culture of western Europe.

When Guy met his end there was one remaining survivor of the family in England: Gwenllian, the daughter of young Eleanor, born in 1282 to a mother whom she never knew.[91] Her mother's cousin, Edward I, had placed her as a baby with the nuns of Sempringham, and there she died, 'a full courteous' lady and an inmate of her house for 53 years, between 6 a.m. and 9 a.m. on 7 June 1337.[92] It was just over 107 years since the first coming of her grandfather to England. The scattered burial places of her family were a broken monument to his ambitions: her mother Eleanor at the Franciscan house of Llanfaes on Anglesey,[93] her grandmother with the nuns of St Antoine's in Paris,[94] her uncle Henry at Evesham, her other uncles in Tuscany and Sicily. The founder of the family's fortunes and misfortunes hardly had a grave in the country where he had fallen, and in his native France few besides the religious of Hautes-Bruyères remembered 'Earl Simon of Leicester, who died in England'.[95] But at the time of Gwenllian's death, on a summer morning in the quiet Lincolnshire countryside, all that was long in the past.

---

[89] *Flores Hist.*, iii, p. 22. The fullest account of the murder will be found in Blaauw, *The Barons' War*, pp. 342–3.

[90] *Inferno*, xii, 118–20. Cf. P. Toynbee, *A Dictionary of Proper Names and Notable Matters in the Works of Dante* (Oxford, 1898), p. 301.

[91] *Florentii Wigorniensis Monachi Chronicon ex Chronicis*, ed. B. Thorpe (2 vols., London, 1848–9), ii, p. 226.

[92] Robert Mannyng's additions to Langtoft's chronicle: Thomas Hearne, *Works*, iii: *Peter Langtoft's Chronicle* (London, 1810), p. 243. Cf. Powicke, *King Henry III*, pp. 684–5 (one of his most elegiac passages).

[93] *Flor. Wig. Chron.*, ii, p. 226.

[94] Or at least her heart: Bémont, *Montfort* (2nd edn), p. 259, n. 2.

[95] *Obituaires . . . de Sens*, ed. Molinier and Longnon, ii, p. 225.

Bibliography

1. MANUSCRIPT SOURCES

A. PUBLIC RECORD OFFICE

Chancery
c. 53 (Charter Rolls)
c. 56 (Confirmation Rolls)
c. 60 (Fine Rolls)
c. 61 (Gascon Rolls)
Duchy of Lancaster
DL. 25 (Ancient Deeds)
DL. 42 (Misc. Books)
Exchequer
E. 101 (King's Remembrancer, Accounts Various)
E. 132 (Transcripts of Deeds and Charters)
E. 159 (K.R. Memoranda Rolls)
E. 368 (L.T.R. Memoranda Rolls)
E. 372 (Pipe Rolls)
E. 403 (Issue Rolls)
Judicial Records
JUST. 1 (Eyre Rolls)
KB. 26 (Curia Regis Rolls)

B. BRITISH LIBRARY

Add. Ch. 47593
Cotton MSS:
    Cleopatra D. III (Hailes chronicle)
    Faustina B. VI, part 1 (Croxden annals)
    Nero C. XII (Burton Lazars cartulary)
    Otho D. III (St Albans cartulary)
    Vespasian E. XXIII (Durford cartulary)
Egerton 3789 (Robert Glover's collections)
Harley 4714 (Biddlesden cartulary)

C. BODLEIAN LIBRARY, OXFORD

Dugdale 15
Dugdale 20
Laud Misc. 625 (Leicester cartulary)
Rawlinson B. 336 (St Radegund's, Bradsole, cartulary)
Rawlinson B. 461 (Transcripts of St Radegund's charters)

D. GLOUCESTERSHIRE COUNTY RECORD OFFICE

D.225/T/7 (Denison Jones deeds)

E. HAMPSHIRE COUNTY RECORD OFFICE

Photocopy Accessions, Ph. 62c.

F. BIBLIOTHÈQUE NATIONALE, PARIS

Clairambault 1021 (Montfort's confraternity letters from St Albans).
Clairambault 1188 (Montfort family documents).

G. VATICAN ARCHIVES

Archivio Segreto Vaticano, AA. Arm. I–XVIII, 123 (Will of Amaury de Montfort).

2. PRINTED SOURCES

Abbreviatio Placitorum (Record Comm., 1811).
Acta Sanctorum: Octobris, Vol. i (Antwerp-Brussels, 1643).
Anglo-Norman Political Songs, ed. I. S. T. Aspin (Anglo-Norman Text Soc., 1953).
Annales Cestrienses, ed. R. C. Christie (Lancashire and Cheshire Rec. Soc., xiv, 1886).
Annales Londonienses, Chronicles of the Reigns of Edward I and Edward II, ed. W. Stubbs (Rolls ser., 1882).
Annales Monasterii de Burton, 1004–1263, Ann. Mon., i.
Annales Monasterii de Oseneia, 1016–1347, Ann. Mon., iv.
Annales Monasterii de Theokesberia, Ann. Mon., i.
Annales Monasterii de Waverleia, A.D. 1–1291, Ann. Mon., ii.
Annales Monasterii de Wintonia, 519–1277, Ann. Mon., ii.
Annales Prioratus de Dunstaplia, A.D. 1–1297, Ann. Mon., iii.
Annales Prioratus de Wigornia, A.D. 1–1377, Ann. Mon., iv.
The Beauchamp Cartulary Charters, 1100–1268, ed. E. Mason (Pipe Roll Soc., n.s. xliii, 1980).

Bond, E. A., 'Historiola de Pietate Regis Henrici III', *Archaeological Journal*, xvii (1860).

The Book of Fees, Commonly Called Testa de Nevill (3 vols., H.M.S.O., 1920-31).

Bracton on the Laws and Customs of England, ed. S. E. Thorne (4 vols., Cambridge, Mass., 1968-77).

The Burton Lazars Cartulary, ed. T. Bourne and D. Marcombe (Nottingham, 1987).

Calendar of Ancient Correspondence Concerning Wales, ed. J. G. Edwards (Cardiff, 1935).

Calendar of Charter Rolls (H.M.S.O., 1916–).

Calendar of Inquisitions Miscellaneous, i, *1219–1307* (H.M.S.O., 1916).

Calendar of Inquisitions Post Mortem (H.M.S.O., 1904–).

Calendar of Liberate Rolls (H.M.S.O., 1916–).

Calendar of Papal Letters, i, *1198–1304* (H.M.S.O., 1893).

Calendar of Patent Rolls (H.M.S.O., 1906–).

Calendar of the Plea Rolls of the Exchequer of the Jews, ed. J. M. Rigg and others (5 vols., Jewish Historical Soc. of England, 1905–72).

Cam, H. M. and Jacob, E. F., 'Notes on an English Cluniac Chronicle', *EHR*, xliv (1929).

Cartulaire de l'abbaye de Porrois, ed. A. de Dion (Paris, 1903).

Cartulaire Normand de Philippe-Auguste, Louis VIII, Saint Louis et Philippe le Hardi, ed. L. Delisle (Caen, 1882).

A Cartulary of Creake Abbey, ed. A. L. Bedingfield (Norfolk Rec. Soc., xxv, 1966).

The Charters of the Anglo-Norman Earls of Chester, c. 1071–1237, ed. G. Barraclough (Lancashire and Cheshire Rec. Soc., cxxvi, 1988).

The Chartulary of the High Church of Chichester, ed. W. D. Peckham (Sussex Rec. Soc., xlvi, 1946).

Chronica de Mailros, ed. J. Stevenson (Bannantyne Club, 1835).

Chronica Johannis de Oxenedes, ed. H. Ellis (Rolls ser., 1859).

The Chronicle of Bury St Edmunds, 1212–1301, ed. A. Gransden (London, 1964).

The Chronicle of Melrose, introduced by A. O. and M. O. Anderson (London, 1936).

The Chronicle of the Monastery of Abingdon, ed. J. O. Halliwell (Reading, 1844).

The Chronicle of Walter of Guisborough, ed. H. Rothwell (Camden ser., lxxxix, 1957).

The Chronicle of William de Rishanger of the Barons' Wars, ed. J. O. Halliwell (Camden soc., 1840).

Chronicon Abbatie de Parco Lude, ed. E. Venables (Lincs. Rec. Soc., i, 1891).

Chronicon de Lanercost, ed. J. Stevenson (Maitland Club, 1839).

Chronicon vulgo dictum Chronicon Thomae Wykes, 1066–1288, Ann. Mon., iv.

Close Rolls, Henry III (H.M.S.O., 1902–).

Close Rolls (Supplementary) of the Reign of Henry III, 1244–66 (H.M.S.O., 1975).

Comptes Royaux (1285–1311), ii, ed. R. Fawtier (Paris, 1954).

A Continuation of William of Newburgh's 'History' to A.D. 1298, Chronicles of the Reigns of Stephen, Henry II and Richard I, ed. R. Howlett (4 vols., Rolls ser., 1884–9), ii.

Councils and Synods, ii, *1205–1313*, ed. F. M. Powicke and C. R. Cheney (2 vols., Oxford, 1964).

Curia Regis Rolls (H.M.S.O., 1922–).

De Adventu Fratrum Minorum in Angliam: The Chronicle of Thomas of Eccleston, ed. A. G. Little (Manchester, 1951).

De Antiquis Legibus Liber. Cronica Maiorum et Vicecomitum Londoniarum, ed. T. Stapleton (Camden Soc., 1846).

A Descriptive Catalogue of Ancient Deeds (6 vols., H.M.S.O., 1890–1915).

Diplomatic Documents Preserved in the Public Record Office, i, *1101–1272*, ed. P. Chaplais (H.M.S.O., 1964).

Documents of the Baronial Movement of Reform and Rebellion, 1258–1267, ed. R. F. Treharne and I. J. Sanders (Oxford, 1973).

Dorset Fines, ed. E. A. and G. S. Fry (Dorset Records, x, 1910).

Dugdale, W., *Monasticon Anglicanum*, ed. J. Caley, H. Ellis and B. Bandinel (6 vols. in 8, London, 1817–30).

Excerpta e Rotulis Finium, 1216–72, ed. C. Roberts (2 vols., Record Comm., 1835–6).

Feudal Aids (6 vols., H.M.S.O., 1899–1920).

Florentii Wigorniensis Monachi Chronicon ex Chronicis, ed. B. Thorpe (2 vols., London, 1848–9).

Flores Historiarum, ed. H. R. Luard (3 vols., Rolls ser., 1890).

Foedera, Conventiones, Litterae et Acta Publica, ed. T. Rymer, new edn, Vol. i, part i, ed. A. Clark and F. Holbrooke (Record Comm., 1816).

Fratris Gerardi de Fracheto, *Vitae Fratrum Ordinis Praedicatorum*, ed. B. M. Reichert, i (Monumenta Ordinis Fratrum Praedicatorum Historica, Rome and Stuttgart, 1897).

Gieben, S., 'Robert Grosseteste at the Papal Curia, Lyons, 1250: Edition of the Documents', *Collectanea Franciscana*, 51 (1971).

Guillaume de Nangis, 'Vie de St Louis', and 'Chronicon', *Recueil des Historiens des Gaules*, xx (Paris, 1740).

Heidemann, J., *Papst Clemens IV: Das Vorleben des Papstes und sein Legationregister* (Münster, 1903).

Historical Manuscripts Commission:
 Fourteenth Report (1896), Appendix 8.
 MSS of the late R. R. Hastings, i (1928).

The Historical Works of Gervase of Canterbury, ed. W. Stubbs (2 vols., Rolls ser., 1880).

Hunt, R. W., 'Verses on the Life of Robert Grosseteste', *Medievalia et Humanistica*, n.s. i (1970).

Layettes du Trésor des Chartes, ed. A. Teulet, H.-F. Delaborde and E. Berger (5 vols., Paris, 1863–1909).

Maitland, F. W., 'A Song on the Death of Simon de Montfort', *EHR*, xi (1896).

Manners and Household Expenses of England in the Thirteenth and Fifteenth Centuries, ed. T. H. Turner (Roxburghe Club, 1841).

Manuscripts at Oxford: An Exhibition in Memory of Richard William Hunt (1908–1979), ed. A. C. de la Mare and B. C. Barker-Benfield (Oxford, 1980).

Matthaei Parisiensis, Monachi Sancti Albani, Chronica Majora, ed. H. R. Luard (7 vols., Rolls ser., 1872–83).

Matthaei Parisiensis, Monachi Sancti Albani, Historia Anglorum, ed. F. Madden (3 vols., Rolls ser., 1866–69).

Memoranda Roll 16–17 Henry III, ed. R. A. Brown (H.M.S.O., 1991).

The Metrical Chronicle of Robert of Gloucester, ed. W. A. Wright (2 vols., Rolls ser., 1887).

Ministers' Accounts of the Earldom of Cornwall, 1296–97, ed. L. M. Midgley (2 vols., Camden 3rd ser., lxvi, lxviii, 1942).

Monumenta Franciscana, ed. J. S. Brewer and R. Howlett (2 vols., Rolls ser., 1858–82).

Munimenta Gildhallae Londoniensis, ed. H. T. Riley (4 vols. in 3, Rolls ser., 1859–62).

Necrologe de l'Abbaie de Notre Dame de Port-Roial des Champs (Amsterdam, 1723).

Nicholas Trivet, *Annales*, ed. T. Hog (London, 1845).

Nicolas, N. H., *Testamenta Vetusta* (2 vols., London, 1826).

Obituaires de la Province de Sens, ed. A. Molinier and A. Longnon (4 vols., Paris, 1902–23).

Odoricus Raynaldus, *Annales Ecclesiastici*, iii (Lucca, 1748).

Les Olim, ed. A. Beugnot (3 vols. in 4, Paris, 1839–44).

Ordonnances des Roys de France de la Troisième Race, ed. E. Laurière, i (Paris, 1723).

Oriel College Records, ed. C. L. Shadwell and H. E. Salter (Oxford Hist. Soc., lxxxv, 1926).

Patent Rolls of the Reign of Henry III (H.M.S.O., 1901–3).

Petrum Vallium Sarnaii Monachi, Hystoria Albigensis, ed. P. Guébin and E. Lyon (2 vols., Société de l'Histoire de France, 1926–29).

Pipe Roll 9 John, ed. D. M. Stenton (Pipe Roll Soc., n.s., xxii, 1946).

Pipe Roll 12 John, ed. C. F. Slade (Pipe Roll Soc., n.s., xxvi, 1951).

The Political Songs of England, ed. T. Wright (Camden Soc., 1839).

Records of the Borough of Leicester, 1103–1603, ed. M. Bateson (3 vols., Cambridge, 1899–1905).

Recueil d'Actes Relatifs a l'Administration des Rois d'Angleterre en Guyenne au XIIIᵉ Siècle: Recognitiones Feodorum in Aquitania, ed. C. Bémont (Paris, 1914).

The Register of Eudes of Rouen, ed. J. F. O'Sullivan (New York and London, 1964).

Les Registres de Gregoire IX, ed. L. Auray and others (4 vols., Paris, 1896–1955).

Les Registres d'Innocent IV, ed. E. Berger (4 vols., Paris, 1881–90).

The Registrum Antiquissimum of the Cathedral Church of Lincoln, ed. C. W. Foster and K. Major (10 vols., Lincs. Rec. Soc., 1931–73).

Registrum Malmesburiense, ed. J. S. Brewer (2 vols., Rolls ser., 1879–80).

Registrum Ricardi de Swinfield Episcopi Herefordensis, ed. W. W. Capes (Canterbury and York Soc., 1909).

'Robert of Boston', *Historiae Anglicanae Scriptores Varii*, ed. J. Sparke (London, 1723).

Roberti Grosseteste Episcopi Lincolniensis, 1235–53, Epistolae, ed. H. R. Luard (Rolls ser., 1861).

Rôles Gascons, ed. Francisque-Michel and C. Bémont (4 vols., Paris, 1885–1906).

The Roll and Writ File of the Berkshire Eyre of 1248, ed. M. T. Clanchy (Selden Soc., xc, 1973).

Rolls of Arms: Henry III, ed. H. S. London (London, 1967).

Rotuli Hundredorum (2 vols., Record Comm., 1812–18).

Rotuli Litterarum Clausarum, ed. T. D. Hardy (2 vols., Record Comm., 1833–34).

Rotuli Selecti, ed. J. Hunter (Record Comm., 1834).

Royal and Other Historical Letters Illustrative of the Reign of Henry III, ed. W. W. Shirley (2 vols., Rolls ser., 1862–6).

Select Pleas, Starrs and Other Records of the Jewish Exchequer, ed. J. M. Rigg (Selden Soc., xv, 1901).

Sir Christopher Hatton's Book of Seals, ed. L. C. Loyd and D. M. Stenton (Oxford, 1950).

Snappe's Formulary, ed. H. E. Salter (Oxford Hist. Soc., lxxx, 1924).

The Song of Lewes, ed. C. L. Kingsford (Oxford, 1890).

The St Albans Chronicle, 1406–1420, ed. V. H. Galbraith (Oxford, 1937).

Statuta Antiqua Universitatis Oxoniensis, ed. S. Gibson (Oxford, 1931).

Statuta Capitulorum Generalium Ordinis Cisterciensis, ed. J. M. Canivez, ii (Louvain, 1934).

Sussex Fines, i, ed. L. F. Salzmann (Sussex Rec. Soc., ii, 1903).

Taxatio Ecclesiastica Papae Nicolai IV (Record Comm., 1802).

Thomas Hearne, *Works*, iii: *Peter Langtoft's Chronicle* (London, 1810).

Three Early Assize Rolls of the County of Northumberland, ed. W. Page (Surtees Soc., lxxxviii, 1891).

Treaty Rolls, i, *1234–1325* (H.M.S.O., 1955).

'Vita Sancti Ludovico auctore Gaufrido de Belloloco', *Recueil des Historiens des Gaules*, xx (Paris, 1740).

Walter of Henley and Other Treatises on Estate Management and Accounting, ed. D. Oschinsky (Oxford, 1971).

Willelmi Rishanger Chronica et Annales, ed. H. T. Riley (Rolls ser., 1865).

Wiltshire Inquisitions Post Mortem, Henry III–Edward I, ed. E. A. Fry (British Record Soc., 1908).

3. SECONDARY SOURCES

Altschul, M., *A Baronial Family in Medieval England: The Clares, 1217–1314* (Baltimore, 1965).

Baldwin, J. W., *Masters, Princes and Merchants: The Social Views of Peter the Chanter and His Circle* (2 vols., Princeton, 1970).

Balme and Lelaidier, *Cartulaire ou Histoire Diplomatique de Saint Dominique* (2 vols., Paris, 1893–97).

Bémont, C., *Simon de Montfort* (1st edn, Paris, 1884).

Simon de Montfort, trans. E. F. Jacob (2nd edn, Oxford, 1930).

Blaauw, W., *The Barons' War* (2nd edn, London, 1871).

Boutaric, E., *Saint Louis et Alfonse de Poitiers* (Paris, 1870).

Boyle, L. E., '*E Cathena et Carcere*: The Imprisonment of Amaury de Montfort, 1276', *Medieval Learning and Literature: Essays Presented to R. W. Hunt*, ed. J. J. G. Alexander and M. Gibson (Oxford, 1976).

Brand, P. A., 'The Contribution of the Period of Baronial Reform and Rebellion to the Development of the Common Law in England' (Oxford D.Phil. thesis, 1974).

'The Drafting of Legislation in Mid-Thirteenth-Century England', *Parliamentary History*, 9 (1990).

The Origins of the English Legal Profession (Oxford, 1992).

Brown, R. A., Colvin, H. M. and Taylor, A. J., *The History of the King's Works: The Middle Ages* (2 vols., London, 1963).

Burton, D. W., 'Politics, Propaganda and Public Opinion in the Reigns of Henry III and Edward I' (Oxford D.Phil. thesis, 1985).

Cam, H. M., *Studies in the Hundred Rolls* (Oxford, 1921).

Carolus-Barré, 'La grande ordonnance de 1254', *Septième Centenaire de la Mort de Saint Louis* (Paris, 1976).

Carpenter, D. A., 'The Decline of the Curial Sheriff in England, 1194–1258', *EHR*, 91 (1976).

'The Fall of Hubert de Burgh', *Journal of British Studies*, xix (1980).

'St Thomas Cantilupe: His Political Career', *St Thomas Cantilupe, Bishop of Hereford*, ed. M. Jancey (Hereford, 1982).

'What Happened in 1258?', *War and Government in the Middle Ages: Essays in Honour of J. O. Prestwich*, ed. J. Gillingham and J. Holt (Woodbridge, 1984).

'King, Magnates, and Society: The Personal Rule of King Henry III, 1234–58', *Speculum*, 60 (1985).

'Simon de Montfort and the Mise of Lewes', *BIHR*, lviii (1985).

'The Lord Edward's Oath to Aid and Counsel Simon de Montfort, 15 October 1259', *BIHR*, 58 (1985).

'The Gold Treasure of King Henry III', *TCE*, i (1986).

The Battles of Lewes and Evesham, 1264/65 (Keele, 1987).

'Chancellor Ralph de Neville and Plans of Baronial Reform, 1215–58', *TCE*, ii (1988).

The Minority of Henry III (London, 1990).

'Simon de Montfort: The First Leader of a Political Movement in English History', *History*, 76 (1991).

'King Henry III's "Statute" against Aliens: July 1263', *EHR*, 107 (1992).

'English Peasants in Politics, 1258–67', *Past and Present*, 136 (1992).

'Peter de Montfort', 'Thomas fitz Thomas', *The Dictionary of National Biography: Missing Persons*, ed. C. S. Nicholls (1993).

Catto, J. I., 'Religion and the English Nobility in the Later Fourteenth Century', *History and Imagination: Essays in Honour of H. R. Trevor-Roper*, ed. H. Lloyd-Jones, V. Pearl and B. Worden (London, 1981).

'Theology and Theologians, 1220–1320', *The History of the University of Oxford*, Vol. 1: *The Early Oxford Schools*, ed. J. I. Catto (Oxford, 1984).

Chaplais, P., 'The Making of the Treaty of Paris (1259) and the Royal Style', *EHR*, 67 (1952).

Chapotin, M.-D., *Histoire des Dominicains de la Province de France* (Rouen, 1898).

Cheney, C. R., *Episcopal Visitation of Monasteries in the Thirteenth Century* (Manchester, 1931).

English Synodalia of the Thirteenth Century (Oxford, 1941).

Medieval Texts and Studies (Oxford, 1973).

Clanchy, M. T., *From Memory to Written Record: England, 1066–1307* (London, 1979).

England and its Rulers, 1066–1272 (Oxford, 1983).

Cockayne, G. E., *Complete Peerage of England, Scotland, Ireland, Great Britain and the United Kingdom*, ed. V. Gibbs and others (12 vols. in 13, 1912–59).

Colvin, H. M., 'Holme Lacy: An Episcopal Manor and its Tenants in the Twelfth and Thirteenth Centuries', *Medieval Studies Presented to Rose Graham*, ed. V. Ruffer and A. J. Taylor (Oxford, 1950).

Coss, P., *Lordship, Knighthood and Locality* (Cambridge, 1991).

Cox, D. C., *The Battle of Evesham: A New Account* (Evesham, 1988).

'The Battle of Evesham in the Evesham Chronicle', *Hist. Res.*, 62 (1989).

Cox, E. L., *The Eagles of Savoy* (Princeton, 1974).

Crook, D., *The Records of the General Eyre* (London, 1982).

Crouch, D., *The Beaumont Twins* (Cambridge, 1986).

William Marshal (Harlow, 1990).

The Image of Aristocracy in Britain, 1000–1300 (London, 1992).

Davies, R. R., *Lordship and Society in the March of Wales, 1282–1400* (Oxford, 1978).

Conquest, Coexistence and Change: Wales, 1063–1415 (Oxford, 1987).

Denholm-Young, N., *Richard of Cornwall* (Oxford, 1947).

'Documents of the Barons' Wars', 'The Winchester-Hyde Chronicle', *Collected Papers* (Cardiff, 1969).

Dondaine, A., 'Guillaume Peyraut: Vie et Oeuvres', *Archivum Fratrum Praedicatorum*, 18 (1948).

Donovan, C., *The de Brailes Hours: Shaping the Book of Hours in Thirteenth-Century Oxford* (London, 1991).

Douais, C., *Les Frères Prêcheurs en Gascogne au XIIIme et au XIVme Siècle* (Paris and Auch, 1885).

Dugdale, W., *The Baronage of England* (2 vols., London, 1675–6).

Dunbabin, J., 'Government', *The Cambridge History of Medieval Political Thought c. 350–1450*, ed. J. H. Burns (Cambridge, 1988).

'The Lyon Dominicans: A Double Act', *Monastic Studies*, ed. J. Loades (Bangor, 1990).

Review of Swanson, *John of Wales*, *Speculum*, 67 (1992).

Duncan, A. A. M., *Scotland: The Making of the Kingdom* (Edinburgh, 1975).

Eales, R., 'Henry III and the End of the Norman Earldom of Chester', *TCE*, i (1986).

Ellis, J., 'Gaston de Béarn: A Study in Anglo-Gascon Relations, 1229–30' (Oxford D.Phil. thesis, 1952).

Emden, A. B., *A Biographical Register of the University of Oxford to A.D. 1500* (3 vols., Oxford, 1957–9).

Farmer, S., 'Persuasive Voices: Clerical Images of Medieval Wives', *Speculum*, 61 (1986).

Farnham, G. F. and Thompson, A. H., 'The Manor of Noseley', *Trans. Leics. Arch. Soc.*, 12 (1921–2).

Farrer, W., *Honors and Knights' Fees* (3 vols., London and Manchester, 1923–5).

Finucane, R. C., *Miracles and Pilgrims* (London, 1977).

Fox, L., 'The Honor of Leicester: A Study in Descent and Administration' (Manchester M.A. thesis, 1938).

'The Honor and Earldom of Leicester: Origins and Descent, 1066–1399', *EHR*, 54 (1939).

Frame, R., 'Ireland and the Barons' Wars', *TCE*, 1 (1986).

Gallia Christiana, xii (Paris, 1770).

Gavrilovitch, M., *Étude sur le Traité de Paris de 1259* (Paris, 1899).

Gibbs, M. and Lang, J., *Bishops and Reform, 1215–1271* (Oxford, 1934).

Gilson, J. P., 'The Parliament of 1264', *EHR*, 16 (1901).

Given-Wilson, C., *The Royal Household and the King's Affinity* (New Haven and London, 1986).

Goering, J. and Mantello, F. A. C., 'The Early Penitential Writings of Robert Grosseteste', *Recherches de Théologie ancienne et médiévale*, 54 (1987).

Golob, P. E., 'The Ferrers Earls of Derby: A Study of the Honor of Tutbury (1066–1279)' (Cambridge Ph.D. thesis, 1984).

Gransden, A., *Historical Writing in England, c. 550 to c. 1307* (London, 1974).

Historical Writing in England, ii: *c. 1307 to the Early Sixteenth Century* (London, 1982).

Hackett, M. B., 'The University as a Corporate Body', *The History of the University of Oxford*, Vol. 1: *The Early Oxford Schools*, ed. J. I. Catto (Oxford, 1984).

Harcourt, L. W. V., *His Grace the Steward and Trial of Peers* (London, 1907).

Henderson, C., *Essays in Cornish History* (Oxford, 1935).

Hinnebusch, W., *The Early English Friars Preachers* (Rome, 1951).

The History of the Dominican Order, i (New York, 1966).

A History of Northumberland (15 vols., Newcastle, 1893–1940), ii, ed. E. Bateson.

A History of York Minster, ed. G. Aylmer and R. Cant (Oxford, 1977).

Holt, J. C., *The Northerners* (Oxford, 1961).

'The Prehistory of Parliament', *The English Parliament in the Middle Ages*, ed. R. G. Davies and J. H. Denton (Manchester, 1981).

Jackson, P., 'The End of Hohenstaufen Rule in Syria', *BIHR*, 59 (1986).

Jacob, E. F., 'A Proposal for Arbitration between Simon de Montfort and Henry III in 1260', *EHR*, 37 (1922).

Studies in the Period of Baronial Reform and Rebellion (Oxford, 1925).
Johnstone, H., 'Poor Relief in the Royal Households of Thirteenth-Century England', *Speculum*, 4 (1929).
Jordan, W. C., *Louis IX and the Challenge of the Crusade* (Princeton, 1979).
Knowles, C. H., 'The Disinherited, 1265–80: A Political and Social Study of the Supporters of Simon de Montfort and the Resettlement after the Barons' War' (Univ. of Wales Aberystwyth Ph.D. thesis, 1959).
Simon de Montfort, 1265–1965 (London, 1965).
'The Resettlement of England after the Barons' War, 1264–67', *TRHS*, 5th ser., 32 (1982).
Labarge, M. W., *Simon de Montfort* (London, 1962).
Saint Louis (London, 1968).
Gascony: England's First Colony, 1204–1453 (London, 1980).
Lawrence, C. H., *St Edmund of Abingdon* (Oxford, 1960).
'The University of Oxford and the Chronicle of the Barons' Wars', *EHR*, 95 (1980).
'The Letters of Adam Marsh and the Franciscan School at Oxford', *Journal of Ecclesiastical History*, 42 (1991).
Legge, M. D., *Anglo-Norman Literature and its Background* (Oxford, 1963).
Le Neve, J., *Fasti Ecclesiae Anglicanae, 1066–1300*, i: *St Paul's London*, comp. D. E. Greenway (London, 1968).
iii: *Lincoln*, comp. D. E. Greenway (London, 1977).
Little, A. G., *Studies in English Franciscan History* (Manchester, 1917).
Franciscan Papers, Lists and Documents (Manchester, 1943).
Lloyd, J. E., *A History of Wales from the Earliest Times to the Edwardian Conquest* (2 vols., 3rd edn, London, 1939).
Lloyd, S., *English Society and the Crusade, 1216–1307* (Oxford, 1988).
Lodge, E. C., *Gascony under English Rule* (London, 1926).
Lunt, W. E., *Financial Relations of the Papacy with England to 1327* (Cambridge, Mass., 1939).
Maddicott, J. R., *Thomas of Lancaster, 1307–22* (Oxford, 1970).
'The Mise of Lewes, 1264', *EHR*, 98 (1983).
'Magna Carta and the Local Community, 1215–59', *Past and Present*, 102 (1984).
'Edward I and the Lessons of Baronial Reform: Local Government, 1258–80', *TCE*, i (1986).
'The Crusade Taxation of 1268–70 and the Development of Parliament', *TCE*, ii (1988).
Maitland, F. W., 'The History of Marriage, Jewish and Christian', *Collected Papers*, ed. H. A. L. Fisher (3 vols., Cambridge, 1911), iii.
McEvoy, J., *The Philosophy of Robert Grosseteste* (Oxford, 1982).
Meekings, C. A. F., *Studies in 13th Century Justice and Administration* (London, 1981).
Mills, M. H., '"Adventus Vicecomitum", 1258–72', *EHR*, 34 (1921).
Moorman, J. R. H., *A History of the Franciscan Order* (Oxford, 1968).
Morris, W. A., *The Medieval English Sheriff to 1300* (Manchester, 1927).

Murray, A., *Reason and Society in the Middle Ages* (Oxford, 1978).

'Confession as an Historical Source in the Thirteenth Century', *The Writing of History in the Middle Ages. Essays Presented to R. W. Southern*, ed. R. H. C. Davis and J. M. Wallace-Hadrill (Oxford, 1981).

Excommunication and Conscience in the Middle Ages (London, 1991).

Nichols, J., *The History and Antiquities of the County of Leicester* (4 vols. in 8, London, 1795–1815).

Orpen, G. H., *Ireland under the Normans* (4 vols., Oxford, 1911–20).

Painter, S., 'The Crusade of Theobald of Champagne and Richard of Cornwall', *A History of the Crusades*, ed. K. M. Setton (5 vols., Madison, Wisconsin, 1969–), ii.

Pape, T., *Medieval Newcastle-under-Lyme*, (Manchester, 1928).

Petit-Dutaillis, C., *Étude sur la Vie et le Règne de Louis VIII (1187–1226)* (Paris, 1894).

Plucknett, T. F. T., *The Legislation of Edward I* (Oxford, 1949).

Pollock, F. and Maitland, F. W., *The History of English Law* (2 vols., 2nd edn., Cambridge, 1952).

Powicke, F. M., 'Loretta Countess of Leicester', *Historical Essays in Honour of James Tait*, ed. J. G. Edwards, V. H. Galbraith and E. F. Jacob (Manchester, 1933).

'Guy de Montfort (1265–71)', *TRHS*, 4th ser., 18 (1935).

'The Archbishop of Rouen, John de Harcourt, and Simon de Montfort in 1260', *EHR*, 51 (1936).

King Henry III and the Lord Edward (2 vols., Oxford, 1947).

The Loss of Normandy (2nd edn, Manchester, 1961).

Prestwich, M., *Edward I* (London, 1988).

Quick, J. A., 'Government and Society in Kent, 1232–80' (Oxford D.Phil. thesis, 1986).

Raedts, P., *Richard Rufus of Cornwall and the Tradition of Oxford Theology* (Oxford, 1987).

Rhein, A., *La Seigneurie de Montfort en Iveline* (Versailles, 1910).

Richard, J., *St Louis: Crusader King of France*, ed. S. Lloyd (Cambridge, 1992).

Richardson, H. G. and Sayles, G. O., 'The Provisions of Oxford, 1258', *Bull. of the John Rylands Library*, 17 (1933), reprinted in Richardson and Sayles, *The English Parliament in the Middle Ages* (London, 1981).

Ridgeway, H., 'The Politics of the English Royal Court, 1247–65, with Special Reference to the Role of Aliens' (Oxford D.Phil. thesis, 1983).

'The Lord Edward and the Provisions of Oxford (1258): A Study in Faction', *TCE*, i (1986).

'King Henry III and the "Aliens", 1236–72', *TCE*, ii (1988).

'King Henry III's Grievances against the Council in 1261', *Hist. Res.*, 61 (1988).

'Foreign Favourites and Henry III's Problems of Patronage, 1247–58', *EHR*, 104 (1989).

'William de Valence and his *Familiares*', *Hist. Res.*, 65 (1992).

Riley-Smith, J., *The Feudal Nobility and the Kingdom of Jerusalem* (London, 1973).

Robert Grosseteste: Scholar and Bishop, ed. D. A. Callus (Oxford, 1955).
Roth, C., *The Jews of Medieval Oxford* (Oxford Hist. Soc., n.s., ix, 1951).
A History of the Jews in England (3rd edn, Oxford, 1974).
Sanders, I. J., *English Baronies* (Oxford, 1960).
Sayles, G. O., *The Functions of the Medieval Parliament of England* (London, 1988).
Sheehan, M. M., *The Will in Medieval England* (Toronto, 1963).
Simpson, G. G., 'The *Familia* of Roger de Quincy, Earl of Winchester and Constable of Scotland', *Essays on the Nobility of Medieval Scotland*, ed. K. J. Stringer (Edinburgh, 1985).
Singer, D. W., *Catalogue of Latin and Vernacular Alchemical Manuscripts in Great Britain and Ireland* (3 vols., Brussels, 1928–30).
Smalley, B., *The Study of the Bible in the Middle Ages* (3rd edn, Oxford, 1983).
Southern, R. W., *Robert Grosseteste: The Growth of an English Mind in Medieval Europe* (Oxford, 1986).
Spufford, P., *Handbook of Medieval Exchange* (London, 1986).
Stacey, R. C., *Politics, Policy and Finance under Henry III, 1216–45* (Oxford, 1987).
'1240–60: A Watershed in Anglo-Jewish Relations?', *Hist. Res.*, 61 (1988).
'Crusades, Crusaders and the Baronial *Gravamina* of 1263–54', *TCE*, iii (1991).
Stevenson, F. S., *Robert Grosseteste, Bishop of Lincoln* (London, 1899).
Stewart-Brown, R., 'The End of the Norman Earldom of Chester', *EHR*, 35 (1920).
Strayer, J. R., *The Administration of Normandy under St Louis* (Cambridge, Mass., 1932).
Stringer, K. J., *Earl David of Huntingdon, 1152–1219* (Edinburgh, 1985).
Stubbs, W., *The Constitutional History of England* (3 vols., 5th edn, Oxford, 1891–98).
Sumption, J., *The Albigensian Crusade* (London, 1978).
Swanson, J., *John of Wales* (Cambridge, 1989).
Thompson, A. H., *The Abbey of St Mary of the Meadows, Leicester* (Leicester, 1949).
Tout, T. F., *Chapters in the Administrative History of Medieval England* (6 vols., Manchester, 1920–33).
'Wales and the March in the Barons' Wars', *Collected Papers* (3 vols., Manchester, 1932–34), ii.
Trabut-Cussac, J. P., *L'Administration Anglaise en Gascogne sous Henry III et Edouard I de 1254 à 1307* (Geneva, 1972).
Treharne, R. F., 'The Mise of Amiens, 23 January 1264', *Studies in Medieval History Presented to F. M. Powicke*, ed. R. W. Hunt, W. A. Pantin and R. W. Southern (Oxford, 1948).
The Baronial Plan of Reform, 1258–63 (2nd edn, Manchester, 1971).
'The Personal Role of Simon de Montfort in the Period of Baronial Reform and Rebellion, 1258–65', addendum to *Baronial Plan*.
'The Battle of Northampton, 5th April 1264', *Simon de Montfort and Baronial Reform: Thirteenth-Century Essays*, ed. E. B. Fryde (London, 1986).
Tyerman, C., *England and the Crusades, 1095–1588* (Chicago, 1988).
Vale, M., *The Angevin Legacy and the Hundred Years War* (Oxford, 1990).

Vaughan, R., *Matthew Paris* (Cambridge, 1958).
Victoria County History: Hampshire, iv, ed. W. Page (London, 1911).
   Oxfordshire, iv, ed. A. Crossley (Oxford, 1979).
   Staffordshire, viii, ed. J. G. Jenkins (London, 1963).
   Warwickshire, iii, ed. P. Styles (London, 1945).
Vincent, N. C., 'Simon de Montfort's First Quarrel with King Henry III', *TCE*, iv (1992).
   'Jews, Poitevins and the Bishop of Winchester, 1231–34', *Christianity and Judaism*, ed. D. Wood (Studies in Church History, Vol. 29, Oxford, 1992).
Wade, M. M. (Labarge), 'The Personal Quarrels of Simon de Montfort and his Wife with Henry III of England' (Oxford B.Litt. thesis, 1939).
Wait, H., 'The Household and Resources of the Lord Edward, 1239–72' (Oxford D.Phil. thesis, 1988).
Williams, D., 'Simon de Montfort and his Adherents', *England in the Thirteenth Century: Proceedings of the 1984 Harlaxton Symposium*, ed. W. M. Ormrod (Grantham, 1985).
Williams, G. A., *Medieval London: From Commune to Capital* (London, 1963).
Wilshire, L. E., *Boniface of Savoy, Carthusian and Archbishop of Canterbury, 1207–1270* (Salzburg, 1977).
Wood, M. A. E. (Mrs Green), *Lives of the Princesses of England* (6 vols., London, 1849–55).
Wordsworth, C. and Littlehales, H., *The Old Service-Books of the English Church* (2nd edn, London, 1910).
Yeatman, J. P., *The Early Genealogical History of the House of Arundell* (London, 1882).
York Minster Fasti, i, ed. C. T. Clay (Yorks. Arch. Soc., Record Ser., cxxiii, 1958).
Zerner, M., 'L'épouse de Simon de Montfort et la croisade albigeoise', *Femmes – Mariages – Lignages, XIIe–XIVe Siècles, Mélanges offerts à Georges Duby*, ed. J. Dufournet, A. Joris and P. Toubert (Brussels, 1992).

Index

Persons are listed by surname, except in the case of major figures (e.g. Richard of Cornwall), where convention dictates otherwise. M. = Simon de Montfort, the subject of this book; H. = King Henry III. In the entries for Montfort's family, the relationships denoted are those to Montfort himself. In some long sequences of undifferentiated entries, page numbers in **bold** have been used to indicate the main discussions.

parliaments and great councils (*cont.*)
  particular meetings: March 1232, 12; Oct. 1234,
    18; Feb. 1235, 22; Jan. 1242, 31, 36; Nov.
    1244, 36; Feb. 1245, 36; July 1248, 125;
    April 1249, 148; May 1252, 115–17, 147;
    Oct. 1252, 119–20, 125; May 1253, 120,
    148; May 1254, 139, 147, 351; April 1255,
    125, 148; Oct. 1255, 144; March 1257, 125;
    April 1258, 146, 152–4; June 1258
    (Oxford), 154, 156–63, 170, 354; Oct.
    1258, 165; Feb. 1259, 178–81, 219; May
    1259, 181; Oct. 1259, 184–6, 360; Feb.
    1260, 193, 195–7, 359; April 1260, 195;
    Oct. 1260, 200–3, 360; Feb. 1261, 207,
    211, 360; Sept. 1261 (St Albans/Windsor),
    213, 215, 360; Oct. 1262, 219; Sept. 1263,
    242–3; Oct. 1263, 244; June 1264, 284–9,
    292, 296, 302, 304; Jan. 1265, 307–9,
    314–20, 322–3, 330, 336; (projected) June
    1265, 333, 364
Pavia, Guido de, 217
Peak (Derby.), 319–24, 326–7
Pembroke, lordship of, 52–3, 127, 145–6, 154,
  196, 332
Percy, Henry, 248
Peter II, king of Aragon (1196–1213), 4
Peterborough, Benedictine abbey, 201, 346–7,
  348; *see also* Caux, John de, abbot
Petronilla, countess of Leicester (d. 1212), 48–9
Pevensey castle (Sussex), 282, 330, 336
Peveril inheritance, 322
Peyraut, Guillaume de, 86, 94, 97–8
Philip Augustus, king of France (1180–23), 2,
  18
Pipton (Brecon), 337
Pitt, William, the younger, 309
Plessis, John de, earl of Warwick, 144, 286
Poitiers, 205
Poitou, 10, 31, 34, 75, 108, 129, 193
Porchester castle (Hants.), 335
Porrois (Port Royal), Cistercian nunnery,
  101–2, 190
Porter, Peter le, 64–5
Portsmouth (Hants.), 10
Powicke, F. M., 258
Prouille (Toulouse), Dominican nunnery, 5
Prudhoe (Northumb.), 56
Pyns, Donatus de, 133

Quincy, Hawise de, countess of Lincoln
  (d. 1243), 167
Quincy, Margaret de, countess of Winchester
  (d. 1235), M.'s great-aunt, 3, 15–16, 62
Quincy, Roger de, earl of Winchester (d. 1264),
  55, 60, 62, 64–5, 69–70, 75, 180n.

Quincy, Saer de, earl of Winchester (d. 1219),
  3, 47, 62

Raimond-Berenger V, count of Provence
  (d. 1245), 205–6
Ranulf, earl of Chester (d. 1232): favour for M.
  (1230–2), 8–9, 12–13, 21, 352; and Hubert
  de Burgh, 11, 13; M.'s debt to, 9, 16, 21;
  his charters, 60–1; death, 13–14, 63; his
  familiares take service with M., 16, 63–6,
  75, 81
Raymond VII, count of Toulouse (d. 1249), 4,
  32
Reading (Berks.), 92, 229, 306
Redesdale (Northumb.), 56, 58
reforms of 1258–9: general aims, 157–9, 163–5,
  180–1, 352; justice as the central
  desideratum, 152, 158, 166–7, 354–6
  reforming institutions: committee of twenty-
    four, 153, 157–9, 164, 170, 361; council of
    fifteen, **158–60**, 163–4, 170, 177, 180, 185,
    190–1, 193, 195–7, 199, 201–2, 204,
    207–8, 215, 240, 248; twelve representing
    the baronage, 159, 178, 248; committee of
    twenty-four to negotiate aid for king, 159
  reforming texts: Petition of the Barons (1258),
    157, 167; Ordinance of Sheriffs (1258),
    165, 168, 210; Ordinance of the Magnates
    (1259), 179–81, 210, 360; Provisions of the
    Barons (1259), 166, 179, 180, 185, 360; *see
    also* Oxford, Provisions of; Westminster,
    Provisions of
Reigate (Surrey), 266
Restormel (Cornwall), 310
Rheims, 220
Rhineland, 138, 349
Richard of Cornwall (d. 1272), H.'s brother:
    wealth of, 30, 55, 104, 310; a womaniser,
    39; not one for a hair shirt, 90;
    appropriates royal rights, 59; negotiates
    with Welsh (1237), 20; rebels over M.'s
    marriage (1238), 21; intervenes with H. on
    behalf of M. and Eleanor (1239), 25; on
    crusade (1240), 30; marriage to Sanchia of
    Provence (1243), 32, 135; fee from H.,
    135–6; influence at court (1244–5), 33, 36;
    loans to H. (1240–58), 33, 35, 126; on
    mission to France (1247), 35; supports M.
    at his trial (1252), 115, 147; given judicial
    protection by H. (1256), 143; elected king
    of the Romans (1257), 138, 143; renounces
    claims in France (1258–9), 155–6, 179;
    returns from Germany (1259), 178; named
    as arbitrator on Eleanor's dower, 182n.;
    secures London for H. (1260), 195;

marriage (1247), 127, 145–6; and Eleanor's
dower, 130, 145; prominence at court
(1255–8), 143–5, 149; advises on foreign
policy (1256), 140; and Sicilian Business,
144; comes to terms with M. (1259), 196;
and Bigorre (1260), 200; returns to
England (1261–2), 208–9, 216; flees to
France after Lewes (1264), 272, 282, 290;
returns to aid Edward against M. (1265),
333–4; *see also* Lusignans; Montfort,
Simon de
Vaux, John de, 227, 244, 248
Vaux de Cernai (Ile de France), Cistercian
abbey, 102
Peter de, 4
Verdun, John de, 248
Vere, Robert de, earl of Oxford (d. 1296), 286
Vernon, Richard de, 326
Vescy, John de, 249
Vielenc, Robert de, 70
Vincent, Nicholas, 11
Viterbo, 370

Wake, Baldwin, 249, 267, 340
Waleran of Meulan, 60
Walerand, Robert, 136, 144, 179, 193, 197, 204,
207, 216, 227, 334–5
Wales: Eleanor's dower lands in, 50, 52–3, 130,
183, 308; failure of H.'s policy towards
(1231–2), 12; peace negotiations with
(1237), 20; H. consults M. and other
councillors about (1244), 35; H.'s
campaign in (1245), 33, 109; Welsh rising
(1257–8), 125–6, 139, 152, 155; William de
Valence accuses M. and Gloucester of
helping Welsh (1258), 146; muster at
Oxford for Welsh campaign (1258), 156;
truce made with, 163; Welsh attack on
Builth (1260), 193, 199; H.'s resentment at
failure of council to deal with (1261), 207;
Welsh rising (1262–3), 220, 222; Cantilupe
negotiates for truce with (1263), 251; H.'s
feigned campaign against (1264), 265;
Isabella de Fors flees to (1264–5), 325;
Gilbert de Clare in (1265), 328; M.'s
alliance with Welsh (1262), 212–13; (1263),
228; (1264), 263, 289, 307; (1265), 337–8,
340; *see also* Llywelyn ap Gruffudd
Wales, John of, 253
Wallingford castle (Berks.), 68, 280, 307
Walton, Simon of, bishop of Norwich
(1257–66), 195, 197, 227, 317
Warenne, John de, earl of Surrey (d. 1304),
203, 209–10, 213, 226, 244, 248, 266, 268,
270, 325, 332, 334

Warwick, 267, 307
earls of, *see* Beauchamp; Plessis
Warwickshire, 55, 58, 65–6, 71, 76, 122, 212
Waverley (Surrey), Cistercian abbey, 42, 44;
annalist of, 42
Wells, Hugh of, bishop of Lincoln (1213–35),
174n.
Wendover, Roger of, 13–14
Westminster, 153; abbey, 115; hall, 320
Provisions of: precursory texts (1258–9), 157,
166; terms and publication of (1259), 185,
211; on conciliar attendance on king, 286;
on sheriff's tourn, 315, 356, 366; M.'s lack
of participation in making, 190–1;
enforcement, 195, 199, 203; and eyre
(1260–1), 211–12, 366; reissued (1263),
221–2, 226, 228 and n., 314; demand for
observance of, in negotiations with legate
(1264), 294, 297, 314, 360; published again
and enforced (1264–5), 314–17;
observance a condition of Edward's
release (1265), 319; largely confirmed in
Statute of Marlborough (1267), 366
Statute of (1275), 366
Weston (Herts.), 46, 50
Wexcombe (Wilts.), 46, 50
Whitchurch (War.), 65
Wigmore castle (Heref.), 263, 332–4, 344
William the Conqueror, king of England
(1066–87), 5
Wilton (Wilts.), Dominicans of, 103
Wiltshire, 122
Winchcombe (Glos.), 331
Winchelsea (Sussex), 269
Winchelsey, Robert, archbishop of
Canterbury (1293–1313), 354
Winchester (Hants.), 209, 339; castle, 239, 247
bishops of, *see* Roches; Valence, Aymer de;
Gervais
countess of, *see* Quincy, Margaret de
earls of, *see* Quincy, Saer de; Quincy, Roger
de
Windsor (Berks.), 148, 213, 229–30, 234, 236,
241, 244, 246–8, 282
Wingham, Henry, chancellor (1255–62),
bishop of London (1259–62), 136, 197, 201
Winton, John de, 255n.
Wintringham (Lincs.), 252
Wissant (Boulogne), 140, 300
Withersfield (Suffolk), 313, 331
Woodspeen (Berks.), 46, 50
Worcester, 211, 227, 263, 307–9, 314–15, 318,
335, 339–40; chronicler of, 261
bishop of, *see* Cantilupe, Walter de
Worcestershire, 332